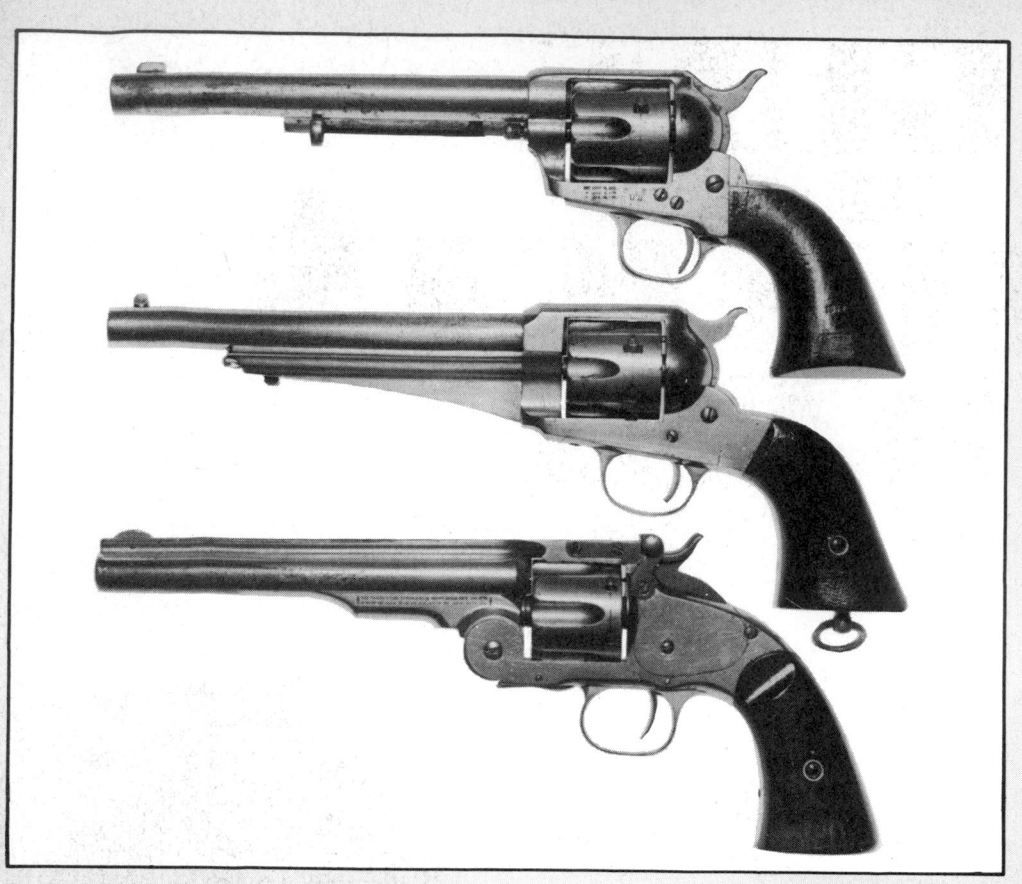

Preceding page: Joseph 'White Eye' Anderson, a friend of Wild Bill Hickok's. Early in his career a burning buffalo chip scorched his eyebrow and turned it white, hence the name. 'White Eye' has a Peacemaker while his friend E. B. 'Yankee' Judd is armed with a Merwin Hulbert revolver. Note the holster and Winchester rifle. (Author's Collection)

Left: Three interesting revolvers: they were all issued to Indian Scouts. As early as 1874 Custer's Indian scouts in the Black Hills expedition were issued with nickel-plated Peacemakers, and it became a standard practice. Top: a U.S.-marked Peacemaker; Second: an 1875; Third: a Second Model Schofield. (By courtesy of Arnold Marcus Chernoff)

Below: Hays City, Kansas, in the late 1870s, some years after the period when Wild Bill Hickok was responsible for its law and order. (By courtesy of the Kansas State Historical Society)

GUNS
OF THE
AMERICAN
WEST

Joseph G. Rosa

a&ap

ARMS AND ARMOUR PRESS
LONDON MELBOURNE CAPE TOWN

Published in 1985 by Arms and Armour Press,
Lionel Leventhal Limited, 2-6 Hampstead High Street,
London NW3 1QQ; 11 Munro Street, Port Melbourne
3207, Australia; Sanso Centre, 8 Adderley Street,
P.O. Box 94, Cape Town 8000, South Africa

British Library Cataloguing in Publication Data
Rosa, Joseph G.
Guns of the American West.
1. Firearms — West (U.S.) — History
I. Title
683.4'00978 TS533.2
ISBN 0-85368-676-9

Edited by Michael Boxall; layout, maps and diagrams
by Anthony A. Evans; typeset by Typesetters
(Birmingham) Limited; printed on Palomar Matt
Coated Cartridge, supplied by Link Publishing Papers
Ltd, and bound by Robert Hartnoll Ltd, Bodmin.

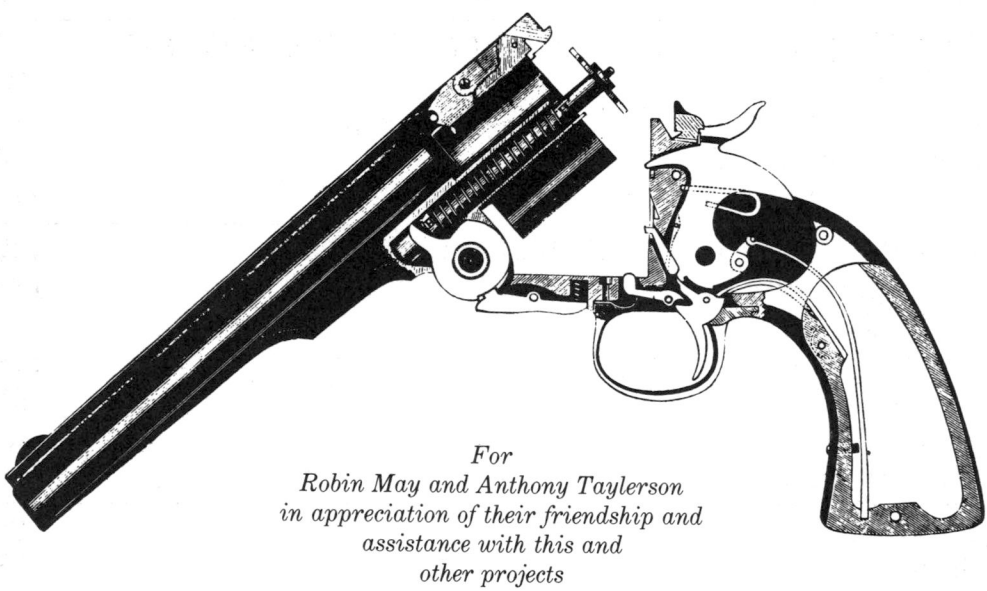

For
Robin May and Anthony Taylerson
in appreciation of their friendship and
assistance with this and
other projects

CONTENTS

CHRONOLOGY

1700-1800 The Pennsylvania-Kentucky rifle gains its reputation

1718 James Puckle's repeating flintlock

1755 Braddock's defeat in Pennsylvania

1759 Wolfe defeats Montcalm, and the British take Canada

1763 British Army is reduced in size

1773 Boston Tea Party

1775 British attacked at Lexington and Concord; Battle of Bunker Hill

1776 April, the Ferguson breech-loading rifle tested at Woolwich; 4 July, Declaration of Independence

1781 October, Cornwallis surrenders at Yorktown

1783 End of the Revolutionary War; the British withdraw

1795 Congress approves a new model musket

1799 Death of George Washington; Edward Howard claims discovery of fulminate of mercury

1803 Lousiana Purchase; introduction of the Model 1803 rifle

1804-6 Lewis and Clark's expedition to the Pacific and back

1805 Battle of Trafalgar and death of Nelson; Alexander Forsyth invents a percussion ignition system

1806 Zebulon Pike's trek west; names Pike's Peak in Rocky Mountains

1807 Jacob Hawken arrives in St. Louis

1812 Pauly's breech-loading centre-fire percussion gun; war with England

1814 The war ends, but news of peace arrives too late to stop the Battle of New Orleans in January 1815

1815 Defeat of Napoleon at Waterloo; Jacob Hawken sets up on his own

1817 Hall's flintlock breech-loading rifle

1818 Wheeler-Collier revolving flintlock patented in England

1822 Joshua Shaw patents the percussion cap in the United States

1833 Formation of the first Regiment of U.S. Dragoons

1835 Colt's revolver patented in England

1836 February, Colt's revolver patented in the United States; March, the fall of the Alamo; Texas becomes a republic

1839 Colt's rifles and revolvers adopted by the Texas Navy

1844 Texas Rangers obtain Colt's revolvers

1845 Texas annexed by the United States

1846 War with Mexico; Colt contracted for 1,000 revolvers

1847 Colt-Walker Dragoon; Colt opens a factory at Hartford

1848 Revolutions in Europe; Prussia adopts the Dreyse needle-gun; Colt redesigns his Dragoon pistol and introduces a pocket model; Christian Sharps patents a breech-loader; end of the war with Mexico; California ceded to the United States; gold discovered in California

1849 California gold-rush; Colt redesigns his pocket pistol

1850 California achieves statehood

1851 Great Exhibition in London; Colt exhibits pistols; gold discovered in Australia; the Colt Navy revolver; Adams revolver

1852 Death of the Duke of Wellington; Colt establishes London factory

1853 Crimean War breaks out; introduction of the Enfield .577 rifle

1854 Sharps improves his breech-loader; the Kansas-Nebraska Act; border warfare in Kansas

1855 Introduction of the Springfield Armory's carbine pistol; formation of two new mounted regiments — first use of the word 'cavalry' in U.S. service; April, Rollin White secures a patent for a bored-through cylinder; June, formation of the Volcanic Arms Company; Smith and Wesson reformed

1856 End of the Crimean War; closure of Colt's London factory; the British Government adopts the Beaumont-Adams revolver

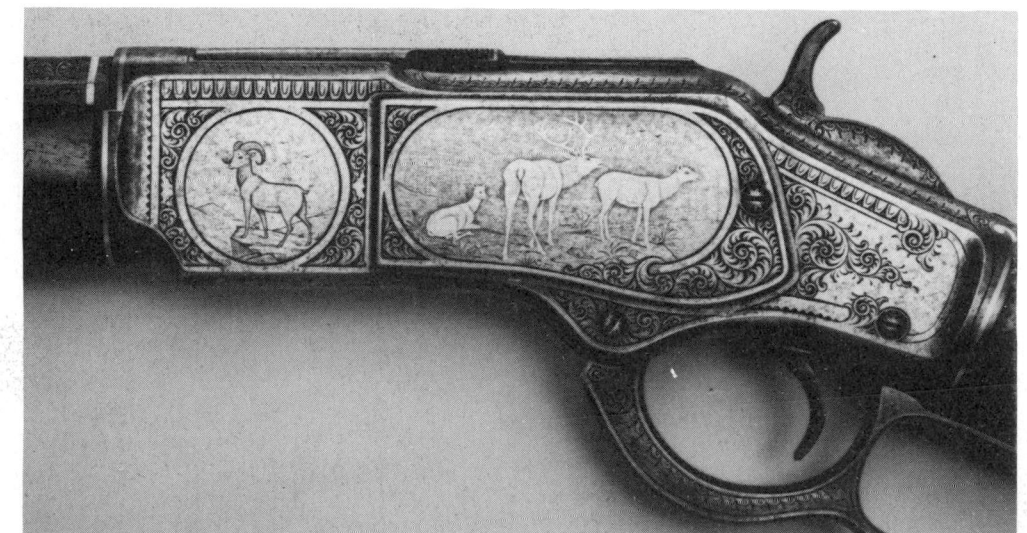

Left: A close-up of the receiver of an ornate Model 1873 engraved by John Ulrich. The gun was shipped to the Paris Exhibition in 1889. (By courtesy of Christie's, London)

Right: Cattle grazing in Kansas. Once they reached a railhead town the cattle were held back and fattened-up while awaiting their turn at the shipping pens. (Author's Collection)

1857 Indian Mutiny; Winchester forms the New Haven Arms Company

1858 Merrill, Latrobe & Thomas carbines on trial with the cavalry; the Remington-Beals revolver

1859 Colt introduces a modified carbine stock for pistols

1860 The Colt New Model .44 Army revolver

1861 April, outbreak of the Civil War; Kansas becomes a state; Colt's New Model Navy pistol; Remington's new Army and Navy pistols; the Springfield Armory's rifled musket; Dr. Gatling's hand-cranked repeating gun

1862 Henry's improved cartridge; death of Samuel Colt

1863 Lincoln frees slaves; new Sharps' breech-loader; new Remington Army and Navy model; Battle of Gettysburg; Berdan's sharp-shooters; Spencer rifle and carbine

1864 June, sinking of *Alabama* by *Kearsarge* off Cherbourg

1865 April, end of the Civil War; May, Quantrill killed by Union troops; July, Hickok shoots Tutt; an improved Spencer; Allin-Springfield conversion

1866 First lever-action Winchester rifle

1867 Cattle shipping point established at Abilene, Kansas

1869 Colt's Theur conversion soundly beaten by the Adams revolver; Rollin White's patent expires; Smith and Wesson's first .44 calibre revolver patented in England

1870 Colt and others commence conversion of percussion arms to metallic cartridge; Smith and Wesson's new revolver accepted by the Ordnance Board

1871 Hickok appointed Marshal of Abilene; Colt's Richards and Richards-Mason conversions; Smith and Wesson deliveries to the army; first 'Russian' models; first Schofield model

1872 Colt's new solid-frame pistol goes on trial

1873 The Peacemaker is adopted; Winchester produce a new rifle; Springfield carbine adopted by the Ordnance Board

1874 Custer's expedition to the Black Hills; gold in the Black Hills; Colt-Forehand and Wadsworth trials

1875 Remington's New Model Army

1876 June, Custer's Last Stand; August, Hickok assassinated; Winchester's Model 1876; Colt-Remington-Schofield trials

1877 Colt's double-action Army revolver; Royal North-West Mounted Police adopt the Winchester Model 1876 carbine

1878 Colt-Merwin and Hulbert trials; Smith and Wesson New Model No. 3

1881 Gunfight at the O.K. Corral; Billy the Kid murdered

1882 Colonel Schofield commits suicide; Jesse James murdered

1883 Formation of Buffalo Bill's Wild West (Cody himself never referred to it as a 'Show')

1889 Colt's first successful double-action revolver adopted by the Government

1890 Remington's last model revolver; Sitting Bull murdered; the Frontier officially declared at an end; Battle of Wounded Knee

1892 Winchester Model 1892

1894 Winchester Model 1894; introduction of the Colt 'Bisley' revolver

1895 John Wesley Hardin murdered

1896 Introduction of the Mauser automatic pistol

1911 Butch Cassidy and the Sundance Kid allegedly killed in Bolivia; Colt-Browning .45 Army automatic pistol

1921 Death of Bat Masterson, at his desk

1924 Bill Tilghman murdered

1929 Death of Wyatt Earp — in bed!

1. Carolina, North (1783)
2. Carolina, South (1783)
3. Connecticut (1783)
4. Delaware (1783)
5. Georgia (1783)
6. Maine (1783)
7. Maryland (1783)
8. Massachusetts (1783)
9. New Hampshire (1783)
10. New Jersey (1783)
11. New York (1783)
12. Pennsylvania (1783)
13. Rhode Island (1783)
14. Virginia (1783)
15. Washington DC (1783)
16. Vermont (1791)
17. Kentucky (1792)
18. Tennessee (1796)
19. Ohio (1803)
20. Louisiana (1812)
21. Indiana (1816)
22. Mississippi (1817)
23. Illinois (1818)
24. Alabama (1819)
25. Missouri (1821)
26. Arkansas (1836)

27. Michigan (1837)
28. Florida (1845)
29. Texas (1845)
30. Iowa (1846)
31. Wisconsin (1848)
32. California (1850)
33. Minnesota (1858)
34. Oregon (1859)
35. Kansas (1861)
36. Virginia, West (1863)
37. Nevada (1864)
38. Nebraska (1867)
39. Colorado (1876)
40. Dakota, North (1889)
41. Dakota, South (1889)
42. Montana (1889)
43. Washington (1889)
44. Idaho (1890)
45. Wyoming (1890)
46. Utah (1896)
47. Oklahoma (1907)
48. Arizona (1912)
49. New Mexico (1912)

Purchases/annexations:

| 1803 | 1819 | 1845 | 1846 | 1848/53 |

INTRODUCTION

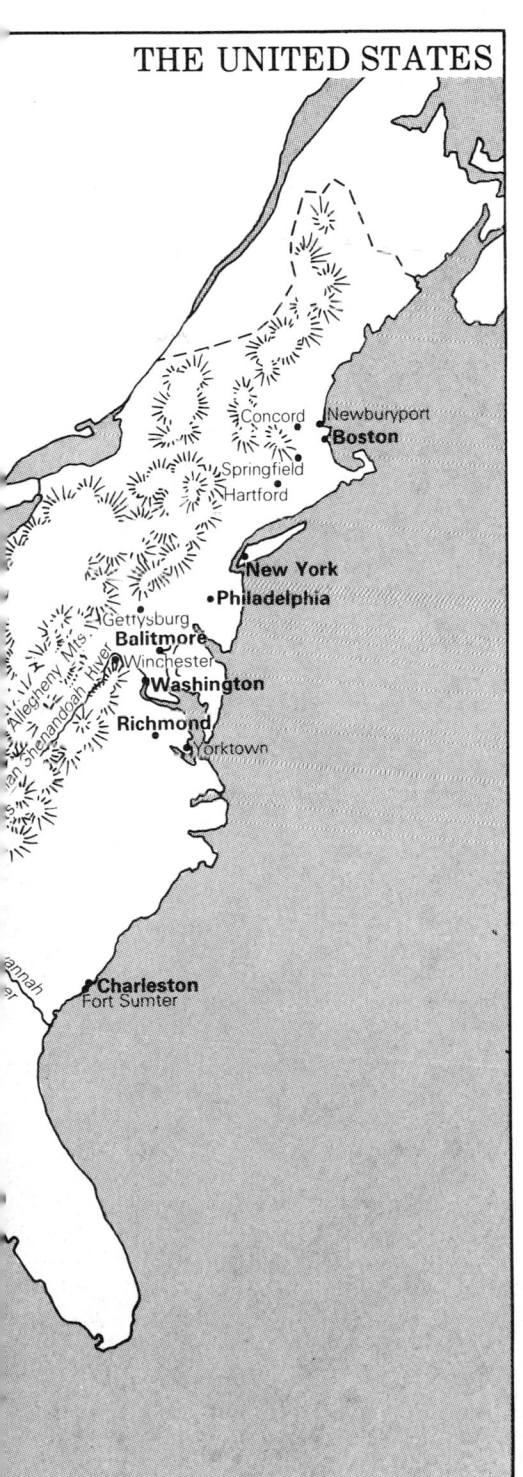

THE UNITED STATES

Newburyport
Concord
Boston
Springfield
Hartford
New York
Philadelphia
Gettysburg
Balitmore
Winchester
Washington
Richmond
Yorktown
Charleston
Fort Sumter

THE United States was born to the sound of gunfire, and she has endured a love-hate relationship with firearms ever since. The Constitution, which gave the individual the 'right to bear arms', has been interpreted by some to mean the right (should they so wish) to keep a 'Bazooka in the basement', or a 'Gatling in the garage'. But the less warlike argue that it really means the 'right' or 'duty' of the individual to bear arms in defence of the Republic in time of war. But whichever interpretation one accepts, fire-arms have played a large part in America's way of life. Outsiders may well view this passion for guns as a regressive rather than a progressive step, but anyone who knows the country and its people will appreciate that underlying their apparent preoccupation with guns, and their right to keep them, is, on the one hand a fierce patriotism in defence of National and individual freedom, and on the other an inborn resistance to governmental interference.

As a life-long student of the American West and of firearms, I never cease to be amazed by the lure of the legendary 'Wild West', for despite the fictions of Hollywood and the novelists, it continues to attract a vast audience. We all have our favourite historical or film characters; most of them encountered as children during many happy hours spent sitting in the dark mesmerised by the spectacle, or perhaps when reading lurid fiction. But for whatever reason, the West has a fascination which time cannot dim.

The Western film and novel are blamed for the public's distorted view of the West and its belief that the Colt Forty-Five and the Winchester Seventy-Three really did 'Win the West'. Despite howls of protest from purists, the film industry (aided by Western fiction) has rarely discouraged that impression. In truth, though, Hollywood is not entirely to blame, faced as it has been with certain problems of practicability. In the first place, early Western films were relatively cheap to produce, time was not at a premium, and there were large quantities of obsolete firearms available. However, it is

one thing to load blank cartridges into metallic cartridge weapons, or to carry stocks of them on location, but to use percussion weapons presents many difficulties; consequently, despite obvious anachronisms it is more convenient to use metallic cartridge arms.

Similarly, the classic gunfight which is an essential part of any Western book or film worthy of the name, is itself highly controversial. Various films have included the legendary 'Gunfight at the O.K. Corral', but none (to my knowledge) have dared depict it as it really happened – seventeen shots fired in a space of thirty seconds! Rather, the fight is drawn out into a lengthy exchange. And the lone man against the mob: we watch with fascination as Gary Cooper in *High Noon* stands alone against four men while terrified townsfolk hide themselves; or Alan Ladd as Shane does battle with an imported 'top gun' who is in turn backed by a number of villains anxious to shoot him in the back if he wins. Despite all odds, our heroes outdraw and out-shoot their opponents in confrontations which are exciting and spectacular. These and similar cinematic exploits have enthralled generations of filmgoers; but in the real west of the 1860s and 1870s, a *High Noon* affair could not have occurred. There were no one-man law-enforcers, for backing every town marshal were at least two deputies (more if required) and most of the male population who, at the first sound of alarm, would arm themselves and rush to the assistance of the police.

As for the gunfights . . . yes, there were a number of face-to-face confrontations, and some of these are mentioned in this book, but few of the real shoot-outs would have made good cinema. For example, when William L. Brooks, generally known as Billy Brooks (although some called him 'Bully Brooks', but not to his face) was Marshal of Newton, Kansas, in 1872, he was attacked by a number of Texan cowboys out on a spree. According to the Wichita *City Eagle* of 14 June the shoot-out took place on Sunday the 9th. When the Texans made it hot for the citizens: 'Brooks had run them out of town, when they turned and fired three shots into him, with what effect may be judged, from the fact that he continued his pursuit for ten miles before he returned to have his wounds dressed. One shot passed through his right breast, and the other two were in his limbs. We hear from a driver here that he will recover. Bill has sand enough to beat the hour-glass that tries to run him out.'

Fights over women were another cause of conflict. On Sunday 19 February 1872 a man named A. M. Sweet made overtures to 'Rowdy Kate' Lowe, the common-law wife of the notorious Joseph 'Rowdy Joe' Lowe, at that time the owner of a saloon in Newton. The Kansas *Daily Commonwealth* of 21 February claimed that Sweet got Kate drunk and took her to a brothel run by Fanny Grey. The next morning, Joe heard that Sweet had threatened to kill him on sight, so he 'went to Fanny's House to see about the matter. As soon as he presented himself, Sweet pulled his revolver; but before he fired, Joe fired two shots, both taking effect in Sweet's body, from the effects of which he died in three hours. Rowdy Joe immediately went to the sheriff and gave himself up.'

The last sentence is important, for despite the apparent ease with which Hollywood's

gunfighters can kill one another off without any form of retribution, the actuality was very different: coroner's courts were active and both police and civilians involved in gun-fights were called upon to enter pleas of 'justifiable homicide in the pursuance of duty' or 'self-defence'.

The relationship between the cowboy and the cow-town police will be discussed later, but here are two contemporary accounts of 'community shoot-outs' from the 1870s when Dodge City rejoiced in the titles of 'Queen of the Cow-towns' and 'Wickedest City on the Plains'. The first comes from the Dodge City *Ford County Globe* of 20 August 1878, which reported:

'Another shooting affair occurred on the "south side" Saturday night [August 17]. It appears the one of the cow boys, becoming intoxicated and quarrelsome, undertook to take possession of the bar in the Comique. To this the bar keeper objected and a row ensued. Our policemen interferred and had some difficulty in handling their man. Several cattle men then engaged in the broil and in the excitement some of them were bruised on the head with six shooters. Several shots were accidentally fired which created general confusion among the crowd of persons present. We are glad to chronicle the fact that none were seriously hurt and nobody shot. We however cannot help but regret the too ready use of pistols in all rows of such character and would like to see a greater spirit of harmony exist between our officers and cattle men so that snarling

coyotes and killers could make their own fights without interesting or dragging good men into them.' And on 10 June 1879, the same paper reported:

THE WORK OF THE PISTOL
'Last night the police undertook to disarm a squad of cow boys who had neglected to lay aside their six-shooters upon arriving in the city. The cow boys protested and war was declared. Several shots were fired, and one of the cow boys was wounded in the leg. The balance of the cow boys made their escape.'

The exploits of the cowboy, the policeman and the gunfighter will be dealt with, together with the role of the Colt and Winchester in relation to their many rivals. And it should also be borne in mind that the majority of firearms used in the West were either originally designed for military use or owed their origin to military-style weapons.

In an endeavour to put the subject into perspective, this book is written for the general reader rather than for the student or scholar. There are innumerable specialist books devoted to almost every facet of the suject, whereas the general reader is less fortunate. I hope, therefore, that by the time he or she reaches the final section (which covers briefly the 'Wild West') they will have a clear understanding of the weapons and their calibres, and of other details which may have baffled or bemused them. Perhaps this informal study may also inspire others to pursue the subject further – I hope so.

Joseph G. Rosa

Ruislip, Middlesex, England.

Below: A faro lay-out at Bisbee, Arizona, in the mid-1880s. The 'dealer' is Harry Emerson; the 'lookout' is George Oakes, and at the left is part-owner of the saloon, Tony Downs. At the right (in the top hat) is 'Sleepy Tom' Thomas. All of these men were noted characters of the time. (Author's Collection)

Part One
FROM FLINT TO CAP
1776-1846

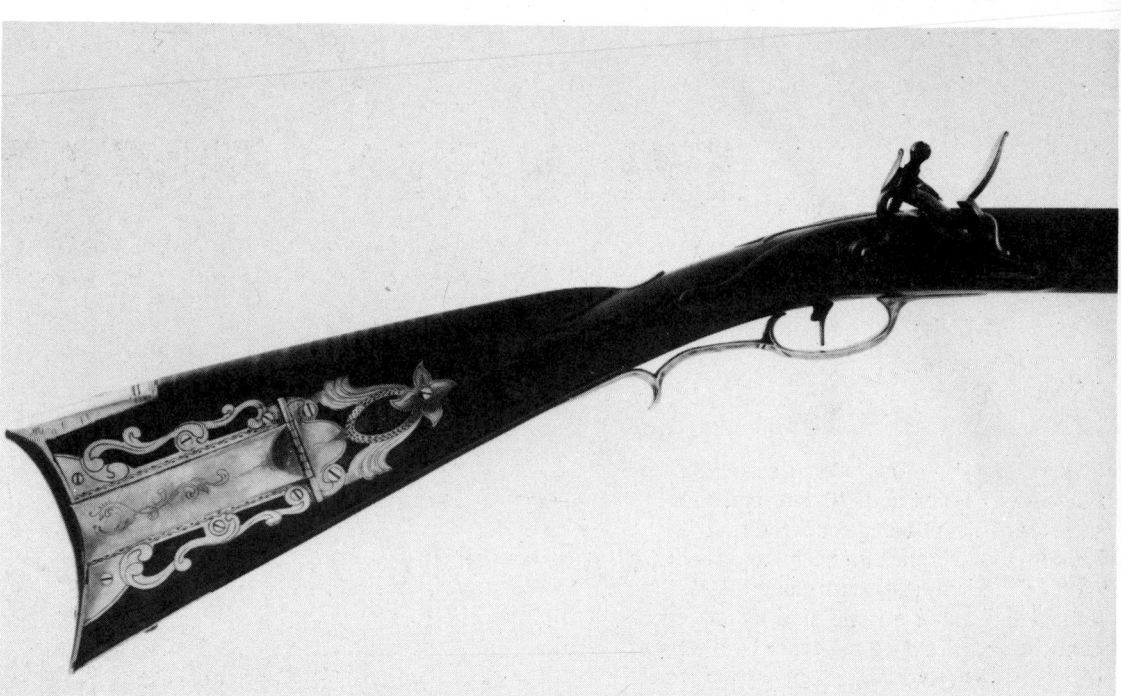

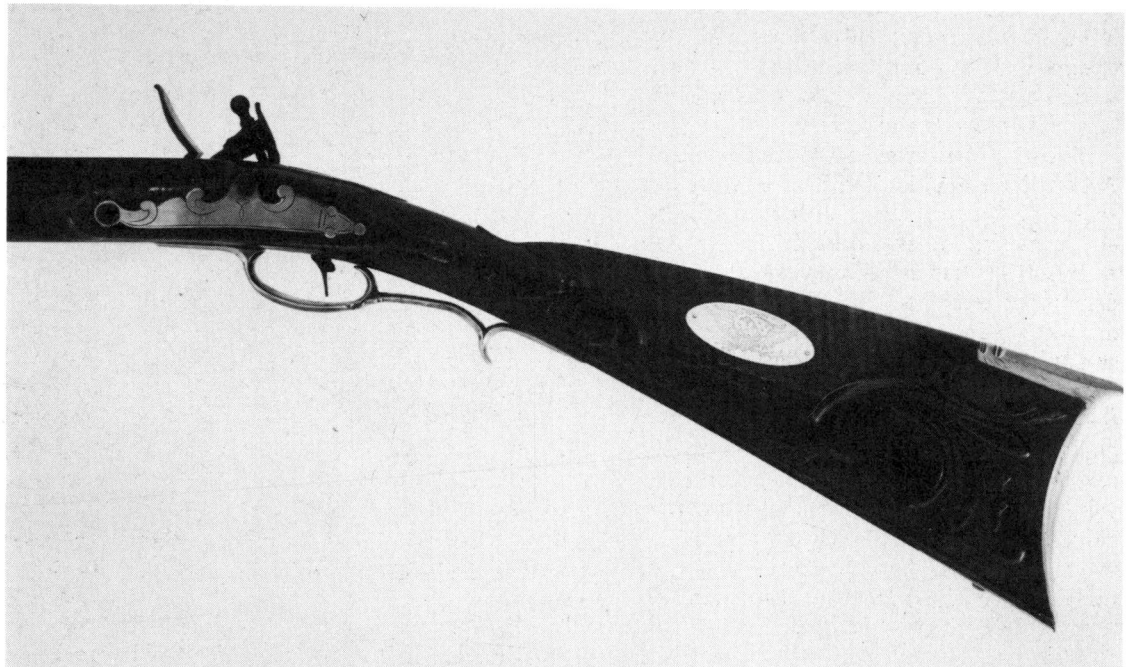

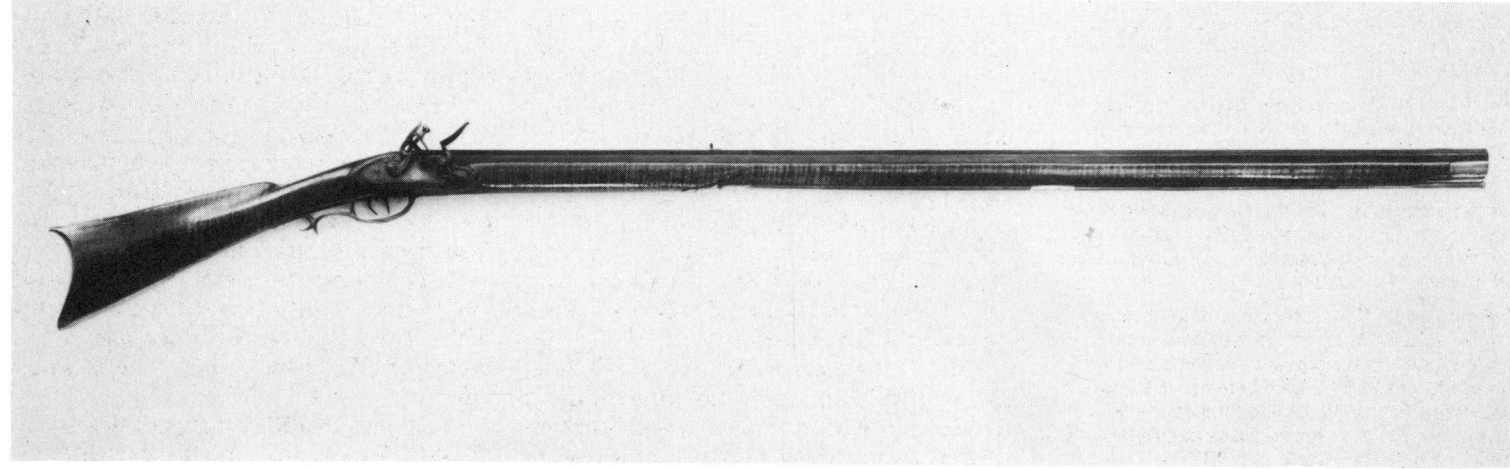

1

THE RIFLEMEN

In such dangerous times, the experienced mountaineer is never without his rifle, even in camp . . . His rifle is his constant friend and protector. – Washington Irving

LONG, long before the Declaration of Independence in 1776, survival to most Americans meant being prepared to fight the Indians or the French (or both), and shooting to eat. The few settlements along the eastern seaboard, flanked on one side by the cruel Atlantic Ocean and on the other by a wilderness of woods and forests in which lurked now friendly, now hostile Indians, were sparsely populated. But with time and the influx of more people, there were those who dreamed of pushing westward into the wilderness to discover just what did lie beyond the woods and forests.

Dreams, however, were not enough. Action, determination and courage were also required. Having survived Indian attacks, and conscious of ever-present danger, the early settlers had armed themselves with all manner of weapons. The flintlock was the most commonly available, and most homesteads had at least one musket or shotgun, and sometimes a pistol or two. Many used the same weapon to defend the home and hunt game. Only when individuals, or perhaps a group decided to penetrate the wilderness in the face of unknown dangers did they deem it necessary to arm themselves with the best available guns, in particular the rifle which was just beginning to make its presence felt.

Far left: This fine Kentucky rifle by C. Hawken is typical of the weapons manufactured during the late eighteenth and early nineteenth centuries. (From the Leonard Collection, by courtesy of the Winchester Museum)

Top left: The Hawken Kentucky's lockplate and finely worked patch box. (From the Leonard Collection, by courtesy of the Winchester Museum)

Centre left: Left side of the Hawken Kentucky showing the finely carved stock and silver inlay. (From the Leonard Collection, by courtesy of the Winchester Museum)

Bottom left: A Kentucky-type smooth-bore long gun in .42 calibre complete with double set-triggers. The weapon bears the name J. THORNTON on the top of its 44½-inch barrel, but the lock is unsigned. The full stock is of striped maple, the most popular wood for weapons of this type. (By courtesy of Messrs Wallis & Wallis)

Then, in April 1775 a shot was fired on Lexington Green that was to be 'heard around the world', and plans for Western expansion were soon forgotten when the colonists found themselves faced with a situation that was to change the course of history, bring tragedy to many of them, but lead eventually to the birth of the United States of America.

Almost from the moment that Columbus discovered the New World (or, as some claim, rediscovered it in the wake of the Vikings and others) in 1492, there were disputes over possession of the new land. After the defeat of the Spanish Armada in 1588, when England became mistress of the seas, she took care to establish a foothold in America. Soon, however, people from France, Spain, Holland, Germany and smaller nations were also anxious to claim a part of it, in a bid to escape from poverty, disease, political and religious persecution.

The first English Colony was at Jamestown in what was to become Virginia. The early settlers found themselves in a hostile land and in 1622 many of them were massacred by Indians, but the survivors were soon joined by more people, other settlements sprang up and the country prospered.

The English Parliament recognized the potential wealth of the country, and certain individuals who had proved helpful in securing some of that wealth, were graced by royal favour and granted vast tracts of land. For instance, Charles I granted to Cecil Calvert (Lord Baltimore) and his heirs almost seven million acres of land – this later became the state of Maryland. The present states of North and South Carolina and Pennsylvania were grants from Charles II. Annual bounties were usually paid to the Crown, some quite large and others very small – Lord Baltimore's contribution was two Indian arrowheads and William Penn provided two beaver skins!

Not all the immigrants were honest 'God-fearing folk', however; many were convicted criminals for whom America was an alternative to gaol. Those who took advantage of

the 'new life' soon found themselves bonded slaves; the cost of passage being repaid by working for a period, sometimes for life. But as the population increased the bondage system declined. With increased prosperity came demands from Britain for a greater share in the country's wealth, and the 'loyal colonists' soon found themselves subject to British taxes.

For their part, and despite an increasing independence, the colonists were generally loyal to the Crown, but additional financial burdens soon led to friction. Some put the blame on Charles II for limiting freedom of trade, but following his death there was a lull until the early years of George III's reign when the Crown again began demanding more support from her American colonies both in coin and goods. Repressive laws were enforced which hampered trade; imports and exports were prohibited except via England and in English merchant ships. Even the manufacture of goods for home consumption was forbidden for fear that English industry might suffer, and there was also an embargo on exports to other Crown Colonies.

Perhaps parliament's most humiliating Act came as a result of problems with the French. A treaty in 1748, ending a war between both countries, was not honoured; the fur trade and French expansionist policies led to conflict culminating in the defeat at the hands of the French and their Indian allies, in 1755 of Major-General Edward Braddock, Commander-in-Chief of the British forces in North America. In this catastrophe the British lost 900 out of a force of 1,300 men. French losses were estimated at about a dozen or less, for unlike the British, who had expected to fight in the open, they used natural cover from which to pour a deadly fire into the redcoats who had little hope of hitting an unseen enemy. Not until 1759 were the British able to restore the balance, when General Wolfe's army scaled the Heights of Abraham and all but destroyed Montcalm's army with a single volley.

Then in 1763, with Braddock's defeat and Wolfe's victory behind it, the British Army suffered a politically-motivated indignity which was to have tremendous repercussions. All line regiments above the 70th Foot, and cavalry regiments above the 18th Light Dragoons, were disbanded, leaving a standing army of 17,500 men, of whom 3,000 were in reserve and derisively called the 'Corps of Invalids'. In the colonies only about 10,000 men were under arms (this excluded 4,000 for Minorca and Gibraltar). True, the East India Company had its own army, nevertheless the British were very much under strength. The Government argued that with Canada safe from the French (although won at great cost) the thirteen American colonies were secure, so there was little need of a large army, but the troops that were kept on American soil were to be paid for by the colonists, and once again the British Government acted without thought.

Instead of using tact and diplomacy when implementing new forms of taxation, parliament simply imposed them. The most outrageous was the Stamp Tax. A value was placed upon all legal documents, almanacs, newspapers, pamphlets and other papers, including packs of cards. Despite their taxation, the American colonists could boast of a greater personal freedom than had most Britons, and when news of the new tax reached America there was a roar of protest. Soon the cry 'No taxation without representation' (a reference to the fact that the American colonists had no representative in the British Parliament) was echoing up and down the country, and the subject of innumerable pamphlets. In December 1773 the colonists manifested their objection to the tea duty imposed by parliament. A large quantity of tea shipped to Boston was seized on arrival and thrown into the harbour by a number of young men disguised as Red Indians – an event remembered as the 'Boston Tea Party'. A worried parliament then repealed the Stamp Act and some of the import duties, but by 1775 the country was seething with talk of revolution.

In Massachusetts, for instance, the British reacted by banning meetings (except with the local governor's permission), and vested in the governor the power to appoint or discharge judges and sheriffs. A quartering act forced householders to accept troops as boarders, and there was trouble when the Quebec Act was passed. This guaranteed the right of the French to follow their own religion and legal customs, together with an extension of the Boundaries of Quebec. Many feared that this would eventually impede Western expansion and that they would be surrounded by a Roman Catholic-dominated absolute province. Other colonists flocked to Massachusetts' aid. In 1774 a meeting was held at Philadelphia to

discuss the problem which was in effect the first gathering of the Continental Congress – all patriots, although a fair cross-section of American opinion. Extremists who would accept no resistance to British rule were excluded from the Congress. With the exception of Georgia, every colony sent at least one delegate.

Despite representations to the British Government to make concessions, parliament would not budge, and when some Philadelphia Quakers petitioned George III he wrote: 'The die is now cast, the Colonies must either submit or triumph.' Submit they would not, so revolution was in the air. Loyalists were shunned; millers refused to grind their corn, their men deserted them and they were denounced as 'traitors'. Parliament then took action, and what happened next was inevitable.

London insisted that the army, depleted though it was, enforce its Acts and, accordingly, General Thomas Gage, married to an American lady but loyal to the Crown and in command of the garrison at Boston, was ordered to seek out trouble-makers and rabble-rousers. Learning that the Massachusetts patriots were alleged to be amassing powder and military stores at Concord, twenty miles away, he dispatched a strong detail on 18 April 1775, with orders to confiscate the munitions and arrest the ringleaders, Sam Adams and John Hancock. Warned of the troops' approach by Paul Revere, a coppersmith and engraver (one of many such men employed by the Congress to watch for British troops), the rebels had time to prepare themselves.

At Lexington on 19 April the British, numbering about 800, found their way barred by perhaps 70 to 80 Minutemen under the leadership of Captain John Parker. ('Minutemen' is a term that crept into general use after 1774, denoting men who could be armed and assembled ready for action within 'minutes' if required.) When the British commander, Major John Pitcairn, Royal Marines, a very experienced officer, ordered the men to lay down their arms and disperse, someone fired a shot. This was the shot 'heard around the world'. The Minutemen opened fire, and were greeted by two volleys which killed eight of them and wounded nine others. The British went on to Concord where they met with resistance. After destroying some of the rebels' munitions, they were attacked by some of the Minutemen and in the course of several engagements both sides sustained losses, including Major Pitcairn. It was decided to retreat to Boston, and on the return journey snipers picked off at least another 65 redcoats.

On 17 June British troops moved into Charlestown, Massachusetts, to occupy

Bunker Hill (also known locally as Breed's Hill after the man who owned it), which was found to be already occupied by the Americans. The British advanced, and despite terrible losses, eventually took the hill. From then on it was open war between the British, aided by loyal Americans, and the rebel colonists. By early 1776 despite numerous setbacks, the Americans' 'Continental Army' with George Washington in command, had become very professional and a force to be reckoned with.

The colonists declared their Independence on 2 July 1776, but the actual Declaration was not signed until the 4th when it was ratified by the Colonial Congress. England, however, refused to recognize it and continued the war, although it was a tremendous drain on manpower and resources. The French joined the Americans and, in 1779, were followed by the Spanish, which made for tremendous odds. By October 1781 when Cornwallis, after a desperate wait for reinforcements, surrendered at Yorktown, England was fighting half of Europe. The battles continued until 1782, by which time the British still held New York, parts of New England and, of course, Canada. The first peace treaty was signed in Paris on 30 November 1782, and on 18 April 1783 – just eight years after British troops had marched on Lexington – the end of hostilities was proclaimed by Congress followed by the signing of a final peace treaty in September. In November, the last British redcoats were removed from American soil, leaving behind them a legendary reputation for courage, discipline and for being the finest fighting soldiers in the world. Even George Washington, who became the first President of the United States, and who in his time had served with Braddock, recalled that the most memorable sight in his career had been to watch an army of British redcoats on the march; firm, upright and in perfect step, colours bravely flying, urged on by the stirring sound of fife and drum.

Most of the men who fought in the war between Britain and the American colonies were armed with the smooth-bore flintlock musket, the standard weapon of the day. The British Army was equipped with a long-barrelled musket commonly called the 'Brown Bess', a name derived partly from its 'browned' finish and from the German *Buchse* meaning 'tube' or 'gun'. It was first introduced into the British Army in the 1720s. By the early 1730s it had been widely adopted by and, with variations, remained the standard infantry firearm for 100 years. Indeed, it has been claimed that as late as 1836 some of the troops who accompanied Santa Anna when he defeated the defenders of the Alamo and later met his own defeat at

San Jacinto, were armed with Besses or weapons of similar design.

Classified during various stages of its development as a 'Land Musket' (to distinguish it from the 'Sea Service' patterns), it had originally a 46-inch barrel with a .750 diameter bore. The barrel was later reduced in length to 42 inches or less, and the ramrod for the weapon was attached by means of 'pipes' set into the stock. In its original state the Brown Bess was five feet two inches long, and weighed (unloaded) ten pounds twelve ounces. The addition of a 17-inch triangular bayonet made it a formidable weapon.

A trained soldier was normally supplied with 50 rounds of prepared paper or linen cartridges, which he carried in a leather pouch slung over his left shoulder so that it hung on his right side. The cartridges contained both powder and ball. The powder charge was six drams (or 163 grains). Experienced troops could load and fire two shots per minute, and some could manage three. Accuracy, of course, varied: at 60 yards the 'Bess' was satisfactory; at 100 acceptable, but beyond that distance it was considered erratic. Complaints by some officers that many of these muskets had been badly made and produced poor results even at close range, carried little weight with officialdom, whose main concern seemed to be a reliance upon 'fire-power'. Among those concerned at the lack of accuracy of existing arms was Colonel George Hanger. In 1814 in his book, *To All Sportsmen and Particularly to Farmers and Gamekeepers*, he noted that: 'A soldier's musket, if not exceedingly ill-bored (as many are), will strike the figure of a man at 80 yards; it may even at a hundred, but a soldier must be very unfortunate indeed who shall be wounded by a common musket at 150 yards, provided his antagonist aims at him; and, as to firing at a man at 200 yards, with a common musket, you may just as well fire at the moon. No man was ever killed by a musket at 200 yards by the person who aimed at him.'

As late as the 1840s, despite the introduction of the percussion cap, the smooth-bore musket was still in service (although it was slowly being replaced by rifled weapons) and its accuracy was again in question. In April and May 1846 tests to establish range and elevation for smooth-bore weapons disclosed that to hit a target at 600 yards the muzzle was elevated almost upright! Ten shots at a target eleven feet six inches high by six feet wide at 250 yards resulted in ten misses, but at 150 yards five hits were recorded. At 200 yards it was necessary to aim at least five feet six inches above the target. It was then officially declared that 150 yards was the maximum range for smooth-bore weapons; anything beyond that range 'would be a mere waste of ammunition'.

It does not require much imagination, therefore, to appreciate the devastating effect of several hundred troops firing in line or as part of a British 'square', when discipline and sustained volleys wrought havoc upon the enemy. But the 'Bess's' moment of supreme glory had come on 13 September 1759, when a thin line of British soldiers had stood like carved statues on the Plains of

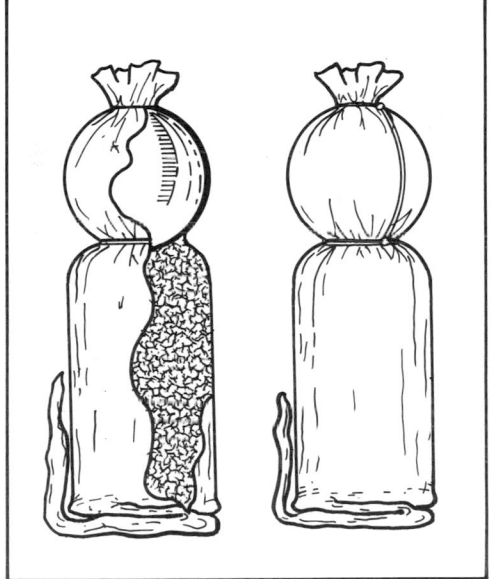

Abraham as Montcalm's troops came running towards them. Not until the French were a mere forty yards away did General Wolfe give the order to fire, whereupon the redcoats delivered the most decisive musket volley in history, and destroyed French Canada.

That the military should continue to rely upon tried and trusted weapons for far longer than would seem practicable is understandable, despite the innumerable experiments by gunmakers and scientists in their endeavour to improve upon existing weaponry or to produce something new. During the eighteenth century a great deal of work was done to improve the flintlock, but apart from improvements in mechanism, pan covers, and yet another attempt to refine gunpowder, success was limited, and it would be thirty years before ignition underwent a radical change and percussion systems gradually replaced the flintlock. Meantime, considerable attention was paid to the bore which, with the introduction of rifling, considerably enhanced not only the performance of the weapons but accuracy as well.

Left: A typical musket cartridge of the eighteenth and early nineteenth centuries. A paper cylinder was tied at one end with string, the ball was dropped in and powder was poured on top of it. The string was then tied around the ball and the end of the cartridge was folded over or twisted. When needed it was torn off and a portion of powder was poured into the priming pan. If a separate powder horn were available, the entire cartridge was pushed into the muzzle and rammed home, which spilled the powder in the breech to accept the flame from the priming pan.

Below: A fine example of the British 'Brown Bess' musket. This specimen is marked with the crowned 'G.R.'. The 'Bess' was the principal weapon of the British Army for almost 100 years and was widely copied. Originally fitted with a 46-inch barrel, this was later reduced to 42 inches or less. Even so, when equipped with a 17-inch triangular bayonet, the soldier's 'reach' was akin to a lancel (By courtesy of Messrs Wallis & Wallis)

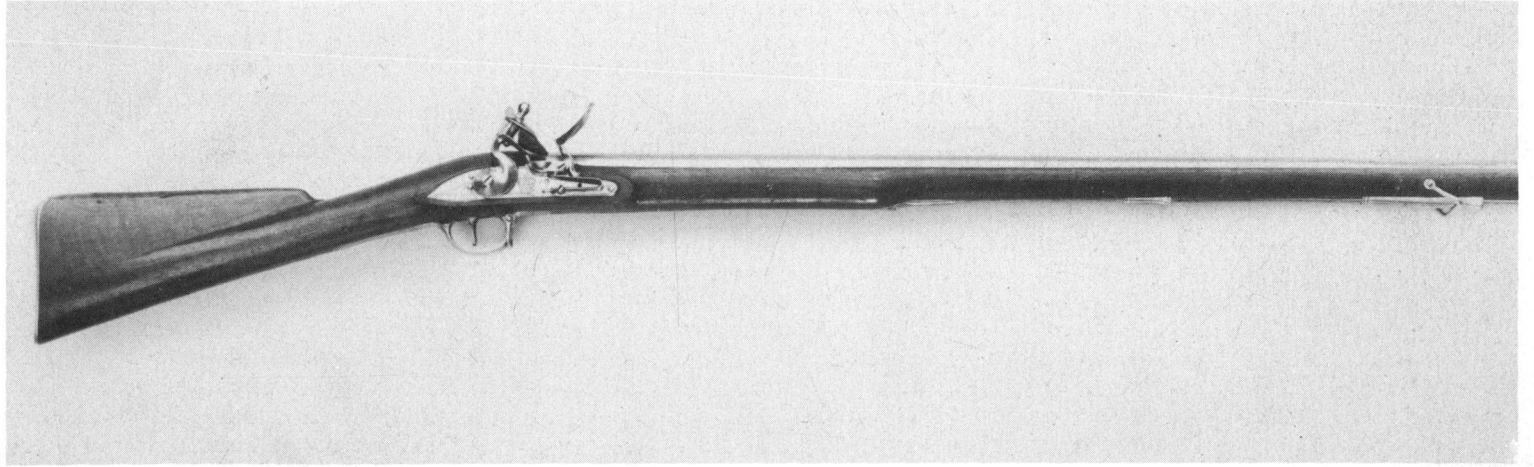

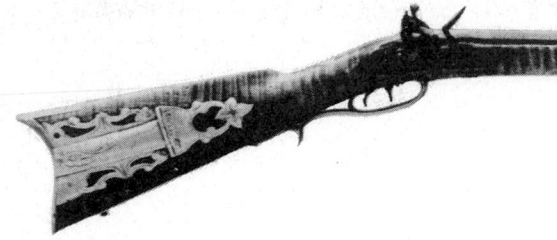

Above: This superb Pennsylvania-Kentucky rifle, complete with set-triggers and an ornate patch box set in the butt, is an excellent example of the work some gunmakers put into their weapons. One can imagine the difficulty of loading such a weapon on the move or in a confined space. (By courtesy of The West Point Museum)

The origin of rifling and by whom it was first used is disputed, but the Germans had experimented with it for many years. Scientists and mathematicians had found it a fascinating study. In 1742 Benjamin Robins, an English gun expert and mathematician, wrote that 'the projectile follows the sweep of the rifles [rifling]; and thereby, besides its progressive motion, acquires a circular motion around the axis of the piece, by which means the bullet discharged from the rifle barrel is constantly made to whirl around an axis coincident with the lines of its flight.'

In America, however, the rifle owes its origin to the German Jaeger, a heavy hunting weapon with a rifled barrel. The Germans had long appreciated the accuracy to be derived from rifled barrels, but they were also aware of the problems of loading such a weapon from the muzzle. The lead ball had to be hammered into the rifling which not only caused damage, but made the process of loading twice as protracted as with the conventional smooth-bore weapons. German immigrant gunsmiths (sometimes called 'Dutch' or 'Deutsch'), many of whom settled in Pennsylvania, gradually overcame the problem by decreasing the size of the bore, equipping the weapon with a longer and lighter barrel, and replacing the heavy stock by a longer, slender piece. This lengthening of the barrel, smaller bore and less powder, increased the velocity of the ball. In fact, experienced frontiersmen could now vary their powder charges and weight of ball, with consequent improvements in performance and accuracy.

The result of these experiments was the now legendary Pennsylvania rifle generally known as the 'Kentucky'. It was so-called because although the typical frontiersman of the period lived west of the Appalachians in territory encompassing Tennessee, the Great Lakes region and the Central Mississippi Valley, he was usually called a 'Kentuckyian', and his rifle was similarly dubbed. Purists, however, can be forgiven when they quite rightly point out that while a great many of the so-called Kentucky rifles can be traced back to Pennsylvania, notably to Lancaster, the state of Virginia, too, can also claim some credit. The gunsmiths of Winchester, Virginia, produced some fine versions of the weapon which owed its origin

to the elegant French and English fowling pieces of the seventeenth and eighteenth centuries. But from whichever state the rifles came, they shared characteristics of design and calibre, and in this the 'Kentucky' scored over all previous rivals.

By the mid eighteenth century the Kentucky-type rifles were being produced in calibres as large as .80 and .45, and down to as small as .30 – the smaller calibres predominating. Where the military established certain guidelines to be followed *verbatim*, the frontiersmen, who were great innovators, yet extremely practical in their approach to the subject by dint of experience and performance, were able to experiment with results which suited them if nobody else, and this 'free thinking' attracted much attention. As late as 1896 Lieutenant-Colonel G. V. Fosbery, V.C., in a talk 'On Pistols', given before the Royal United Services Institution in London, declared that another reason for the reduction in Kentucky bore sizes was because the weapons 'were intended for the use of hunters and Indian fighters, who only visited the settlements at long intervals, the calibre was kept down to enable the man to carry enough lead about his person to last him for a long time'.

A secret of the Kentucky's success was in the quality of the gunpowder used, and this depended a great deal upon the ingredients used in its manufacture. Special attention was paid to the granulation of the powder: the main charge might be quite coarse grained, but for fast ignition only the finest grains were used for priming. The established manufacturers, both in Europe and the United States, devoted a great deal of time and energy towards improving the powder and its performance, but the quality of their products and the results achieved were quite diverse. The British, for instance, determined that military powder should contain 75 parts of saltpetre, ten of sulphur, and fifteen of charcoal. The Belgians and French, on the other hand, preferred 75 per cent saltpetre and 12½ per cent charcoal and sulphur. Other European countries differed yet again. Austria and Prussia preferred 76 parts of saltpetre, fourteen parts of charcoal, and ten parts of sulphur. But of all these ingredients, it was the quantity of saltpetre used that was altered most frequently.

On the frontier the main concern was whether the finished product would burn 'wet' or 'dry'. Powder which burned dry tended to cake-up the bore, whereas 'moist' powder assisted in lubrication and lessened the need for constant swabbing out and oiling. Curiously, it was not until the latter part of the nineteenth century that American manufacturers were able to compete with their European counterparts, whose sales, particularly among the buffalo hunters, were impressive, despite the higher price. Most frontiersmen, however, managed to manufacture their own powder and cast their own lead balls. Lead was readily available, but in some areas quite expensive, so if possible bullets were recovered and recast. Powder could pose problems. In the late eighteenth century the ingredients for making powder could be found at a number of sites in the eastern half of the United States. Large quantities of saltpetre were to be found in limestone caves in Virginia, Georgia, Tennessee and Kentucky. Once extracted it was refined by leaching with wood ash and subjected to a process of evaporation which rid it of salts and other unwanted substances. Still too crude for use, it next underwent a series of washing, straining and melting processes to make it, when finally crystallized, ready for drying, sifting and packing into barrels or moulding into 'cake' form.

Top right: Believed to be a boy's Kentucky, the overall length of the weapon is 36 inches and of the barrel, 21½ inches. The calibre is .400 with eight-groove rifling. The barrel is engraved N. STONER'S RIFLE and W. AVERY in script. The stock is striped and, with the addition of silver inlay and a fretted brass patch box, it is a fine weapon. (By courtesy of Messrs Wallis & Wallis)

Centre right: Two views of a most unusual Kentucky-type. Its overall length is 59½ inches, and the barrel is 43½ inches long, but although it looks like a rifle it is in fact a smooth-bore. Even more curious is the fact that it bears no maker's name, but the lock plate is engraved PARTRIDGE WARRANTED. Howard L. Blackmore confirmed that the name 'Partridge' appeared in the 1830s, and the use of the word 'Warranted' suggests that it was a lock made for export. Evidently the gun was made at the very end of the flintlock era. (By courtesy of Matthew E. Taylor)

Bottom right: A close-up of the Partridge Kentucky showing his name and some very light engraving. (By courtesy of Matthew E. Taylor)

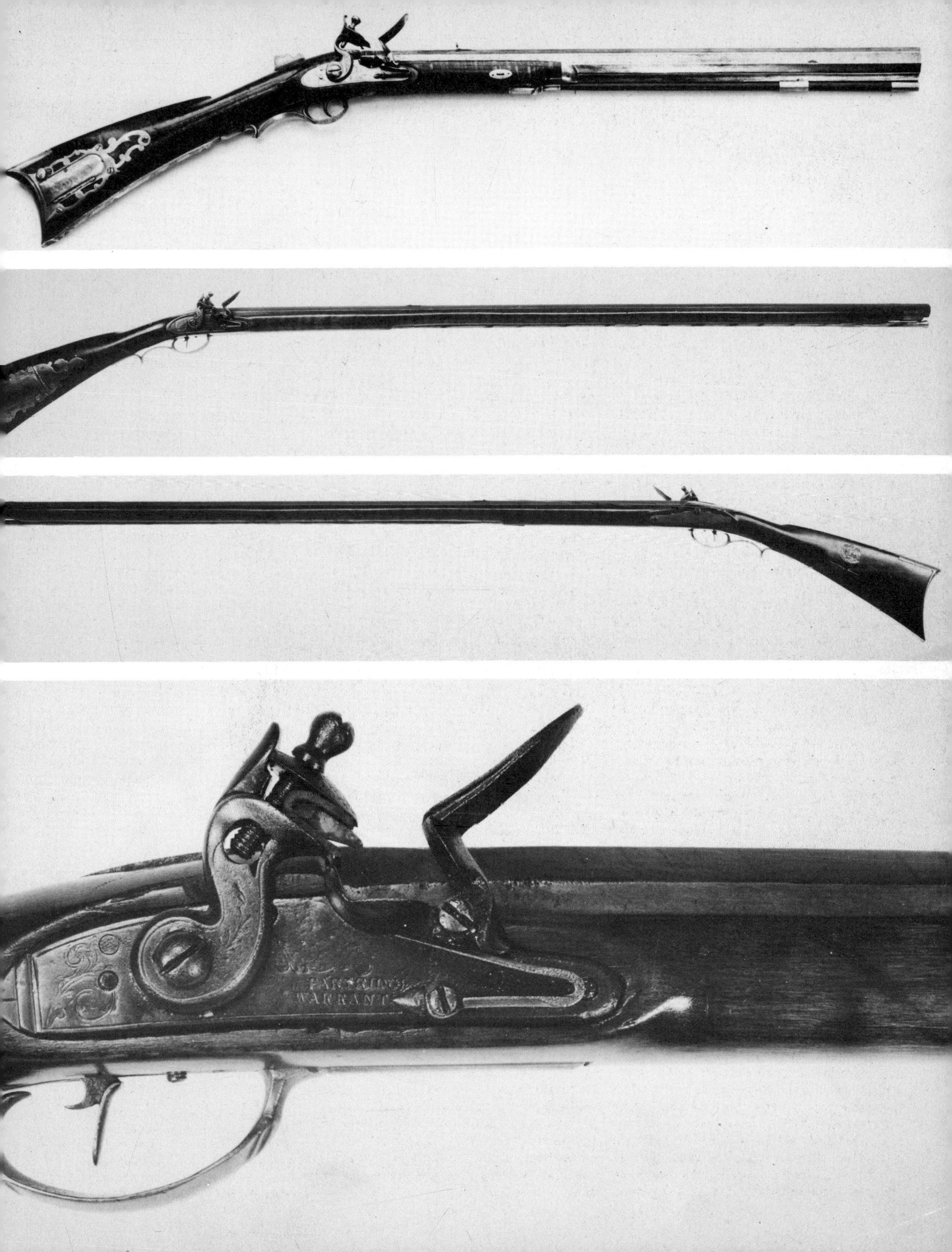

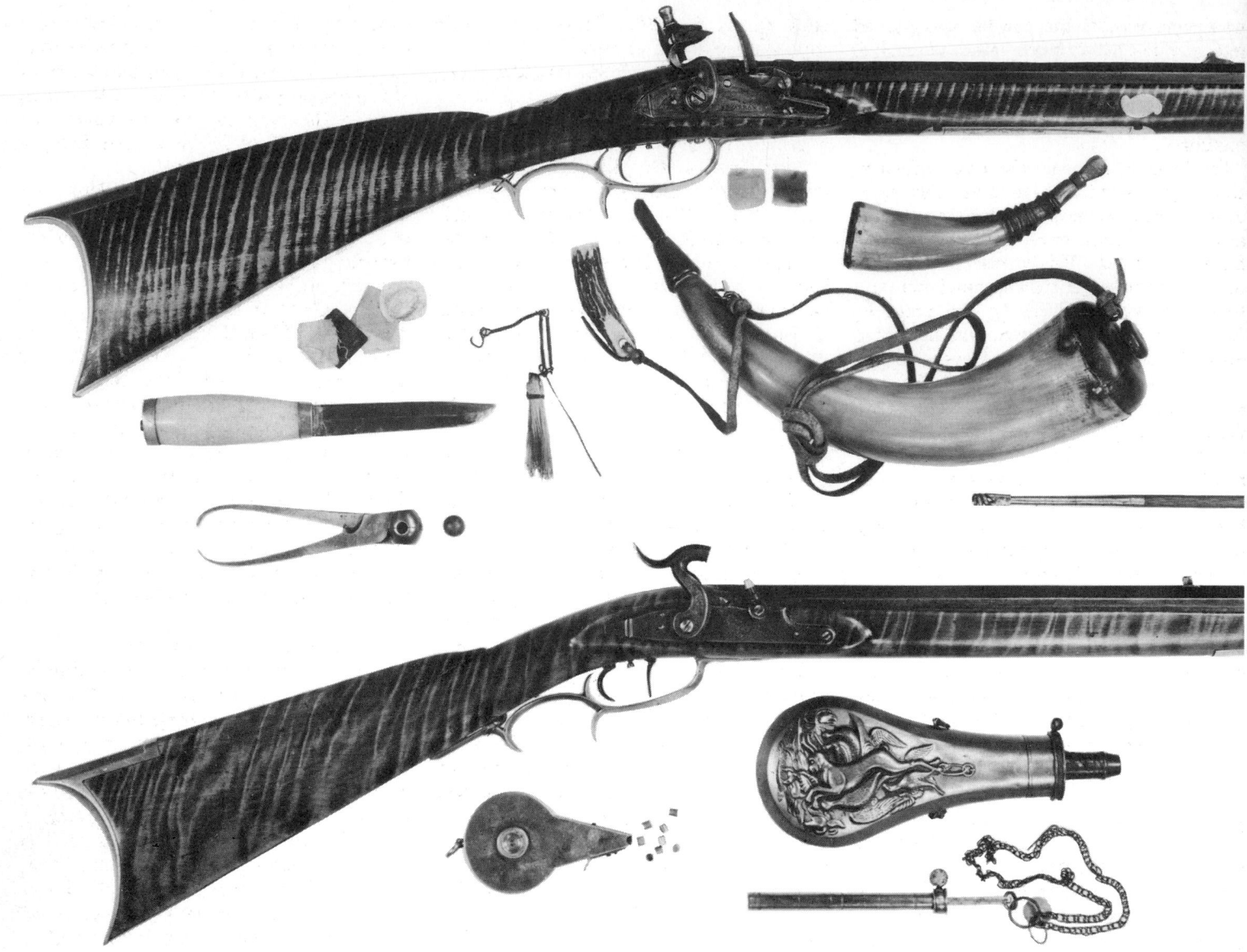

Above: Two Kentucky-type rifles. Top: a typical fully-stocked flintlock Kentucky complete with accessories. The lock is marked WARRANTED. Bottom: a similar weapon converted to percussion, also complete with loading accessories. Note the mechanical capper. (By courtesy of the Winchester Museum)

The addition of sulphur, obtained from volcanic areas and processed by vaporizing and cooling into what is generally termed 'flowers of sulphur', resulted in a solid-state which in turn was melted and moulded. Lastly came the third ingredient – charcoal. Favourite and easily obtainable woods for this purpose were willow, poplar and alder. Small pieces or 'chips' were packed into iron containers and sealed; the only exit a flue which allowed the gasses to escape when the containers were placed in a furnace or on a fire. The subsequent ash or charcoal was then ready for use. The three ingredients were mixed in the proportions previously mentioned, and ground to various sizes of granule to suit priming or main charges. Various methods were employed to establish

the right mixture; but on the frontier, where necessity dictated speed, sometimes crude methods proved the simplest, and generally worked well. The outcome was that the frontiersmen were now in a position to kill game at long range with limited risk to themselves, and the respect shown by Indians when confronted by such men, who could easily keep them out of arrow range, was comforting.

But gunpowder and its manufacture was only one of the many problems faced by the frontiersmen. The carrying of it and its subsequent use inspired much thought. The British and French armies were provided with various forms of prepared paper cartridges which were widely copied. The French loaded up with 189 grains of powder; the British with 163 and the Americans 160. The cartridges were simple: a prepared paper 'tube' with one end tied, against which the ball nestled, and the charge was then poured in. The open end was twisted to seal in the powder. Prior to loading, the twisted end was torn or bitten off, the pan was

primed from the cartridge powder, and the remainder was rammed into the barrel. Where prepared ammunition was unavailable, the soldier or frontiersman relied upon loose powder and ball. Balls were usually cast in large numbers in specially made moulds and carried in a pouch. Powder was normally contained in a stoppered flask or horn – on the frontier the latter was most common; fashioned from cattle horns, these were crude but efficient. Accounts differ, but one of the commonest forms of establishing the right charge for a rifle or musket was for the shooter to place a ball in his hand and cover it with powder. Other methods tried included a trial and error shot on a snowy day to see how much unburned powder was strewn around as the charge was increased – the object being to reduce or increase the charge to ensure that as much as possible was burned in the barrel. Once the right charge had been decided, a measure (either a hollowed-out horn or a small dipper) was prepared and attached to the flask by a rawhide thong. When required, the flask stopper was removed and the powder was poured into the measure. Much later, of course, powder horns included a proper charger, and by the mid nineteenth century they were manufactured in metal with precise measures.

On the frontier the new breed of 'riflemen' were men apart. Where most folk were content with the uncomplicated smooth-bore arms, the riflemen were continually looking for improvements. This concern for accuracy instead of fire-power soon elevated them to a legendary status which, by the time the Revolutionary War started, was bordering upon the miraculous. It was even claimed that the British Army in North America lacked recruits from England for fear of the deadly riflemen of the woods and forests. So worried were the British that the government ordered that an American rifleman, complete with weapon, be captured unharmed and brought to London. According to the story, a raiding-party captured one Corporal Walter Crouse, of York County, Pennsylvania, who, together with his rifle, was promptly dispatched to London and lodged in the Tower. To his surprise, he was not 'beheaded' as he at first had feared, but was invited to demonstrate his marksmanship publically before King George III. This he did willingly, and daily hit targets at 200 yards, four times the effective range of the conventional smooth-bore musket. The King was so shocked, it is said, that he hurriedly hired Hessian rifle companies to boost his redcoats' fading morale.

It is true that King George did hire Hessian troops, but not because his own troops were afraid to fight the American

riflemen. At that time the rifle in British service was practically non-existent, whereas Hessians and Brunswickers were already trained and equipped with rifles which also owed their origin to the Jaeger – in fact they were frequently referred to as 'Jaeger Troops'. Of the large number of German troops used in the war, however, only about 4,000 were riflemen. Their numbers were increased slightly by loyalist riflemen who acted as scouts, guides and snipers. The remainder of Washington's Continental Army were armed with muskets similar to the British Brown Bess and the French Charleville. This latter weapon, or rather its name 'Charleville', is today a generic term for the French Model 1763 flintlock musket, first manufactured at the Royal Manufactory at Charleville, but generally produced by the armouries at Maubeuge and St. Etienne. It was the 1763 version that was selected as a pattern by the United States Government when it set up a number of national armouries after the war.

Despite the marvellous accuracy of the Kentucky riflemen, the British, too, had what could almost be called a 'secret weapon' which not only matched the Kentucky-type arms, but in one respect at least, was its superior, for it was equipped with one important refinement that the American weapon lacked – it was a breech-loader. The rifle was the work of a Scotsman from Aberdeenshire, Patrick Ferguson, formerly a captain in the 70th Regiment of Foot. Aware of the earlier work of the Frenchman, Isaac de la Chaumette, Ferguson had examined his original design, noted its faults and improved upon it. The result was extremely effective,

consisting of a plug with a quick thread screwed vertically through the breech end of the barrel, the base being joined to the front of the trigger guard. One turn of the guard lowered the plug so that the bullet and powder charge could be poured into an aperture on top of the barrel.

At first the British Board of Ordnance were sceptical, but on 27 April 1776, a trial was held before the Master General of the Ordnance at Woolwich. Despite high winds and rain, Ferguson amazed the officials by hitting a target 200 yards away. He set up a steady rate of fire of four shots per minute for five minutes, then, in an extra minute of rapid fire, he fired six shots. Not content with an already impressive performance, he began to walk towards the target maintaining a steady rate of four shots per minute. He even poured water into the pan and down the barrel of the piece to dampen the charge, but within half a minute he was firing again. His final accomplishment was to lie on his back and hit a target 100 yards away. During the whole performance he missed only three times!

The Ordnance ordered 100 rifles on Ferguson's pattern, and he was permitted to supervise their construction. In 1777 he was placed in charge of 100 hand-picked marksmen and shipped to America where the war was at its height. He and his men, clothed in green instead of red, were attached to the Hessian General Knyphausen's column under the command of General Sir William Howe. Soon afterwards, near Germantown, it is reported that Ferguson found a figure wandering about the lines and demanded that he identify himself. It was Washington!

Right: A Ferguson-type weapon, marked VERNCOMB on the lock plate. The weapon is a 14 bore, 53 inches overall with a 36-inch, eight-groove deeply rifled barrel. It is equipped with a flip-up, concealed, three-peep rearsight and the butt cap contains a spring-operated cavity housing a 5-inch steel socket bayonet. (By courtesy of Messrs Wallis & Wallis)

Below: A rare 28 bore Ferguson-type breech-loading flintlock rifle. The weapon is 49 inches overall with a 33-inch barrel with eight-groove rifling. The maker was Leah of London. The number of makers who manufactured Ferguson-type weapons is unknown, but it is evident that his principle was much admired. (By courtesy of Messrs Wallis & Wallis)

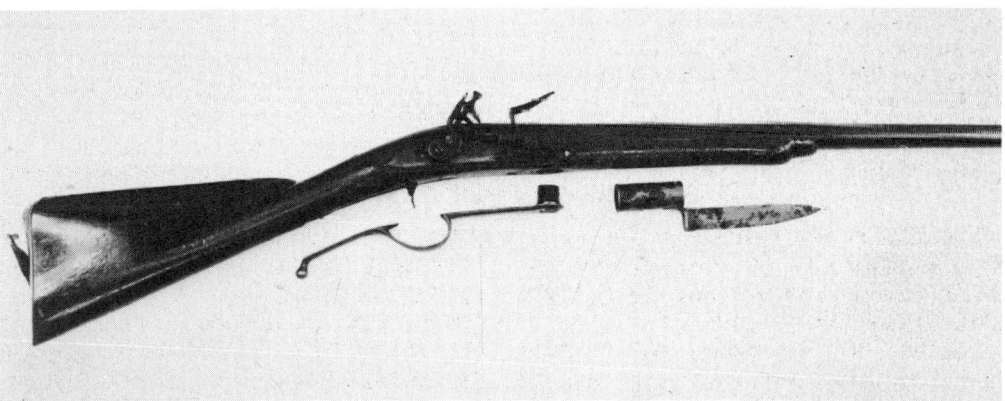

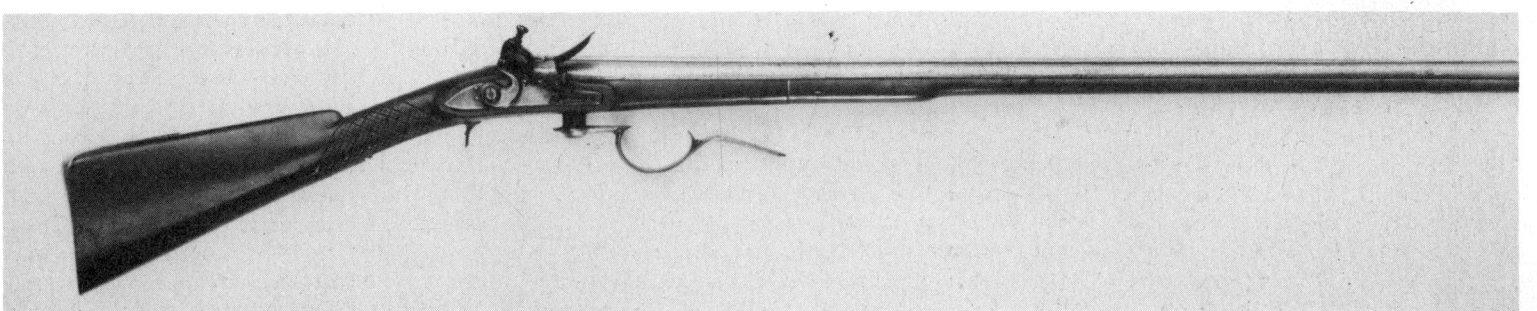

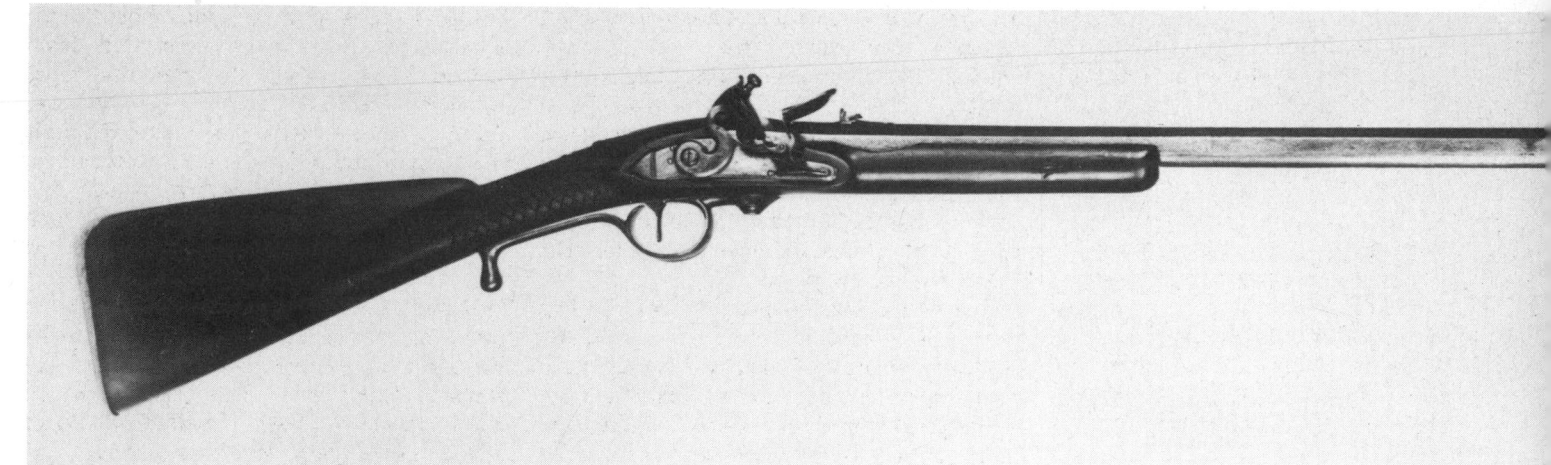

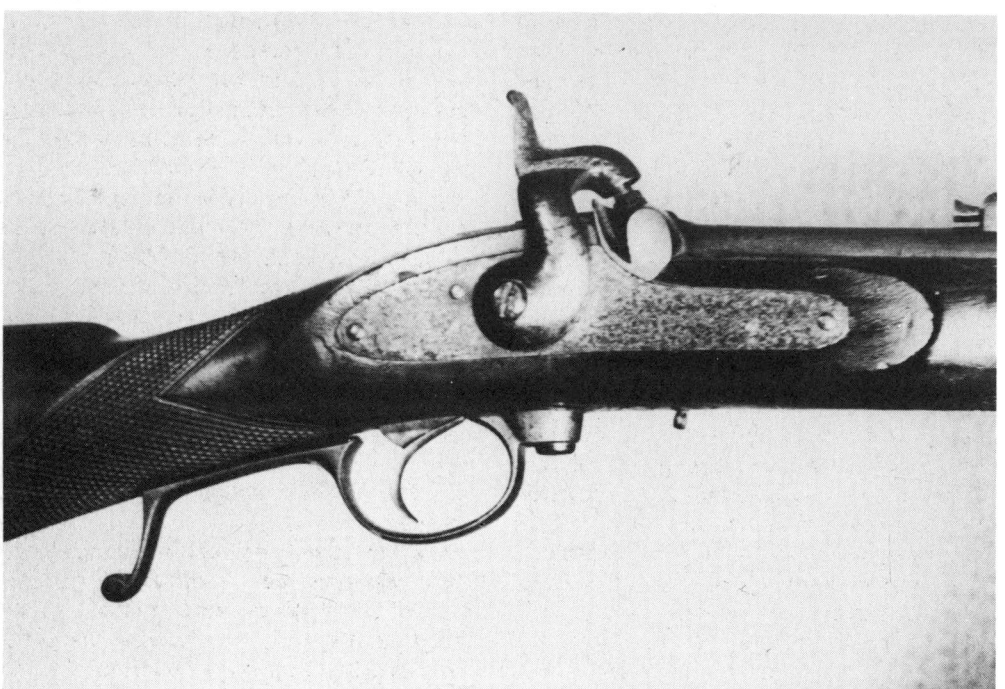

Above: A most interesting Ferguson-type officer's carbine complete with a triangular bayonet, but with no provision for a ramrod. A number of similar weapons without ramrods have been found – evidently, apart from cleaning, it was not thought necessary for a breech-loader. (By courtesy of West Point Museum)

Left and below: A Reeve's patent carbine, made in the 1840s or 1850s, which owes much to the Ferguson. (Private Collection)

What he was doing there is not known, but it is claimed that the General simply stared disdainfully at the muzzle of the rifle and at the officer behind it, turned, and walked away.

Ferguson's further career was one of excitement and achievement. He and his company of the 71st Highlanders performed well at Chadd's Ford, where he was hit in the arm, which fortunately was saved, although he could hardly move it thereafter. On 7 October 1780 at King's Mountain, on the boundary between the Carolinas, Ferguson, in command of 1,100 Loyalist militia and his riflemen, was attacked by about 900 patriotic riflemen from the Carolinas and Tennessee. American estimates state that eight British redcoats died for every rifleman killed, and that when Ferguson exposed himself to the enemy's fire in an effort to rally his men, he was killed, pierced by seven rifle balls.

Of the original 100 rifles issued to him and his men, very few are known to have survived, but it is a frontier tradition that as recently as the early years of this century, 'Hillbillys' and others in the Appalachian and Ozark mountains were armed with, in addition to the usual collection of shotguns, Winchesters and Kentuckys, a handful of 'breech-loader Fergusons' that great-grand-pappy had liberated from the British back in the War of Independence. If even a part of that tradition is true, it is understandable, for the Ferguson rifle was a most remarkable weapon.

But with Ferguson's death, so, too, died (for the time being) any further interest in rifles by the British Army. The truth was

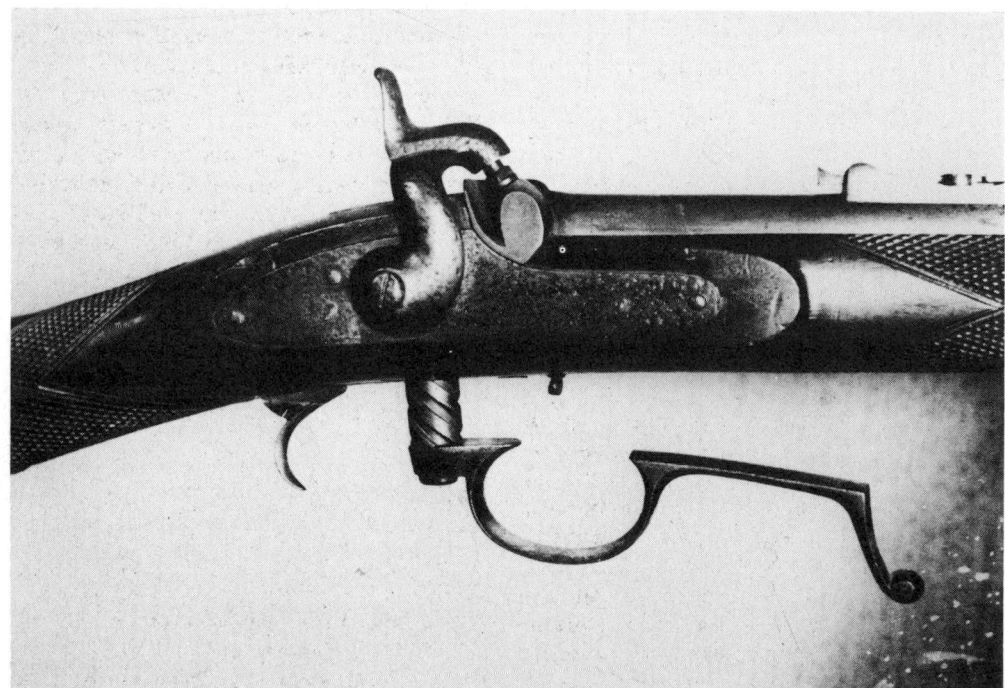

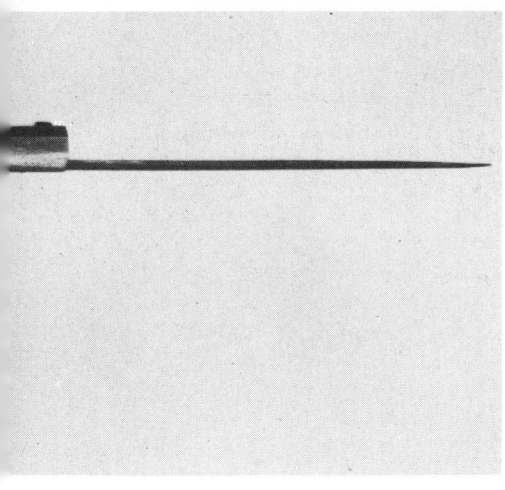

that neither the Americans nor the British placed much faith in rifles, for they were really far ahead of their time. On both sides the average soldier was practically illiterate, and little attempt was made to encourage the introduction of anything more sophisticated than the easy-to-load-and-fire musket. As a result, both armies followed the European preference for massed fire-power, and left the riflemen to take care of skirmishing and sniping.

But the legends abounded, and over the years the early long riflemen have emerged very much as men apart, equalled only in status by the later gunfighters. For these men were different. They had learned to live off the land; to survive in a wilderness where the ability to hunt and trap animals for food became second nature. And most important, they knew how to survive in hostile Indian country, where discretion was often the better part of valour. Bitten by wanderlust, a sense of adventure and the age-old desire to see just what did lie over the hill, the result of their lonely existence was a characteristic individualism which survived in legend long after they were gone. For words, like shots, were never wasted, and a man's reputation depended as much on his taciturnity among equals as on his marksmanship when put to the test.

Among the legendary riflemen of the early West was Lewis Wetzel, a noted Indian-killer from the Western Virginia Panhandle, which is now a part of West Virginia. Between 1770 and the 1790s Wetzel is reputed to have killed about 100 Indians. What prompted this extreme behaviour is not clear, and one cannot help disbelieving some of the more lurid deeds credited to him. One story, however, persists. It is claimed that he was ambushed in Ohio by a band of Indians and reloaded his long rifle three times while on the run, dodging from trunk to trunk as he fled. Three more scalps were added to his belt!

One of the most famous of American Frontiersmen, Daniel Boone (1734–1820)

was reputed to have been able to hit a target at 200 yards every time with his rifle. Perhaps there was some truth in this, for it is reliably reported that his obsession with hunting, exploring and any kind of challenge made him very self-reliant. Legend ever asserts that his dislike of 'civilization' was so intense that if he saw the smoke from a fire, no matter how distant, he moved 'before the place gets too crowded'.

The Kentucky rifle has been described as the 'All American Weapon'. Although evolved primarily as a hunting gun, it was a vast improvement upon available German- and Austrian-inspired sporting and military rifled arms of the time. As we have pointed out, its design was influenced by many factors. The shape can be traced back to French and English fowling pieces of the seventeenth and eighteenth centuries, and the immigrant German gunsmiths who settled in Pennsylvania and Virginia pioneered and perfected it. But the most important part of the Kentucky's success was in its method of loading. The arduous practice of pouring powder down the barrel followed by a ball which had to be hammered home (the most serious disadvantage of the Jaeger) became a thing of the past when American gunsmiths developed a simple and effective improvement. Once the powder had been poured down the barrel, it was followed by a greasy patch made of cloth or buckskin. This was placed on the muzzle, greasy side down, and the ball was pushed on to it until both had cleared the mouth of the muzzle. Next, the rammer was employed to force down the ball and patch sealing them against the powder. When the rifle was fired, the soft lead bullet expanded forcing the greasy patch into the rifling, thereby lubricating the passage of the bullet out of the gun. This also helped clean the bore, a most important factor at a time when indifferent powder led to fouling which caused many problems. Despite all these improvements, however, even a highly skilled rifleman could only load his weapon twice a minute, whereas a trained soldier of the line could, on occasion, manage three rounds per minute – and we should not forget Ferguson's four rounds per minute!

The combination of the patch and the freedom to experiment, which was lacking in military arms, led to many civilian-oriented refinements. Special compartments were fitted in the stock for patches and became regular features. Early patch boxes were made of wood, but later, brass became common and some of these were engravers' works of art. The heavy German stock gave way to the slender and graceful version now so familiar to the collector and historian. Some early Kentucky stocks were probably made from straight-grain American walnut,

but by the time of the weapon's heyday, the commonest stocks were fabricated from striped maple, which became the most popular.

But it was the long, rifled barrel that was most important. Trial and error determined the best charge and calibre to suit the individual, and the increased accuracy and velocity contributed greatly to its legend. It has even been claimed that George Washington boasted that his sharp-shooters could 'hit a sheet of notepaper (about eight inches by ten inches) three times out of five shots at a quarter of a mile'. Such accuracy and at such a distance is immediately suspect and raises the questions: 'How accurate was the Kentucky and what was its range?' Modern tests conducted in the 1950s in Arizona were impressive. An original rifle firing a .457 calibre ball reached a muzzle velocity of 2,410 feet per second, and tests for penetration, range and accuracy with an original flintlock rifle loaded with a ball weighing 159 grains and backed by 56 grains of black powder penetrated 2½ inches through chestnut planks at fifty feet. With an initial velocity of 1,600 feet per second, the penetration at 300 yards was three-quarters of an inch.

Tests at long range, at a man-sized target, produced the following results:

at 100 yards out of ten shots, ten hit the target

at 200 yards another ten hits were recorded

at 300 yards only five hits were registered

The rifle used was fitted with a spirally-grooved barrel which, when tested against straight-grooved or smooth-bore weapons, was found to be infinitely superior – in the latter's case they tended to tail off, one out of ten shots at 100 yards.

A vital consideration, regardless of calibre, rifling or other refinements was, of course, the gunpowder used and in what quantity. Opinions differ, and no two experts agree. Old wives' tales about using enough black powder to cover the round ball if one didn't know the correct load may well have some truth, but for accurate measurement a more scientific approach was necessary. *The American Rifleman* for November 1949, cited Ned H. Roberts (author of *The Muzzle-Loading Cap Lock Rifle*) who advocated three grains of powder for each seven-grain weight of ball, and produced the following table:

Calibre	Ball Weight		Powder
.31 ball	60 grains	=	25 grains
.36 ball	90 grains	=	38½ grains
.44 ball	118 grains	=	50 grains
.50 ball	198 grains	=	85 grains

Similarly, tests carried out by others, notably the University of California in 1935, revealed some quite startling results. A .45

calibre flintlock rifle was loaded with a 135-grain ball (complete with a grease patch) and various powder charges from thirty grains to 100. Its most efficient charge was forty grains. The 100-grain charge increased the muzzle velocity considerably, but accuracy declined. Thus it is understandable why the Kentucky rifle gained such a reputation, especially among those who had no idea of the science of ballistics, but cared much about the effects of stopping power and accuracy at long and short range.

So, in summary, a Kentucky rifle in the hands of an expert is capable of producing 2- and 3-inch groups at 100 yards; but over 200 and 300 yards is erratic, and its accuracy declines. At 100 yards, however, the Kentucky has been able to hold its own against many modern arms. Despite its great reputation and the many legends built up around it, its role as a destructive force against the British was inspired not by the Revolutionary War but by the War of 1812.

The declaration of war between England and America in 1812 could not have come at a worse time for the British. Already stretched to the limit in the Peninsular, where Wellington was combating Napoleon's designs on Spain and Portugal, the arrogance of the British Government in stopping American vessels from trading with the Continent unless they first put into British ports, infuriated the Americans. The situation was further aggravated by the practice of British warships in stopping American vessels to remove forcibly alleged deserters from the British Army and Navy. Unfortunately, the decision to repeal the Acts which permitted these actions, came too late to prevent the United States from declaring war – with disastrous results for the British.

The American Navy, although much smaller, had better armed and larger ships than those ranged against them. British captains, convinced that they could destroy any other ship at sea, were frequently defeated by their better equipped adversary, and not until Captain Broke of the *Shannon* defeated the *Chesapeake* was honour satisfied. None the less, these naval actions were of minor importance compared to the events on land. There was a great deal of fighting on the Canadian frontier, and a large number of British regulars, veterans of the Peninsular army which, according to Wellington, could go anywhere and do anything, were sent out to fight in 1814. Wellington himself did not go, partly because his presence was still much in demand in Europe, and because he appreciated all too clearly the hopelessness of the task. But by 1814 the fervour of war had moderated and on both sides of the Atlantic people were tired of fighting, and the respective governments were resentful of the drain on resources.

In December 1814 the Commissioners of both sides signed the Treaty of Ghent which restored the pre-war boundaries, but settled no other issues. Tragically, news of peace did not reach New Orleans in time to prevent Lieutenant-General Sir Edward Pakenham, Hero of Salamanca, from leading his veterans against Andrew Jackson, who was defending the place from behind a barricade of cotton bales, cypress logs and anything solid that could be found.

Jackson's army consisted of a motley crew of local militia, a few hundred United States Army regulars, mostly armed with smooth-bore muskets, and a determined band of Gulf Coast pirates led by the legendary Lafitte (whom legend credits with the supply of flints and powder), together with about 200 Kentucky and Tennessee riflemen, whose loyalty to Jackson bordered upon open adulation, and more than made up for their lack of military training. Against this 'rabble' as some of the British officers called them, were ranged some of the toughest troops in the British Army. Pakenham's object was to seize New Orleans, thus securing permanent control of the Mississippi Valley, whose economic survival depended upon the port of New Orleans.

When the battle commenced, Jackson's army, outnumbered by more than two to one, relied upon his cannon to wreak havoc among the British forces. Despite the terrible slaughter, their rigid discipline held, and heedless of the swampy terrain, the most formidable fighting force in the world advanced, colours bravely flying and each man prepared to fight or die. It was a very moving yet tragic sight. Jackson, who had no love for the British, but admired courage when he saw it, realized that unless he stopped them all would be lost. Turning to his frontier riflemen he ordered them to shoot, preferably at the officers, as soon as the British were in range.

Standing four deep, the riflemen poured a withering fire into the British ranks. As one man fired he stepped to the rear and another took his place. The result was predictable. Pakenham was killed, as were most of his senior officers, and it is claimed that the highest ranking officer left alive was a major who called the retreat. The British losses were about 2,000 while the Americans claimed only eight killed and about thirteen wounded. Historians have debated the issue for years; some concluding that Jackson won because his men were well protected by their bales and logs, and that his initial devastating cannon fire had won the day. Others, however, believe that he owed victory to his riflemen. An anonymous ballad composer paid the following tribute to the riflemen in the fifth stanza of an eight-verse broadside entitled *The Hunters of Kentucky, or the Battle of New Orleans* which established the name 'Kentucky' for all time:

But Jackson he was wide awake,
    And wasn't scar'd at trifles,
For well he knew what aim we take,
    With our Kentucky rifles.
So he led us up to a cyprus swamp,
    The ground was low and mucky,
There stood John Bull in martial pomp,
    And here stood old Kentucky.

Ironically, the Americans had lost almost every land engagement of the war – even Washington was abandoned and partly burned. The Presidential Mansion was hastily repaired and painted white to hide the scars (and today retains the name 'White House'). But that one last battle established the legend of the long riflemen, and for years after the two wars between England and America, veterans of both continued to enthral audiences with stories of their own or others' heroics. Some were dispassionate enough to praise the courage of both armies, while others brightened many a winter's evening in the local tavern with stories of

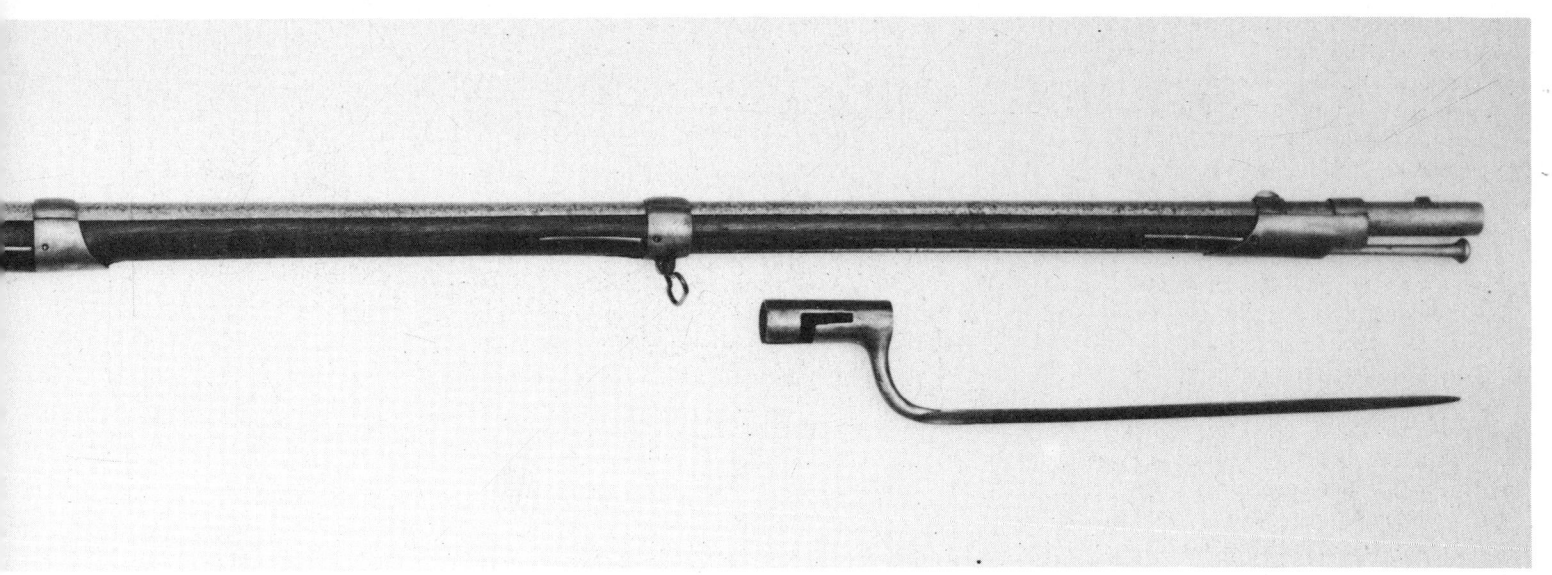

Above: A fine Model 1795 smooth-bore musket complete with bayonet. (By courtesy of the Winchester Museum)

how they or friends had killed British officers. The American rifleman was a force to be reckoned with, and he would soon make his mark.

When England and the United States had resolved their differences in the Peace Treaty of 3 September 1783, and the last redcoat had left New York on 25 November, the following years, up to their final confrontation (the War of 1812), saw a growing fascination on the part of Americans with what lay beyond the Appalachians to the West. Lewis and Clark's expedition to the Pacific in 1804–06 followed by Zebulon Pike and others, had opened up the frontier West to a breed of men who, in their way, greatly influenced American exploration and inspired changes in existing firearms. These were the legendary 'Mountain Men'.

As a type they were unique, for they flourished during a time of economic expansion and for almost forty years they were a law unto themselves. Bitter rivalries between fur companies and nationalities – notably American and British – which had huge investments in the trapping business, also led to rivalry among individuals. Then, abruptly, during the 1840s, it all came to an end, largely because of increased Western migration, and to a lesser but significant extent because public taste had changed. Silk hats were replacing 'beavers' in popularity, and the annual wholesale destruction of the beaver and other fur-bearing creatures had set pelts at a premium too high for a market which demanded a quick turnover and quick profits. But during the heyday of the trapping and hunting business, famous names like the Hudson's Bay Company (which still exists) and the American Fur Company, and others long gone and forgotten, vied with one another for territory and contracts, and left behind an image of a breed of men who can reasonably be regarded as the toughest frontiersmen of them all.

By the 1830s, when the trade was in decline, and the various companies were at loggerheads, they were becoming increasingly perturbed by the number of so-called 'free trappers' or 'mountaineers' who had forsaken the companies and joined various bands or brigades, and worked their way into the Rocky Mountains. A typical mountain man of the early 1840s was described by Rufus B. Sage in his book *Rocky Mountain Life* (published in 1857): 'His waist is encircled with a belt of leather, holding encased his butcher-knife and pistols, while from his neck is suspended a bullet-pouch securely fastened to the belt in front, and beneath the right arm hangs a powder-horn transversely from his shoulder, behind which, upon the strap attached to it, are affixed his bullet-mould, ball-screw, wiper, and &c. With a gun-stock made of some hard wood, and a good rifle placed in his hands carrying from thirty-five balls to the pound, the reader will have before him a genuine mountaineer, when fully equipped.'

In 1825 the mountain men began staging an annual rendezvous at Henry's Fork on the Green River, to which place they brought their pelts, sometimes worth several thousand dollars. They sold their goods to the traders and then indulged in a round of gambling, drinking, fighting and anything else that was going until their money or credit ran out and they were forced to return to the mountains. The last rendezvous was held in 1840, by which time the beaver trade was almost dead, the Indians increasingly hostile, and the emphasis was on the buffalo as a source of vast profits.

When Lewis and Clark, and later Pike, prepared to march off into the wilderness that was the West, the matter of which guns to take was an important consideration. The early explorers and trappers were armed with a wide assortment of weapons. Some contented themselves with standard military-style or issue muskets, a popular version being the Model 1795, which was on a par with the Brown Bess of the day. This was an important weapon, for it had been copied almost part-for-part from the French Charleville Model of 1763. Unlike the Brown Bess, which had a calibre of .75, the Charleville/Model 1795's calibre was .69 – a 370-grain bullet and a powder charge of 189 grains compared to the 500-grain Brown Bess bullet backed by 163 grains.

In trials the Model 1795 proved so popular that it was produced in large numbers at a new National Armoury set up at Springfield, Massachusetts. Fitted with a black walnut stock, 56⅜ inches long and a 44¾-inch barrel, the unloaded weapon weighed almost nine pounds. Like most military weapons, it was not really suited for frontier use where its lead ball, although ideal for stopping elk or deer at close range, was useless beyond sixty yards so that many hunters loaded with shot.

From Canada came another weapon, one that was very popular with the French-Canadian trappers. This was the 'fuzee', a light musket or carbine properly called a 'fusil'. Its success among the hunters was short-lived, because most of them soon expressed an interest in 'them new-fangled rifles' about which they had heard so much, particularly now that it was becoming more acceptable to the United States forces.

The demise of the rifle in military service following Ferguson's death had in no way affected its development, for by 1800 it was again being given serious consideration. Among the arms taken on the Lewis and Clark expedition was the brand-new Model 1803 rifle. The party carried fifteen of them, together with the same number of powder horns, pouches, bullet moulds and other accessories and spares, plus 200 pounds of best 'rifle powder'. These weapons proved their worth and indicate that the superiority of the rifle was already gaining steadily over that of smooth-bore weapons.

Congress also recognized the value of the rifle: in 1800 they authorized the establishment of a regiment of riflemen in the U.S. Army, but it was 1803 before the Secretary of War decided that such a weapon should be standardized. Developed at Harpers Ferry, the Model 1803 underwent a degree of experimentation before it was available for issue to troops. The army's preference for shorter barrels had been noted by the War Department and the production model had a barrel of 32½ inches. The calibre was .54. The original specification called for a steel rather than a wooden ramrod, and the barrel was to be round from the muzzle to within ten inches of the breech, which was octagonal in form. The weapon was half-stocked (that is, the stock ended in front of the breech, leaving the barrel and rammer exposed) and fitted with a patch box in the butt similar to the Kentucky style.

The Ordnance Department decided that the calibre should remain at .54 and the powder charge was to be between 90 and 100 grains of fine-grain powder suitable for rifles. A paper cartridge was prepared, and the bullet, wrapped in linen, was in turn sheathed in thin leather covered in tallow. The weapon's recoil was thought to be excessive, but it was popular among the troops despite criticism from the Ordnance, and more than 4,500 of the Model 1803s were manufactured between 1804 and 1808. Those issued to Lewis and Clark were among the earliest manufactured.

Generally, however, military-style weapons were not favoured by plainsmen

and mountain men of the period. The individual, relying as he so often did upon himself or a mere handful of companions, demanded custom-built weapons of proven reliability and equipped with refinements that made them safe to handle in confined spaces, whereas the army was more concerned with mass fire-power in the open which tended to overlook shortcomings in design.

To protect it from the elements it was customary to carry ammunition in lead-lined kegs or boxes, but these were inordinately heavy – Lewis and Clark recorded that each of their sheet lead canisters weighed eight pounds, twice as much as the weight of powder in each canister! Most mountain men travelled in small bands and carried sufficient ammunition for their immediate needs on their persons, the remainder being carried by pack animals. Included also were spare flints, mainsprings, frizzen springs, and an assortment of screws, mainspring clamps and other items, for each man had to be as self-sufficient as possible.

Since few mountain men would willingly part with their favourite weapon, the problem of trade with Indians for skins and furs, often in exchange for arms and ammunition, was solved by the introduction of 'trade guns'. As early as the seventeenth century both the French and the English had 'traded with the natives' when it suited them, and distributed guns. And those who fondly believe that the white man was superior because the guns he traded to the Indians were poorly made are very much mistaken. Long before the turn of the eighteenth century the Indians were becoming proficient with firearms. As early as 1736 Auguste Choteau had noted that the Chickasaw Indians were armed with 'rifles' and were generally thought to be good shots. It is believed that the rifles referred to were

Kentucky- or Jaeger-type arms captured from or traded from the whites, because at that time no specific weapons had been designed for Indian use. This was rectified by the development of the 'trade gun'.

The trade gun was evolved from a number of different types of weapon, and was manufactured both in Europe and in the United States. It was generally lightweight, short-barrelled and cheaply made, usually with brass mounts, the latter an attraction to most of the tribes. Gauged for the most part to shoot a one-ounce ball (sixteen gauge or .66 calibre), specimens have been found in smaller calibres. The trigger guard was made extra large to permit the user to fire the weapon while wearing gloves or mittens, and the gun was generally designed for use in the northern part of the country, hence its close association with the Hudson's Bay Company.

Many of these weapons were made under contract in Britain for the Hudson's Bay Company by Thomas Barnett and by Bond & Company, among others. Both companies (and their mid nineteenth-century successors) were active in the provision of contract

Below left: The Model 1803 Harpers Ferry Rifle. This weapon was chosen by Lewis and Clark when they set out upon their epic expedition to the Pacific in 1804, and is also believed to have inspired the later Hawken plain (or plains) rifles. (By courtesy of the Winchester Museum)

Top right: A typical Indian trade gun of the early nineteenth century. (By courtesy of the Winchester Museum)

Centre right: Close-up of the lockwork. (By courtesy of the Winchester Museum)

Below right: Left side of the stock. Note the dragon-like ornamentation on the sideplate, typical of early trade guns, particularly those made by Barnett of London. (By courtesy of the Winchester Museum)

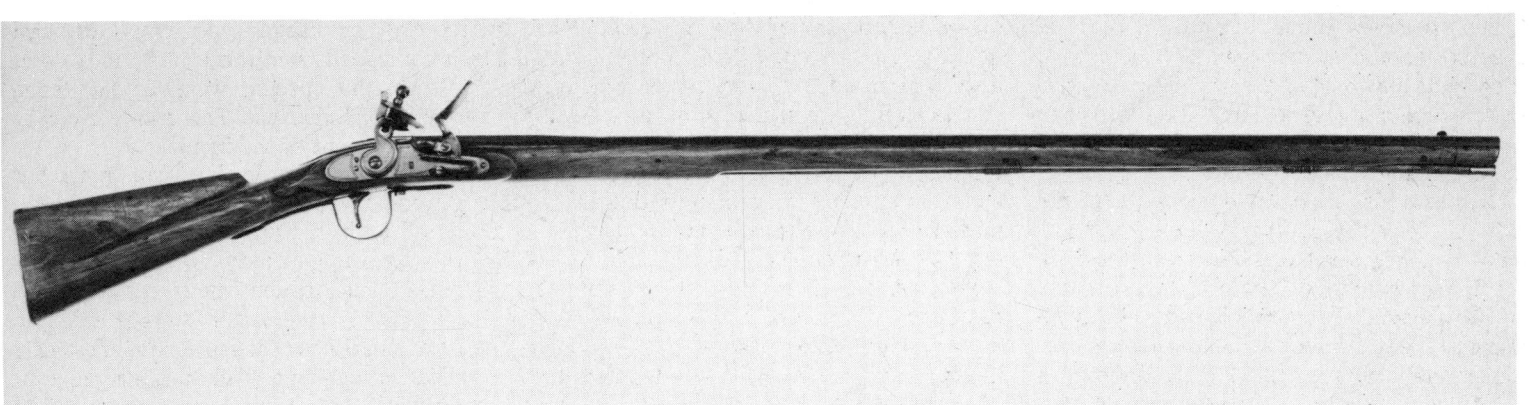

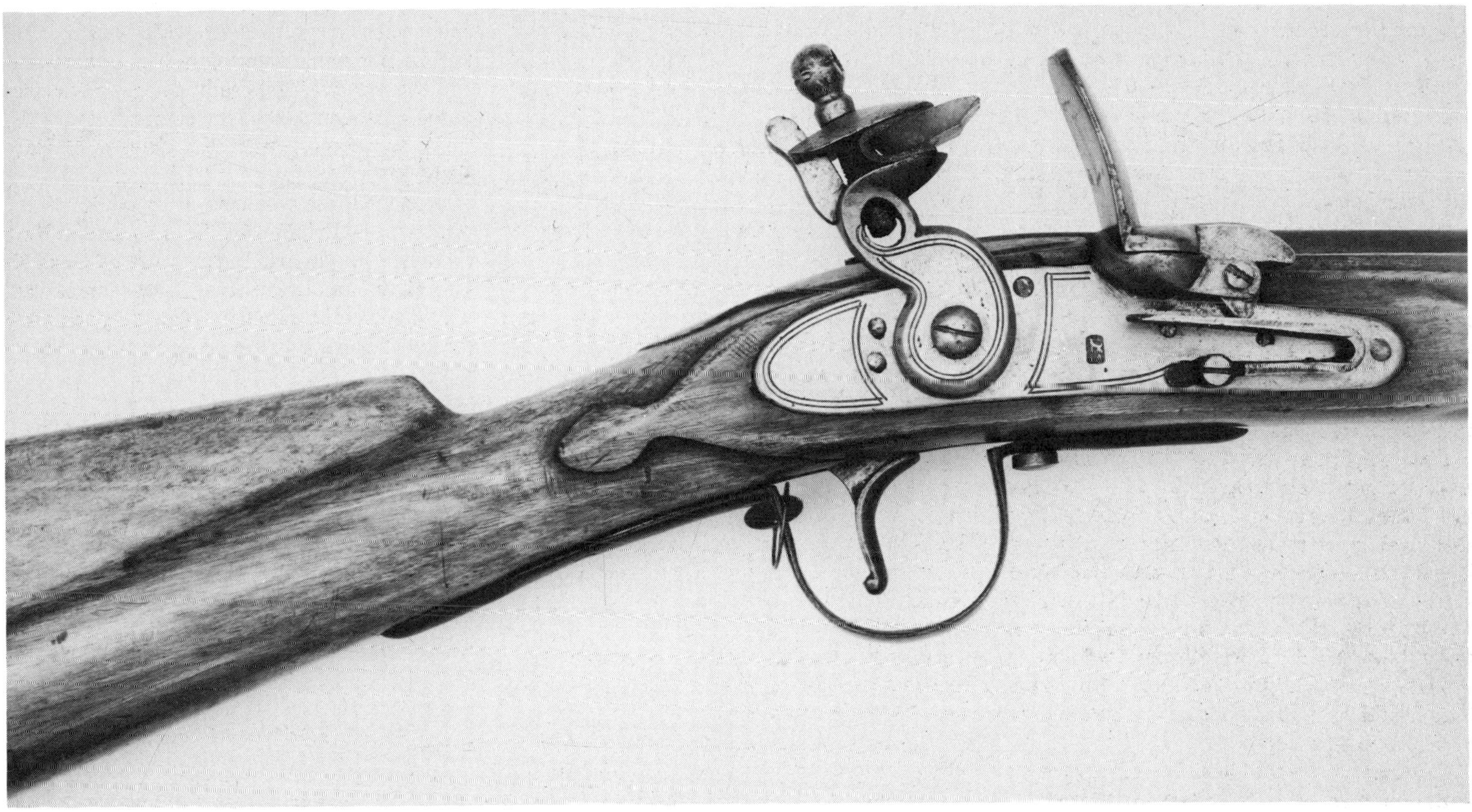

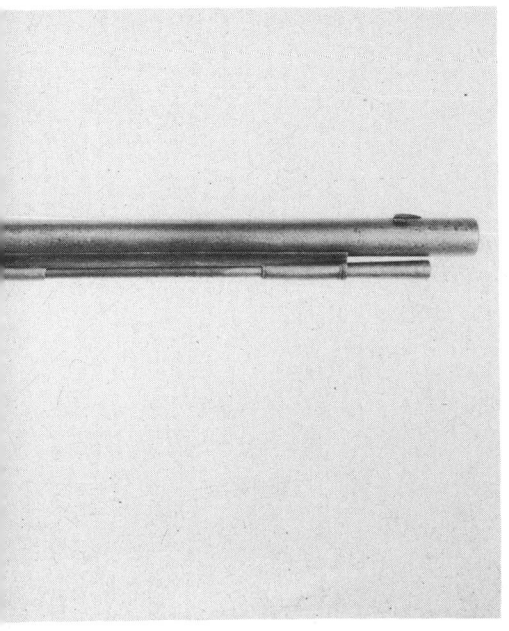

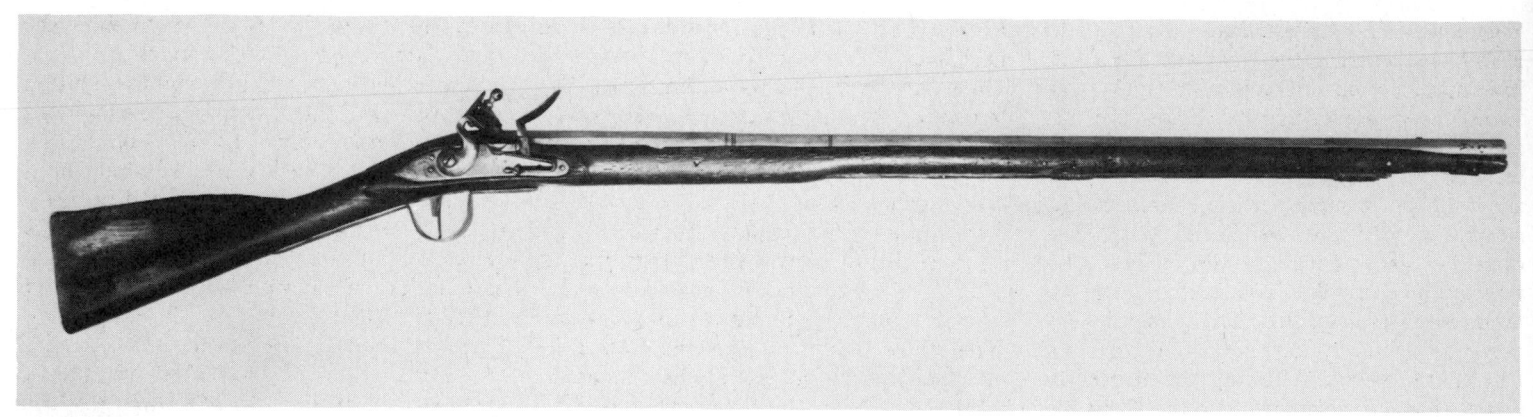

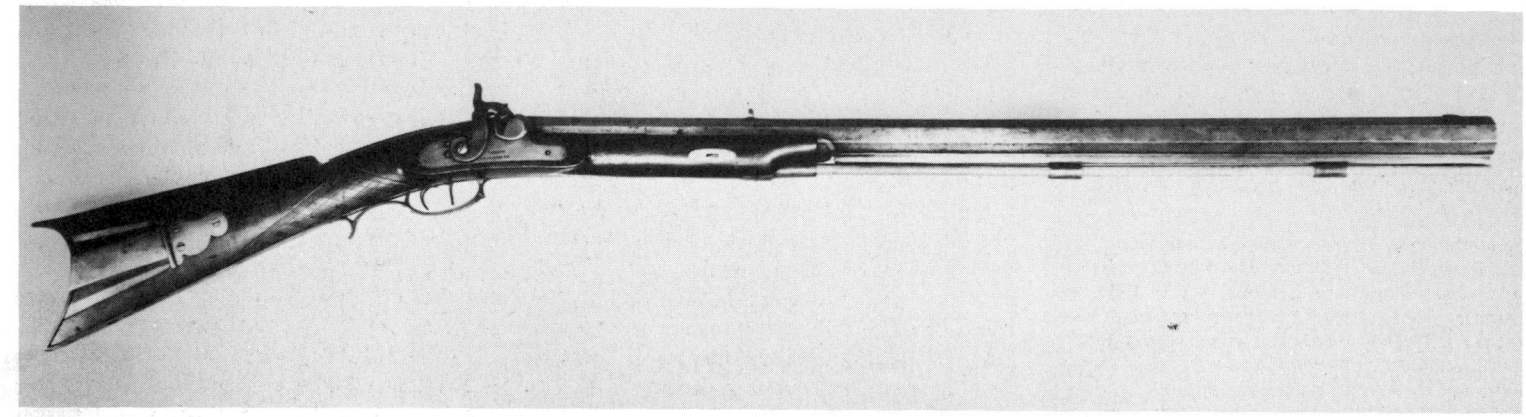

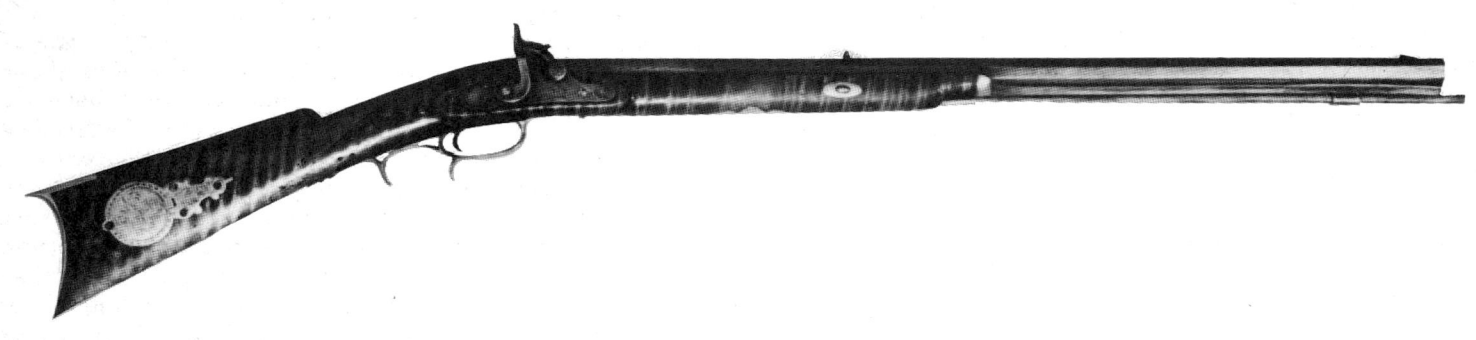

weapons to the United States and also to Britain's colonies in the Near and Far East. The most famous of the trade guns was known as the 'Hudson's Bay Fuke', and has an interesting history. The 'Fuke' ('fusil') was a light-weight, generally short-barrelled smooth-bore weapon, cheaply made but sturdy. It fired a one-ounce ball, which was classified as 16-gauge or .66 calibre. The trigger guard was made extra large to accommodate a gloved hand, for it was designed primarily for use in cold climates. During the period following the American Revolution, Canadian rivals to the Hudson's Bay Company, in particular the 'North West Company', opposed to Hudson's Bay in its far-western aspirations, appropriated the 'Fuke' as their own. Thus in their own territory it was called the 'North West Gun', and the British rival, the 'Mackinaw Company', sold the identical weapon to

Top left: Trade muskets for the Indians were usually well made and there was a lively trade. Following the 'Indian Intercourse Act' of 1834, the number of makers involved in supplying such weapons doubled. Henry E. Leman, who manufactured this weapon, was very active in the 1830s and 1840s and established a good relationship with the Indian Bureau. (By courtesy of West Point Museum)

Centre left: A late, half-stocked Leman .58 calibre plains rifle. Marked H. LEMAN LANCASTER PA. on the lock plate, the weapon also has set-triggers. (By courtesy of West Point Museum)

Left: An unmarked plains rifle (similar to the Hawken) that owes its general appearance to the Kentucky. Its set-triggers and open sights are typical of the period. The gun belonged to a Kansas pioneer who used it years after the introduction of more up-to-date weapons. (By courtesy of the Kansas State Historical Society)

Below: A plains half-stocked rifle made by Gemmer. (By courtesy of the Winchester Museum)

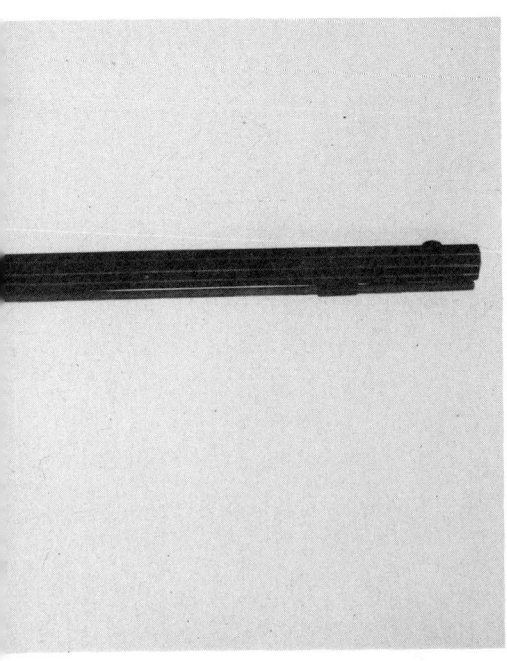

trappers for trading purposes as the 'Mackinaw Gun'. In 1808 when John Jacob Astor formed his famous 'American Fur Company', he quickly added the popular Hudson's Bay 'Fuke' to his inventory. Some claim that he tried to introduce inferior weapons as substitutes, but the Indians rejected them, for already the tribes were able to recognize quality and were beginning to realise that a maker's mark counted for much in a highly competitive market. By the 1820s many American makers had joined the increasing market in trade guns, and in the North West, in exchange for furs and pelts, the Indian was infinitely better armed than his bow-wielding cousins on the plains.

The Indian quickly appreciated the value of the gun and vied with the whites in its use against bear and buffalo. It is reported that they, too, like Lewis Wetzell, could reload on the run, and on horseback, for which latter accomplishment they preferred short-barrelled weapons. Reports of burst barrels among Indian-owned arms have been attributed by some to the poor quality of the arms supplied, but it is more likely that improper loading was the main cause. Without ramming, there was a danger that the ball would roll away from the powder charge, and leave a gap between it and the charge. This would create a 'pocket' which could lead to an explosion on ignition and burst the barrel at this point, sometimes with the loss of a hand or worse.

Most of the arms supplied to the Indians were smooth-bore, but it is on record that during the early years of the nineteenth century a number of rifles were also supplied. Of plain construction, they were none the less sturdy, for as we have already pointed out, the Indians knew what they wanted. Rounded barrels proved more popular, but octagonal were acceptable. The majority of the rifles were fitted with barrels ranging from 36 to 42 inches in length, and in calibres approximating to .52, but the Indians themselves were apt to cut down the barrel length to suit individual preference.

At various periods throughout the early years of the last century, the American Government expressed grave doubts about supplying guns to the Indians, particularly after the War of 1812; but by 1834, with the passing of the 'Indian Intercourse Act', which provided the basic authority necessary for the later procurement of such arms, the trade became extremely lucrative and some of the best known names among gunmakers are to be found on government contracts. It is ironic, therefore, that in its attempt to appease, patronise or simply pacify the Indian, the American Government, aided by innumerable individuals with diverse motives, placed in his hands the very instrument that could put him on a par with the

white man. And time alone would show the rights and wrongs of such a move.

Among the mountain men and the hunters and trappers of the plains, weapons followed a similar pattern, but the swivel gun (originally a piece of ordnance mounted on a turning pivot; eventually blunderbusses, muskets or rifles, on a yoke or swivel) was preferred to the long rifle by the beaver men and by that other tough breed, the keelboat men, who plied the mighty Mississippi and Missouri rivers. They earned their name from the nature of their employment. In ascending the rivers (before the arrival of the steam-boat) most cargo boats were propelled by poles often against a fast-flowing current. Each man was stripped to the waist (in winter and summer) and he placed his shoulder against his pole. His whole strength was then devoted to 'walking' towards the stern of the vessel along a plank or running-board. By the time he reached the stern, his head was almost level with the plank. The pole was then withdrawn, and the man ran forward to commence the operation all over again. It was tiring and thirsty work, and at the end of the day, vast quantities of raw whisky and whatever food was available were consumed before they dropped into an exhausted sleep till dawn.

Swivel guns were usually mounted prominently in the bow of a keel-boat; some in fact, were miniature cannon, firing a one-pound shot from a 30-inch barrel with a bore of about $1\frac{7}{8}$ inches. Swivel guns were often mounted atop palisades of trading-posts, serving as defence or signal guns. Lewis and Clark favoured these weapons and recorded that they put one to good use on 25 September 1804 when a band of Teton Sioux threatened to disrupt the expedition; sixteen musket balls were fired in lieu of the normal, single heavy ball.

The mountain and riverboat men were also apt to arm themselves with the so-called 'blunderbuss', the bell-mouthed scourge of many an eighteenth-century highwayman who attempted to stop a mail-coach on the King's highway. But times were changing, and the disappearance of the true Mountain Man, and the influx of hunters and others to the plains, heralded yet another innovation, one which would leave its mark long after it had disappeared, the so-called 'Plains Rifle'.

By the 1820s, as more and more men moved into the hunting areas, they brought with them an assortment of arms, prominent among them the Kentucky style which survived long after the demise of the flint-lock. When percussion ignition achieved a state of practicality that made it easy to copy, and the percussion cap (a small copper 'cup' filled with fulminate and placed upon a hollow tube or nipple, and struck by the hammer) became generally available, all

manner of weapons were produced to cater for a growing need. A number of Pennsylvania gunsmiths, including Henry Deringer (maker of the legendary 'Deringer' pistol), began to experiment with various types of weapon and to export so-called 'trade rifles' to the West. An initial success during the last days of the flintlock had established certain styles, based primarily upon the Kentucky rifles, but by the 1820s the plainsmen were demanding heavier and more robust arms

than were immediately available, and from this demand evolved what was to become the celebrated 'Plains Rifle'.

Various sources have credited its development to individual makers, but it is clear that one man in particular played a great part in it. This was Jacob Hawken. The Hawken family were well known in the gunmaking world. Of Dutch origin, the family name is thought to have been Wee Hawken, but some members anglicized it to Hawkins. Henry

Hawkins, the father of Jacob (b 1776) and his brother Samuel (b 1792), is thought to have worked for some time at the Harpers Ferry Arsenal. At some point in early life, Jacob and Samuel decided to revert to the original spelling of the family name, which has caused some difficulty for scholars and others when confronted with the various spellings of their names and of their rifles. Both brothers are credited with producing the best of all the so-called 'plains rifles',

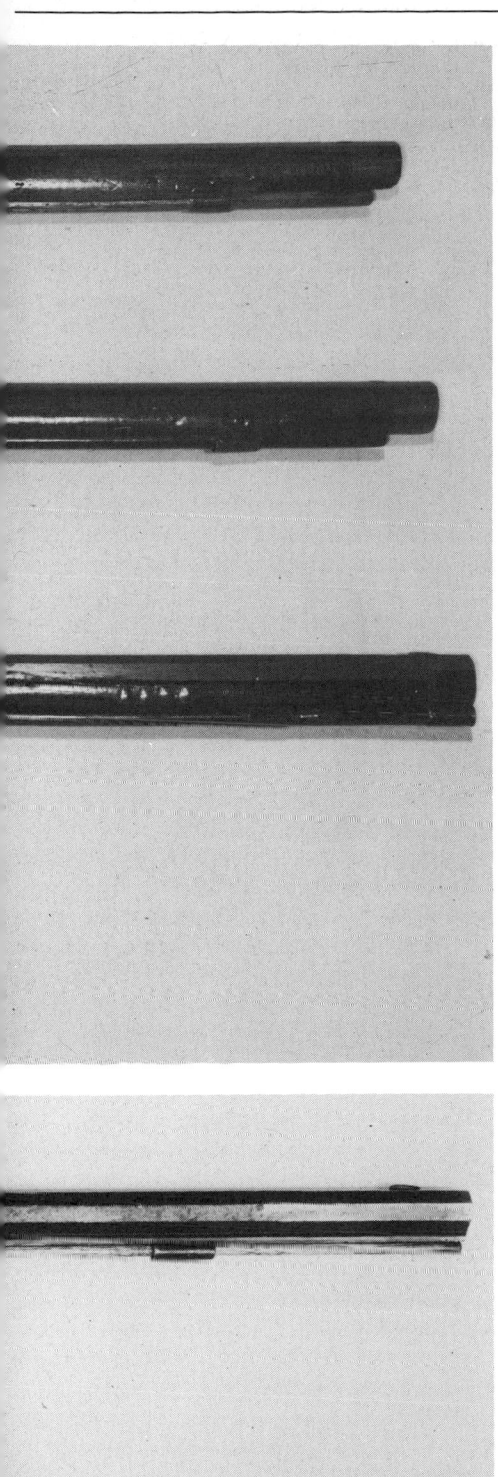

Top: Three fine specimens of the Henry E. Leman percussion rifles manufactured for Indian use. All three weapons have been repaired with buckskin or rawhide; note the brass tacks along the stock, a favourite decorative device of the Indians'. (By courtesy of Arnold Marcus Chernoff)

Above: A typical Hawken plain (or plains) rifle, circa 1840. (By courtesy of the Winchester Museum)

sometimes called 'mountain rifles', a frontier noun for a heavy muzzle-loading weapon. But by whatever name the rifles were known, they were without doubt the best available and in continuous demand.

Jacob arrived in St. Louis in 1807 and soon found employment for his mechanical skill. He opened his own shop in 1815. St. Louis was a bustling, rapidly-growing community, ideally suited for the Missouri river trade and as a jumping-off point for would be explorers and the large number of traders, trappers and others whose livelihood depended upon weapons.

Jacob Hawken was a good listener as well as a good craftsman. He met many of the veterans of earlier expeditions, including some who claimed to have been with Lewis and Clark. While repairing their weapons, he carefully noted their criticisms and needs. If a man wanted changes to trigger, sights, length of stock, or any other modification, Jacob questioned him closely to establish the source of dissatisfaction. Many of the changes involved simple repair or replacement, but major work was always a serious concern with Hawken, and from these modifications sprang ideas for new weapons. The Model 1803 soon attracted his attention, and he became expert at the rectification of its faults. He learned that the length of the barrel of most Kentucky-type arms was a hindrance when crawling around in brush or through confined spaces, and the heavier calibres demanded by the Western hunters and trappers called for shorter barrels. Most of these were fully stocked, but a large number were turned out with half-stocks. By the early 1820s Jacob Hawken's reputation was second to none, and when he was joined by his brother Samuel in 1822, the partnership proved very fruitful. Within ten years they were renowned for their rifles, and produced large-calibre guns, some as big as .70, which became the chosen weapons of a new breed of plainsmen – the buffalo hunters. Later generations of hunters (notably Buffalo Bill Cody) had the advantage of cartridge weapons; but the buffalo hunters were restricted to slow-loading muzzle-loaders, and so were particularly concerned with reliability as well as accuracy, especially when 'buffalo running'.

Patched bullets were rarely used; time being an essential factor. Instead, several extra balls were carried in the mouth. Spittle helped stick the powder to the ball when it had been rammed home. Few men carried rifles, mainly because of the difficulty of loading while mounted; the shorter the barrel the better, and better still if it was a smooth-bore.

Once a herd was sighted and the riders gave chase, it was essential not to slacken pace. Once the gun had been discharged, it was held in the crook of the left arm, the flask taken in the right hand and the stopper removed by the teeth. The ponies were trained to respond to knee pressure to allow the rider maximum use of his hands. The stopper was retained on the flask by a cord. A charge of powder was shaken into the left hand, and the stopper replaced in the flask or horn which was swung back across the shoulder or slung from the belt or saddle-bow. The gun was then held rigidly in the right hand and the powder was poured down the barrel, with a final slap from the left hand to ease it down. A ball was then removed from the mouth with the left hand and dropped into the barrel. Smooth-bore weapons were preferred to the rifle because there was no need of a rammer. Similarly, flintlocks were preferred to percussion arms because it was difficult to extract a percussion cap from the pouch and place it on the nipple at full gallop. But whichever method was used, the hunter got as close to the animal as possible, and fired at its heart.

Big game shooting had its problems. Old-timers jokingly recounted tales of companions who, rather than risk a miss, were prepared to get so close to a grizzly bear that the muzzle of the gun could almost be placed in its mouth before discharge: 'Yer may not kill the old gal first shot, but yer sure give 'er a coughin' fit in time fer yer next un!'

When the percussion system finally overhauled the flintlock, the Hawken rifle really came into its own. A typical weapon of the late mountain man-early plainsman period was impressive. The barrel was usually octagonal, about 34 to 40 inches long, and the calibre .35 (a half-ounce round ball averaging 214 grains of lead). The sights were low, and there was usually a set-trigger. This consisted of two triggers; the second or rear one was pulled or 'set' which eased the pressure on the main trigger allowing a gentle 'let off'. The percussion lock included a steel basket (the 'snail', so called because it resembled one) which enclosed the nipple. Such a weapon was usually half-stocked, with metal or brass pipes attached beneath the barrel to carry the ramrod, while the crescent-shaped heel of the sturdy stock was fitted with heavy brass plates. Sometimes a patch box, similar to that found on Kentucky rifles, was set in the side. The average weight of these splendidly balanced weapons was ten and a half to twelve pounds. Curiously, it was the lack of embellishment on the majority of Hawken rifles which led to the suggestion that what we today call the 'plains rifle' was in fact known in its own time as a 'plain rifle'. If this is true, it will explain the confusion over names.

Old-time mountain men swore by the Hawken rifle, and for them it was the *ne plus ultra.* Jim Bridger, possibly the most famous of them, carried a Hawken rifle for years, as did Colonel Christopher 'Kit' Carson and Joseph Meek – the latter called his rifle 'Sally'.

For more than twenty years the Hawken brothers had little competition despite the influx of a number of British-made and other foreign weapons. Some of these were extremely well-made, but were so similar in appearance to the Hawken that it was generally believed that their looks owed more to copy than to an independent evolution of design. Among the better weapons were some fitted with set-triggers, sturdy, walnut half-stocks, steel rather than brass furniture, ramrod pipes and calibres ranging from .45 to .50, although it is claimed that some appeared in six bore (.92)! Some of these weapons were turned out by such great names as Joseph Manton, which impressed the natives 'some'.

The old-timers' concern for accuracy and stopping-power led to as much controversy in establishing the true worth of the Hawken as had been the case with the Kentucky. Improved ignition and manufacturing techniques obviously helped, and it is claimed that as recently as 1960 an original Hawken was fired at 200 yards in an 'off-hand' manner and the marksman still managed to place his shots within a 12-inch bull. If this is true, then a buffalo, grizzly or even a man, stood little or no chance at that long distance.

After the death of Jacob Hawken, victim of an outbreak of cholera, in 1849, others moved into the field, and although Samuel continued to produce excellent rifles, he was soon rivalled by such notables as Trisman Campbell, J. F. Diettrich (who specialized in buffalo rifles), and Horace A. Dimick, who remained active in St Louis long after the era of the mountain and early plainsmen had

passed. Dimick became a dealer for many of the leading revolver manufacturers of the 1850s and 1860s, in particular Samuel Colt, whose voluminous correspondence includes details of parts of arms shipped to Dimick in the mid 1850s.

By 1860 Sam Hawken's health was beginning to fail, and in 1862 he sold the business to J. P. Genmer, who had worked for him for years and who had been one of his best workmen. Genmer continued to make Hawken-style rifles, but the trend was towards smaller weapons for target shooting. He remained in business until 1915. Sam Hawken died in 1884 aged 90, and it seems fitting that the very last true Hawken rifle was made by him in retirement. He outlived most of the great names associated with his and his brother's guns; weapons made for a time and a place when a good gun was an essential means of survival and worth its weight in gold.

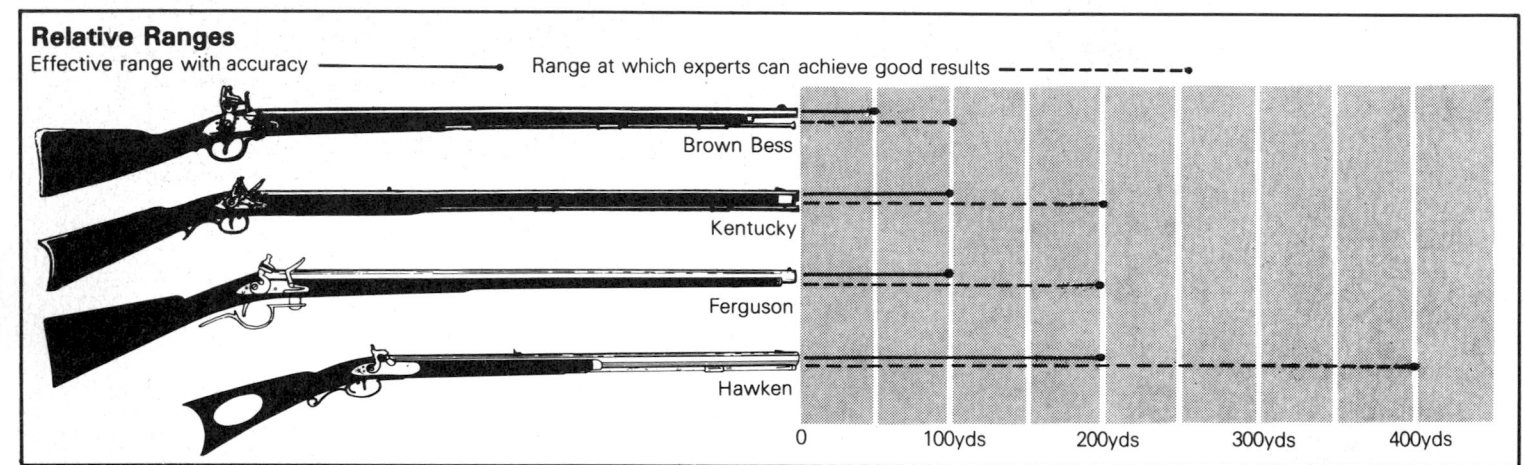

Relative Ranges
Effective range with accuracy ⟶   Range at which experts can achieve good results ⤏

Brown Bess

Kentucky

Ferguson

Hawken

0   100yds   200yds   300yds   400yds

Above: Top, an American 100 bore seven-shot hand-rotated percussion revolving rifle marked D. COON ITHACA with a 27¼-inch barrel, circa 1850. Bottom, a 70 bore seven-shot hand-rotated percussion revolving rifle, circa 1850, marked C. MILLER (possibly of Ontario County, New York). The barrel is 28½ inches long, half-round, half-octagonal. Weapons of this type were common during the period and are graphic examples of how Colt's mechanism simplified existing systems. (By courtesy of Messrs Weller & Dufty)

2
PISTOLS AND REPEATERS

It [the 'pepperbox'] was a cheerful weapon . . . Sometimes all its six barrels would go off at once,
and then there was no safe place in all the region roundabout but behind it. – Mark Twain

Above: An American flintlock pistol by A. Whiting of New Orleans. Note the downward sweep of the butt. (By courtesy of the Winchester Museum)

IT is ironic that at the very time when rifles had reached a state of sophistication undreamed of by the earlier mountain and plainsmen, little or no attention seems to have been paid to improvements in handguns. The pistol in various forms had been in use for several hundred years by the time the United States was born, but it was considered a secondary weapon to the musket or rifle. Few troops were armed with a pistol, whereas on the frontier it formed an essential part of every man's equipment as a backup weapon for emergencies. Single- and double-barrelled pistols were carried by many hunters, trappers and mountain men, although they did not place the same reliance upon them as did later generations. As with contemporary flintlocks – both rifles and

muskets – they, too, had their problems, but since most pistols were carried in pairs, there was, perhaps, a slight psychological edge over their large single-shot rivals.

The so-called 'Kentucky' pistols, however, did not make an appearance until long after the rifle, and some authorities believe that they did not achieve any popularity until after the French and Indian wars. The makers of rifles certainly had the capacity to manufacture pistols, but demand was limited, and few of them had the inclination to compete with the well-made imports from England and the Continent. The outbreak of the Revolution, however, changed all that. The demand for arms of every description and the lack of British-made weapons and parts, compelled the local gunsmiths to

produce weapons from scratch and, as a result, they evolved the weapon we now call the 'Kentucky' pistol.

Unlike its contemporaries, which were smooth-bore and in calibres as large as .60, the Kentucky followed the tradition of its larger namesake. Produced in calibres ranging from .36 to .50, the barrels, which were made of iron (and, but very rarely, of brass) were rifled and fitted with sights. The stocks were of striped maple and capped with brass or silver, and the side plates, too, reflected the skill of the maker and engraver. Octagonal barrels were very popular and

Above: At the left is an all-brass English flintlock pistol complete with an 8-inch snap bayonet on the right side. Missing is the weapon's trigger guard and one of the ramrod pipes. At the right is an English box lock, Queen Anne period, brass flintlock pistol marked JOYNER LONDON, but proved in Birmingham. Weapons of this type abounded out West and in the southern states, sometimes years after the introduction of more up-to-date arms. (By courtesy of Richard A. Bourne Co. Inc.)

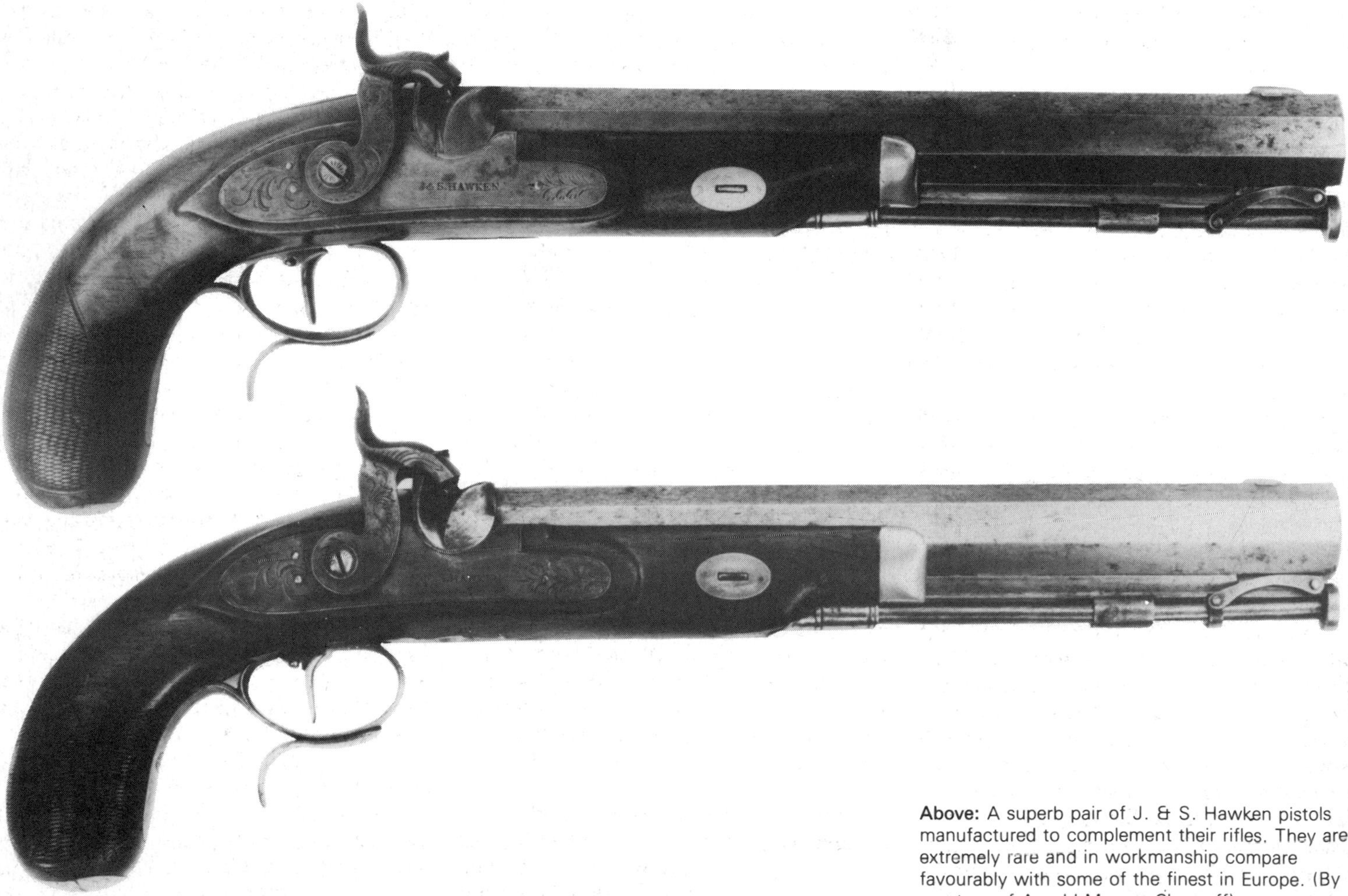

Above: A superb pair of J. & S. Hawken pistols manufactured to complement their rifles. They are extremely rare and in workmanship compare favourably with some of the finest in Europe. (By courtesy of Arnold Marcus Chernoff)

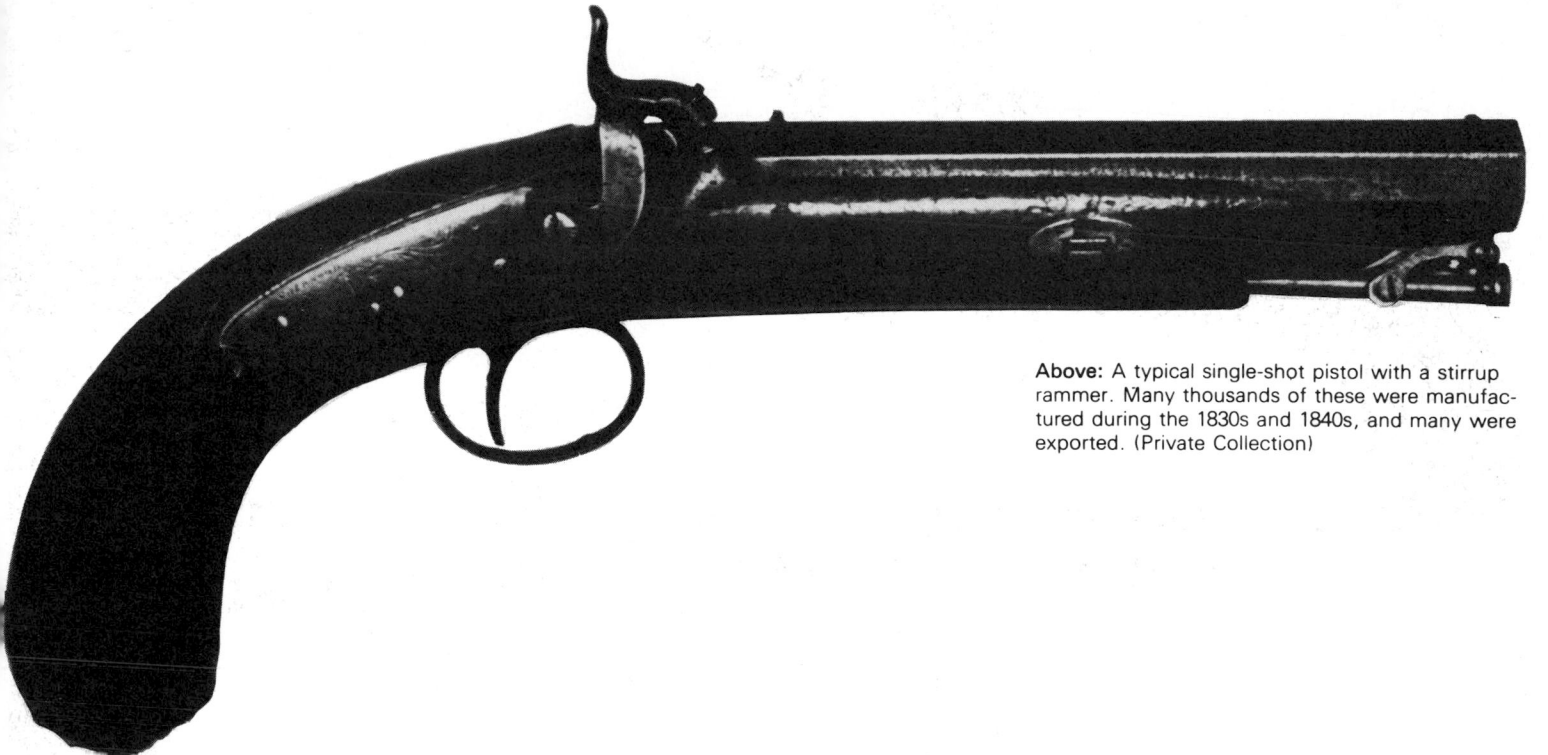

Above: A typical single-shot pistol with a stirrup rammer. Many thousands of these were manufactured during the 1830s and 1840s, and many were exported. (Private Collection)

ranged in length from six to twelve inches, the shorter sizes predominating.

By the early 1800s the Kentucky pistol was well established and was a popular weapon with Easterners and Westerners alike. Carried in belt scabbards (now called holsters) or slung from shoulder cross-belts, singly, or in pairs, they were an ideal back-up for anyone venturing alone into the wilderness. By 1820, however, when the percussion system began to make inroads into the realm of the flintlock, makers of the Kentucky pistol either gave up altogether or attempted to compete with the cheaper rivals which began to flood the Western states. Either way, the passing of the flintlock firearm marked the end of an era and the birth of a new one.

The Kentucky-type pistols established a reputation and are now highly sought-after collectors' pieces. Among some of the more desirable are those produced by such makers as Constable, Philadelphia; W. Wurrfflein, Philadelphia and several others in the New England states. Some of these makers remained in business until the early percussion era. Recent tests on some of the pistols have produced some interesting results. Weapons in .45 calibre with rifled barrels and firing similar loads to those used in mid nineteenth-century percussion revolvers proved to be comparable, if lacking in range, and even smooth-bore weapons were impressive. A .44 calibre, flintlock smooth-bore pistol was loaded with a charge of 40 grains of very fine black powder, and a patched round ball weighing 120 grains. When fired,

the weapon produced a muzzle velocity of 1,050 feet per second and 290 foot-pounds of energy; an efficiency slightly over seven foot-pounds per grain of propellant, which compares very favourably to a Colt Dragoon! Such weapons, however, without sights and designed for close-action work, soon lost velocity, yet were ideal in the purpose for which they were intended.

In place of the Kentucky pistols there appeared weapons with larger bores, shorter barrels and less ornamentation; although such makers as the Hawken brothers did manufacture some finely ornamented weapons with attached stirrup-operated rammers. These were fixed to the muzzle end of the barrel by a crossbolt, the arms or 'stirrups' were attached to the rammer which could be removed from its pipes, used and replaced yet remain attached to the weapon at all times. Dimick, too, produced some excellent weapons, and by the late 1840s and early 1850s the pistol was rapidly overtaking the knife as the individual's personal weapon.

Washington Irving noted a reliance upon pistols for effect and use, and wrote that a so-called 'free trapper', dressed in a 'blanket of scarlet, or some other bright color', had 'around his waist . . . a red sash, in which he bestows his pistols, knife, and the stem of his Indian pipe; preparations either for peace or war'.

The majority of the pistols carried by the mountain and plainsmen were well-made and powerful. The advent of the percussion system did more for the pistol than any other

innovation, and by 1846 such leading lights as Francis Parkman were impressed enough even to consider tackling the mighty buffalo with one. In his classic book *The Oregon Trail*, first published in 1849, he decided to 'run buffalo', and wrote that:

'I separated another from the herd and shot him. The small bullet of the rifled pistol, striking too far back did not immediately take effect, and the bull ran on with unabated speed. Again and again I snapped the remaining pistol at him. I primed it afresh three or four times, and each time it missed fire, for the touch-hole was clogged up. Returning it to the holster, I began to load the empty pistol, still galloping by the side of the bull . . . as I looked back, his neck and shoulders were exposed to view; turning in the saddle, I shot a bullet, through them obliquely into his vitals. He gave over the chase and soon fell to the ground.'

By this time, of course, the change in ignition from flint to cap was one of the most talked of events on the plains. It was a radical change, and although it was to lead to innumerable improvements, it was not so rapid as hindsight suggests it should have been, and there were some who viewed the new-fangled cap locks with deep suspicion. None the less, its significance changed the whole concept of firearms, and, in a sense, the development of the percussion system is as interesting as the result.

The change from flintlock to percussion took less than twenty years; a period fraught with problems both for the inventor and for those who sought to develop the idea, for the

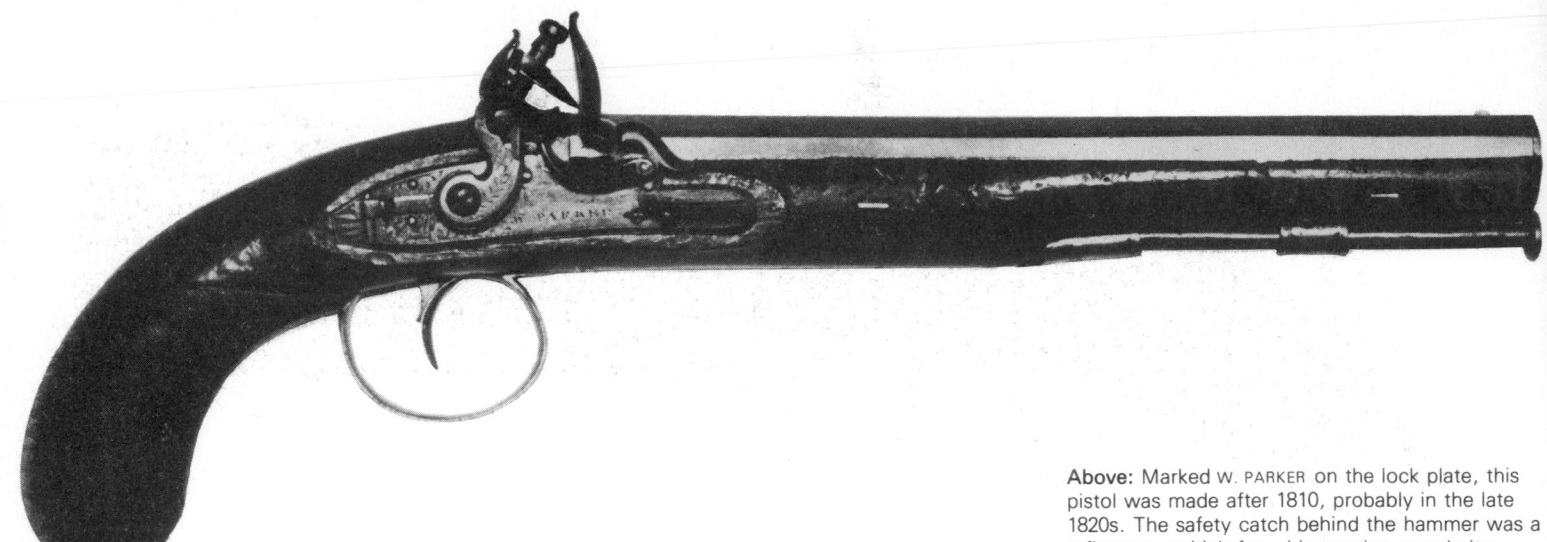

Above: Marked W. PARKER on the lock plate, this pistol was made after 1810, probably in the late 1820s. The safety catch behind the hammer was a refinement which found increasing popularity during the early 1800s. (Private Collection)

fulminates involved were highly combustible, and if mishandled the results could be disastrous. A cursory glimpse into the history of firearms will show that two factors dominated the field right from the earliest times: ignition and multiple discharge. It was ignition, however, which received the greatest attention, and it was an obscure Scottish minister who was to change dramatically the whole concept of arms.

The Reverend Alexander John Forsyth practised Christianity at Belhelvie in Aberdeenshire. He was also an amateur chemist, of mechanical bent, and as a further diversion from his religious duties, he was an ardent hunter. It was this latter passion which led to one of the most important discoveries of the age. Some claim that he was inspired by the fact that birds dived with the flash, when the priming powder was ignited, which caused even the most accomplished marksman to 'miss the mark'. Whether this story is true or not Forsyth applied himself with great dedication to the problem and soon gained a working knowledge of the various fulminates then in common use.

Here he encounted many difficulties which would have discouraged a lesser individual, but he persevered. Most of these fulminates were salts produced by dissolving metals in acid. When struck they exploded violently and so required great care in handling. As early as the seventeenth century, gold, silver and potassium chlorate had been used as fulminates, and the English scientist, Edward Howard, had successfully produced fulminate of mercury in 1799. But no one had seriously considered them as a potential source of ignition for firearms – no one, that is, until the Reverend Forsyth.

His frequently perilous experiments, some of them conducted at the Tower of London, to control fulminate of mercury by reducing the amounts to safe, workable proportions,

reached fruition in 1805. He was at last able to control the explosion and devise a simple system to employ it. He produced a pivoted magazine designed to contain deposits of fulminate of mercury which, when struck by the hammer, sealed the escape of the flame, and in turn touched off the powder in the bore and discharged the weapon. It is claimed that in 1806 Napoleon endeavoured to acquire the 'secret' of Forsyth's experiments, but failed. As it was, government experiments at Woolwich were not successful, and Forsyth's talents were then directed toward the commercial world.

He was followed by others who continued to improve upon the idea. There was the 'pill lock', a device in which fulminate, mixed with gum arabic, was rolled into pellets, placed inside touch-holes and struck by a sharp point set in the face of the hammer which ignited the main charge. Another scheme embraced the 'tube lock', a metal tube filled with fulminate inserted into a touch-hole, the top end of which rested on an anvil. When the hammer struck it the flame was sent into the bore. Unfortunately, it was prone to flash back (during discharge the flame from the chamber sometimes 'flashed back' at the shooter) often with disastrous results. But by far the most successful was the percussion cap – this more than anything revolutionized guns throughout the world.

It is not known who invented the cap, although some authorities claim that credit belongs to the English artist, Joshua Shaw (1776 – 1860), who first introduced a practical cap to replace existing methods. Shaw found that by mixing the various materials into a paste, and placing a small amount of it in a minute steel cup (or cylinder) sufficient power was generated to set off the main charge. Further experiments led to the introduction of the cone or

nipple, a hollow tube screwed into the breech, on top of which was placed the 'cap'. When struck by the hammer, the flame flashed to the charge and the gun fired. Unlike the flintlock, the percussion lock worked in all weathers and was a vast improvement. The erstwhile hesitation between the flash from the priming pan and the main discharge, a common problem with the flintlock, was almost eradicated, so that by the mid 1840s the flintlock was already becoming a relic of the past.

Having modified ignition, would-be inventors turned their attention to multi-shot weapons. All manner of experiments were conducted in an endeavour to find a safe and practical method of employing such systems. The majority of these proved to be impracticable – and dangerous! In 1718, the Englishman, James Puckle (1667–1742), had patented a weapon loosely described by some as a 'machine gun', which, of course, it was not. Yet this remarkable weapon provided others with food for thought. It consisted of a single barrel to which was attached a cylinder bored out with varying numbers of chambers. Although the cylinder was revolved by hand, a crank at the rear was used to screw it up tightly to the barrel. Each chamber mouth was coned to form a gas-tight fit in the countersunk breech of the barrel. According to contemporary accounts it was possible to fire 63 times in seven minutes – a miraculous performance for the time! Would-be purchasers were informed that the weapon was available with cylinders that fired either round balls for use against Christians, or square ones for use against Infidels or Turks!

In 1818, however, Elisha Collier of Boston, Massachusetts, perfected what he considered to be a reliable, revolving-breech flintlock pistol. He freely admitted that he owed much to the earlier work of

Above: A true 'traveller's friend', this double-barrelled side-by-side pistol is also equipped with a spring-loaded bayonet centrally mounted. (Private Collection)

Below: A typical tap-action pistol of the early 1800s. The superimposed barrels are fired by one hammer, but the tap-like device seen on the left sealed off one barrel while the other was being fired. This was one of many systems tried prior to the appearance of revolving breeched firearms. (Private Collection)

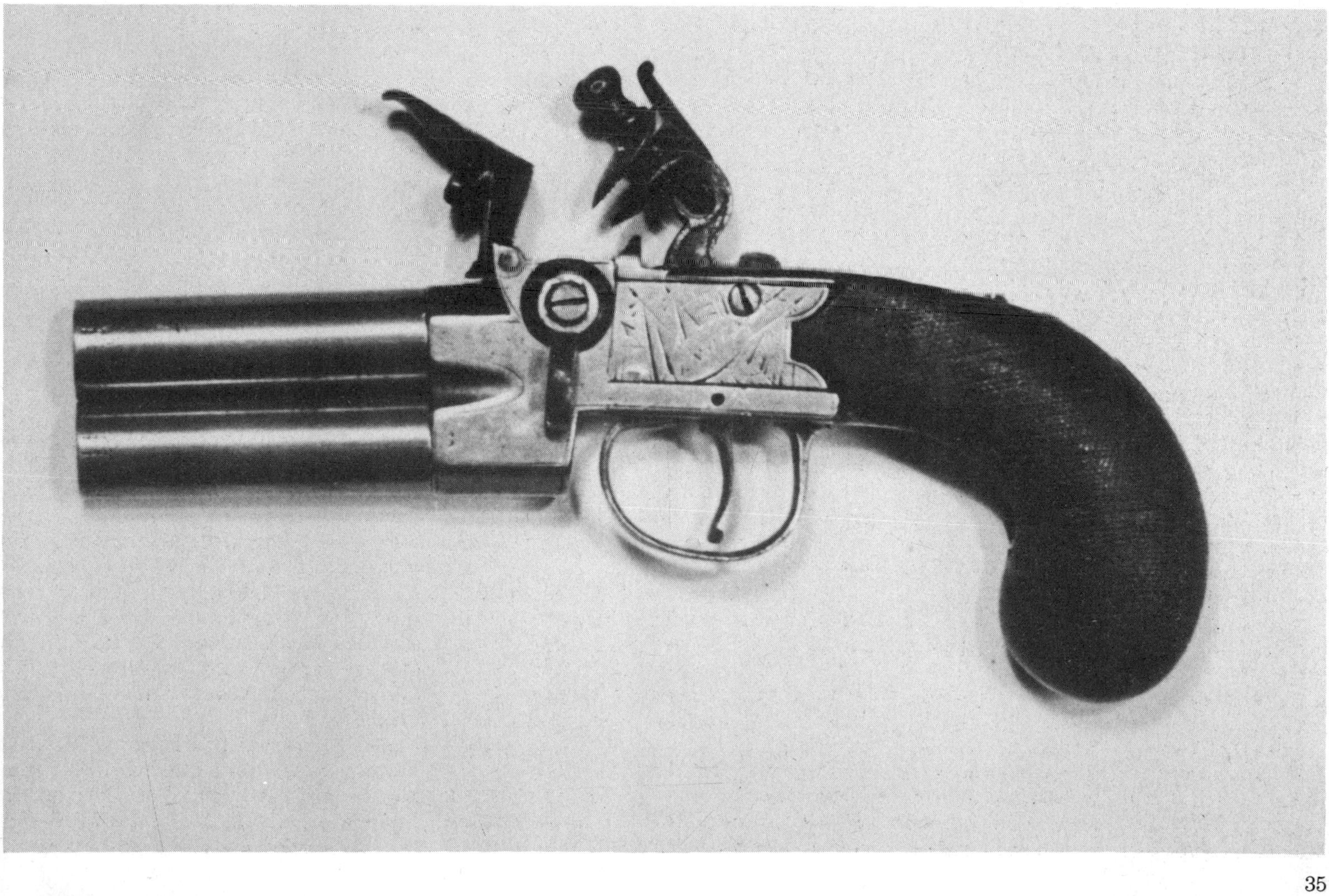

Captain Artemus Wheeler of Concord, Massachusetts, who in his turn may well have been influenced by Puckle. On 24 November 1818 Elisha Collier secured an English patent for his firearm which combined a 'single barrel with several chambers to obtain succession of discharges from one loading', which was, in effect, almost identical with the weapon that had been designed by Captain Wheeler, with some assistance from Collier and finance from a Boston merchant named Cornelius Coolidge. The Collier flintlock 'revolver' incorporated an automatic priming pan which, when the frizzen was closed, allowed powder from a container in its top to filter into the pan. Rotation of the cylinder was achieved by means of a coil spring linked to the hammer, which first had to be activated by hand. Despite interest in the weapons by

no less a person than Field Marshal, His Grace the Duke of Wellington, they failed to attract much attention from the Board of Ordnance who regarded them as interesting but far too complicated for general use. Later, when a company was formed to produce the weapons incorporating a percussion system, a number of them were sold to the public, but again, the weapons were considered too cumbersome for military use and interest lapsed.

By the late 1830s, however, the percussion system had inspired a number of multi-shot weapons, the commonest of these being the 'pepperbox', so-called because in appearance it resembled the pepper-shakers of the time. It consisted of a handle attached to a frame which in turn was attached to a rounded block of metal with fluted surface and around its central axis were drilled four, five or six

'chambers' at the rear of each was placed a percussion nipple or cone. To operate it, the trigger was pulled, which raised the hammer (sometimes a bar with a rounded flattened striker), and as the cylinder turned, it struck the cap on the nipple of the next chamber in line.

Already popular in Europe, the 'pepperbox' soon found its way across the Atlantic, where Ethan Allen is credited with patenting the system in the United States in 1834. By the early 1850s these weapons were common, and had reached a surprising degree of sophistication, and the finish and quality were designed to suit all pockets. Some were finely made, engraved and well finished, while others were cheap and best termed 'serviceable', the calibres ranging from as small as .26 to as large as .50 (perhaps even larger), yet they were considered clumsy in

Above and below: A Collier flintlock revolver with an automatic priming pan. Serial No. 23, this weapon was of the type produced after 1818 and until the early 1820s. Trials before the Board of Ordnance aroused a great deal of interest, but no orders; the weapons were considered too complicated for service use. (By courtesy of the Victoria and Albert Museum)

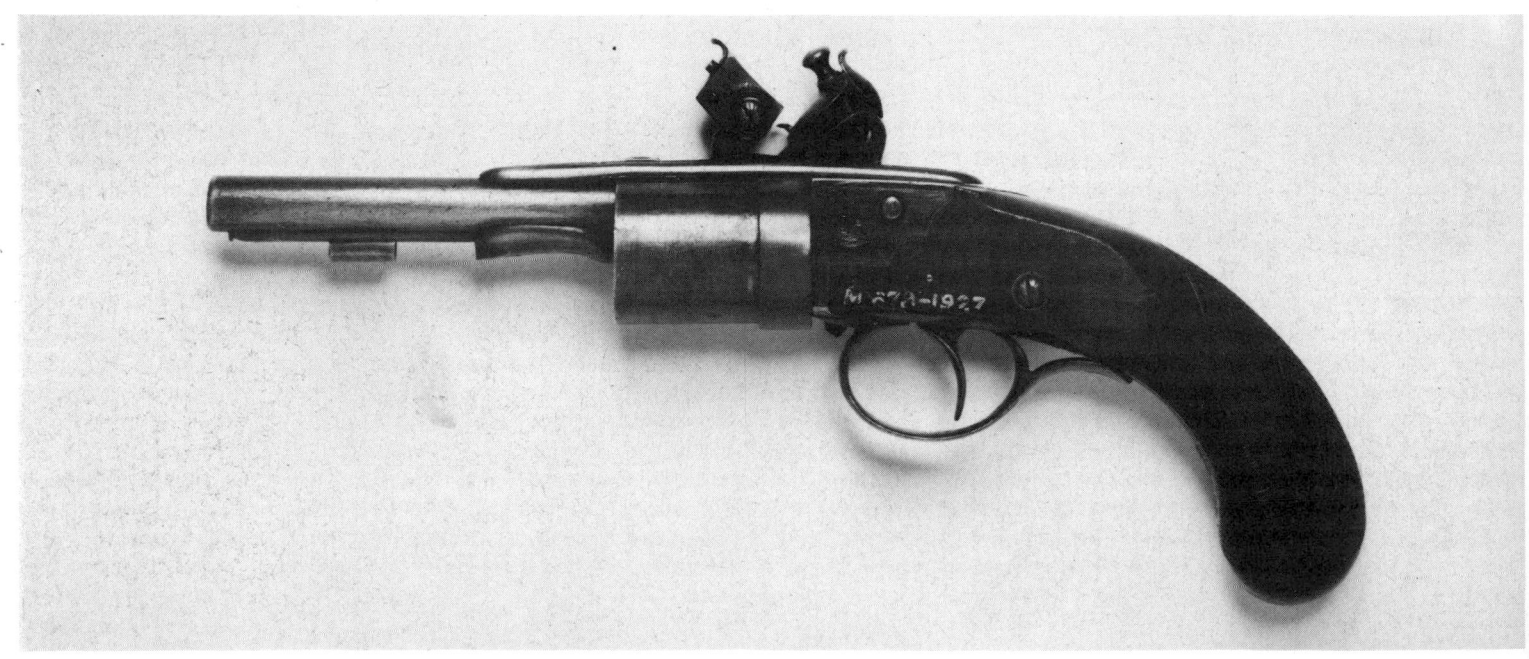

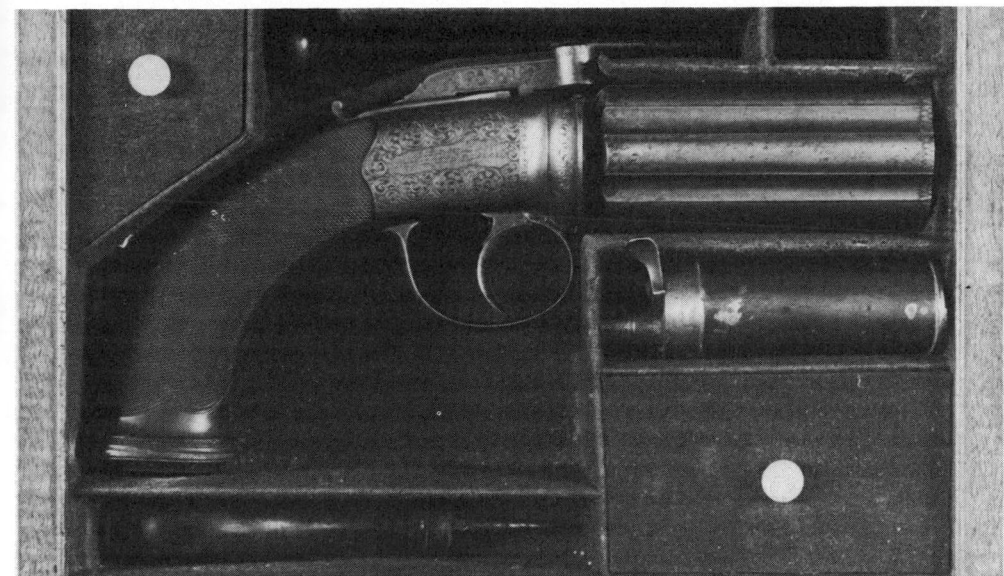

Left: The 'pepperbox' revolver was extremely popular in Europe, and thanks to Ethan Allen (who patented the design in the United States) it was also welcomed in the New World. This example is a good-quality Birmingham-proved 52 bore six-shot bar hammer self-cocking version retailed by Wilkinson & Son in about 1840. It is complete with a mould, copper-bodied three-way flask, percussion caps, wooden cleaning rod and a nipple wrench. (By courtesy of Messrs. Weller & Dufty)

Below: Two views of the Collier flintlock revolvers — the fluted cylinder bears a close resemblance to those that followed some forty years later. This weapon also has an automatic priming pan which operates when the pan (and combined frizzen or frizzel) is closed enabling a small amount of powder to filter into the pan. (By courtesy of the Victoria and Albert Museum)

the extreme. No less a person than Mark Twain (Samuel L. Clemens) in his classic *Roughing It*, recounted the experience of a fellow traveller, George Bemis, when demonstrating his 'pepperbox' during a stagecoach trip West in 1861:

'He wore in his belt an old original "Allen" revolver, such as irreverent people call a "pepperbox". Simply drawing the trigger back, cocked and fired the pistol. As the trigger came back, the hammer would begin to rise and the barrel to turn over, and presently down would drop the hammer, and away would speed the ball. To aim along the turning barrel and hit the thing aimed at was a feat which was probably never done with an "Allen" in the world. But George's was a reliable weapon, nevertheless, because, as

one of the stage drivers afterwards said, "If she didn't get what she went after, she would fetch something else." And so she did. She went after a deuce of spades nailed against a tree, once, and fetched a mule standing about thirty yards to the left of it. Bemis did not want the mule; but the owner came out with a double-barreled shotgun and persuaded him to buy it anyhow. It was a cheerful weapon – the "Allen". Sometimes all its six barrels would go off at once, and then there was no safe place in all the region roundabout but behind it.'

Despite these setbacks, multi-shot pepperbox-type pistols were common and popular out West, especially during the heyday of the fur trade and the early goldrushes to California. It is estimated that

these pistols outnumbered the Colt and other true revolvers for some years, particularly in the South (where they were available in quantity up to the Civil War).

Below: Four views of the percussion version of the Collier revolver. Marked with the barrel address: COLLIER & CO. 54 STRAND LONDON, this is a true percussion version and not one altered from flintlock. The pistol dates from about 1824, and is a fine example of its type. It was years ahead of its time, and despite the interest of the Duke of Wellington, the company never obtained government orders. (By courtesy of Robert Q. Sutherland)

Right: Colonel Samuel Colt in later life. Colt's inventiveness and genius in implementing ideas and modifications kept him ahead of most of his rivals during his lifetime. Despite his critics, he never did claim to have invented the revolver; rather, he made an existing system both practicable and simple. (Author's Collection)

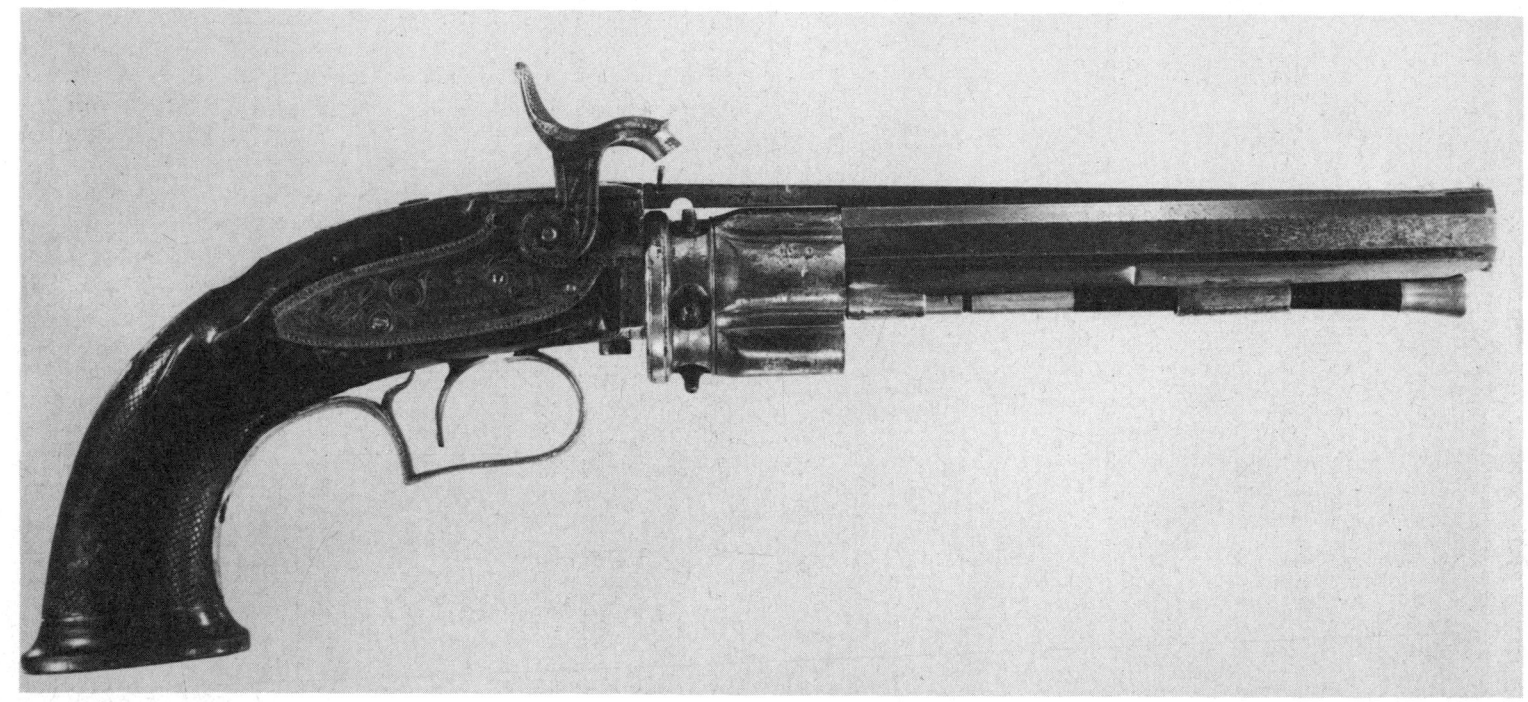

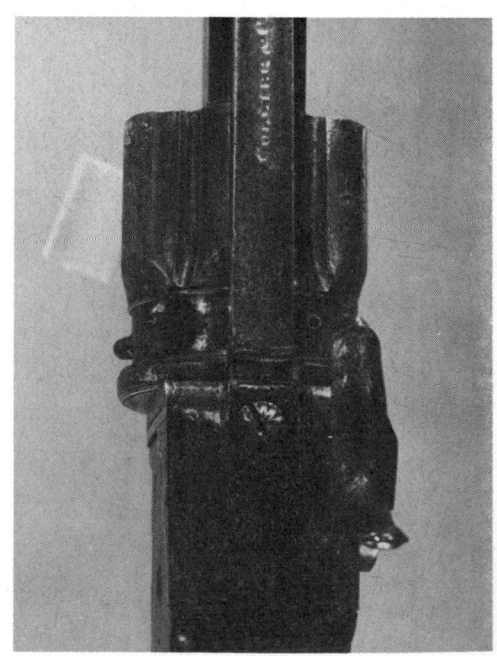

3
THE REVOLVER
– A GREAT 'CIVILIZER'

Be not afraid of any man, no matter what his size; just call upon me and I shall equalize.
– Anonymous Frontier tribute to the six-shooter or 'Equalizer'.

WE have already seen that the Wheeler-Collier flintlock and percussion lock 'revolving breeched' pistols met with a limited success in the early 1800s, although they were still regarded as novelties when Samuel Colt patented his own version in England in 1835 and in the United States early the following year. But Colt's revolver was much more practicable and aroused a great deal of interest, particularly in the United States which was to become the 'spiritual home' of the revolver.

Those who belittle the part played by the revolver in history tend to be influenced by its mythical rather than its practical accomplishments. Its role as a useful piece of equipment cannot be denied, and historians recognize the part it played in 'civilizing' the frontier regions of the American West. Until its arrival, the white man was at a great disadvantage in his endeavours to share the land with the native Indian tribes. This was particularly true in Texas where the Comanche Nation, perhaps the finest light cavalry in the world, waged ceaseless war against invaders, regardless of nationality. And faced by the Indians' speed and skill on horseback, together with an amazing ability to fire up to a dozen arrows to the white man's one or two shots, the settlers realized that without a superior weapon they stood little chance against the Red man.

During the late 1830s and early 1840s, the Indians' principal opponents were the Texas Rangers, that formidable body of men who had been formed in 1823, some thirteen years before the 'Texians' won their independence from Mexico in 1836. Their one-time commander, John S. 'Rip' Ford, said in 1846 that a typical Ranger 'can ride like a Mexican, trail like an Indian, shoot like a Tennesseean, and fight like the very devil'. Then as now, they had no official uniform, and were dressed in assorted coats, trousers, hats and boots. Some wore their hair long and 'matted' which, with the addition of the fashionable 'full set' of whiskers, gave them a particularly cutthroat-like appearance. They were a tough crowd, but they treated their Indian adversaries with respect.

The Rangers appreciated the need of fast horses and the importance of sticking close together come what might, for in that country a lone man stood little chance against the Indians. Two, three or more disciplined men, armed with single-shot rifles or muskets and perhaps a single-shot pistol or two, could put up a good fight. Reloading time was at a premium, for the Indians knew that they had the upper hand. So the Texans developed a form of 'British Square' when they were attacked by Indians. They would dismount immediately (to charge Indians would have been fruitless) leave a guard with the horses, and form into a platoon. When one man had fired another was ready to take his place while he reloaded. The Indians either became discouraged and rode away, or, as sometimes happened, the defenders ran out of ammunition and the Indians closed in for the kill.

Understandably, it was with great enthusiasm that the Rangers greeted the news that the Republic of Texas had invested in Colt's revolvers, and looked forward to the day that they, too, would be issued with them. Sam Colt's detractors have long claimed that he did not invent the revolver, but simply improved upon the ideas of others. It is true that he did not invent the revolver, but what he did do was to perfect the first reliable version of a principle that was both simple and practical. Indeed, Sam would have been the first to admit that the concept of 'revolving breeched' arms was far

from new, for specimens of such weapons had been known for several hundred years. But each lacked something that the others had, or were impracticable for one reason or another. Colt finally collated all known systems and, with the addition of a few ideas of his own, produced the first true 'revolving pistol'.

Tradition has it that in 1830, Sam Colt, then aged sixteen, embarked as a hand in the vessel *Corvo*, bound for India and England. During the visit to England he is said to have seen repeating arms in London gunshops, and back at sea whittled away at a piece of wood and produced what was to become the basic idea for his revolving pistol. In fact, the *Corvo* never reached England (her voyage took her from Boston to Calcutta and back), and if Colt saw any repeating arms it was in Calcutta where a number of quality gunsmiths were in business. Consequently, when Colt obtained his first patent in London in 1835, it was the first time that he had visited the place that was to dominate his life and work for the next 25 years.

Colt was granted his English Patent on 22 October 1835, for what was described as a 'Revolving Breeched Pistol'. Similar patents were granted in France and Belgium and, on his return to the United States, he patented his pistol on 25 February 1836. Ironically, on 6 March 1836, just one day after Colt had succeeded in persuading some New York capitalists to put up the money to organize the Patent Arms Manufacturing Company of

Paterson, N.J., to produce 'revolvers' (as the weapons were soon to be called) on his principle, the Alamo fell. We can only assume that had James Bowie, Davie Crockett and all the other heroes of that tragic siege, been armed with a brace of Colt's revolvers apiece, they would have taken more of the 'greasers' with 'em. Racial insults being common at the time, Spanish-speaking peoples called the whites 'Gringos' and honour was satisfied! But Colt's revolver was a thing of the future when the gallant defenders of the Alamo gave their lives so that their fellow 'Texians' could prepare themselves to meet the army of Santa Anna, and defeat him just ten days later at San Jacinto.

Colt's negotiations were successful, and despite some initial setbacks and design faults which required modification, the prototype pistols and rifles were in production by early 1837. Unlike later arms, the early Colt pistols were not fitted with conventional triggerguards, but with folding triggers of the kind used on pocket-pistols, commonly found in Europe, but rarely in the United States. Only when the hammer was pulled back to full-cock by thumb pressure did a spring activate the trigger so that it dropped down into position ready for firing. But the one significant advantage Colt's revolver had over most of its predecessors was that not only did the hammer cock the weapon and turn the cylinder, by means of a hand or pawl attached to it, but it also released a bolt which locked the cylinder in position ready for firing, and this made the weapon a practicable and reliable proposition.

Colt soon approached the government in the hope of arousing interest in his revolver, but Washington was not completely convinced of its practicability. Parts of it were liable to breakage, and while Colt's ingenuity was admired, details of that kind were not. Fortunately, many of the officers who had witnessed the weapon on trial were impressed enough to purchase it personally or recommend its adoption by the government. When the Seminole War broke out in 1838 many of these same officers ordered his pistols, and Sam, quick to react to any sales possibilities, went south armed to the teeth with his pistols and rifles, determined to interest the army in the weapons. Among those who favoured Colt's revolving arms was Colonel William S. Harney, who persuaded Major-General Thomas Jessup to order 50 rifles. These were the early ring-lever rifles produced in .34, .36, .38, .40 and .44 calibres. The cylinders were eight-shot, but occasionally ten-shot versions were available. Faults in design, however, and the prejudice of those who failed to understand the worth of such arms, did little to improve

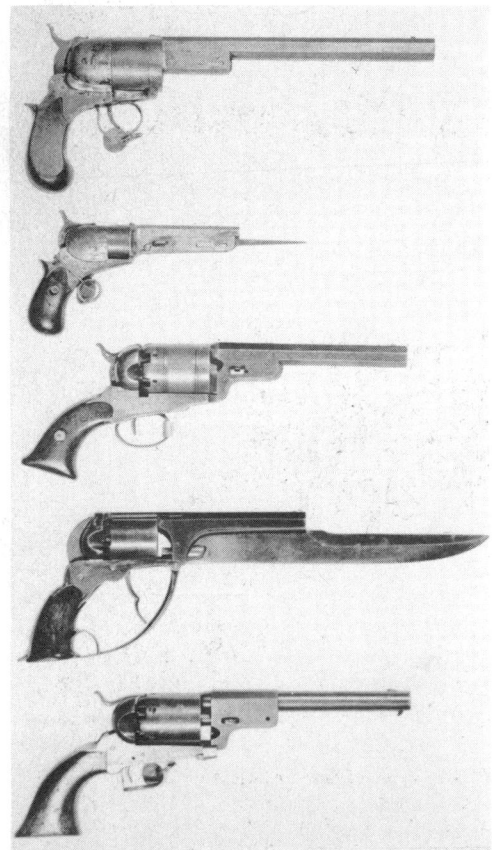
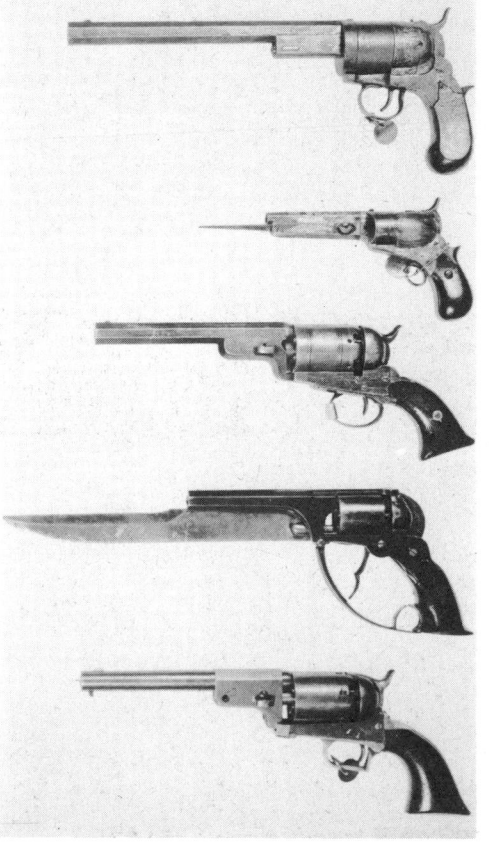

sales. One Ordnance officer even expressed the opinion that Colt's weapons 'will ultimately all pass into oblivion', a view fortunately not shared by many of his colleagues. Colt himself appreciated the faults and continued to modify his weapons and, although by 1839 he was still unable to sell the rifle and carbine versions in large numbers in the East, it was the West, predictably, that showed most interest, particularly in Texas.

Following the fall of the Álamo and the subsequent defeat of Santa Anna the new Republic of Texas displayed a remarkable farsightedness. In 1839, 180 holster-size pistols (intended for use in saddle holsters) were purchased from Colt by the Republic of Texas, together with 180 of the new carbines. These were issued to the Texas Navy. Later that year, the Texans purchased 100 of the ring-lever rifles. Many of these arms were later re-issued to the Rangers. Both troops and Rangers used them with some effect against Indians. In November 1840, the Texas newspaper the *Telegraph and Texas Register* reported: 'In the late Indian fight, Captain Andrews used one of Colt's patent rifles which he discharged ten times while a comrade could discharge his rifle only twice. He believes that these rifles in proper hands would prove the most useful of all weapons in Indian warfare.' It was the revolver, however, which aroused most interest. In 1844, fifteen Rangers, under the command of Colonel John Coffee Hays, fought a running fight with about eighty Comanches; armed with their Paterson pistols, the Rangers killed 42 of them. On 30 November 1846 Captain Samuel Walker, one of the Rangers involved in the fight, wrote to Sam Colt giving his opinion of Colt's pistols and his recollection of the fight:

'The pistols which you made for the Texas Navy have been in use by the Rangers for three years, and I can say with confidence that it is the only good improvement that I have seen. The Texans who have learned their value by practical experience, their confidence in them is unbounded, so much so that they are willing to engage four times their number. In the summer of 1844 Col J. C. Hays with 15 men fought about 80 Comanche Indians, boldly attacking them upon their own ground, killing & wounding about half their number. Up to this time these daring Indians had always supposed themselves superior to us, man to man, on

Opposite page: Right- and left-hand views of an assortment of Colt's revolvers from the earliest experimentals to production pistols. Top to bottom: a prototype made (it is believed) for Colt by John Pearson, a Colt-Pearson prototype complete with spring-loaded 'bayonet', a prototype Walker made by Blunt & Syms of New York in 1847, Colt's 1842 self-cocking Bowie-knife pistol and a partially-completed Third Model Dragoon. (By courtesy of the Connecticut State Library).

Above, top: Colt concentrated upon revolvers, but he never lost sight of the fact that rifles and carbines were also essential. This is the Model No. 1 ring lever rifle, produced in calibres of .34, .36, .40 and .44. The chamber capacity was about forty grains and the weapons were either eight- or

ten-shooters. A number of these rifles were purchased for use in the Seminole Wars of the late 1830s, but they were not a great success. Lateral muzzle flash from the cylinder (a fault with all Colt revolving long arms) did not endear them to the troops. (By courtesy of the West Point Museum)

Above, centre: This .44 calibre eight-shot Dragoon rifle has a 30-inch barrel, and a 2½-inch cylinder (about the same length as the Walker). The model never went into production, but a modified version with a creeping-lever rammer was produced in the early 1850s. This specimen is circa 1847–48. (By courtesy of the Connecticut State Library)

Above: A fine Texas Paterson Colt with the later-addition rammer. The stock inscription was evidently added some years after the event. (By courtesy of the West Point Museum)

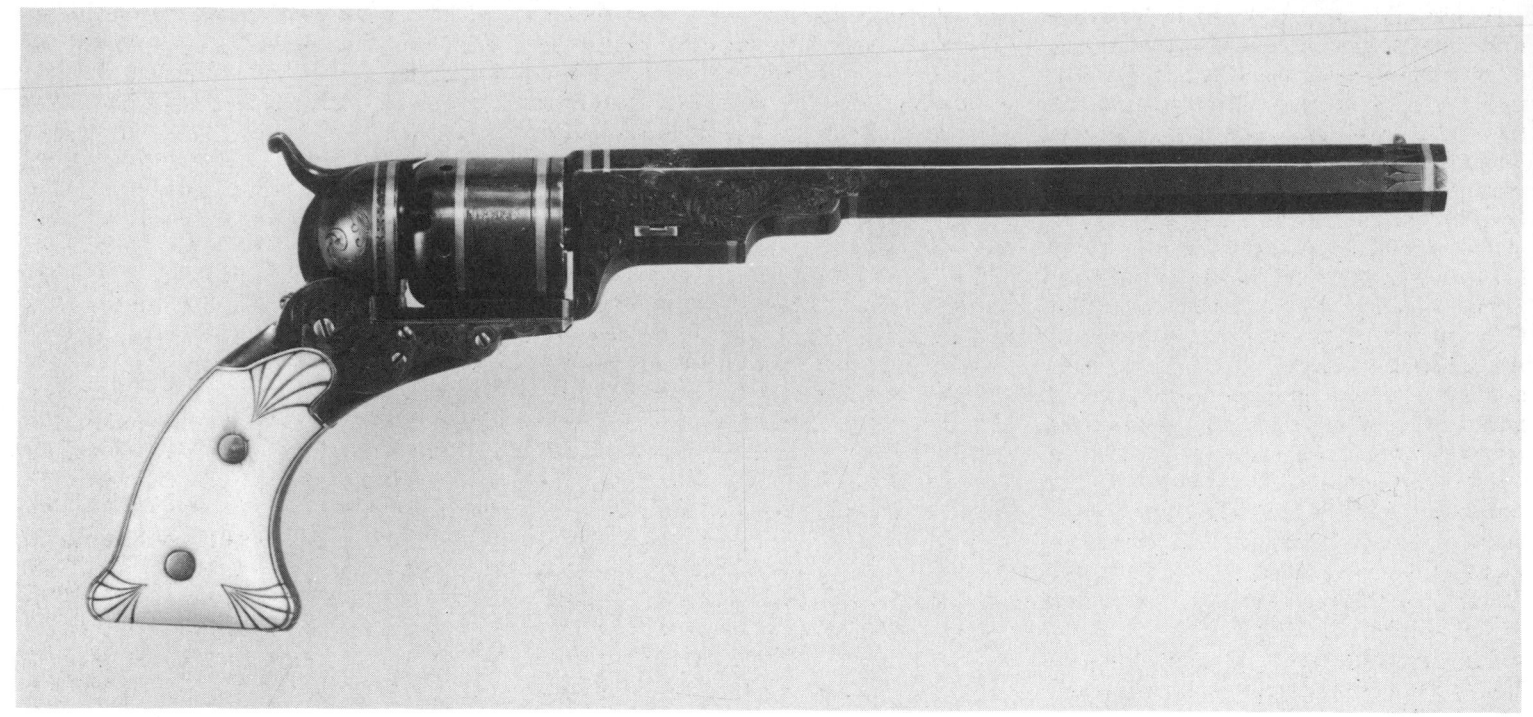

horse – at that time they were threatening a descent upon our Frontier Settlements – the result of this engagement was such as to intimidate them and enable us to treat with them. Several other Skirmishes have been equally satisfactory, and I can safely say that you deserve a large share of the credit for our success. Without your Pistols we would not have had the confidence to have undertaken such daring adventures . . .'

The tribes were learning the hard way that bows and arrows were no match for multi-shot weapons.

A similar reaction was experienced on the plains when Colt's and other repeating rifles and revolvers became available. Kit Carson was particularly taken with Colt's revolving rifles, and it is reported that he advised Fremont that a number of men armed with such weapons were more dangerous than a small army equipped with the old-fashioned single-shot weapons. During the late 1830s and early 1840s, however, the shortcomings of the revolving rifles and carbines outweighed their obvious advantages, and it was the single-shot rifles and muskets that held sway. None the less, it is claimed that a caravan of wagons attacked by Indians 175 miles from Taos in the autumn of 1841 was saved when Kit Carson and some of his men hid among the wagons to await a dawn attack. Soon after first light when the Indians appeared, they were greeted by a sporadic burst of musket fire. True to form, the Indians swept in to attack while the defenders reloaded. Their charge, however, was met by a withering and repeated fire from Carson and his men, who were armed with the latest Colt's repeating rifles and revolvers.

Above: A fine example of the Texas Holster pistol, serial No. 984. This was the model most popular with the Texas Rangers from about 1840 until 1848 (before it was replaced by the Walker and the later Dragoons). This .36 calibre pistol was fitted with a 7½-inch barrel. (By courtesy of the Wadsworth Atheneum)

Below: Captain Samuel Walker, who did so much to promote and improve Colt's revolver. His death is said to have affected Colt very deeply; one of his proudest possessions was one of the pair of Walker pistols he had presented to the gallant captain, and which was returned to him by Walker's family. (Author's Collection)

Despite the interest shown in his arms, Colt had problems with his stockholders concerning money owed to and by him. Furthermore, the U.S. Marines, while satisfied with the principle of the 1839 model carbine, found the weapon itself lacking in certain respects and recommended that it be no longer used. The inevitable happened: a lack of government orders and shortage of money led to bankruptcy and in 1842 the Patent Arms Company went into liquidation. For Colt the next four years was a period of frustration and determination. His ingenuity seemed boundless. He experimented with all manner of things, including underwater mines and, at one point, even produced a self-cocking knife-pistol which, with its cutlass-like handle and Bowie-type blade, made it a fearsome-looking weapon. But it was not the answer. Then in 1846, the United States and Mexico went to war, with dramatic results for Sam Colt.

The United States' relationship with Mexico had been worsening for some years, and the amnesty between Mexico and the Republic of Texas was precarious to say the least. The problem was partially solved in 1845 when, by joint resolution, Texas was annexed by the United States; but on 8 May 1846, the Battle of Palo Alto saw the opening round of a war between the United States and Mexico which lasted until February 1848, when the two sides signed a peace treaty.

During the early months of the war, when the United States Government concerned itself with establishing a ready supply of arms, reports were coming in of the effectiveness of Colt's revolvers in the hands of mounted troops. On 25 April 1846 an American patrol under the command of Captain S. B. Thornton, of the 2nd Dragoons, who was armed with a pair of his own Paterson pistols, shot their way out of an ambush with the loss of fifteen men. News of the incident swept the army, and there were demands for more revolvers. Major-General Zachary Taylor, who commanded the American forces, which included a number of Texas Rangers, was aware of the great attachment the Texans had for their Colt's pistols (many of them fought throughout the war using their, by now, well-used Paterson arms), and encouraged the use of such weapons.

This was the sort of encouragement for which Sam Colt yearned and he wasted no time in trying to gain access to influential members of the Senate in the hope of re-establishing himself in the arms business. The news that former Ranger, Captain Samuel Walker, had been newly-commissioned into the United States Mounted Rifles Regiment prompted him to write to the gallant captain to remind him of the value his revolvers had been to the Rangers, and to point out that there was still a lot of prejudice against his arms among the military. He hoped Walker and Colonel Hays would be instrumental in convincing their superiors of the value of Colt's repeating arms (rifles and revolvers). He also asked Walker for his honest opinion of the existing weapons and for any suggested improvements. Walker's reply of 30 November, which we have mentioned, made no reference to faults; but when, on 1 December Colt offered to supply 1,000 revolvers at $25 each, and decrease the cost with each succeeding thousand pistols, Colt and Walker met and in successive correspondence thrashed out the weapons' faults and suggested improvements. Walker was able to persuade the Ordnance Department to purchase 1,000 pistols; but on 7 December he warned Colt that the Ordnance doubted whether Sam could produce such an order within three months. Should he be successful, however, another order would follow. In any event, Walker was convinced that Colt could sell pistols in Texas or New Orleans without any difficulty.

Colt's biggest problem was to find someone to manufacture the revolvers for him. At one point it was recommended that he approach Eliphalet Remington of Ilion, New York, who would one day be Colt's biggest rival, but he did not do so. Instead, he approached Eli Whitney, Junior, of New Haven, Connecticut, and eventually persuaded him to manufacture the weapons at his factory under Colt's supervision. Finally, following long discussions with Walker and a part-by-part acceptance or rejection of Colt's existing revolver, a new weapon was designed, and on 4 January 1847, Colt and Walker (the latter acting on the authority of the Secretary of War) drew up a contract for the manufacture of 1,000 pistols for the U.S. Government. The steel for the manufacture of the barrels and cylinders was purchased from Naylor & Company of Sheffield, England, through their Boston office. This company continued to supply materials to Colt until the early 1850s when he switched to another Sheffield firm, Thomas Firth & Sons.

The contract called for the weapons to be produced to the following specifications: the barrel was to be nine inches long and rifled; of best cast steel and of a bore suited to carry round balls (50 to the pound) and strong enough also to fire an elongated ball weighing 52 to the pound. Although not stated, the actual calibre was .44. The six-chambered cylinder was also to be constructed from hammered cast steel and the length was to be sufficient to accept round or elongated (conical) bullets. The lockwork (except the hammer) to be made of the best cast or double-sheet steel and the parts to be made interchangeable with little or no refitting. The hammer and the lock frame were to be of the best gun iron and case-hardened. Finally, the stock was to be of sound black walnut, bound and secured by a strong strap of brass or iron. The contract price per pistol was agreed at $25.

Above: If pistoldom ever had a 'Big Bertha' this was it! The Colt-Walker Dragoon or Holster pistol of 1847 was formidable in many ways: it was too big, too powerful, and in danger of blowing up. But it paved the way to better arms, and ensured Sam Colt's return to armsmaking. (Private Collection)

Despite many problems with Whitney's work-force, who were unfamiliar with the manufacture of firearms, Colt was impressed by the finished product, for it was indeed a formidable weapon. The 9-inch barrel was manufactured with the forepart round and the breech end part octagonal. The cylinder bolt notches were oval, and around the periphery of the cylinder was a rolled-on engraving of a Ranger-Indian fight scene with the inscription MODEL U.S.M.R. COLT'S PATENT in a cartouche. The cylinder itself was $2\frac{7}{16}$ inches long and was fitted with one safety or locking pin set in the rear. A corresponding notch in the lower face of the hammer allowed the weapon to be carried with the hammer set down between chambers. The loading lever was retained by a T-shaped spring which slotted through a channel cut into the lever lug. The mainspring was a V-type which fitted into a lug set in the lower part of the grip strap, and instead of fitting flush as in later models, the head of the stock was rounded to conform to the rounded rear portion of the frame.

As with all succeeding models, Colt ensured that his name was prominently displayed, and the barrel address read: ADDRESS SAML. COLT NEW-YORK CITY. The finish of the weapon followed previous models – blued barrel, case-hardened frame, hammer and loading lever, but for some reason the cylinders were left in the white. The trigger guard was of polished brass and had a squared back. The backstrap, however, was iron and blued. The barrel foresight was of German silver, and the rear sight a slot cut into the hammer lip (a feature carried over from the Paterson period, and continued in all succeeding percussion models except for the Root side-hammer). The unloaded pistol weighed a staggering four pounds nine ounces and was a veritable 'Big Bertha'!

In addition to the pistols, Colt was to supply one set of springs for every ten pistols; an entire lockwork set, a spring clamp and an extra set of cones and screws for every 25 pistols. One bullet mould for casting one elongated bullet was to be supplied with every ten pistols, and one double-cavity mould with every fifty pistols. The contract also called for powder flask, screwdrivers and nipple wrenches.

Thanks to Whitney and various subcontractors, Colt was able to complete his contract for the government, and produced an extra 100 pistols, many of which were presented to deserving individuals for services rendered or in pursuit of fresh contracts. Tragically, Captain Walker, who had been instrumental in influencing Colt and paving the way for his re-entry into the firearms field, never saw the results of his efforts, for he was killed in action at Huamantla in October 1847. One of the new 'Walker-Colt' revolvers which he carried was returned to Colt, who prized it highly, and the other one was retained by Walker's family.

Although provision was made for loading the Walker revolvers direct from a flask, the weapon was designed to use either round or conical bullets. The round ball was 146 grains (48 to the pound) or a ½-ounce conical bullet. The round ball was never made up into cartridge form. Standard cartridges (when available) were made up from the conical bullets (128 grains or 32 to the pound) and 1½ drams (40 grains) of rifle powder. Unfortunately, the base of the bullet created problems in loading, and this fault was not rectified until 1851 when the base was rebated to enable it to fit into the mouth of the chamber, to ensure accurate loading.

The success of the new revolver was not total; it was really too powerful, and far too big and heavy. The chambers could actually accept a powder charge of 57 grains, which gave the pistol a muzzle velocity of 1,300–1,500 feet per second when firing a 140-grain lead ball. A number of the pistols blew up, partly because of the material used in construction (some authorities blame the treatment it received during manufacture) which caused problems. Writing from Vera Cruz, Mexico, on 8 May 1848, to Colonel G. Talcott of the Ordnance Department in Washington, Captain John Williamson informed him that only 191 of the 280 new revolvers issued to the Texas Rangers under the command of Colonel Jack Hays, had been handed in, and of these only 82 were considered serviceable, the remainder having been lost in battle or burst.

Talcott was no lover of Colt and was frequently critical of the man and his pistols. On 5 April, prior to receipt of Williamson's letter, he wrote to the Secretary of War and reviewed the previous purchases of Colt's revolvers, rifles and carbines. In addition to the recently purchased 1,000 revolvers used in the late war, another thousand had been ordered, but he felt it necessary to add that 'Whoever supposes that placing a Colt's Pistol in the hands of an ordinary soldier, will make him a "Jack Hays" will be disappointed.'

Colt however, was undeterred. By now he was well aware of his pistol's failings and was convinced he could rectify them. The cylinders were the main problem. A few weapons which had suffered from muzzle damage were re-worked and the barrels shortened, but the cylinder required some further thought. While admitting the faults, Colt, in promising to rectify them, also prepared to set up a factory in his home town of Hartford, Connecticut. This he did late in 1847. Here, he believed, he would be best able to control every phase of production and ensure that the shortcomings of the Walker–Colt revolver were eradicated.

For the prototype of his new improved revolver, Sam replaced the iron backstrap by one made of brass. The weak T-spring used to keep the rammer lever in place through a slot cut in the lever, was replaced by a more substantial latch. He solved the cylinder problem by reducing its length from $2\frac{7}{16}$ inches to $2\frac{1}{16}$ inches and cut the powder charge down to a maximum of 40 grains. The barrel length was reduced to 7½ inches; but the weapon's weight was reduced by only seven ounces to four pounds two ounces.!

It was a start, and the next step was to improve the materials used in manufacture. Following a visit to London in 1849, where he patented his new revolvers in England and on the Continent, he went to Sheffield. Naylor & Company again supplied some forged parts, but it was Thomas Firth & Sons who received the contracts to supply iron and steel to the Hartford (and later London) factory. Firth were to remain Colt's sole suppliers until the late 1860s.

By 1850 Colt had modified his original Walker revolver until it was a Model in its own right, and from then until 1861, it underwent the following changes.

The single safety-pin on the rear of the cylinder was increased to six; and the grips and frame were finished flush, a feature which became standard on all succeeding models. Colt was aware that the oval or rounded bolt stops on the cylinder were weak, and on 10 September 1850 he patented a rectangular version with guide grooves to prevent the cylinder from over-shooting during cocking. A flat spring replaced the V-type mainspring, and a bearing wheel was added to the base of the hammer to prevent wear and ease pressure when cocking. Late in production, about fifty pistols were produced with 8-inch barrels, bevelled bullet cuts (to facilitate the loading of the foil cartridges introduced in 1855) and rounded trigger guard. The lever latch was improved to conform to that used on the Navy and Pocket pistols introduced in the early 1850s, and a number of these large revolvers were equipped with carbine stocks. The finish was standardized to a charcoal blued barrel, cylinder and, occasionally, iron grips and straps (the majority were in fact of brass, plain or silver-plated); case-hardened frame, hammer and lever assembly. Finally, the stocks were made from American walnut, which on civilian arms was shellac varnished, but on military arms was plain or oil-finished.

Colt's confidence in the revolver, which he now called the 'Army' or 'Holster' pistol (but which soon became known simply as the 'Dragoon') was such that he showed it at the Great Exhibition in London in 1851, where it received great acclaim, attracted many

Above: A fine First Model 1848 Dragoon or Holster pistol. This specimen is marked US beneath the COLT'S PATENT stamping on the frame. It turned up in Kansas many years ago and may well have once been issued to one of the dragoon regiments stationed at Fort Leavenworth. (By courtesy of the Kansas State Historical Society)

Below: A woodcut published in an illustrated guide to the Great Exhibition of 1851. Colt's revolver received a great deal of publicity in England during the 1850s; in 1852 he opened a factory in London which closed in 1856 at the end of the Crimean War. (Author's Collection)

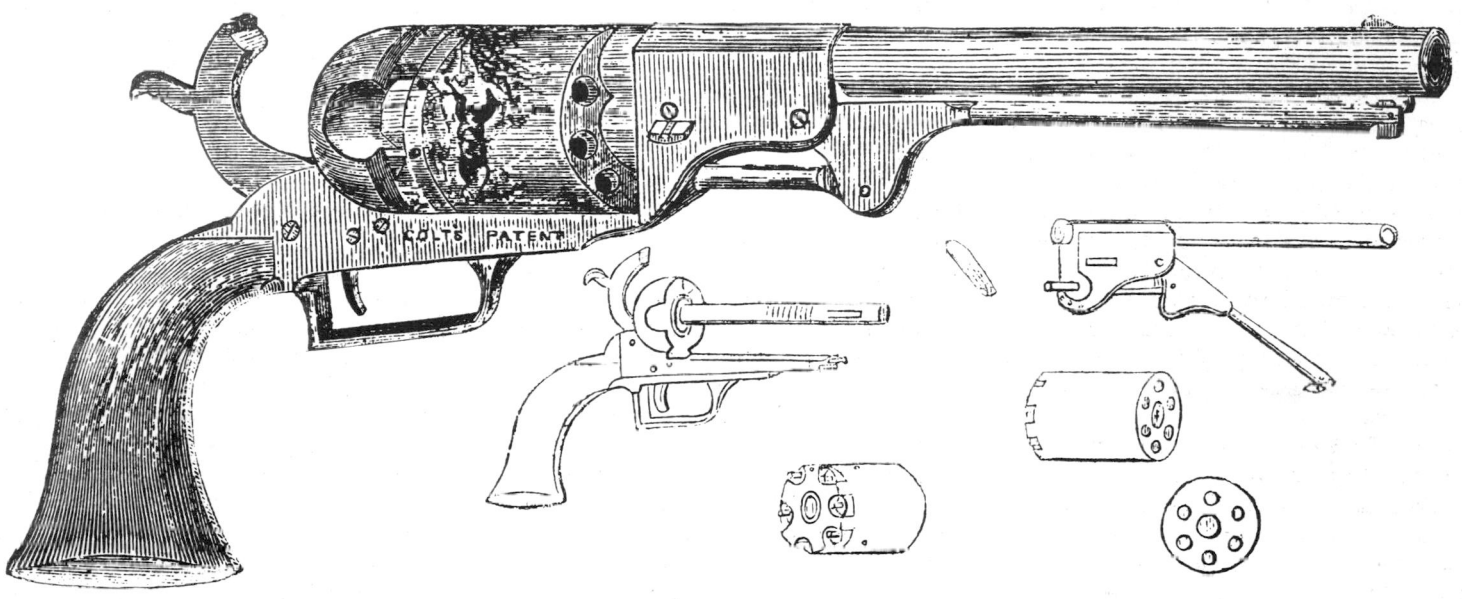

COLT'S REVOLVER.

purchasers and inspired Colt to set up a factory in England in which to manufacture his arms.* Tests conducted by the British Board of Ordnance confirmed what the Americans already knew – the Dragoon was extremely accurate at long range and, according to one British source, 'there is no weapon like it for Cavalry'. Even so, perhaps because of its size and great weight, the pistol was never purchased in any large quantities in England.

The Americans, however, were very much taken with the weapon. On 8 January 1849, 1,000 Dragoon revolvers were ordered, and on 4 February 1850, another 1,000 were purchased for military use. By 1851 more

*For a full account of Colt's British aspirations and the story of his London factory, see: Joseph G. Rosa, *Colonel Colt London*, 1976.

weapons were required, and on 8 May a further 2,000 were purchased. But between 1851 and 1861, when the model was discontinued, government purchases were very small, and its total production (which included the 1,100 Walker–Colt revolvers, and approximately 700 pistols made up in London) was only about 20,000.

Despite its comparatively short life and small production, due largely to its great weight, the weapon was popular in use. Of course, it was not a belt weapon; most troops carried one or a pair in saddle holsters, but whereever the pistol went so did its reputation. In Africa, it struck terror into the hearts of slave-traders, Arabs and others who encountered it. On many of his treks in Africa and across the United States, Captain Richard Burton carried Dragoon pistols and

some of these were fitted with stocks; he noted that they easily doubled as rifles. When confronted by one of these 'she-devils' native opposition wilted. Kaffirs who witnessed them in action were said to be almost reverent in their description of them as 'God's pistol!' Burton also noted that during his American trip in 1861 he was told that when going up against Indians, 'the Dragoon is universally preferred'. Anyone armed with such a weapon commanded respect – and envy.

George Catlin, the artist, owed his life to a Dragoon when his rifle failed to kill a large bull buffalo which promptly chased him. 'Fortunately', he recalled, 'I had one of Colt's [Dragoon] revolvers with me. I drew it and turned and fired at his head. Instantly, to my great surprise and relief, he fell dead

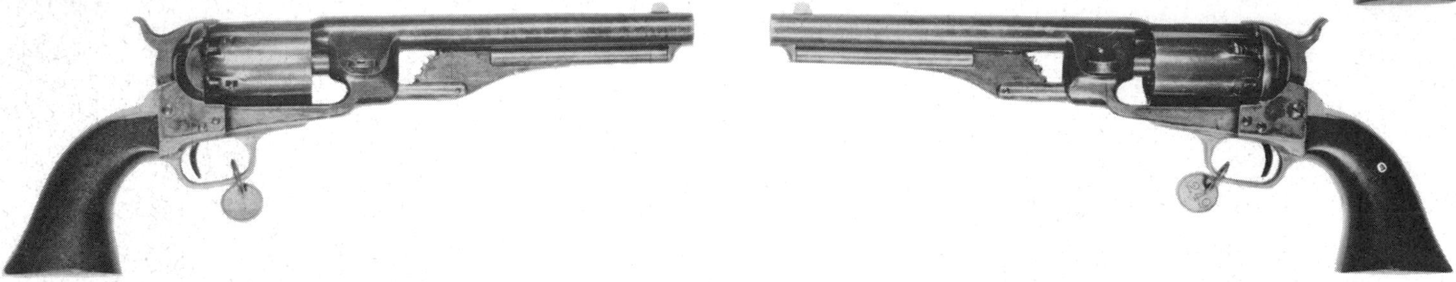

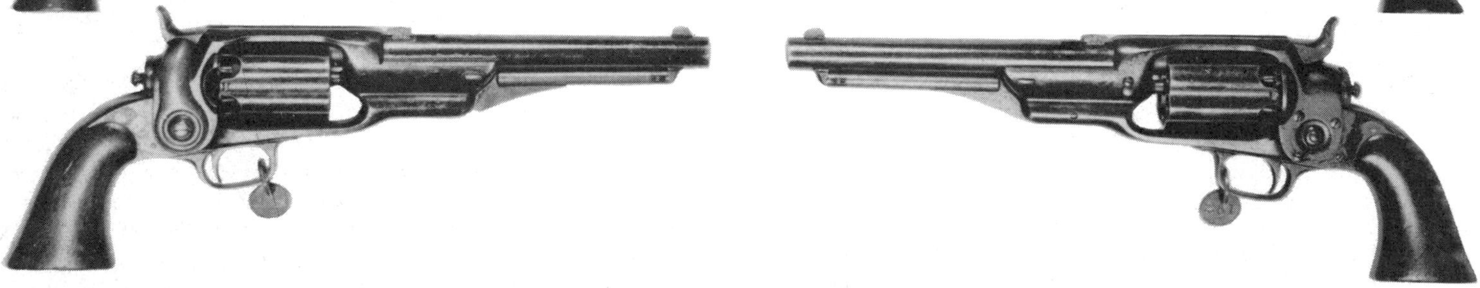

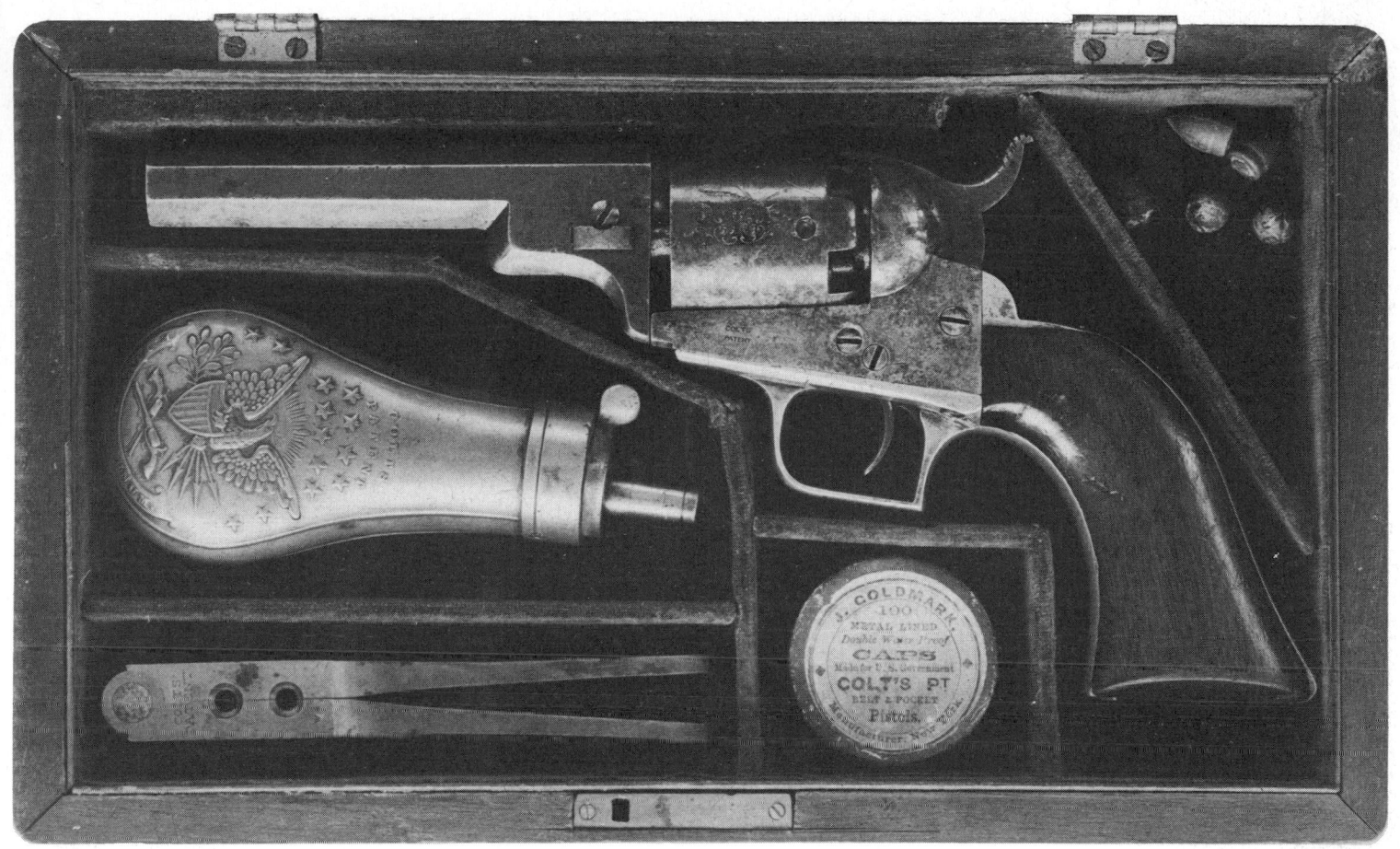

Top left: Right- and left-hand views of a group of Colt experimental revolvers. Top to bottom: Whitneyville-Hartford Dragoon (the first modification following the Walker contract) complete with belt hook. Late-production Old Model Navy (1851) with rounded instead of octagonal barrel; note the finely-carved grips. A third Model Dragoon which has been machined down to save weight, and fitted with a creeping-lever rammer. A late-production six-shot 1849 pocket-pistol. When so-called 'silver steel' was introduced in 1860, Colt deemed it safe to produce six-shot pocket models, whereas hitherto he had produced only five-shot versions. One of the few experimental pistols to have survived the fire of 1864, the Roots side-hammer type was intended to replace the Dragoon, but fortunately the 1860 Army pistol was adopted instead. (By courtesy of the Connecticut State Library)

Below left: George Catlin, the notable nineteenth-century artist, was also an avid hunter and keen shot. He had hunted in most of South America and was well known on the plains. This illustration from an early lithograph, was also reproduced in the *Illustrated London News* of 11 April 1857, where it was noted that buffalo hunting was a 'sport indulged in both by the Indians (with bow and arrow or spear) and the whites with the rifle-pistol'. (Author's Collection)

Top right: A Second Model pocket-pistol of 1848. These early pistols were often called 'Baby Dragoons', and proved to be very popular. By 1850, however, the cylinder bolt notches had been made rectangular and most weapons were produced with a rammer. This version is cased with all accessories. (By courtesy of William H. Myers)

at my feet, the ball having passed through his skull and entered the brain. So near was he when I fired the revolver, that the fire from its muzzle singed the curly hair on his pate.'

In 1858 Colt received from the U.S. Government belated contracts for Dragoon pistols. Some 924, together with 462 stocks (one per pair) were ordered at $50 per set. By May 1860 another 128 had been purchased, some of these with the 8-inch barrel we have previously mentioned, complete with folding rear sights. To boost sales, Colt even machined down some of the pistols to further reduce weight, but they were not really a success. Nevertheless, the Dragoon had made its mark. Loaded with 40 grains of black powder and a 140-grain bullet, it achieved a muzzle velocity of 1,100 feet per second, almost on a par with the Walker. With the same powder charge and a 212-grain bullet the velocity dropped to between 820 and 920 feet per second – but still powerful enough to stop anything that got in its way!

Colt, of course, had long realized that the weight of the Dragoon was the drawback, and he continued his search for a successor. Several pocket-pistols were produced between 1848 and 1850, but they were no match for the Dragoon. Then, in 1850, he got out a prototype for a pistol which, more than any other of his 'family' manufactured during his own lifetime, would ensure his

fame and fortune. This was the pistol he originally called the 'New Ranger Size Pistol' in honour of Jack Hays and the Texas Rangers.

Designed as early as 1847 (according to a surviving sketch), the new revolver was thirteen inches overall with a 7½-inch octagonal barrel. The calibre was .36, which was generally called 'Navy calibre' and identical with that used in the original Texas Paterson pistols. The cylinder was six-shot and around its periphery was a rolled-on scene depicting the battle between Mexican and Texas Navy ships which took place on 16 May 1843. The most important feature, however, was the pistol's weight – two pounds nine ounces, an improvement on the Dragoon's four pounds two ounces.

When the new pistol was submitted to the United States Board of Ordnance they were much impressed with it. On a single day it was fired 1,500 times, cleaned only once during that time, and yet continued to function properly. In penetration tests the balls went through six pine boards, propelled by a powder charge of twenty grains and firing an 83-grain bullet. The chamber capacity was about thirty grains, but the Board was more concerned with recoil than with accuracy and the weapon was underloaded.

It was during these tests or soon afterwards, that the original 'Ranger' title was

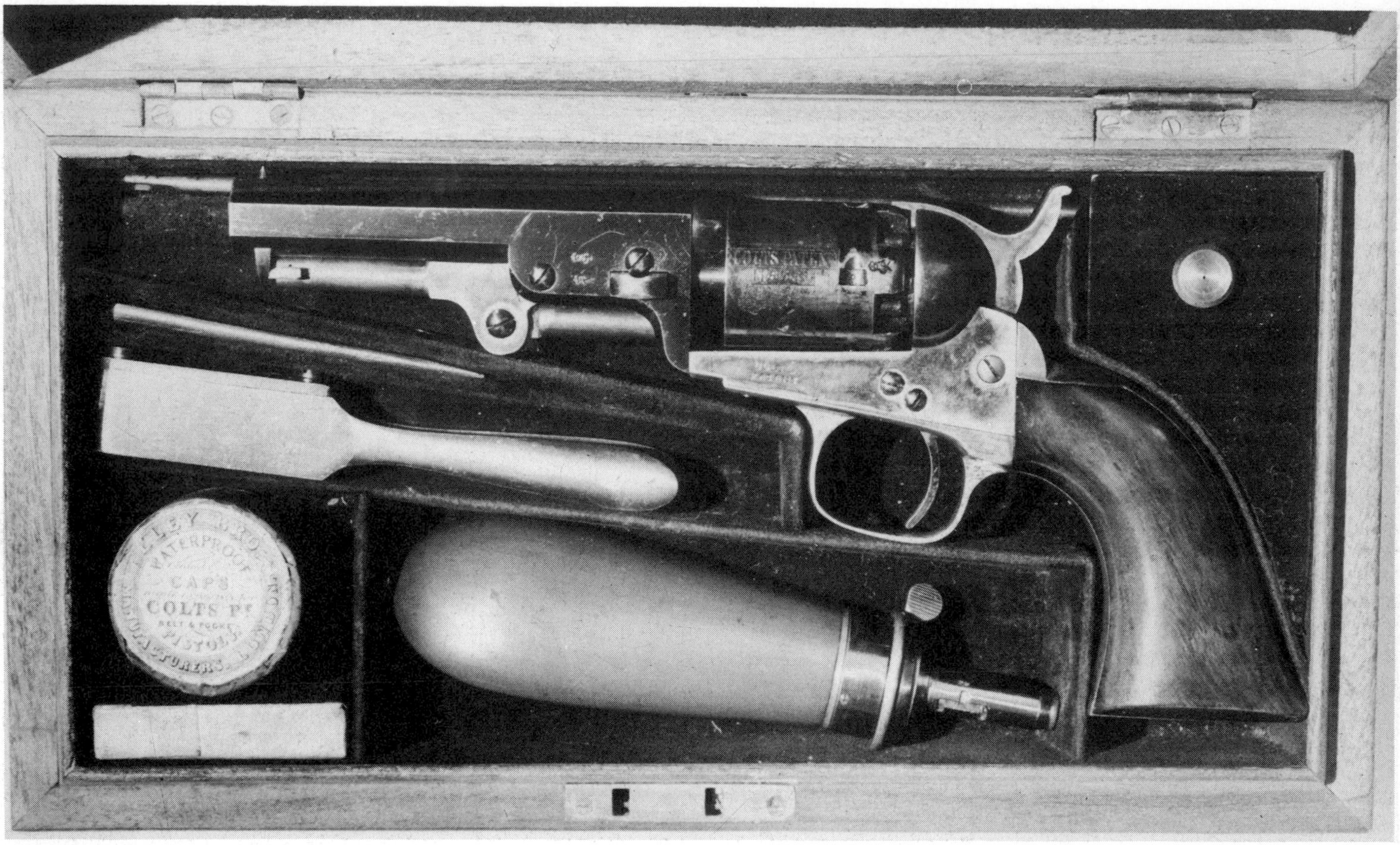
WATERPROOF
CAPS
COLTS Pt
PISTOLS

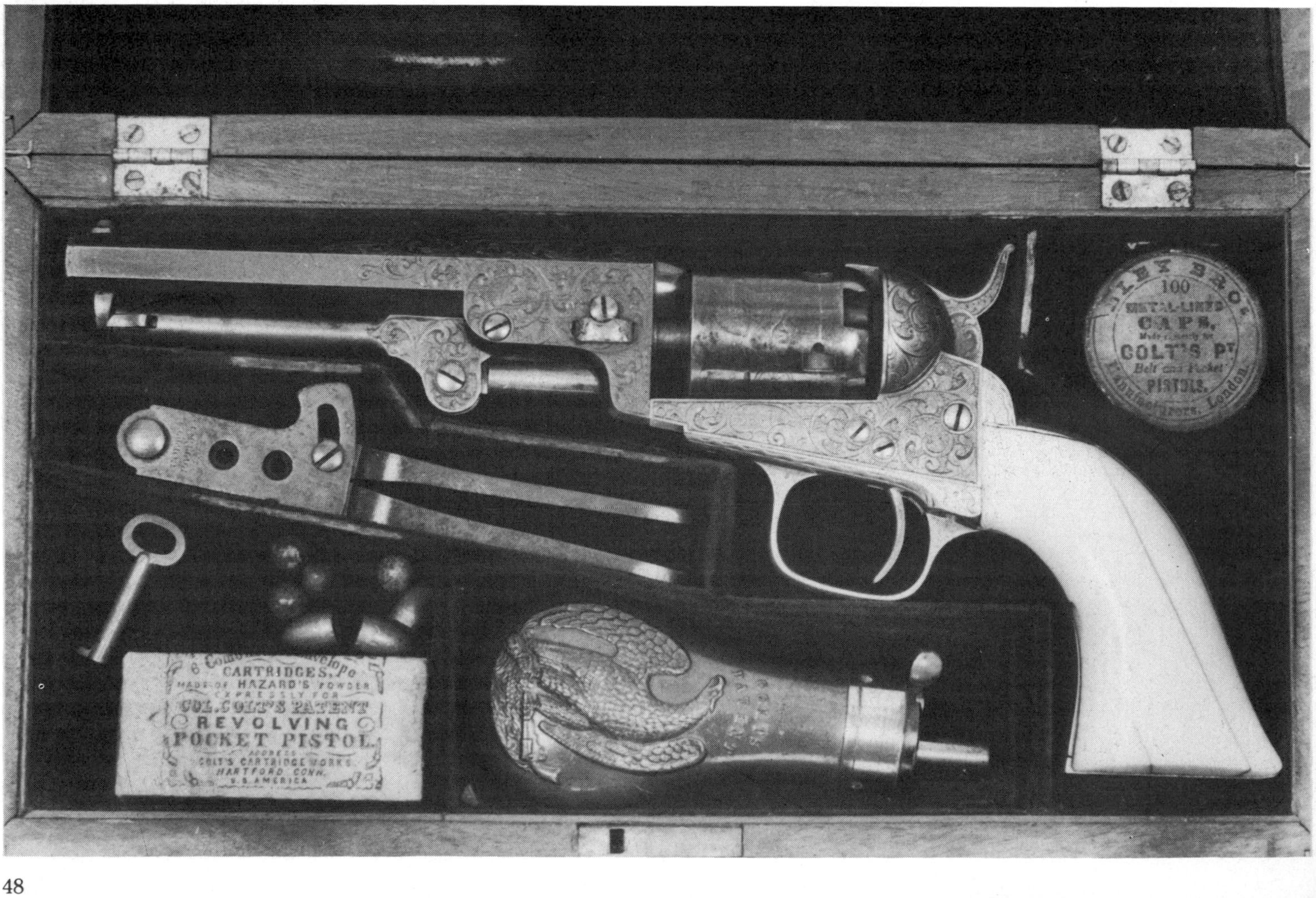
100
METAL-LINED
CAPS
COLT'S Pt
PISTOLS
London
CARTRIDGES
HAZARD'S POWDER
REVOLVING
POCKET PISTOL
HARTFORD CONN.

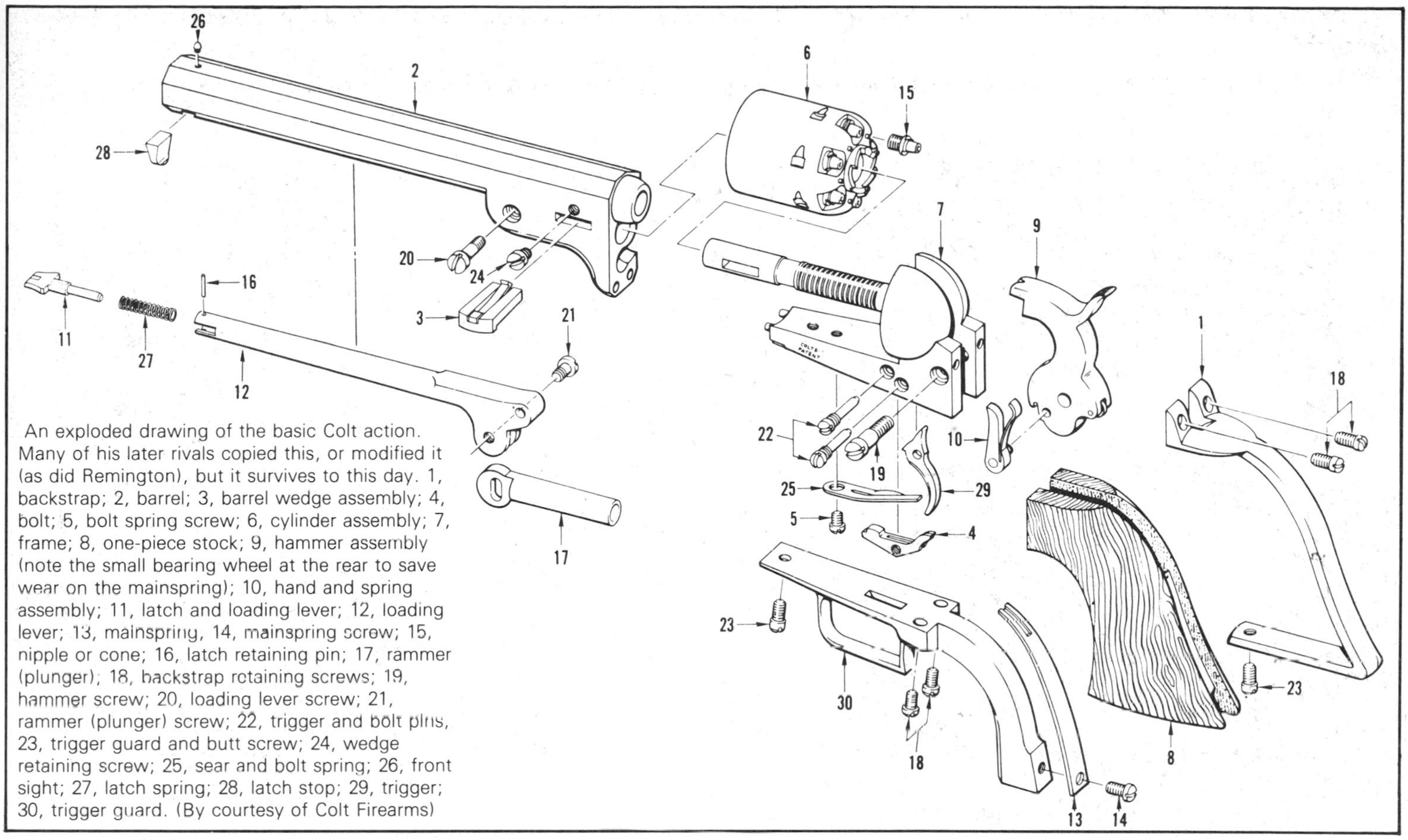

An exploded drawing of the basic Colt action. Many of his later rivals copied this, or modified it (as did Remington), but it survives to this day. 1, backstrap; 2, barrel; 3, barrel wedge assembly; 4, bolt; 5, bolt spring screw; 6, cylinder assembly; 7, frame; 8, one-piece stock; 9, hammer assembly (note the small bearing wheel at the rear to save wear on the mainspring); 10, hand and spring assembly; 11, latch and loading lever; 12, loading lever; 13, mainspring, 14, mainspring screw; 15, nipple or cone; 16, latch retaining pin; 17, rammer (plunger); 18, backstrap retaining screws; 19, hammer screw; 20, loading lever screw; 21, rammer (plunger) screw; 22, trigger and bolt pins; 23, trigger guard and butt screw; 24, wedge retaining screw; 25, sear and bolt spring; 26, front sight; 27, latch spring; 28, latch stop; 29, trigger; 30, trigger guard. (By courtesy of Colt Firearms)

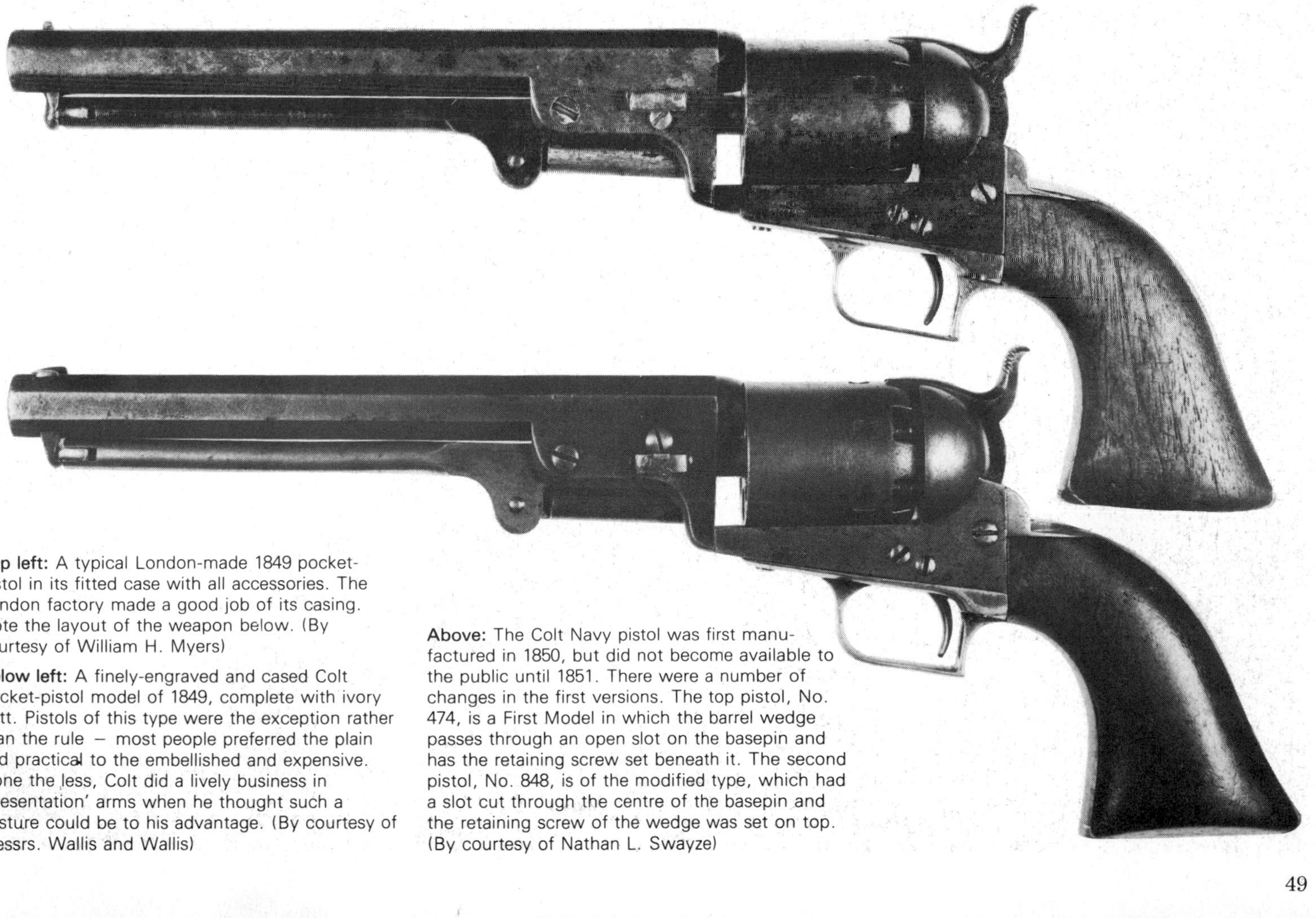

Top left: A typical London-made 1849 pocket-pistol in its fitted case with all accessories. The London factory made a good job of its casing. Note the layout of the weapon below. (By courtesy of William H. Myers)

Below left: A finely-engraved and cased Colt pocket-pistol model of 1849, complete with ivory butt. Pistols of this type were the exception rather than the rule — most people preferred the plain and practical to the embellished and expensive. None the less, Colt did a lively business in 'presentation' arms when he thought such a gesture could be to his advantage. (By courtesy of Messrs. Wallis and Wallis)

Above: The Colt Navy pistol was first manufactured in 1850, but did not become available to the public until 1851. There were a number of changes in the first versions. The top pistol, No. 474, is a First Model in which the barrel wedge passes through an open slot on the basepin and has the retaining screw set beneath it. The second pistol, No. 848, is of the modified type, which had a slot cut through the centre of the basepin and the retaining screw of the wedge was set on top. (By courtesy of Nathan L. Swayze)

dropped in favour of 'Navy'. Whether this was because of its calibre or the cylinder scene, or perhaps because the Board had contemplated purchasing some of the new pistols for the U.S. Navy is unclear, but the 'Navy' tag stuck, and the weapon has become immortalized as the Navy Colt.

Colt was as impressed with the new pistol as was the Board, and it remained in production from late 1850 until 1873, by which time more than 215,000 had been produced (excluding the 41,000 made at or finished by the London factory and sold from the London Agency between 1853 and 1861). The pistol underwent several modifications, the most important being the addition of a round-barrelled version in 1860–61. In general, however, the most important changes concerned the replacement of the original barrel key or wedge (which entered through the top of the cylinder pin) by one secured by a slot cut through the centre of the pin, the employment of enlarged trigger guards and the introduction in London of iron instead of brass for the trigger guard and backstraps. It was the latter which prompted the then General William S. Harney, in 1855, to order revolvers so fitted from Colt. By the outbreak of the Civil War, a number of the later Navys were cut for a shoulder stock, but by the end of the conflict this feature had been discontinued.

The Navy was popular as soon as it became available. Its lightness, balance and accuracy were soon appreciated and it became a favourite of Westerners in general, and for anyone who relied upon a pistol for survival. By 1850, when the supply for revolvers was outstripping demand, especially in California, all manner of weapons were shipped to the region, where the discovery of gold increased the local population three-fold.

Gold was discovered at Sutter's Mill on 24 January 1848. Fortunately, at that time it aroused only a local interest, because nine days later, on 2 February, the Treaty of Guadalupe Hidalgo was signed and Mexico ceded California to the United States. Had the discovery not been made until decades later, California would have assumed a normal territorial status, but within a year, when news of it had spread, people from all over the world were *en route* to California. The 1849 gold-rush was responsible for one of the most amazing migrations in history. Soon, doctors, dentists, princes and paupers jostled with one another in their feverish attempts to reach the precious metal, many of them deserting their families to join the frantic throng.

Getting to California, however, posed problems. Both Europeans and people from the Eastern states normally took the sea route around Cape Horn, a 168-day trip

which was both tedious and expensive. Some tried the short-cut across the Isthmus of Panama (the canal had not yet been built), their greed overcoming natural caution in a region notorious for its lethal diseases. Others came through Northern Mexico, risking daily attacks from bandits, but the truly hardy headed West across country to St. Louis, and from there followed the Oregon Trail, a gruelling 2,000-mile trip which took months. The climate was unpredictable as were the wild animals and even wilder Indians who resented such intrusions into their homelands. But whatever their route, the determination of the would-be gold-seekers was matched by the determination of those anxious to help get them there and (at a price) provide for their needs upon arrival.

The gold-seekers were soon joined by crowds of gamblers, aspiring politicians, prostitutes and every kind of speculator. By the early 1850s, California was, by contemporary standards, densely populated, and following resolutions from the citizens and some dead-locked debates in Congress, primarily concerning whether the territory should be a slave or a free state, statehood was granted on 9 September 1850. So without any formal territorial status, the region had leapt ahead to statehood, thus creating a paradox. The United States was now almost two nations separated by two thousand miles of largely unsettled territory, but few of the gold-seekers concerned themselves with such technicalities. There was 'gold in them thar hills', fortunes to be made, and everyone was anxious to stake a claim to his fair share – or somebody else's.

When preparing for the trip, people took care to pack plenty of clothing and other easily transportable items, and they were also very careful to be properly armed. Some relied upon a rifle and a brace of pistols, others preferred just the pistols. Initially, the demand was met by the innumerable single- and multi-shot versions readily available. Despite their increasing reliance on vigilance committees, the miners were well aware of their own vulnerability and soon there was a big demand for Colt's revolvers. Those who had armed themselves with the multi-barrelled Allen and similar weapons were now anxious to acquire Sam's products. For Colt it was an opportunity not to be missed.

Along with other makers, Colt of course had followed events very closely. The military success of the modified Dragoon pistols had soon led to a civilian demand, but he was also aware of the need for smaller, lighter weapons, especially for the civilian market. Prior to the Navy he had produced a range of small .31 pocket-pistols which had proved to be very popular, but they were only five-shot weapons. So it was the Navy on which he pinned his hopes for the future.

Getting arms to California had its problems, because one had to rely on others to transport them. When the gold-rush started the military were still in control of the region. Sam kept a jaundiced eye on the activities of John Ehlers, a former stockholder in the Paterson company. When Colt's original Paterson venture had failed, there was a great deal of animosity between Colt and Ehlers, a New Jersey hardware merchant, who had assumed control of the Patent Arms Manufacturing Company during the early 1840s and, following a court order, had acquired parts for several hundred pistols and long arms. Some of these post-Colt Paterson arms were sold by Ehlers to the U.S. Government. The Mexican war and the California gold-rush led to further limited sales, but, as the following advertisement (surmounted by a woodcut of a Paterson pistol), originally published in *The American Flag* in 1847 and as late as April 1848, clearly indicates, Ehlers was very wary of Sam who was again in a position to fight him if necessary:

'COLT'S PATENT REPEATING RIFLES, CARBINES AND PISTOLS

With the latest Improvements of 1844, 1845, 1846 Special permission having been granted to Mr. Ehlers, to sell his "Colt's Repeating Fire Arms", under certain restrictions – officers of the army are respectfully informed that these Arms are now for sale at the offices of the subscriber, (casa de John Andreas Saldana,) on the street leading out south, at the south-west corner of the Plaza de Hidalgo. Private soldiers and American citizens can also be accommodated with them, but must produce written permission; the soldiers from their commanding officers, and the citizens from the commander of this city, Col. Davenport, Matamoporos, June 23, 1847.

John Ehlers.'

Ehlers had nothing like a monopoly, and once the lure of gold gripped the world, California's population, estimated at the end of 1848 to be 20,000, had by 1850, leaped to 100,000, and in 1851 was estimated at a quarter of a million. So there was no shortage of would-be customers or importers of Colt's and other arms. Once itinerant merchants and speculators realized the potential, weapons which sold for a few dollars in New York doubled and trebled in price by the time they reached 'the diggings'. Available Colt Dragoons were sold for as much as $300 each and the pocket-pistols for about $150–200. It was indeed a sellers' market, but while individuals were prepared to gamble on a swift return for their initial outlay, there were merchants who were reluctant to take that gamble. Some felt that

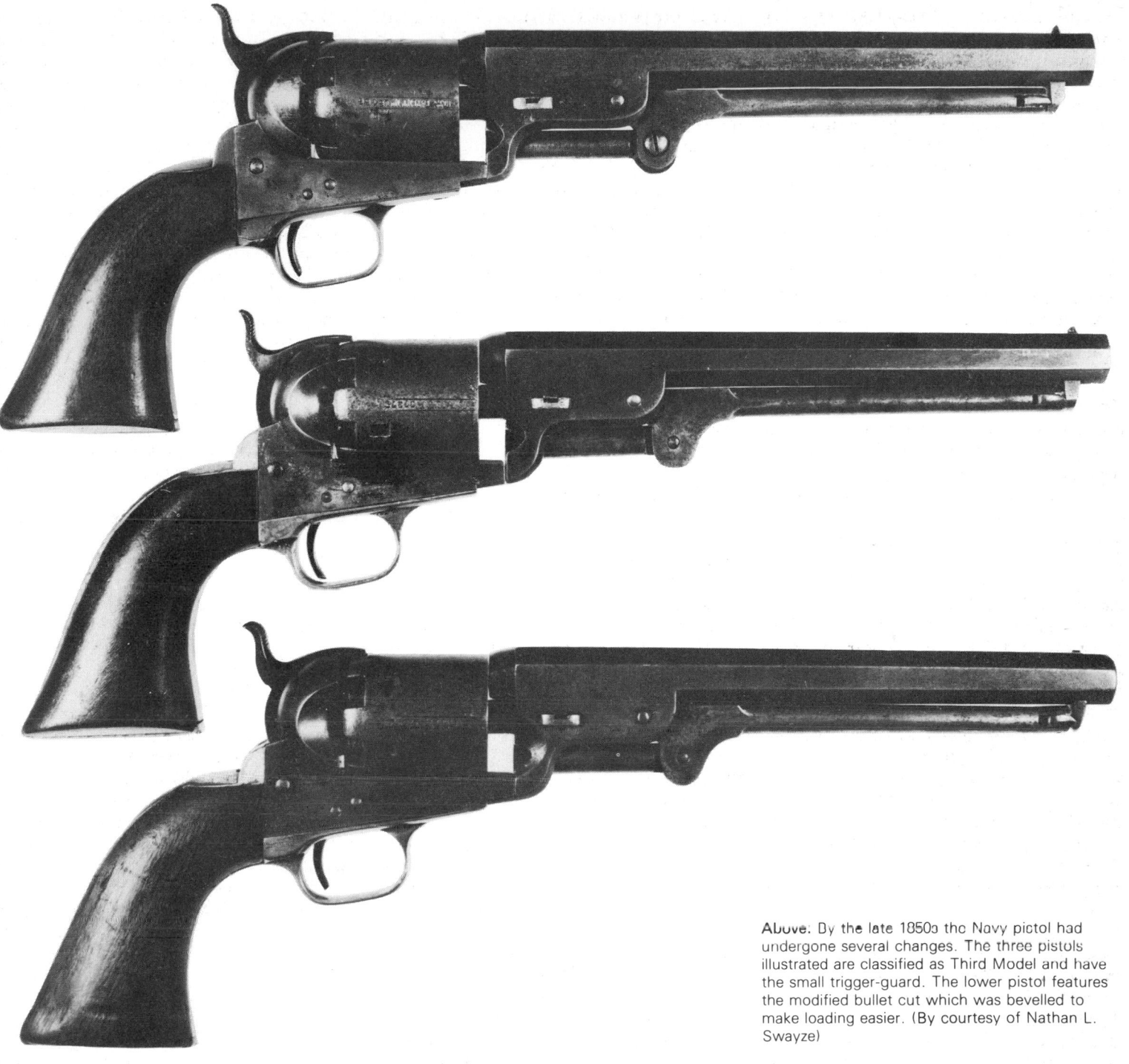

Above: By the late 1850s the Navy pistol had undergone several changes. The three pistols illustrated are classified as Third Model and have the small trigger-guard. The lower pistol features the modified bullet cut which was bevelled to make loading easier. (By courtesy of Nathan L. Swayze)

the rigours of the trip, the possibility of shipwreck and the chance that they might not make the gains they expected, were not worth the risk. However, the true speculator was unperturbed and many people took along extra pistols just to make a quick sale.

By January 1850, Colt was gaining ground in the arms race to California. The earliest pistols to arrive seem to have been 3- and 4-inch barrelled pocket models, to be followed by a limited number of Dragoon pistols. One of Sam's cousins, Elisha Colt, arranged with the help of business colleagues to get Sam's pistols to California, and by 1851, the following advertisement which

appeared in the Alta *Californian* of 16 March indicated which arms were available:

'COLT'S PISTOLS. – A complete assort- ment of these valuable firearms, 3 & 4 in. and United States Dragoon size, brass and silver mounted with appendages, powder flask, bullet moulds, extra cones, main springs, percussion caps, etc., received by the *Prince de Joinville* and for sale by Macandry & Co.'

Sales of the few available Dragoons and more abundant pocket-pistols were brisk, but soon word reached California of the new Colt's revolver – the Navy – and the demand for it was such that Colt introduced a night-

shift to meet it. It is probable that the first Navys to reach California came in during January or February 1851. The pocket- pistols were then retailing for $18.30–$19.30 (dependent upon barrel length) and the Navy retailed at $31.00 – a considerable improvement on the inflated prices of two years before! This led to a steady stream of arms, and within a year almost 2,000 assorted Colt's pistols had been sold through his own outlets.

Compared to the situation in the gold regions of Australia, Colt's prices within the United States were very reasonable. Weapons reaching 'down under' were

Above: Two contemporary views of the California 'diggings' showing how hard it really was to gather 'dust' in the face of tremendous competition. A hard day's work could also mean a hard night guarding claims from would-be 'jumpers' and others anxious to obtain their riches the easy way. (Author's Collection)

Left: Women were scarce in the days of the early gold-rushes and the miners had to make their own entertainment — as can be seen from this tongue-in-cheek cartoon 'Lady's Claim!' (Author's Collection)

grossly overpriced. One man writing from the Bendigo Diggings, about 100 miles north-west of Melbourne, declared: 'Colt revolvers fetch £25 at the diggings and are quite in common use. A 26 shilling brace of pistols will here bring £5.'

During the early months of 1853 it was reported that the 'yield of fine gold from California is as great as ever, and the supply seems to be really exhaustless'. That same year, *Gleason's Pictorial Drawing Room Companion* reported that wages in California 'are now $4 a day. Provisions and miners' tools are very high, and it costs double to live than it did last year at this time'. And Colt's fortunes, too, were the subject of some speculation: 'He is rapidly becoming a millionaire, from the immense demand for his revolvers in all parts of the belligerent world.'

But, gold, vigilantes and climate were not all that California had to offer, for despite innumerable books and comment to the contrary, she produced more than her share of dangerous men who could match shot-for-shot many of the better-known 'pistoleers' and 'shootists' who crowd today's history books, yet many of the California characters remain curiously obscure.

Take Will Hicks Graham, a Philadelphia-born newspaperman who spent time in New York before following the gold trail to California in 1850, where he found employment in the law offices of Probate Judge R. N. Morrison. When the judge was insulted in print by William Walker, editor of the San Francisco *Herald*, and a noted duellist, it was Graham who issued a challenge in defence of the judge's honour. Both men were to fire Colt's Navy revolvers at ten paces, and advance one step after each shot. Graham fired first and put a bullet through Walker's 'pantaloons' and then through the fleshy part of the thigh, at which point the duel was terminated.

Graham went on to achieve considerable fame as a duellist, vigilante and lawyer, but he was well aware of the dangers of his existence. Of his reputation as a fighting man, he declared: 'Such a reputation is a curse to anyone. Every reckless fool who wants to get his name up as a desperado thinks he is duty-bound to have a difficulty with you, while you are expected to resent every grievance, real or imaginery, with knife or pistol.' Any one of a half dozen top-notch gunfighters of a later era would have said 'Amen' to that!

By 1857, however, there were many Californians (and others) who, while appreciating the 'civilizing' effect of the revolver in the right hands, regretted its abuse in the hands of the lawless. On 15 September 1857 the *Illustrated London News* published the following long letter from a San Francisco correspondent which is graphic in its condemnation of the latter:

'CRIME IN CALIFORNIA. – The crime of homicide continues to prevail all over the country to an extent which in any other country than this would be taken as proof that civil society was completely disorganised. Our "Homicide Calendar" for June, lately published in the *San Francisco Chronicle*, the "total of Killed" for the first six months of the present year is set down at 219 persons; and in the same period, "Hung [sic] by the sheriff, 2; hung by the mob, 24.2. But whether the two judicial and the twenty-four lynch executions are included in or are in addition to the 219 I am not able to determine from the calendar. The number of "killed" in the month of June was twenty – a fact which it is sincerely to be hoped may be taken as an evidence that the homicidal epidemic is abating. Were it not for the atrocity of the deeds, the causes which produce all this murder would appear ludicrously trivial. I attribute nearly all the crime of this character committed to the universal and cowardly practice of carrying revolvers. For instance, it appears that in June four men were killed by two of the officers employed in collecting the foreign miners' tax, one of the collectors having "killed" a Mexican miner at Tuttletown, and another of them having "shot and killed" three Chinamen in Mariposa county. These four murders were perpetrated by the too ready use of the ever-handy revolver on a slight resistance to the payment of the tax which, to my own knowledge, Mexicans and Chinamen have often been made to pay twice over the extortion of unauthorised rascals, who laid them under contribution by assuming the office of collector. Several instances, even more striking than the foregoing, have occurred throughout the country, as given in the public papers during the last fortnight, showing the trivial causes which produce murder. I will take two or three examples at random: – A man was shot in his own house because he "refused to serve out liquor" to a riotous customer late at night; while another man was killed for "refusing to drink" with a "gentleman" who could not brook a refusal. These two cases occurred at different localities; the disputes were short and sudden, and followed a speedy death. Another affair appears to have ended as tragically on equally slight provocation. In a crowd assembled in the Northern Mines (on the South Salmon River) one man "rubbed against or pushed" another several times. This offense was expatiated [sic] with the offender's life, for the man "pushed" struck him "on the head with a bar of steel" which he suddenly seized, and he "died about four hours afterwards." The murderer "slipped from the crowd and made his escape." Both were known and their names are given, but not a word as to any prospect of punishment for so barbarous a deed. This case is the more remarkable from the novelty of the weapon being anything else than a revolver. At Cave City, "in a row at a gaming-table, two Chillians were killed and two more badly wounded." On the Fresno, in a "difficulty over a game of cards, a man was shot dead." In Tuolumne a blacksmith unluckily asserted that one of his neighbours knew rather too much about a robbery recently committed not far away; and from this "a dispute arose, angry words ensued, both were armed, and the quarrel ended" by the poor blacksmith being "shot dead in his own shop." In a case of attempted resistance to an officer of the law, the man resisting, although he had no firearms, only a knife, was shot down by a looker-on, who seemed determined neither to "take a prisoner nor give quarter" if one may judge from the report of the case. To these cases may be added the melancholy one of a young gentleman who was shot dead in a duel fought with double-barreled guns loaded with ball, distance forty paces, for writing a newspaper critique on a 4th of July oration, in the Northern Mines.'

Five years earlier, the vigilante committee would have taken care of a number of the murderous thugs mentioned, but California was becoming more civilized and democratic. Any preoccupation the citizens of California might have had with the six-shooter and its justice (or injustice), however, was overshadowed by the events taking place in the East: war was in the air, and in some parts of the country, particularly in the South, there were many who wondered which way the Californians would jump if it did break out. Thanks primarily to the support she had received from Congress when pushing for statehood, California eventually came out for the North. But the 2,000 miles which separated her from the conflict presented little more than moral support. None the less, she, like her fellow Western states, found herself fighting minor wars of her own – this time against the lawless elements who freely roamed regions where military influence had been curtailed because of the Civil War, or was too limited to be effectual.

In the ten years between 1850 and 1860, the revolver came into its own: in Europe it was recognized as a military asset, and in the United States (and in Australia which had similar problems to California) both its military and civil potential were much appreciated. Consequently, Colt's initial success, backed by his patent, gave him a monopoly over would-be rivals, but with the expiration of his basic patent in 1857, there was no shortage of competition. Colt soon learned that some of it was quite formidable.

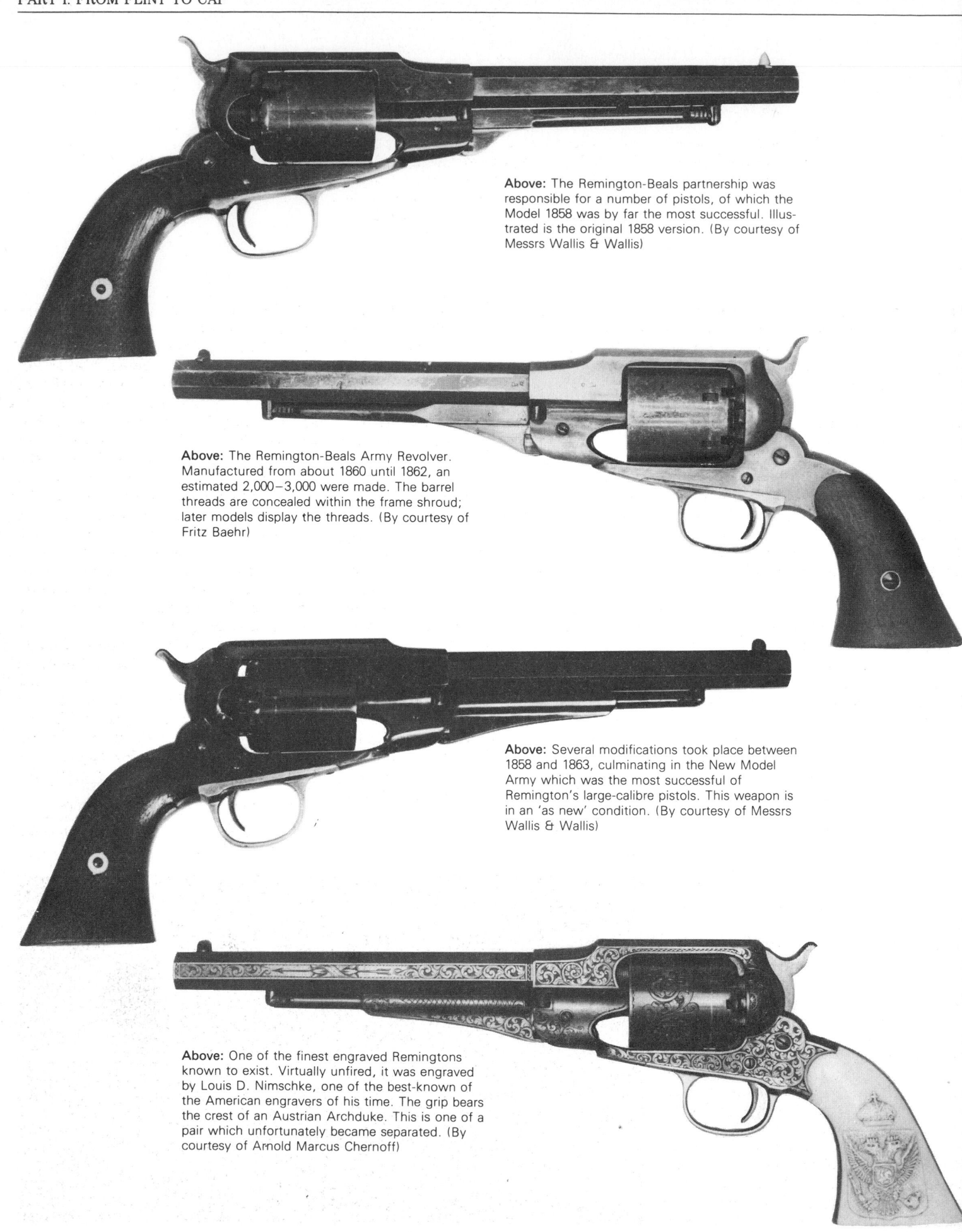

Above: The Remington-Beals partnership was responsible for a number of pistols, of which the Model 1858 was by far the most successful. Illustrated is the original 1858 version. (By courtesy of Messrs Wallis & Wallis)

Above: The Remington-Beals Army Revolver. Manufactured from about 1860 until 1862, an estimated 2,000–3,000 were made. The barrel threads are concealed within the frame shroud; later models display the threads. (By courtesy of Fritz Baehr)

Above: Several modifications took place between 1858 and 1863, culminating in the New Model Army which was the most successful of Remington's large-calibre pistols. This weapon is in an 'as new' condition. (By courtesy of Messrs Wallis & Wallis)

Above: One of the finest engraved Remingtons known to exist. Virtually unfired, it was engraved by Louis D. Nimschke, one of the best-known of the American engravers of his time. The grip bears the crest of an Austrian Archduke. This is one of a pair which unfortunately became separated. (By courtesy of Arnold Marcus Chernoff)

REVOLVER RIVALS

*Revolvers have been known to discharge several of their charges (by accident) at the same
time, thus rendering them unfit for troops formed in two ranks, for the reason that the
front-rank men would be more in dread of those behind them than of the enemy . . .*
– Colonel H. K. Craig at Washington, D.C., on 6 February 1861 to the
Honourable J. Holt, Secretary of War.

THE enormous sales of Colt's revolvers during the early part of the 1850s did not go unnoticed by his rivals, both at home and abroad. In Europe, the English gunmaker, Robert Adams, proved formidable: in 1851, just in time for the Great Exhibition, he patented a self-cocking five-shot 54 bore (.442 calibre) revolver that was to be a thorn in Colt's side for several years; when it was modified in 1855, the British Government adopted it in preference to his own arms. But it was Sam's American rivals who caused him most concern, and the most important of these during the percussion era was Remington, who came quite late to the revolver business.

Eliphalet Remington, Junior (1793–1861), made his first gun at Ilion, New York, in 1816 and during the following years built up a good reputation as an armsmaker. Assisted by his father, Eliphalet, Senior, the young Remington soon established a thriving business in custom-built rifles and gun parts for sale to the trade. When his father died in 1828, the company moved to larger premises, where young Remington carried on by himself. By the 1840s his son Philo had joined him and the company's name was changed to E. Remington & Son.

In 1845 the firm's fortunes changed dramatically when another gunmaker failed to fulfill a government contract for 5,000 U.S. Model 1841 rifles. Remington successfully completed the order which led to further contracts, and by the 1850s his other sons, Eliphalet and Samuel had joined the company and the name was now changed to E. Remington & Sons.

In 1856 Remington's turned their attention to revolvers. Hitherto they had interested themselves only in long arms, but the pending expiration of Colt's basic patents may have prompted their decision to expand, although the weapons they produced were not entirely of their own design. Remington had formed a partnership with Fordyce Beals, a professional firearms designer who had also worked with Eli Whitney, Junior, to produce a suitable design. The result was the Remington-Beals single-action revolvers of

1856 and 1857, which were moderately successful. But it was the combined Remington-Beals design of 1858 which paved the way to a large share of the revolver market. This solid-frame revolver, produced both in .44 and .36 calibres, went into production in 1860 and, with modifications in 1861 and 1863, became Colt's greatest percussion rival.

Remington's employment of a solid-frame was quite revolutionary within the United States. Most of Colt's customers accepted his continued use of the open-frame (the exceptions being the Roots side-hammer model of 1855, and various side-hammer rifles and carbines) because they were satisfied with it. The new-style revolvers from Remington, however, quickly gained attention. Unlike Robert Adams, who had pioneered the solid-frame revolver in 1851 and concentrated upon self-cocking mechanisms (the pistol was cocked and fired simply by pulling the trigger), Remington stuck to single-action. Colt's solid-frame revolvers necessitated a side-hammer to permit the removal of the cylinder pin, but the Remington version was removed from the front and secured in place by the loading lever which had to be lowered to enable the pin to be pulled forward for removal.

The Remington-Beals revolvers underwent a number of modifications before the design was standardized, but the basic shape and style of the revolvers remained unchanged. The .44 calibre Army pistol was fitted with an 8-inch octagonal barrel, and the .36 version with a 7½-inch barrel. The loading lever was held in place by a spring-loaded catch which fitted into a stud beneath the barrel, and the lever was provided with a web to create a streamlined appearance. The forepart of the frame, into which the barrel was screwed, also housed the rammer and lever in a portion that was machined into a shroud-like formation. The grip straps were a part of the frame formation and the brass trigger guard was retained by a tang at its rear and a screw on the plate.

Between 1861 and 1863 a number of minor changes were made, but the 'New Model Army' of 1863 was to become their most popular weapon. The front sight was standardized as an iron pin which had scooped sides and screwed, instead of being dove-tailed, into the barrel. The cylinder was

Below: A pair of fine nickel-plated Remington 1863s with gold-washed cylinders; they were a Civil War presentation. (By courtesy of the Kansas State Historical Society)

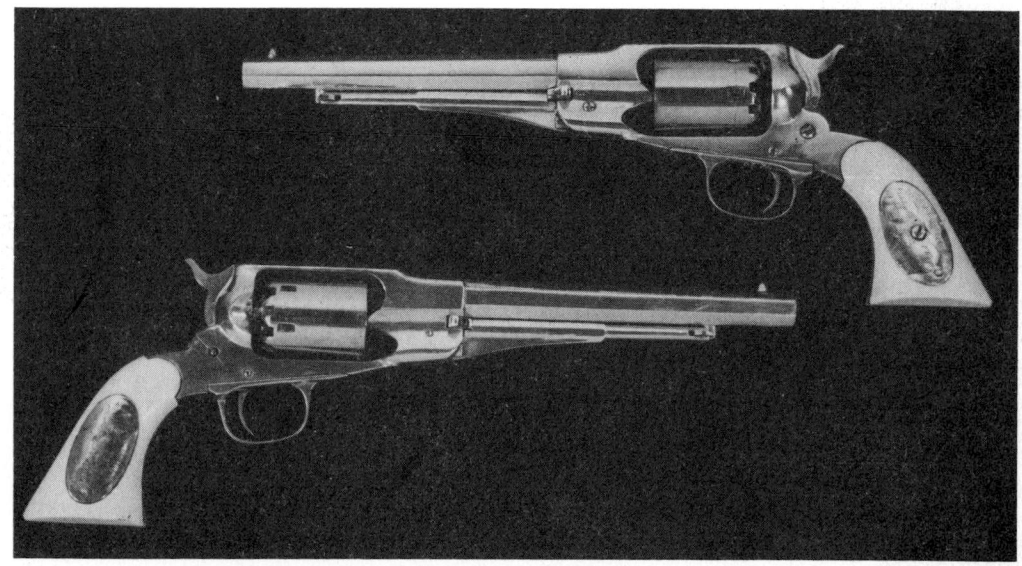

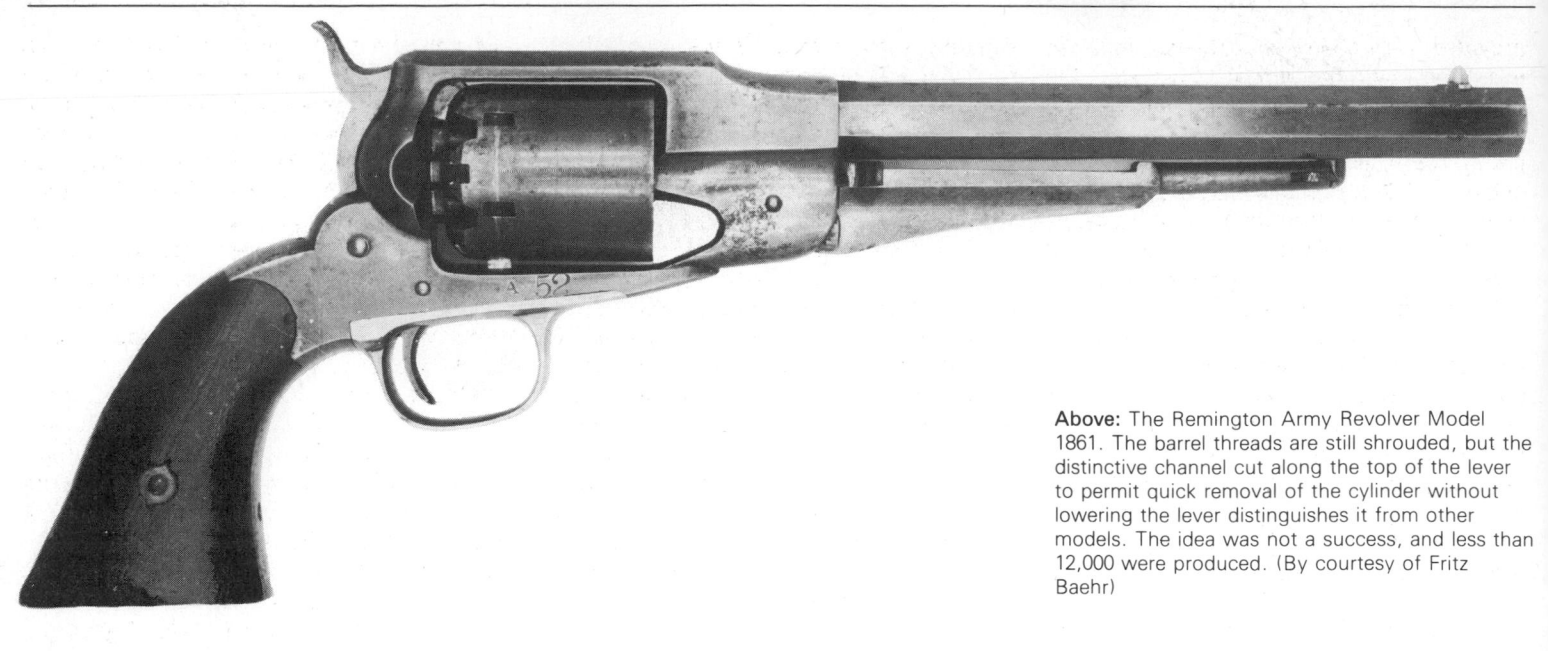

Above: The Remington Army Revolver Model 1861. The barrel threads are still shrouded, but the distinctive channel cut along the top of the lever to permit quick removal of the cylinder without lowering the lever distinguishes it from other models. The idea was not a success, and less than 12,000 were produced. (By courtesy of Fritz Baehr)

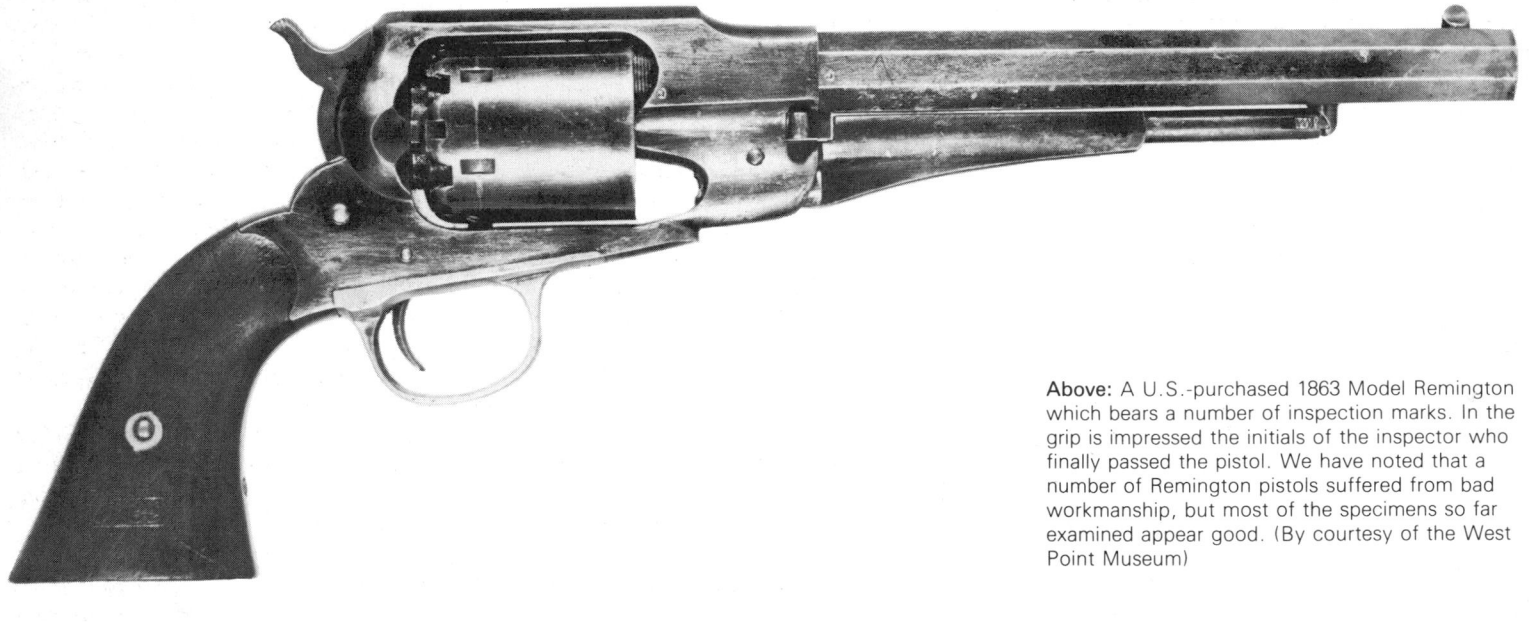

Above: A U.S.-purchased 1863 Model Remington which bears a number of inspection marks. In the grip is impressed the initials of the inspector who finally passed the pistol. We have noted that a number of Remington pistols suffered from bad workmanship, but most of the specimens so far examined appear good. (By courtesy of the West Point Museum)

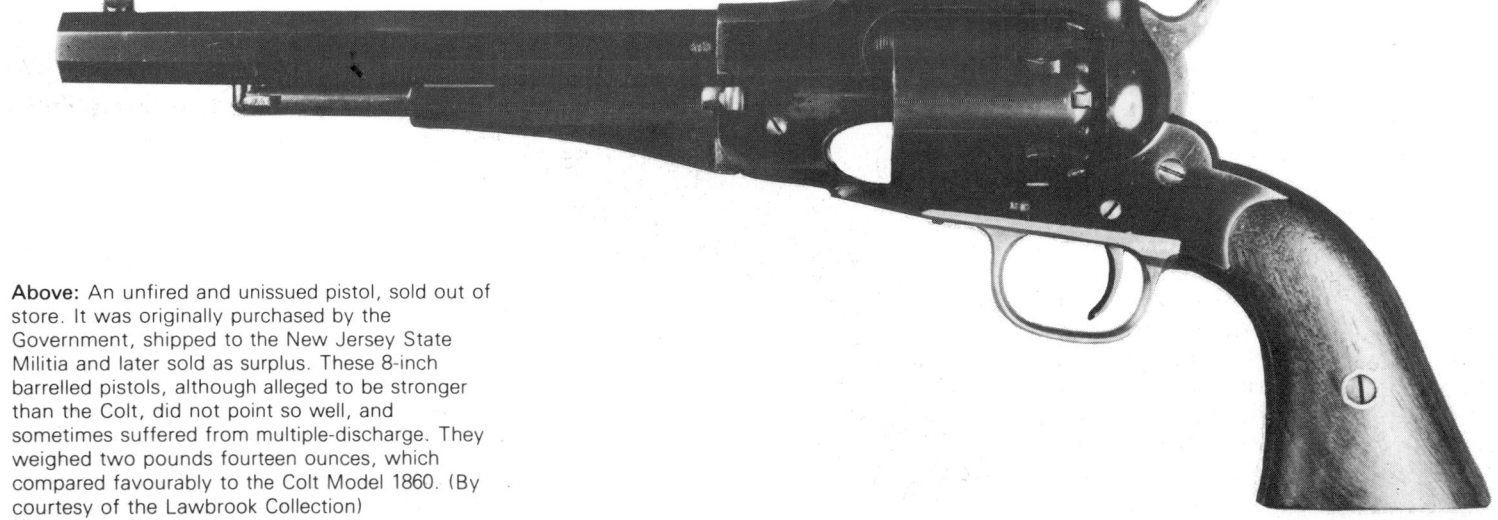

Above: An unfired and unissued pistol, sold out of store. It was originally purchased by the Government, shipped to the New Jersey State Militia and later sold as surplus. These 8-inch barrelled pistols, although alleged to be stronger than the Colt, did not point so well, and sometimes suffered from multiple-discharge. They weighed two pounds fourteen ounces, which compared favourably to the Colt Model 1860. (By courtesy of the Lawbrook Collection)

provided with safety notches cut into the metal between the nipples to enable the hammer nose to rest without contact with the nipples (a great improvement over Colt's pin system); the nipple channels were also enlarged. The barrel was marked: PATENTED SEPT. 14, 1858. E. REMINGTON & SONS, ILION NEW-YORK U.S.A. NEW MODEL. A double-action version of the Navy-size pistols was available, designed by Joseph Rider, but they were not as successful as the single-action pistols. The finish on all Remington revolvers (except those silver-plated or otherwise embellished) was a standard blued barrel and frame; case-hardened hammer and loading lever and rammer, and the trigger guard was either left plain brass or plated. Civilian arms were provided with shellac varnished two-piece walnut stocks, but the military version was oil-finished.

Remington's also invoked techniques that had been pioneered by Colt's to enable them to produce their pistols more cheaply. The construction of the frame and backstraps in one piece was an advantage over Colt's separate frame, trigger guard and backstrap, and where the Colt required two pins to hold the cylinder stop and trigger, the Remington needed only one. But it was the cylinder pin which maintained Colt's lead. He employed an oil-groove – a spiral anti-fouling thread – on the majority of his weapons, whereas Remington's had no such refinement, and it was not uncommon to find that their pistols suffered from 'frozen' cylinders as a result of fouling. This was not considered a major fault, however, and the new weapon was generally popular; an estimated 132,000 1863 New Model Army revolvers were manufactured between that year and 1875. During the Civil War, the U.S. Government purchased 125,314 of both the 1861 and the 1863 versions at $13 (some batches were purchased for $12) per pistol. The government also purchased 4,901 Navy pistols at the rather inflated price of $30 each. The chamber capacity of the Remington was about on a par with its contemporary Colt rivals, but was adjusted according to military (or civilian) requirements.

Despite its present day reputation as Colt's greatest percussion rival, the Remington in the 1860s had a poor reputation in some branches of the army, notably the cavalry. When the company negotiated with the government on 13 May 1864, to supply 5,000 pistols at $12 each, an examination of contract pistols caused some alarm. On 6 June the Office of the Inspector of Contract Arms reported that on some pistols the front sight orifice had been drilled straight into the bore; frames contained slag; the machining was poor and some other parts were equally inferior.(stocks, for instance, were made of poor timber and roughly finished). In con-

demning these pistols, it was pointed out that some of the components were good; but the company's insistence upon being paid the full contract price of $12 or, failing that, being given permission to export the arms for $15 to make up the loss incurred by the recent increase in duty on materials, did not impress Colonel A. W. Thornton:

'If it is imperative to accept arms composed of *defective* parts assembled with good works, then as the *rejected* pieces cost the contractors less for workmanship, a deduction in price should be such as to offer no inducement in manufacturing such arms. I think *ten dollars* would be a fair valuation for the pistols, with the usual appendages, and in their acceptance they should be inspected to determine that the parts are sound & that the barrels have been proven.'

The issue of Remington revolvers to certain cavalry regiments following the Civil War brought further complaints. On 31 January 1867 General C. C. Augur, commanding the Department of the Platte, wrote to Major-General A. B. Dyer, Chief of Ordnance to advise him of the receipt of a number of dispatches and letters of complaint:

'Referring to a number of Remington revolvers in the hands of the 2nd Cavalry, and on which a previous complaint he was directed to make a careful report, Bvt Brig Genl I. N. Palmer at Fort Laramie says "Defects of Remington pistols are as follows, they are made of very poor material as shown by the great number burst at ordinary exercise, in some companies ten (10) or twelve (12) burst in one (1) year, Capt. Ball took three (3) of them out for trial with the ordinary charges they all burst at the trial. The springs are not strong enough in many cases to burst the cap, and in many of them the hammer is not long enough to reach the cap, this may be remedied in part by filing away the shoulder so as to let the hammer further down. Many of them will burst the cap but not discharge the barrel. At a firing

drill on the twentyseventh (27) forty (40) pistols were loaded carefully, and out of the two hundred and forty (240) loads not more than one hundred and fifty (150) could be discharged at all. All this has so disgusted the company commanders here that they prefer to have no pistols at all; they consider them almost a useless weight for the men to carry. There are however some of them that appear to be good: on the whole I think if it were left to Company commanders, they would not take them into the field. . .

'The defects reported in the Remington revolvers are of great consequence, and destroy the confidence of the men in their arms, which in view of the approaching Indian campaign is to be avoided by all means. Some of the revolvers tried were on hand at Fort Laramie and were probably sent there during the war. Some of them were recently sent the Cavalry from Leavenworth Arsenal. Is there any quick way of remedying these evils? The Cavalry should by all means have revolvers and these should of course be reliable. Colts have never to my knowledge been found fault with in any important particular, and it is possible as Colts cannot be supplied that there are on hand at some convenient arsenal a sufficient quantity of Remingtons which have been thoroughly tested and found perfect to replace those found deficient . . .'

Understandably, government interest in the Remington declined, and a number of them were sold off as surplus, many of them reaching Europe and the Middle East. In London they were sold for as little as eight shillings each.

During Remington's rise to fame, Colt's other rivals had not been idle. Robert Adams had found a manufacturing outlet for his revolvers in the United States. These weapons were based upon the so called 'Beaumont-Adams' model of 1855, which utilized Lieutenant Frederick Beaumont's improvement on the existing Adams lockwork. Adams' self-cocking system was trans-

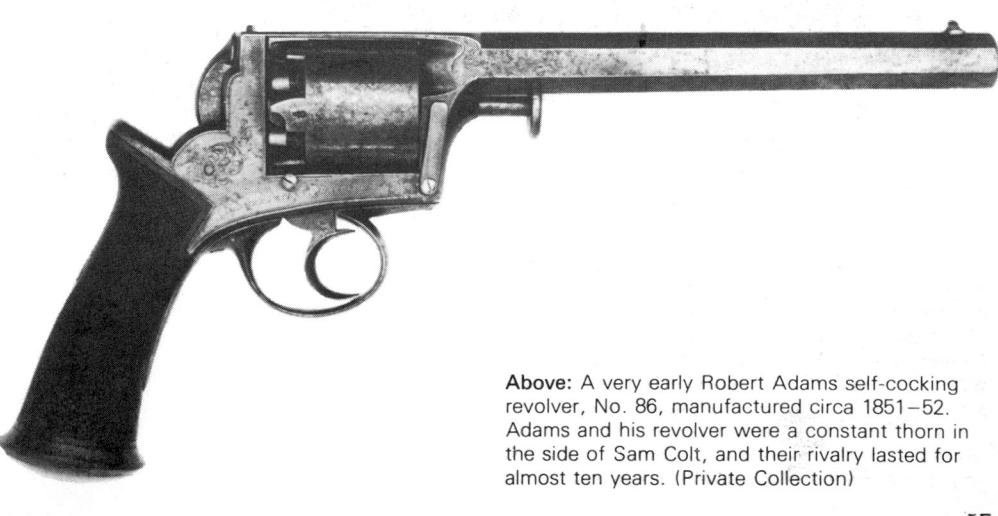

Above: A very early Robert Adams self-cocking revolver, No. 86, manufactured circa 1851–52. Adams and his revolver were a constant thorn in the side of Sam Colt, and their rivalry lasted for almost ten years. (Private Collection)

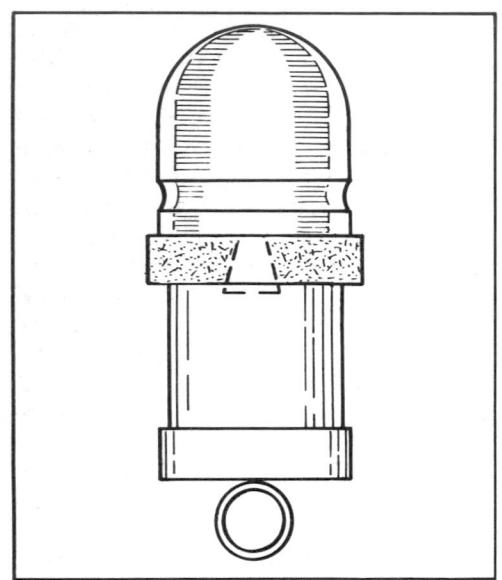

Above left: Paper, foil and skin cartridges were the commonest available during the 1850s and the 1860s. Plainsmen treated them with caution because they were easily damaged, and the army constantly complained they got damp or broken up when carried in belt pouches. (Private Collection)

Above right: D. C. Sage & Co., of Middletown, Connecticut, were a well-known makers of skin and foil cartridges. This pack contains the six cartridges set in a wooden frame cut to receive and protect them. Original boxes of cartridges are now rare and eagerly sought by collectors. (Private Collection)

Left: The Adams 'dustbin' cartridge. This consisted of a spiked ball, the spike passing through a felt wad. A sheet copper cup or chamber was riveted to the spike, and powder was placed inside the container, sealed with thin blue paper. To protect this, a lid containing a ring was placed firmly in position. The ring enabled a number of cartridges to be strung together. It was removed prior to loading.

Opposite page, top: The Beaumont-Adams revolver of 1855. When Lieutenant Beaumont of the Royal Engineers designed a simple mechanism to transform the Adams self-cocking revolver into a true double-action (that is a self-cocker and a single-action similar to the Colt and activated by cocking the hammer), the British Government at last took the Adams revolver seriously. In 1856 it was adopted into the service in preference to the existing Colt revolvers, but problems with ill-fitting nipples meant that many of these pistols were returned to store and the Colt was re-issued. (By courtesy of John Darwent)

Opposite page, centre: This Beaumont-Adams, which bears the Liège, Belgium, proof marks and the King William Street, London Bridge address of Deane, Adams & Deane, was alleged to have been used by Wild Bill Hickok, but its only connection with Wild Bill is that it was in the possession of one of his biographers, Frank J. Wilstach, whose wife presented it to the Society when he died. (By courtesy of the Kansas State Historical Society)

Above: When Robert Adams patented his revolver in the United States, its manufacture was undertaken by the Massachusetts Arms Company which had lost a court battle with Colt over patent infringements, and probably thought this would be a way of getting back at him. The pistol illustrated was sold to the United States Government and bears the accepting inspector's initials in its stock. (By courtesy of Messrs Wallis & Wallis)

formed into a double-action by an additional bent or notch on the hammer which enabled the pistol to be fired by trigger pressure (as previously), or cocked as a single-action (like its Colt rivals) by means of a thumb spur on the hammer. These modified revolvers were manufactured by the Massachusetts Arms Company of Chicopee Falls, Massachusetts. This was the same company that had been taken to court by Colt in 1851 for alleged patent infringements. Colt won his case, and historians believe that it influenced the company's decision to manufacture Adams' revolvers. The Massachusetts Arms Company had also been of assistance to Adams when he set up his own London factory in 1852, and the companies enjoyed a good relationship.

The Massachusetts Arms Company produced an estimated 6,000 Adams revolvers in .31 and .36 calibre; some were sold to the Confederacy, and the Government is believed to have purchased about 600 of them. British-made 54 bore (.442) Adams revolvers had also sold in the late 1850s, and at least 115 of these were purchased for $18 each by the Government during the Civil War.

Ammunition for the Adams revolvers underwent a number of changes. In 1851 Robert Adams patented a design for a wadded bullet, and later modified it to include a metallic container attached to the spigotted ball, which in shape and size was soon dubbed the 'dustbin' cartridge. These were expensive to make, however, and eventually were replaced by an Adams-Eley design which proved popular, and consisted of a membrane or skin container covered in paper. But the drawback to any Adams ammunition was its limited powder charge. The big 38 bore (.50) was powered by fourteen grains and the 54 bore (.442) by twelve grains. These loads were almost impotent compared to the Colt's and Remington's 30–40 grains of powder.

At this point something should be said of Colt's paper and foil cartridges. By 1850 he

Above: In 1858 James Kerr, formerly manager of the London Armoury Company, patented a single-action side-hammer revolver (there are believed to be some double-action versions) which was designed to make the care and repair of the weapon comparatively simple. In fact, actual lockwork is identical with the existing muskets of the time. The weapon found little favour in England, but it was welcomed in parts of Europe and the Confederacy. Illustrated is pistol No. 12, with a rakish slant to the grip and a brass trigger guard, and (Bottom) a standard issue weapon of the type purchased by the Confederacy. No. 12 is now in the armoury at the Tower of London. (Private Collection)

was already experimenting with a form of foil, but in 1854, in partnership with William Eley, he patented a paper cartridge. It consisted of skin membranes glued to a conical ball and enclosed in a paper envelope to which was attached a piece of black tape. When required for use the tape was torn off to remove the paper and expose the bullet and skin container. The powder was then exposed to the flash of the cap when the cartridge was rammed into the chamber.

In 1856, when Captain John Montague Hayes patented a skin cartridge, similar in design to the Colt-Eley version, the British Board of Ordnance was concerned at the similarity between them. By 1861, however, it was reported that the Eley version now had a thinner skin on the base than on the body, and there was no danger of either maker infringing the other's patent. The Hayes cartridges, manufactured by Brough and Moll, London, were extremely popular

both in the United Kingdom and the United States. Supplied in bundles of eighteen, and wrapped in waterproof bags, they were used both with Colt and Adams revolvers, and in the United States were sold in packets of six bearing the 'Broux' blue label.

Skin and paper cartridges, however, suffered from climate. The Royal Navy had had trouble with them on the China Station and in the earlier cited Fosbery lecture 'On Pistols', one of the later speakers, Captain Applin, who had been serving in Japan, had been present when 120 rounds were fired from several Colt weapons and reported that 90 were misfires caused by damp. Consequently, Sam Colt's introduction of tinfoil cartridges in 1855 was especially welcome. The bullet was cast with a rebate and an annular groove at its rear end. A sheet-foil case filled with powder was then cemented to the bullet under pressure, and a layer of grease was run around the cartridge at the

junction of the powder-case and the bullet. Most of them were then enclosed in a paper envelope with an attached tape (similar to the earlier paper cartridges). Many thousands of these cartridges were sold to both the British and American Governments.

Colt's old ally, Eli Whitney, Junior, also appreciated the sales potential of the revolver, and during the late 1850s he produced a number of pistols under his own name and in collaboration with others. His association with Beals, who later joined Remington, has been noted, but perhaps the most important of the Whitney revolvers were those produced from the 1850s until about 1865. His Navy pistol was a .36 six-shooter, of solid-frame form which resembled the current Remington arms. The screwed-in octagonal barrel was 7½ inches long, but 8-inch and 4-inch versions are known. The cylinder was round with no flutes and bore a rolled-on engraving depict-

Above: The Whitney .36 calibre six-shot Navy revolver was a well-made and efficient weapon. Whitney utilized the basic Colt action (which after 1857 was no longer subject to patent protection) and with the addition of a solid frame, produced a weapon which had the best of both Colt and Remington designs. However, his combined cylinder pin and rammer, retained by a turn-screw (shown on the left of the frame), was considered superior to the Remington version. (By courtesy of the Kansas State Historical Society)

Above: Another fine Whitney Navy revolver. A large number of these were purchased by the Government during the Civil War, but few of them made their way out West, and today are generally found to be in good condition. (By courtesy of Messrs Wallis & Wallis)

Above: A fine Rogers & Spencer Army Holster pistol. These .44 calibre six-shot pistols were fitted with 7½-inch barrels. They bear a strong resemblance to the contemporary Freeman revolvers and to the Whitney. The U.S. Government ordered 5,000 of them in November 1864, but none was issued. In 1900 they were sold for scrap! (By courtesy of the Lawbrook Collection)

Top: The Freeman single-action Army revolver. Austin T. Freeman had worked at the Starr Armory and his revolver bears a superficial resemblance to the 1863 model, but it also owes a debt to Remington, and there is some evidence that Freeman negotiated with Rogers & Spencer for parts in return for the design. About 2,000 were made but none was purchased by the Government. (By courtesy of Messrs Wallis & Wallis)

Above: Benjamin Joslyn's bulky side-hammer revolver. These .44 calibre five-shots were produced during the early years of the War, but none was purchased by the Government. (By courtesy of Messrs Wallis & Wallis)

ing an eagle, a lion, and a naval engagement, together with a shield bearing a rib and marked 'WHITNEYVILLE.' The iron frames were machined to cut down weight as much as possible, and like the Remington, the grip straps were an integral part of the frame; the brass silver-plated trigger guard was attached separately. Like the Remington, too, the top strap was grooved to form a rear sight; but the pistol's most interesting contribution to the solid-frame breed was its combined cylinder pin and ramming assembly, held in place by a key or moveable pin permanently fixed in the frame and machined on one side to allow it to lock into a groove on the cylinder pin so as to hold it firmly in place. The frame, barrel and cylinders of these weapons were blued and the hammer and lever assembly were case-hardened.

During the Civil War, Whitney sold approximately 11,214 Navy-size pistols to the Government. In 1861, the Ordnance Department purchased 360 Whitneys from Shuyler Hartley & Graham of New York for $17 each, which was thought to be high. On 15 May 1862, however, the Ordnance dealt with the company direct, and 600 were purchased for $15.03 each. Later, on 9 June, a contract was drawn up for 6,000 pistols, the contract price being $10; but when the first 1,000 pistols were delivered on 27 June 1862, the price paid was $12 not $10. By 28 February 1863, when the contract expired, Whitney had delivered 7,002 revolvers. It is clear that the price per arm must have reached a firmer figure, because according to Colonel Berkeley R. Lewis, by the close of the war the contract price for Whitney Navy pistols was set at $12.50.

Cartridges for the Whitney Navy revolver were supplied by D. C. Sage & Company, and were manufactured under the Hotchkiss

patent. They consisted of 'waterproof skin' or 'seamless skin' membrane, similar in some respects to the Colt-Eley skin cartridges of the mid 1850s. They were interchangeable with the Colt Navy revolver, and were officially described as having a bullet weight of 139 grains, the powder charge varying from as low as fourteen grains up to 28 grains.

Purchase of the Whitney Navy pistol was not confined to the Ordnance and many thousands were bought by various states for militia use. The pocket version of the Whitney solid-frame revolver was a five-shot .31 calibre pistol which resembled it in all respects, and approximately 32,000 of these were manufactured. An interesting deviant from the pocket model was a stud-trigger revolver, produced in 1860, which closely resembled the Colt-Roots side-hammer pistol, except that the hammer was centrally mounted. By the time production ceased in 1867, less than 2,000 of them had been produced and few of them turned up in the West. In fact, few Whitney Navy or pocket-pistols found their way Westward; most of those encountered today are in a reasonable condition. They were well-made and reliable weapons.

A number of other U.S. revolver-makers produced a variety of revolvers, good, bad and indifferent. Among them were the Rogers & Spencer; the Pettengill; the Joslyn and the North & Savage. Each weapon featured characteristics of existing Colt and Remington arms, and a glance at the official records reveals that with the exception of the North & Savage (14,287 purchased for $19.50 each) the remainder were purchased in lots of 1,000 or fewer.

Besides the British Adams, other foreign-made weapons were imported, including the

LeFaucheux pin-fire revolver. According to official returns, the U.S. Government purchased two types – the Army in .427 calibre (12mm) and the Navy in .35 (9mm). Approximately 12,374 were purchased for $13.50 each, but whether they were used in action is debatable. Many of the LeFaucheux revolvers, called the 'French Tranter' by some (a dubious compliment to Britain's

Below: An advertisement for the Cooper Fire Arms Manufacturing Company, circa 1863. The Cooper closely resembled contemporary Colt revolvers, but was fitted with a double-action mechanism. It was popular as a personal weapon among troops during the War. This specimen is a five-shot .31 calibre pistol. (Author's Collection)

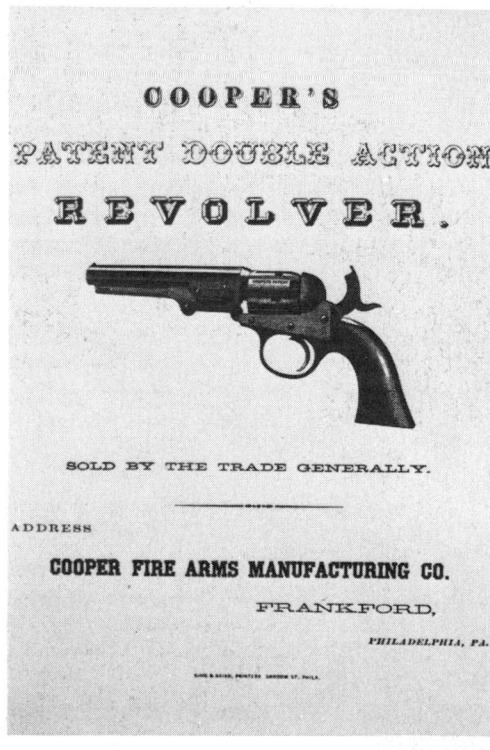

COOPER'S
PATENT DOUBLE ACTION
REVOLVER.

SOLD BY THE TRADE GENERALLY.

ADDRESS

COOPER FIRE ARMS MANUFACTURING CO.
FRANKFORD,
PHILADELPHIA, PA.

famous gunmaker), were issued to state militia or volunteer regiments. The troops themselves were not very impressed. For one thing, the ammunition, with its pin primer sticking out of the side of the cartridge at the base, necessitated careful handling, and when a number of these pistols were issued to Kansas regiments of Volunteer Cavalry (together with some Union units stationed along the Kansas–Missouri border) there were several complaints.

The 5th Kansas was one of the chosen regiments. Having originally been issued with Sharps' carbines and some obsolete muskets (which had soon been modified into musketoons by the men) in September 1862, the order came to hand in all existing weapons and take delivery of some Hall's carbines, sabres, and the LeFaucheux revolvers. Sergeant August Bondi, who served in Company K, was frankly disgusted with the new revolvers. In his diary he wrote: 'The LeFaucheux were worthless, would not carry a ball over fifteen steps, [and] were condemned French arms,' an opinion apparently shared by the majority of the regiment. On 16 July 1862, however, the regiment traded in their pin-fires for Colt's Navy revolvers. At least the 5th Kansas had had one advantage over their colleagues in the 2nd Kansas who were issued with LeFaucheux revolvers on 20 April 1862, but had no cartridges – none had been ordered!

Another rival to Colt during the closing years of the Civil War was the Metropolitan Arms Company of New York City. One of Colt's basic patents ran out in 1857 which allowed companies such as the Metropolitan

Above: Three Civil War rivals. Top: the North & Savage .36 Navy revolver (some of which were purchased by the Army); Centre: a Rogers & Spencer; Bottom: a very early Colt 1860 Army with the fluted cylinder and fourth screw or 'stud' for attaching a stock. (By courtesy of Messrs Weller & Dufty)

Above: Two views of a Lefaucheux Model 1853 12mm six-shot pin-fire revolver of the type purchased by the U.S. Government and issued to some troops, particularly volunteer and militia units. This specimen was discovered some years ago and its history is not known. It is marked LEFAUCHEUX PARIS in a semi-oval on the left side of the frame and its serial No. is 29133. Note the crude loading gate on the frame and the simple but effective rod ejector. (By courtesy of Gregory Hermon)

to produce almost identical copies of his own arms. The disastrous fire which destroyed the Hartford factory in 1864 enabled them to cash in on the Colt Company's predicament, and an estimated 7,000 revolvers similar to the Colt 1851 Navy, together with a limited number resembling the Model 1861, and about 3,000 revolvers similar in appearance to the Colt police pistol of 1862 were manufactured.

Apart from Remington, Colt's most important rival was undoubtedly the Starr Arms Company which was also situated in New York City. This company produced a semi-solid frame pistol in .36 and .44 calibres. A cross-bolt or screw secured the top strap and forepart of the frame. The bolt was fitted with a knurled head for quick removal, which allowed the barrel and top strap to drop forward. Like the Colt, the loading lever and rammer were hinged to the front of the frame, and the barrel was screwed in as on the Whitney and Remington arms. The finish was simple: a case hardened hammer, with all the other metal parts blued. The one-piece grip was walnut and oil-finished.

The Starr was produced in three basic models: the self-cocking six-shot .36 calibre Navy Model of 1858, with a 6-inch barrel; the .44 Army Model, which was identical with the Navy pistol in all other respects; and the 1863 single-action Army model with an 8-inch barrel. These .44 calibre pistols were designed to replace the 1858 models which had proved difficult and expensive to make. Production of the Navy pistol was about 3,000; of the 1858 Army about 23,000, and of the 1863 Army an estimated 32,000. Of

Above: Typical pin-fires of the mid nineteenth century. The top weapon is a fearsome ten-shooter! (By courtesy of Messrs Weller & Dufty)

these, 25,000 1863s and 22,925 self-cocking Army and Navy pistols were purchased by the U.S. Government for war service, at a contract price of $15.25 per pistol. The 1863 model was by far the most successful and was the one chosen by the French Government in 1870 for conversion to five-shot

centre-fires. Many of them were issued during the Franco–Prussian War, but their use in the West was limited.

During the rise of their rivals, Colt's, of course, had not remained complacent. Indeed, the success of the Navy pistol had proved to the company that there was a firm

Above: The 1858 Model Starr .44 double-action army pistol. To dismantle the weapon, the knurled knob on the rear of the frame is loosened and the cross-bolt withdrawn, which enables the barrel to tip forward and release the cylinder. The double-action model was expensive to manufacture and the trigger pull was excessive. This specimen, in fine condition, was purchased by the U.S. Government and sold out of store years later. (By courtesy of Messrs Wallis & Wallis)

Above: The Starr Model 1863. This six-shot, single-action pistol with an 8-inch barrel was the most popular of the Starr revolvers, but after the Civil War there was little demand for it until the Franco-Prussian War when a number were converted to five-shot centre-fires. (By courtesy of Messrs Wallis & Wallis)

Below centre: Another group of Colt experimental pistols covering the period 1858 – 1872. Left- and right-hand views of: 1. a .36 calibre experimental Navy revolver, circa 1860; 2. a Dragoon, with a hinged frame and top strap — the cylinder pin extends only as far as the front of the chamber to allow quick removal; 3. a Root side-hammer revolver with a zig-zag revolving system which proved impractical; 4. an early cartridge conversion of the 1849 pocket-pistol, and 5. an early .44 rim-fire that was close to the final 1872 open-frame pistol. (By courtesy of the Connecticut State Library)

Below left: Four Civil War rivals. Top to bottom: .36 Starr Navy double-action, .44 Army double-action, .36 Whitney Navy, .36 Savage Navy revolver. (By courtesy of Richard A. Bourne Co. Inc.)

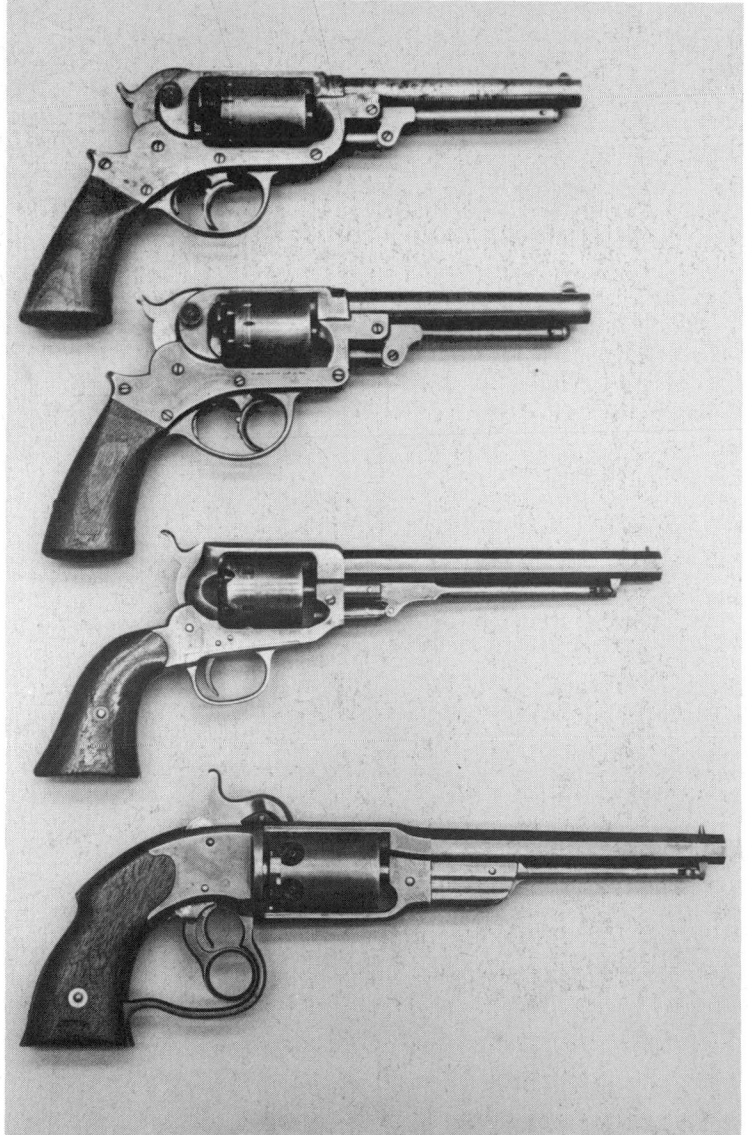

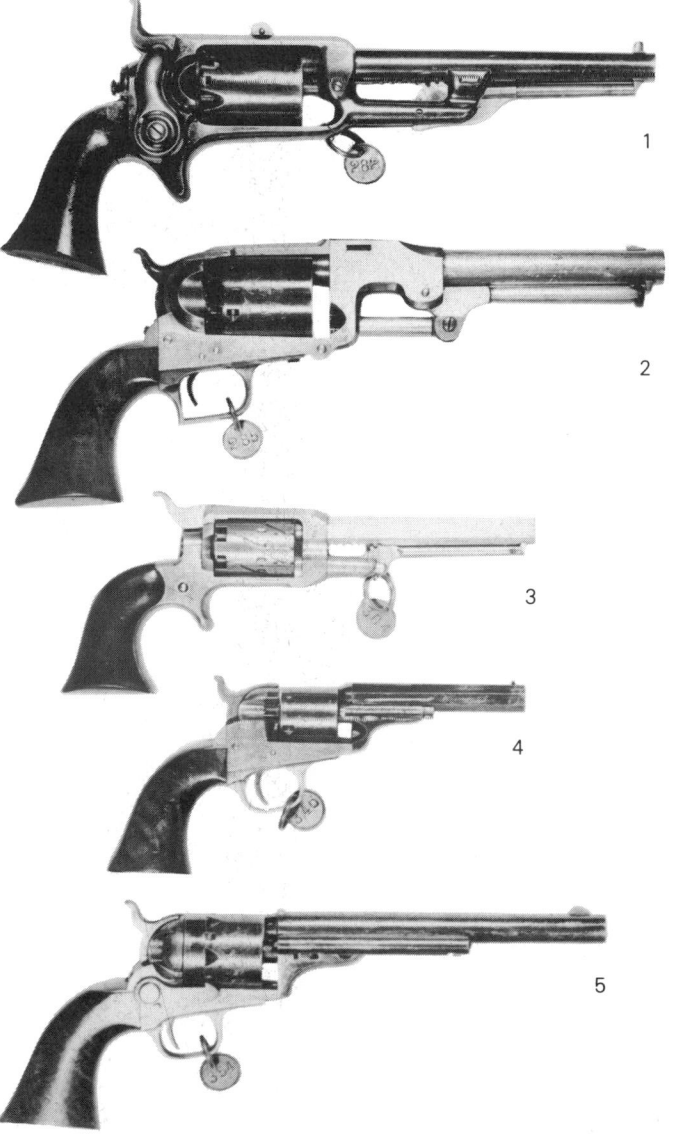

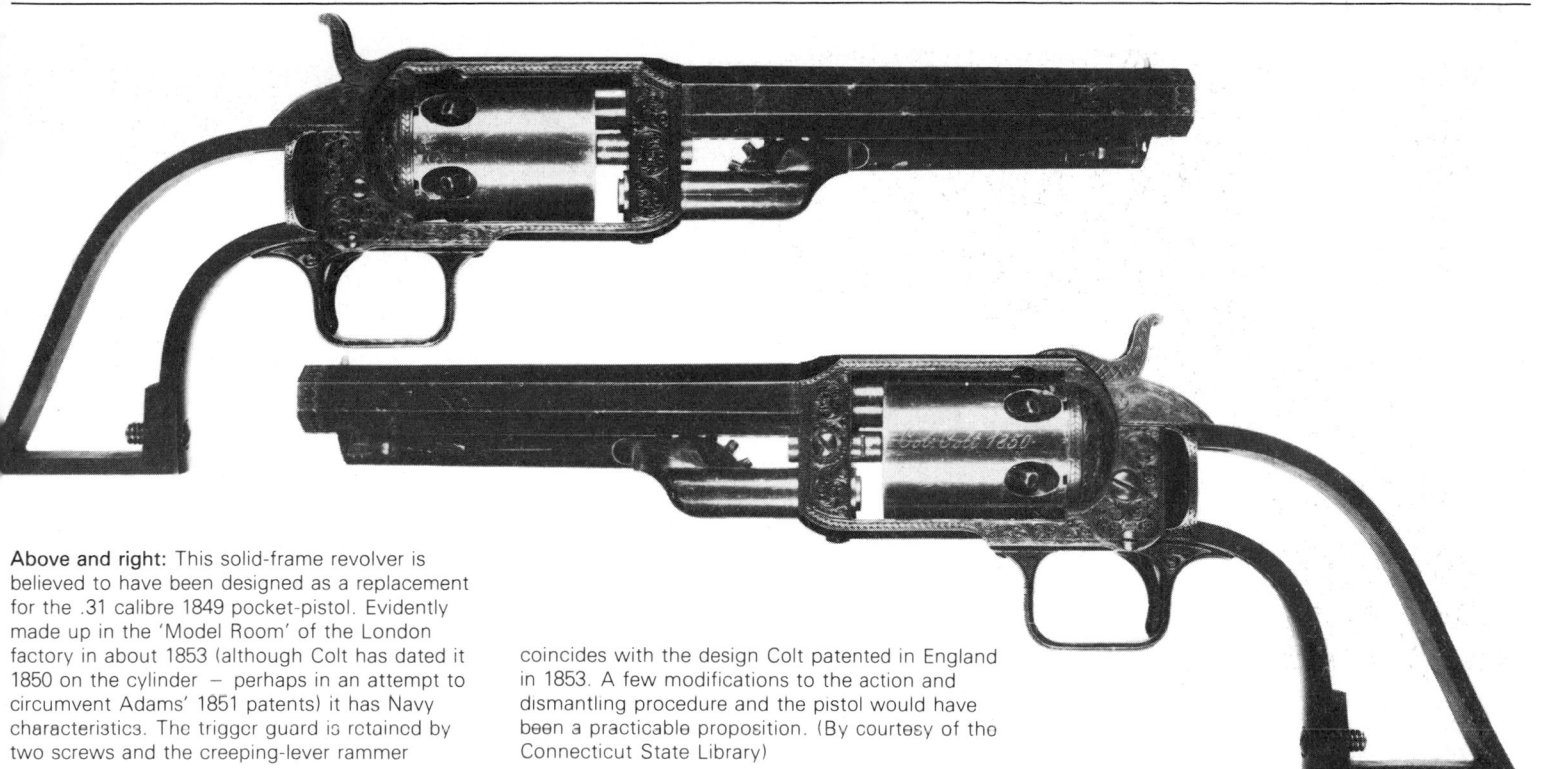

Above and right: This solid-frame revolver is believed to have been designed as a replacement for the .31 calibre 1849 pocket-pistol. Evidently made up in the 'Model Room' of the London factory in about 1853 (although Colt has dated it 1850 on the cylinder — perhaps in an attempt to circumvent Adams' 1851 patents) it has Navy characteristics. The trigger guard is retained by two screws and the creeping-lever rammer coincides with the design Colt patented in England in 1853. A few modifications to the action and dismantling procedure and the pistol would have been a practicable proposition. (By courtesy of the Connecticut State Library)

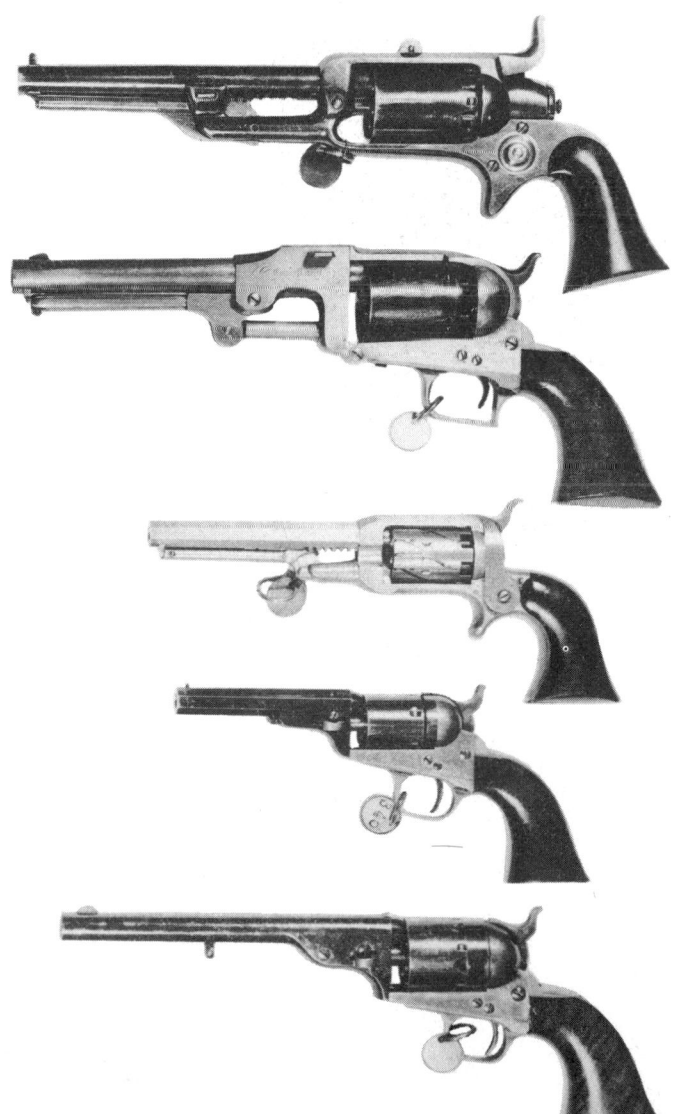

Above: George Armstrong Custer as a Cadet at West Point in about 1859. The Colt-Root pistol grasped firmly in his left hand is of the first type with an octagonal barrel and produced in .28 calibre. These pistols enjoyed good sales, but never surpassed the more popular pocket and Navy revolvers. (By courtesy of Dr. Lawrence A. Frost, M.D.)

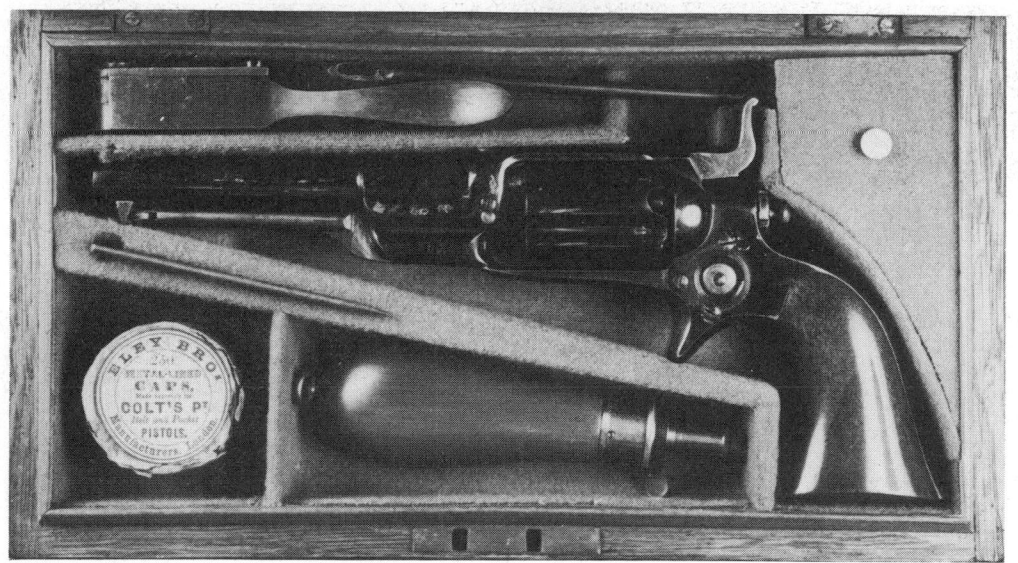

Left: Elisha Root is generally credited with designing the 1855 side-hammer pocket-pistol, but it now appears that he actually designed the creeping-lever rammer, the remainder of the design being Colt's. This fine cased specimen of the round-barrelled version introduced in about 1861, was made in the mid 1860s and exported to London for sale through the Agency. (By courtesy of the Lawbrook Collection)

Right: One of the few 1860 Army revolvers to get through to the London Agency during the Civil War. The fire in 1864 severely cut back exports, and only twelve Army pistols were sent over that year. The pistol is complete with its original bullet mould, but the flask is designed for the Navy. (Private Collection)

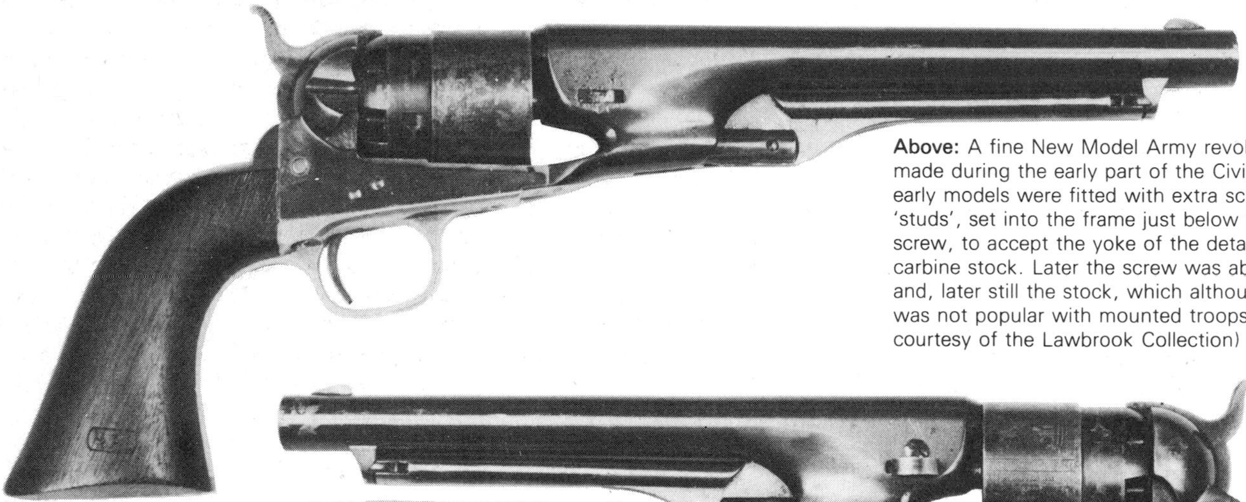

Above: A fine New Model Army revolver of 1860 made during the early part of the Civil War. The early models were fitted with extra screws or 'studs', set into the frame just below the hammer screw, to accept the yoke of the detachable carbine stock. Later the screw was abandoned and, later still the stock, which although effective, was not popular with mounted troops. (By courtesy of the Lawbrook Collection)

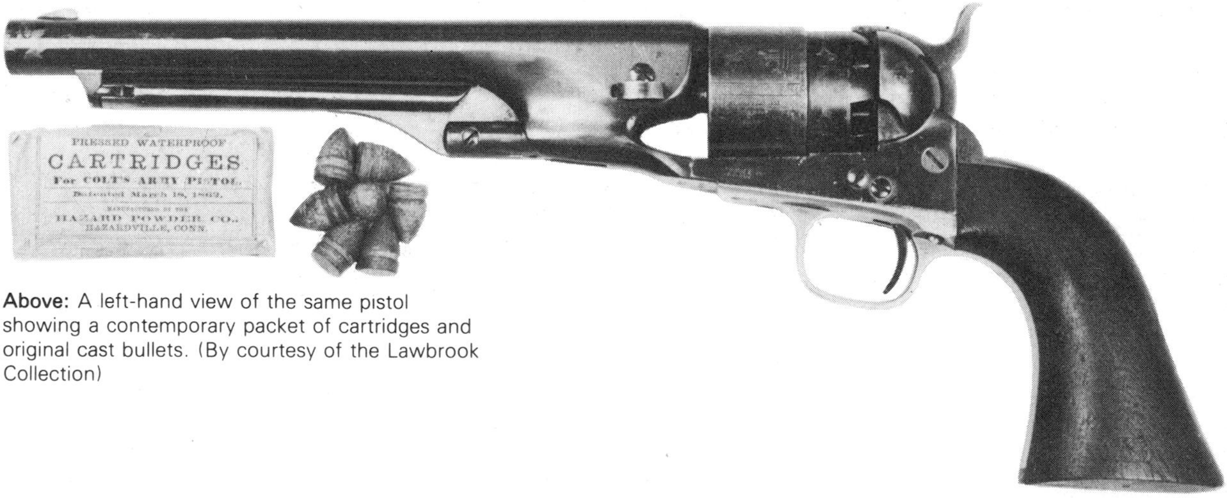

Above: A left-hand view of the same pistol showing a contemporary packet of cartridges and original cast bullets. (By courtesy of the Lawbrook Collection)

Above: A fine example both of the 1859 demountable carbine stock and the contemporary Navy pistol, serial No. 68203. (By courtesy of Jackson Arms, Dallas, Texas)

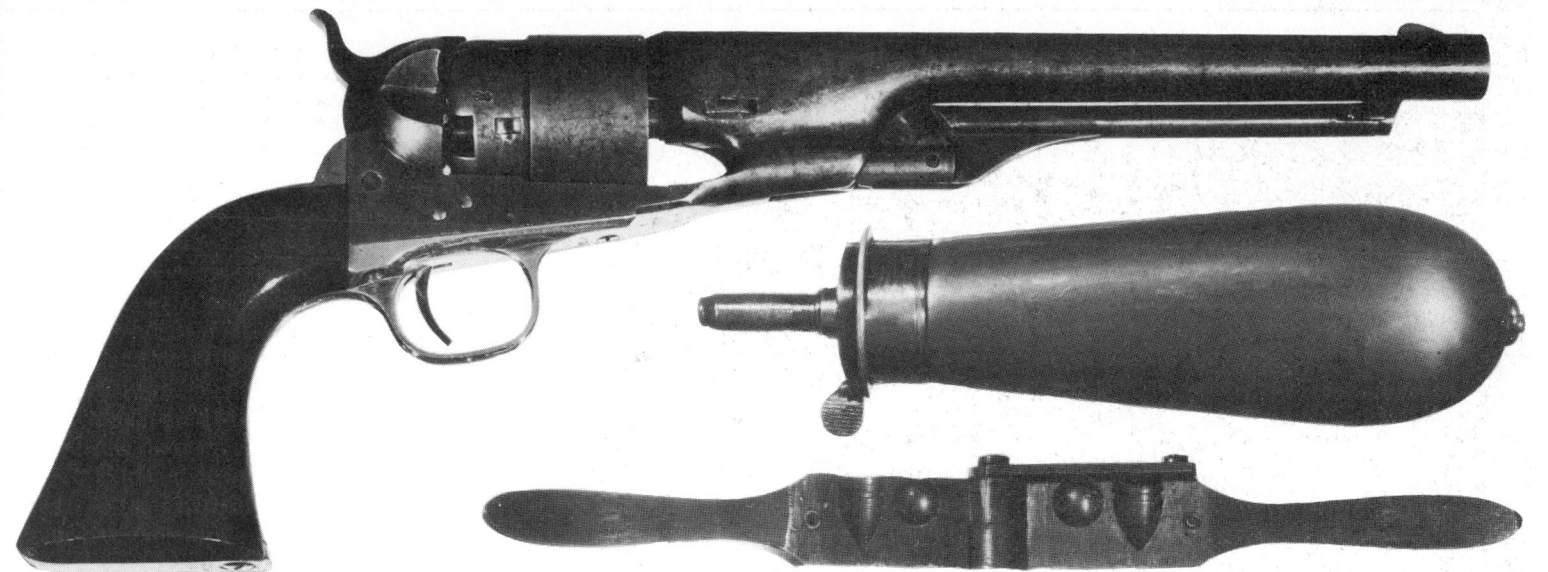

market for lightweight but heavy-calibre weapons, and Sam's search for a successor to the Dragoon had involved him in many experiments. There still exist in Hartford a number of solid-frame .44 calibre weapons which are best described as 'abominations', for they all resemble cut-down side hammer rifles and are fitted with creeping-lever rammers. Their weight equalled or surpassed the Dragoon. It is a pity that the documentation for these curious pistols was destroyed in the 1864 fire.

As early as 1850 Colt produced a pilot for a solid-frame revolver which had great potential. One of its features was the creeping-lever rammer first patented in England in 1853, which was, in fact, the brain-child of Colt's friend and mentor, Elisha K. Root. The five-shot .31 calibre pistol in part resembles an 1851 Navy, but has no practical lockwork mechanism, and for reasons best known to himself, Sam discarded this pistol and turned instead to existing designs. It is now preserved at the Connecticut State Library.

During the late 1850s Sam produced several Navy revolvers in .40 calibre, but he found that although the barrel had sufficient metal to accept .44 calibre, the cylinder did not. Colt's Navy revolver was a 'six-shooter', so the suggestion that he introduce a .40 calibre five-shot version did not appeal to Sam or to his engineers, but someone came up with a much better idea.

A prototype pistol, No. 2, incorporating a round barrel, a hinged rammer and a rebated, fluted cylinder which would accept the .44 cartridge, is the first clue to Colt's thinking. By stepping down the front of the Navy frame to take the rebated cylinder, he solved the problem of calibre with little increase in weight. Next, the conventional hinged lever was replaced by the creeping-lever version housed inside the barrel lug, and the weapon, best remembered today as

the '1860 Army', was born. Sam advised the United States Government of its existence even before he had put the pistol into production.

As a part of Sam's sales ploy, he informed the Government that the new pistols were to be manufactured from 'silver spring steel', claiming that it had qualities not present in existing materials, which enabled barrels and cylinders to be manufactured with less metal – a technique hitherto thought to be dangerous. The validity of Colt's claim, or for that matter, the true worth of the material, is debatable, but since it did demand greater attention both in manufacture and treatment during arms production, the Board was impressed enough to arrange trials.

Late in 1859 a trials board met at Washington to test the 'New Model Army Pistol'. Colt submitted two weapons: one with a 7½-inch, the other with an 8-inch barrel. The latter was half an ounce heavier, which was considered negligible. The Board tested the new pistols against a Dragoon, and concluded that it was more accurate and had greater penetration, but there were criticisms. The 8-inch barrel was preferred, and if the grips were extended, perhaps by a quarter of an inch or more, it would help absorb recoil. Colt promised to incorporate both suggestions and they became standard.

The belief that the 1860 Army was ballistically superior to the 1848 Dragoon is debatable, and experts still argue the point. By measurement the chamber of the Dragoon is 1½ inches long, and that of the 1860 Army, 1$\frac{11}{16}$ inches long. In theory, this gives the Dragoon an advantage in powder content, but not necessarily in practice. Even allowing for a full chamber capacity, however, black powder is slow-burning, occasionally a percentage of it is discharged unburned, and as was well known, it was vulnerable to damp.

The reported muzzle velocity of the Dragoon was 1,100 feet per second when loaded with forty grains of powder and a 140-grain round ball. It dropped to between 820 and 920 feet per second when a 212-grain conical bullet was used. Therefore, the real question is: did the Army and the Board test the Dragoon under full load or to accepted military-issue ammunition? It is important to remember that in 1861 the official load for the 1860 Army was thirty grains of powder and a 216-grain conical bullet. This produced a muzzle velocity of about 740 feet per second – which was weak, but considered adequate for the purpose.

One important change did, however, come about with the 1860 Army: Colt decided to modify the conical bullet used with his .44 calibre arms. He added a grease groove which the Ordnance readily recognized as a valuable anti-fouling measure.

By the early 1860s the New Model Army was the most popular revolver in the country and, unlike its forebears, underwent few changes before becoming standardized. The barrel was rounded, its lug machined down to a minimum and incorporating a shroud into which the rammer fitted. The teeth of a ratchet or creeping-lever meshed into holes machined inside the lug recess. Both parts were held in place by a small screw linking the lever to the rammer plunger.

The fluted cylinders originally supplied were abandoned at about the 8,000 serial range, and replaced by conventional rounded cylinders complete with the same battle scene used on the Navy pistols, together with the patent date of 10 September 1850. The frame was identical with the standard Navy version, except that the fore-part had been machined or 'stepped' down to accept the enlarged portion of the new rebated cylinder. Military pistols included a notch on the recoil shield to accept the detachable stock, and a notch in the heel of the backstrap for the

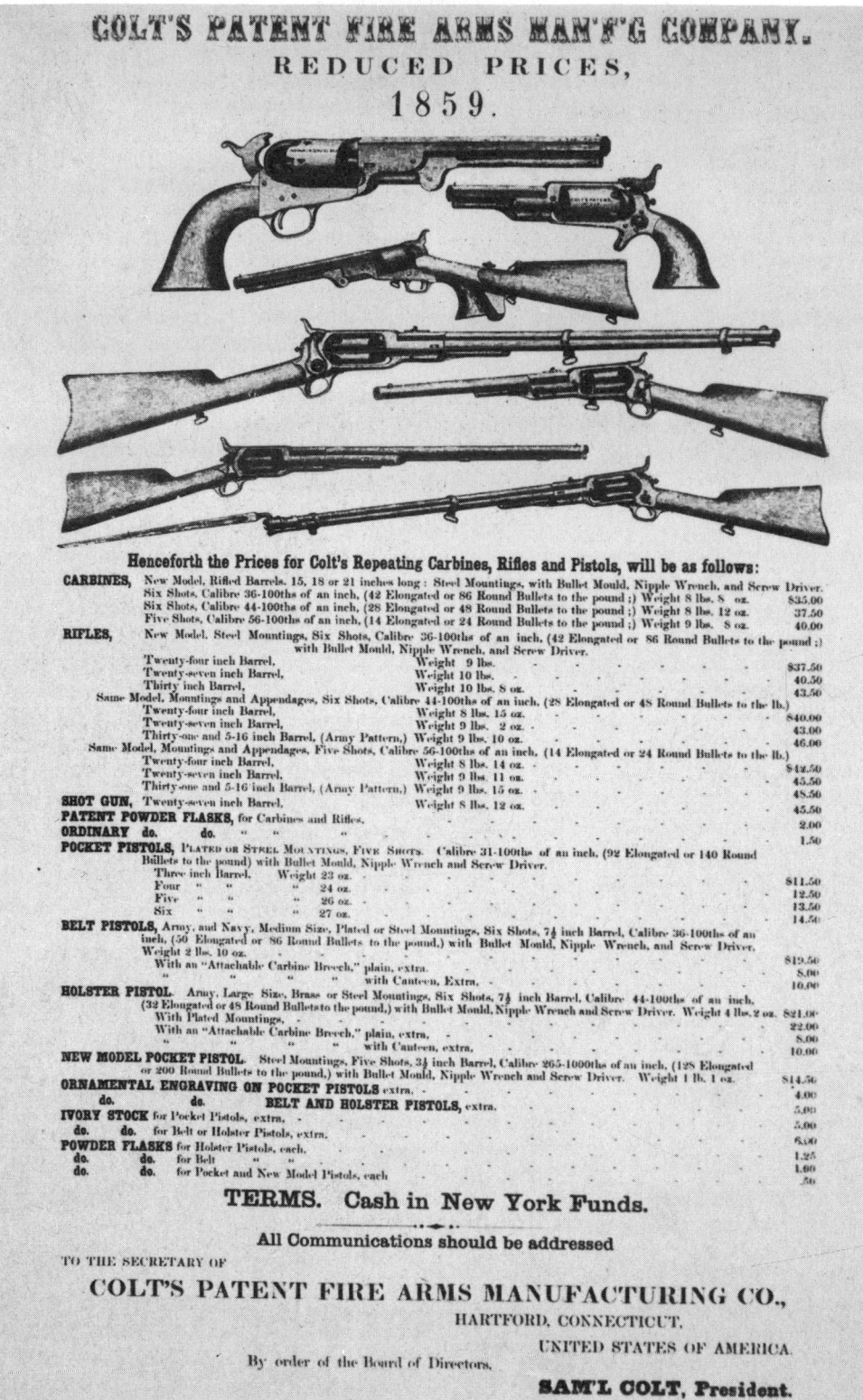

especially at the bolt notches. To rectify this, Colt increased the periphery size and tapered the inside of the chambers slightly. Military reaction to the addition of a carbine stock was less than enthusiastic, but others found that the pistol equipped with a stock doubled quite effectively as a carbine. By 1863, however, the army abandoned them altogether.

News of the new Colt pistol soon reached the South, and just prior to the outbreak of the Civil War on 12 April 1861, a number of them got through quite legally. Between 28 March and 8 April 1861, about 1,100 pistols were shipped to Kitredge & Folsom in New Orleans, and another 500 were dispatched via express to Peter Williams of Richmond, Virginia – on 5 April 1861, the very day on which Lincoln called for troops. Once the war began, however, supplies were cut off, and most of the pistols reaching the South were either contraband or the spoils of war.

Sam Colt's death on 10 January 1862, could not have come at a worse time for his family, his factory and for the United States, for despite the inventive genius of Elisha K. Root, who succeeded him as President of the Company, no new revolver designs were introduced until the early 1870s. So Sam's untimely death effectively brought experiments to an end. Several attempts had been made during Colt's last years to replace the 1860 Army, which had been a 'stop-gap' pistol, and all that remains are several sketches upon which the accompanying drawing is based. Evidently, it was Colt's intention to hinge the barrel and cylinder in a manner that kept the frame and barrel together when the cylinder was removed.

Purchasers of Colt's and other makes of revolver during the Civil War faced several problems, chief of which was the availability of suitable caps. Those designed for Colt's pistols did not necessarily function as well when used in other makes. The problem was discussed in a letter from Major R. H. K. Whitely, writing from the New York Arsenal on 5 July 1862, to Brigadier-General J. W. Ripley, Chief of the Ordnance Department in Washington:

'First, a cap suitable for Colt's pistol does not suit either Savage's or Starr's, because the main spring is too weak to explode it.

'Second, a cap suitable for Savage's or Starr's pistol does not suit Colt's, because

same purpose. Early weapons had extra screws or 'studs' fitted to the frame to seat the stock, but when it was found that they were unnecessary they were discontinued. The recoil shield cut-out was channelled to make capping easier.

To absorb increased recoil, the backstraps were manufactured in iron and blued, but the trigger guards continued to be made from brass. The exceptions were some weapons made up for sale in England where the preference was for iron. The finish of the new pistols was simple: blued barrel, cylinder and backstrap, and a case-hardened rammer assembly, frame and hammer. Military-issue weapons were fitted with plain brass guards and oil-finished stocks, but civilian arms had shellac varnished stocks.

Soon after the 1860 Army reached military arsenals, Colt received complaints about burst cylinders, and it was discovered that drastic machining tended to weaken them,

ELEY
LONDON
PISTOL CAPS
ELEY BROS
LONDON
ELEY BROS
250
METAL-LINED
CAPS,
Made expressly for
COLT'S P^T
Belt and Pocket
PISTOLS.
Manufacturers, London.
ELEY BROS
250
CAPS.
Made expressly for
COLT'S P^T
Belt and Pocket
PISTOLS.
Manufacturers, London.

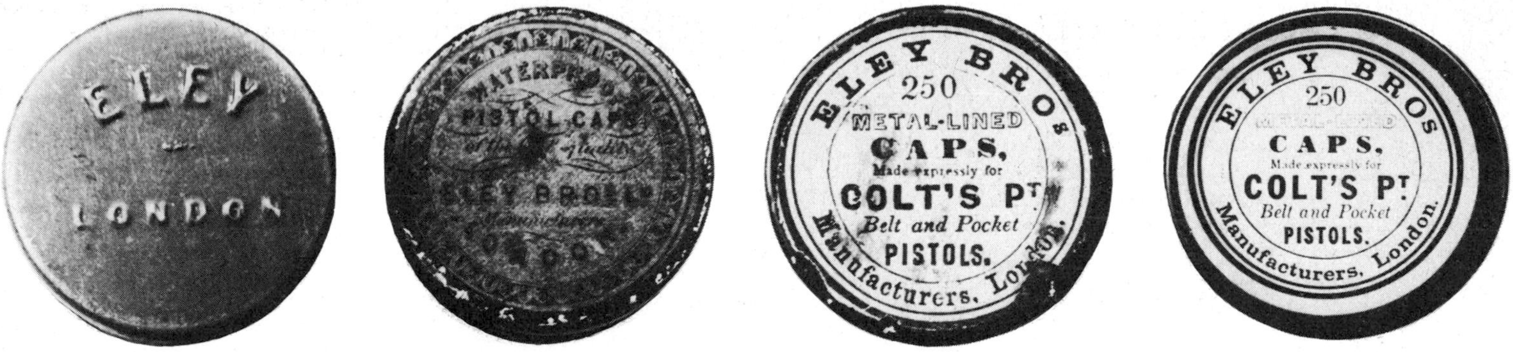

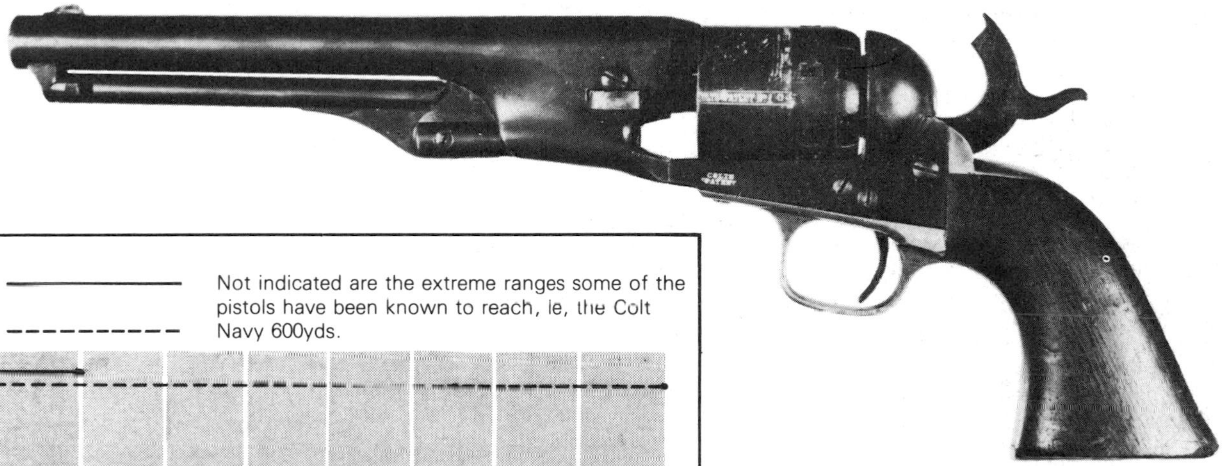

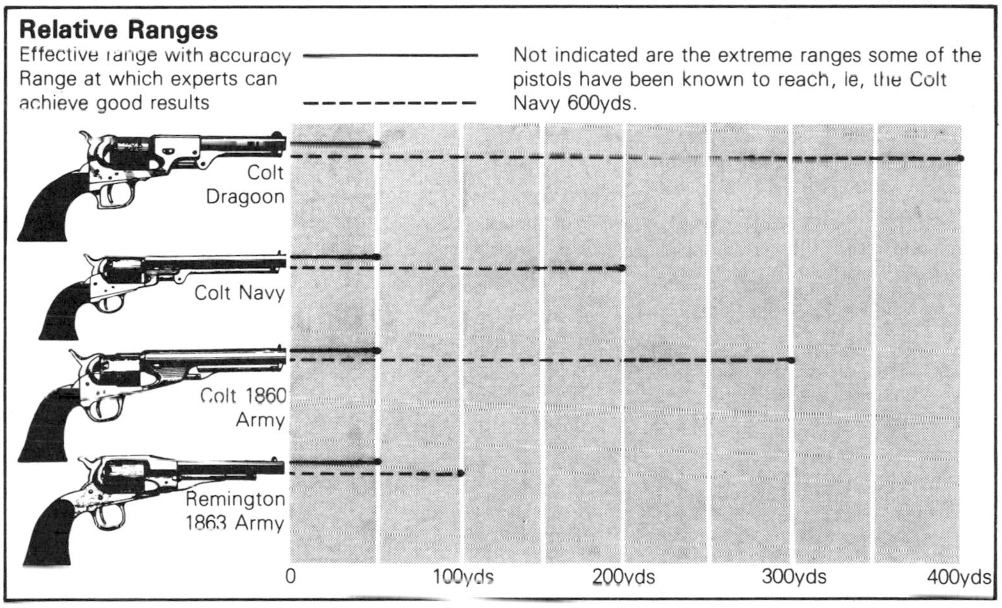

Relative Ranges
Effective range with accuracy
Range at which experts can achieve good results
Not indicated are the extreme ranges some of the pistols have been known to reach, ie, the Colt Navy 600yds.
Colt Dragoon
Colt Navy
Colt 1860 Army
Remington 1863 Army
0
100yds
200yds
300yds
400yds

Above: The New Model Navy (generally called the Model of 1861) was introduced late in 1860. Colt was able to save on material, by utilizing the same forgings as used on the 1860 Army barrels and machining them down. The 1861 version is basically the same as the 1851 model except for the barrel and assembly, but it never received the same attention as the old model. (By courtesy of the Kansas State Historical Society)

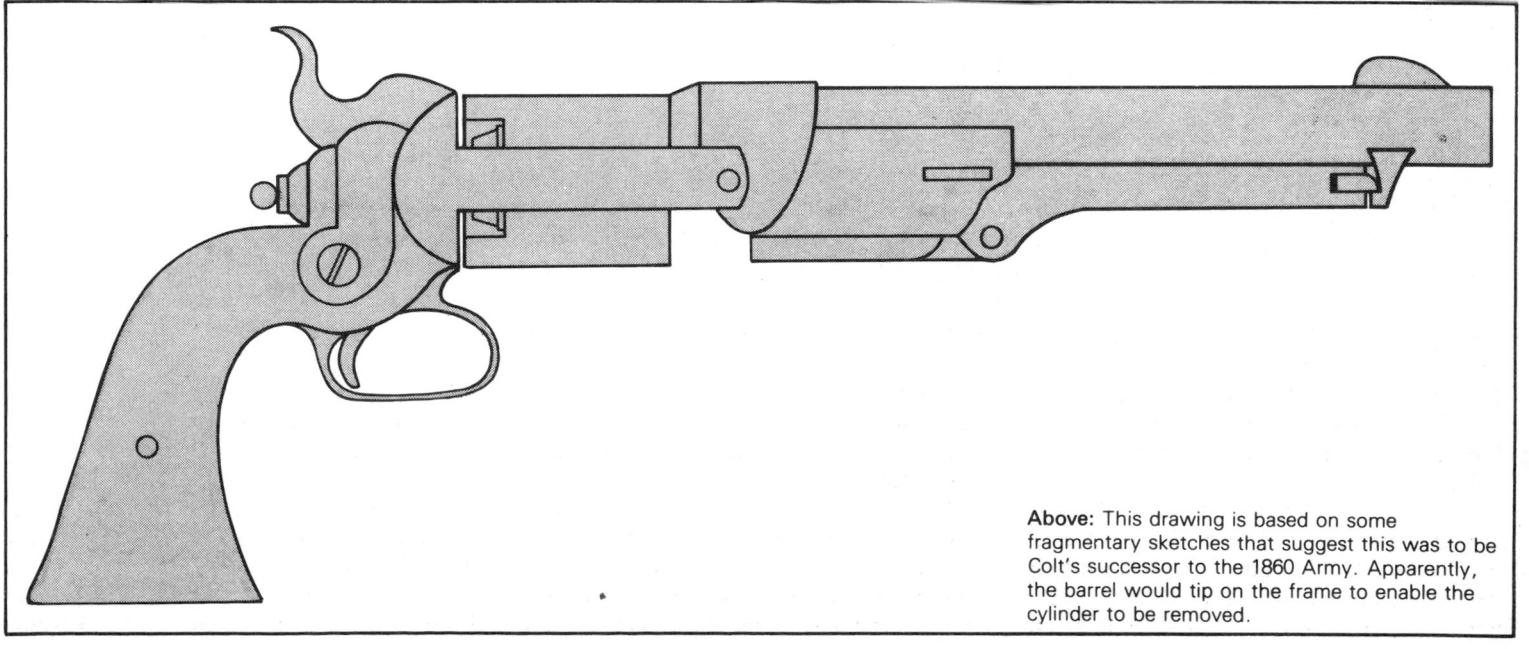

Above: This drawing is based on some fragmentary sketches that suggest this was to be Colt's successor to the 1860 Army. Apparently, the barrel would tip on the frame to enable the cylinder to be removed.

the hammer drives it in pieces, a fragment often lodges in front of the cock, and renders the arm useless after the first fire. On this account our spies carry two pistols, and have had to depend on the second for safety for the reason above stated. Therefore, I am compelled to have two qualities made, one for Colt's answering in thickness of copper to Eley's double waterproof, and the other for Savage's and Starr's to Eley's metal-lined.'

Ripley forwarded the letter to Major W. A. Thornton at the West Troy Arsenal and requested that he 'please see that all revolvers made for this Department are suited to fire the same caps as Colt's army pistols.'

The identity of the actual revolver supplied to 'spies' is not disclosed; presumably it was either a Savage or a Starr, but it is interesting to learn that non-Colt or Eley-type caps were liable to jam pistols when bits lodged inside the hammer channel or the mechanism. This is a common occurrence today, mainly because few of the available commercial caps meet the standards demanded by Colt and others in the 1850s and 1860s. Indeed, if one compares the quality of an original Eley-made cap to some of those manufactured today, the latter is inferior.

Colt's sales during the Civil War were impressive. Some 17,010 Model 1851 and 1861 Navy pistols were purchased for a price of $27.50 each, but it was the combined sales of the Dragoon (several thousand still on hand at the factory, together with 200 sent over from London) and the 1860 Army which accounted for the largest number. The combined purchase was 129,800 revolvers at $17.50 each. In its annual report in April 1865, the Colt company stated that but for the 1864 fire, they would have manufactured an additional estimated total of 50,000 Army

pistols, which would have put paid to some of their lesser rivals who had benefitted from their misfortune.

When in 1871 the Ordnance Department decided to introduce cartridge pistols, 1,000 Armys were ordered to be returned to Colt's for conversion to .44 centre-fire pending an as yet undecided replacement for all existing percussion arms in service or in store.

The 1860 Army has been the subject of debate among engineers and historians for decades. Some claim that it was weaker than the contemporary 1851 Navy pistol, and that the hardened teeth on the rammer soon wore out the unhardened notches in the barrel. It is true that after considerable use (or abuse) these weapons do tend to 'loosen up', but in new condition they were quite adequate and well able to hold their own against most of their rivals.

The New Model Army also inspired Sam Colt to modify the Navy. Here little work was required: barrel forgings for the 1860 Army were machined down to conform to Navy size, and except for the round barrel and rammer assembly (the latter was interchangeable with the Army except for the tapered rammer to fit the Navy-size chambers), the weapon closely resembled its 1851 counterpart. A few pistols were manufactured to accept carbine stocks, but the majority were left plain.

The so-called Model 1861 Navy was actually available late in 1860, but it was 16 April 1861, before any of them were sold commercially. On that date twenty of them left the factory for Colt's New York Agency, all under serial No. 33. A limited number were also shipped to London during the war years, and available ledgers indicate that at the beginning of 1864 the serial range was about 17,000. When production stopped in about 1873, it had only reached approxi-

mately 38,843. This small production run was due partly to the fire at Colt's factory in 1864 and partly because the 1861 model never achieved the fame of its predecessor of 1851. There was a glut of these weapons at the end of the Civil War, so new pistols were only got up on demand. A number of them were sold in Europe and the Middle and Far East, and they were popular in the Western states.

In Europe, where cartridge weapons were fast overtaking percussion arms, sales of these and other such pistols were limited. During the middle 1870s, however, when Russia and Turkey made angry noises at each other and eventually went to war, sales picked up a little. Writing on 28 January 1875, Frederich von Oppen, Colt's London Agency manager, reported that his customers had definite preferences: 'We sent before New Model Navy pistols instead of Old Model ones to Turkey, but our Customers greatly complained, and insisted upon Old Model ones after that . . .' Prices differed. The 1851 model sold for £1.9.0.d.; and the 1861 model for £1.8.0d.; but by October 1875 the 1851 model had dropped to £1.8.0d. and the 1861 even lower, some as low as 22 shillings. Why the weapon should have lost favour can perhaps be explained by the prejudice on the part of those familiar with the original octagonal barrels and 'black' mountings.

These then, were some of the revolvers available during the period 1851–1861, when America became embroiled in border conflicts, Civil War and the emergent Western expansion which followed it.

Below left: A plain cased 1861 Navy lacking its flask. (By courtesy of Messrs Wallis & Wallis)

Below right: A de luxe cased 1861 Navy complete with all accessories. Serial No. 11784, the cylinder was not numbered. (By courtesy of R. Larry Wilson)

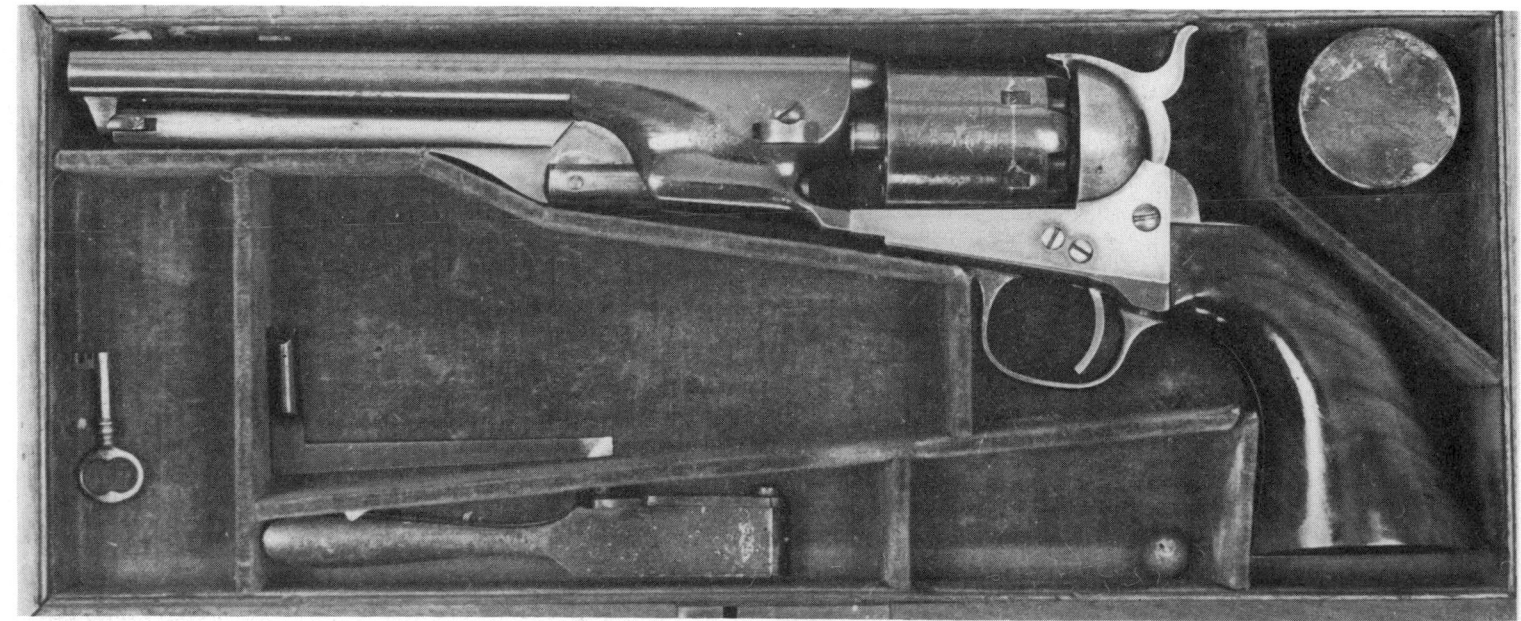

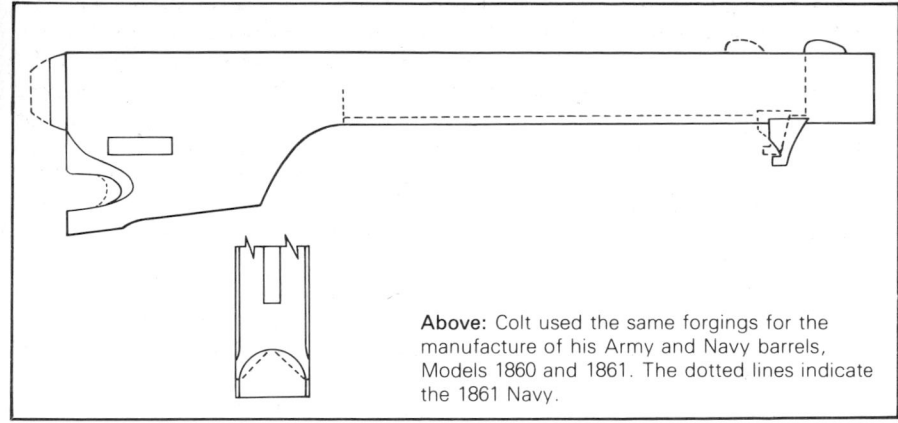

Above: Colt used the same forgings for the manufacture of his Army and Navy barrels, Models 1860 and 1861. The dotted lines indicate the 1861 Navy.

Right: A contemporary advertisement for Schuyler, Hartley & Graham, published in *Harper's Weekly* in 1863. The pistol illustrated is the 1862 Colt Police. (Author's Collection)

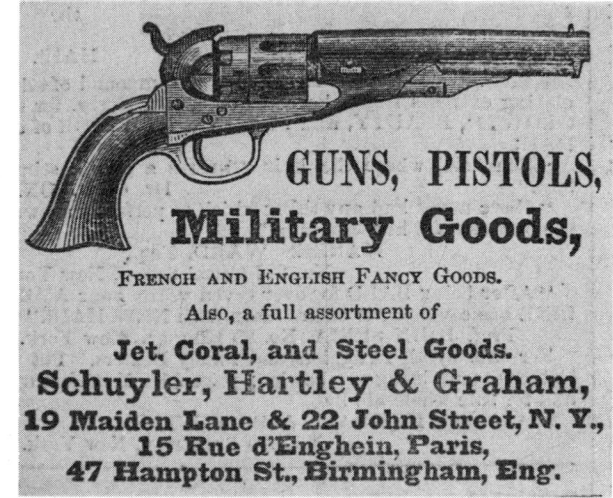

GUNS, PISTOLS, **Military Goods,**
FRENCH AND ENGLISH FANCY GOODS.
Also, a full assortment of
Jet. Coral, and Steel Goods.
Schuyler, Hartley & Graham,
19 Maiden Lane & 22 John Street, N. Y.,
15 Rue d'Enghein, Paris,
47 Hampton St., Birmingham, Eng.

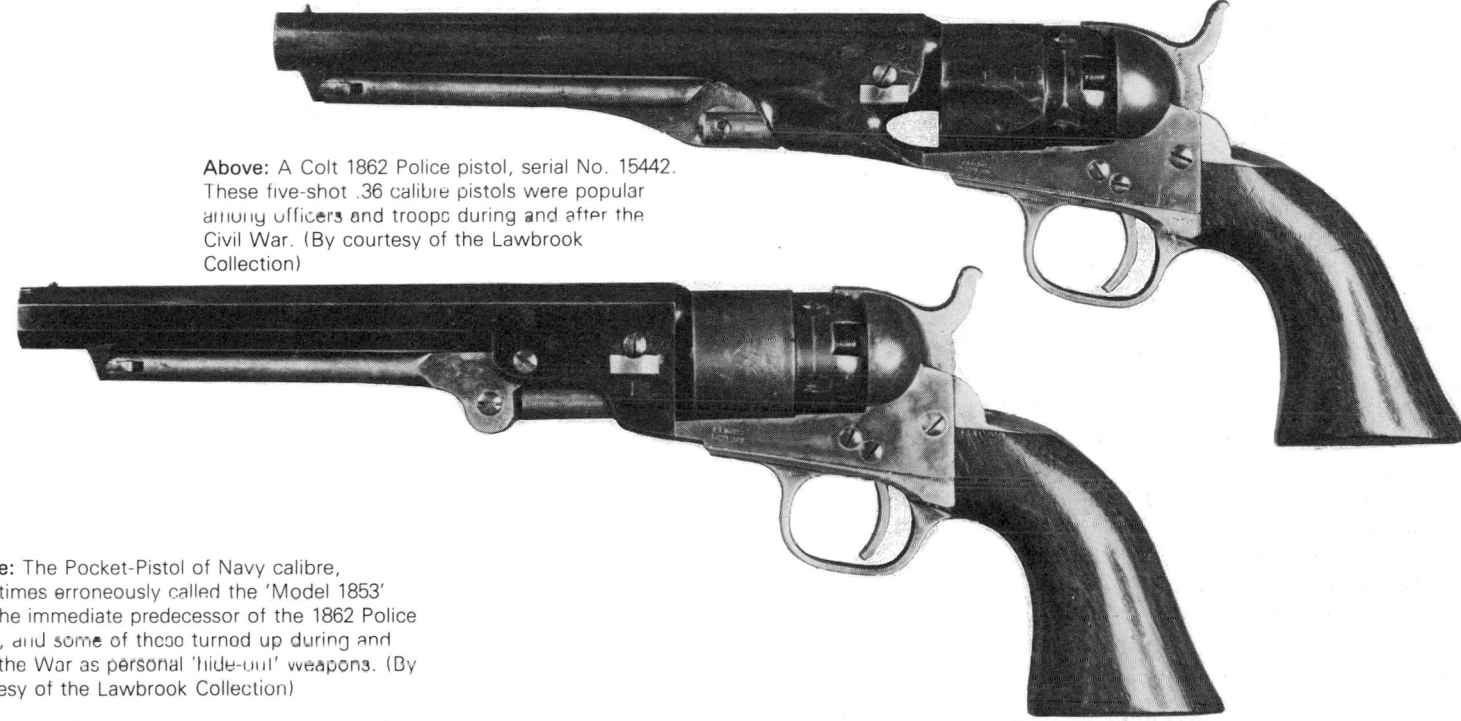

Above: A Colt 1862 Police pistol, serial No. 15442. These five-shot .36 calibre pistols were popular among officers and troops during and after the Civil War. (By courtesy of the Lawbrook Collection)

Above: The Pocket-Pistol of Navy calibre, sometimes erroneously called the 'Model 1853' was the immediate predecessor of the 1862 Police pistol, and some of these turned up during and after the War as personal 'hide-out' weapons. (By courtesy of the Lawbrook Collection)

Above: Left, top to bottom, Continental Arms Co. .22 pepperbox revolver, Remington-Elliot .32 rim-fire Deringer, Frank Wesson .32 rim-fire Deringer (second type), .41 'Southerner'. Centre, top to bottom, Reid .22 'knuckleduster' revolver, Minneapolis Firearms Co. palm pistol, National Arms Co. .41 No. 1 Deringer (note all-metal construction), Allen & Wheelock centre-hammer .25 lip-fire pocket-revolver. Right, top to bottom, European .22 rim-fire six-shot revolver with folding trigger, Allen .22 side-hammer revolver, Philadelphia-style Deringer in .41 calibre, Morgan & Clapp single-shot .32 rim-fire pistol, Stevens .22 single-shot pistol. (By courtesy of Richard A. Bourne & Co. Inc.)

Left: An interesting selection of Deringer pistols. Left, Butterfield .38 pistol with 2-inch barrel. It is fitted with the Butterfield patent priming device. Priming pellets were fed into the tube when the knurled knob on the bottom was removed. .41 Remington double Deringer No. 303. The lever on the side just above the stub trigger is moved downward to permit removal of the barrels which swing upwards on a hinge fixed to the top of the frame. Right, Frank Wesson .22 two-shot 'vest-pocket Deringer', Remington-Elliot .22 Deringer with mother-of-pearl grips and 'Little All Right' .22 palm pistol, manufactured by the All Right Fire Arms Co., Lawrence, Massachusetts. (By courtesy of Richard A. Bourne Co. Inc.)

5
THE DERINGER AND OTHER 'HIDE-OUT' PISTOLS

A shooting affray occurred this morning on First Street, between two men . . . words passed between them, when one drew his revolver, and No. 2 remarked 'You know you have got the advantage of me'. No. 1 then put back his weapon, whereupon No. 2 drew a Deringer and fired at No. 1 who also managed to draw his six-shooter. Each fired two shots; one was hit in the wrist and the other in the shoulder . . . to fire at a man when you know that he is defenceless and can't return the compliment, is next to the lowest species of cowardice known among men. – Abilene, Kansas, *Chronicle*, 22 June 1871.

DURING the middle years of the nineteenth century, the frontiersmen came to rely upon the rifle and large pistol; but there was also an increase in that most sinister of firearms, the 'hide-out' gun, commonly called a 'Deringer'. The Deringer is an essential part of the Western myth. Any character worthy of a reputation is reputed to have carried one or a pair of these small but deadly large-calibre weapons tucked into his waistcoat, coat pocket, trousers or even boot tops, as a back-up when a full-size pistol was unavailable or impracticable. Yet these arms were not designed simply for the gun-toting fraternity; they were an attempt to conserve weight and space, while remaining as effective as their big brothers.

Pocket-pistols were by no means uncommon, for these and 'muff' pistols had been in use long before the close of the flint-lock era, by which time the English, in particular, had produced a fine selection of turn-off barrelled box-lock pistols which sold in their hundreds at least until the 1840s. But it was the Philadelphia gunmaker, Henry Deringer, who produced the pistol which more than any other inspired public interest in small, large-calibre weapons.

Deringer made his name and reputation supplying contract arms to the U.S. Government, notably the Model 1817 flintlock rifle (Deringer and several others produced more than 26,000 such arms from about 1817 to the 1840s). A notable gunmaker in his own right, he produced a fine range of conventional pocket-pistols which were very popular. The little pistol which immortalized him was, in fact, a late addition, and a good description of it and the other weapons from the same stable is found in the transcript of an action against infringers of his trade mark

brought by his executors in 1868. There were about six basic types with barrel lengths ranging from six to nine inches for the 'duelling'-type or 'ordinary' version, down to 1½ to three inches for the small pocket-pistols – the latter being the most popular and 'notorious'. Various calibres have been reported, but the majority of pistols were produced in .41 calibre – the size most favoured by many of his competitors. Henry began making his small pocket-pistols in the late 1830s, but it was not until the late 1840s that their reputation led to the bulk demand that encouraged many imitators.

The shorter-barrelled pistols were not provided with a ramrod, but this does not seem to have caused many problems. The barrels were constructed in two parts (the barrel was screwed into a breech-plug), made of iron with seven-groove rifling. They were machined to an oval shape, but flattened

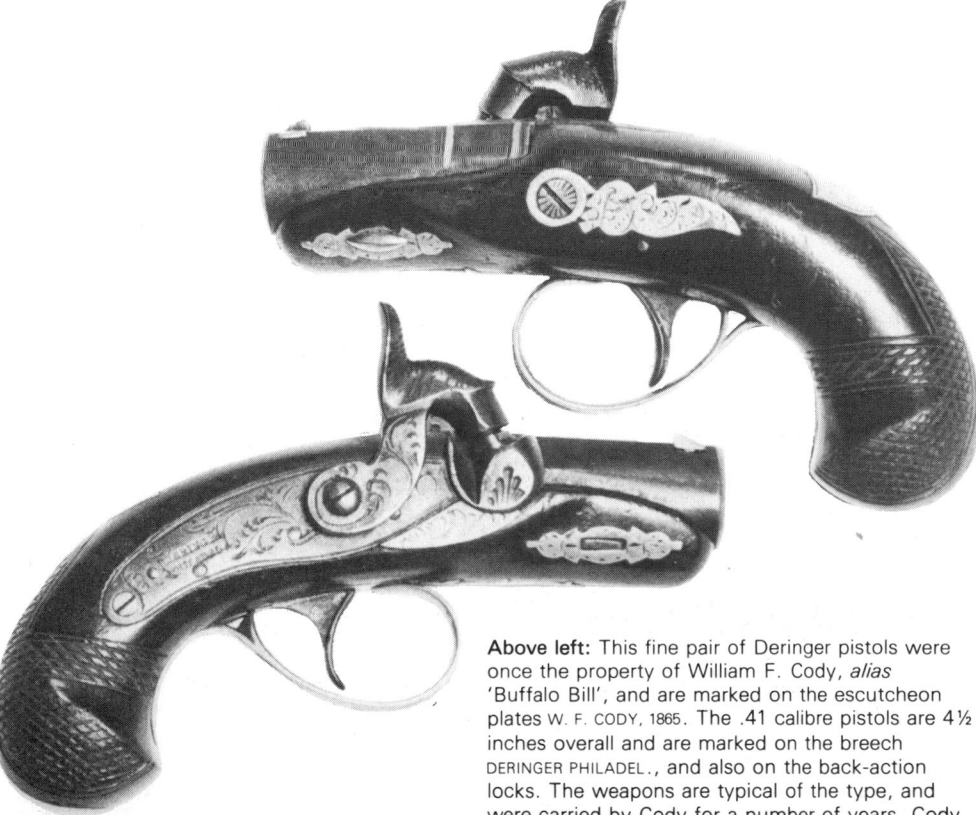

Above left: This fine pair of Deringer pistols were once the property of William F. Cody, *alias* 'Buffalo Bill', and are marked on the escutcheon plates W. F. CODY, 1865. The .41 calibre pistols are 4½ inches overall and are marked on the breech DERINGER PHILADEL., and also on the back-action locks. The weapons are typical of the type, and were carried by Cody for a number of years. Cody

later gave them to Louis A. Barker, who in turn presented them to W. G. Renwick. The pistols are now in the Buffalo Bill Museum, Cody, Wyoming. (By courtesy of Sotheby & Co.)

Above right: A close-up of the escutcheon plate of one of the Cody pistols, showing the inscription. (By courtesy of Sotheby & Co.)

along the top. The stocks were of varnished walnut with a coarse chequered design. The barrels were finished with a pseudo-Damascus effect (that is, copper streaks in a browned finish); the locks were case-hardened and other iron parts were blued. Some pistols had silver-plated brass trigger guards and escutcheons. Most were fitted with German silver front sights, but occasionally other materials were used, and silver or gold bands were placed around the barrel mouth or breech. A cap box was normally provided in the butt. The overall effect was very pleasing to the eye.

Deringer's pistols varied in price and, of course, fluctuated with demand. Between 1849 and 1851 they rose from as little as $3.25 to $5, and once the demand increased, particularly during the California gold-rush, Eastern prices had doubled and trebled by the time the pistols reached the West. Competition from such rivals as Slotter & Company (Slotter was a former employee of Deringer) who were making their barrels from steel rather than iron, forced a price war. One rival from Philadelphia actually signed his pistols 'J. DERINGER' which confused many people until it was established by the late John E. Parsons that he was in fact unrelated and was a tailor who had allowed the use of his name! The arms companies' infighting, however, meant little to the men who relied upon these small pistols, and they eagerly purchased whatever was available.

Despite the demand for pistols of any sort in California, there is little evidence to indicate that Deringer-type weapons reached the states in any great numbers prior to 1852, but once they did, they swiftly established themselves as a part of frontier life. With rooms in San Francisco costing as much as $200 to $1,000 a month at one period, it is not surprising that Deringer or Deringer-type pistols could sell for $20 or more.

It has long been alleged that the misspelling of the name Deringer as 'Derringer' owes its origin to the assassination of Abraham Lincoln on the evening of 14 April 1865, at Ford's Theatre, Washington. His assassin, John Wilkes Booth, used a Deringer pistol, and the press described it as a 'derringer'. Perhaps it was the Lincoln murder which established the term, but as early as 1856 in California, the word 'derringer' had appeared in print.

The elevation of California to statehood had also brought with it the problems of all societies – corruption in high places. By the spring of 1855, San Francisco was afflicted by an openly corrupt city administration, and there were demands for a return to the 'uplifting' days of the Vigilante lynch-mobs. On 17 November 1855, General William H.

Richardson, the United States Marshal for the Northern District of California, quarrelled with Charles Cora, a saloon-keeper and noted 'ballot-box rigger'. The Marshal objected to the presence of Cora's mistress, Arabella Ryan, at a performance at the American Theatre. Both men continued their argument on the street. Suddenly, Cora pulled his Deringer pistol and shot the unarmed Richardson dead. The local press described the murder weapon as a 'derringer', which established the use of the second 'r' prior to Lincoln's murder. Thanks to a divided verdict, Cora escaped justice, but he was later lynched by irate Vigilantes following the murder of one newspaperman by another. The mob had decided that it was time for a general 'clean-up' anyhow.

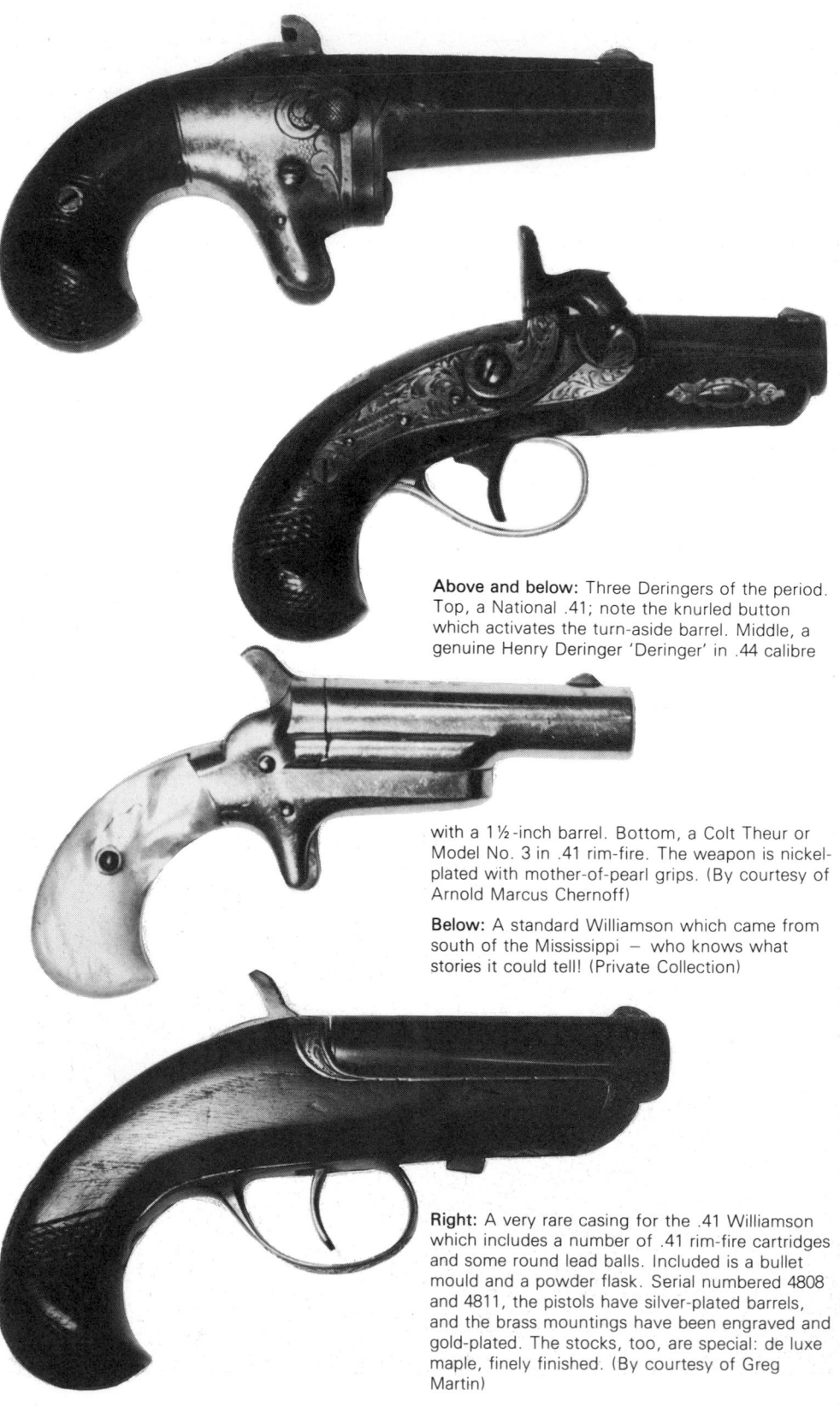

Above and below: Three Deringers of the period. Top, a National .41; note the knurled button which activates the turn-aside barrel. Middle, a genuine Henry Deringer 'Deringer' in .44 calibre with a 1½-inch barrel. Bottom, a Colt Theur or Model No. 3 in .41 rim-fire. The weapon is nickel-plated with mother-of-pearl grips. (By courtesy of Arnold Marcus Chernoff)

Below: A standard Williamson which came from south of the Mississippi — who knows what stories it could tell! (Private Collection)

Right: A very rare casing for the .41 Williamson which includes a number of .41 rim-fire cartridges and some round lead balls. Included is a bullet mould and a powder flask. Serial numbered 4808 and 4811, the pistols have silver-plated barrels, and the brass mountings have been engraved and gold-plated. The stocks, too, are special: de luxe maple, finely finished. (By courtesy of Greg Martin)

In the wake of Henry Deringer and his innumerable imitators, came a whole breed of metallic-cartridge Deringers, the most important being the Williamson, the Remington and, eventually, the Colt. The first was the brain-child of David Williamson of New York, who patented it on 2 October 1866, and put it into production soon afterwards. Some think that the pistols were made for Williamson by David Moore or the National Arms Company. There is some truth in this, because Moore's Patent Fire Arms Company, formed in 1864, was succeeded by the National Arms Company in 1865. In 1870, National, in turn, were bought out by Colt's who continued to manufacture National's later range of Deringers as their own First Model.

Williamson's agreement with Moore or National is unknown, but from 1866 until about 1870 an estimated 3,000 of his pistols are believed to have been manufactured (and recent observations have disclosed weapons with serial numbers as high as 7,000). The advantage of the Williamson over many of its rivals was its dual ammunition; rim-fire cartridges or a percussion tube insert, complete with a percussion cap nipple in order to use loose powder and ball.

In appearance, the Williamson resembled the original Henry Deringer pistols, except that the hammer was centrally mounted and the barrel was moveable. When the pistol was set at half-cock, a catch in front of the trigger guard was depressed enabling the barrel to slide forward to load fixed rim-fire .41 calibre ammunition or the percussion insert. Like most pistols of this type, the Williamson was less than six inches overall (in fact, five inches). It was constructed as follows: barrel, 2½ inches long with broad three-groove rifling. Impressed upon the left side is the legend WILLIAMSON'S PAT. OCT. 2, 1866, NEW-YORK. The rear portion of the barrel is rounded, but the muzzle is finished in a semi-oval form with the top portion left flat. Along the top flat is engraved a fletched arrow (some pistols have two) and the front sight is a small blade of German silver.

The calibre of these weapons has been stated as both .41 and .36, but I have never encountered one in .36 – all those so far examined were in .41 calibre. The frames and trigger guards were of cast brass. Some were left plain, but the majority were either silver- or gold-plated. All weapons so far encountered had engraved frames and trigger guards. A blade-type firing-pin in the nose of the hammer took care of the fixed ammunition, and a small stud set beneath it accounted for the percussion cap. In each instance, the pin or stud engaged with its case or cap through holes cut in the frame. The rear sight was a 'V' cut into the hammer lip. The stock, made from straight-grain American walnut, was machine-made, flat-sided and bevelled to curve down to a pleasing bird's-head grip which was chequered, and the whole treated to a coat of shellac varnish.

The Williamson Deringer was popular with many of the gambler gunfighters of the day. Wild Bill Hickok is alleged to have carried a pair of them in his waistcoat during his period in Kansas City and New York when conventional pistols would have aroused comment and caused concern. A Williamson pistol, gold-plated and engraved and alleged to have been one of the Hickok-owned pair is known, but it lacks documentation. However, the genuine Deringer 'Deringers' owned by his life-long friend, Buffalo Bill Cody, are better documented. Marked W. F. CODY, 1865, on the escutcheon plates, they were carried by Cody for a number of years, but late in life he presented them to a man named Louis A. Barker in appreciation of services rendered.

When Colt's took over the National Arms Company, for a short period they continued to manufacture the company's top-selling Deringer, an all-metal, .41 calibre rim-fire weapon with a stud trigger and a side-swung barrel for loading and ejection. The Second (Colt) Model, however, had a better-designed bird's-head wooden grip. Later, both models were replaced by the Model No. 3, designed by F. Alexander Theur, and generally called the 'Theur' model. Although this was a vast improvement upon its predecessors, Colt's made no further effort to introduce other models. Instead, the Theur version remained in production until about 1910, by which time, approximately 45,000 of them had been manufactured.

Remington's, on the other hand, devoted much time and effort to the production of their Deringer-type pistols, as can be seen from the accompanying woodcuts from contemporary sales brochures. Between 1860 and 1865, several semi-prototype 'pepper box' six-barrelled .22 rim-fire pistols were produced with ring triggers. These had varying degrees of success, and were followed by several single-shot .30, .32, and .41 rim-fire pistols which aroused interest. But it was the 1866 'over-and-under' or 'double Deringer' pistol which attracted most attention. From 1865 until about 1935, an estimated 150,000 were made.

Remington's 'over-and-under' proved to be the most popular of all metallic-cartridge Deringers. The 3-inch superimposed barrels tipped upwards for loading and extraction, and were held in place by a pivoting key or latch placed on the right side of the frame. In operation, the firing-pin automatically switched from barrel to barrel (similar in some respects to the Sharps' four-barrel pistols which will be discussed later). The finish on most of these pistols was nickel, although some have been found fully-blued. The stocks were available in rosewood, chequered hard rubber or, if required, ivory.

The popularity of this weapon, which kept it on the market for 69 years, says much for its design. Gamblers and others who travelled around a lot, especially in areas where the display of pistols would not only have been unsociable but unlawful, found them a boon. Furthermore adverse publicity came with the assassination of President James Garfield by the fanatic, Charles Guiteau, on 12 July 1881. Guiteau was reported to have been armed with a double-barrelled Remington Deringer (although it has since been claimed that the weapon was in fact a pocket-pistol made by Iver-Johnson). But the unsavoury reputation of

the Deringer was finally established on 6 September 1901, when Leon Czolgosc shot President McKinley: his weapon was a double-barrelled Remington Deringer.

During the 1850s and 1860s, the period that saw the 'wildest' of the Old West, the true Deringer had many 'piratical' imitators and rivals. Even the talents of Christian Sharps were turned toward the production of these pistols, together with a limited range of percussion revolvers. The latter were produced in .25 calibre and were six-shot weapons which resembled the Smith & Wesson .22 pistols; but they were nowhere near as successful and only about 2,000 of them were made. Between 1859 and 1874, however, the Sharps' Deringer-types sold in their thousands. In 1862 Sharps joined forces with William Hankins and the Sharps & Hankins partnership was responsible for some fine weapons. Licensed copies were also manufactured in Birmingham, England, by Tipping & Lawden.

The Sharps' four-barrelled pistols were available in rim-fire in .22, .30 and .32 calibres. Barrel lengths were 2½–3½ inches. The barrels were set in a cluster, which slid forward for loading or extraction. The four barrels were fired from the one hammer by

Below: A series of Remington advertisements for Deringers and vest-pocket pistols. (Author's Collection)

means of a rotating firing-pin set at the rear of the barrels or in the frame. Some of the weapons had silver-plated brass frames and others had iron which was blued. The grips were either walnut or gutta-percha. A stud trigger replaced the conventional version. Despite their small calibres, the Sharps four-barrel pistols enjoyed large sales.

An interesting Deringer-type was the 'Southerner', a .41 calibre rim-fire pistol manufactured from about 1869 until 1873 by the Brown Manufacturing Company, Newport, Massachusetts. Total production amounted to only a few thousand, but it was popular in the West and, predictably, in the South. The 2½-inch octagonal barrel pivoted sideways to facilitate loading and unloading. The extractor was mounted in the barrel, and a catch set in the base of the frame released the barrel for loading and unloading. An earlier version of the pistol, made by the Merrimack Arms & Manufacturing Company of Newburyport, Massachusetts, was marked SOUTHERNER on the top flat of the barrel. These pistols were produced between 1867 and 1869 when Brown took over. Among the later Brown-produced specimens were some with 4-inch octagonal barrels and an extended bag-shaped grip, but they were not as popular as the smaller versions.

Forehand & Wadsworth, who are best remembered for revolvers, also produced a

single-shot Deringer from about 1871 until 1890. This was in .41 rim-fire and bore a superficial resemblance to the Southerner. The barrel was machined to conform to the flat-sided frame, but the fore-end was rounded. Fitted with a bird's-head grip, only a few hundred were produced.

The Connecticut Arms Company of Naubuc, Connecticut, produced the Hammond 'Bulldog' single-shot Deringers and pocket-pistols from 1866 until 1868. These curious pistols with a 4-inch barrel, sold in calibres varying from .22 to as high as .50 (although the .44 version was the most common) and were popular in some areas. The smaller calibres were also used in some specimens that were produced with 8½-, 10-, 12- and 18-inch barrels, complete with carbine stocks for target work. Wild Bill Hickok is reported to have carried a Hammond; the weapon is in a collection in Berryville, Arkansas, but its connection with Hickok is hearsay rather than documented fact.

The 1880s witnessed the end of the Deringer era, for already most of the manufacturers were producing small, reliable five- and six-shot pocket-pistols that were comparable to the Deringer in size. The Deringer, however, both in its original form and in its numerous imitators, had established itself as the true 'hide-out' pistol, as the term implies.

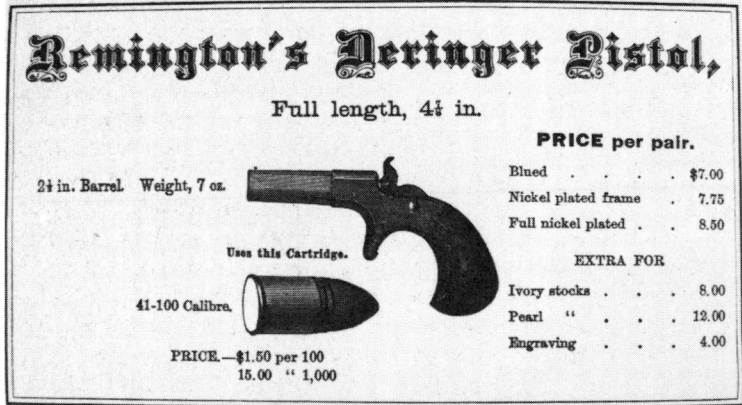

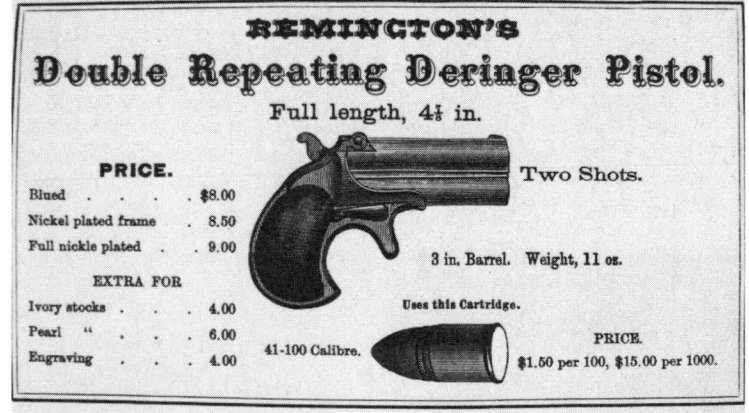

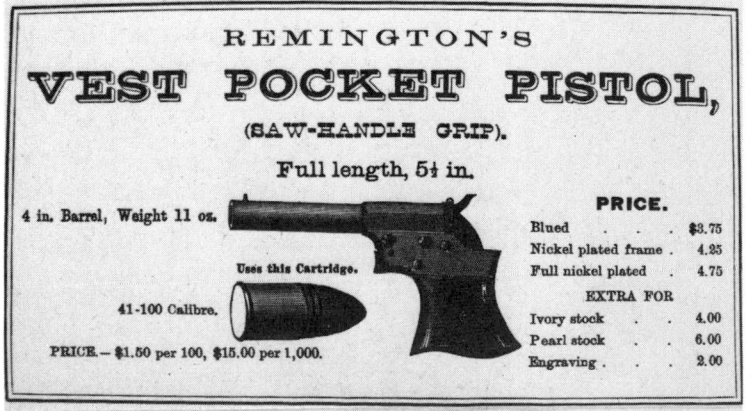

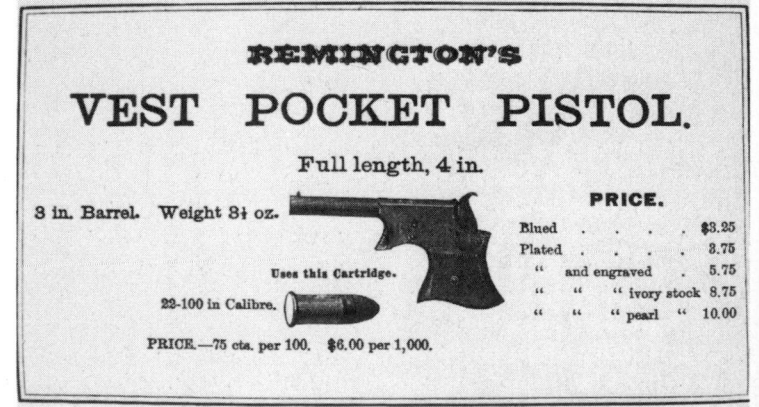

6
BORDER CONFLICT – A PRELUDE TO WAR

The Border Ruffian . . . when in the minority, like the savage Indian, [is] the most sneaking, cringing coward of the plains. But when in the majority, the most braggardly, overbearing, insolent, tyranical of creatures . . . and they were a menace to Kansas, particularly along her eastern border, for more than four years . . . – William W. Denison.

THE success of the revolver during California's early years was matched in Kansas and Missouri. On 30 May 1854 President Franklin Pierce signed the Kansas–Nebraska Act and the pro- and anti-slavery factions fought each other to determine the new territory's future. Pierce had applied a slow-burning fuse to a powder keg which was to smoulder for the next seven years, for the conflict in Kansas presaged what would happen when it did explode – the Union would split asunder and plunge the nation into civil war.

Slavery, the South's 'peculiar institution', was a root cause of the conflict, for despite extremist views as to the real issues involved, it was slavery which dictated each state or territory's future. Slavery had been officially outlawed by England in 1807, but it continued to play a major role in the economics of the southern states of the Union. Because Southern economy was based almost entirely upon slavery, moral issues counted far less than monetary values. It was a trap of the South's own making, and one for which she would eventually pay a terrible price.

In the North, where industrialists had looked objectively at the shortage of skilled craftsmen and the high wages they commanded, they saw the answer in the employment of machinery which, combined with the available skills, had revolutionised manufacturing techniques. The South, however, had remained feudal, it being cheaper to breed large numbers of slaves to perform manual tasks than to purchase machinery, plus the additional cost of employing someone to run it and someone else to repair it. The possibility that the slaves, if freed, would jeopardize the whole Southern economy, or unleash a work-force that would work for far less than even the poorest whites, was both abhorrent to the poor whites (who feared for their own future) and unacceptable to those whose fortunes were tied-up in the system. So slavery had to stay, and a balance be struck between 'free' and 'slave' states.

In order to preserve the balance, each new state or territory was admitted to the Union as either 'slave' or 'free'. Missouri was admitted in 1820 on a 'compromise' vote which allowed her to become a slave state, but forbade the exclusion of freed Negroes and mulattos (which she had wanted), and the agreement that all slavery would be forbidden in United States territories north of parallel 36° 30' which was the state's southern boundary. This left the South free to admit Arkansas and Florida as slave states, but the North gained much of the unsettled territory west of Illinois as slave-free.

In 1849, however, when California applied for admission to the Union, the balance would again be upset because she wished to be slave-free. The South immediately argued against it, for it destroyed the existing balance. But with 2,000 miles separating her from her sister states, and a determined population prepared to go it alone, there was a further compromise in California's favour. She was admitted as a free state, but because Utah was entirely above parallel 36° 30', the new compromise repealed the one of 1820 so that when the Kansas–Nebraska Act was passed, conflict was inevitable.

The Kansas–Nebraska Act, passed in 1854, established the boundaries of Kansas on the east of the Missouri state line, and on the west at the crest of the Rockies (present-day Colorado was at that time a part of the territory). The Act provided for popular sovereignty; that is, the voters would decide for themselves whether Kansas should enter the Union as a free or slave state. It was this issue that was to lead to seven years of turmoil and bloodshed.

Senator Stephen A. Douglas, the 'little giant', was the architect of the Kansas–Nebraska Act, and while it is clear that his ambitions were far-sighted, historians still debate his motives. Railroads were his passion and doubtless he envisaged the eventual linking of East and West by rail, he died in 1860 – nine years before this was accomplished. Douglas was a shrewd man, and had long realized that the issue of slavery needed careful handling. Following several disappointments and revisions, the final Act, which enabled the people of the new territory to decide for themselves whether they wished to adopt slavery or otherwise, was acceptable to the South, but even before it was passed, pro-slavery Missourians and others had been poised to cross into Kansas to claim territory for the South.

The territory of Kansas, was mostly grassland, some 200 miles long by nearly 700 miles wide. A few buffalo still roamed, mostly in the western parts of the territory. At this time the white population numbered less than 1,000, and there were Indian tribes, some indigenous and others who had been moved there when their own lands were annexed by the whites. Before the Indians had time to protest, their leaders were summoned to Washington to be informed officially that their lands now belonged to the Government. Many of the Indians were moved farther west to 'Indian Territory' in what is now Oklahoma.

At first there was little sign of what was to come. A few Missourians crossed the border and established pro-slavery townships, among them Leavenworth, Kickapoo and Atchison, before returning home, but once word had reached the eastern states that the new territory was open for settlement and that good farming land was available, more people began to move in. The territory's first Governor, Andrew H. Reeder, arrived in October, but his term was short-lived – between 1854 and 1860, Kansas had had no less than six Governors!

Governor Reeder set the first territorial election for 30 March 1855, and it was a fiasco. Armed Missourians crossed the border and under threat of death forced many of the electorate, and judges, to vote along with their pro-slavery opponents. Similar results were recorded at succeeding elections, and everyone knew that it could be only a matter of time before there was open conflict.

The majority of incoming settlers were anxious to establish a new life for themselves and their families without slavery, but slave-owning Missourians were equally determined that Kansas should be a slave state.

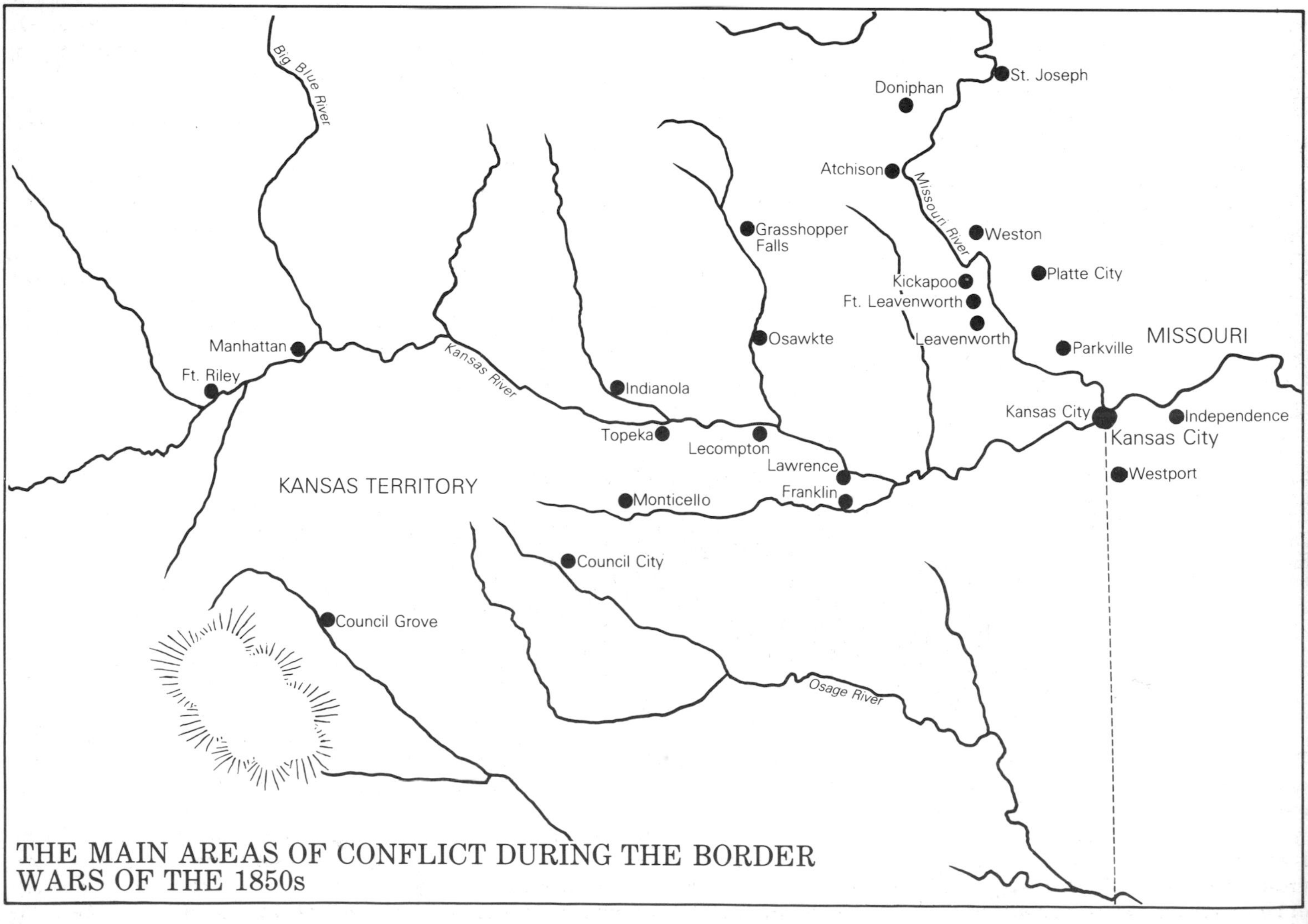

THE MAIN AREAS OF CONFLICT DURING THE BORDER
WARS OF THE 1850s

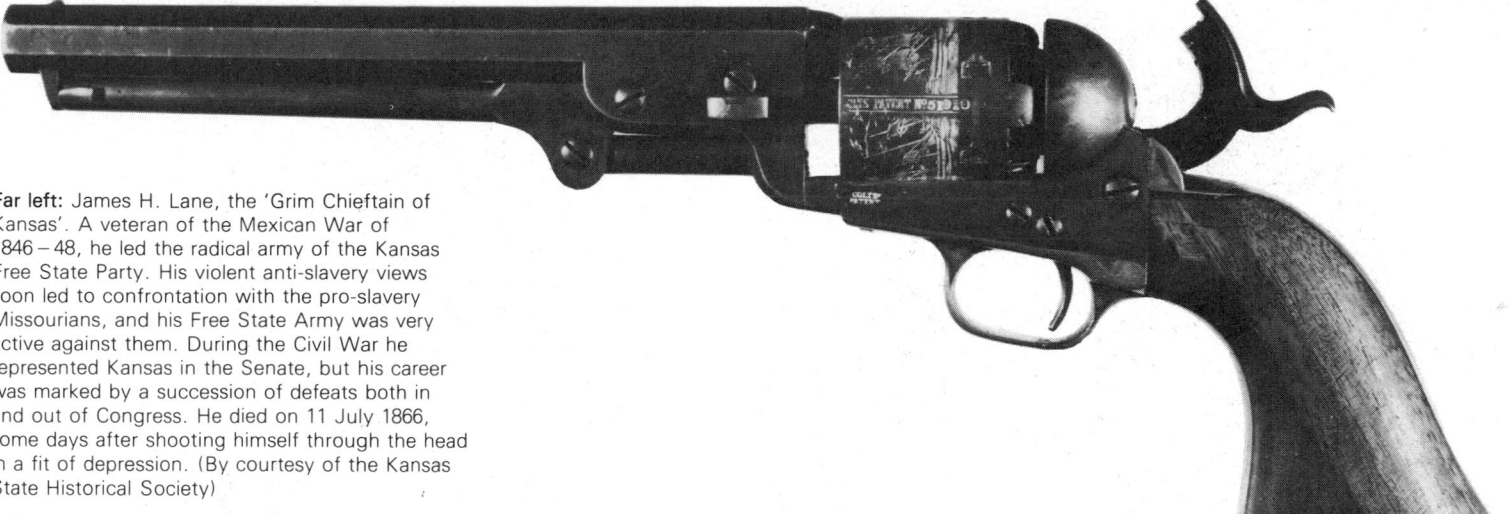

Far left: James H. Lane, the 'Grim Chieftain of Kansas'. A veteran of the Mexican War of 1846 – 48, he led the radical army of the Kansas Free State Party. His violent anti-slavery views soon led to confrontation with the pro-slavery Missourians, and his Free State Army was very active against them. During the Civil War he represented Kansas in the Senate, but his career was marked by a succession of defeats both in and out of Congress. He died on 11 July 1866, some days after shooting himself through the head in a fit of depression. (By courtesy of the Kansas State Historical Society)

Left: John Brown, the self-styled 'Saviour' of Kansas, though dogged by failure. A rabid Abolitionist he is believed to have been tainted by hereditary insanity. On 23 May 1856, accompanied by four of his sons and three other men, he set off for Pottawatomie Creek, where he murdered five pro-slavers and mutilated their bodies, thereby starting a border war. Brown's raid on Harpers Ferry in 1859 was foiled by Colonel Robert E. Lee (who later commanded the Army of Northern Virginia) and Brown was hanged on 2 December. His 'soul goes marching on'. (By courtesy of the Kansas State Historical Society)

Above: John Brown's Colt Navy revolver, No. 51010, made in about 1856. Brown is alleged to have carried this pistol during some of his raids against pro-slavery Missourians. (By courtesy of the Kansas State Historical Society)

Below: Missouri Border Ruffians as depicted in a woodcut published in Bryant & Gay's *A Popular History of the United States*, 1883. (Author's Collection)

armed men against the 'Border Ruffians' (the Missourians). His 'Free State Army' was involved in a number of conflicts and both it and its illustrious leader are established in the annals of Kansas history.

Lane was only one among several who influenced events during those turbulent years. The most notorious was John Brown, whose 'soul goes marching on' both in history and legend. Brown arrived in Kansas in 1855 and was soon a leading light among the abolitionists. Many believed that he was tainted by hereditary insanity, and that he believed his actions were divinely inspired. Following an attack on Lawrence by Border Ruffians on 21 May 1856, Brown, intent on revenge, set off for Pottawatomie Creek where he knew a number of pro-slavery men were to be found. Accompanied by four of his sons and three other men, he attacked without warning, murdering five of the Missourians. It was his declared intention to strike terror into the hearts of the pro-slavers. When news of the massacre became known, a hunt began for Brown and his followers.

Federal troops were rushed to the area. The newly-appointed Governor, William Shannon, resigned on 21 August and was replaced, temporarily, by Daniel Woodson, Territorial Secretary, and a pro-slaver. Woodson proclaimed that the territory was now in open rebellion. John Brown fought off a brief attack by a 'Grand Army' of Missourians led by David R. Atchison. He escaped and they were turned back by the Federal troops. In the meantime, Lane and his men marched on Lecompton, but were prevented from joining battle with the Missourians by troops from Fort Leavenworth. On 11 September John W. Geary, the new Governor arrived. He promptly disbanded Woodson's militia and joined with the military in persuading Atchison and his companions to leave the

Washington, worried by what it thought could escalate into a constitutional issue, ordered troops into the territory charged with the task of 'cooling tempers' and keeping the warring factions apart. Their presence, however, did little to stem the tide of bitterness that was engulfing the region.

In June 1855 the 'Free Soilers' held a convention at Lawrence and repudiated the bogus election results, declaring that the abolition of slavery was their prime task. James H. Lane, a veteran of the Mexican War, became the leader of the radical arm of the Free State party, and organized bands of

territory, but not before Colonel James A. Harvey had fought a minor engagement with the pro-slavery men at Hickory Point.

The antics of both the pro- and anti-slavery factions did little credit to either. Each displayed the characteristics and total disregard for life and property that would later be the hallmark of the Civil War guerrillas. The Kansas faction were generally referred to as 'Jayhawkers', which was meant to imply that they were thieves. Since it was the ambition of most Kansans to rid themselves of the Missourians, to kill a Border Ruffian was considered a service to the community. As late as 1926 William W. Denison, in an article in the Kansas State Historical Society's *Collections,* was still unable to write dispassionately about the men who had invaded Kansas so many years before. A typical Border Ruffian he noted was:

'. . . rather undersized than oversized, dirty rather than dark; he wore long, straight, greasy hair, and had a small head, grey eyes, small hands and feet; his favourite animal was a good horse. He never smiled, but grinned; never laughed, but chuckled.

'Tobacco to him was a natural luxury, to which he took as easily as a duck to water. His native drink was corn whiskey as much so as New England rum was to a Yankee. Profanity was born in him; an oath was ready to pop out every time he opened his mouth. He prefaced every sentence with an oath and ended in the same way. He never sat on his horse, he just hung there; his feet ornamented with spurs, a pair of Navy revolvers and a large knife attached to his belt; a skillful rider, an excellent shot and I might say when in the minority, like the savage Indian, the most sneaking, cringing coward of the plains. But when in the majority, the most braggardly, overbearing, insolent, tyranical and brutal of creatures. And the border country was full of just such fellows as I have described, and they were a menace to Kansas, particularly along her eastern border, for more than four years. . . .'

One visitor from the East added a few more details to the above description which in truth could be ascribed equally well to the Free Staters and Jayhawkers:

'Imagine a man standing in a pair of long boots, covered with dust and drawn over his trousers, the latter made of a coarse, fancy-colored cloth, well-soiled; the handle of a large Bowie knife projecting from one of the boot tops; a leathern belt buckled around his waist, on each side of which is fastened a large revolver; a red or blue shirt, with a heart, anchor, eagle, or some other favourite device braided on the breast and back, over which is swung a rifle or carbine; a sword dangling by his side; an old slouch hat, with a

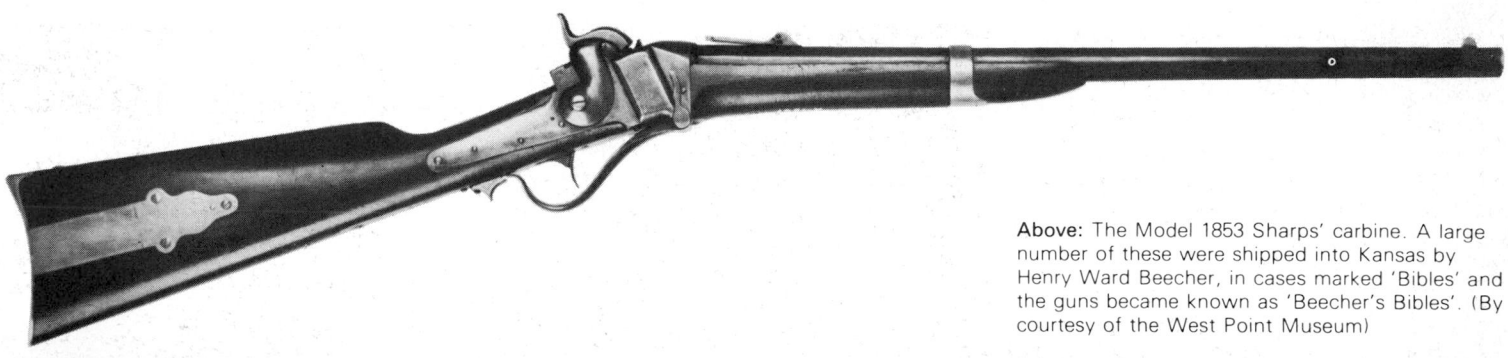

Above: The Model 1853 Sharps' carbine. A large number of these were shipped into Kansas by Henry Ward Beecher, in cases marked 'Bibles' and the guns became known as 'Beecher's Bibles'. (By courtesy of the West Point Museum)

Opposite, top left: Border Ruffian ballot-riggers at Kickapoo, Kansas, in the mid 1850s. (By courtesy of the Kansas State Historical Society)

Opposite, centre: A Free State cannon photographed in 1856. Note the coloured facings on the shirts. (By courtesy of the Kansas State Historical Society)

Opposite, bottom: A fine ambrotype (that is the image reproduced on glass; if placed upon a dark image it appeared as a positive image, or the plate could be used to make paper prints) depicting the rescuers of Dr. John Doy of Lawrence (seated) who was kidnapped into Missouri and tried for stealing slaves. He was rescued from a gaol in St. Joseph and returned to Kansas where this and one other photograph were made. (By courtesy of the Kansas State Historical Society)

Above left: One of the last acts of violence during the Kansas-Missouri border wars was the Marais des Cygnes massacre in Linn county, when in May 1858, Missourians murdered five Free State men – some claimed in reprisal for John Brown's action at Pottawatomie Creek two years earlier. The site is now a memorial state park. (By courtesy of the Kansas State Historical Society)

Right: James Butler Hickok, from a tintype made in about 1863 when he was a contract scout for the Union Army. One pistol butt can be seen poking from an open-top holster under his coat. This Navy pistol may be one of a pair, but the bag in his right hand obscures the other. (By courtesy of Ethel Hickok)

cockade or brass star on the front or side, and a chicken, turkey, or goose feather sticking to the top; hair uncut and uncombed, covering his neck and shoulders; an unshaven face and unwashed hands. Imagine such a picture of humanity . . . and you will have a pretty fair conception of the border ruffian, as he appears in Missouri and Kansas.'

The battles of the Kansas–Missouri Border Wars were fought with a variety of weapons, ranging from flintlock to cannon. By 1856 it was unsafe to enter the territory without a weapon and many of the settlers came armed to the teeth. Money was solicited in the East to buy rifles, and the famous Henry Ward Beecher's congregation even subscribed to buy each member of the Wabaunses colony a rifle and a Bible. Some

of the arms were shipped in cases marked BIBLES and were referred to grimly as 'Beecher's Bibles'. Many of these weapons were Sharps' rifles and carbines; even John Brown is said to have believed fervently in the 'miraculous powers' of the Sharps. He and his men carried them on their abortive raid on Harpers Ferry Arsenal in 1859. Brown was captured, tried and hanged at Charleston, South Carolina on 2 December 1859. In view of his sometimes vicious behaviour, it is ironic that his death rather than his life was to affect so much the events that were soon to split the nation.

In 1856, among the new arrivals who came in peace but got mixed up in the fight, was a 19-year-old named James Butler Hickok. Not yet known as 'Wild Bill', he planned to farm, but his talent for peace-keeping became

apparent and he was appointed Constable of Monticello Township, Johnson County, instead. Soon after his arrival he wrote to his mother and advised her that Kansas was a terrible place for drinking and fighting, with no law at all, adding: 'This is no place for women and children yet . . . if a man fights in Kansas and gets whipped, he never says anything about it. If he does he will get whipped [again] for his trouble.'

As the government and military in Kansas grew stronger, the fighting diminished, and by the end of the decade, the pro-slavery Missourians realized that they had lost. Yet even when Kansas achieved statehood in 1861, there were still those who harboured bitterness which was to continue well into the Civil War, by which time former Jayhawkers and Border Ruffians were now

following as guerrillas the flags of the Confederacy or the Union. In the South, John Singleton Mosby's celebrated band of guerrillas wrought havoc among Union forces pushing towards Virginia and other southern states, and Mosby became a legend. He and General George Armstrong Custer, then in command of the 7th Michigan Brigade, clashed over an incident on 23 September 1864, when Mosby attacked a Federal wagon train at Front Royal, Virginia where a number of his men were captured. General Grant ordered: 'Hang them without trial', and Custer obeyed, but many local people believed the executions (they deemed them murders) were carried out on Custer's own initiative.

When news of the hangings reached Mosby he was furious, and with the full agreement of General Lee ordered 27 Federal prisoners to draw lots to see which seven of them would hang in reprisal. The unlucky ones were taken to a local turnpike where two of them managed to escape; the remainder were hanged. One of Mosby's men attached the following placard to one of the bodies:

'These men have been hung [sic] in retaliation for an equal number of Colonel

Mosby's men hung by order of General Custer at Front Royal. Measure for measure.'

On 11 November 1864 Mosby wrote to General Philip Sheridan and advised him that unless Custer and his brother officers curtailed such acts he would be forced to take 'a line of policy repugnant to humanity'. Sheridan took the point and there were no further incidents. In later years, a monument was erected to Mosby's murdered men which infuriated Mrs. Custer, and she complained to Mosby. In his reply of 5 August 1910, he stated that he had not visited Virginia for thirty years and had no knowledge of the monument, adding 'I would have no control over it as I am not responsible for it.'

James J. Williamson, who fought with Mosby, and in 1895 published the first edition of his classic *Mosby's Rangers*, noted that the sabre was considered obsolete, and to carry one, which clanked and rattled most of the time, was an open announcement of their presence. Rather, the 'carbine was for long-range shooting', and at 'close quarters' the revolver was 'used with deadly effect'. Williams also disclaimed the term 'guerrilla'

when referring to Mosby's men – he preferred 'Ranger' because they were an official arm of the Confederate army.

Writing in *Munsey's Magazine* for September 1904, John W. Munson claimed that each of 'Mosby's men was armed with two Colt's .45 calibre muzzle-loading revolvers. Long practise had made a good shot of every man in the command and each was sure with his revolver just as every cowboy is sure with his six-shooter. The Colonel admonished his men never to fire a shot until the eyes of the enemy were visible. It was no uncommon thing for a Mosby man to gallop by a tree at full tilt and drop three bullets into its trunk in succession.'

The .45s were, of course, .44s, but one would like to have optical proof of such shooting! Similarly, Bill Stewart, an ex-Quantrill guerrilla, claimed in old age that 'We always kept right at revolver practice. All of us had two, some more, all of them .44 calibre cap and ball Dragoon revolvers – captured, of course.'

Colonel Mosby survived the war to become a very famous lawyer. In his old age he grew very caustic and at times could be as rough as a corn cob, but his integrity and sense of the truth never let him flinch from action. This was never better expressed than when copies of England's premier newspaper, *The Times*, reached him in 1915 with some disturbing comments. A certain George Haven Putnam had written to the editor on the vexed question of 'German Practice and Some Precedents' relative to 'sniping', and his remarks were published on 14 November. He claimed that under the 'accepted rules of modern warfare it is permissible to execute a person who, being without a uniform, takes the responsibility of joining in the fight. . . In the Shenandoah Valley, for instance, in 1864, the "crippled" old farmers whom we saw in the daytime hobbling around their fields became at night active raiders with Mosby, and rarely troubled themselves to change their garments . . .' Putnam was careful to remark that unlike the Germans, during the Civil War unless a man was proved to be a spy, his actions were accepted as a means of defending his home.

Opposite page: Colonel John Singleton Mosby and some of his men photographed c. 1862 during one of his quieter moments. The colonel is seated in the centre and has a fine feather in his cap. (By courtesy of David Jeffcoat)

Below right: This drawing of Mosby and his men preparing to attack the enemy was among a number widely circulated in the South during the Civil War. (By courtesy of David Jeffcoat)

Bottom: Lawrence, Kansas, two years after the Quantrill raid of 21 August 1863, when 150 civilians were murdered. The 'false fronts' were a feature of most early Western towns. (By courtesy of the Kansas State Historical Society)

Mosby's reply was published on 30 December 1915, and provides us with an interesting insight into the activities of the guerrillas and the reaction of others:

'The homes of a large portion of my command were not in the region where we operated; many of my men were from Maryland. There were some Canadians who joined us from love of adventure. I was never in the Shenandoah Valley before the war; my home was more than a hundred miles away. The Union cavalry knew the country as well as I did. When my men were captured they were sent to Fort Warren, near Boston; all who saw them know that they wore grey uniforms. His (Putnam's) statement shows that the writer was never in the Shenandoah Valley as a soldier; or, if he was, that he was prudent enough to keep out of sight of us. My own uniform can be seen in the National Museum. A sniper, I believe, shoots under cover with a long-range gun. The foes we often met by daylight in open combat knew that my men always fought with pistols in a mounted charge; and I am sure that our antagonists would not admit that they had ever met defeat from a band of cripples. The published records of our war show the relations of my command to the main Confederate Army; and refute the implications of your correspondent's letter. An English

officer, Captain Hoskins, who had the Crimea medal, served with us. He had passed through the fire of the Redan and the Malakoff and fell by my side in a skirmish. A German officer, Baron von Bassow, was also in my command until he was disabled by a wound and returned home. A few years ago he wrote me that he then commanded the 9th German Army Corps. If you were to ask Bassow if he was ever a sniper in the Shenandoah Valley he would answer from the mouth of a Krupp gun.'

Mosby's reference to fighting with pistols is borne out in many accounts, and the British officer, Captain A. H. East, during some after-speech comments following Colonel Fosbery's previously cited paper 'On Pistols', described how a band of 'Southern irregulars' were attacked by a troop of Federal Cavalry armed with sabres. The Confederates had none. 'It was really a case of swords *versus* pistols – and the pistols won . . .'

William Clark Quantrill was a legend of a different kind from Mosby. His deeds more than anyone else's invested the term 'guerrilla' with a far more sinister meaning than it deserves. His punitive raid against Lawrence, Kansas, on 21 August 1863, allegedly in reprisal for a similar raid by General James Lane on Oseola in 1861 (some

claim that it was really because a Union prison had collapsed in Kansas City killing a number of Confederates) left nearly 150 people dead and most of the town destroyed. Similarly, a raid on Olathe, where a number of people were killed, inspired a great hatred of Quantrill and all those who followed his 'black flag'.

Quantrill the man has fascinated and repulsed those who have attempted to understand what it was that motivated him. To some he was a latter-day cavalier, a hero, cunning and brave, but few who encountered him found him appealing. Indeed, some officers of the Confederacy would willingly have shot him out of hand, but he was tolerated as a necessary evil. Historians regard him as a bandit with pro-Southern sympathies. A man of great intelligence, his military skill was evident, as was his courage and power of command, but he was marred by a total lack of scruples. He was a treacherous opportunist and was to some extent paranoiac – characteristics later credited to one of his lesser lights, Jesse James.

James Lane, the 'Grim Chieftain of Kansas' was more active during the pre-war conflict than during the Civil War proper, but his influence was still very strong. Some have credited him with the organizing of the famous 'Red Legs' guerrilla band during the Kansas–Missouri border wars, but this is incorrect. That organization was a Civil War outfit and ranked at one stage with Jennison's Jayhawkers (officially known as the 7th Kansas Volunteer Cavalry Regiment) under the command of Colonel C. R. Jennison.

Available records indicate that the 'Red Legs' were formed in 1861 and they got their name when a number of Jennison's Jayhawkers raided the shop of a cobbler in Independence, Missouri, and stole a number of sheepskins which had been dyed red; they fashioned some leggings from these and the name was swiftly coined. Colonel William S. Oliver, of the 7th Missouri Volunteers, is believed to have been their first commander, and he employed a number of 'Red Legs' in his efforts to hunt down Quantrill. By 1862, however, they were under the command of Captain Nathan L. Stout, Provost Marshal under Brigadier-General James G. Blunt. Stout was later replaced by George Hoyt who had achieved notoriety as the counsel for John Brown following his arrest and imprisonment after his abortive raid on Harpers Ferry.

The exploits of the real and bogus 'Red Legs' and other guerrilla bands eventually became a serious problem and General Blunt finally disbanded them. Some joined various cavalry regiments, others joined a newly-formed band of 'buckskin scouts' led by Captain William S. Tough. In addition to the LeFaucheux revolvers previously mentioned, Colt's 1860 Armys, revolving rifles and some Henry repeaters found their way into the hands of regular and irregular troops who fought on the borders of Kansas and Missouri during the war; it was essential that the men be well-horsed and well-armed and ready for immediate action. Despite Bill Stewart's claim that he and the others who rode with Quantrill carried .44 calibre Colt's Dragoon pistols, the favoured weapon of most guerrilla outfits was the Colt Navy revolver. Quantrill's best biographer, William E. Connelley, wrote in his *Quantrill and the Border Wars*, published in 1910, that 'the guerrillas and other irregular forces rarely carried any other arm. Quantrill and his men never used anything but the Colt's Navy, and their superior marksmanship came from the mastery and application of its principles. The pride to-day of the survivors of the Civil War is the Colt's Navy revolver carried by him through that period of strife . . .' As many as eight pistols or spare loaded cylinders were carried, and one can easily imagine just how formidable a band of determined guerrillas could be!

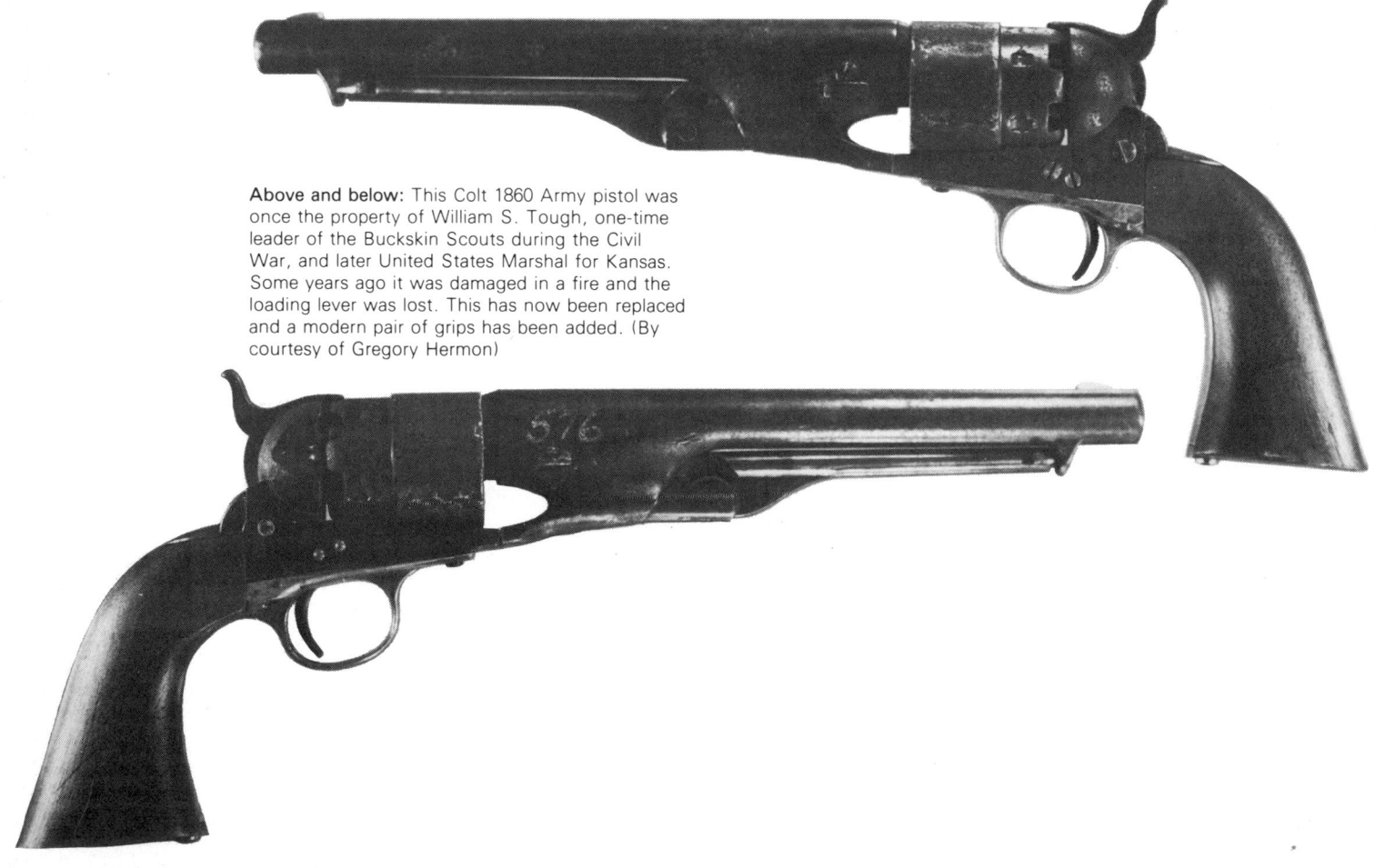

Above and below: This Colt 1860 Army pistol was once the property of William S. Tough, one-time leader of the Buckskin Scouts during the Civil War, and later United States Marshal for Kansas. Some years ago it was damaged in a fire and the loading lever was lost. This has now been replaced and a modern pair of grips has been added. (By courtesy of Gregory Hermon)

Part Two
RIM-FIRE, CENTRE-FIRE AND RAPID FIRE 1846-1866

Below: Seven famous United States rifles. Top: Model 1803 in .54 calibre; second: Model 1814 in .54 calibre (this specimen manufactured by H. Deringer, Philadelphia; third: Model 1817 'Common Rifle', manufactured by N. Starr, calibre .54; fourth; the Hall Rifle, Model 1819 (the first type with barrel springs), dated 1824 and in .54 calibre; fifth: Model 1841, made by Tryon, calibre .54; sixth: Model 1855 Harpers Ferry Rifle in .58 calibre, and seventh: Model 1861 Springfield Rifle in .58 calibre. (By courtesy of the Winchester Museum)

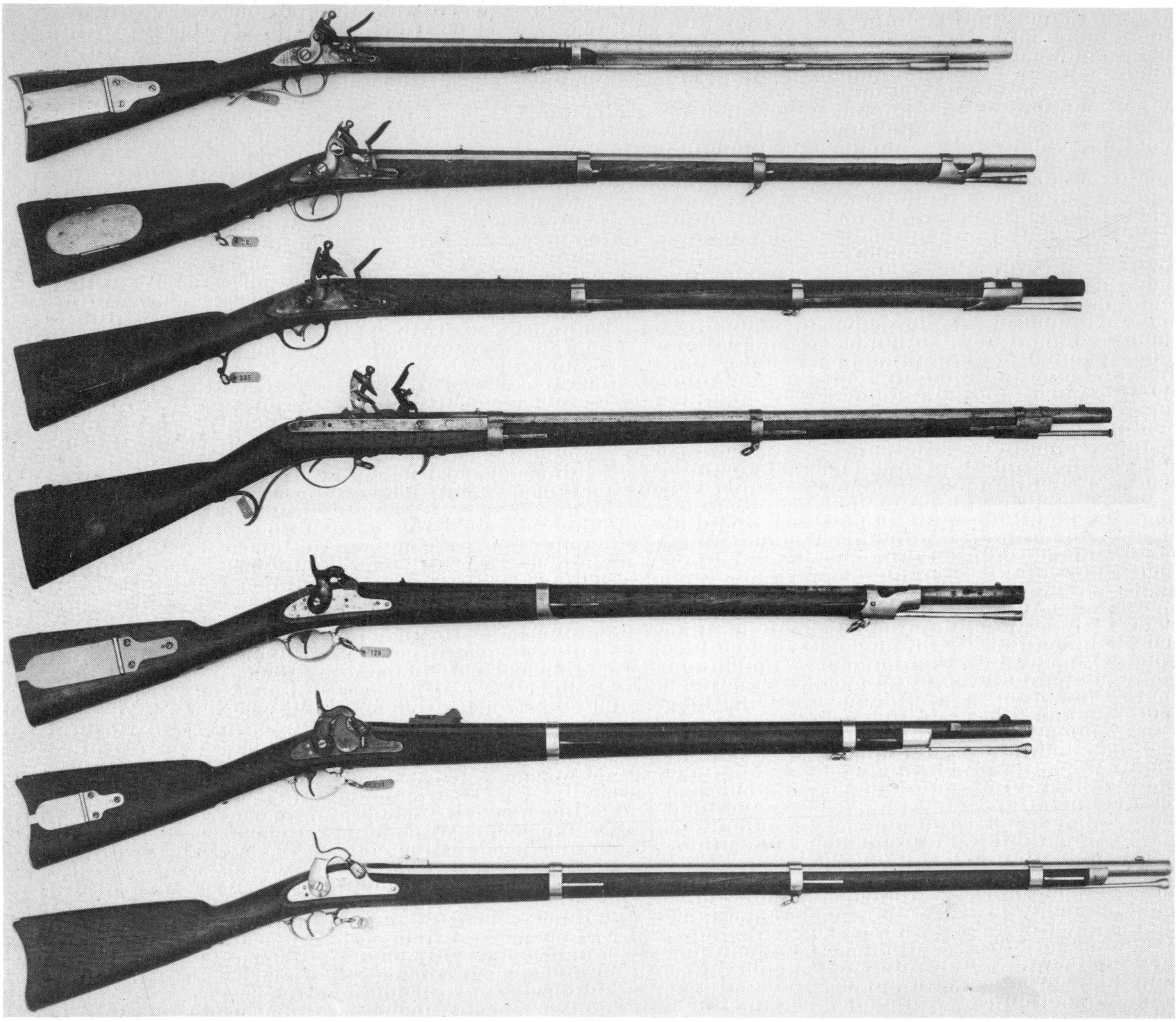

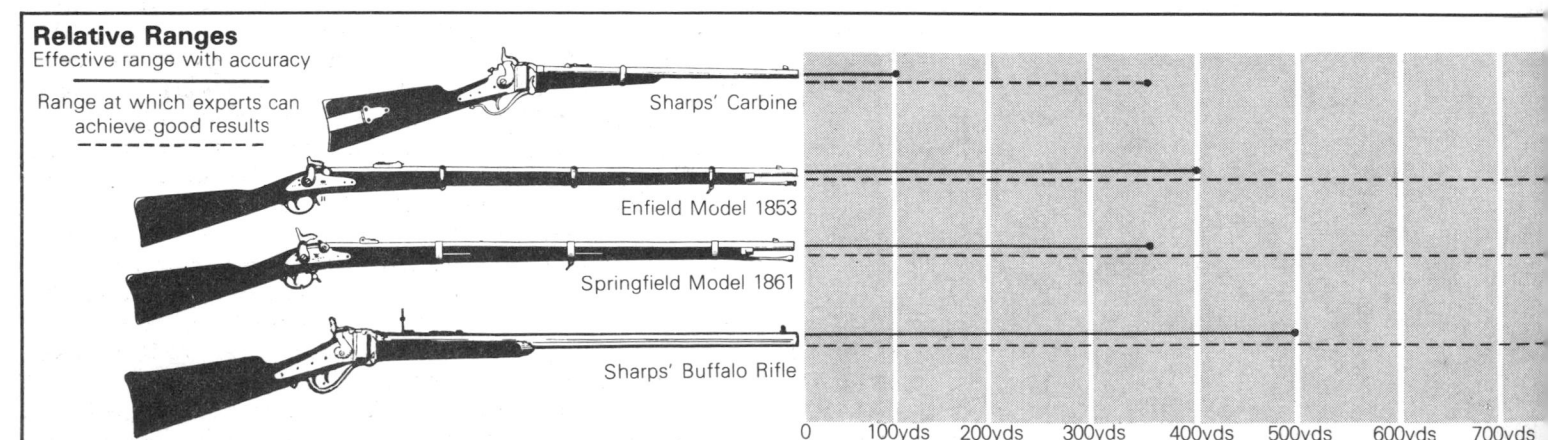

Relative Ranges
Effective range with accuracy

Range at which experts can achieve good results

Sharps' Carbine

Enfield Model 1853

Springfield Model 1861

Sharps' Buffalo Rifle

0   100yds   200yds   300yds   400yds   500yds   600yds   700yds

7

THE BREECH-LOADERS

Sharps' . . . carbine was tried at various distances, from 100 to 500 yards, the result proving it to be an effective weapon . . . – United Service Gazette, 17 February 1855.

ON 12 April 1861 the Confederate batteries opened fire on Fort Sumter, and the American Civil War began. The turmoil of the Kansas–Missouri border wars had done little to prepare the American nation for the carnage to come – an estimated 204,000 killed in action on both sides, and about 400,000 victims of disease and sickness – in a war that had come as no surprise. Both North and South had known it was inevitable, but each blamed the other for starting it.

The South, deeply suspicious of the industrialized North and paranoiac and protective about slavery, was steeped in feudal traditions of property and possessions; a society in which a gentleman's word was his bond, and honour was all. Many outsiders, particularly in England, tended to overlook the evils of slavery and instead applauded the Southerner's British-style gentility and chivalry toward women (so long as they were white). In turn, the South genuinely believed that England would eventually come to her aid despite the issue of slavery. England did not do so but many in England and other parts of Europe willingly supplied arms, ammunition and other essential supplies in exchange for cotton. When the Union naval blockade of Southern ports eventually stopped these shipments, *matériel* only became available if an enterprising blockade-runner risked his life and his ship to run the gauntlet of the Yankee guns.

The North, long-used to industrial mechanization, was better prepared for war than the South, and the Lincoln administration, being the legally elected Government of the United States, commanded greater attention from outsiders. But initially one event nearly cost the North the war, and for a period they faced the grim possibility of another war with England. On 8 November 1861 Captain Charles Wilkes, in command of the U.S.S. *San Jacinto*, stopped the British mail-packet *Trent* one day out from Havana, bound for England, and forcibly removed two confederate Commissioners, Mason and Slidell, and took them to Fort Monroe. This act of piracy almost brought the two countries to war, but some high-powered diplomacy by Prince Albert (ironically, within days of his death on 14 December) and William H. Seward, resolved the problem. The diplomats were released and both sides breathed a sigh of relief, but many believe that the insult to the British flag was the main reason why the Confederacy received so much sympathy in England.

Despite the prominence of slavery in the dispute, few Union veterans in later years considered it to have been the reason why they fought in the war, some openly declaring that had that been the only motive they would not have fought. Rather, it was Southern treachery and the threat to the Union itself which had inspired them; most taking the view that slavery was only a factor, not the direct cause, of the war. None the less, Lincoln's shrewd proclamation freeing the slaves in 1863 had a two-fold effect: as an act of humanity it impressed England and the other anti-slavery powers, and it further hampered the South's already dwindling economy by removing much of its labour force. The Confederacy managed at great cost to continue the struggle until April 1865, by which time she was defeated, though not in spirit.

In 1861, of course, all this was yet to come. Of immediate concern to both sides was the type of armaments they would need. Before pursuing this, however, it is essential that we review the development of rifled long arms

from the early years of the century, when they began to make headway in military and frontier circles. The decades prior to the Civil War witnessed many improvements in firearms, particularly in Europe. Some were a success, others are now lost in obscurity, but the desire to find a new form of ignition to replace the percussion cap, and a safe, reliable breech-loading system was paramount.

Ferguson's short-lived but successful breech-loading flintlock rifle was followed by others. During the early 1800s Henry Nock, a famous London gunmaker and military-contractor, and Durs Egg, whose family made many guns for royalty, both contributed to the development of the breech-loader. On the Continent, French and Austrian gunmakers vied with one another to produce a successful breech-loader; but the United States was the first to adopt a breech-loader for military use. This was the invention of John Hancock Hall.

Born in Portland, Maine in 1778, Hall was a mechanical genius. He admitted in later years that when he started his experiments he was 'but little acquainted with rifles', and totally ignorant of breech loaders. Although he claimed never to have seen any of the European examples, his tip-up breech design did bear some resemblance to existing weapons. Hall learned that a young Washington architect named William Thornton was similarly engaged, and after a meeting the two decided to join forces. Hall contributed most of the design, but Thornton's suggestions made the system practicable. A joint patent was obtained in 1811 for a rifle in which the entire breech-block, including the lock, tipped up to load. When closed, it was held in place by a simple spring catch. Despite the pressing needs of the War of 1812, it was 1817 before Hall's breech-loader was introduced into United States service following extensive tests. The first 200 were delivered that year and, in 1818, Hall was employed by the Government to supervise the manufacture of his rifles at Harpers Ferry Arsenal. By 1826 the armoury was producing rifles with all parts

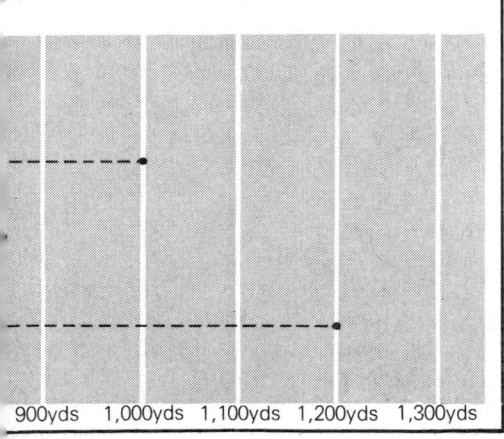

900yds 1,000yds 1,100yds 1,200yds 1,300yds

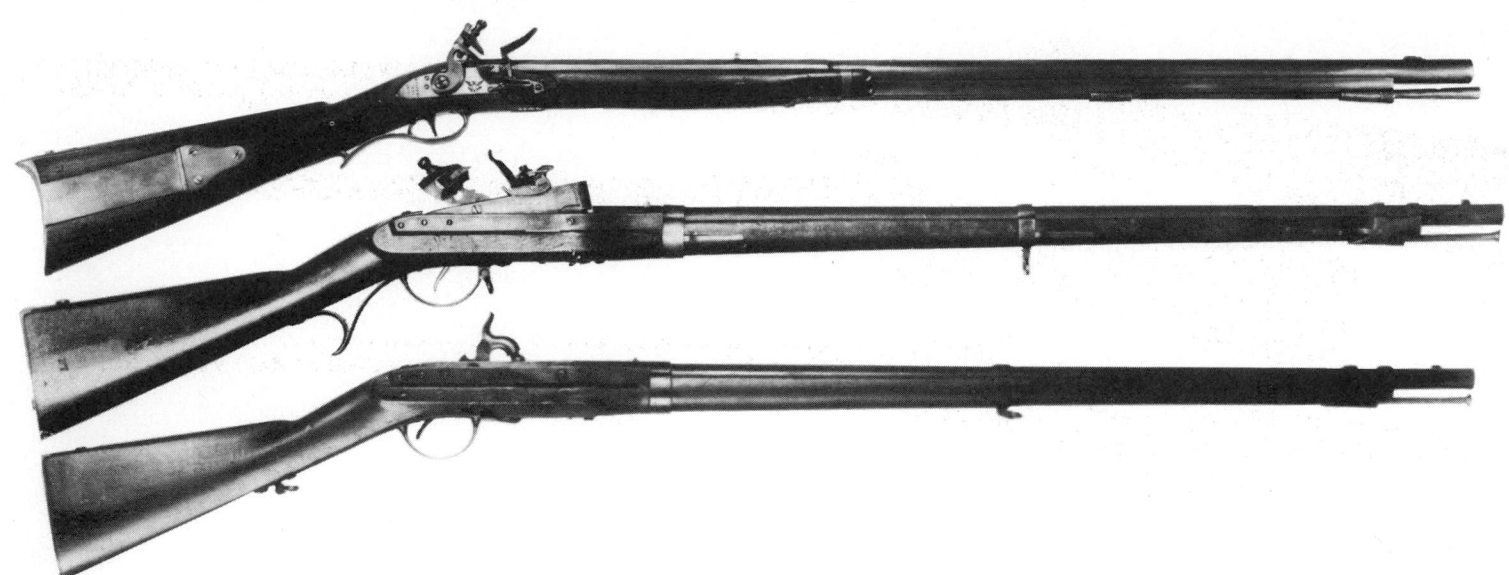

uniform and interchangeable, the first government establishment to do so. (The method had been tried successfully by Eli Whitney, of cotton gin fame, and the father of the man who produced Colt's Walker pistols, and by Simeon North, who had supplied many weapons to the United States Government. North completed many of his arms with all American-made parts, but others were equipped with parts, especially locks, imported from England.)

Hall's rifles and later carbines remained in service alongside such rivals as Jenks's flintlock carbines, and eventually many of Hall's weapons were converted to percussion. Some converted weapons saw service on the frontier with their more modern percussion rivals, especially during the Mexican War. During the Civil War a number were reissued after having been reamed out and recalibred to .58, the same calibre as the issue Springfield Armory's rifled musket.

One deadly facet of the percussion version of the Hall carbines was soon appreciated by the troops who used them during the Mexican War: if removed, the breech-block could be used as a pistol. Without the barrel it was impossible to hit a barn door from the inside, and the flash from the cap frequently caused bad burns, but it was comforting to have such a weapon in one's pocket or waistband when in a Mexican bordello or cantina where, according to one veteran of the War, 'The ratio of greaser to gringo was sometimes ten to one, but the Hall's even things up "some"!'

In Europe, interest was centred on the work of Johannes Pauly, a Swiss gun inventor and notable balloonist. Aware of the work of Forsyth, Pauly endeavoured to produce a breech-loader employing the new percussion compounds. He was granted a patent on 29 September 1812, for a breech-loading, centre-fire percussion arm that was ingenious – but years ahead of its time.

Pauly's system was impressive: it incorporated an internal firing-pin cocked by an outside lever. The break-open breech was closed by a lever on the long guns and by a tip-down barrel on the pistol, but more important was its cartridge. Where existing cartridges were simply paper tubes containing both powder and ball, Pauly's version had a brass head and a paper body. A small compartment at its base contained a fulminate (caps had yet to be invented) which, when struck by the hammer, flashed through a small channel to the main charge, the force of the explosion simultaneously expanding the metal to form a gas seal. It was far from perfect, however, and despite interest shown by various governments (including the Russian and, of course, the French) it was thought not rugged enough for military service, especially in the hands of raw recruits.

Pauly's successor was undoubtedly Johann Nikolaus von Dreyse who had worked in Paris for Pauly as a lock-maker. A Prussian by birth, he returned to Soemmerda and opened a percussion-cap factory under the name of Dreyse & Collenbusch. His knowledge of Pauly's guns and the use of a firing-pin were the inspiration for his experiments with a considerably lengthened pin which led to the 'needle' gun. Basically, he produced a cartridge which consisted of a hollow-based lead bullet in which was placed the percussive compound. Attached to this was the actual cartridge containing the powder. When the gun was fired the long firing-pin penetrated the base of the casing and struck the fulminate. The effect was revolutionary, but perhaps von Dreyse's most important contribution was the bolt action. Prussia officially adopted the system in 1848, and somehow managed to keep the construction details secret long enough to win their war with Denmark in 1864, and the war with Austria in 1866 (which lasted seven weeks).

The needle rifle played a major role in the unification of Germany.

In 1866, the French inventor, Antoine Alphonse Chassepot, developed an improved bolt-action rifle that was quickly adopted by the French Army. It differed from Dreyse's system by having a shorter firing-pin which struck a percussion cap set in the base of the cartridge. Its advantage over the Dreyse was quickly appreciated. Dreyse's long firing-pin was liable to break and because it was at the centre of the explosion of the cartridge, corrosion hastened its deterioration. The Chassepot's firing-pin suffered no such damage. The impact of the Chassepot was such that during the Franco–Prussian War of 1870, the Saxon Army also adopted it and altered it to accept their own cartridges.

In England the breech-loader was a slow starter. Field Marshal the Duke of Wellington, hero of the Peninsular War and

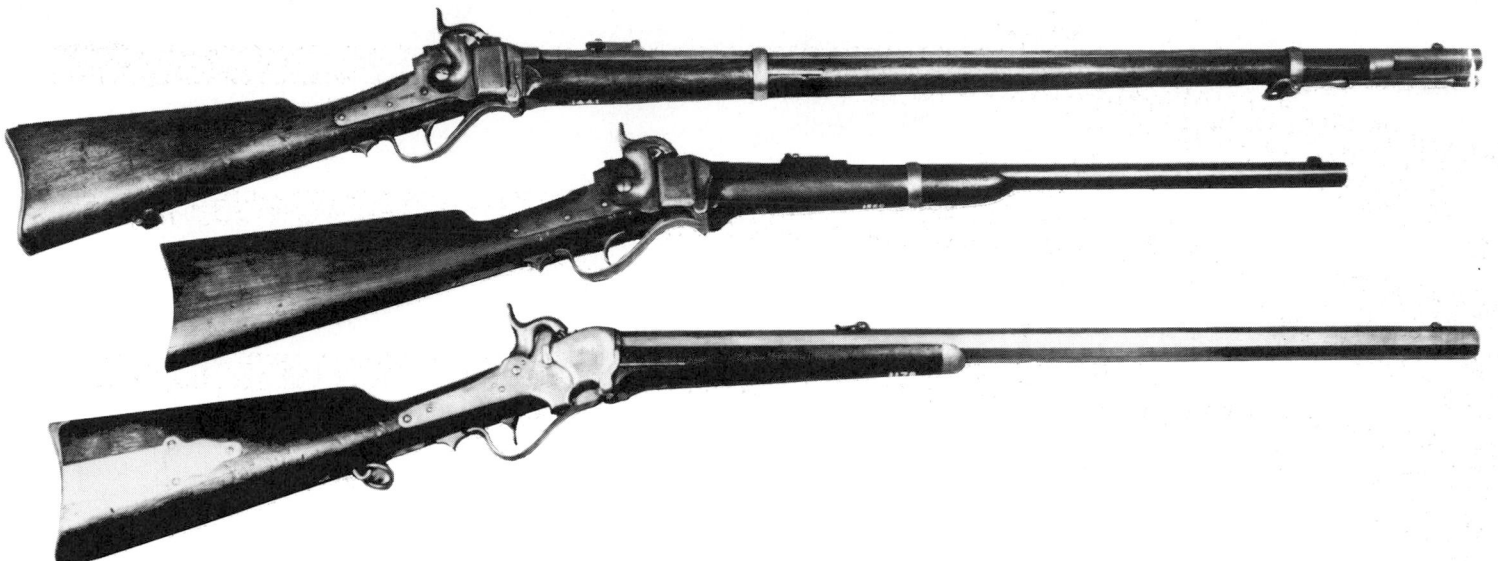

Above: Three famous models of Sharps' long arms. Top: New Model Rifle of 1859, which underwent several improvements in 1863 and 1865; Centre: Model 1863 carbine minus a patch box. Approximately 25,000 (some 40,000 with the patch box) of these were manufactured. Bottom: a circa 1851 sporting rifle with an octagonal barrel. These arms were available in both .44 and .52 calibre. This weapon is fitted with a Maynard tape primer. Note the hammer is mounted inside the lock. (By courtesy of the West Point Museum)

the victor of Waterloo, although satisfied with existing weapons (he particularly liked the dramatic effect on the enemy when his troops fired their flintlock muskets *en masse*) was sympathetic to new ideas. Despite its short-comings, he liked the Collier flintlock revolver and its successor in percussion, but accepted the Board of Ordnance's view that it was not suited to military service.

The Crimean War (1853–56) was a proving ground, particularly for the new British service rifles. At the Battle of the Alma, and just prior to the 'Charge of the Light Brigade', Sir Colin Campbell's 93rd Highlanders, armed with the Pattern 1851 rifle, successfully withstood repeated Russian cavalry charges. Later, when the Pattern 1853 became the standard rifle of the British Army, it was designed to accept the hollow-based bullet of Captain Minié and became possibly the most successful single-shot, muzzle-loading rifle of its day.

In the United States, meanwhile, interest was concentrated upon the new Sharps breech-loaders which were so successful that the British Government ordered 6,000 of them. Despite problems with cracked stocks (during shipment) and the need to have the weapons converted to accept the British .577 calibre cartridge, the military were enthusiastic about them. On 17 February 1855, the *United Service Gazette* carried the following news item:

'Hythe School of Musketry. – Last week Sharpe's [*sic*] breech self-loading and

priming carbine was tried at various distances, from 100 to 500 yards, the result proving it to be an effective weapon. 60 shots were fired in seven minutes (at 100 yards), of which 47 struck the bull's eye. 160 rounds were fired from the piece during the trial with the greatest ease, no oiling or cleaning from fouling being required. The same piece, after the trial, was loaded and left all the following day, when, after placing the carbine under water, and putting to other severe tests before firing it, it was discharged, after missing fire twice, the wet having got into the caps . . .'

On 3 March, the journal expressed the hope that the carbine would be adopted for the Cavalry Service, but problems with gas escape, and military prejudice combined with political red tape meant that few of these arms were issued. Instead, experiments were made with various other breech-loaders, including the Leetch, the Prince and Calisher & Terry arms, but none of these weapons was adopted in large numbers.

The United States took the subject far more seriously. Christian Sharps had worked at Harpers Ferry and was familiar with every model of the Hall carbine and rifle, together with assembly-line production techniques. He left Harpers Ferry in the early 1840s and set up in business on his own at Cincinnati, Ohio. Following numerous experiments with breech-loading mechanisms, he obtained a patent for one in 1848 which was simple but very strong. The Sharps' breech block slid vertically in a mortise cut in the receiver, and the trigger guard was designed to act as a lever; when it was depressed the lock was also lowered to expose the chamber. A paper cartridge was pushed into the breech, and as the guard was returned to its normal position, a knife edge cut off the base of the cartridge exposing powder to the flame of a bursting cap or, in some models, a disc-fed cap which was placed

automatically on the nipple just as the hammer struck it.

The correct ammunition and priming for Sharps' weapons was crucial. In 1859 and again in 1864, the Sharps company issued the following instructions on how to manufacture ball cartridges:

'Take proper cartridge paper or linen cloth of proper length, of width sufficient to form a cylinder on the cartridge stick with a lap of three-sixteenths of an inch, secure the lap with gluten or paste, withdraw the stick, place a piece of thin paper or gauze three-fourths of an inch square on the reverse end of the stock, form it to size, apply the paste or gluten to the part which overlies the circumference of the stick and insert to form the rear end of the tube. When dry, charge with the requisite powder and insert the rear end of the ball moistened with an adhesive preparation.'

When the company introduced a capping tube device, 'Sharps' Primes', it was

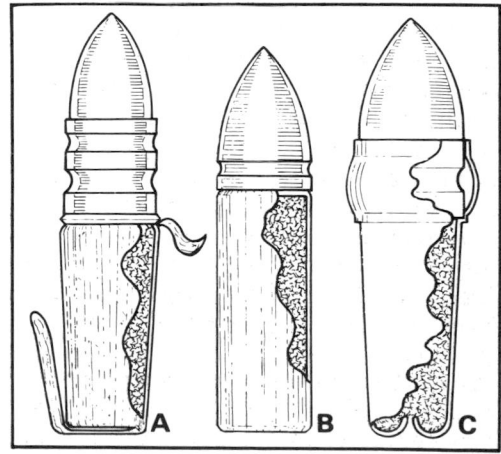

Above: A. paper cartridge for the Sharps' carbine. B. linen cartridge for the Sharps' rifle, and C. foil cartridge for the Burnside carbine. The base of the Sharps' cartridge was cut when the breech closed, whereas the flash of the cap was sufficient to discharge the Burnside version.

welcomed. The magazine cover on the top surface of the lock plate was pushed back, and the primer end of the charging tube was placed in the magazine with the slot in the tube facing rearwards toward the breech. It was pressed down as far as the spiral spring would permit and the primer holder was pushed forward by means of a spur projecting from the inner side of the lock plate. The tube was then withdrawn. An additional feature was that the primer holder could be shut off if required and ordinary caps substituted, which must have been a boon to troops anxious to avoid constant repriming, yet comforted in the knowledge that they had something in reserve.

The Sharps could be loaded and fired about five times a minute, which was a considerable improvement over the muzzle-loaders then in use. This was demonstrated with deadly effect at Gettysburg one hot July day in 1863. The Confederate General Longstreet launched a fierce attack on the Union Army's left flank. Had it succeeded, it would have split the Union force and opened the way for a Confederate victory. Longstreet, a highly successful and experienced General, was gambling on this move, believing that his 30,000 men would overrun General Sickles' numerically inferior force grouped at the Round Top. But Longstreet reckoned without the Sharps. Although only an estimated 300 men faced his initial onslaught, about two-thirds of whom were armed with standard muzzle-loaders, 100 men were armed with Sharps' rifles.

Under the command of the legendary Colonel Hiram Berdan (himself a gun inventor), they used the Model 1859, .52 calibre, paper-cartridge breech-loader to such good effect as to ensure a great Union victory, which was to prove a turning-point of the war.

Berdan, a rifleman of great skill, had formed an élite corps of sharpshooting skirmishers at the outbreak of the war. In a manner similar to the British Rifle Brigade, his men were dressed in a camouflage uniform of a green texture, and were recruited from the best available riflemen. Most of the men who applied were frontiersmen, from woods, forest and plain, whose lives had been devoted to shooting well and economically. Berdan's standard was very high. Each man had to be able to put ten consecutive shots into a five-inch bull's-eye at 200 yards. There were many applicants, but an estimated two-thirds were rejected! Berdan also rejected weapons in the standard .58 calibre, believing that a smaller calibre coupled with a light, well-balanced and highly accurate weapon was more important than firepower. And, of course, he was proved right.

But breech-loaders were in the minority, for military weapons were still dominated by the percussion rifle. Union forces relied largely upon the Springfield musket, Models 1861 and 1863. The .58 calibre was only three-thousandths of an inch difference in diameter from the British Enfield's .577 calibre. As the Union also imported large numbers of Enfields as their 'second weapon', for an emergency, an American bullet could be used in it, but fouling was a problem. In the South, however, the Enfield, made by a number of English contractors, became the principal weapon of the Confederate Army. Despite the Union naval blockade of Southern ports, thousands of Enfields were imported, and troops on both sides argued the relative merits of the Enfield and its Springfield rival. Official records reveal that the Springfield Armory and its contractors produced at least 1,476,219 Model 1861 and 1863 rifles by 1865, and the U.S. Government imported more than 428,292 Enfields for issue during the tooling-up period.

The Enfield was well made and extremely accurate. Ironically, the machinery used in its manufacture was copied or purchased from the U.S. Government! During the middle 1850s the British Government was much concerned at the deplorable state of the supply of arms for the Crimea. Colt's machine-made revolvers, in particular his interchangeable parts system, made a great impression and following negotiations with the Americans, a number of machines were purchased from Springfield, together with some drop-hammers from Colt, and these were installed at Enfield Lock, the Government's main small arms factory.

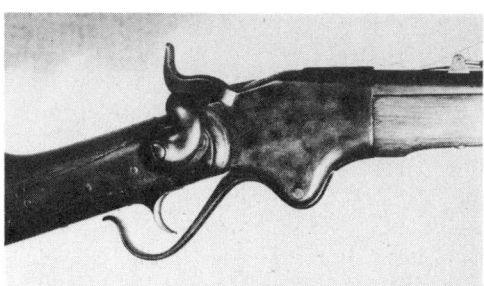

Below: Two views of the Spencer action. This specimen is a carbine made in about 1863. An estimated 144,500 rifles and carbines were manufactured by the Spencer Repeating Rifle Company of Boston, Massachusetts, of which about 107,372 rifles and carbines were purchased by the U.S. Government. The calibre was .52, and the weapons were seven-shooters, loaded through a tube inserted into the butt of the weapon. In 1867, the Springfield Armory altered many of these weapons to .50 calibre and added the Stabler cut-off – a device fitted ahead of the trigger to enable the weapon to be used as a single-shot, but keeping a full magazine in reserve. (Private Collection)

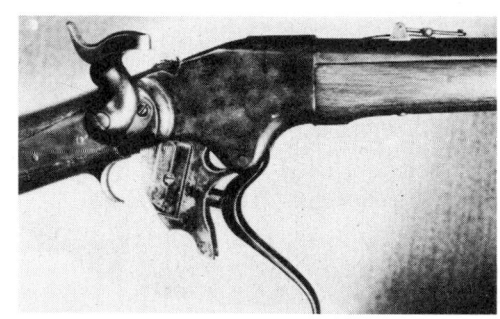

In 1953, to test the alleged superiority of the Enfield, 2,000 rounds of carefully-prepared ammuniton was used in tests to compare the relative merits of the Springfield and the Enfield. It was discovered that at 100 and 400 yards, the Enfield was more accurate than the Springfield, and quite noticeably so at the crucial anti-field gun range of 1,000 yards. Even the short Enfield carbine held its own against the breech-loading carbine and rifle – this was the carbine adopted after 1862 by Nathan Bedford Forest's mounted infantry.

An important rival to the single-shot rifles, and one which rivalled the Sharps, was the Spencer, a seven-shot breech-loading repeater chambered for the .52 rim-fire

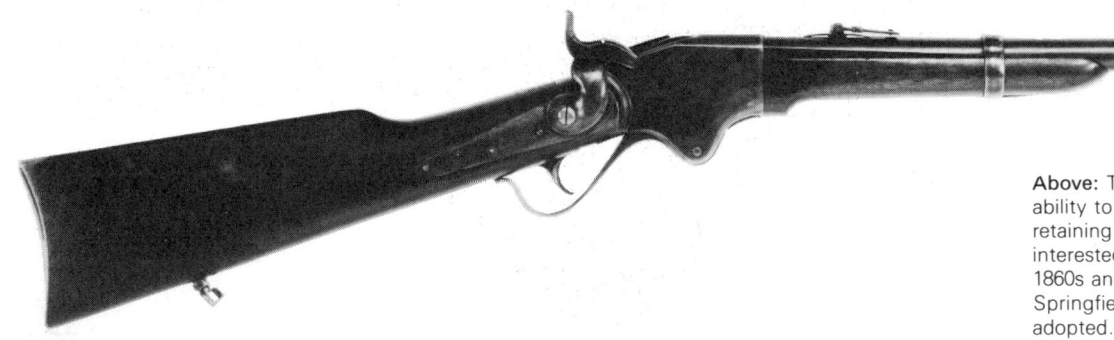

Above: The Spencer carbine, Model 1865. Its ability to operate as a single-shot weapon while retaining a loaded seven-round tube in the butt, interested many Ordnance officers in the late 1860s and early 1870s; but it was the inferior Springfield Model 1873 rifle and carbine that was adopted. (By courtesy of the Winchester Museum)

cartridge. This weapon incorporated an ejector attached to the trigger guard. When depressed, it ejected the spent case and fed a fresh round into the chamber from a tube set in the stock. The hammer had to be cocked for each shot, but the tubes could be changed at speed, and the weapon was popular with the troops lucky enough to get one.

Christopher Miner Spencer, its inventor, developed it after numerous experiments with magazine weapons. The weapon was in great demand and he received an order for 10,000 from the U.S. Government, and delivered the first batch in December 1862. Spencer's ambition was to see the entire Union Army issued with his weapons. He had several meetings with President Lincoln, who was suitably impressed and even fired a few rounds himself, but the weapons were not purchased in bulk. The Confederacy, which also had a few captured Spencers, but had difficulty in acquring ammunition, soon grew to dislike and fear 'that damned Yankee gun they load on Sunday and shoot all week!' Ammunition was also a problem for the North. Official records disclose that the majority of the rim-fire ammunition purchased for use in the Spencer carbines came from private contractors, but some of it was supplied by the Frankford Arsenal. The .52 calibre carbine fired a 410-grain lead bullet backed by forty grains of black powder. However, the popularity of the Spencer was such that Wilder's Spencer-armed Lightning Brigade contributed greatly to the Battle of Chicamauga in 1864. It was their Spencers that broke Longstreet's charge (shades of Gettysburg and the Sharps!), and Wilson's Cavalry Corps even incorporated their beloved Spencer into their regimental insignia.

Specialist weapons were also used; typical of these was the British Whitworth rifle. This excellent weapon was employed primarily by Confederate snipers (surviving records disclose that in 1863, thirty of these hexagonal-bored .451 calibre weapons were purchased, complete with telescopic sights – the combined weight of the gun and tele-scope brought it up to 30 pounds!), but the weapon was not generally introduced.

In 1857, tests of the Whitworth and the 1853 Pattern .577 Enfield rifle were con-ducted by the British School of Musketry at Hythe, which concluded that the Whitworth rifle was infinitely superior at any range over 1,000 yards, and in some tests at distances below that figure it had proved more efficient. There seems to have been a curious fascination with long-distance shooting on the part of the British military. Colt's revolvers had been tested to their utmost at long range, and in *The Times* of 27 December 1854 we find a comment by one Charles Shaw, in a letter to the Editor (which takes

up almost two columns) on 'Modern Warfare, or Minié *Versus* Cavalry and Field Artillery', in which he states that infantry armed with Minié rifles 'have the power of shooting down the artillerymen at their guns at a distance of 1,000 yards long before they can make use of their guns with effect'.

Apart from the predominance of rifles and muskets, the appearance of breech-loading small arms foretold in stark reality the shape of warfare in the future. But another weapon was even more sobering. In 1861, a certain Dr Richard Gatling, a prolific inventor of farming machinery, pneumatic powered systems and related concepts, turned his attention to firearms. The result was amaz-ing. Late that year he produced a prototype of a six-barrelled 'revolving' percussion gun with a cyclic rate of fire of 200 rounds per minute. The barrels were fed from a hopper mounted on top of the gun. There were six separate breech-bolts, one for each barrel, which revolved with them. The hopper con-tained a large number of individual steel charges loaded with ball, powder and a per-cussion cap on the nipple. The bullet and charge was identical with the standard musket load. The barrels were turned by a hand-operated crank, and as they turned, a charge was dropped onto a steel hump or block within the breech during firing, which created a gas-tight fit. The strikers for each barrel were housed inside the breech-blocks and were cocked by a spiral cam which carried each in turn into the firing position. Tests of the weapon proved highly success-ful, and a number of them were employed by General Benjamin Butler at the Battle of Seven Pines near Richmond, Virginia. Their devastating fire inflicted terrible casualties among the Confederates, yet the true worth of the gun was not appreciated even by those who used it! Some even regarded the

'artillery-like' contrivance as little more than a speedy means of delivering grapeshot against massed formations. In May 1865, however, a new Gatling was patented which was a considerable improvement on the original. The barrels were reduced to four; the calibre was .58 and rim-fire ammunition containing a 565-grain bullet and between 60 and 85 grains of powder replaced the paper cartridges introduced in 1863.

The new Gatling maintained its 200 rounds per minute, but would soon be replaced by yet another version built by the Cooper Fire Arms Company. By this time, of course, the war was over, but the Gatling was now in demand. In 1867, the good doctor formed a liaison with the company which, in its own way, was about to change the face of the West. On 26 August 1866, the Ordnance Department had given Gatling a contract for fifty 1-inch calibre guns, and fifty in .50–70 calibre. He approached Colt's Patent Fire Arms Manufacturing Company who under-took the manufacture of the guns and they were delivered in 1867. The true machine-gun was still some time off, but such was the efficiency of the mechanism that in 1893 Gatling himself patented an electric version capable of 3,000 rounds per minute. In 1945, an 1886 Model Gatling was field-tested and found capable of 5,800 rounds per minute. In fact, the Gatling principle survives in the Gatling-Vulcan aircraft machine-gun.

The Gatling, of course, was years ahead of its time. What had impressed the troops and their commanders most had been the breech-loaders. The Civil War had begun with a limited issue of these remarkable weapons (together with the 'miraculous' fifteen-shot Henry repeater which will be discussed later) and by its end it was realized that the days of the single-shot muzzle-loading rifle as a military arm were numbered.

Below: The Gatling gun underwent numerous changes and improvements from 1861 until the late 1890s; the weapon illustrated is the Model 1883 in .45 calibre. This ten-barrelled version has a drum magazine, and like all Gatlings, is hand-cranked. (By courtesy of the West Point Museum)

Above: A fine Volcanic rifle. The forerunner of the Henry and Winchester rifles, the Volcanic was considered a 'marvel of the age' when it first appeared in the early 1850s. (By courtesy of the Winchester Museum)

Below: A Volcanic Lever Action Pistol. These weapons were similar to those previously manufactured by Smith & Wesson and in most respects had actions identical with the Volcanic lever-action rifles. (By courtesy of the Winchester Museum)

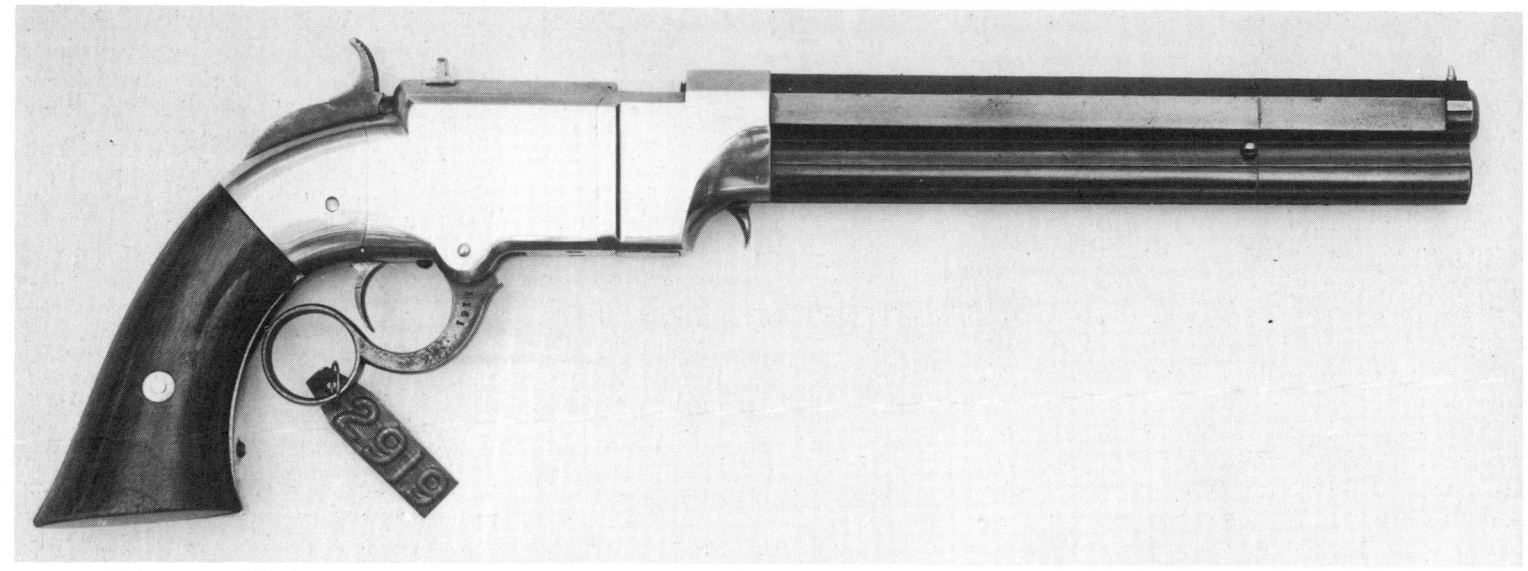

Above: A fine Volcanic pistol. Similar in design to the Smith & Wesson type made prior to the change of ownership and name to the Volcanic Repeating Arms Company, these weapons were produced in various calibres and barrel lengths. (By courtesy of Lieutenant-Colonel William S. Brophy from the collection of David R. Burghoff)

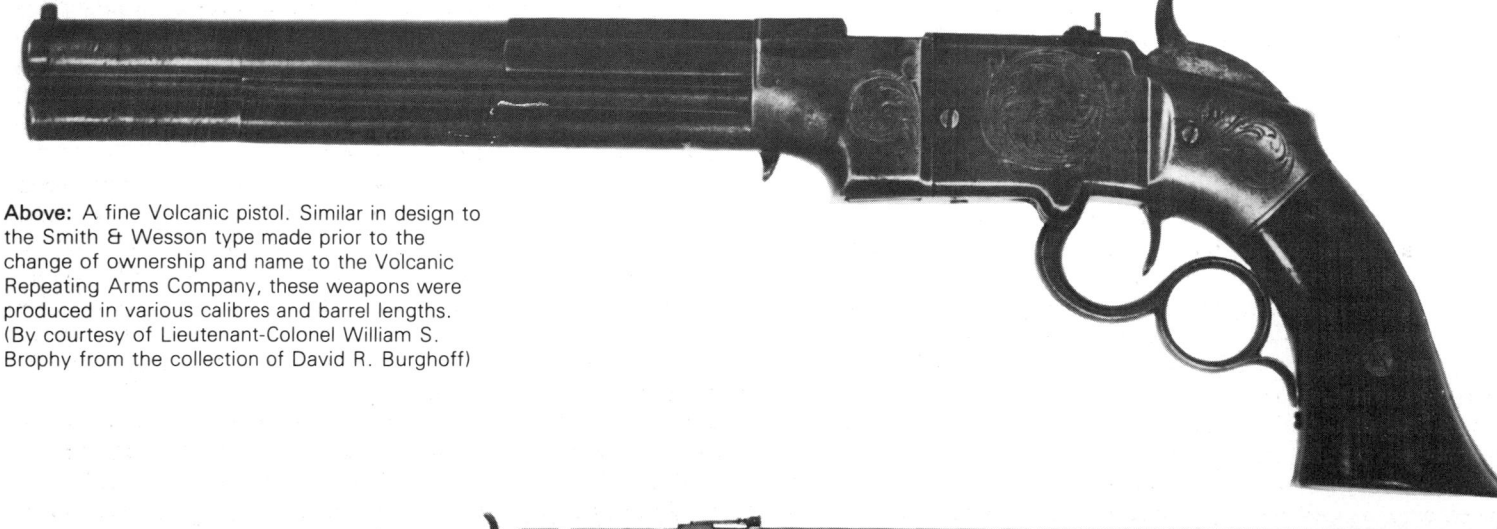

Above: A good example of the Henry rifle. To load this model (and the previous Smith & Wesson and Volcanic arms) the spring-loaded catch at the bottom of the barrel is pushed towards the muzzle and catches in the 'charge cap' (a hollow tube attached to the muzzle which houses the spring during loading and is turned aside to allow the cartridges to be loaded into the tube). Once the cartridges are loaded, the 'charge cap' is returned to position, and the spring released to exert pressure on the cartridges. An estimated 13,000 Henry rifles were manufactured from 1860 until 1866. (By courtesy of the West Point Museum)

8
THE LEVER ACTIONS: VOLCANIC TO WINCHESTER

No enemy can withstand, in open field action, a charge of a line of men armed with the Henry Rifles, and no line or lines of battle can drive even a line of skirmishers armed with them. – Major David C. Gamble, 66th Illinois Vet. Infantry Volunteers to O. F. Winchester, 1 June 1865.

ANY reference to a lever-action rifle immediately suggests a Winchester; but that remarkable weapon was by no means the first of its kind, and at this late date it would be difficult to establish the true origin of such mechanisms. Flobert's ammunition was well known in Europe during the late 1840s, and the appearance of a number of saloon pistols and rifles of Italian origin marked VENDETTI BREVETTATO (Vendetti Patent) has inspired the theory that magazine weapons were known in Europe prior to the arms of Smith & Wesson and later Volcanic.

The Volcanic Repeating Arms Company was formed in June 1855, and continued to manufacture the magazine pistols first produced by Smith & Wesson (whose story is told on page 116). The Volcanic arms varied only slightly from those produced by Smith & Wesson. Although William B. Edwards in his classic *Civil War Guns* (published in 1962) suggests that the American manufacturers of lever-action arms owed a debt to Vendetti, more recent research suggests that his weapons did not make an appearance until the early 1860s. Curiously, the toggle-action was never patented within the United States, but that country did more to promote the lever-action system than any other.

B. Tyler Henry, who had assisted Smith & Wesson while still employed by Robbins & Lawrence, is credited with modifying the toggle-link, and when the Volcanic Repeating Arms Company was formed, Henry was employed by them, and made responsible for a number of improvements to existing arms. The company produced rifles and carbines as well as pistols, but the latter predominated. From June 1855 until 15 March 1857 (when the company went into liquidation), pistols were available in calibres of .30 or .38, and fitted with 4- or 8-inch barrels. Some 8-inch barrelled pistols were fitted with carbine stocks. Rifles and carbines with 16½-, 21- and 25-inch barrels were also available. Curiously, only days after the company went into liquidation, it received favourable comment from the press. The New Haven *Journal-Courier*

(which copied the item from the New York *Tribune*) noted that the 'Volcanic pistols and rifles seem the very perfection of firearms, and must be favourites with the public when they are fully known. We understand that orders crowd in upon the company from all quarters.' On 17 November the *Journal-Courier* (again quoting the *Tribune*) under the heading 'Tall Pistol Shooting' noted an alleged feat of arms by a Colonel Hay of the 'British Army' who was using an 8-inch barrelled Volcanic loaded with nine cartridges which were fired with great rapidity. The paper added that 'The colonel fired shots which would do credit to a rifle-man. He fired at an 8-inch diameter target at 100 yards further, a distance of 300 yards from the mark, and placed five of the nine balls inside the ring, and hitting the bulls-eye twice. The man who beats that may brag.'

Such shooting with such a weapon, using greatly underloaded ammunition, is immediately questionable. Winchester's experts examined the ballistic potential and concluded that the odds were very much against the Colonel, but any publicity was good and at least it served to keep the Volcanic before the public.

Oliver F. Winchester, a very successful shirt-maker, formed the New Haven Arms Company in April 1857 and chose B. Tyler Henry to manage it. The weapons they produced were the Volcanic arms, which retained their original name, but included the name of the new company as part of the barrel markings. From 1857 until 1860, about 3,200 weapons were manufactured. They were available in .30 and .40 calibre in varying barrel lengths; a number of .40 calibre pistols in varying barrel lengths; and a number of .40 calibre 16½-, 21- and 25-inch barrelled carbines and rifles.

The magazine capacity of these weapons was: No. 1, 4-inch barrelled pocket-pistol, six cartridges; No. 1; 6-inch barrelled 'Target' pistol, ten; No. 2, 6-inch barrelled Navy pistol, eight; No. 2, 8-inch barrelled Navy pistol, ten; No. 2, 16-inch carbine, twenty. Additionally, the No. 2, 20- and 24-inch barrelled carbines held 25 and 30 cartridges

respectively. An 1859 broadside states that the ammunition for these arms was packed in tin cases, 200 each, and the 'powder and cap is contained in a loaded 'minnie' [Minié] ball of the best form and proportions, and is as sure as the best percussion caps'.

Volcanic also followed the practice of the time and produced circulars made up of alleged comment from satisfied purchasers. According to a C. F. W. Behm 'late of the Clipper ship *Stag Hound*', he considered the Volcanic Repeating pistol to be the: '*ne plus ultra* of Repeating or Revolving Arms, and far superior in many respects to Colt's much extolled Revolver. I have fired, myself, over 200 shots from it without even wiping the barrel – this is an advantage which no other arm I know of possesses. I have had the pistol with me at sea for more than eighteen months, on a voyage around the world, and find that, with the most common care, it will keep free from rust far more so than Colt's. I find the Balls as good now as when I left New York. I have shown the pistol to my friends in San Francisco, Hong Kong, Manila, Canton, and Shanghai, and they were much pleased with it.'

Oliver Winchester, however, was never happy with the Volcanic arms, or their ammunition. He set Henry the task of improving both it and the weapons. Henry substituted brass for the iron used in the receivers and generally improved the overall finish of the weapons. But ammunition was another problem. When Winchester purchased some of the original Smith & Wesson patents prior to setting up the Volcanic Repeating Arms Company, he was able to invoke a number of their ideas. Instead of utilising them to the eventual detriment of the now independent Smith & Wesson Company, however, he instead chose to concentrate upon the ammunition, and it was here that Henry really came into his own. On 16 October 1860 he was granted a patent for an improved cartridge. This led to a metallic cartridge which greatly increased the power and reliability of the arms. By 1862 the Henry cartridge consisted of a 216-grain bullet and 25 grains of powder; but by the end of the Civil War it had undergone a number of changes. The copper-cased cartridge was much improved; a flat-lipped bottom was filled with fulminate and detonated when struck anywhere on the rim by the hammer. The new rim-fire was an immediate attraction. When loaded with a solid ball and up to forty grains of black powder, it had, according to a contemporary broadside, a penetration of eight inches, at 100 yards, and five inches at 400, and carried 'with a force sufficient to kill at 1,000 yards'. The latter comment was tongue-in-cheek, of course, but the round was very potent for its time, and the rim-fire survives today as the .22.

Henry also applied his genius to the existing lever-action and toggle system. The result was a greatly improved action, and this, combined with the new ammunition, resulted in a brand-new rifle – the Henry. It was fitted with an octagonal barrel ranging in length from sixteen inches for the carbine, to 25 inches for the rifle. The carbine's tubular magazine held fifteen rounds and the rifle's, sixteen.

Government interest in the Henry rifles, however, was slow to develop. On 9 December 1861 Brigadier-General James W. Ripley, Chief of Ordnance, wrote to the Secretary of War, Simon Cameron, on the subject of breech-loading weapons. Having examined both the Henry and the Spencer rifles, he admitted that they had made a good impression. He was, however, concerned at their weight when fully-loaded, and their repairability and reliability under battle conditions. He also objected to their specialized ammunition – he would have preferred that they could be adapted to accept loose powder and ball if necessary. There was also the possibility of damage when carried on horseback – indeed, would they still function if damaged? He concluded that in view of the already extended budget for the purpose of purchasing nearly '73,000 breech-loading rifles and carbines, to the amount of $2,250,000, I do not consider it advisable to entertain either of the propositions for purchasing these arms.'

By June 1863 Ripley had relented enough to purchase 250 Henry rifles, but as late as 5 April 1864 he was still of the opinion that although repeating arms might be a favourite with the army, he considered them expensive and delicate. In what must have been a reference to Colt's revolving rifles, he remarked that the 'Colt's is both expensive and a dangerous weapon to the user'. As for the Spencer, it was the 'cheapest, the most durable, and most efficient of any of these arms'. Nevertheless, it is believed that the Federal Government purchased 1,731 Henry rifles and 4,610,400 cartridges during the period from 23 July 1863 until 7 November 1865.

A number of these rifles were issued to volunteer and State troops, and an as yet undisclosed number were issued to State militia units in Kansas. General James Blunt, who commanded the Kansas District of the Frontier, was presented with a finely engraved Henry rifle. Some claim that this was the reason he decided to arm select units of his volunteer cavalry with them. It was also reported in the Leavenworth *Daily Conservative* of 8 April 1863, that a bodyguard was being picked to protect the General. The paper noted that: 'The soldiers will be armed with Henry's Volcanic repeating rifles and two revolvers, and will be mounted on picked horses. Only good shots and good horsemen are wanted, for the guard will always hold the place of honor, and must be composed of the most efficient and gallant men.'

Various Union forces were impressed with Henry's rifle and the Company (and the Government) were inundated with requests for them. Like most weapons, however, it had its problems. On 20 January 1865, Colonel Lafayette C. Baker of the 1st Washington, D.C., Cavalry, Provost Marshal of the War Department, wrote from a camp outside Richmond, Virginia, to Major-General A. R. Dyer, Chief of Ordnance:

'I would beg leave to make the following remarks in regard to the merits and demerits of Henry's Repeating Rifle, as an arm for the cavalry soldier:

'My regiment has been fully armed with these rifles, ever since their first organization, which was in June, 1863. The rifles now in use in my command are the same that were issued to us at the time of our organization, and since that time they have been in constant use, most of the time in active service in the field, and they are now with very few exceptions as serviceable and efficient as they were placed in the hands of the regiment . . .'

The Colonel then listed a number of battles and raids in which his regiment had been involved, concluding with the following description of the Henry rifle in use:

'From the experience I have had with this rifle, in the engagements above-mentioned, and in numerous other affairs and skirmishes on the picket lines, I have no hesitation in saying that I consider it one of the most effective weapons now in use in the Army.

'The remarkable rapidity and accuracy with which the gun can be discharged renders it an invaluable weapon to the Army. Under ordinary circumstances, I believe, it utterly impossible to make a successful charge on troops armed with them. At the battle of Reams's station on the 25th August [1863] repeated attempts were made by the enemy in large numbers to charge a position held by my regiment (they being dismounted) and at each attempt they were repulsed with heavy loss. On one occasion there were

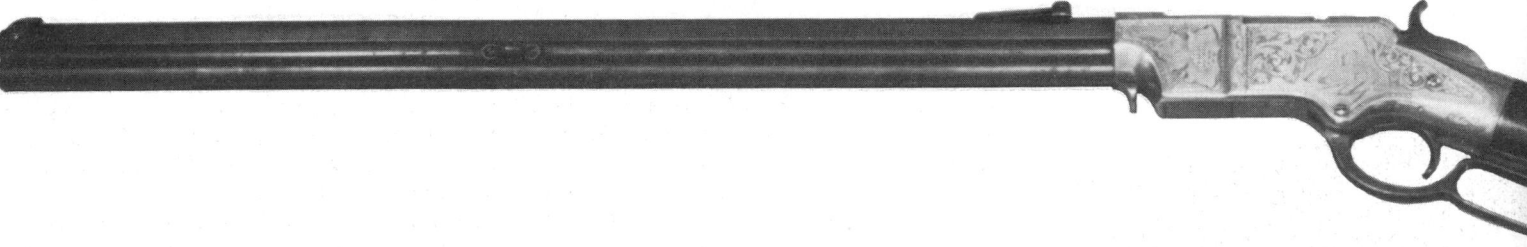

Above: This Henry presentation rifle was given to General James G. Blunt when he commanded the Kansas District of the Union Army's District of the Frontier. With the presentation went an order for Henry rifles to arm his bodyguard! (By courtesy of the Kansas State Historical Society)

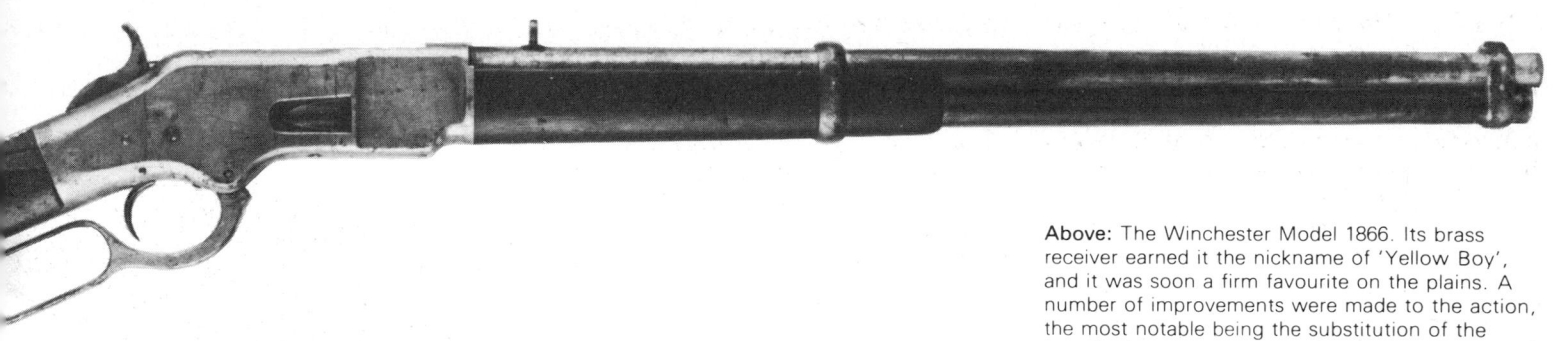

Above: The Winchester Model 1866. Its brass receiver earned it the nickname of 'Yellow Boy', and it was soon a firm favourite on the plains. A number of improvements were made to the action, the most notable being the substitution of the muzzle charge cap to a slot-in-the-side, which was easier and faster. The rifle version had a 24-inch barrel and the carbine a 20-inch. The total of rifles and carbines manufactured from 1866 until 1898 is estimated at 170,101. (By courtesy of the West Point Museum)

several officers of high rank from the Cavalry Corps, and the 2nd Army Corps present, and noticed the destructive effect of my fire upon the enemy. But notwithstanding my high opinion of this arm when in the hands of dismounted men, I do not think it a suitable weapon for cavalry. I consider it too heavy; the spring used in the magazine is also liable in the cavalry to become fouled with sand and mud, and this, for the time being, renders the arm unserviceable. I do not think they get out of repair any more easily than most of the carbines now in use in the Army.

'They carry with great accuracy; in target practice I have ascertained that an ordinary marksman can put two balls out of the three inside a ring two feet in diameter at a distance of from six to seven hundred yards.

'For the Cavalry service I prefer arms of calibre .44 in preference to those of larger calibre.'

Baker's favourable view of the Henry rifle was shared by many. As early as 1863 Oliver Winchester had been gathering material for the company's first catalogue which was published later that year. Copies of it even found their way to Europe and it was translated into German and French. Perhaps the most graphic advocacy to appear was by James M. Wilson, a captain in the Kentucky Cavalry. He lived in what was regarded as a 'disloyal' section of the State and had several

times been threatened by his neighbours. To protect his family he kept a Henry rifle and a Colt's revolver on hand in a log crib a short distance from his house. When seven guerrillas attacked his home (their first shot smashed a glass of water from his wife's hand) he begged the men to leave his family out of the fight and if he was to be killed to let him come out alone. They agreed. He emerged from the door and sprang for cover; a fusilade of shots removing his hat and tearing through his clothing. Reaching the crib, he grabbed his Henry rifle, cocked it, and opened fire. Five rapid shots killed five guerrillas in as many seconds; the remaining two ran for their horses. As one man swung himself into the saddle, Wilson's sixth shot took off four of his fingers as he grasped the pommel, and the seventh shot killed him. In an almost leisurely fashion, the captain killed the seventh man with his eighth shot! Not surprisingly, his own company were armed with the Henry.

The Henry was an expensive weapon: the list price in October 1862, was $42, and the ammunition cost $10 per thousand. Discount for dealers was not very high – the Company expected $34 and for the ammunition, $8. None the less, there was no shortage of customers. Among the rifle's great weaknesses was the exposed magazine spring and the need to load the magazine tube from the muzzle end. This was rectified in 1866 when a slot was placed in the side of the receiver and spring pressure from the muzzle end of the magazine maintained tension. Unfortunately, this modification came too late for the Henry, but it worked well on its successor, the first Winchester rifle, the Model 1866.

Perhaps the Henry's greatest triumph, and certainly one of its main attractions, was its rim-fire ammunition which placed it in the forefront, indeed ahead of most of its rivals. Henry, unfortunately, did not share his rifle's success; his early death robbed the company of a great designer and Oliver Winchester of one of his dearest friends. To commemorate the part Henry played in the

development of his own and the Winchester rifle and its ammunition, Oliver ordered that the initial letter H be stamped on the base of all the company's rim-fire cartridges – it is there to this day on their .22s.

The Henry rifle taught Winchester a great deal, and when he established the Winchester Repeating Arms Company on 30 December 1866, the company implemented many of Henry's proposed improvements. Problems with the cartridge extractor demanded a number of changes before the introduction of the Model 1866, commonly called 'Yellow Boy' because of its brass receiver. In 1867, the company's catalogue was careful to remind potential customers of the new rifle's origins, and stated:

'The Winchester rifle remains in the mechanism for loading and firing precisely the same as the Henry, except the cartridge extractor. The latest improvements consist of an entire change in the magazine and the arrangements for filling it. By these changes, the gun is made stronger yet light; the magazine is closed and strongly protected; it is more simple in operation, requiring few motions in the one case and fewer pieces in the other. Not only can this gun be fired thirty times a minute continuously as a repeater, but it can be used as a single loader without any attachment to be changed for the purpose, retaining the magazine full of cartridges to be used in an emergency, when the whole fifteen cartridges can be fired in fifteen seconds, or at the rate of sixty shots a minute, or in double-quick time, in seven and a half seconds, or at a rate of one hundred and twenty shots per minute, or two shots per second, loading from the magazine – an effectiveness far beyond that of any other arm.'

Naturally, such a blurb caught the attention of military and Westerners alike, but whereas the military failed to adopt the weapon, on the frontier it became a great favourite. Produced in several versions, including two sporting rifles and a military musket, the rifle held seventeen rounds and

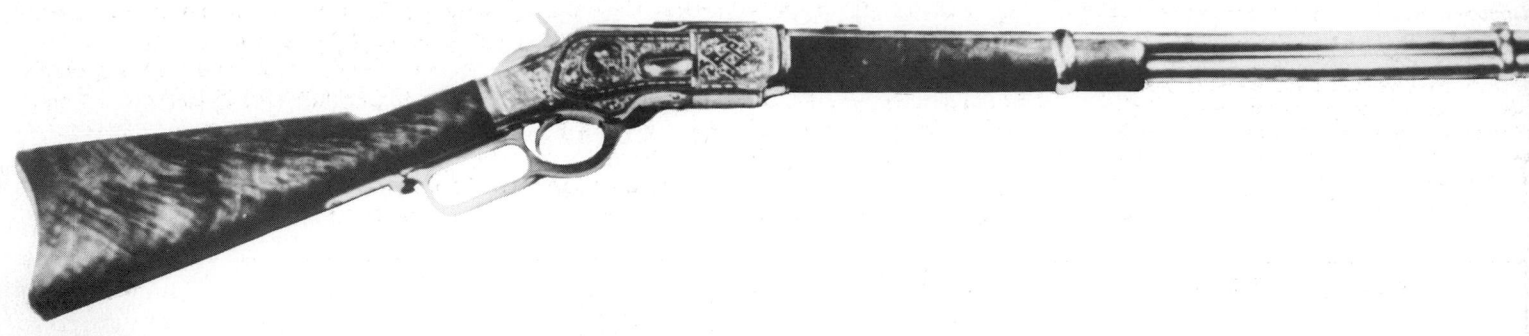

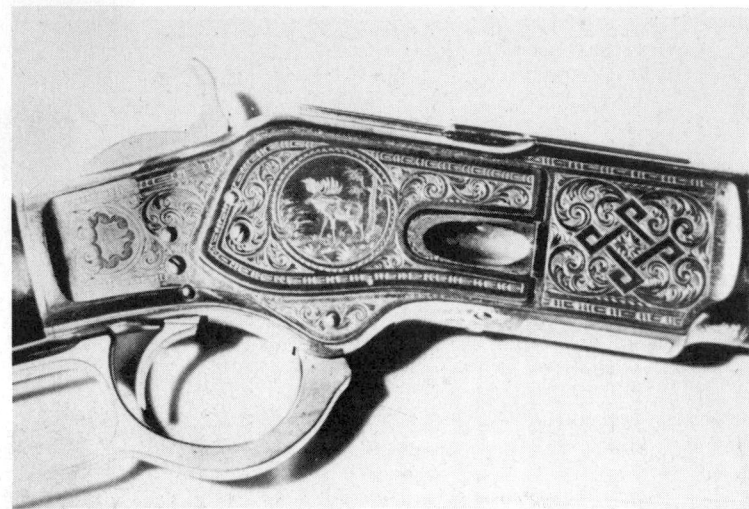

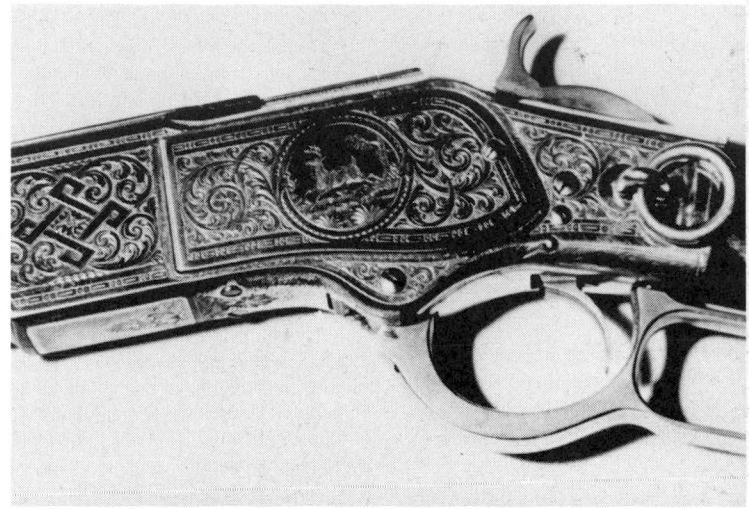

the carbine twelve (these figures it will be noted, differed from those quoted in the 1867 catalogue). The ammunition was essentially the same as the later Henrys. The actual round, a 200-grain conical or pointed bullet (or, if required, flat-nosed) backed by 28 grains of black powder, was a puny load for a rifle, but the weapon's strength lay in its ease of loading and its magazine capacity.

During this period, the company moved from New Haven to Bridgeport, Connecticut, and when all the machinery had been set up, Winchester decided that no further Henry rifles would be produced. Insofar as the company was concerned, the Henry had been a prototype; it had proved the superiority of repeating weapons over single-shot arms, and the need now was to convince the military. Fears that the repeater would encourage troops to waste ammunition were greeted by Winchester with scorn. In the company's catalogue he declared: '. . . where is the military genius that is to grasp this whole subject and so modify the science of war as to best develop the capacity of this terrible engine – the exclusive control of which would enable any government (with resources sufficient to keep half a million men in the field) to rule the world?'

Unfortunately, although the Government was impressed with the repeaters, it was more concerned with breech-loaders in general. There was also an enormous number of muzzle-loaders on hand following

the war. These could be converted to rim- or centre-fire much more cheaply than the purchase of brand-new weapons. Also, there were complaints that the Henry and Winchester repeating rifles were underloaded.

By 1872, however, the Government was concerned with improved breech-loaders, and the Ordnance Department requested that $150,000 be spent on development at the Springfield Arsenal. Wisely, the Government insisted that the money would be granted on the understanding that trials would be held of weapons submitted by civilian manufacturers and inventors. A military board was set up to judge and choose the weapon best suited for military use. Tests began in the September, and continued for another year. The requirements set out by the Board were strenuous:
1. Rapidity of fire with aim; the number of shots fired in one minute at a target six feet by two feet at a distance of 100 feet. The test would start with an empty magazine or chamber, and the misfires would be checked to establish why they failed to explode.
2. Rapidity; the number of shots fired in one minute with no attempt at accuracy.
3. Endurance; each weapon to be fired 500 times without cleaning, the magazine or breech-mechanism to be examined after every 50 rounds.
4. Defective cartridges; each weapon was to be tried with a variety of defective cartridges to test for gas escape.

5. Dust; the weapon to be exposed to fine dust for a number of minutes, removed, fired fifty times, placed in a box of sand for another five minutes and then fired fifty times.
6. Rust; the breech mechanism and receiver to be degreased and the chamber of the barrel greased and plugged. The butt to be inserted to chamber height in brine for ten minutes, exposed to the open air in a rack for two days and then fired another fifty times.
7. Excessive charges; a bullet weighing 450 grains backed by a charge of 86 grains of powder to be fired, followed by one backed by 90 grains and, finally, two balls and 90 grains of powder. The weapon to be examined after each discharge.

Undaunted, Winchester produced a specially modified Model 1866 which fired a .44 calibre 360-grain lead bullet backed by 70 grains of powder. This weapon went for trial on 2 February 1873, and passed the first test satisfactorily, although the stock was split. When the gun was subjected to a blast of fine sand-dust, however, problems arose. The Board noted that: 'After the first exposure the utmost exertion in working the lever and other parts failed to clear the piece of dust sufficiently for the movement of the carrier and the arm was dropped from further competition.'

Winchester took heart from the fact that none of the other lever-action weapons submitted for trial was successful. It was the

Opposite: Three views of an ornately engraved Winchester '73 in .38-40 calibre. This is the carbine version and was shipped from the factory in 1879. The weapon is blued and gilded. Until 1964 it was on view in the Birmingham Museum of Science and Industry and was believed to have been presented by Buffalo Bill during one of his European tours, but this may be hearsay. (By courtesy of Messrs Weller & Dufty)

Springfield Model 1873 carbine that was adopted, chambered for the powerful .45–70 cartridge. This single-shot weapon became the mainstay of the United States Army for some years, and the bullet weight of 405 or 500 grains backed by 70 grains of powder became the standard by which any future rifle would be measured. No potential military rifle or carbine would be considered unless it could handle similar loads.

On the plains, however, the military's reaction to the 1866 Winchester carried little weight, for most plainsmen were more concerned with day-to-day survival than ballistics. Naturally, the more powerful the gun the better, but without readily available

The Development of Ammunition

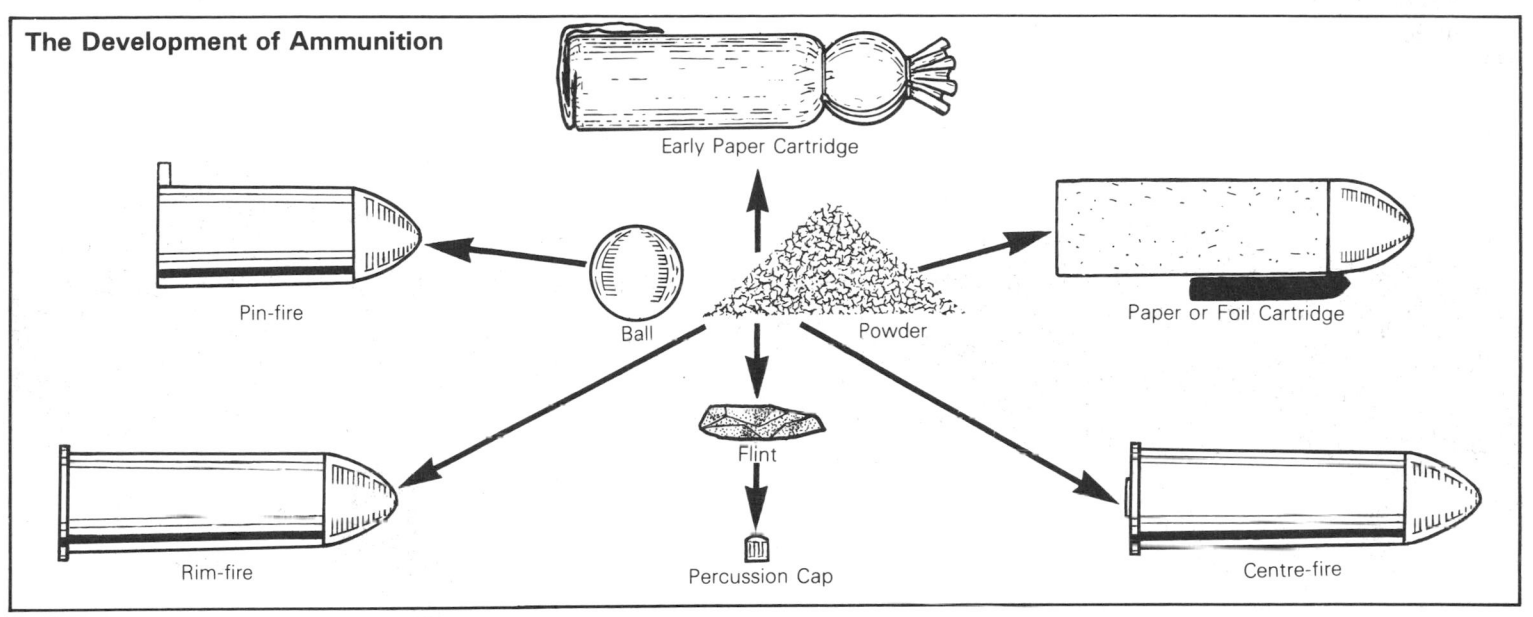

Early Paper Cartridge

Pin-fire

Ball

Powder

Paper or Foil Cartridge

Rim-fire

Flint

Percussion Cap

Centre-fire

Relative Ranges

Effective range with accuracy ———————— Range at which experts can achieve good results – – – – – – –

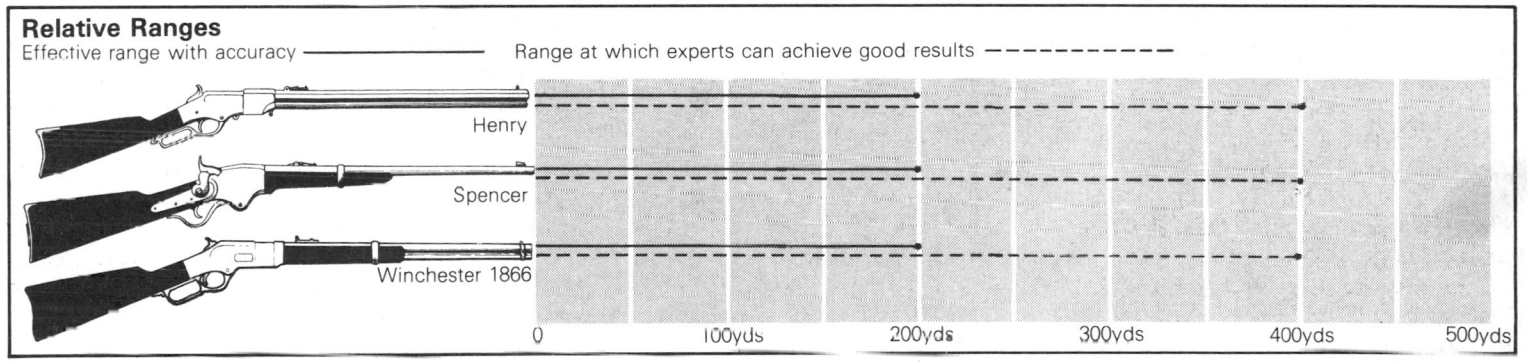

Henry

Spencer

Winchester 1866

0   100yds   200yds   300yds   400yds   500yds

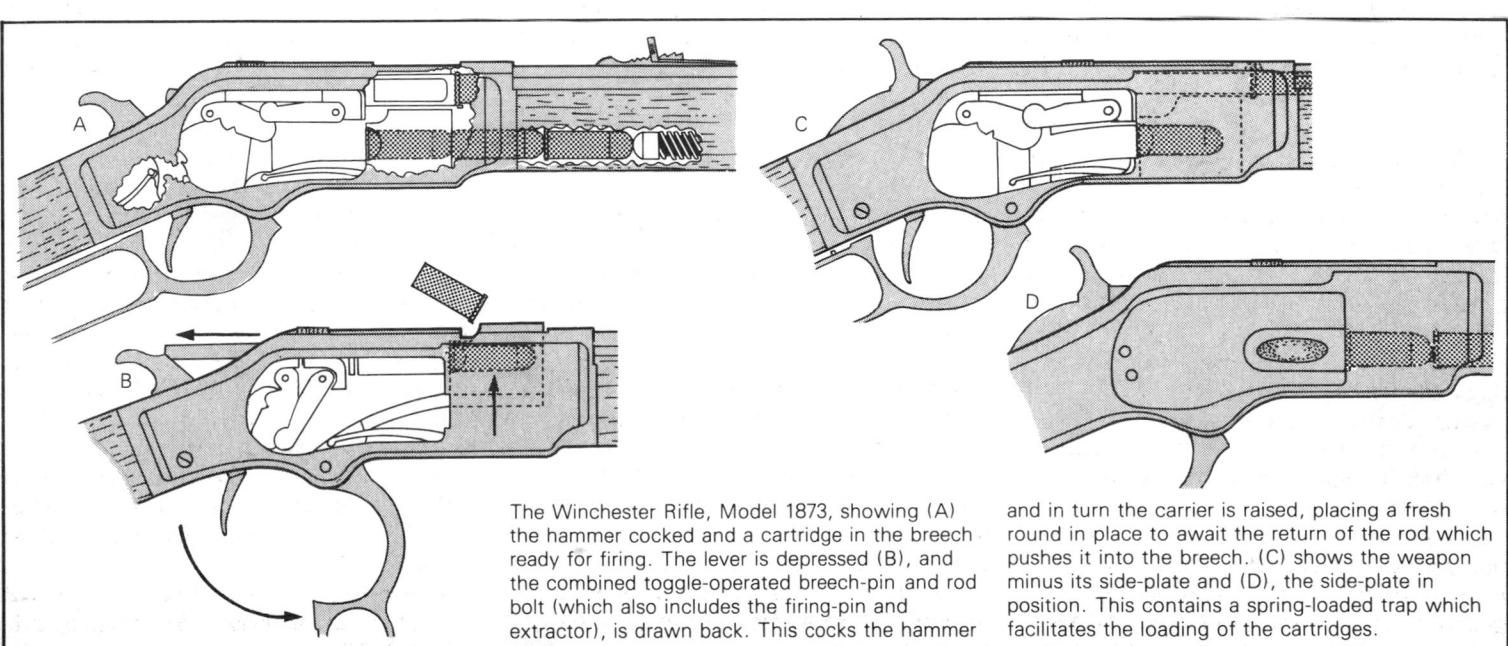

The Winchester Rifle, Model 1873, showing (A) the hammer cocked and a cartridge in the breech ready for firing. The lever is depressed (B), and the combined toggle-operated breech-pin and rod bolt (which also includes the firing-pin and extractor), is drawn back. This cocks the hammer and in turn the carrier is raised, placing a fresh round in place to await the return of the rod which pushes it into the breech. (C) shows the weapon minus its side-plate and (D), the side-plate in position. This contains a spring-loaded trap which facilitates the loading of the cartridges.

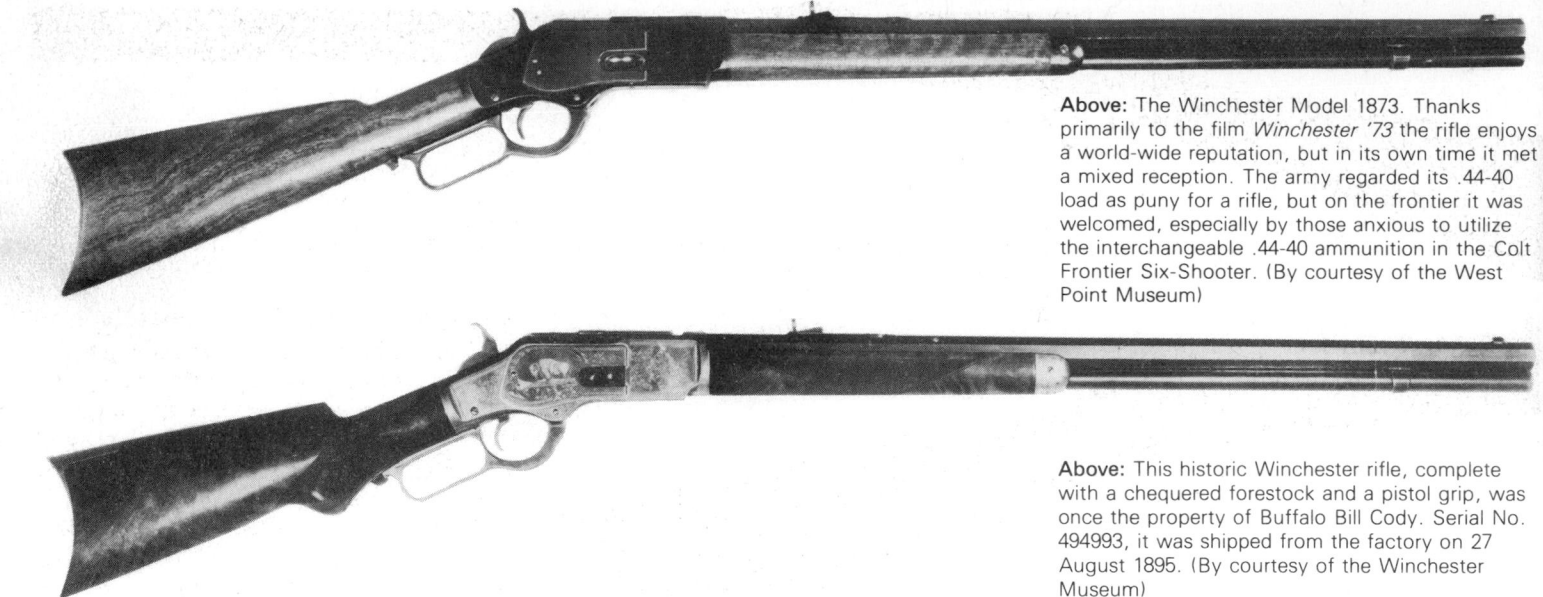

Above: The Winchester Model 1873. Thanks primarily to the film *Winchester '73* the rifle enjoys a world-wide reputation, but in its own time it met a mixed reception. The army regarded its .44-40 load as puny for a rifle, but on the frontier it was welcomed, especially by those anxious to utilize the interchangeable .44-40 ammunition in the Colt Frontier Six-Shooter. (By courtesy of the West Point Museum)

Above: This historic Winchester rifle, complete with a chequered forestock and a pistol grip, was once the property of Buffalo Bill Cody. Serial No. 494993, it was shipped from the factory on 27 August 1895. (By courtesy of the Winchester Museum)

ammunition this meant little. So while Winchester concentrated on foreign sales (particularly to Middle East governments) and the U.S. Army retained its single-shot breech-loaders, out West the repeating rifle was much prized. Thus assured of sales, Winchester set about improving the existing rifle, and came up with one that was to become world famous – the Model 1873.

The Model 1866 had confirmed the company's belief that, given improvements in ammunition and mechanisms, they could do even better – at home and abroad. Rim-fire ammunition was easier to manufacture than centre-fire, so it occupied the company's attention for perhaps longer than it should have done; but by the early 1870s, when centre-fire ammunition was being adopted world-wide, the company's designers looked closely at existing weapons to determine where improvements could best be made. An initial move was to replace the brass receiver with one made from steel. Next, the toggle-link action was modified to include a firing-pin. This was now activated by the action instead of by a spring, as in earlier models, and this solved a previous problem: accidental misfire. To protect the action from dirt and moisture, a sliding cover was placed over the carrier-block. Other minor changes were made to reduce weight – the butt plate was changed to iron instead of brass, and a cleaning rod and oil bottle compartment was bored out at the base of the stock. The Model 1873 was produced in two barrel lengths: the rifle had a 24-inch octagonal barrel and a magazine capacity of fifteen rounds, while the carbine had a 20-inch round barrel and a magazine capacity of twelve rounds.

In operation the new Winchester was very simple. When the combined lever and trigger guard was depressed, the toggle-operated breech-pin and rod bolt was drawn back, forcing the hammer to full cock. The carrier block also moved up to bring a cartridge in line with the chamber. When the lever was closed it forced the cartridge forward into the chamber. At that instant, the carrier-block dropped to accept another cartridge from the tubular magazine. Once fired, the lever was depressed, which operated the ejector mechanism and the gun was again ready for loading.

Winchester knew full well of course, that the new rifle was too weak to accept military ammunition, but perhaps they were more concerned with their civilian and overseas markets. Nevertheless, for a rifle the weapon was underpowered. Despite its reputation as a man-stopper, the .44–40 was basically a pistol cartridge, and consisted of a .44 calibre lead bullet weighing 200 grains backed by a black powder charge of 40 grains, which gave the rifle a maximum range of about 600 yards. Colt's Dragoon pistol, firing the same loading (albeit loose powder and ball or a fixed paper or tinfoil cartridge) was effective up to 400 yards. Indeed, military tests of the .44–40 indicated that it had a muzzle velocity of 1,300 feet per second, but the drop in trajectory over 300 yards was about twelve feet. To hit a man at that distance required a sight elevation of twice his height!

Despite these shortcomings, the .44–40 proved to be one of the most popular rounds on the frontier. No less a person than Buffalo Bill Cody testified to its worth when he wrote to Winchester from Fort McPherson, Nebraska: 'I have been using and have thoroughly tested your latest improved rifle. Allow me to say that I have tried and used nearly every kind of gun made in the United States, and for general hunting, or Indian fighting, I pronounce your improved Winchester the best.' Anxious, perhaps, to receive just a little more than a letter of thanks from the company, Buffalo Bill added:

'An Indian will give more for one of your guns than any other gun he can get. While in the Black Hills this last summer I crippled a bear, and Mr. Bear made for me, and I am certain had I not been armed with one of your repeating rifles I would now be in the happy hunting grounds. The bear was not thirty feet from me when he charged, but before he could reach me I had eleven bullets in him, which was a little more lead than he could comfortably digest. Believe me, that you have the *most complete* rifle now made.'

Buffalo Bill's letter was published in the company's 1875 catalogue at a time when he was not generally known for his stage and later 'Wild West' exhibitions. By then, of course, the Model 1873 Winchesters he used on stage were specially loaded with shot and only twenty grains of powder.

Colt's rejoined the .44–40 market in 1878 when they started chambering some of their single-action Armys for the round; these they called the 'Frontier Six-Shooter' (which will be discussed elsewhere). The pistols were welcomed by those anxious to use inter-changeable ammunition, but the .44–40 was too limited for some, and Winchester received many letters complaining about it. The company considered the matter and admitted that the round had its shortcomings, but was generally popular and they saw no reason to discontinue it. However, they determined to improve their ammunition – if not for the Model 1873, then for another rifle.

The Government cartridge was 2¾ inches long, or almost twice the length of the .44–40. This meant that to chamber the 1873 for such a round would mean drastic

Above: A late-production Winchester '73, manufactured in September 1907. (Private Collection)

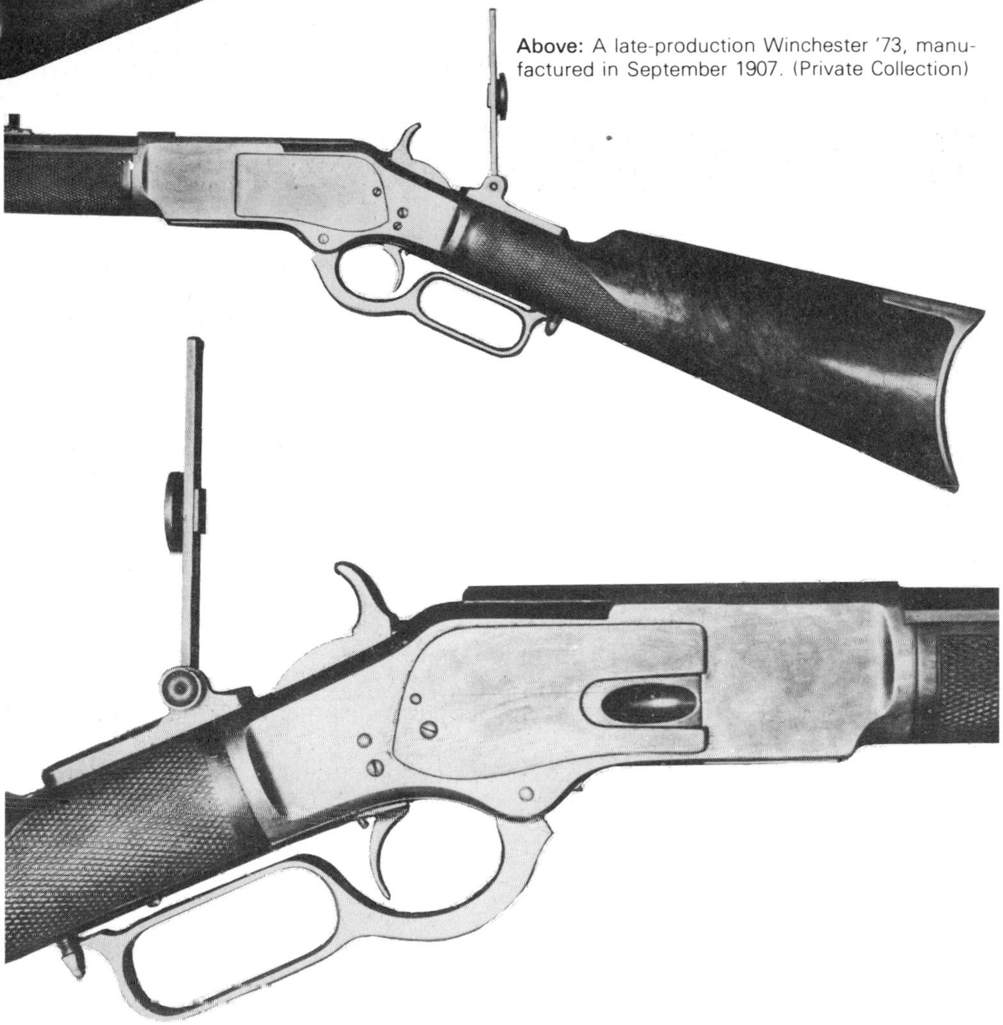

Below: Numbered 7559, this Winchester '73 is marked as being 1 OF 1,000, but R. Larry Wilson has confirmed that the latter is the addition of a clever workman. None the less, it is a fine rifle and is fitted with both normal barrel rear sight and tang sight. (By courtesy of Messrs Weller & Dufty)

redesigning of the mechanism and the receiver, which would result in a weapon too heavy for conventional use. Additionally, the toggle-action was just not strong enough to withstand the strain of pressures exerted by the .45–70. Just in time for the Centennial Exposition of 1876, a solution was found in the form of a weapon, modified and improved to the point where it could take an even more powerful cartridge than the Government round. The Model 1876 was chambered for a .45 calibre 350-grain bullet backed by 75 grains of powder, which was as close as the company could get to the Government version, while still managing to cram in an extra five grains of powder to give it a little edge over its rival. The Model 1876 never received the adulation of the Model 1873, but it was to become the favoured weapon of the North-West Mounted Police (later called 'Royal' and later still, The Royal Canadian Mounted Police), who adopted the carbine version in 1877, and retained it in service until 1914.

On the frontier, however, the popularity of the Model 1873 was unabated, and overseas sales were encouraging. Certain specimens of the Model 1873 are eagerly sought today. These are the celebrated 'One of One Thousand' and 'One of One Hundred' rifles which were got up for special presentation. Periodically, a barrel was produced that was considered 'perfect' and it was made up in a weapon itself said to be flawless. Only about 136 of these rifles are known to have survived. The Winchester rifle may not have 'Won the West', but it certainly contributed towards the taming of it. From 1873 until 1919 (when production stopped) an estimated 720,610 Model 1873 rifles and carbines were produced in calibres ranging from .44–40 down to .22.

In 1886, another high-powered lever-action rifle was produced by Winchester, and this was the most powerful of them all. Chambered for .45–90, it also appeared in .50–110–300 Express, which many claim was its most popular calibre. This was folowed by the Model 1887, the Model 1892 and the Model 1894 – the latter still listed as in production. Ironically, it is the Model 1894, produced in such diverse calibres as .25–35; .32–40 and the celebrated .30–30 (the 'thutty-thutty'), which features in so

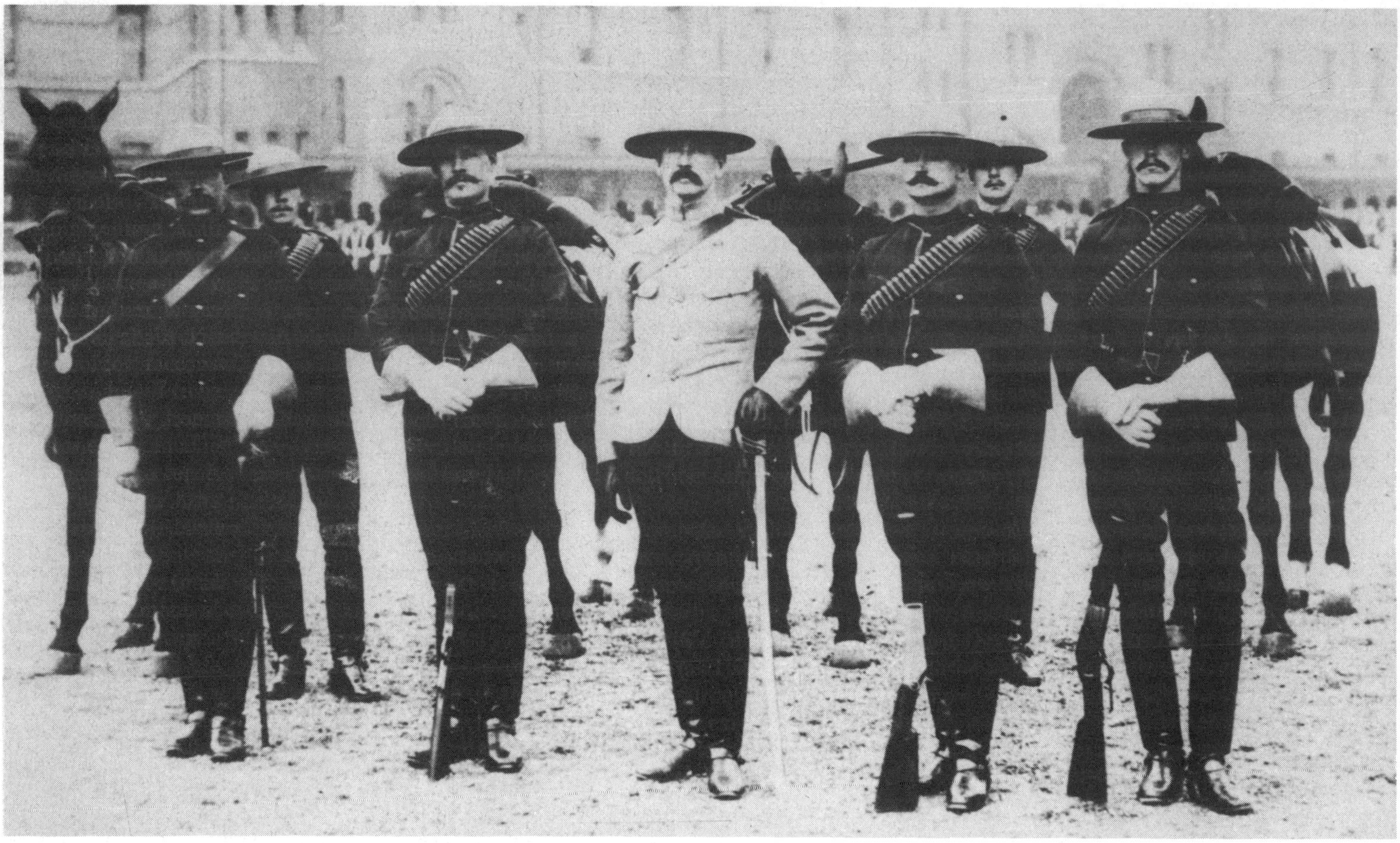

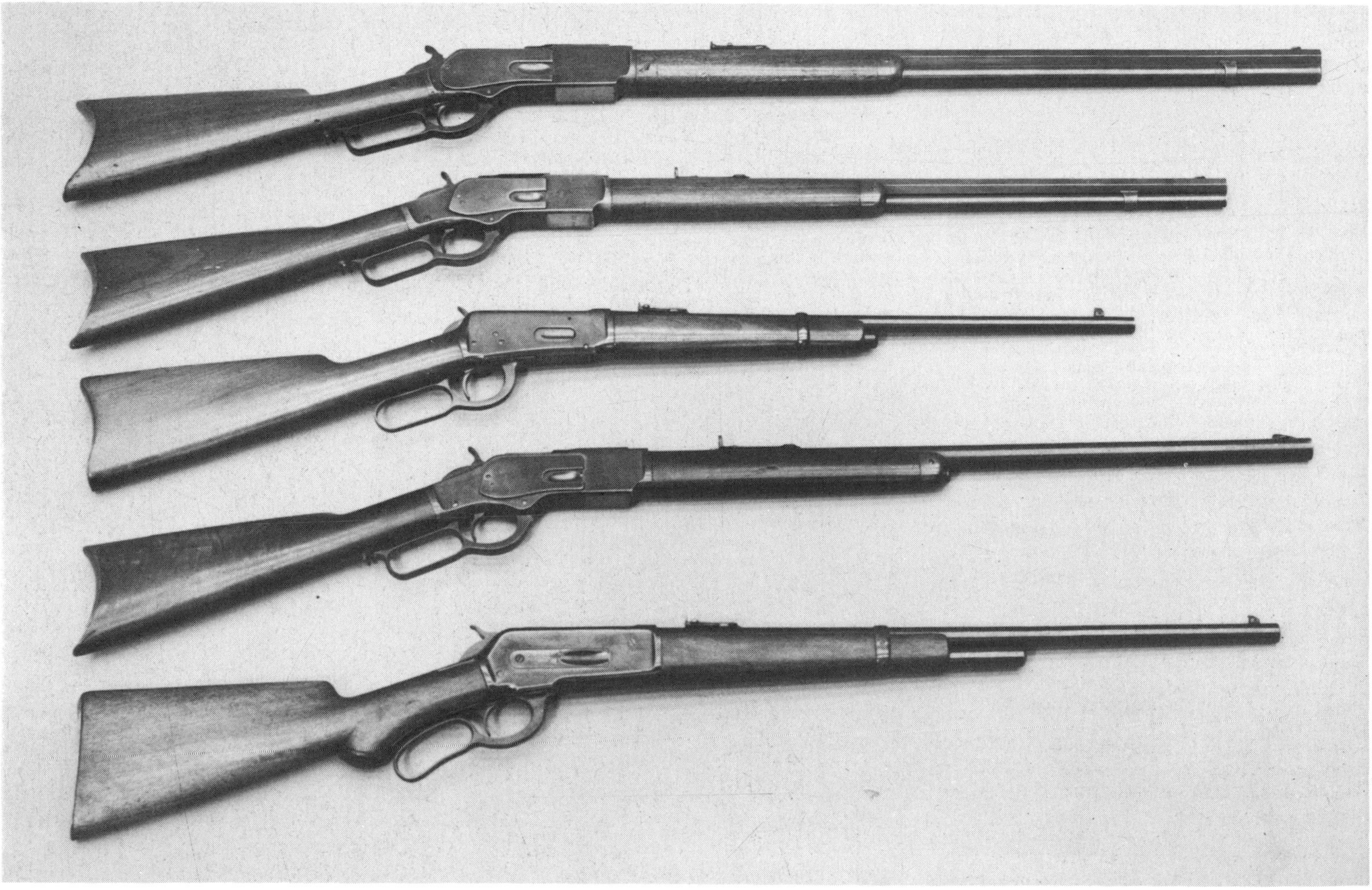

many Western films, where the uninitiated can be forgiven for believing that they are in fact Model 1873s!

In 1883, Colt's produced a lever-action rifle under the Burgess Patent. This .44–40 calibre 15-shot rifle (the carbine held twelve shots) was an attempt to broaden the company's range. Its appearance upset Winchester who believed it could damage their sales. It is alleged that, in reprisal, they were prepared to unleash a series of revolvers, some designed by William Mason, who had worked at Colt's on the Peacemaker, which in turn would have depleted Colt's sales. Tradition asserts that officials of both companies got together and reached a 'gentlemen's agreement' to discontinue products which could be detrimental to each other.

Other lever-action rifles competed with the Winchester during the closing years of the nineteenth century, most importantly those manufactured by J. M. Marlin of New Haven, Connecticut. From 1881 until the early years of this century (and in some models until recently) the company competed with Winchester and earned a great reputation of their own. None the less, as we pointed out earlier, thanks to legend and, in recent years, the film *Winchester '73*, it is the Winchester rifle that is best remembered.

Top left: Members of the North-West Mounted Police at Chelsea Barracks in 1897. They were in London to take part in Queen Victoria's 60th anniversary celebrations. The carbines are Winchesters Model 1876 — used by the force until 1914 — and the pistols are either the 1872 Model Adams or the Enfield replacements. (By courtesy of the Royal Canadian Mounted Police)

Bottom left: A group of Winchester lever-actions. Top: 1876 Model rifle in .40-60 calibre, with a 28-inch fully octagonal barrel and fitted with a set-trigger. Second: 1873 Model rifle in .32 calibre with a 24-inch barrel. Third: Model 1894 saddle carbine complete with carrying ring in .30 calibre. Fourth: 1873 Model rifle with a 24-inch round barrel. Fifth: Model 1886 rifle in .38-56 calibre with a 22-inch round barrel. The magazine has been shortened to thirteen inches and the weapon is fitted with a carbine-style fore-end, a pistol grip and a saddle ring. (By courtesy of Richard A. Bourne Co. Inc.)

Top right: The bogus '1 OF 1,000' on Winchester No. 7559. (By courtesy of Messrs Weller & Dufty)

Bottom right: Legend has it that the Winchester company and Colt had a gentlemen's agreement in the early 1880s: Winchester would stop experimenting with revolvers and Colt would cease production of the Colt-Burgess lever-action rifles. True or not, the company did produce a number of experimental revolvers from the early 1870s until the early 1880s. The top specimen is the work of William Mason and closely resembles his Peacemaker design for Colt; the lower three pistols are credited to Stephen W. Wood and Hugo Borchardt who had also worked for Colt. He subsequently worked for Sharps before returning to Germany where he designed the link mechanism which evolved into the semi-automatic Luger pistol. (By courtesy of the Winchester Museum)

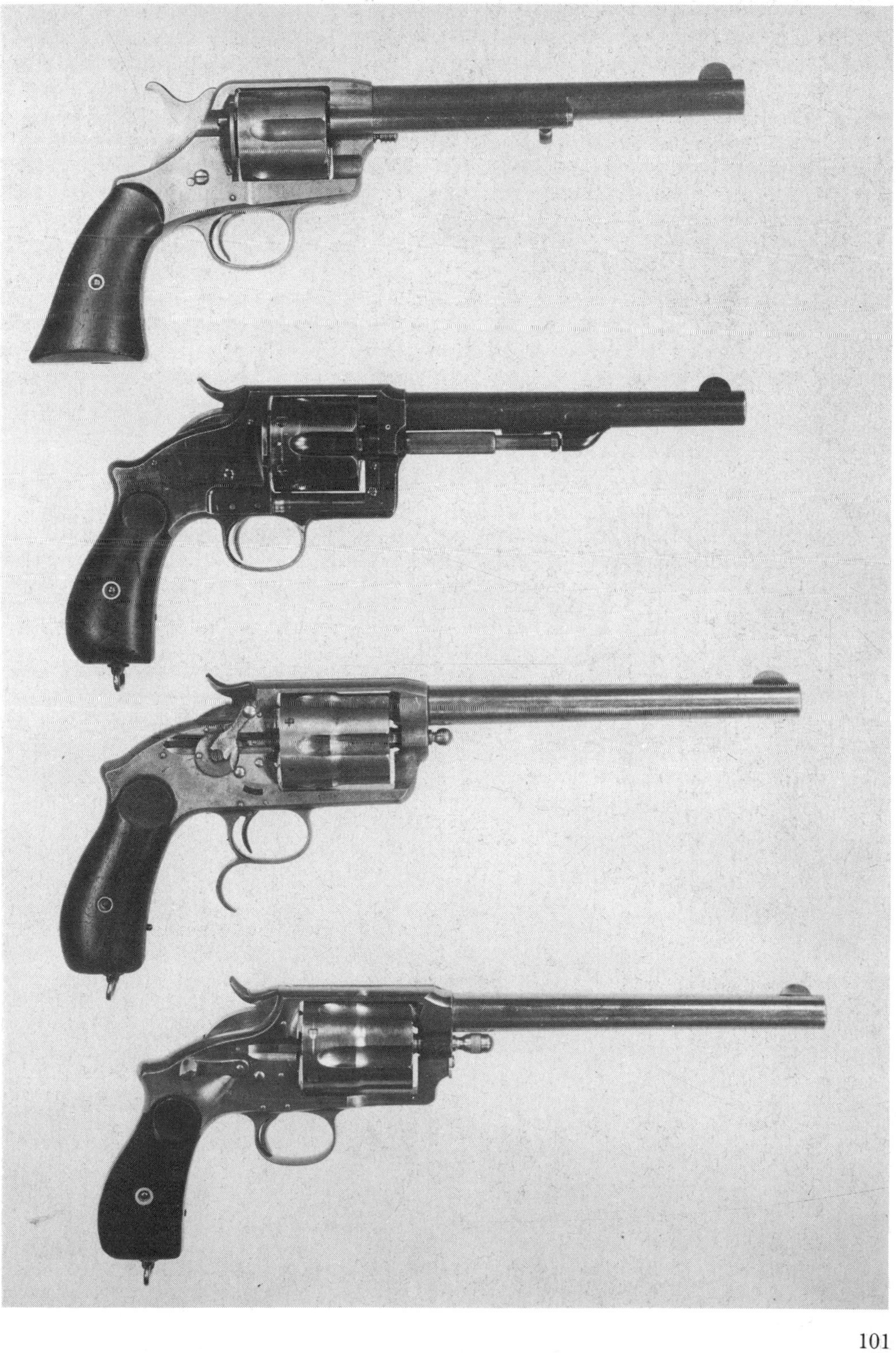

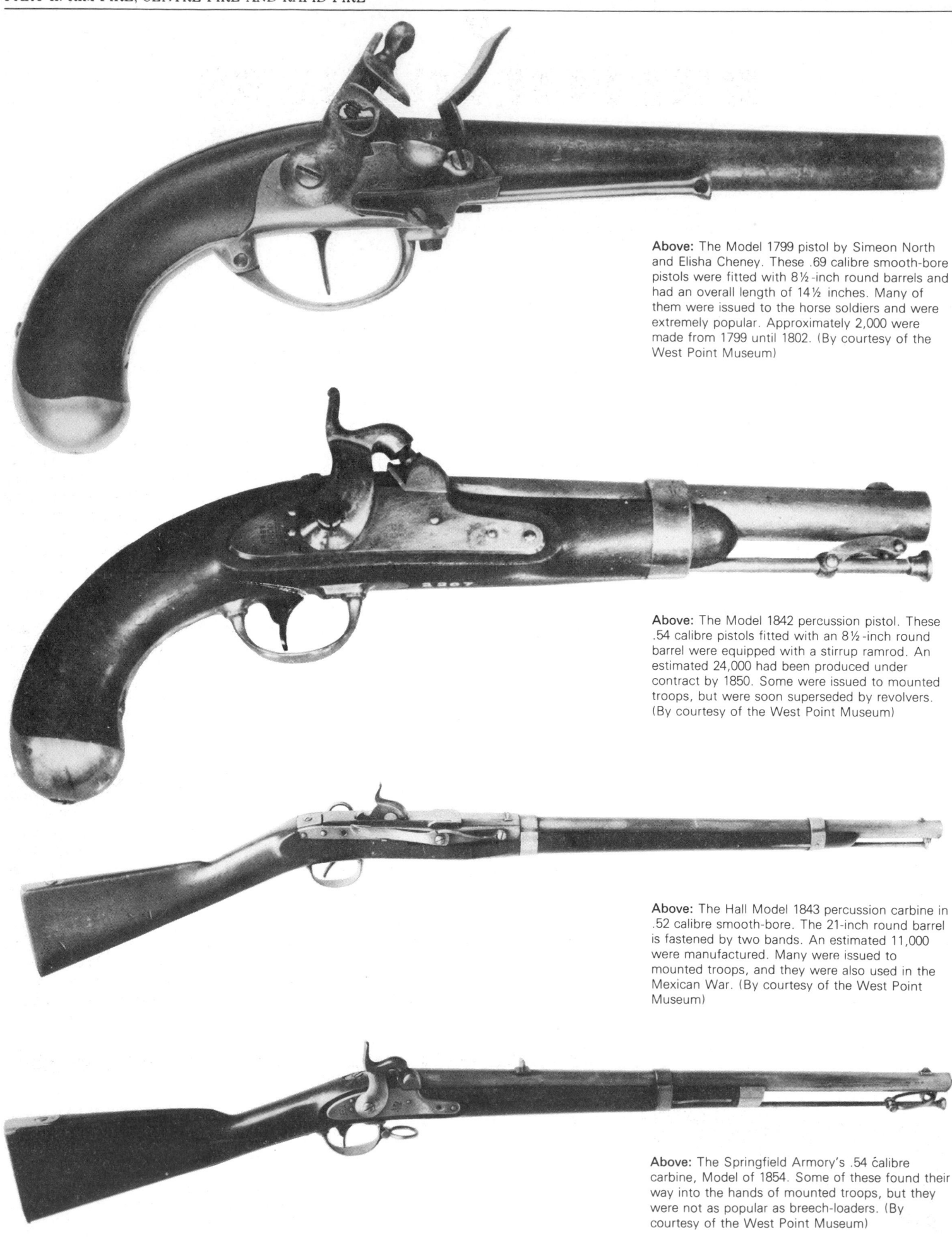

Above: The Model 1799 pistol by Simeon North and Elisha Cheney. These .69 calibre smooth-bore pistols were fitted with 8½-inch round barrels and had an overall length of 14½ inches. Many of them were issued to the horse soldiers and were extremely popular. Approximately 2,000 were made from 1799 until 1802. (By courtesy of the West Point Museum)

Above: The Model 1842 percussion pistol. These .54 calibre pistols fitted with an 8½-inch round barrel were equipped with a stirrup ramrod. An estimated 24,000 had been produced under contract by 1850. Some were issued to mounted troops, but were soon superseded by revolvers. (By courtesy of the West Point Museum)

Above: The Hall Model 1843 percussion carbine in .52 calibre smooth-bore. The 21-inch round barrel is fastened by two bands. An estimated 11,000 were manufactured. Many were issued to mounted troops, and they were also used in the Mexican War. (By courtesy of the West Point Museum)

Above: The Springfield Armory's .54 calibre carbine, Model of 1854. Some of these found their way into the hands of mounted troops, but they were not as popular as breech-loaders. (By courtesy of the West Point Museum)

9
BREECH-LOADERS FOR THE CAVALRY

The [breech-loading] carbine is the best weapon yet known . . . for a cavalry soldier . . .
dragoon soldiers have more confidence in it than any other weapon . . . – Captain
J. W. Davison, 1st Regiment of Dragoons, to the U.S. Ordnance Department, 1858.

THE United States Cavalry was involved in the civilizing and settling of that vast region west of the Mississippi long before the period which marks the latter part of this present study, but rarely does it receive due credit. Rather, it is portrayed in fiction and on film as an interfering or semi-incompetent force which either gets it all wrong, or redeems itself by arriving in time to save the hero or besieged settlement in the last reel. This is nonsense, of course, in reality the U.S. Army (both infantry and cavalry) played a major role in the 'Wild West'.

The first 'horse soldiers' in the United States service were the 'Continental Dragoons', based loosely on European dragoon regiments. In November 1776 a committee was appointed by Congress to organize and provide arms and equipment for 3,000 horsemen. Initially, only four Continental regiments were formed and they were never up to full strength. In 1780, when it was pointed out that some regiments were supplied with carbines in order that they could better defend their camps as did the infantry, the tradition was established of arming mounted regiments with long arms as well as swords and pistols.

Most of the pistols were .69 calibre, single-shot flintlocks patterned after the British version, but a number of Kentucky-style weapons in smaller calibres, were also used. The issue carbines varied from captured British .65 calibre 37-inch barrelled 'musketoons' to weapons with shorter barrels and better suited to horseback use. By the 1820s, however, the pistol and sabre were more common, and with the formation of the United States Regiment of Dragoons on 2 March 1833, greater attention was paid to specific arms. From 1833 until the early 1850s the Dragoons were armed with various models of Hall's carbine. From 1836 (when the 2nd Regiment was formed) the Dragoons were issued with the percussion version of these remarkable weapons, together with a sabre and a single-shot, muzzle-loading pistol which was carried in a saddle holster. Hall's contribution to military arms has been mentioned elsewhere, and the Model 1833, based on his design was also manufactured under contract by Simeon North. These Hall-North carbines were originally made in .579 calibre, but from 1836 the calibre was .52 smooth-bore. The weapon had a 26-inch barrel and provision for a rod bayonet.

A number of weapons were also produced in .69 calibre, carrying a ball weighing one-eighteenth of a pound, but the .52 calibre weapon with a ball weighing one-thirty-second of a pound was more common. In 1836 a 21-inch barrelled version of the Hall carbine was produced in .64 calibre and this was ordered for the 2nd Regiment of Dragoons. From 1840 until 1843 several other versions of the weapon appeared in .54 calibre. The 1843 model, in .54 calibre with a 21-inch barrel, was the last of these fine weapons to be introduced into dragoon service.

Sam Colt also had an eye on the cavalry service long before his revolvers were adopted. During the Seminole wars of the late 1830s, 100 Paterson .525 calibre smooth-bore six-shot 24-inch barrelled carbines were purchased for the use of Lieutenant-Colonel William S. Harney's 2nd Dragoons. But Colt's revolving rifles and carbines did not enjoy the reputation of his pistols, and by the 1850s they were replaced by the Model 1847 smooth-bore 'musketoon', which was later rifled and re-issued when the elongated (conical) bullet was introduced.

From 1853 until 1861 a number of carbines were tried and issued to mounted troops. The Model 1848 .52 calibre Sharps (some fitted with Maynard tape-primers) were issued to the 1st Regiment of Dragoons in 1853, and later a number were also issued to the 2nd Regiment. The cartridge for these weapons contained a 450-grain ball backed by 55 grains of black powder.

The success of the Sharps can be gauged by the correspondence which passed between the Ordnance and serving officers, and between officers and the Sharps company. In 1858 a number of officers of the 1st Regiment of Dragoons, stationed at Fort Buchanan, New Mexico, wrote to the Ordnance Department praising the Sharps carbines in service with the regiment. 'I am satisfied from trial and experience,' wrote Captain J. W. Davison, in command of Company B, 'that the Sharps' carbine is the best weapon yet known in our country for a cavalry soldier. Its range and accuracy are greater than those of the musketoon. It is a stronger arm; the soldier can make it last longer . . . The range of the Sharps' is as great as that of the new carbine pistol – its accuracy of fire greater. The Sharps' can be loaded at full speed; the carbine pistol cannot without great inconvenience. I am satisfied

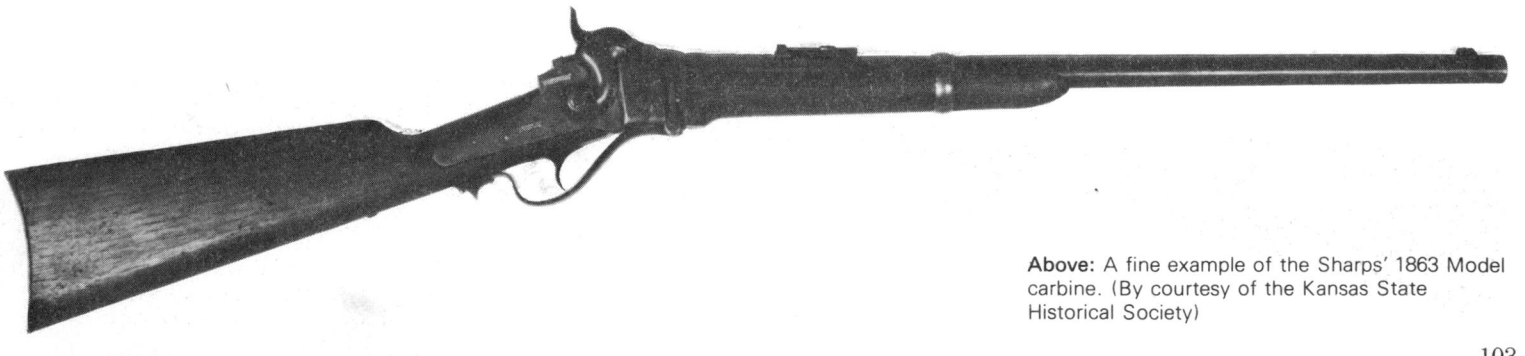

Above: A fine example of the Sharps' 1863 Model carbine. (By courtesy of the Kansas State Historical Society)

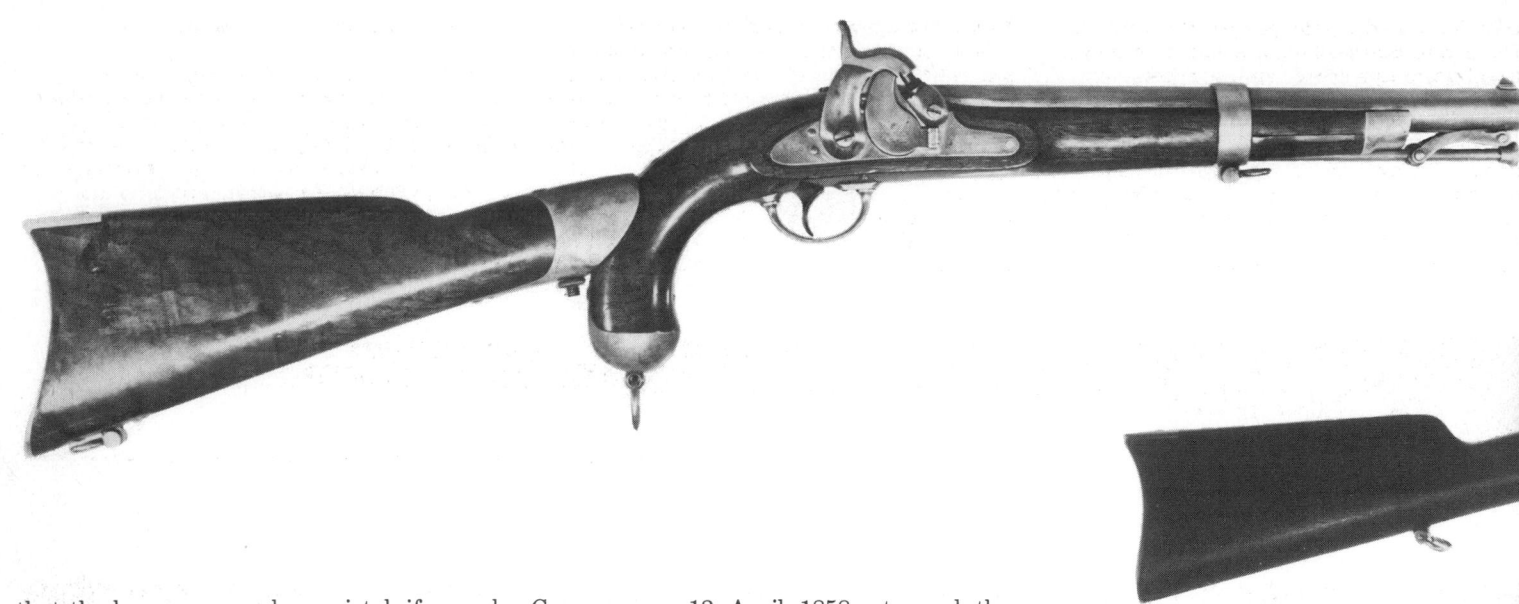

that the horseman needs no pistol, if armed with Sharps' carbine and a light and *sharp* sabre . . . dragoon soliders have more confidence in it than any other weapon I have ever seen put into their hands; and I have seen them use the musketoon, carbine pistol and Minié rifle. Give your soldiers but confidence in the effectiveness of their weapons, and they will give a better account of themselves than with those they cannot trust.'

The captain's comments were backed by other officers, and he later remarked that he believed that a 'wounded man on the ground can load and fire and use as effectually one of these carbines as he could a revolver'.

The 'carbine pistol', which had aroused the captain's ire, was the Springfield Model 1855 'Pistol-Carbine' issued that year for trial. The cartridges for these weapons were paper or linen and were composed of a .58 calibre 450-grain bullet backed by forty grains of black powder. The load was effective enough, but the weapon itself was the problem. These cumbersome single-shot percussion pistols (which must surely have ranked with the British Army's accursed 'Victoria Carbines' and described officially as 'worse than useless') had detachable carbine stocks, and were also fitted with the Maynard tape-primer. This latter additon consisted of sixty primers in a row on a paper tape (similar to today's toy cap pistol) which moved under the hammer when the weapon was cocked. This ingenious idea was popular, but improved ammunition and the advent of the true breech-loader saw its demise.

The 1855 pistol-carbine had been designed to replace the single-shot pistols and carbines then in service, but it was not a success. Troops, who already had experience of the Sharps or other breech-loading arms or even Colt's revolvers, found them cumbersome and 'old-fashioned'. As for the Colt revolving rifles then in service, General C. C. Hornsby, writing from Washington to the Sharps Company on 12 April 1858, stressed the superiority of the Sharps rifle over the Colt rifle and carbine. The Sharps was superior in range and accuracy and was much safer to handle – he admitted a prejudice against Colt's rifles which were prone to accidental discharge. The General also noted that they were liable to get out of order; they were difficult to load, and 'furthermore the soldiers used them in fear'. This latter comment was obviously directed toward the fearsome blast between chamber mouth and breech, which caused severe burns.

This tendency to 'inflame' more than just tempers, prompted a great deal of comment. In England, although Colt's revolvers were greatly admired, the same could not be said for the long weapons. One man who did admire Colt's long arms was Hans Busk (1815–1882), a barrister and a leading light in the Volunteer Movement of 1859. In that year England feared a French invasion, and hundreds of men answered the call to arms. The Volunteers eventually became the Territorial Army. Busk wrote glowingly of the long arms and their accuracy, but neglected any reference to their faults. This was left to John Scoffern, who was as anti- as Busk was pro-Colt. In his *The Royal Rifle Match on Wimbledon Common*, published in 1860, he wrote:

'Fire a revolving pistol at night; observe the escape of lateral flame like the halo around the head of a saint. How would you like your arm to be in that burning halo of flame? Colt tells you his carbines need not be held with two hands. I tell you they *cannot* be held with two hands; the coat sleeve would be burned through presently. And see how manufacturers of revolver long arms steer clear of big or moderately big bores; a condition which would speedily try out conclusions. They stick to thick barrels and small bores and low charges. I tell you revolving full length arms are a failure.'

Left: The infamous pistol-carbine, Model of 1855. These .58 calibre single-shot weapons, fitted with the Maynard tape primer, were equipped with 12-inch barrels, and a two-leaf rear sight graduated to 400 yards (more in hope than in expectation). They were not popular with the troops, and fewer than 5,000 were manufactured. It is claimed that Colt's detachable shoulder stock owes its origin to this pistol, but he was using a similar device at least two years before. (By courtesy of the West Point Museum)

Below: Colt's revolving rifles were normally reliable, but unpractical weapons. An unfortunate side-effect was the lateral flash between cylinder mouth and breech which could burn the shooter's hand if he were not wearing gloves. First, Model 1855 rifle with bayonet; second, the rifled musket complete with bayonet; third, 'First Model' 1855 sporting rifle; fourth, Model 1855 carbine; fifth, Model 1855 half-stock sporting rifle, complete with rammer and cleaning rod; sixth, Model 1855 half-stock sporting rifle converted to metallic cartridge.

(By courtesy of the Winchester Museum)

Bottom: A Colt revolving carbine, circa 1859. These side-hammer weapons were the mainstay of Colt's long arm revolving-cylinder models, and despite some glowing reports in the press (and from his friends), he was well aware that the lateral flame from the cylinder frightened the troops. None the less, a large number were in service. (By courtesy of the Kansas State Historical Society)

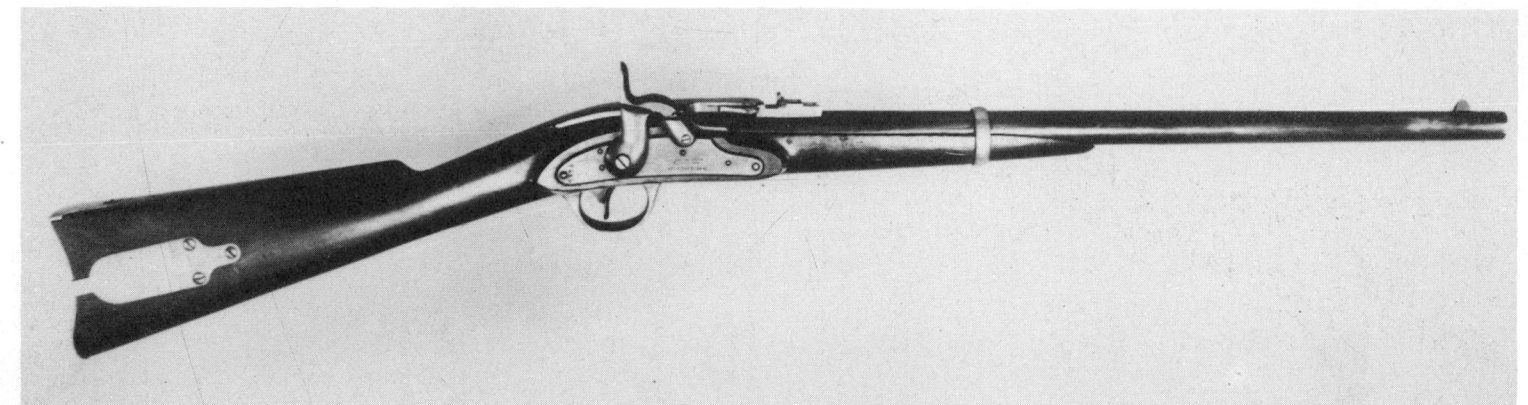

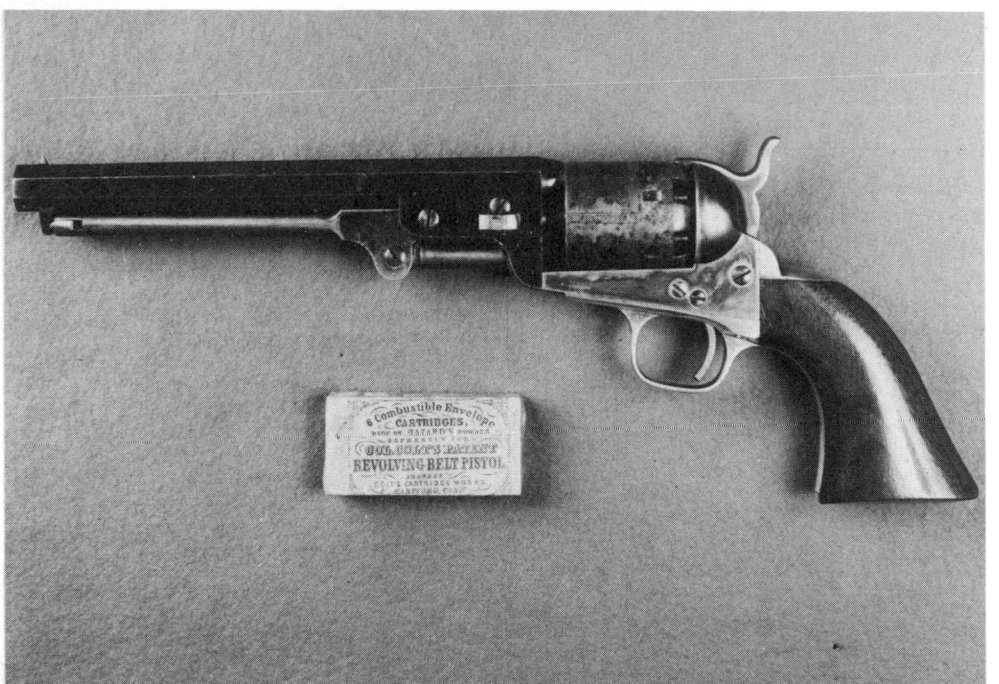

Above: A Merrill First Model carbine in .54 calibre. These percussion breech-loaders underwent several modifications and a number of them were issued to dragoon regiments for trial. An estimated 14,495 of the first model were manufactured, most of them going to the Government. (By courtesy of the West Point Museum)

Left: A late Fourth Model Navy pistol, called by Colt the Old Model because by the time this one was produced there was a round-barrelled version which is now generally called the Model 1861. This specimen was manufactured circa 1863 – 64. (By courtesy of the Lawbrook Collection)

Top right: Ambrose E. Burnside was a man of parts: he was a famous Union General during the Civil War, and he invented a popular carbine. Illustrated is a typical example of the weapons he manufactured from 1857 until 1865. These .54 calibre percussion weapons were similar to the Sharps in that the trigger guard acted as a lever to lower the breech-block for loading. The weapon fired a bullet made of copper or of tapered foil – the latter being the more common. Some weapons were also fitted with a tape primer, and the design underwent several modifications. About 60,000 were produced. (By courtesy of the Kansas State Historical Society)

On 3 March 1855 Congress authorized the formation of two new regiments of infantry and two of cavalry – this was the first time that the term 'cavalry' had been officially applied to mounted troops. The 1st and 2nd Cavalry were issued with several types of weapons, including Merrill breech-loading percussion carbines and Colt Navy pistols. Some of these revolvers were made up with iron backstraps and trigger guards from the London factory on the orders of General Harney, but the majority of weapons from Hartford continued to use brass for these parts. The Merrill, Latrobe & Thomas carbine was a .54 calibre weapon, and 170 were ordered for trial. The Perry breech-loading carbine and the U.S. Model 1854 cavalry carbine, a .58 calibre weapon, were also issued on a trials or permanent basis.

The Civil War, however, put an end to trials, and on 10 August 1861, the Government decided to standardize the horse soldier regiments. The 1st Dragoons became the 1st Cavalry; the 2nd Dragoons the 2nd Cavalry; the U.S. Mounted Rifles became the 3rd Cavalry; the original 1st

Cavalry now became the 4th Cavalry; the 2nd Cavalry the 5th, and the 3rd Cavalry became the 6th Cavalry. All very confusing to those involved, but, presumably, perfectly logical to the Government!

From 1861 until 1865, a variety of weapons were issued to the cavalry regiments. Some retained the Old Model Colt Navy revolver (now known as the Model 1851) issued to the original first and second cavalry regiments from 1855. The majority of troops, however, were issued with the .44 calibre Colt New Model Army revolver of 1860, or the .44 calibre Remington revolvers, Models 1861 and 1863. The different makes of carbine were far more numerous and included the Burnside in .54 calibre, which fired a bullet crimped into a special copper cartridge tapered at its rear; the Model 1863 Sharps, which used the Lawrence primer system and was chambered for .52 calibre paper cartridges. After the war, however, many of these arms were converted to cartridge and rivalled the Springfield rifles and carbines. These were converted from percussion to the Allin system at the Springfield

Armory (which will be discussed later). As we have already noted, one of the more successful and popular arms was the Spencer seven-shot carbine with the Blakeslee quickloader; it took only a few seconds to remove an empty tube and replace it by a new one. The carbine version of the Spencer was produced in 1863 and the first 1,000 were delivered on 3 October. By the end of the war, an estimated 90,000 carbines had been issued to the army, together with 12,000 rifles. In 1865, Spencer produced a .50 calibre carbine equipped with a magazine cut-off which enabled it to be used as a single-shot weapon if required. Thus a full magazine could be kept in reserve. This fact was not forgotten by serving officers when, during the middle 1870s, the decision was made to standardize cavalry carbines.

The Spencer found itself at the centre of a storm when in some areas it was reported that ammunition for the weapon was defective. Late in January 1867 General C. C. Augur, commanding the Department of the Platte with headquarters at Omaha, Nebraska, ordered his Inspector General's

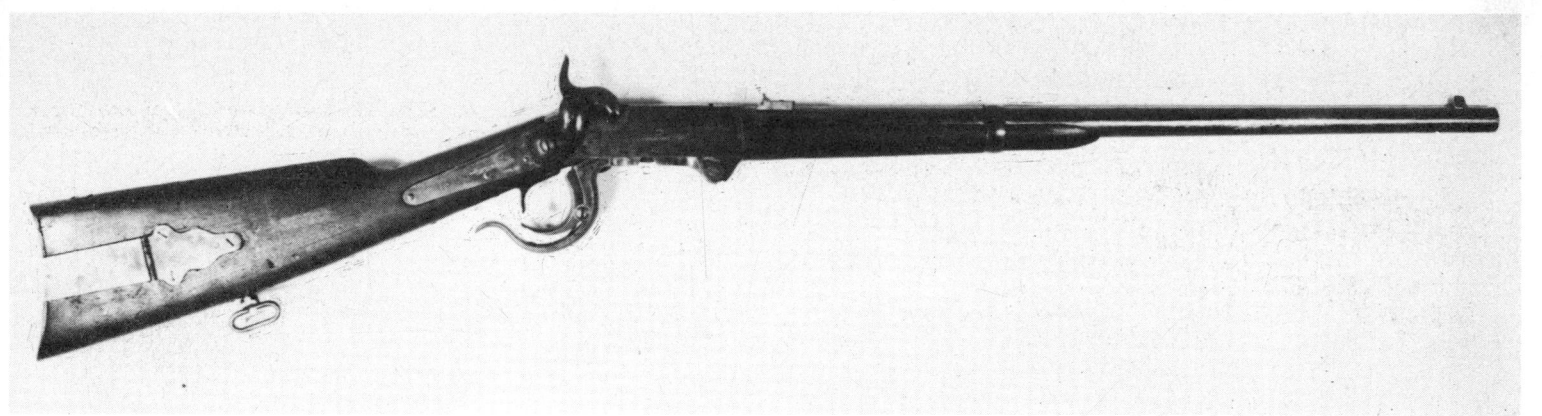

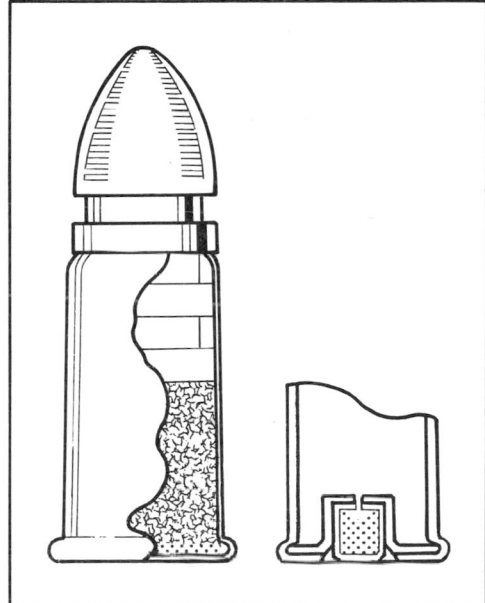

Above: Spencer's rim-fire cartridge, and Brevet Colonel Benét's central-fire priming of 1865.

Department to investigate. In a report dated 31 January General Augur was informed:

'I went yesterday to the Quartermaster's Depot and made a careful inspection of the Spencer carbines there, and the ammunition for them. I found the carbines to be the improved Spencer, model of 1865 calibre .50 with Stabler's attachment or cut off and the ammunition furnished for them to be the correct calibre, several officers of the staff accompanied me and the ammunition was thoroughly tested with the following results – Of two hundred and fifty rounds fired, only one cartridge failed to explode at once, and that did explode after having a new part of the rim turned under the hammer. In a number of instances the base of the shell (at the rim containing the fulminate) burst out in firing and blew grains of powder and bits of copper out at the junction of the breech slide and barrel, in one instance when this occurred the quantity was sufficient to sting severely and blind me for a moment and I think if I had not had on spectacles to have perhaps temporarily injured the eye. In every instance it blew grains of powder into the face of the person firing – enough to sting severely for a moment.

'I find that there are two different calibres of Spencer carbines issued – calibre .50 (which was the one tried) and probably calibre .52; some of the officers thought calibre .56 at any rate the calibres differ enough to make different ammunition necessary.

'The opinion of every officer present was that the Spencer model of 1865 with Stabler's attachment was the most perfect carbine they had ever seen, and that with reliable ammunition is nearly a perfect arm. My own opinion (in which the others coincided) is that the shell of these cartridges is made too thin at the rim, and is carelessly made, – the accident which occurred with them being one which in the experience of every officer there they had never known to occur before, and that this is a serious defect in the ammunition.

'The ammunition inspected was made by J. Goldmark New York – some ammunition of the same kind made by Crittenden and Tibball, New Coventry, Conn. had none of this defect. . .'

In forwarding this report to Major-General A. B. Dyer, Chief of Ordnance, General Augur included similar complaints from other officers:

'. . . the Thirtieth Infantry were, at Washington, armed with Spencer carbines and furnished with ammunition for them. They were not used or tried until the regiment reached Fort Sedgwick, where the following reports were made by Bvt Brig Genl I N Potter Commanding the regiment. Telegram of 27th inst.

"The ammunition furnished this command is defective and unfit for service, of *473* cartridges expended in practice – *177* failed to explode, *250* would not fit the carbines. I request a supply of suitable ammunition."
Letter of 28th Inst.

"I cannot imagine why such worthless stuff was issued to troops ordered on active service, *197* cartridges out of *477* tried were found worthless. Twenty of the number were too large for the carbines.

If a cartridge is too large for the chamber and force is applied it will get wedged, and the carbine is disabled for the time necessary to force it out with a rod. I request that suitable ammunition may be furnished me as early as practicable."
Telegram of 31st inst.

"Sir, ammunition is of different kind, some Spencer Rifle, some Spencer and Jocelyn, some calibre .56 some cal .50, but little of the latter, the Spencer and Jocelyn was made by Crittenden and Tibbal's Coventry Conn. This does not fail as the other does, carbines are of 1860, ammunition marked new model from New York Arsenal April 15th 65."

'There was on hand here a quantity of ammunition which has been sent with the carbines, sent from Columbus Arsenal. And desiring to replace what General Potter had with reliable ammunition, I directed an inspection and tests of the ammunition before sending it. Of this inspection and test I enclose the report of the assistant Inspector General of the Department [quoted above]. . . The remedy for the defective and imperfect ammunition will suggest its self. There are in the hands of troops in this department, about two thousand Spencer carbines probably half of them of the model 1865, and I have to request that a supply of reliable ammunition sufficient to meet all probable contingencies during the coming summer, be forwarded to the Assistant Inspector General of the Department in reason to permit him to distribute to the posts where needed by the middle of March. The amount I would suggest should be not less than two hundred rounds to the arm . . .'

None the less, the superiority of the breech-loader over muzzle-loaders was not lost upon Government or military, but having survived a war which had all but destroyed the country's economy, there was little enthusiasm for drastic change. With most of the arsenals chock-full of perfectly good Springfields or Enfields, the logical course was to convert them – an expedient but short-sighted measure. The system eventually decided upon was that of Erskine S.

Allin, the Master Armorer at the Springfield Armory, which could be employed at a minimum of cost to the Government. A moveable breech-block, which included a firing-pin, was hinged at the forward end, enabling it to be flipped up to expose the chamber for loading, or to eject a spent case. The system was soon dubbed the 'trap-door' and the name stuck. Once the breech was opened it was a simple matter to slip a cartridge into the chamber, snap the block shut, and cock the side-hammer for action.

Conversions began in 1865, when several thousand muzzle-loading Springfields were converted to .58 rim-fire. Similarly, experiments with weapons made by Remington, Ward Burton, Spencer, Ballard, Sharps and Starr, also came under scrutiny. In 1867 a Board was set up to examine existing systems. The Remington rolling-block was considered superior to the existing Allin-converted Springfields, and some of its rivals, but it was not generally adopted, and few were purchased. The Government, however, authorized the Springfield Armory to set up 313 carbines using the 1865 conversion for trial in the field. Later, in 1871, an estimated 259 Model 1870 Springfield carbines in .50 centre-fire were issued for trial, together with a number of Remingtons, Sharps and some Ward Burtons, but it was the .50–70 Springfield that was adopted.

The new breech-loading carbines came into their own in 1867, but not before the shortcomings of muzzle-loading weapons had been high-lighted in tragic circumstances. The establishment of a line of forts along the Bozeman trail in 1866 angered the Sioux and led to confrontations between the military and the Indians. Colonel Henry Carrington, the commander of Fort Phil Kearny in Dakota Territory, repeatedly advised his superiors that Red Cloud's Sioux were unsettled, and reported a number of Indian attacks that left seventy whites killed or wounded and the loss of stock. The most notorious incident, however, involved men of his own command. On 21 December 1866 Brevet Lieutenant-Colonel Fetterman insisted on heading the detail sent out to bring in the fort's wood supply; he had frequently boasted that with 80 men he could ride through the whole Sioux Nation, but no one had taken him seriously.

Carrington ordered Fetterman and his 81 men to follow the established route because Red Cloud's warriors were highly disciplined and dangerous. Fetterman ignored the warning; he chose his own route and was ambushed and his entire command wiped out. Carrington, of course, was blamed for the loss of so 'brave' an officer, and it took him twenty years to clear his name. The army had its revenge on 2 August 1867 at Piney Island, where troops escorting a number of wagons were attacked by Red Cloud's warriors. The soldiers and civilians quickly formed their wagons into a box, with the animals inside, and prepared to fight to the death. The Indians, used as they were to slow-loading arms, and accustomed to sending in a second wave of warriors before the soldiers could reload, received a severe shock when the troops, backed by a number of civilians armed with Henry rifles, opened fire with their .58 calibre breech-loading Allin-converted Springfields. The 'Wagon Box Fight' as it was afterwards called, lasted for four hours, during which time Red Cloud, watching with his women and children from nearby hills, saw his young men mown down by a continuous withering fire. But for the arrival of reinforcements, complete with cannon, however, the Indians might well have won, for the defenders were rapidly running out of ammunition. Indian losses were estimated at 67 killed and about 120 wounded; troop losses were minor in comparison, but many of them were found to be suffering from nervous exhaustion. Some months later Red Cloud had the satisfaction of seeing the troops leave. Under the terms of a treaty signed in April 1868, the forts along the Bozeman trail were abandoned and later burned by the tribes.

Conscious of the need for well-armed troops on the frontier, the Government at last took a serious interest in its army's weapons. On 6 June 1872 an Act of Congress was passed authorizing the selection of a breech-loading system for muskets and carbines. The existing Allin conversions, weapons mostly converted to .50–70, or the Model 1870 in that calibre, were thought to be too large, and it was decided to reduce the calibre to .45–70. The weight of the bullet was 611 grains (much later this was reduced to 600). After much experimentation, the ensuing weapon weighed seven pounds and had a rate of fire of twelve or thirteen rounds per minute. The carbine version, with a

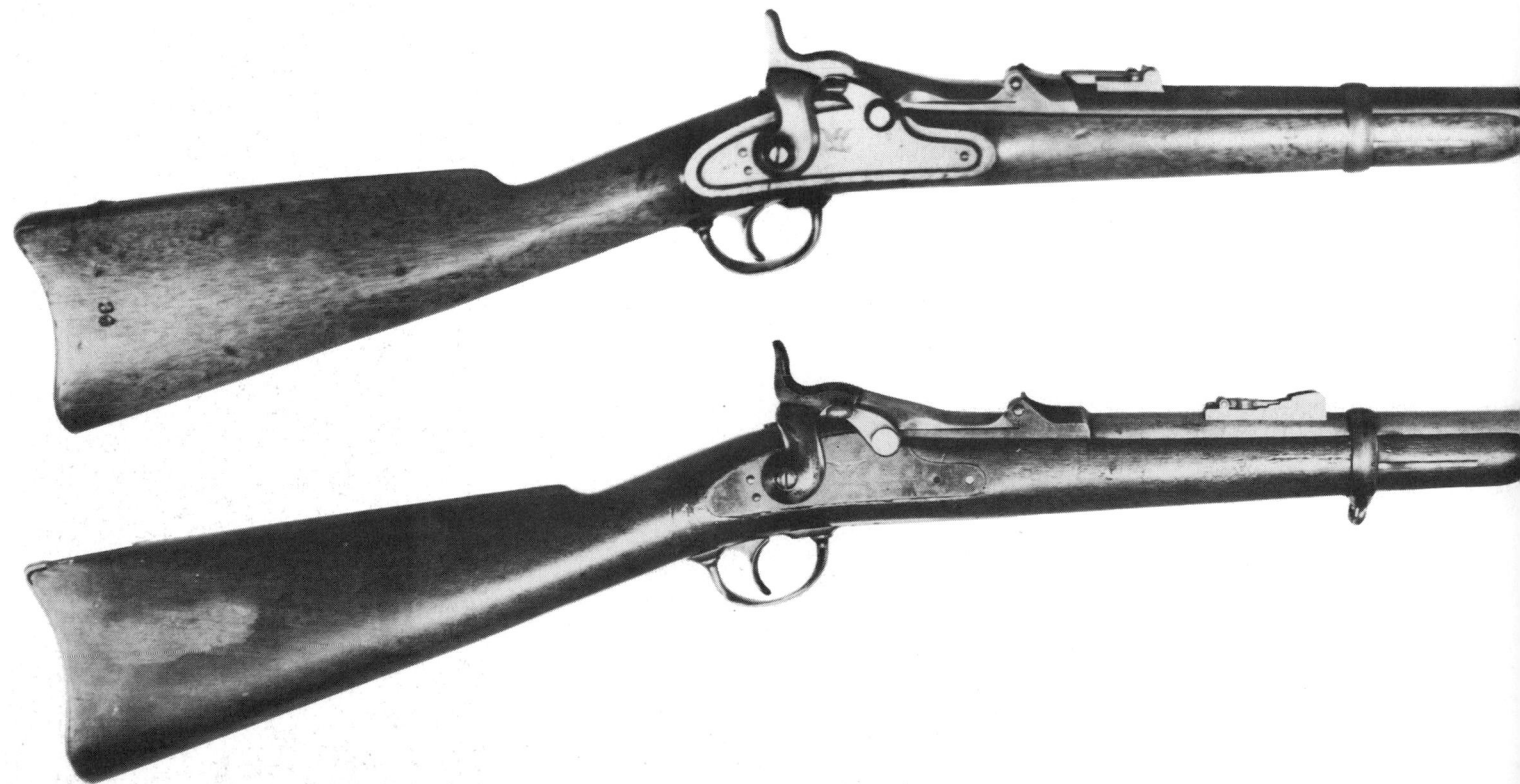

22-inch barrel (against the rifle's 32-inch) was reported to be accurate at 700 yards. According to Government tests, however, the best recorded groupings for the rifle at 500 yards were 2.8 inches, and for the carbine, 3.4 inches. Shooting beyond that distance was considered best suited to the rifle.

There were those, however, who thought that the choice of the Model 1873 was unwise. An estimated 99 other weapons, some of them of foreign make, were tested, but the Board was adamant in favour of the Springfield. In view of what eventually happened, many bitterly rued the day that the 1865 Model Spencer with the cut-off magazine was discarded.

The new 'trap-door' Springfield was issued in four basic models or versions: 1873, 1879, 1884 and the 1889. The additional weight and barrel length of the rifle was satisfactory to the infantry, but the carbine suffered from heavy recoil and a muzzle blast that caused cavalrymen to flinch. Problems with ammunition during the early years of production were not helped by Government economies which forbade the liberal use of ammunition for practice. On 5 August 1874 the War Department issued General Order No. 103 which restricted the number of .45 calibre rounds to ten per month per man. Later, on 23 September 1875 Order No. 83 increased this figure to fifteen, but the extra rounds were for cavalry use only!

The lack of practice and familiarization with the new weapon was a matter of some concern among serving officers. In 1874 following complaints about recoil, the charge in the carbine ammunition was dropped from 70 grains to 55. This, it was hoped, would reduce recoil and solve the problem of jamming and fouling during rapid fire; unfortunately, it did not. The ammunition for the new weapons was manufactured at the Frankford Arsenal. The cartridges were made of copper and were fitted with Benét cups and inside primers. These had been invented by Colonel S. V. Benét: the fulminate was held in place at the base of the cartridge case by a 'cup' or 'anvil'. Outwardly, the cartridge resembled a rim-fire except for indentations in the lower case wall which anchored the inside primer system.

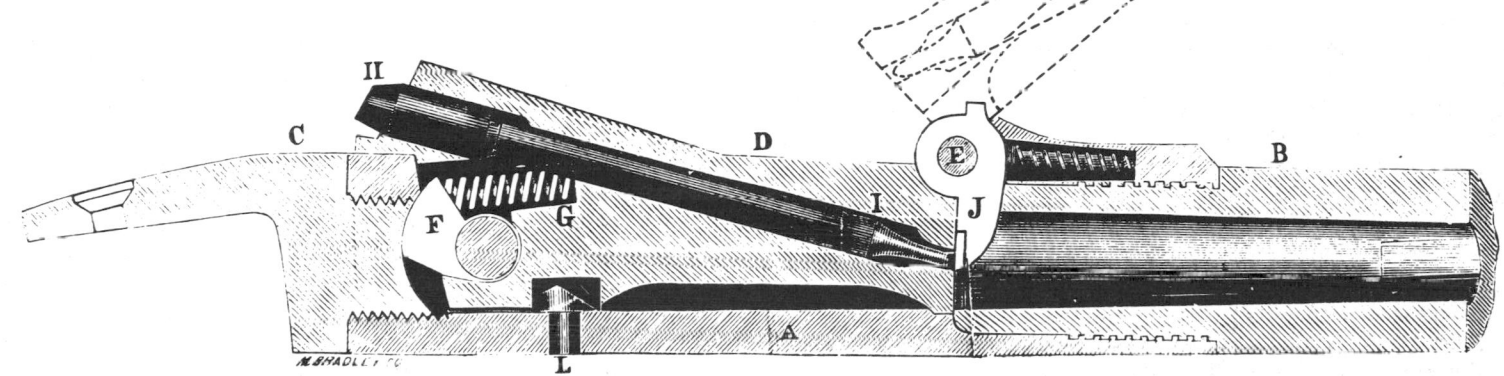

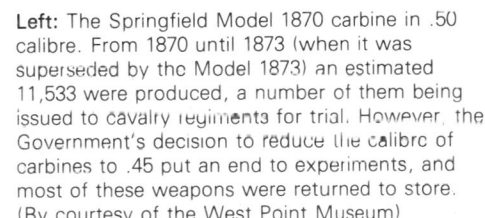

Left: The Springfield Model 1870 carbine in .50 calibre. From 1870 until 1873 (when it was superseded by the Model 1873) an estimated 11,533 were produced, a number of them being issued to cavalry regiments for trial. However, the Government's decision to reduce the calibre of carbines to .45 put an end to experiments, and most of these weapons were returned to store. (By courtesy of the West Point Museum)

Below left: The Model 1873 Springfield carbine. A number of faults were found with this weapon, in particular with its ammunition which was rectified, but too late to save Custer. (By courtesy of the West Point Museum)

Above: A diagram of the Springfield trap-door action, taken from the 1898 edition of Description and Rules for the Management of the Springfield Rifle, and Army Revolvers, Caliber .45. A: the bottom of the receiver; B: the barrel; C: the breech-screw, with its circular recess to receive the cam-latch; E: hinge-pin around which the breech-block (D) turns; F: cam-latch, which locks the breech-block in place; G: cam-latch spring — to press the cam-latch into the recess; H: firing-pin; J: the extractor; K: ejector spring and spindle. (Author's Collection)

Right: An unknown cavalry trooper wearing an issue bandolier and armed with a Peacemaker and an 1873 Model carbine. This illustration is from an original tintype, so therefore appears in reverse. (By courtesy of Herb Peck, Junior)

The casing, however, was thin and problems in manufacture resulted in a lack of uniformity. Reports of swollen cases and parts stuck in the mechanism when the heads were torn off during extraction were common, but attention was directed towards getting the weapons into the hands of the troops.

When news of the new carbines was circulated to the frontier army, the War Department received numerous requests for them. By February 1874 orders had been issued from General Terry's headquarters at St. Paul, Minnesota, directing commanding officers to 'requisition for Springfield breech-loading carbines calibre forty-five (45) and Colts revolvers and ammunition for same when shipped; the old ammunition and arms to be transferred to Rock Island Arsenal . . .' General George A. Custer, Lieutenant-Colonel of the 7th Cavalry Regiment, is reported to have delayed his Black Hills Expedition pending his own request for an issue of the new carbines.

Under the terms of the 1868 treaty, nearly 43,000 square miles of land had been set aside as a Sioux reservation. Part of this land embraced the Black Hills in what later became Dakota Territory and is now a part of South Dakota. The Sioux placed great emphasis on the region's spiritual aspect; they held the Hills sacred and believed that it was 'bad medicine' for outsiders to trespass, but the military mind viewed the matter in a different light. Despite the treaty, Indians and whites were still engaged in sporadic skirmishing and war was inevitable; but where and when it would begin was a matter of speculation in military and political circles. General Philip H. Sheridan decided upon a military survey of the Black Hills; the establishing of a post might inhibit the warlike behaviour of the Indians. After much soul-searching and legal wrangling, an expedition was mounted under the command of Custer, to explore and reconnoitre. The party returned late in 1874, bringing confirmation that there was gold in the Black Hills, and within months bands of illegal gold-seekers were invading the area. By 1876 even the army was unable to stem the tide, and such places as Custer, Deadwood and other boom towns sprang up. The Indian had lost the Hills for ever, but before he finally relinquished his hold, he put up a fight.

When Custer's 1874 expedition was being prepared, he had written to General Terry on 23 May 1874 advising him that he could proceed with the forces he had, but that 'two companies of infantry with their Springfield guns would be a powerful support'. On 31 May Terry advised him that 'New revolvers for your ten (10) companies with ammunition were to be shipped from Rock Island Arsenal yesterday via St. Paul. I am trying to get new carbines also.' On 15 June Custer received a telegram advising him that the Ordnance Department could not furnish the ammunition for the new carbines, therefore none of the weapons would be issued to his command, but on the 22nd he was told that the Department had received telegraphic notification that the Rock Island Arsenal had after all been instructed to issue arms and ammunition. General Terry's headquarters then ordered Custer to 'delay starting a day or two, if necessary in order to get them. He especially wants your command armed with the new carbines'. The weapons finally arrived at Bismark on the 27th and were transferred to Fort Abraham Lincoln and issued to troops on 1 July.

Some days before, on 23 June, and in anticipation of the weapons' arrival, Custer issued a circular to his troops which stated: '. . . Springfield carbines Cal .45 have been ordered for this command. This will necessitate a change in the waist belts already prepared to carry cartridges of 50 calibre. All Springfield muskets, and the various patterns of carbines now in the hands of the men belonging to the cavalry companies of this post, will be stored at this post, until the return of the expedition.' Ironically, it was this expedition that was ultimately responsible for his own 'last stand' in June 1876, when the Indians fought to retain what they rightfully believed was theirs.

Despite complaints from troops and commanding officers that the new ammunition was faulty, no real effort was made to improve it. Instead, procedures were laid down which, with hindsight, seem ludicrous. If the ejector failed to remove a spent case it could be removed by the forefinger. Failing that, a cartridge would 'fall to the ground if the muzzle [of the carbine were to] be elevated with the breech open'. Similarly, if the head of a cartridge were torn off by the extractor, the trooper was advised to prise the ball from another cartridge, pare with a knife so as to be able to insert it in the muzzle, and then ram the 'ball hard with the ramrod when the breech is closed; this will upset the ball and fill the headless shell. Open the breech-block and the ball and shell can be easily pushed out with the ramrod.' With only one wooden cleaning rod between ten men, this sort of advice was unhelpful.

When Custer's command faced Crazy Horse and Gall's Sioux and their Indian allies on Sunday, 25 June 1876 at the Little Big Horn, each soldier was armed with the Springfield carbine and the Colt's single-action Army revolver (the Peacemaker). Their sabres had been left behind with the supply train, for despite popular belief, the sabre had not been used in plains warfare for some years.

Once the battle commenced, it was soon realized that the quality of the ammunition left much to be desired and none of the suggested methods of dealing with awkward extraction would work. With better ammunition Custer's men might have given a much more telling account of themselves than they did. In his report of the battle, Major Marcus A. Reno (who was made a scapegoat for not going to Custer's aid, although it would have been useless and would have meant a further loss of life) explained that he had managed to avoid falling into the same trap as Custer, but had suffered serious casualties all the same. He gave the following reasons for arms failure:

'. . . out of 380 carbines in my command six were rendered unserviceable in the following manner, (there were more rendered unserviceable by being struck with bullets) failure of the breechblock to close, leaving a space between the head of the cartridge & the end of the block, & when the piece was discharged, & the block thrown open, the head of the cartridge was pulled off & the cylinder remained in the chamber, whence with the means at hand, it was impossible to extract it. I believe this a radical defect, & in the hands of hastily organized troops, would lead to the most disastrous results. The defect

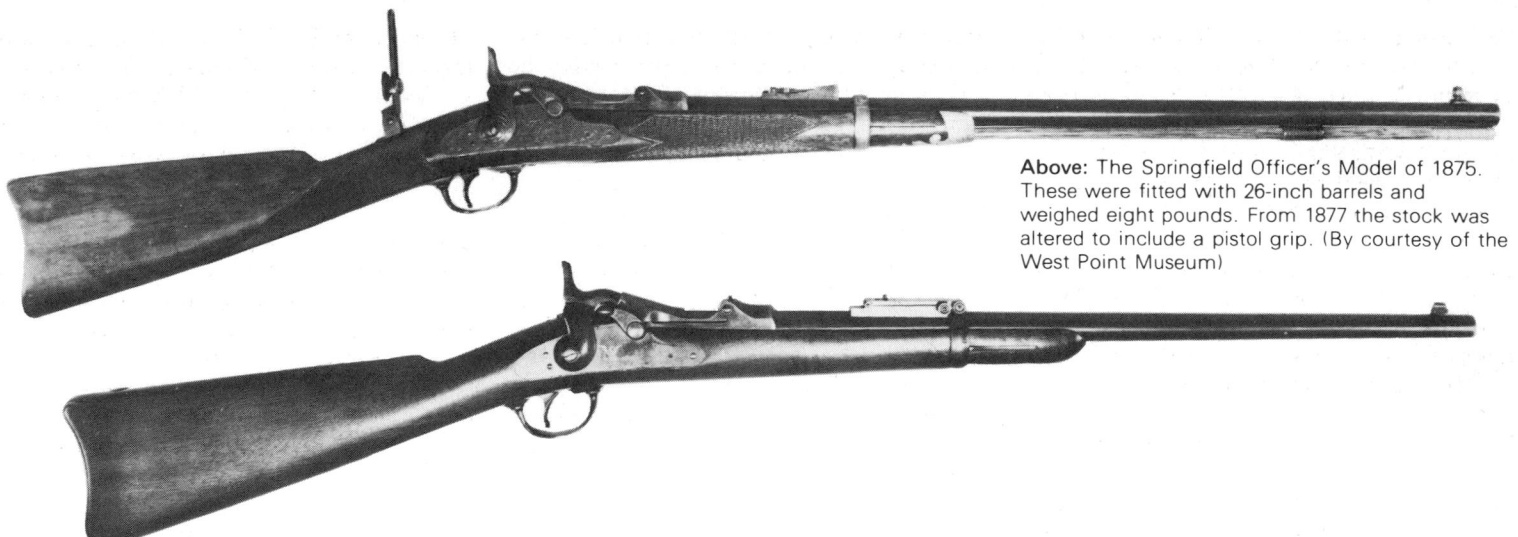

Above: The Springfield Officer's Model of 1875. These were fitted with 26-inch barrels and weighed eight pounds. From 1877 the stock was altered to include a pistol grip. (By courtesy of the West Point Museum)

results in my opinion in two ways – the manufacture of the gun the breechblock is in many instances so made that it does not fit snug up to the head of the cartridge after the cartridge is sent home, & it has always been a question in my mind whether the manner in which it revolves into its places does not render a close contact almost impossible to be made – another reason is that the dust, always an element to be considered in the battlefield, prevents the proper closing of the breechblock, & the same result is produced. There may be want of uniformity in the flange of the head of the cartridge, which would also render the action of the extractor null, in case it was too small, altho' when the shell was left in the chamber, the head would not be torn off. I also observed another bad

Above: The Springfield Model 1884 carbine, which included some of the modifications demanded after the defeat of Custer. (By courtesy of the West Point Museum)

Below: J. Mulvany's 1881 painting of Custer's Last Stand, is somewhat romanticized: Custer did not have a sword, and his revolvers are believed to have been .450 Webley 'Bulldogs'. None the less, the artist has captured the drama of the occasion. (By courtesy of the Library of Congress)

Above: Three Indian guns circa the Custer massacre. All three show signs of much wear and repair and are decorated in the usual Indian fashion. Top and second are a pair of Springfield 1870 .50 calibre weapons, the third is a Springfield .45-70. (By courtesy of Arnold Marcus Chernoff)

Below: The Gatling Model 1873 in .45-70 calibre. (By courtesy of the Winchester Museum)

Above: General George A. Custer was carrying a pair of Webley 'Bulldog' .45 calibre pistols when he was killed, and others out West liked some of the British makes. This Model 1867 Webley R.I.C. (Royal Irish Constabulary) pistol in .442 calibre (54 bore) was owned by John Hunton, Post Trader at Fort Laramie. Even as an old man he could still shoot straight with it: in the 1920s he shot off the head of a rattlesnake as it reared to strike at a little girl. (By courtesy of the late L. G. 'Pat' Flannery)

Left: Two types of ammunition available for the Model 1873 rifle and carbine. The folded-head cartridge consisted of a copper case containing 70 grains of musket powder, an exterior primer containing a half-grain of percussion composition, and a lubricated lead bullet weighing 500 grains (circa 1898). The case was tapered and the primer was struck against an anvil by the firing-pin. The folded-head cartridge contained only 55 grains of powder and a bullet weighing 405 grains. Both illustrations from *Description and Rules.* (Author's Collection)

fault of the system, altho' it did not render the guns unserviceable – viz. the weight of the breechblock is such that the hinge on which it revolves is very soon loosened, giving to the block a lateral motion, that prevents its closing.

'I can also state the blowing up of the breechblock was a contingency that was patent to members of the Board which adopted the system & induced strong opposition to it on the part of a minority. . .'

Major Reno went on to report that an Indian scout with Custer stated that he had seen soldiers sitting down under fire, working at their carbines, and officers later reported finding a number of knives with broken blades lying beside dead troopers. A year later a special instruction sheet was issued dealing with headless cartridge extraction; but it came too late for Custer. The Springfield remained in service until replaced by the Krag rifle in 1892, but it was still the subject of an official manual as late as 1898. The real irony must surely be that among the officers who sat on the Board which selected the weapon in 1872 and 1873, were Brigadier-General A. H. Torry and Major M. A. Reno, 7th U.S. Cavalry – although in the latter's case one suspects he was one of the 'minority' who originally faulted the system.

The revolver, rifle and carbine remained the main armament of the frontier army, but there were other and more sinister weapons which became prominent in the closing years of the frontier, among them so-called 'machine-guns'. The Gatling gun was often referred to as a machine-gun, but since it was hand-cranked the term was erroneous. According to legend, Custer was reported to have turned down the offer of three Gatlings for use in his last campaign. On the face of it, it seems incredible that he would have ignored the potential fire-power of three weapons capable of 150 rounds per minute minimum, but the answer lay in mobility. The Gatlings available in 1876 were a vast improvement on the version produced during and after the Civil War. They now had ten barrels of musket calibre and were mounted on cumbersome cannon-like four-wheeled carriages, complete with limber and ammunition box. On the march, however, the guns were each drawn by four condemned cavalry horses, which did not inspire confidence, especially when the troops were well aware that the Government was more concerned about the national economy than about the safety of the frontier.

Custer's decision not to include Gatling guns was doubtless influenced by his experience in 1874, when he had requested that two Gatlings accompany his Black Hills Expedition. Later, however, he reported that they had proved unsuitable for fast-moving cavalry in rugged country. After his death, the development of even more powerful weapons was soon well advanced. By the 1880s the Gatling was rivalled by the Hotchkiss and Gardner guns. Of these, the Hotchkiss is the best remembered, for this was the gun used by the United States Cavalry in its last confrontation with the Indians at Wounded Knee in 1890.

The gun was the brain-child of Benjamin Berkley Hotchkiss, inventor of small arms cartridges, projectiles and artillery. He first began experiments after the Franco–Prussian War of 1870, where he witnessed the successes and failures of available rapid-fire weapons. Having devised a simple mechanism for his gun, he turned his attention to its ammunition and decided that it should fire explosive shells. Although the European Powers were bound by the Congress of St. Petersburg to limit explosive shells to 450 grains, Hotchkiss rounded up the figure to 455. His shell was 37 millimetres (1.45 inches) in diameter and was in fact the ancestor of the 'one-pounders' of the First World War.

Below left: Geronimo, a name much feared by the whites. He led the U.S. Army a lively dance across Arizona before he surrendered in 1886. This photograph was made by A. Frank Randall in 1886. The old chief died on 17 February 1909 at Fort Sill, Oklahoma. His grasp on the Springfield Model 1873 and determined look suggest that he wished he also had some ammunition! (By courtesy of the Smithsonian Institution)

Below right: Buffalo Bill Cody and Sitting Bull photographed in 1885 when the old chief was a member of his 'Wild West'. Had the Indian Bureau allowed Cody access to Sitting Bull it is possible the old man might not have been killed. As it was, his death caused world-wide outrage. (Author's Collection)

The Hotchkiss available to the army in the 1880s and 1890s, bore a superficial resemblance to the Gatling, and had a similar cluster of barrels turned by a hand-crank. The Hotchkiss's five barrels were fed from a gravity magazine. Where the Gatling barrels turned constantly, those of the Hotchkiss were designed to index during one-half of each turn of the crank and were held stationary as it completed its cycle. At each pause one barrel was loaded, one was fired, and one had its empty case extracted, the entire operation being conducted with only one firing-pin, extractor and loading mechanism. The saving in weight made it possible to use a larger round than in the Gatling, but it did not have the same rate of fire of its rival. None the less, it was a terrifying weapon and was widely adopted in various parts of the world. So it was that in 1890, the 7th U.S. Cavalry found themselves armed with breech-loading carbines, revolvers and a number of Hotchkiss 'revolving cannon' when late in the December, they were called into action at Wounded Knee.

The events which led up to that final and tragic confrontation were many. Fourteen years after Custer's defeat at the Little Big Horn, feelings still ran high. Although Sitting Bull was no longer 'Public Enemy Number One' (it had long been realized that he had not personally killed Custer), his continued presence irked some of the die-hard, anti-Indian extremists both in the Army and in the Government. Then the Ghost Dance Craze, inspired by the 'dreams' of a Paiute medicine-man named Wovoka, which declared that the buffalo would return and the Indian regain his place as master of the continent, incited many of the Indians to take part in ceremonies that could only lead to trouble. Sitting Bull realized this and did his best to dissuade his young men from joining in the dances. The Government, however, feared that there might be an uprising,

and the Indian Agent at Standing Rock, Nebraska, James McLaughlin, blamed Sitting Bull and ordered his arrest as a part of the Indian Bureau's plan to destroy the power of the chiefs – and of Sitting Bull in particular.

Buffalo Bill Cody had just returned from Europe where he had been on tour with his 'Wild West', and when he heard that his old friend Sitting Bull was in trouble (the chief had appeard in the Exhibition for a brief period) he offered to help. General Nelson A. Miles thought it would be a good idea if Cody talked to the old man, and authorized Cody to remove him from his reservation into military custody for protection. If Buffalo Bill had been able to do this the bloodshed which followed might have been prevented, but McLaughlin and his cronies managed to get him side-tracked. On 14 December the Indian police moved into the reservation and on the morning of the 15th Sitting Bull was killed when a number of his followers resisted them. A number of Indians and police died in the ensuing fracas. About 250 of Sitting Bull's people fled to the camp of the Miniconjou Sioux Chief Siteka ('Big Foot'), on Cherry Creek, about 70 miles from Grand River (now South Dakota). Some of the Indians were intercepted by the army and persuaded to surrender, others managed to reach Big Foot.

Negotiations with the army and the movement of the Indians toward Pine Ridge almost succeeded. The Indians numbered about 300 (including women and children) and the troops about 470, well-armed and backed up by the Hotchkiss guns. When the troops began to disarm the Indians under a flag of truce, a medicine-man named Yellow Bird gave a sign and the young Indians began to fire on the troops. The troops returned fire and when the Hotchiss guns, backed by pistols and carbines were finally silent, about 200 Sioux and 25 soldiers had

died, the snow-covered ground being strewn with bodies lying in pools of blood.

Eye-witness and later accounts differ. Some assert that although most of the Indians had readily given up their guns, Big Foot had not been anxious to hand over his Winchester, which he had concealed in his blanket. Not all the army casualties were the result of Indian action; some troops were killed in the cross-fire of their own men. Even the Hotchkiss guns are the subject of dispute. Claims that they were the single-shot, lanyard-operated version were refuted by those who alleged that they were in fact rifled cannon – and to this date the controversy continues. But it is academic: the carnage was complete.

John Y. Nelson, Junior, son of the famous frontiersman, and friend of Buffalo Bill, was one of the seventeen Indian scouts attached to the army. He described the attack as the 'foulest trick white soldiers ever pulled' on disarmed Indians. The army, however, claimed that they were fired upon by 'hostiles' and were forced to defend themselves under fire. Whatever the cause and effect, there were those who believed that Custer had been avenged and that the Indian was no longer a threat to the white man in his determination to rule the continent.

Wounded Knee marked the end of the Indian wars, and, ironically, 1890 was also the year when the Government declared the 'frontier' officially ended. From now on the West was to become more and more entwined with myth; legend became history, and romance replaced reality. But as we shall see, that most grim reminder that it all really happened – the gun – remained.

Below: 7th Calvary troopers at Wounded Knee, January 1891, soon after the massacre. Most of them are armed with Springfield carbines, but a few have pistol butts in evidence. (By courtesy of the Smithsonian Institution)

10
REVOLVERS: THE COLT AND ITS POST-WAR RIVALS

There are as many . . . revolvers and repeaters as there are breech-loading rifles, but . . .
Colt's and Remington's Army Pistols are still the best we have for the service. . . – Army
and Navy Journal, 16 March 1868.

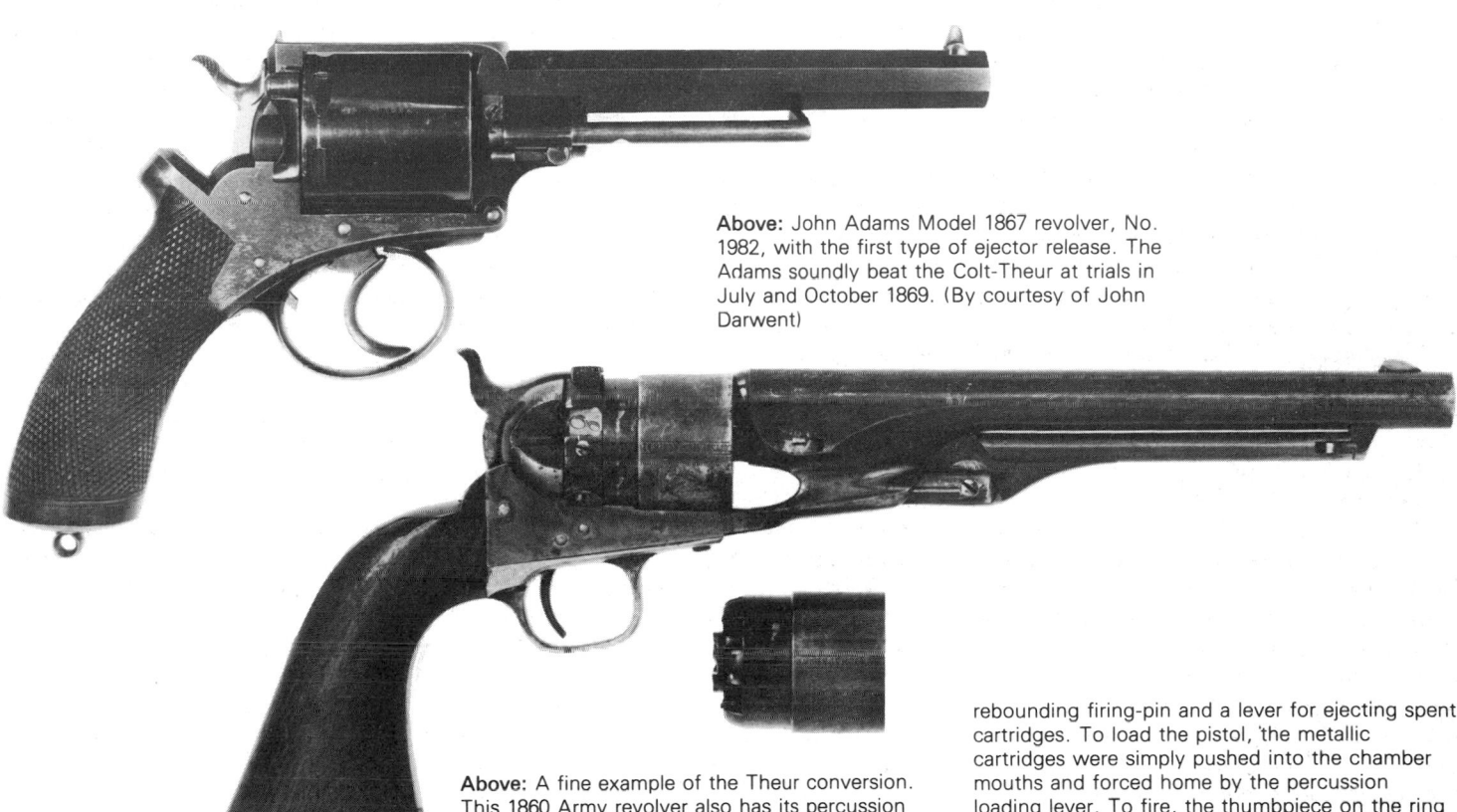

Above: John Adams Model 1867 revolver, No. 1982, with the first type of ejector release. The Adams soundly beat the Colt-Theur at trials in July and October 1869. (By courtesy of John Darwent)

Above: A fine example of the Theur conversion. This 1860 Army revolver also has its percussion interchangeable cylinder. The rear of the cylinder was cut off leaving a spindle-like projection containing the turning ratchet. Over this was slipped the collar or ring that was independent of the cylinder. Contained in the ring was a rebounding firing-pin and a lever for ejecting spent cartridges. To load the pistol, the metallic cartridges were simply pushed into the chamber mouths and forced home by the percussion loading lever. To fire, the thumbpiece on the ring was moved to the right of the hammer, and to eject, it was moved to the left — each cartridge was ejected by snapping the hammer which forced the empty shell out of the chamber. It was a slow and cumbersome system. (Private Collection)

AFTER the War the glut of arms was huge; the major manufacturers vied with one another to find outlets at home and overseas. Colt's scored over their rivals by having a London Agency through which many thousands of Navy, Army and other pistols, and at least 12,000 Springfield muskets converted to cartridge, were sold to Middle and Far East countries. But this was a short-term solution, for already Europe was replacing the percussion cap by various forms of fixed metallic ammunition, and by 1867 Colt's was being compared unfavourably with Smith & Wesson.

Colt's problem was not eased when, on 8 July 1868, the United States Ordnance Department circulated a memorandum which declared that although there was no urgency for metallic cartridge weapons, the

Board would, however, consider weapons 'altered on the two systems of loading at the front and rear of the cylinder, respectively', and would also be 'prepared for further trials at the Springfield Armory'. In an effort to avoid infringement of the Smith & Wesson's patent Colt's gave F. Alexander Theur, a long-time employee, the task of producing a front-loading metallic cartridge pistol. The result was the so-called 'Theur conversion'. Existing percussion revolvers were fitted with an interchangeable cylinder which accepted front-loaded metallic cartridges. Although popular in some parts of Europe, it was not favoured in the United States, and in 1869 the system was soundly defeated when tested against the British .450 calibre Model 1867 Adams Army revolver. This weapon fired centre-fire metallic ammunition and

was unaffected by Rollin White's patent (which will be discussed shortly). The Theur conversion did not answer their need, so Colt's had to think again.

A limited number of Remington .44 calibre New Model Army revolvers were converted from percussion to .46 calibre five-shot pistols by the U.S. Government at the Springfield Arsenal, but they were expensive, and Smith & Wesson were determined to maintain their monopoly. Here it is necessary to explain the complications experienced by Colt's, Remington and others when confronted by the Rollin White-Smith & Wesson monopoly.

The story really starts back in the early 1850s when the development of metallic ammunition in the United States was a slow starter. Sam Colt had little faith in the existing types, but a young man (who is reputed to have worked for Sam and offered him his idea which was refused) pursued the subject and on 3 April 1855 was granted a patent. His name was Rollin White.

His many talents were directed at whatever happened to interest him at the time but he was not a firearms man. So it was fortunate for him when, on 31 October 1856, he received a letter from Daniel B. Wesson of New Haven, Connecticut, asking for permission to utilize his system in the manufacture of firearms. This letter led to a revolution in firearms ammunition and ignition in the United States and to fifteen years of squabbling between White and his rivals, and it is still controversial.

Daniel B. Wesson and his elder brothers, Frank and Edwin, together with others, had been involved in the manufacture of firearms in Massachusetts for many years. In 1852 Daniel joined with Cortland Palmer of Norwich, Connecticut, and Horace Smith to manufacture firearms. Smith, who had worked at the Springfield Armory for eighteen years, met Daniel when they both worked as barrel makers for Allen, Brown & Luther, and they were fast friends. Smith patented a breech-loading rifle in 1851, and together with Palmer was anxious to produce a magazine rifle which they had both worked on, but it was not until 20 June 1854 that Smith & Wesson was in a position to manufacture a unique magazine pistol.

The weapon, protected by several patents, was manufactured at Norwich, and was produced in .30 calibre with a 4-inch barrel or .38 calibre with a 6- or 8-inch barrel. A few now extremely rare pistols were made in .44 calibre with 8- and 16-inch barrels, the latter provided with detachable stocks. The combined trigger guard/loading lever loaded and ejected ammunition placed in a tubular magazine set beneath the barrel. The ammunition consisted of a hollow-nosed bullet which contained its own primer and propellant. This owed its origin to the Frenchmen Houiller and Louis Flobert – the latter invented the BB cap, a small-calibre ball inserted into an oversized percussion cap. In 1849, Flobert had produced a metallic cartridge which contained powder and ball, and the rim was filled with fulminate which exploded when struck by the hammer. Thus was born the 'rim-fire' cartridge.

About 1,100 Smith & Wesson lever-action pistols were manufactured before the partners incorporated the firm under the name Volcanic Repeating Arms Company of New Haven, Connecticut in July 1855, turning over their machinery, parts, stock and patents. Smith remained for a period as factory manager before returning to Springfield, Massachusetts where, for a time, he ran a livery stable. Daniel Wesson in the meantime, continued as factory superintendent until February 1856, by which time the former partners had received a block of shares in the new company as a part payment from the recent sale. The Volcanic Repeating Arms Company (as we have noted) became a part of the New Haven Arms Company and eventually Winchester. But Smith and Wesson had reformed their own company and had plans of their own, and it was here that White really came into the picture.

The partners had developed an improved version of their rim-fire cartridge, but Colt's basic revolver patents were not due to expire until 1857, and they needed a weapon to accept their cartridge. They succeded in producing a prototype and were then confronted by White's patent. It was then that Wesson wrote to White. Within weeks the parties had met, and on 17 November 1854, White entered into an agreement with Smith & Wesson granting them exclusive rights to his system.

I suspect that Sam Colt was one of the first to obtain details of White's patent, and I imagine that he had a chuckle to himself when he examined it. Its only valid claim was the bored-through cylinder; the rest appears useless. But the bored-through cylinder was its strength. I doubt if Sam Colt was much concerned, for there is no evidence that he really contemplated centre- or rim-fire ammunition at this time. Rather, I think he was primarily concerned with protecting his patents and improving existing arms. Smith & Wesson, however, had other ideas. A combination of White's patent and the partners' joint revolver and cartridge design culminated in the first of their pistols which was produced in 1857, and despite legal attempts to disprove the validity of the claim, the company maintained a virtual monopoly of bored-through cylinder revolvers until April 1869 when the Rollin White patent expired.

The first weapons produced were a series of seven-shot .22 calibre revolvers. Termed the 'Model No. 1' they were born out of caution rather than competition with such as the large-calibre Colt and other makes of revolver. Experiments had revealed that the available copper cases could not take the pressures exerted by heavier loads. Indeed, even with the 2.6-grain loads prepared for the pistols, there were problems – some cases actually bulged from pressure! This frequently jammed the cylinder, and to prevent it, the company added a recoil shield on the rear of the chamber to stop it binding against the frame. In time, of course, the ammunition was improved and the problem diminished, but the small calibre remained a problem.

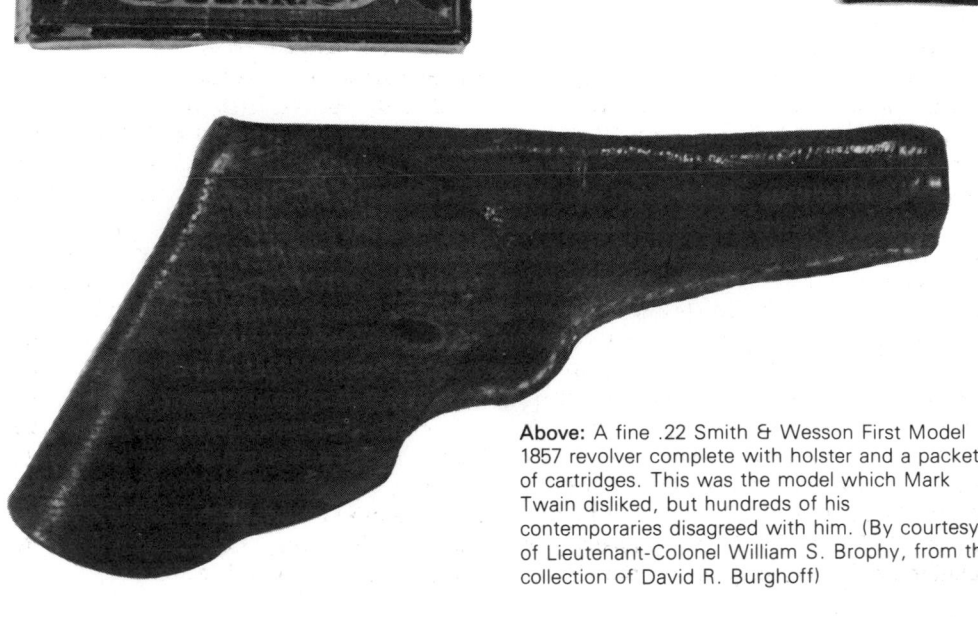

Above: A fine .22 Smith & Wesson First Model 1857 revolver complete with holster and a packet of cartridges. This was the model which Mark Twain disliked, but hundreds of his contemporaries disagreed with him. (By courtesy of Lieutenant-Colonel William S. Brophy, from the collection of David R. Burghoff)

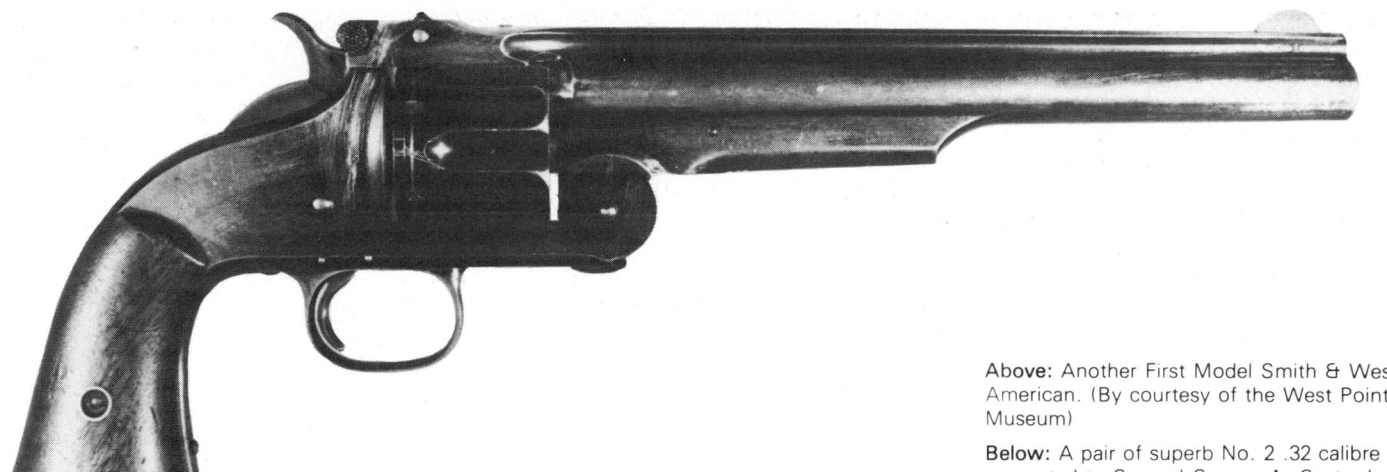

Above: Another First Model Smith & Wesson American. (By courtesy of the West Point Museum)

Below: A pair of superb No. 2 .32 calibre revolvers presented to General George A. Custer by J. B. Sutherland in 1869. Finely engraved and fitted with pearl grips, they were much prized by the General. (By courtesy of Dr. Lawrence Frost, M.D.)

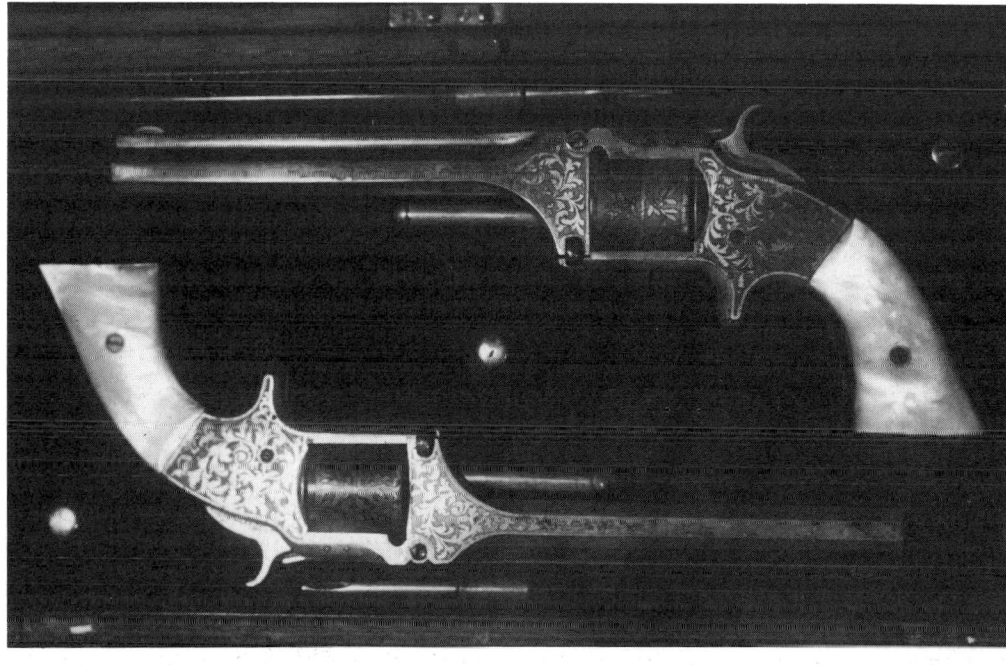

In principle, the .22 seven-shot Smith & Wesson revolvers were excellent. The frame and gripstraps were constructed in one piece (a brass casting which was either silver- or gold-plated), with the barrel hinged from the top of the frame and retained in position by a catch at the lower part. Attached to the $3\frac{3}{16}$ inch barrel was a rod for use as an ejector when the cylinder was released. With minor variations in grip shape (flared or bird's head), the .22 remained in production until 1881, and met with considerable success, although one disgruntled individual found fault with it. This was Mark Twain, who recalled his objections in *Roughing It*:

'I was armed to the teeth with a pitiful little Smith & Wesson's seven-shooter, which carried a ball like a homeopathic pill, and it took the whole seven to make a dose for an adult. But I thought it was grand. It appeared to me to be a dangerous weapon. It only had one fault – you could not hit anything with it. One of our "conductors" [shotgun guard] practiced a while on a cow with it, and as long as she stood still and behaved herself she was safe; but as soon as she went to moving about, and he got to shooting at other things, she came to grief.'

The early Smith & Wesson revolvers are confusing to record because they were not named, but numbered. The 'Model No. 1', used by Mr. Twain, appeared in several variants between 1857 and 1881, featuring improvements in the cylinder-turning ratchet, the shape of barrel, frame and grips (bird's head or flared – the latter probably the most popular). Many of these weapons were put up in pairs in wooden or gutta-percha cases, and were very popular with travellers and people who wanted something small as a 'hide-out' weapon, for despite the calibre, the .22 was deadly at close range.

From 1865 until 1892, the company also manufactured what they called the 'Model No. 1½' in First, Second and 'Old Model', in .32 calibre. In general they resembled the Model No. 1 and enjoyed large sales. In competition with this version was the 'Model No. 2' in .32 calibre, first introduced in 1861 and manufactured until about 1874, by which time an estimated 77,155 had been manufactured. During the Civil War this particular model was popular with officers and has often been called the 'Army' model, but this was not a company definition. It was one of these revolvers, serial No. 30619 that was alleged to have been found on Wild Bill Hickok's body when he was killed at Deadwood. According to the family in Canada who owned it as late as 1961, it was given by Charlie Utter to a Captain Willoth, and, following his death, it passed through several hands before ending up in Canada. No real evidence, however, has been found to connect the pistol with Hickok.

The No. 2 differed from its contemporaries from the Smith & Wesson stable in that it had a wrought iron frame, and it was produced in barrel lengths of four, five and six inches, the last size being the most popular. Enlisted men as well as officers expressed an interest in the No. 2 and sales were brisk, but the calibres were still too small. As early as 1862 it was decided to produce a .44 calibre version, although a suitable design was not evolved until 1869.

In the immediate postwar years, Smith & Wesson (as we have noted) permitted the conversion under licence of a number of Remington pistols to .46 calibre five-shooters, the existing frame being too small to accept six-shot cylinders in that calibre. There was no ejector and the conversion was not a great success. But an estimated 4,541 Remingtons were converted before the patent expired.

Smith & Wesson had wrestled with the problem of producing their own large-calibre pistol before their patent expired, and their decision to settle for the .44 was calculated. The .44 calibre had been popular in long arms and pistols for years, but Sam Colt's use of it in his revolvers firmly established it as a 'man-stopper'.

As early as February 1864 Smith & Wesson were negotiating with Eli Whitney, Junior, to produce 3,000 revolvers for military use which had been ordered from them by Cooper & Pond. Smith & Wesson were prepared to supply cartridges, but before the project could get started, Rollin White raised objections about licensing and the idea was shelved. White, meantime, through his own company, the Rollin White Arms Company, developed a prototype revolver which greatly impressed Smith & Wesson who tentatively agreed to manufacture 5,000 of them. White was agreeable, but this time it was William C. Dodge, the designer of the extractor, who posed problems. Before any firm decision could be made the Civil War ended and with it the demand for large-calibre military revolvers.

Undaunted, by 1866 the partners had placed before the Board of Ordnance a revolver which they described as 'too heavy' for general military use but ideal for the cavalry service. The Ordnance, however, were not impressed. The Paris Exhibition for 1867 was looming, and in his book *Smith & Wesson Revolvers*, the late John E. Parsons noted that the company got up a prototype 'No. 3 Model' revolver in .41 calibre. The four-shot weapon weighed just one pound, and the sample was dispatched to Paris, but although admired, none was sold.

In 1869 the tide turned against Smith & Wesson in one respect, but spurred them to

Below: An almost 'as new' No. 2 Smith & Wesson .32 complete with its original holster and a box of cartridges. The No. 2 was extremely popular with troops and officers during the Civil War (some writers have even dubbed it the 'Officer's Model') and after the war it became popular out West as a 'hide-out' gun. Wild Bill Hickok was alleged to have been carrying one of these when he was killed, but the evidence is not conclusive. (By courtesy of Lieutenant-Colonel William S. Brophy, from the collection of David R. Burghoff)

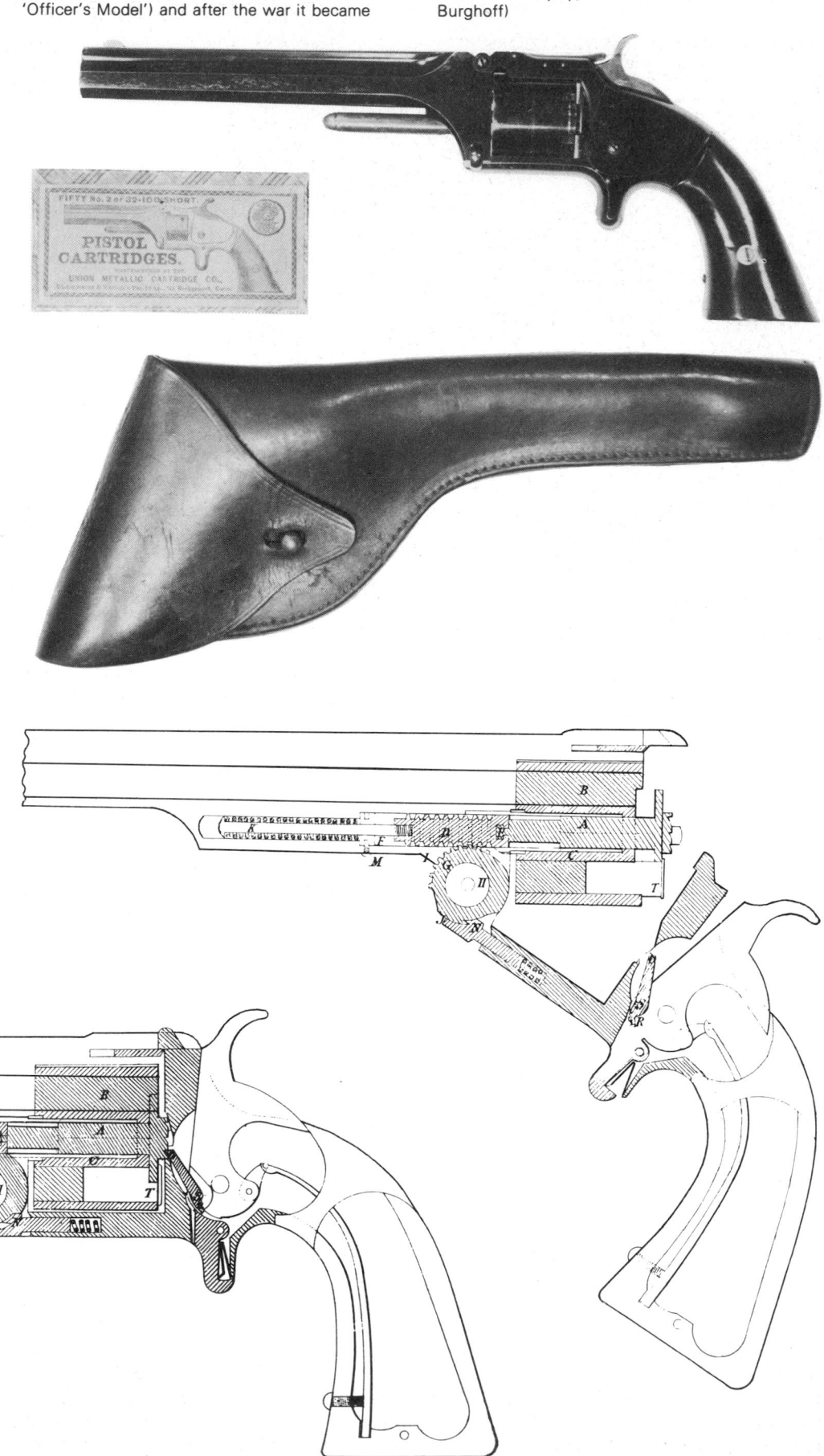

Above: The Smith & Wesson break-open action of 1869, from the British patent granted on 17 May of that year. The break-open action shows how the ejector rides up the ratchet to eject spent cases before snapping back into position.

Above: A most interesting relic of the Old West. John B. Omohundro, *alias* Texas Jack, acquired this pistol when he was living at Cottonwood Springs, Nebraska, and as was common at the time, had his name, location and the date engraved on it (evidently there was not room for the 's' in springs). Many years later Herschel C. Logan acquired the pistol and as a result wrote the only known biography of this intrepid plainsman and Indian scout (*Buckskin and Satin*, 1954). The barrel is marked U.S. and the serial No. is 2008, which suggests that the pistol was an Army issue, possibly presented to Jack for services rendered. (By courtesy of Herschel C. Logan)

Left: Texas Jack Omohundro photographed in stage costume, circa 1872–73. His pistols are a pair of fine ivory-butted Colt Navys. (By courtesy of Herb Peck, Junior)

greater efforts to produce a practicable 'No. 3'. In April their patent expired, and the Government refused to renew it. It was claimed that this was on the direct orders of President Grant who felt that to pay 'parties already well paid a large royalty for altering its revolvers to use metallic cartridges', was unreasonable and would cost the Government money. Besides, it was believed in Washington that Grant had been influenced by the Ordnance Department who had not forgiven Smith & Wesson for their refusal to make full use of their system during the late war. The way was now clear for Colt's, Remington's and others to produce their own metallic cartridge revolvers, and neither company wasted any time.

Despite the loss of their monopoly, Smith & Wesson continued their efforts to produce a large-calibre revolver and after further experiments and problems with patents (many of which were bought out), the final version of the 'No. 3' was ready early in 1869. On 17 May a British patent was filed which clearly shows the hinged barrel and ratchet-operated extractor which was the brain-child of Charles A. King, superintendent of the Smith & Wesson factory from 1867 until 1874. The No. 3 prototype was ready in May 1870 and was submitted to the Board of Ordnance for trial. In its report the Board concluded: 'The Smith & Wesson is decidedly superior to any other revolver

submitted. It should be modified as follows, viz: Made center fire; the cylinder lengthened so as to close the space in front of the breech-block, and counter-sunk to cover the rim of the cartridge, caliber increased to standard.'

The company made several modifications, and on 30 July they quoted a price of $14.25 each to make 2,000 revolvers for military use. One thousand pistols were ordered on 28 December 1870, and two completed revolvers were supplied for use as inspection models. In the meantime, specimens of the new revolver were also sent to representatives of foreign governments – despite the expiration of the Rollin White patent on 3 April 1869, they still had the advantage over most of their rivals.

The army order revolvers were shipped on 16 March 1871, following inspection at the factory. About 200 of them were nickel-plated and the remainder blued. This was the first bulk issue of centre-fire revolvers to the United States Army, and Smith & Wesson were delighted at its success. Mr. Parsons quotes a number of comments (he told me that there were enough to fill a volume) praising and criticising the weapons, all of which were duly noted by the company. Captain Robert H. Young of the 7th Cavalry, wrote from Louisa, Kentucky on 18 May 1872, and complimented them upon the 8-inch barrelled version, which shot very

well, but he wondered if they could also supply a 5- or 6-inch model. Apparently, the long barrel tended to 'punch' against his horse's back and the saddle, and the captain only wanted a pistol for use at very close quarters, 'say not more than ten yards distance . . .'

Probably the most important feature of the No. 3 was its method of loading and ejecting. By releasing a catch in front of the hammer the barrel dropped forward. Thus the pistol could be loaded at speed, or ejected in the same manner, for as the barrel tipped down the ejector rose and ejected all the shells in the chambers, before springing back into position. The only problem, of course, was that should one fire only one or two rounds and decide to reload, all the cartridges would be ejected, and end up spread across the prairie if one were on the back of a galloping horse!

These were minor problems when set against the overall worth of the pistol. Its reputation was soon established, and orders for it were received from all parts of the West. Buffalo Bill Cody ordered a pair of No. 3s, as did his scouting friend and stage companion, Texas Jack Omohundro, and there is evidence that Wild Bill Hickok was also a customer, or at least the recipient of a pair of No. 3s. To date, however, no correspondence has been found in the company's files concerning Hickok, or from

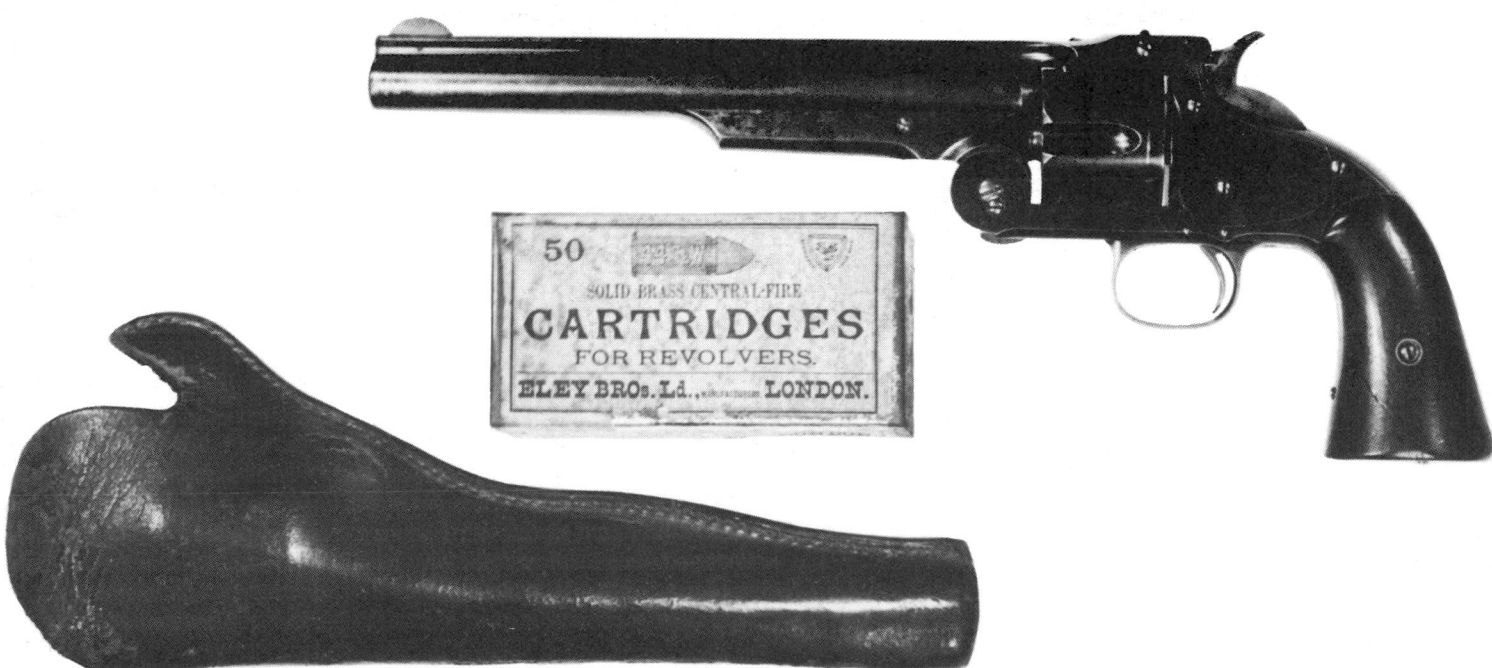

Top: In 1872 Buffalo Bill Cody formed a theatrical combination which toured the Eastern states. In September 1873 he persuaded his old friend, Wild Bill Hickok, to join him and this photograph was made in the autumn of that year. Left to right: Elisha Green, Wild Bill, Buffalo Bill, Texas Jack Omohundro and Eugene Overton. Despite the theatrical costume, the five men are armed with up-to-date Colt and Smith & Wesson revolvers. Cody and Omohundro are holding Remington rolling-block rifles. (By courtesy of the Denver Public Library, Western Collection)

Above: The original No. 3, later called the 'American' model, first by those anxious to distinguish it from contemporary Russian-issue weapons, and later by Smith & Wesson. Trials in 1870 resulted in its adoption into Government service. Note the box of Eley Brothers cartridges (a real rarity!) and the reverse-draw holster to allow the pistol to be worn butt forward on the right hip. (By courtesy of Lieutenant-Colonel William S. Brophy, from the collection of David R. Burghoff)

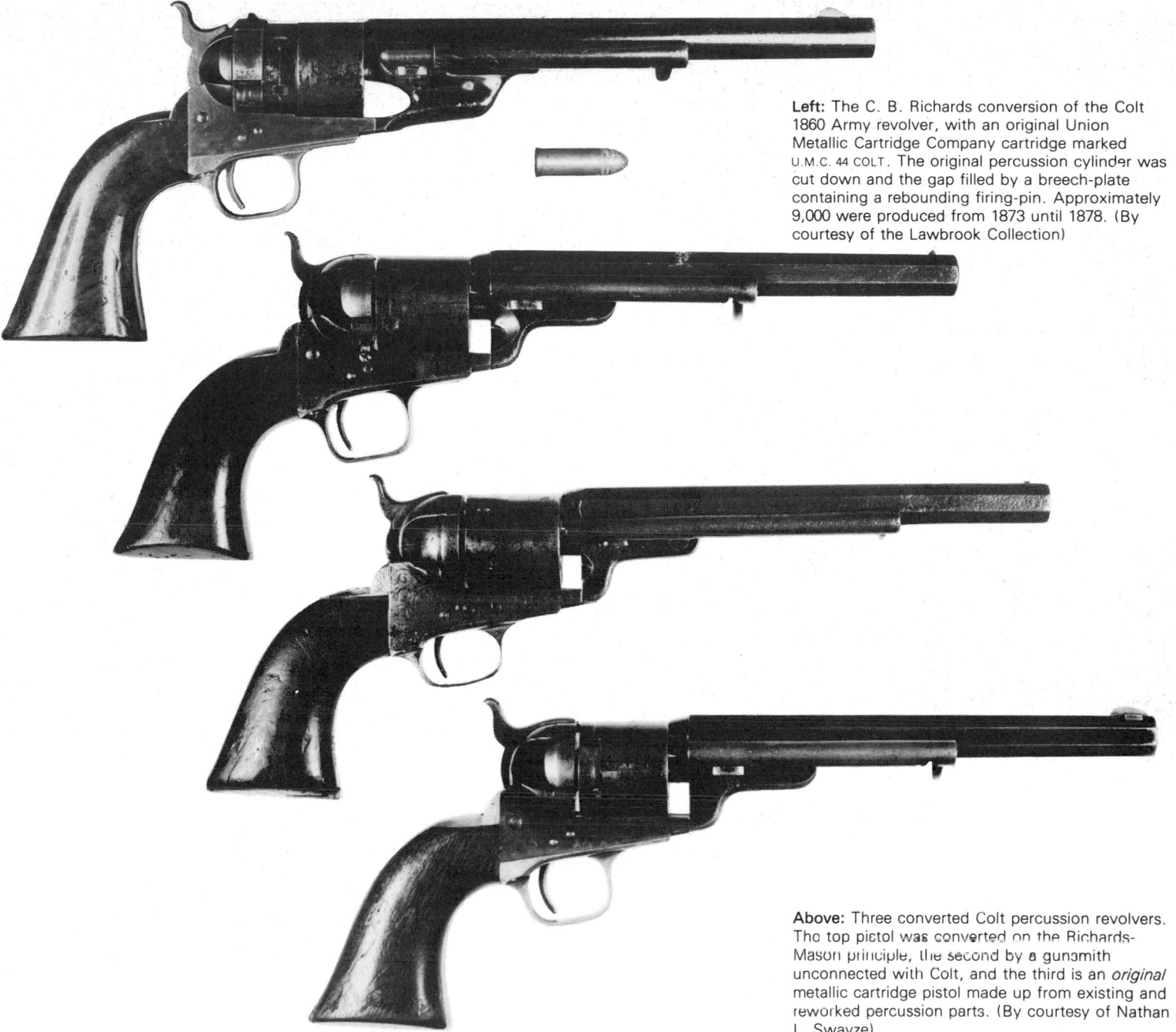

Left: The C. B. Richards conversion of the Colt 1860 Army revolver, with an original Union Metallic Cartridge Company cartridge marked U.M.C. 44 COLT. The original percussion cylinder was cut down and the gap filled by a breech-plate containing a rebounding firing-pin. Approximately 9,000 were produced from 1873 until 1878. (By courtesy of the Lawbrook Collection)

Above: Three converted Colt percussion revolvers. The top pistol was converted on the Richards-Mason principle, the second by a gunsmith unconnected with Colt, and the third is an *original* metallic cartridge pistol made up from existing and reworked percussion parts. (By courtesy of Nathan L. Swayze)

him, and much of the old correspondence has been destroyed in recent years. However, we do know that when he quit Cody's theatrical 'Combination' at Rochester, New York in March 1874, Wild Bill was presented with two pistols, one from Cody and one from Omohundro. Months later an as yet unidentified newspaper claimed that he had been interviewed in Colorado and was then carrying a 'pair of heavy Smith & Wesson revolvers, which shoot nearly as accurately as rifles'.

Smith & Wesson's initial advantage over their rivals was short-lived, for both Colt's and Remington's were now hard upon their heels. Following the Theur disaster and the expiration of White's patent, C. B. Richards and William Mason, engineer-designers employed by Colt's individually or in joint ventures, converted existing Colt percussion revolvers to accept metallic ammunition in both rim- and centre-fire. These modifications culminated in the famous open-frame Model 1872; a weapon which was soon superseded by the Model 1873, though an estimated 7,000 of them were produced and were well received out West. Today they are eagerly sought by collectors.

A major problem which confronted both Richards and Mason was that they were confined to existing concepts, and their modifications were restricted to loading and unloading systems rather than actions or other changes. Consequently, Sam Colt's original 1846 single-action mechanism was retained with little change. In 1872, how-ever, the Ordnance Department expressed an interest in 'strap' pistols (that is, with cylinders enclosed in a solid frame), and it was then that William Mason came up with the ideal compromise. He retained the original Navy frame, but built it up into a solid form; the recoil shield was enlarged to conform to a cylinder of greater diameter, and a screwed-in barrel was fitted. A spring-loaded 'gate' was let into the side of the recoil shield to facilitate loading and unloading the metallic cartridges, and ejection was achieved by a spring-loaded plunger contained in a tube screwed alongside the barrel. Finally, a minor but important change affected the hammer spur: the shape of the percussion hammers was altered from a right-angle to an almost in-line spur. Thus, a

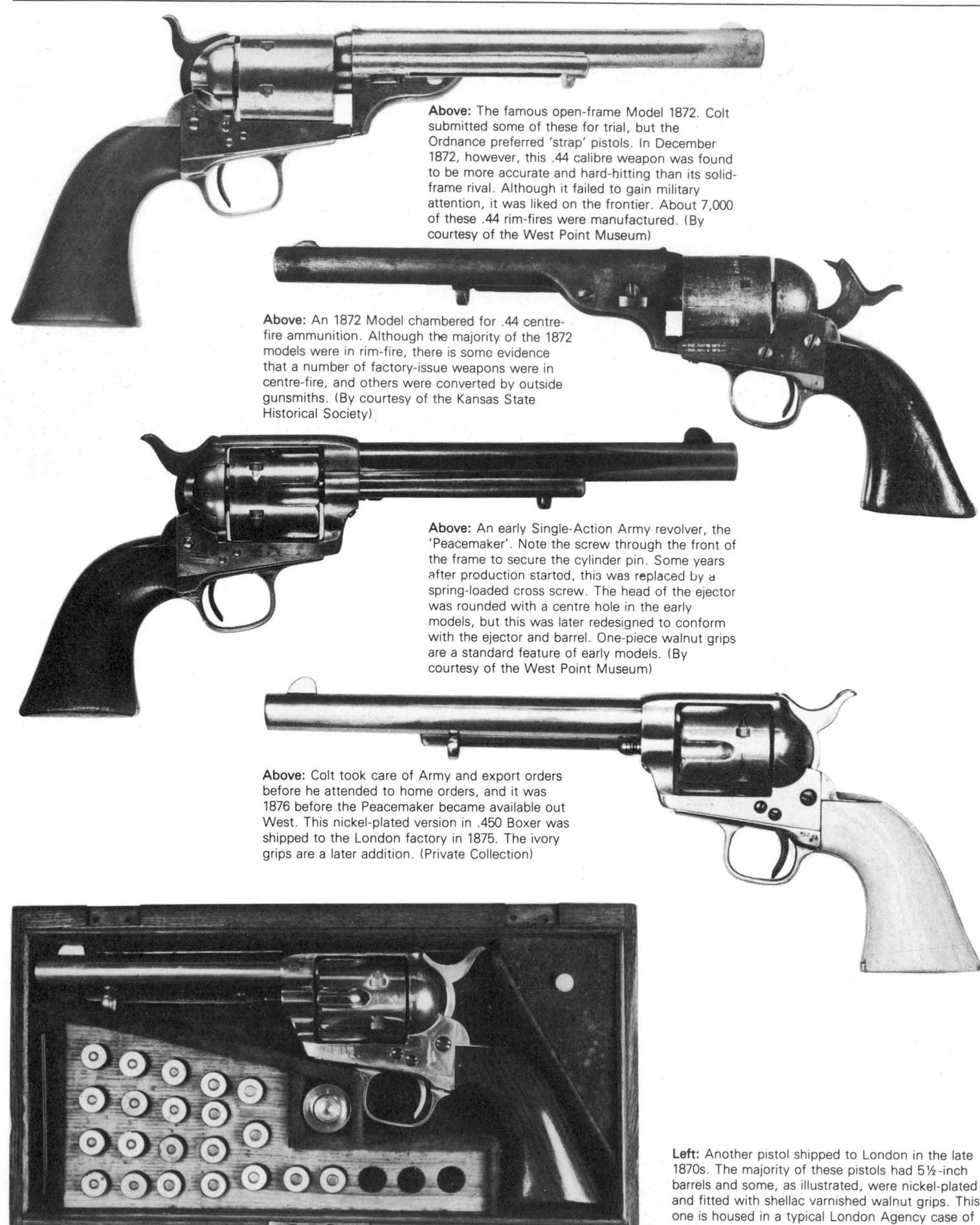

Above: The famous open-frame Model 1872. Colt submitted some of these for trial, but the Ordnance preferred 'strap' pistols. In December 1872, however, this .44 calibre weapon was found to be more accurate and hard-hitting than its solid-frame rival. Although it failed to gain military attention, it was liked on the frontier. About 7,000 of these .44 rim-fires were manufactured. (By courtesy of the West Point Museum)

Above: An 1872 Model chambered for .44 centre-fire ammunition. Although the majority of the 1872 models were in rim-fire, there is some evidence that a number of factory-issue weapons were in centre-fire, and others were converted by outside gunsmiths. (By courtesy of the Kansas State Historical Society)

Above: An early Single-Action Army revolver, the 'Peacemaker'. Note the screw through the front of the frame to secure the cylinder pin. Some years after production started, this was replaced by a spring-loaded cross screw. The head of the ejector was rounded with a centre hole in the early models, but this was later redesigned to conform with the ejector and barrel. One-piece walnut grips are a standard feature of early models. (By courtesy of the West Point Museum)

Above: Colt took care of Army and export orders before he attended to home orders, and it was 1876 before the Peacemaker became available out West. This nickel-plated version in .450 Boxer was shipped to the London factory in 1875. The ivory grips are a later addition. (Private Collection)

Left: Another pistol shipped to London in the late 1870s. The majority of these pistols had 5½-inch barrels and some, as illustrated, were nickel-plated and fitted with shellac varnished walnut grips. This one is housed in a typical London Agency case of the period. (By courtesy of the Lawbrook Collection)

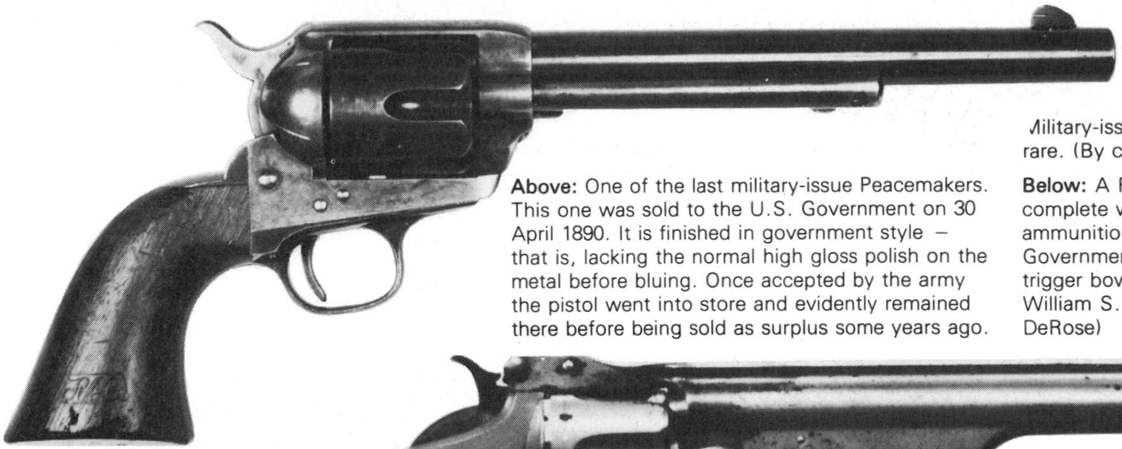

Above: One of the last military-issue Peacemakers. This one was sold to the U.S. Government on 30 April 1890. It is finished in government style – that is, lacking the normal high gloss polish on the metal before bluing. Once accepted by the army the pistol went into store and evidently remained there before being sold as surplus some years ago. Military-issue pistols in this condition are extremely rare. (By courtesy of the Lawbrook Collection)

Below: A First Model 'Russian' Smith & Wesson complete with cross-draw holster and a box of ammunition. Later versions sold to the Russian Government had the distinctive spur added to the trigger bow. (By courtesy of Lieutenant-Colonel William S. Brophy, from the collection of Peter DeRose)

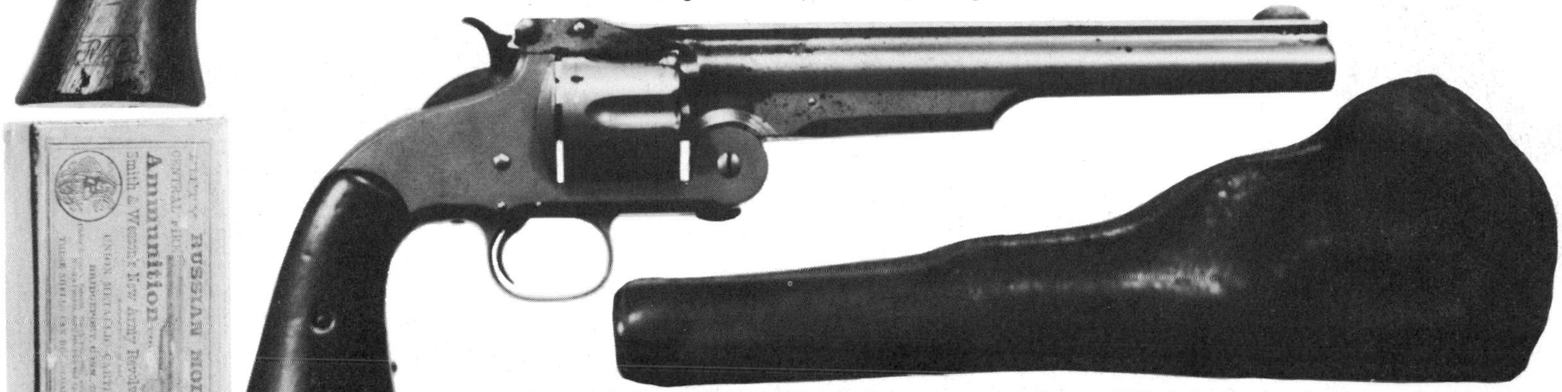

Below left: The 1873 Model 'Russian' complete with trigger bow spur and a lanyard ring. The holster is either left-handed or a cross-draw, and the box of cartridges indicates how popular the .44 'Russian' round was as several makers produced them. (By courtesy of Lieutenant-Colonel William S. Brophy, from the collection of David Burghoff)

Below right: A contemporary Colt broadsheet, circa 1873. (Author's Collection)

COLT'S

New Model Army Metallic Cartridge Revolving Pistol.

The Drawing is one-half the size of the Pistol.

It has been adopted by the War Department for the Cavalry Service of the United States.

cal. .45 inch. PRICE, $20.00

The length of the pistol is 12½ inches; length of barrel, 7½ inches; its bore or calibre, .45 inch. Weight, 2 lbs. 5 oz. Rifling, six grooves, one revolution in 16 inches; depth of groove, .005 inch. Number of chambers in cylinder, six. *It has a solid frame, case hardened.*

CARTRIDGE. Weight of powder, [illegible] grains; weight of lead, 250 grains. Central fire, external priming.

IT DIFFERS FROM OTHER REVOLVERS IN THE FOLLOWING POINTS, VIZ :

The hand, or finger, or pawl, which revolves the cylinder has two points, one above the other. The upper engages the ratchet of the cylinder when the revolution begins. But before the necessary sixth of a revolution could be made, as the pawl moves in a plane, and the ratchet tooth in the arc of a circle whose plane is perpendicular to the pawl's plane of motion, the pawl would lose its hold on the tooth, and the revolution of the cylinder would stop. To prevent this, the second point is added, and just as the first point will disengage from the ratchet, the second or lower point engages another tooth of the ratchet and completes the revolution. By this arrangement the pawl actuates a larger ratchet than it could otherwise, and therefore exerts more force upon the cylinder, by acting upon a longer lever-arm. This permits a smaller sized cylinder for the same diameter of ratchet.

The cylinder has a bushing, which projects in front of it, and gives three surfaces upon which the cylinder revolves, thus diminishing the chance of sticking from dirt or rust, and also giving a very small axis upon which to revolve, decreasing the moment of friction.

When the ejector is used it springs back to its place and is ready for use again, avoiding the necessity of putting it back.

TO TAKE APART THE PISTOL. Half-cock the pistol, loosen the catch screw which holds the centre-pin, draw out the centre-pin, open the gate, and the cylinder can then be withdrawn.

To remove the ejector, turn out the ejector tube screw, then push the front end away from the barrel and pull it towards the muzzle. The barrel can then be unscrewed.

The stock can be removed by turning out the two screws just behind the hammer and that at the bottom of the strap. All the parts of the lock are then displayed and can be readily separated.

The cylinder bushing should be pushed out for cleaning.

To remove the gate, turn out a screw in the lower side of the frame, (hidden by the trigger guard,) then the gate spring and catch can be withdrawn, and the gate can be pushed out. The best sperm oil should be used for oiling the parts.

TO LOAD THE PISTOL. 1st motion; holding the pistol in the left hand, muzzle downwards, half cock it with the right hand and open the gate. 2d motion: insert the cartridges in succession, with the right hand, close the gate, cock and fire it, (taking it in the right hand,) or bring the hammer to the safety notch, as may be desired.

TO EJECT THE CARTRIDGE SHELLS. 1st motion: holding the pistol in the left hand, half cock with the right hand and open the gate. 2d motion: eject the shells in succession with the ejector pushed by the right hand, moving the cylinder with the thumb and forefinger of the left hand. When the shells have been ejected, the pistol is ready for the 2d motion of loading.

N. B. There are three notches in the hammer of this pistol. The first is the safety notch, the second is the half cock notch, and the third is the cock notch. The pistol cannot be fired when the hammer rests in the safety notch or half-cock notch, and can be fired by pulling the trigger when the hammer rests in the cock notch. The pistol should be carried habitually with the hammer resting in the safety notch.

COLT'S NEW .22 PISTOL, SEVEN SHOT.

PRICE, $8.00

TERMS CASH.

All Communications must be addressed to

Colt's Patent Fire-Arms Manufacturing Company,

HARTFORD, CONN., U. S. A.

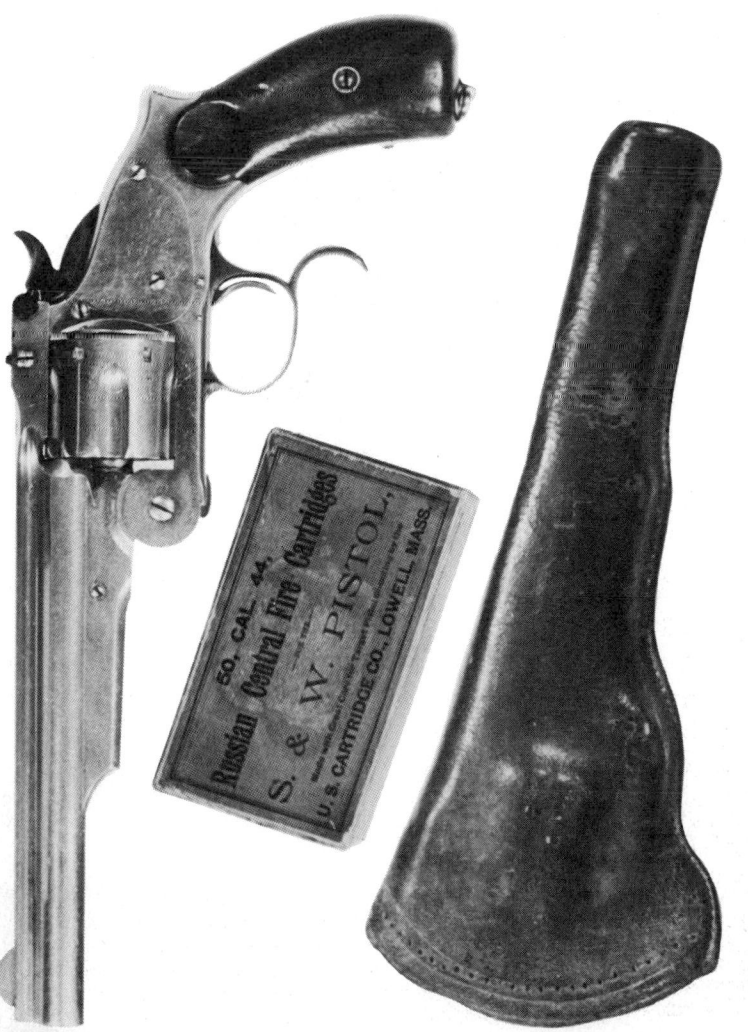

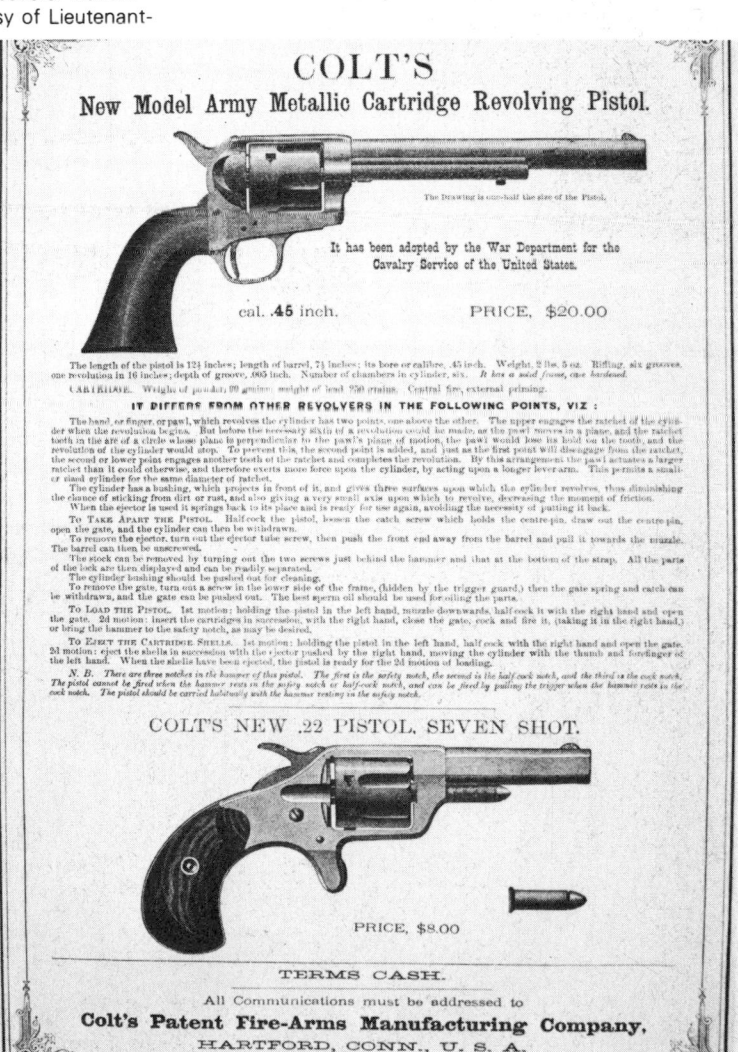

horseman merely had to bring his rein hand down to cock the pistol, rather than backwards, which might jerk the reins.

Initially, some thought was given to including the grip length of the 1860 Army, but finally it was decided to retain the Navy-size grips, and tests confirmed the decision. When unloaded the pistol weighed three pounds, but its balance and ease of handling made it seem lighter. Years later, Mason intimated that he would have altered the action also, but he did not have the time. The company was pleased with the result, and promptly informed the Board of Ordnance that the pistol was available for trial. The Board expressed interest, and in November 1872, two pistols were dispatched to Washington. Unfortunately, when they arrived it was found that they had been chambered for .44 Smith & Wesson 'Russian' ammunition (which we will discuss later) rather than the standard .44 then in service. Once the mistake was realized, Colt's hastily dispatched replacement pistols, and by December the substitute weapons were ready for trial against the Smith & Wesson No. 3.

During the tests, both weapons were fired more than 800 times. The Colt functioned well, but the Smith & Wesson tended to clog and proved difficult to dismantle. The Colt, with fewer parts, was more rugged and was unaffected by fouling. The No. 3's principal advantage was its means of ejection at speed, whereas the Colt required both hands and the rod ejector was slow.

Accuracy tests from a rest indicated that at 50 yards the Colt had a radius (or 'grouping within the circle') of 3.11 inches compared to 4.39 inches for the Smith & Wesson. Penetration at 25 yards was 4.1 inches for the Colt and 3.55 for the Smith and Wesson. Ironically, during the trials, the Board also included a .44 calibre Colt Model 1872 open-frame pistol, which proved to be more accurate and capable of greater penetration than its 'strap' rivals! The Board, however, preferred the strap pistol, stating that it was a great improvement; it was stronger and it was 'more readily dismounted for cleaning'. That conclusion heralded the end of an era; the open-frame was now obsolete.

During the following months Colt's negotiated with the Board to gain orders. On 15 May 1873 the Ordnance came up with a revolutionary request: could the new pistol be chambered for .45 instead of .44 calibre? Colt's readily agreed, and advised the Ordnance that they had been experimenting with some new rifling. Up to that time, the majority of Colt's revolvers had been manufactured with a left or right twist, seven-groove 'gain twist' rifling. This means that the number of turns in the rifling increases

as it nears the muzzle. Now, however, the company had produced a six-groove version giving one turn in sixteen inches with narrow lands (these are the raised part of the rifling as opposed to the grooves). The change was approved by the Ordnance Department, and by June production of the 'Model 1873' was well advanced.

On 26 June 1873 the U.S. Government accepted the Board's findings that the new Colt revolver was superior to those tried against it, and the 'Chief of Ordnance has been authorized by the War Department to purchase 8,000 of these arms for the cavalry arm of the service'. A contract was drawn up on 23 July and by November 1,000 revolvers had been produced, but it was late in 1874 before the first government contract was completed. Chambered for the .45 centre-fire long-cased cartridge, the bullet weight was 230 grains, and the charge was forty grains. But the army, concerned about recoil (and on the orders of the War Department) underloaded the cartridges to 28 grains which was considered adequate for their needs – the pistol was still capable of imparting a good 'punch' at normal pistol ranges.

Early specimens of the new revolver were fitted with German silver front sights, but when the army showed a preference for steel, the machinery was modified so that the barrels were slotted to accept blanks which were then machined to shape when in position. The pistols were then sighted in for 25 yards.

In August 1874, the Board seriously considered shortening the barrel of the Model 1873. Colt's were requested to supply two pistols with 5½- and 6½-inch barrels for test. Following trials for penetration and accuracy, it was decided that 'the entire performance of the 7½-inch' was best suited for military use.

Late in 1874 when most of the military contracts had been filled, Colt's started advertising the new pistols to the trade and the public. It was at this point that the name 'Peacemaker' began to appear in advertisements. The factory may have coined the name (perhaps someone recalled that Sam Walker had once described Sam Colt as a 'peacemaker'), or perhaps it was one of their 'allies' (dealers). However, the term 'Peacemaker' had a much more romantic ring to it than 'Colt's New Model Army Metallic Cartridge Revolving Pistol'. The 'Peacemaker' was an immediate success in name and popularity, and the name today is generic for all Colt Single Action Army revolvers.

Despite the great demand for their new pistol, Colt's concentrated upon the army and overseas orders before satisfying home demand. The retail price of the pistol was $17.00, but the 'allies' were able to purchase them for $10.50, an agreement which caused

friction with the Government who were paying $13. However, when it was explained that the 'allies' paid for Colt's advertising, the authorities were mollified, especially when their orders took precedence over civilian demand until 1876.

Colt's were surprised to learn that when the new pistol reached England it was not popular. The London Agency manager, F. C. von Oppen, ordered about 1,000 pistols between 1874 and 1877. Sales were never brisk, but he did manage to sell a number of them to army officers, many of whom also purchased the metal skeleton stocks which the company produced to convert the pistols to carbines. The real problem, von Oppen reported, when a pistol he had submitted for trial was returned unfired by the British Government, was that single-action pistols were no longer viable in Europe where 'double-acting, self-extracting' weapons were very much the norm.

But Europe was not America where double-action pistols were in the minority in the 1870s. In many parts of the continent, especially in the Western states, they were viewed with deep suspicion. However, the problem of improved actions, although a priority, did not concern Colt's quite so much as did improving available ammunition. By 1878 it was considered reliable enough for them to contemplate the introduction of pistols in .44–40 calibre to accept the Winchester rifle cartridge or vice versa. The pistols chambered for this ammunition were easily identifiable by the words FRONTIER SIX-SHOOTER etched on the left side of the barrel. So perhaps at this point we should clarify the proper definition of a 'Peacemaker'. This was the 'Cavalry' revolver with a 7½-inch barrel and chambered for the .45 long Colt cartridge. In 1895 (and until about 1903) a number of these pistols were returned to the company, repaired and refinished, with the barrels cut back to 5½ inches. They were known as the 'Artillery' model. From the late 1870s until now, pistols fitted with 4¾-inch barrels (the same length as the ejector housing), and regardless of calibre, are called 'Civilian' models. Therefore, a true 'Peacemaker' is in .45 calibre, and a 'Frontier Six-Shooter' in .44–40.

Outside the United States, the term 'Peacemaker' was rarely used, it being more usually referred to as 'Colt's Government Revolver', whereas the .44–40 was described as the 'Frontier Revolver' – inspired no doubt by the barrel etching. By 1902, however, Colt's English and American catalogues described the model as the 'Single Action Army', and listed eight available calibres from .32 to .45. During its long career the pistol was chambered for the smallest .22 and the largest, the .476 calibre Eley.

Meanwhile, Smith & Wesson had not been idle. Their concern for foreign sales led eventually to a contract with the Russian Government that was one of the largest the company ever won. Following negotiations with Major-General Alexander Gorloff, the Russian military attaché in Washington, a contract for 2,000 revolvers was drawn up in March 1871, which was later extended for several years. The initial contract stated that the weapons were to be supplied for $13 each in gold within ten months. This was cut down to seven months when the Russians agreed to advance $50,000 for tooling, *et cetera*. A further contract was signed for 20,000 pistols at $13.02 gold per weapon.

The Russians were very thorough: a special barrel stamping was requested and the additon of a lanyard swivel. Later, as work progressed and the further contract was negotiated, a number of changes were requested, the most important being the addition of a spur to the trigger guard. The Russians thought this was of 'great value', and with the creation of a special .44 'Russian' cartridge, the pistol was established as a distinct model in its own right. Mr. Parsons reports that although the bore of the Russian Model barrel was identical with the standard No. 3 revolver (.419 inches between the lands), the chamber of the cylinder was of a greater diameter – .433 to .458. In 1873 the specification drawn up for the Russian round showed cartridge: total weight 369 grams, length 1.448 inches; bullet: diameter .429 inches, length .775 inches, weight 275 grams plus 23 grains of powder.

On 7 December 1871 the Grand Duke Alexis visited Smith & Wesson's factory. He was the guest of the United States Government and a visit to the factory was considered of importance. In honour of the occasion, the company presented him with a fine cased No. 3 revolver, described by the local press as 'inlaid with gold, having a pearl butt upon which were the coats of arms of America and Russia, and inclosed into a rosewood case, bearing the inscription "From S & W to A. A." ' Some weeks later, when the Duke, accompanied by General Custer and coached by Buffalo Bill, went on a buffalo hunt, he fired all six shots from his pistol, but failed to bring down a 'beastly bison'.

Curiously, some years ago, the writer was advised by the late Escott North, a former cowboy and gun collector, that he believed he owned the original pistol presented to the Archduke, and described it as a 'Russian Model' complete with engraving and ivory grips. When I tactfully pointed out that the original presentation pistol had been fitted with pearl grips engraved with the two coats of arms, he retorted that he found no reason to think that his informant was in error, and besides: 'The artist who could engrave the Russian coat of arms on one side of the ivory grips, and the U.S. coat of arms on the other would be a miniaturist's dream of an artist!'

The success of the Russian Model and the continuing demand for the No. 3 led to a designation of the latter that the company thought was good for sales. Once news of the 'Russian' model got about, intending purchasers defined their requirements by the simple use of the words 'Russian' or 'American' Models. The company eventually appreciated the compliment, and by 1874 (the last year that the original No. 3 was sold direct from the factory) they, too, began calling it the 'American' Model.

An unlikely publicist for Smith & Wesson emerged in the early 1870s. This was Brevet Colonel George W. Schofield, a major in the 10th Cavalry, stationed at Fort Leavenworth. He was the younger brother of General John M. Schofield, who presided over the Small Arms Board in 1870 which had tested the No. 3 and recommended its adoption. His enthusiasm for the pistol affected his younger brother, who not only purchased one, but attempted to persuade his brother officers to buy it too. Smith & Wesson were impressed by his enthusiasm and offered to supply pistols to him wholesale; soon, he had sold more than 100 of them. But the Colonel was also inventive. Between 1871 and 1875 he made a number of

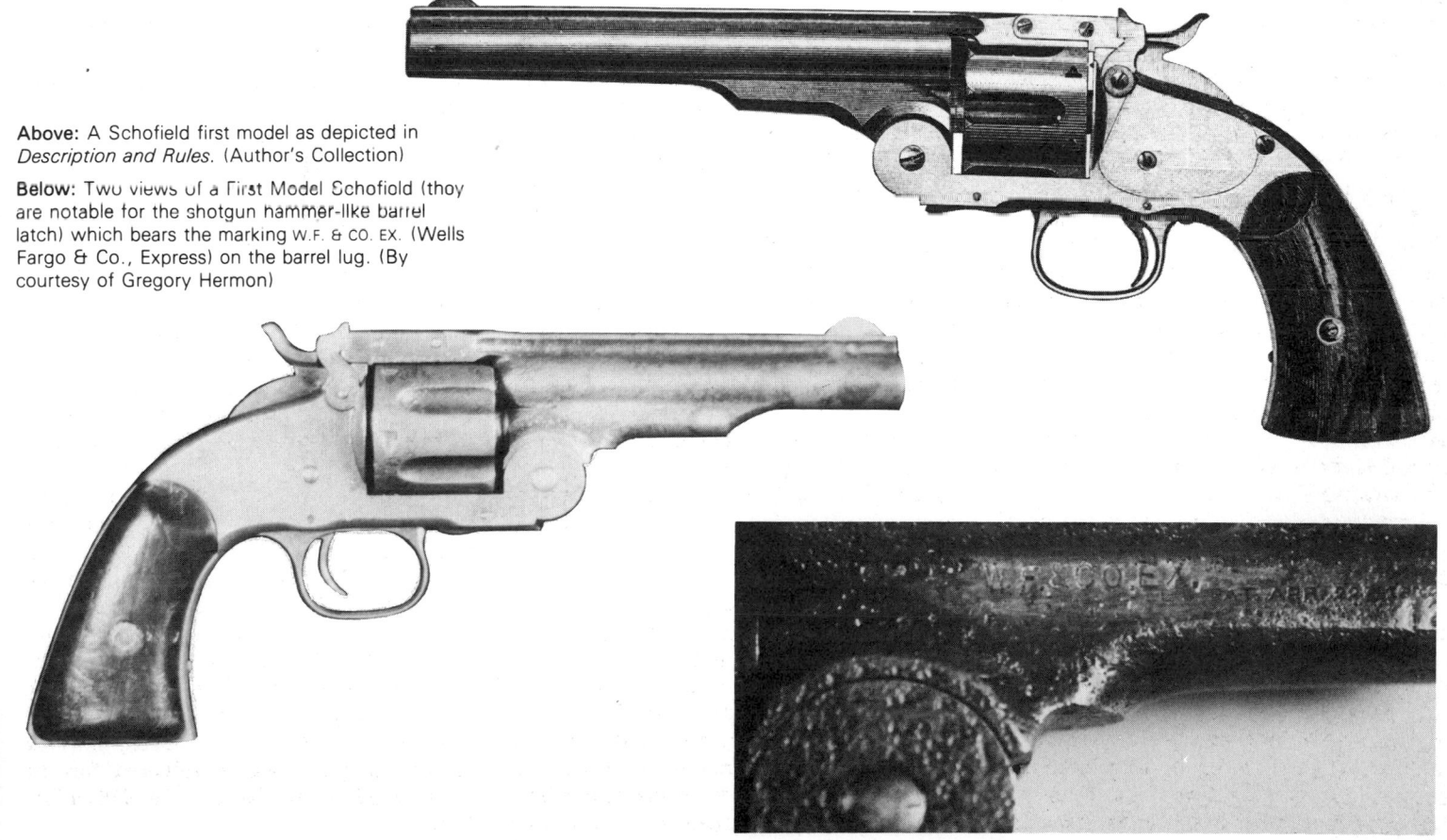

Above: A Schofield first model as depicted in *Description and Rules*. (Author's Collection)

Below: Two views of a First Model Schofield (they are notable for the shotgun hammer-like barrel latch) which bears the marking W.F. & CO. EX. (Wells Fargo & Co., Express) on the barrel lug. (By courtesy of Gregory Hermon)

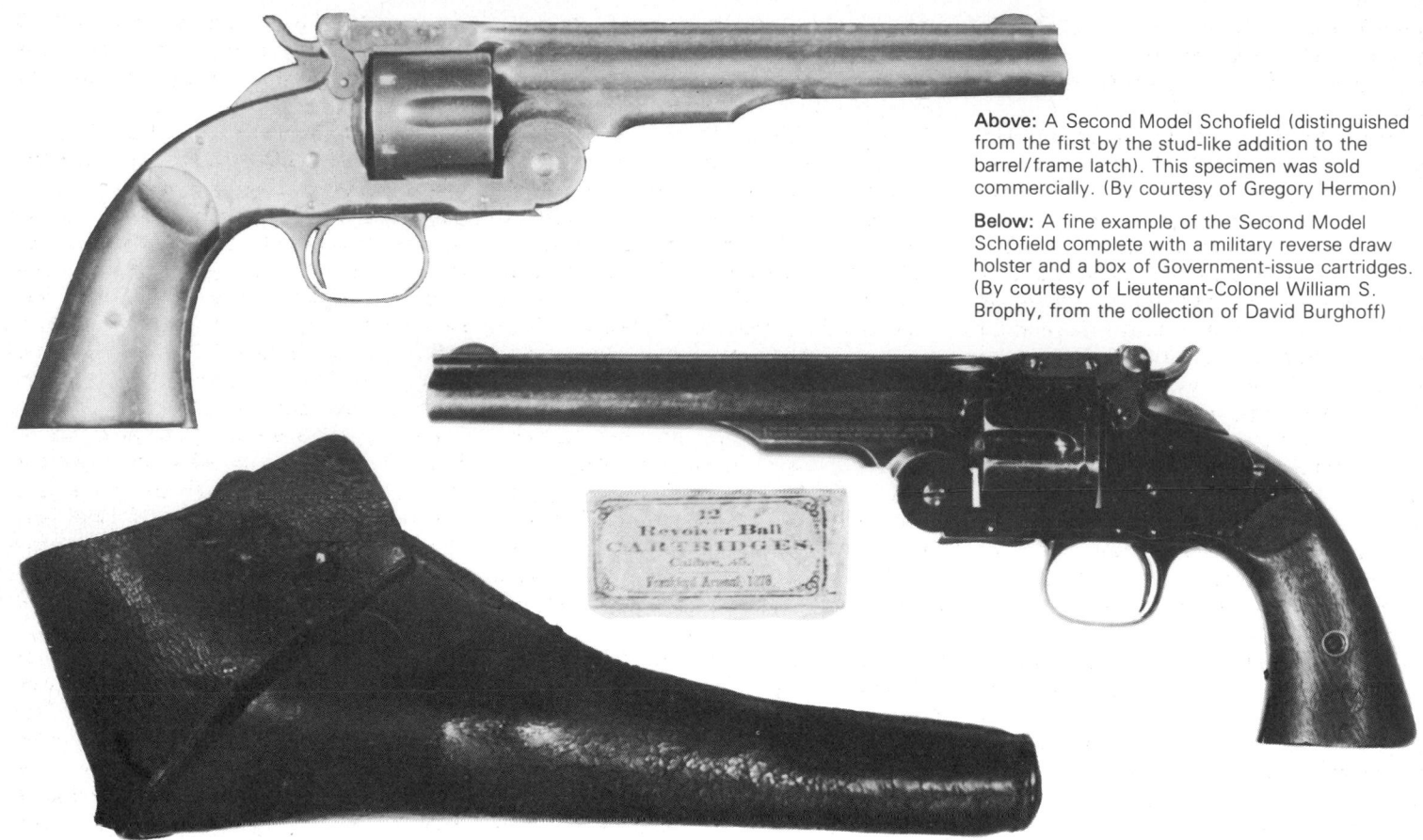

Above: A Second Model Schofield (distinguished from the first by the stud-like addition to the barrel/frame latch). This specimen was sold commercially. (By courtesy of Gregory Hermon)

Below: A fine example of the Second Model Schofield complete with a military reverse draw holster and a box of Government-issue cartridges. (By courtesy of Lieutenant-Colonel William S. Brophy, from the collection of David Burghoff)

modifications to the pistol and patented several of them. Six Model No. 3s were altered by the company to the Colonel's specifications and tested by the Board of Ordnance before production started. The principal difference between his version and the company's standard product was the placement of the barrel latch. The company's latch pivoted from the top strap, whereas the Colonel's version was attached to the frame. In appearance it resembled an external hammer (similar to a side-hammer shotgun); not particularly attractive but functional. An estimated 3,035 Schofield First Model revolvers were produced, of which 3,000 were purchased by the U.S. Army.

The second version had a rounded barrel latch, knurled on top, and a longer base pin. Steel replaced iron for the frame, which obviated the need of a recoil plate. About 5,934 of these pistols were manufactured, all except 649 being sold to the army. The Colonel received no royalties for his first model, but received fifty cents a pistol for the second one. He also modified the Russian model. Following some disappointing results of trials conducted by the Board in March 1874 of his own and other Smith & Wesson arms, the news that his alteration to the Russian pistol (which allowed the cylinder to be removed more readily) must have cheered him considerably. No further military orders were forthcoming, but Schofield continued his experiments.

In 1876 Remington's, Colt's most formidable rival during the percussion era, decided to take on both Colt's and Smith & Wesson in the contest to gain military contracts. Since the end of the war, they had experienced a very lean time insofar as revolver sales were concerned. The last delivery of their percussion revolvers to the United States Government had been in March 1865, and most of those had gone straight into store. Since then they had concentrated upon other types of arms. The introduction of the Remington–Ryder single-shot cartridge pistols (the lockwork was similar to the Joseph Rider 'Rolling Block' action used on rifles manufactured by the company) aroused military interest. The 'rolling block' was simply a breech-block which rotated about a pivot and was slotted in its upper surface to allow a heavy hammer to turn in the slot to strike the exposed edge of a rim-fire cartridge. When the hammer was cocked the breech-block could be opened or closed as required, but once the hammer was lowered it was locked firmly in place. Subsequently, 10,000 percussion Remington revolvers were sold out of store to make way for 5,000 of the new single-shot pistols. Produced in .50 calibre, the pistols were extremely successful and popular despite being single-shot, and by the early 1870s several versions in different calibres were known. It was one of these pistols that did so well in the rapid-fire section of a trial at Woolwich in the mid

1860s that the British Board of Ordnance requested confirmation of its performance! However, it was not adopted.

In the United States, however, the Government was impressed with the Remington rolling-block pistol and about 6,500 were purchased by them. But it was the revolver which really interested Remington, for apart from its military use, there was a growing Western market, and they were anxious to get back into it. One unnamed army officer complained that while a lot was being done to perfect rifles and carbines, very little was being done to improve army pistols. On 16 March 1867 *The Army and Navy Journal* published his comments. He said, in part:

'There are as many different pocket pistols, revolvers and repeaters as there are breech-loading rifles, but most of them are poor affairs for troops, and Colt's and Remington's Army pistols are still the best we have for the service; but we greatly need a better weapon of this kind. We want a pistol to use the metallic cartridge, of the calibre to be adopted for the new carbines (.45 or .50); or the Colt and Remington pistols might be altered to use metallic explosive cartridges, by cutting off the rear of the cylinder, so as to make it similar to Smith & Wesson's pistol cylinders; shortening the space in which the cylinder plays, and altering the hammer slightly. Every one in the Army knows the great inconvenience of loading and capping an army pistol while in motion on horseback, and also the great number of pistol cartridges that are destroyed in the cartridge box, and in the loading . . .'

When the Rollin White patent expired, Remington's joined Colt's in the rush to produce metallic cartridge pistols. By September 1869 a number of their existing percussion arms had been converted to .46 calibre five-shot, similar to those that had originally been converted under the licence granted by Smith & Wesson. Complaints were received from the frontier army that the improved weapons, although a vast improvement on the existing arms, were just not available and demanded to know why. On 25 September 1869 the editor of *The Army and Navy Journal* agreed that 'The Remington revolver of *recent* issue is an undeniably good weapon. Its range is great and it can be relied on for accuracy. It is the old issue to which exceptions are taken'.

In fact, the army had good cause for complaint: the continued reliance upon percussion revolvers when metallic cartridge weapons were available, but hampered by patent restrictions, led to many requests and complaints to the Government. But Remington's were able to rectify the matter. By 1872 they had improved their conversions and produced a number of what might be termed sub-models culminating in the celebrated Model 1875 Army revolver. And once news of this weapon reached the frontier army, the War Department was besieged with requests for the weapon. Remington's, of course, were, delighted, especially when the Government decided that since no comparative trial had yet been held between the Colt and the Schofield Smith & Wesson, it would be necessary to conduct trials of all three pistols.

The Board convened on 23 February 1876 and lasted for several days. Each weapon was tested for rapidity of fire, and the trial commenced with each pistol's cylinder unloaded. The Schofield took 59 seconds to load, fire and eject eighteen cartridges; the Colt 1 minute 54 seconds, and the Remington about the same. The Colt was unaffected by dust tests, but the Schofield had some difficulty in loading, and the Remington's ejector was difficult to operate. During dismantling, the Colt's centre pin, which had become fouled, had to be removed with a vice. When stripping each pistol down completely, it required five minutes for the Colt, 7½ minutes for the Schofield and seven minutes for the Remington. Assembling the rival revolvers required seventeen minutes for the Colt, nineteen for the Schofield and 24 minutes for the Remington – the latter because of problems with its mainspring. It should be clarified, of course, that the stripping down meant every part, not just the action.

At the conclusion of the trials, the Colt again proved itself to be superior, and the Board recommended its continued use in service. The Remington was found to 'fall so far short of improvements as to condemn the arm for military service', whereas the Schofield, despite its workmanship and fine mechanism was not considered suitable for military service, although it would no doubt be in demand 'by a large class of commissioned officers in time of war'. Evidently, the Board was unaware that several thousand Schofields had already been purchased for military use! But the most damning comment came when it was suggested that the Remington revolver closely resembled the Colt. Remington's promptly retorted that it was in fact the Colt that closely resembled the Remington!

The lack of Government support did not affect Remington's commercial and overseas sales. They supplied an estimated 10,000 revolvers in .44 Remington calibre to the Egyptian Government (but whether these were of their own manufacture or only part manufacture is debatable), and sales of the new revolver out West were impressive,

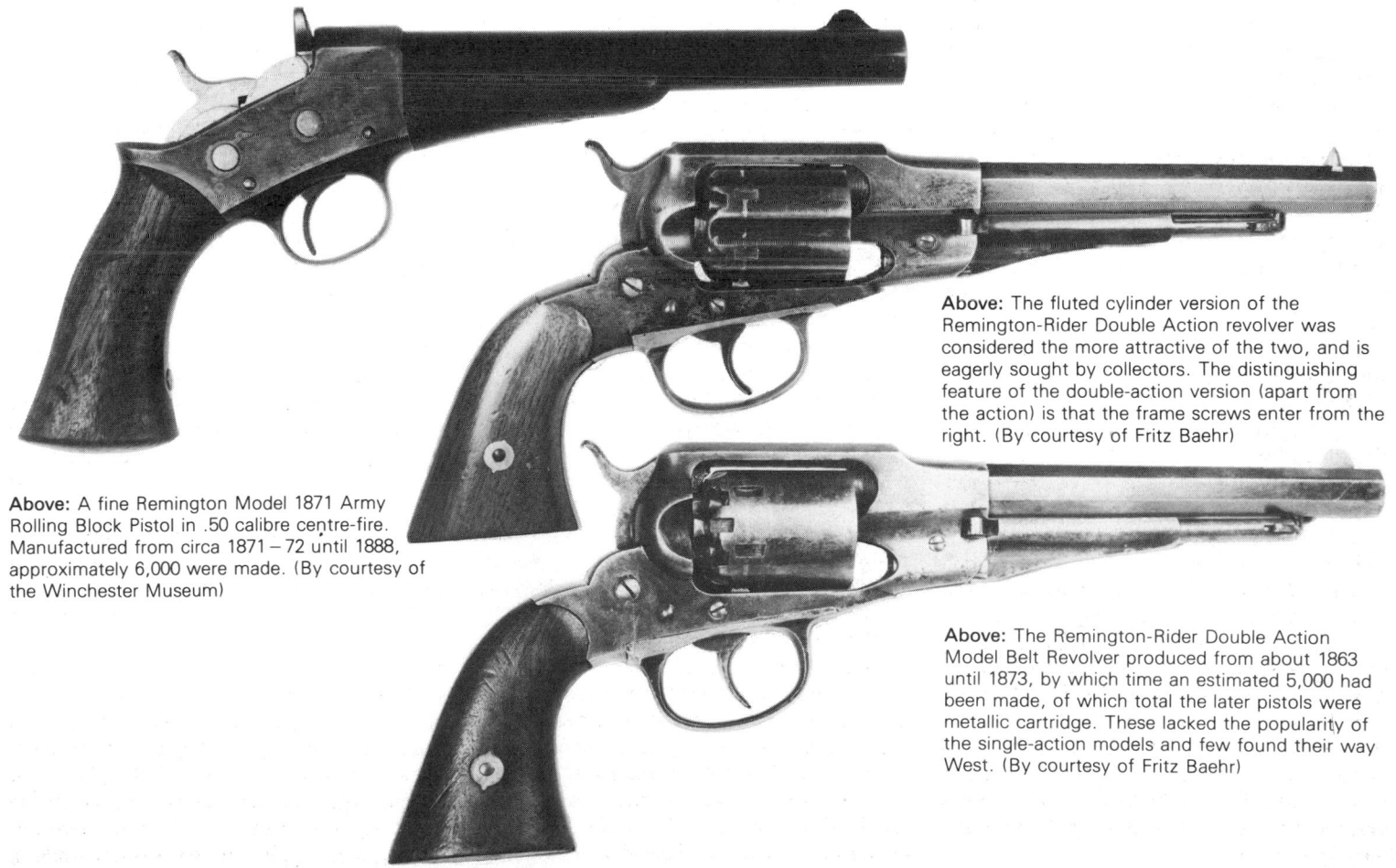

Above: A fine Remington Model 1871 Army Rolling Block Pistol in .50 calibre centre-fire. Manufactured from circa 1871 – 72 until 1888, approximately 6,000 were made. (By courtesy of the Winchester Museum)

Above: The fluted cylinder version of the Remington-Rider Double Action revolver was considered the more attractive of the two, and is eagerly sought by collectors. The distinguishing feature of the double-action version (apart from the action) is that the frame screws enter from the right. (By courtesy of Fritz Baehr)

Above: The Remington-Rider Double Action Model Belt Revolver produced from about 1863 until 1873, by which time an estimated 5,000 had been made, of which total the later pistols were metallic cartridge. These lacked the popularity of the single-action models and few found their way West. (By courtesy of Fritz Baehr)

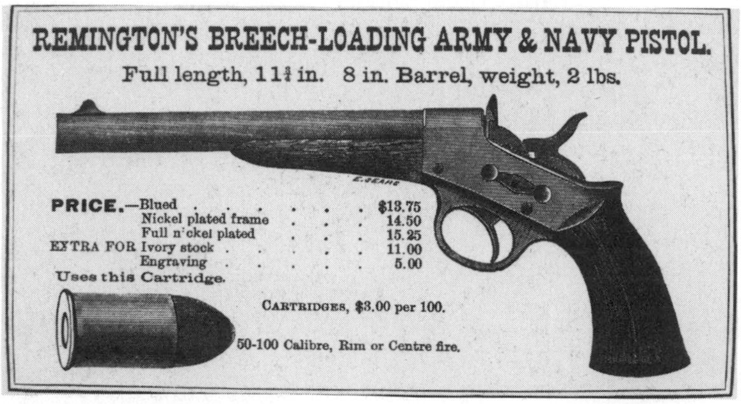
REMINGTON'S BREECH-LOADING ARMY & NAVY PISTOL.
Full length, 11¾ in. 8 in. Barrel, weight, 2 lbs.
PRICE.—Blued $13.75
Nickel plated frame . . . 14.50
Full n'ckel plated . . . 15.25
EXTRA FOR Ivory stock 11.00
Engraving 5.00
Uses this Cartridge.
CARTRIDGES, $3.00 per 100.
50-100 Calibre, Rim or Centre fire.

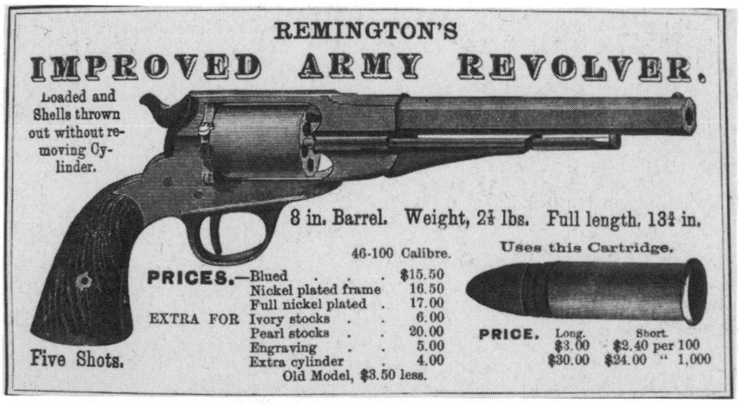
REMINGTON'S
IMPROVED ARMY REVOLVER.
Loaded and Shells thrown out without removing Cylinder.
8 in. Barrel. Weight, 2⅞ lbs. Full length, 13¾ in.
46-100 Calibre.
PRICES.—Blued . . . $15.50
Nickel plated frame 16.50
Full nickel plated . 17.00
EXTRA FOR Ivory stocks . . 6.00
Pearl stocks . . 20.00
Engraving . . 5.00
Extra cylinder . 4.00
Old Model, $3.50 less.
Five Shots.
Uses this Cartridge.
PRICE. Long. Short.
$3.00 $2.40 per 100
$30.00 $24.00 " 1,000

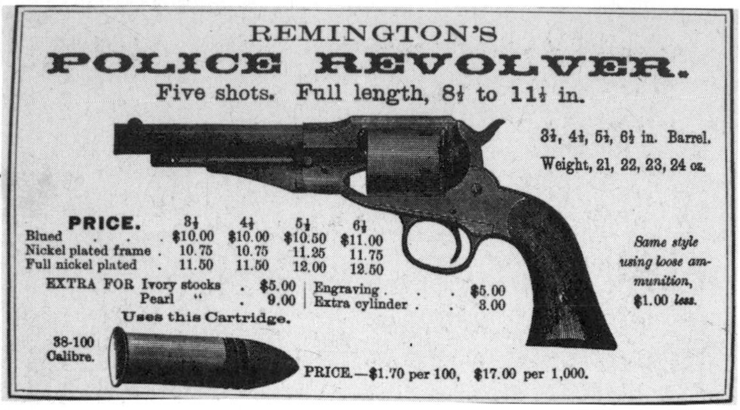
REMINGTON'S
POLICE REVOLVER.
Five shots. Full length, 8½ to 11½ in.
3½, 4½, 5½, 6½ in. Barrel.
Weight, 21, 22, 23, 24 oz.
PRICE. 3½ 4½ 5½ 6½
Blued . . . $10.00 $10.00 $10.50 $11.00
Nickel plated frame . 10.75 10.75 11.25 11.75
Full nickel plated . 11.50 11.50 12.00 12.50
EXTRA FOR Ivory stocks . $5.00 | Engraving . . . $5.00
Pearl " . 9.00 | Extra cylinder . . 3.00
Same style using loose ammunition, $1.00 less.
Uses this Cartridge.
38-100 Calibre.
PRICE.—$1.70 per 100, $17.00 per 1,000.

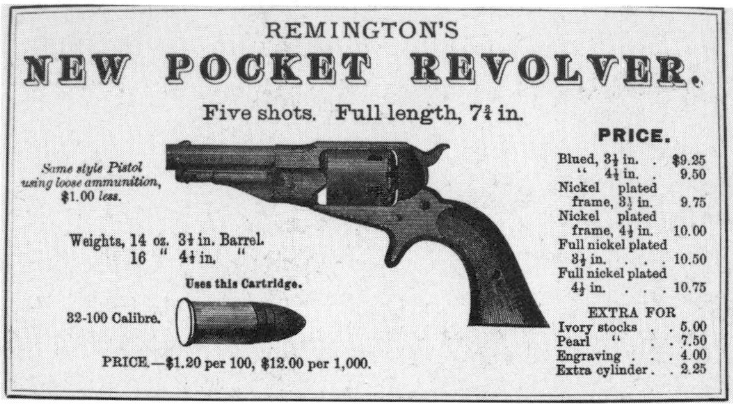
REMINGTON'S
NEW POCKET REVOLVER.
Five shots. Full length, 7¾ in.
Same style Pistol using loose ammunition, $1.00 less.
Weights, 14 oz. 3½ in. Barrel.
16 " 4½ in. "
Uses this Cartridge.
32-100 Calibre.
PRICE.—$1.20 per 100, $12.00 per 1,000.
PRICE.
Blued, 3½ in. . $9.25
" 4½ in. . 9.50
Nickel plated frame, 3½ in. 9.75
Nickel plated frame, 4½ in. 10.00
Full nickel plated 3½ in. . . . 10.50
Full nickel plated 4½ in. . . . 10.75
EXTRA FOR
Ivory stocks . . 5.00
Pearl " . . 7.50
Engraving . . . 4.00
Extra cylinder . . 2.25

despite its chambering for .44 Remington ammunition only. In 1877, however, the company did chamber a pistol for trial in .45 Government (a cartridge which fitted both the Colt and the Remington revolvers). To accept the enlarged calibre the cylinder had to be increased by $\frac{1}{16}$-inch in diameter. The results of the trials were little changed, however, and the company continued to sell weapons at home or abroad. Between 1875 and 1890, an estimated 25,000 1875 Model revolvers were manufactured and sold.

In 1886 the Remington company went into receivership, and the Remington family no longer had any controlling interest. The company was reorganized in 1888 by Hartley & Graham of New York as 'The Remington Arms Company'. Revolvers were no longer a prime concern, and the last one produced bearing the Remington name of interest to us was the Model 1890 in .44–40 calibre. The Model 1875 had had a standardized barrel length of 7½ inches (a limited few were produced in 5½-inch lengths), but the Model 1890 was provided with both 7½- and 5½-inch barrels on demand. The 1890 model differed only slightly from the 1875 model, the most noticeable feature being the removal of the distinctive barrel/ejector web found on the earlier model. Only about 2,000 of the 1890 model were produced, however, and production ceased in about 1894.

Other makers of American revolvers, of course, rivalled the Colt, Smith & Wesson and Remington arms, the most important being the Forehand & Wadsworth and the Merwin & Hulbert revolvers. Forehand & Wadsworth were an interesting partnership. Sullivan Forehand, the senior partner, had been employed in the early 1860s by Allen & Wheellock in an administrative capacity. His career took an upward spiral when he married one of Ethan Allen's daughters. The couple had two sons, both of whom later joined their father in the business. By a curious coincidence, Henry C. Wadsworth, a Union Army officer during the Civil War, married another of Allen's daughters, and on his discharge from the army he, too, joined the firm. In 1865, the company's name was changed to Ethan Allen & Co., and following Allen's death in 1871, it was continued as Forehand & Wadsworth, the partners continuing to manufacture the line of weapons established by their joint father-in-law.

The early examples of the company's metallic ammunition revolvers are uninspiring, but by 1874 the company had produced an army or 'Frontier' revolver which they wanted accepted by the Government. The company submitted it for trial through Shuyler, Hartley & Graham, arms dealers of New York, and noted for their association with the Colt company. The weapon was tested against the Peacemaker at the Springfield Arsenal in December 1874. It had been intended to include the Smith & Wesson Schofield, but a specimen was not readily available.

Forehand & Wadsworth's revolver was a solid-frame weapon with a hollow retractable

Top left: A contemporary advertisement for the Remington single-shot breech-loading rolling block pistol. This weapon went on trial in England in the mid 1860s and its rapid-fire performance outshone most of the revolvers put up against it (loading and unloading at speed was a feature), but no orders were placed. The U.S. Government ordered 5,000 of them however, and sold 10,000 percussion Remingtons to make way for them. (Author's Collection)

Top right: A contemporary advertisement for the 'Improved Army Revolver' manufactured by Remington in the early 1870s. It was, however, identical with the .46 calibre five-shot conversions carried out under licence in the mid 1860s. (Author's Collection)

Above left: The expiration of the Rollin White patent in 1869 brought a new lease of life to many existing percussion arms, and Remington's, more than most, did a lively trade in conversions. (Author's Collection)

Above right: The stud trigger pocket-pistol had been popular as a percussion arm, and enjoyed a renewed interest when converted to rim-fire. (Author's Collection)

Opposite, top left: By 1872, Remington's were busy converting many of the larger pistols to accept rim- and centre-fire ammunition. The conversions necessitated changes in the frame size when the calibre went above .38. (Author's Collection)

Opposite, top right: The 1872 'Belt Revolver' in double- and single-action was popular, but the single-action sold better. (Author's Collection)

Opposite, above left: The Remington double-action pocket-pistol was hideous, but apparently effective. (Author's Collection)

Opposite, above right: The 'Repeating Pistol' is regarded by many as a form of Deringer, and indeed one could be forgiven for accepting it as such! (Author's Collection)

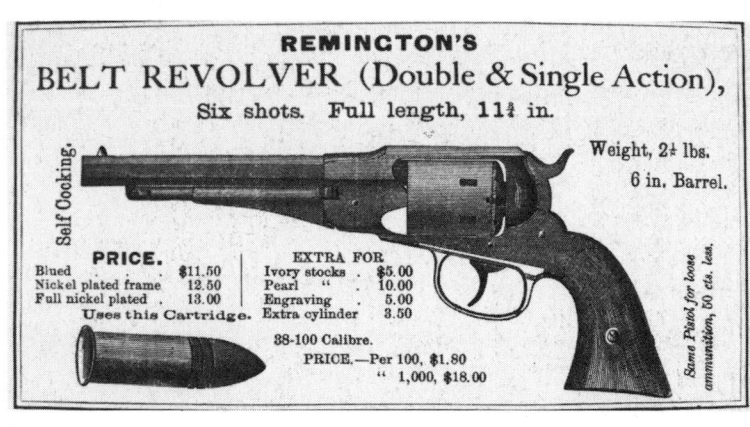

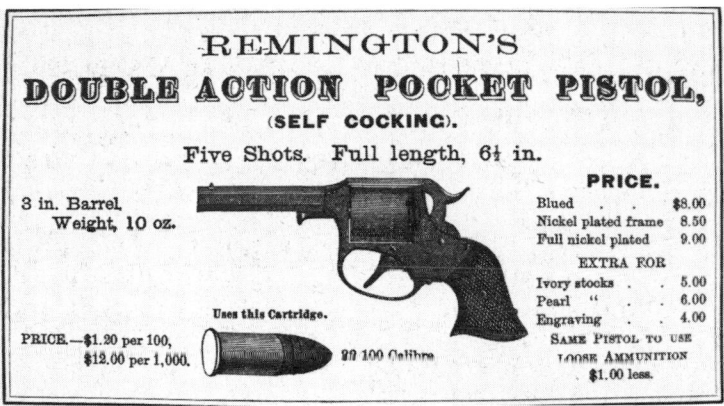

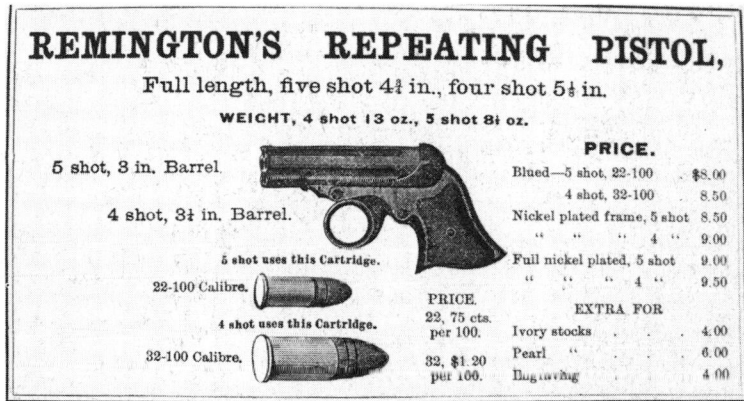

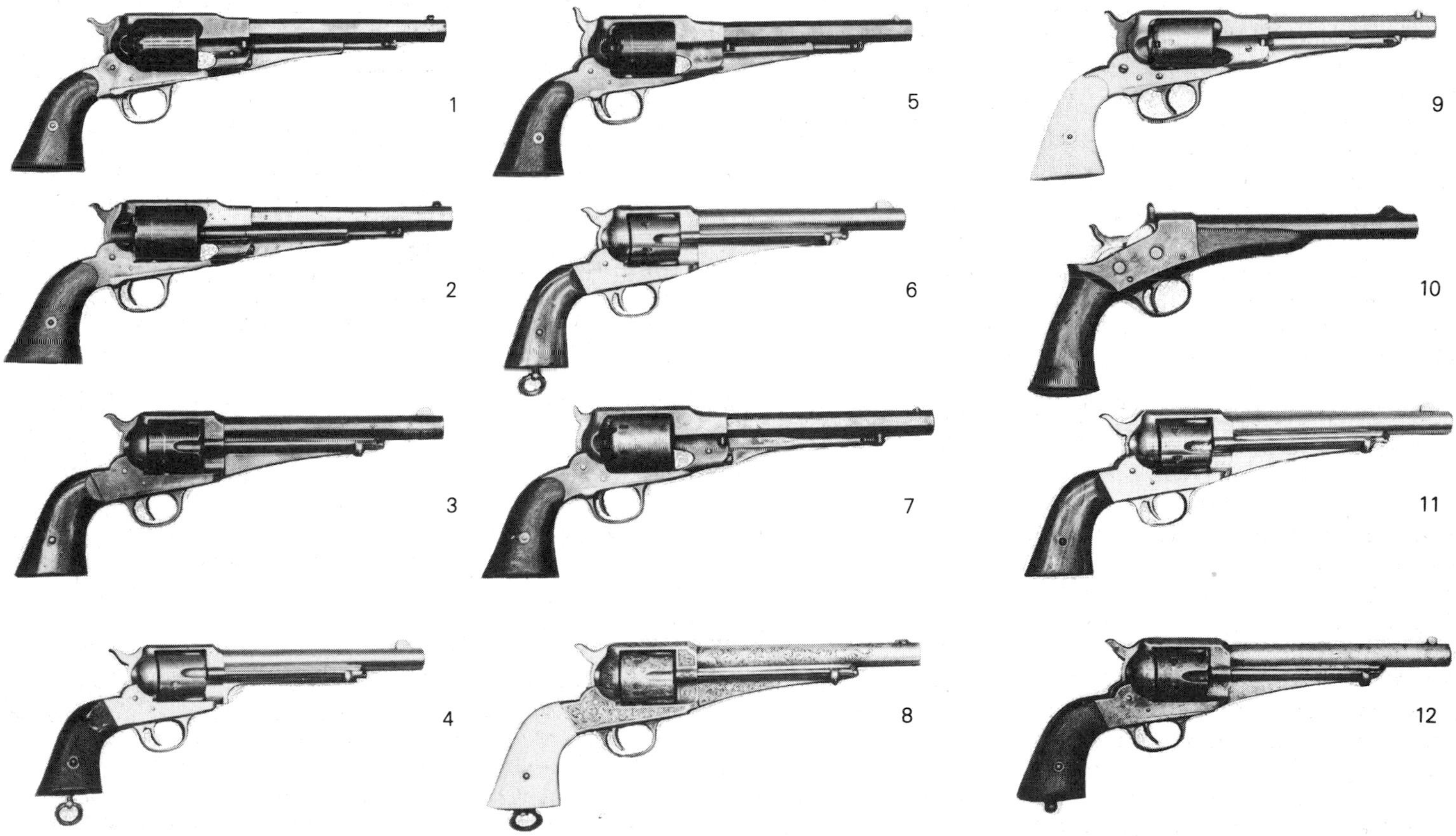

Above: The Remington Army revolver — from percussion to cartridge. 1, .44 New Model Army 1863 (complete with U.S. markings); 2, New Model Army converted by the factory to a .46 calibre five-shot; 3, an 1875 Single Action Army in .44 Remington calibre. 4, the rare Model 1890; 5, Model 1861 .44 Army; 6, a fine nickel-plated 1875 Model Army. Note that both this pistol and the 1890 model have lanyard rings. 7, an early Remington-Beals .44 Army revolver; 8, a very fine engraved ivory-butted 1875 Army revolver complete with lanyard ring. Weapons of this quality are rare. 9, a Remington-Rider double-action New Model belt revolver, nickel-plated with ivory grips; 10, an 1871 Army Rolling Block Pistol in .50 calibre, centre-fire. About 6,000 of them were manufactured and despite the preference for revolvers, the design survived as a target pistol until the 1890s. 11, another 1875 Model Army. Note the distinctive web on the extractor which is not present on the Model 1890; 12, a well-used version of the Model 1875. (By courtesy of Richard A. Bourne Co., Inc.)

centre pin which held the cylinder in place. An ejector rod, when not in use, was housed inside this pin. The ejector rod also passed through the shoulder of a ferrule which turned between the barrel and the frame, so that when pulled forward, and moved to one side, the rod could be used to eject cases from the chambers when a hinged gate was open. The pistol was considered neat and impressive, but during the trial a number of faults were detected. The Board criticised the frailty of the ejector system and there were problems with the cylinder. When the weapon was set at half-cock, the cylinder tended to revolve backwards or forwards, obstructing the ejector rod. The hand or pawl which controlled and rectified this fault on the Colt and Remington, evidently did not fulfil the same function in the Forehand & Wadsworth arm.

The revolver submitted for the trial was chambered for .45 (they are normally found in .44 calibre) and there were a number of misfires and complaints that the cylinder did not index properly, but it was the rusting test that was the pistol's downfall. After 24 hours in the rusting tank, the ejector rod could not be removed without a vice, the cylinder stop refused to function and the

Below: 'The Merwin Hulbert & Co.' Army revolvers failed in their trial against the Colt, but they were quite popular out West. This pistol was issued in calibres of .44-40; and .44 M & H. The pistol was produced from 1876 until 1880 and only a few thousand were made. (By courtesy of Messrs Weller & Dufty)

Above: A very fine 1875 Model Remington chambered for .44-40 Winchester, complete with an original UMC 44 WCF (Winchester Centre-Fire) cartridge. Approximately 25,000 Model 1875s were produced from 1875 until about 1889. (By courtesy of the Lawbrook Collection)

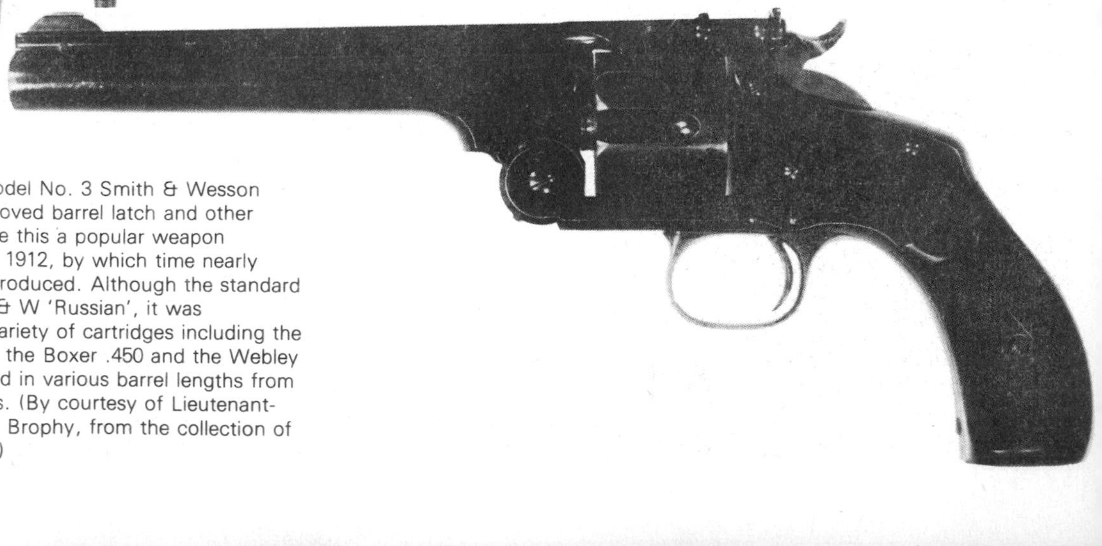

Above: A New Model No. 3 Smith & Wesson revolver. The improved barrel latch and other modifications made this a popular weapon between 1878 and 1912, by which time nearly 36,000 had been produced. Although the standard calibre was .44 S & W 'Russian', it was chambered for a variety of cartridges including the Henry .44 rim-fire, the Boxer .450 and the Webley .45, and was issued in various barrel lengths from 3½ to eight inches. (By courtesy of Lieutenant-Colonel William S. Brophy, from the collection of David R. Burghoff)

Left: A typical broadsheet issued by Remington in 1875. Note their own definition of the 1875 model as the 'No. 3' revolver. The lower pistol competed with the available Colt pistol of similar design. (Author's Collection)

Below: 'Wild Ben' Raymond, a friend of Joseph 'White Eye' Anderson, seen in about 1879. Little is known of this man, and it is possible that he was a local (Leadville, Colorado) character. In his right hand he is holding a Merwin Hulbert revolver. Strung around his neck is a beaded chain which was fashionable when individuals 'dressed up' for the camera. (Author's Collection)

loading gate would not close. Even when fired the pistol proved troublesome, for many of the parts failed to work properly. The Colt, however, had few problems, and the Board concluded that: 'The material points of difference between the Forehand & Wadsworth pistol and the Colts pistol, are decidedly in favor of the latter. The ungainly appearance of the ejecting rod of the Colt pistol is sought to be improved, in the Forehand & Wadsworth . . . to eject a single shell requires seven distinct motions, while one motion in the Colt model accomplishes the same end . . .'

Although the report concluded that the arm was unsuitable for military service it is estimated that several hundreds were sold from the middle 1870s into the 1880s, but the company's other small frame pocket-pistols enjoyed far greater success.

By 1878 the Peacemaker had successfully bested its rivals, but during that year one more weapon was presented to challenge its supremacy. This was the Merwin & Hulbert Army revolver. Located in New York City, the company entrusted the manufacture of the revolvers to Hopkins & Allen of Norwich, Connecticut. The pistols were pleasing in appearance and the ejection and loading technique was interesting, the barrel being twisted sideways and pulled forward with the cylinder still attached. They were produced in .44–40 calibre and the company's own .44 calibre. Fitted with a 7-inch round barrel, the early pistols had an open frame, but later versions were fitted with a top strap. When tested against the Colt and the 1875 Remington revolver, the Board discovered that initial velocity tests revealed a mean of 656 feet per second, which was one foot per second better than the 1875 Remington. Penetration and recoil were recorded at 45 and 74 respectively, as opposed to 43 and 53 for the Remington – both weapons being tested in .44 calibre instead of the Service .45. During endurance, fouling and dust tests (being covered with sand) the pistol worked well, but when submitted to the usual rusting processes it did

Above: Possibly the most 'notorious' New Model No. 3 of them all! This is alleged to be the revolver used by Robert 'Bob' Ford to kill Jesse James in 1882. Despite some alleged material that links the gun with Ford, I prefer to accept the evidence of the Kansas City *Daily Times* of 5 May 1882, which published the text of a sworn affidavit by Robert N. Ford that he used a .45 Colt Peacemaker, No. 50432. The Colt Company subsequently confirmed that the pistol left the factory in September 1878, and was one of 150 purchased by the Government. (Author's Collection)

not function at all well. The base pin could not be removed without the aid of a vice, and twenty minutes were spent in restoring the pistol to working order. The Board, however, did note that despite its shortcomings the weapon 'worked very satisfactorily'.

At the close of the trials, the Board concluded that the Merwin & Hulbert's failings in comparison with the Colt were its greater weight (about five ounces); its balance (the centre of gravity was too far forward); cylinder rotation and the fact that there were too many parts and too many different screw heads necessitating several screwdrivers to take it apart. It was also not so rigid in construction as was the Colt. None the less, it was deemed a 'very good pistol', having endured many of the tests. No orders were placed by the Government, but commercial sales were satisfactory, and the company also produced a number of double-action revolvers. By 1886 Merwin & Hulbert had abandoned the manufacture of the .44 single-action Army revolvers and were concentrating on other models.

By 1878, the official 'let off' pressure for the trigger pull on the Colt was between 6 and 8 pounds and for the Smith & Wesson 9 pounds with limits of between 8 and 10 pounds. More Smith & Wessons, however, exceeded the pressures than did the Colt 'on account of the trigger being so close to the guard that a portion of the force is expended upon the latter'. Springfield Armory also noted that this was acceptable because a mounted trooper needed to 'steady the revolver before he fires'. It was especially true of 'the Smith & Wesson revolver on

131

account of the faulty shape of the stock'. This fault did not deter the military, but some civilian purchasers had complained to the company about the grip shape and they also objected to the pistols' short hammer spur. But such criticisms had no detrimental effect on sales.

The Smith & Wesson–Schofield relationship came to an end in 1882 when, on 17 February, following what his brother officers believed was a temporary bout of insanity brought on by worry over an invention, the Colonel shot himself with one of his own revolvers at Fort Apache, Arizona. The revolver continued to sell well out West, where it was popular among some of the better-known of the gun-toting fraternity, including Jesse James. His Schofield pistol is now in a private collection.

Apart from the Schofield models in .45 calibre, Smith & Wesson updated the No. 3 in 1878 and it remained in production until 1912. Chambered for the .44 'Russian' cartridge, it was also available on limited demand

in other calibres. Barrel lengths differed from as small as 3½ inches to the original eight inches. The finish was blued or nickel with a variety of grip materials including ivory. During its long life, the No. 3 appeared in three basic versions. The first model, the celebrated 'American' was chambered for .44 Smith & Wesson or .44 Henry rim-fire. The 8-inch barrel was machined round, but with a ribbed section at the top which housed the German silver blade foresight, while the rear sight was fitted just ahead of the barrel release catch. Later, some barrels were shortened to six inches on demand, and the barrel lug contained the ejector mechanism, and was machined to fit into the fore part of the frame. The cylinders had three-quarter flutes and rectangular bolt stops (the latter fitted with hardened steel shims to prevent bolt wear). The iron frame included the gripstraps, and there was a side plate to allow access to the mechanism. The iron trigger guard was formed separately and inlet into the frame. These pistols were blued

or nickel plated, but some special order pistols were engraved and plated, and fitted with ivory stocks, or made to order variations.

The second model differed from the first in that barrel lengths varied from the normal eight inches to as short as 5½ inches. A steel blade replaced the German silver foresight, and it was during the production of this model that the Russian contracts were drawn up. Although most of the pistols were accepted (and are referred to) as the Old Model Russian, the suggested change in trigger guard shape to include the spur had taken place, together with the special .44 Smith & Wesson 'Russian' cartridge. A few pistols, rejected during the life of the contract, were sold commercially. From 1873 until 1878 the company produced the Russian Model chambered for both the .44 Smith & Wesson Russian cartridge and the .44 Henry rim-fire. The barrel length was seven inches and the finish was blued or nickel. There are several variations in design

Above: A New Model No. 3 Smith & Wesson American which was once the property of George Sprigg, City Marshal of Jetmore, Kansas in the 1880s. (By courtesy of Gregory Hermon)

Above: A pair of .41 calibre 'Thunderer' revolvers (the 'Lightning' models were in .38 calibre and the 'Thunderers' in .41) presented to H. C. Lindsey (sometimes spelt Lindsay) in 1893 when he was appointed Chief of Police in Topeka, Kansas. The backstrap of each pistol is inscribed H. C. LINDSEY. CHIEF. TOPEKA, KAS. Lindsey had served during the Civil War and later during the 1867 Indian War, and was a great friend of Wild Bill Hickok and the other scouts and guides. (By courtesy of Dr. Richard C. Marohn, M.D.)

in this series and barrel inscriptions in both English and Cyrillic have been found.

The No. 3 'American' and its successor, the New No. 3, were probably the most successful of the early Smith & Wesson revolvers and are the two most eagerly sought by collectors. The second model was available as late as 1912, despite the fact that Colt's Peacemaker maintained its supremacy as the most popular single-action revolver on the market, but both companies realized that the day of the single-action was numbered, as did other American manufacturers. The problem was what form should a double-action pistol take? Smith & Wesson went on to produce a fine line of double-action revolvers suitable for the American market, but Colt's lagged behind; for some reason they were unable to look beyond the single-action concept.

In 1875 a prototype double-action pistol was designed (and now, alas, is lost to history) which by late 1876 was almost ready for production. Sam Colt had dismissed the double-action (or self-cocker, as they had

Top right: Three double-action Colt 'Lightning' revolvers in various barrel lengths (the smallest without an ejector), all used by the American Express Company. Not only did American Express think that the 'Lightning' would 'do very nicely', but other security-minded organizations also favoured them. (By courtesy of Dr. Richard C. Marohn, M.D.)

Above right: Thunderer, No. 73728 was owned by John Wesley Hardin; its finish is well worn, but the pearl grips are fine. Hardin was carrying this gun on 1 May 1895, when he entered the Gem Saloon in El Paso and took part in a dice game. He lost, pulled the pistol and walked out with the $95 he had lost. He was later arrested and fined. On 19 August 1895 as he stood at the bar of the Acme Saloon he was shot through the head by John Selman, and died instantly. (By courtesy of Dr. Richard C. Marohn, M.D.)

Above: This Colt .41 calibre 'Thunderer' was presented by President Theodore Roosevelt to Pat Garrett, the slayer of Billy the Kid, following his appointment as Collector of Customs for the El Paso District. It was shipped in the white from Colt's on 29 October 1902, to Hartley & Co., and engraved, a two-piece sterling silver grip added and the entire gun given a gold wash. The backstrap is inscribed: PAT F. GARRETT FROM HIS EL PASO FRIENDS; on the left grip: LINCOLN, DONA ANA, EL PASO, and on the right grip: CUSTOMS COLLECTOR. The serial No. is 138671. (By courtesy of Dr. Richard C. Marohn, M.D.)

been called in his day) as impracticable, but great strides had been made since the 1850s and 1860s. Nevertheless, when Colt's announced the arrival of their first model in 1877, those who expected a radical change were disappointed. The brain-child of the prolific William Mason, the pistol was simply a modified version of the single-action, but with a smaller frame, enlarged trigger guard (to accept the new action) and a bird's-head grip. The Peacemaker's gate and rod ejection was retained, and this was not welcomed in Europe. Produced in two calibres, .38 and .41, the model has been generally known as the 'Lightning', but when originally advertised by B. Kittredge & Co., the 'Lightning' referred to the .38 calibre model, and the .41 calibre pistol was called the 'Thunderer' – a term rarely used today except by collectors and historians.

The new pistols were produced in various barrel lengths ranging from 3½ to six inches (and some special flat-top target versions with 7½-inch barrels). In general, the Lightning and Thunderer pistols relied upon their resemblance to the Peacemaker to encourage sales, and no doubt this was a factor; between 1877 and 1909 an estimated 167,000 were manufactured and sold, which is remarkable when one considers the problems associated with the pistols and their action. They were prone to breakage, re-assembly was a chore, and gunsmiths cursed them – yet they did have a following. Among the frontier characters who are reported to have favoured the 1877 models, were John Wesley Hardin, whose documented .41 calibre pistol is now in a private collection, and Henry McCarty, alias William Bonney, 'Billy the Kid'. The 'Kid's' alleged pistol was once in the collection of Western film actor, the late William S. Hart, and is now in an Arkansas museum. It is numbered 57821 which, according to available Colt's records, makes its year of manufacture about 1887 – six years after Billy was shot dead by Pat Garrett during the night of 14/15 July 1881! Few .38 or .41 double-actions found their way West; for the most part their use was confined to American police or similar organizations, and the few overseas customers who found them acceptable.

Colt's produced their first double-action .45 calibre Army revolver in 1878. Again, it bore a strong resemblance to the Peacemaker (the barrels and extractor rod assemblies were interchangeable), but it was bulkier and it retained the bird's-head grip introduced with the Lightning and Thunderer models. Initially it attracted much attention, but there were soon problems. The heavy trigger pull necessitated the use of a weaker mainspring than was desirable, and this led to misfires and accidental discharges. The action was

Above: Joseph 'Rowdy Joe' Lowe, one of the sights of early-day Ellsworth, Wichita and later Denver, Colorado. Joe engaged in gambling, saloon- and brothel-keeping and one of his most famous fights was with a rival saloon-keeper, into whom he emptied both barrels of a shotgun. He was murdered in Denver in 1899, being unarmed at the time. (Author's Collection)

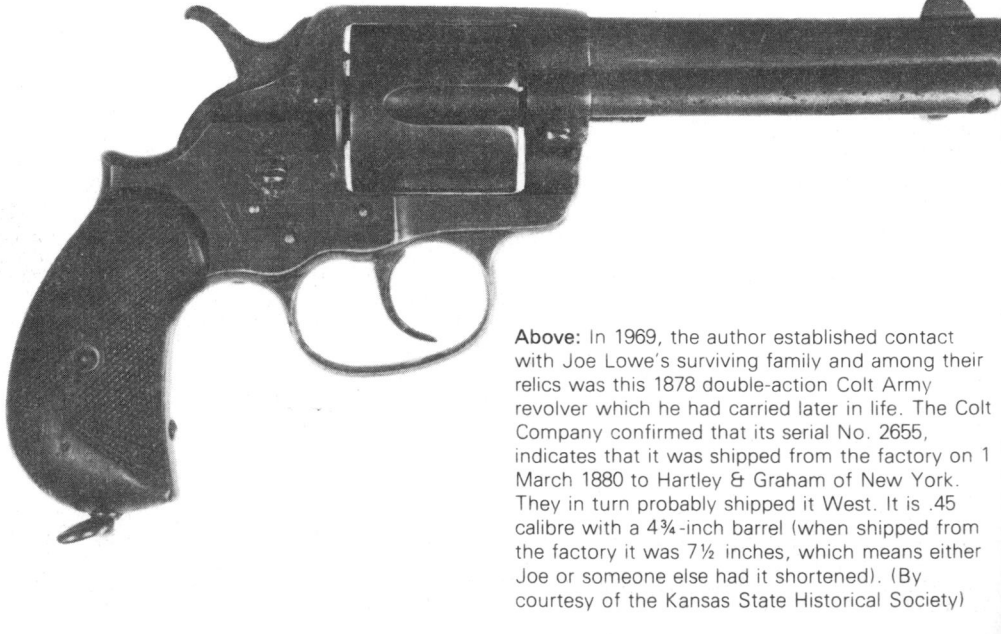

Above: In 1969, the author established contact with Joe Lowe's surviving family and among their relics was this 1878 double-action Colt Army revolver which he had carried later in life. The Colt Company confirmed that its serial No. 2655, indicates that it was shipped from the factory on 1 March 1880 to Hartley & Graham of New York. They in turn probably shipped it West. It is .45 calibre with a 4¾-inch barrel (when shipped from the factory it was 7½ inches, which means either Joe or someone else had it shortened). (By courtesy of the Kansas State Historical Society)

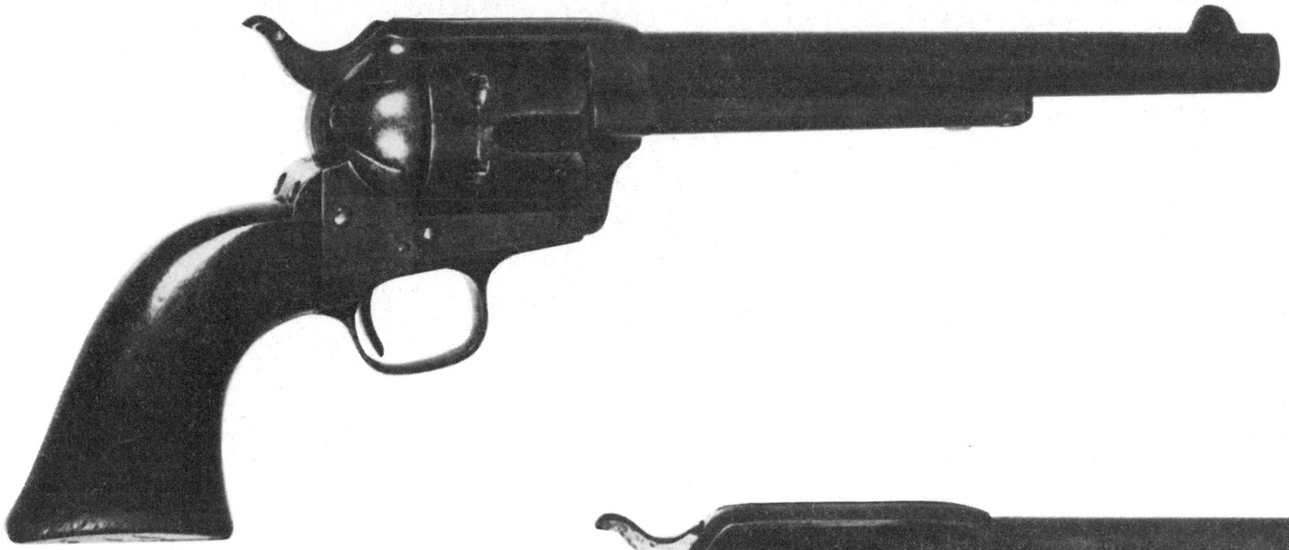

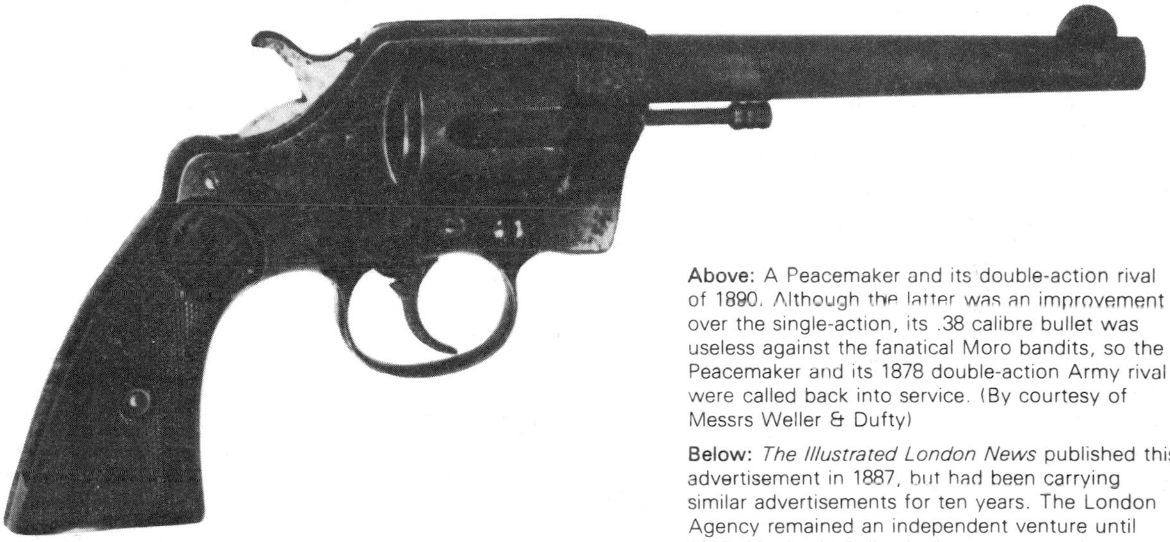

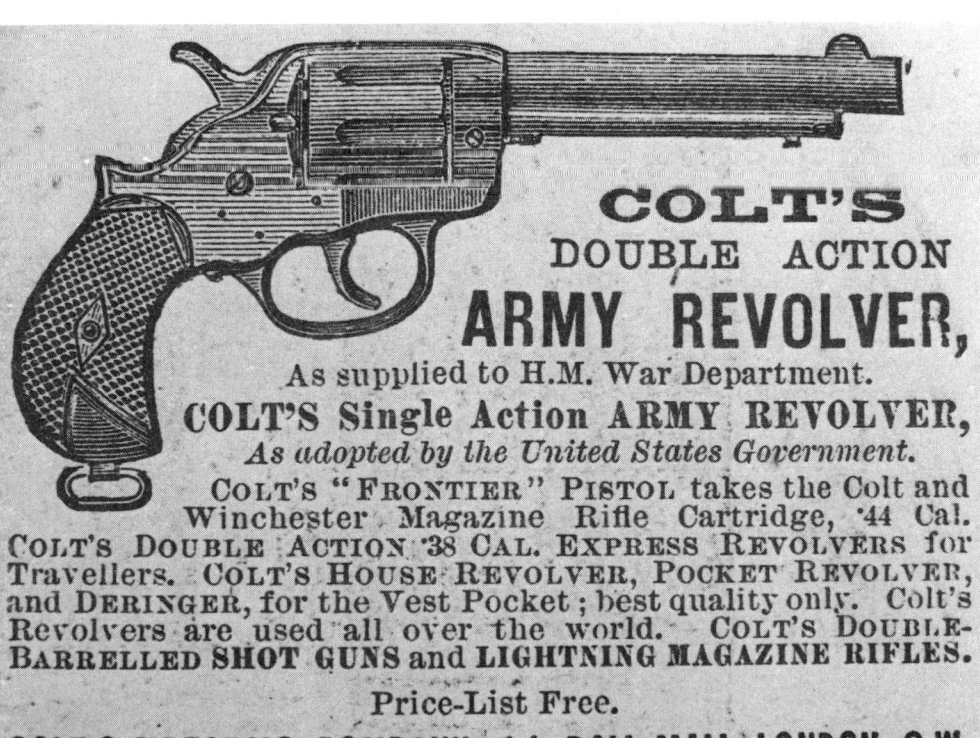

Above: A Peacemaker and its double-action rival of 1890. Although the latter was an improvement over the single-action, its .38 calibre bullet was useless against the fanatical Moro bandits, so the Peacemaker and its 1878 double-action Army rival were called back into service. (By courtesy of Messrs Weller & Dufty)

Below: *The Illustrated London News* published this advertisement in 1887, but had been carrying similar advertisements for ten years. The London Agency remained an independent venture until 1913. (Author's Collection)

COLT'S
DOUBLE ACTION
ARMY REVOLVER,
As supplied to H.M. War Department.
COLT'S Single Action ARMY REVOLVER,
As adopted by the United States Government.
COLT'S "FRONTIER" PISTOL takes the Colt and Winchester Magazine Rifle Cartridge, '44 Cal. COLT'S DOUBLE ACTION '38 CAL. EXPRESS REVOLVERS for Travellers. COLT'S HOUSE REVOLVER, POCKET REVOLVER, and DERINGER, for the Vest Pocket; best quality only. Colt's Revolvers are used all over the world. COLT'S DOUBLE-BARRELLED SHOT GUNS and LIGHTNING MAGAZINE RIFLES.

Price-List Free.

COLT'S FIREARMS COMPANY, 14, PALL-MALL, LONDON, S.W.
Agents for Ireland—JOHN RIGBY & Co., Gunmakers, Dublin.

cumbersome and it was susceptible to breakages. In this respect, the sale of about 150 of these weapons to the British Government was only achieved after the staff of the London Agency had worked all night to ensure that each pistol had as good an action as possible in order to pass the tests! But the rod ejector militated against a favourable reaction in Europe, although enough weapons were sold to justify its continued export. Out West, most cowboys took one look at the 1878 model and, as one concluded, declared that it was not 'worth a can of beans'. None the less, as late as 1902, the U.S. Government purchased about 4,600 of them for use against the Moro bandits in the Philippines. Fitted with an enlarged guard (to accept a redesigned trigger to ease pressure on the mainspring), they were sometimes misnamed the 'Alaska' model.

In 1889 Colt's introduced a superior double-action .38 calibre pistol which soon attracted military attention. It was adopted by the Government in 1892 to replace the Peacemaker, and within a year 5,000 of them had been issued. The new double-actions, while better designed, were not man-stoppers. Officers and men alike complained

135

Left: General George S. 'Blood and Guts' Patton purchased this Colt single-action in about 1916 when he was with Pershing's punitive force fighting Pancho Villa. It stayed with him through the remainder of his career, and during the Second World War he wore this pistol and a Smith & Wesson revolver wherever he went. Someone is alleged to have mistaken the weapons' grips for pearl, and the General is reputed to have snorted: 'They are ivory — pearl is for pimps!' (By courtesy of the West Point Museum)

Relative Ranges

Effective range with accuracy ————————
Range at which experts can achieve good results — — — — — —

Not indicated are the extreme ranges some of the pistols have been known to reach, ie, the Colt Navy 600yds.

Smith & Wesson 'American'

Colt 'Peacemaker'

Remington

0　　　100yds　　　200yds　　　300yds　　　400yds

that when they shot it out with the Moros in the Philippines it took as much as a full cylinder load to bring down the fanatics (shades of the maddened Sepoys of the Indian Mutiny), and sometimes even that did not stop them. This worried Washington, already concerned by insurrection in the Philippines which were to drag on until the early years of this century, and the War Department ordered the Ordnance to refurbish as many .45 calibre pistols as possible for use in the Philippines. A large number of the .45 double-actions were dispatched, and with them went a batch of refurbished single-actions, some with barrels cut down to 5½ inches. Once received, many of the pistols were issued to the local constabulary, who were supplied with black powder ammunition. This was a calculated move; it was reasoned that if any policemen decided to desert, they would be unable to use the weapon in the jungle because the smoke would disclose their position.

Although the Peacemaker failed to arouse much military interest in Europe, it was welcomed as a target pistol. To meet the demand, Colt's produced a limited number of weapons modified for this purpose. Some were even provided with longer handles, flat top straps and target sights, and special triggers were another attraction. They performed well at Bisley, and encouraged Colt's to further modify the weapon and the 'Bisley' model of 1894 was the result, both as an ordinary revolver and as a target pistol. The Bisley Colt differed from the normal single-action in that the hammer spur was swept down to allow ease of cocking, and the handle was curved down and forward. These changes were possibly motivated by the demands of precision shooting and perhaps because the normal hammer spur tended to

pinch the skin between the index finger and the thumb when the pistol was at full cock, which is why most shooters hold the Peacemaker low down on the grip.

On 24 November 1909 the Peacemaker was officially declared obsolete by the United States Army, but its career as a symbol of an era was only just beginning. Western films, books and magazine articles depicting the real and imaginary West gave new life to the old warrior, so Colt's decided to keep it in limited production, but even they were surprised by the demand. Between 1909 and 1939, a further 40,000 single-action revolvers were produced in a variety of calibres and barrel lengths, and production only stopped when the company needed the machinery for war work in the 1940s. The British Purchasing Commission obtained 108 of the remaining revolvers, some in .357 magnum calibre, and these are known to collectors as the 'Battle of Britain Colts'. When production officially ceased in 1941, almost 360,000 single-action Army pistols had been made. In 1947 a number of pre-war parts were made-up for a limited order. Curiously, when challenged a few years later, Colt's denied manufacturing this batch of pistols, but finally admitted they did exist. Then, in 1955 Colt's announced that to cater for the demands of collectors and shooters, they would reintroduce the Peacemaker, and it is still available on limited demand.

Like its famous ancestor, the 1860 Army, experts have argued about the Peacemaker's strengths and weaknesses for years. Some

express surprise that no improvements were made to the basic action, or that the third notch on the hammer (which acted as a safety catch) was not replaced by a more efficient system. Old-timers, of course, solved that problem themselves: they carried their pistols with the hammer on an empty chamber. Similarly, the flat mainspring could have been replaced by a coiled spring (as was adopted in many of its modern copies). Colt's considered these questions academic. The pistol was popular as it was, and any changes of a drastic nature could prove prejudicial to sales.

One question, however, remains: how effective was the Peacemaker in action, and I mean aside from bar-room shoot-outs? During the period when it served as the principal side-arm of the United States Army (from 1873 until 1892) the Peacemaker was confined to frontier warfare, mainly against Indians armed with bows and arrows, ancient muskets and a limited number of more up-to-date weapons. There was a brief revival in the Philippines, and, despite some early sales to the Prussians in 1874, possibly the New South Wales Police in the same year (this has never been officially confirmed), the North-West Mounted Police and a few other organizations, its record is not impressive. There were no major wars whose records one could examine to see how the Peacemaker stood up to the rigours of battle, so we must examine its performance in the hands of the man who more than anyone else immortalized it — the gunfighter.

Part Three
THE 'WILD WEST'
1840-1900

Above: This rifle was presented in 1882 by the grateful citizens of Caldwell, Kansas, to Henry Newton Brown, the City Marshal who brought order out of chaos (see plaque). The citizens were soon shaken to the core when, in May 1884, Brown and his Assistant Marshal, Ben Wheeler, were captured when they and others tried to rob the Medicine Lodge Bank. The President and cashier were killed. The gang escaped, but were soon captured and later removed from jail by an armed mob. The prisoners attempted to escape;

Brown was riddled by buckshot and Wheeler and a cowboy named Wesley were hanged. The rifle disappeared for almost 90 years but recently, with the help of R. Larry Wilson, it was found and presented to the Society. (By courtesy of the Kansas State Historical Society)

Below: This photograph of Henry Brown and his gang was made on the day of their capture. Left to right: John Wesley, Henry Brown, Billy Smith and Ben Wheeler (whose .45 Colt Peacemaker

turned up in Liverpool about twenty-five years ago). Brown and Wheeler, accompanied by Wesley and Smith (described as 'cowboys') had obtained leave of absence from Caldwell to go in pursuit of an alleged murderer. Instead, they themselves ended up dead. (By courtesy of the Kansas State Historical Society)

Below right: The Medicine Lodge Posse which captured Brown and his gang. (By courtesy of the Kansas State Historical Society)

A TRADITION OF VIOLENCE

. . . the practice of drawing deadly weapons, except as a last resort for the defense of life,
being dangerous to society and in numerous instances leading to affrays and bloodshed,
notice is hereby given that the same is prohibited and offenders against this regulation will
be summarily dealt with. . . – Vigilante Committee, Virginia City, Montana,
23 September 1865.

IN Western parlance, the 'Frontier' meant a place apart; untamed, largely unsettled and little known. Those who were courageous enough to venture there were a rare breed of self-sufficient individuals, well aware that once they crossed the boundaries of so-called 'civilization', survival was in their own hands. In such a harsh, largely hostile region, each man made his own decisions. The mountain and plainsmen had their own codes of conduct and generally lived by them, but as more people moved West in their wake and townships blossomed, violence might be accepted, but the citizens yearned for law and order, and thereby created a paradox. Despite attempts to civilize parts of the early West, there was no guarantee that the laws of the United States would be implemented. In some territories they proved almost impossible to enforce, and for years the region harboured wanted men, guaranteeing them hide-outs. Only when the railroads, the telegraph and the telephone reached the more remote areas were people able to establish law and order and bring civilization to the places that hitherto had known only the law of the gun.

But long before the six-shooter achieved its reputation as an 'equalizer' and a 'civilizer', there were some who were alarmed at the number of weapons in private hands, and sought ways to disarm the population. Others believed, just as fervently, that without any form of protection the individual was helpless. The arguments rage as vehemently today. Such simplification, of course, is deceiving; there are times when firearms are necessary in the struggle to preserve law and order and the rights of the individual. But what concerned most law-abiding people between the early 1800s and the outbreak of the Civil War, when the flintlock and percussion lock single- and multi-shot weapons gave way to Colt's five- and six-shot revolvers, was the ease with which some individuals were able to invoke a specious 'code of conduct' when settling personal disputes. One's honour and pride, particularly in the Southern states, counted far more than one's responsibility to the local community, and as a result the 'Code Duello' became a passion and almost a pastime.

Fortunately, the situation was never allowed to deteriorate into mass murder, for the authorities made numerous attempts to part antagonists from their pistols although with varying degress of success. Tennessee, for example, in as early as 1801, made it illegal for persons to 'publicly ride or go armed to the terror of the people, or privately carry any dirk, large knife, pistol or any other dangerous weapon, to the fear or terror of any person'. Ten years later Louisiana made it unlawful for people to carry weapons concealed 'in their bosom, coat or any other place', permitting peace officers to search anyone they suspected of being so armed. Free blacks could, with a permit issued by a justice of the peace, carry weapons, but no slave was allowed near one. And with variants, most of the Southern states tried various means of disarming the population, but with little success.

The frontier regions, and those over which State or territorial law had little jurisdiction, or where, for all practical purposes, the law was unenforceable, suffered most from lawlessness. All men went armed, and took care not to be caught alone or taken unawares by the numerous gangs that roamed the territory. Travellers in other parts of the East and West during the 1830s and 1840s also experienced similar evidence of lawlessness. The English traveller, Alexander Marjoribanks, noted that the Bowie knife and the pistol were common sights in

Cincinnati, and expressed the opinion that Queen City was also a tough town, and fast outstripping New Orleans. Another Englishman, James Logan, who had travelled extensively within the United States, recalled that in New Orleans there were many stalls selling pocket-knives, pistols and other weapons that were soon 'scattered in all directions'. In fact, it was supposed that most white men had either carried a knife or played with a pistol before they 'learned to swim'.

Many foreigners were under the impression that all over America the populace were busily snuffing out one another's lives in duels, scrapes and community violence, while pleading self-defence. Given the time and the place, this view is understandable, but there were those that protested vehemently against indiscriminate slaughter and were prepared to involve themselves in establishing law and order – if they had to invoke vigilante justice to do it.

Vigilantes were as much a part of frontier tradition as the cowboy or the gunfighter. Their sometimes drastic action in the face of lawlessness was fiercely criticised, but they achieved results that the more liberally minded wished for yet lacked the courage or inspiration to achieve. The origins of the Vigilante movement in America can be traced back at least to the 1760s, at the time when the British were maintaining a firm hand both militarily and politically, and it lasted in various forms until about 1909, during which time it achieved a notoriety that even today arouses controversy.

Some argue that the British 'regulators' of early eighteenth-century London were a form of vigilantes, but they were legally empowered to act, whereas vigilante 'committees' were locally inspired and frequently motivated by emotion rather than cold-blooded logic. It would be unfair, however, not to point out that vigilantes arose again and again in response to an absence of effective law enforcement. Some such organizations received the blessing of the local community – as did the Vigilante Committee in Hays City, Kansas, in 1869 – while in other places they were a cover enabling the hard-headed and the ruthless to achieve by force that which they could not do via the ballot-box.

In the context of law and order, however, by far the best example of the vigilance committee could be found in San Francisco during the early 1850s, and again in Nevada – both places, incidentally, where gold- and silver-mining were the main industries, and where vigilante organizations assumed the status of unofficial police. In some areas, these arrangements effectively served to deter rather than detain wrongdoers, who learned the hard way that 'civilization' was a

lot closer than they thought. In San Francisco, for instance, it became almost political to cultivate the vigilance committee which rapidly achieved world-wide fame. On 3 September 1851 London's *The Morning Chronicle*, reporting the hanging of a man by order of the vigilantes, declared:

'If the state of society in California demands the existence of a "Committee of Vigilance", the action of that body should be in co-operation with the officers of justice. Acting in defiance of the law, it perpetrates abuses more dangerous than those which it seeks to remedy . . . it "over-rides the law and sets the Constitution at defiance". Its organization is extending itself by branches throughout the whole of California.'

Besides the lack of organized law enforcement – and it should be remembered that in remote areas even English law (which formed the basis of American law) was almost unenforceable – there also existed an economic situation that inspired lawlessness. Having attracted people to a region with promises of boundless riches in gold and silver, some Western states were faced with large-scale unemployment during seasonal recessions. That kind of situation, coupled with rot-gut whisky, gambling and prostitution, soon erupted in violence.

Gamblers, of course, abounded. On the Mississippi and other great rivers where the steamboat was Queen, it was common for captains to allow gambling so long as they received a share of the profits. Indeed, the Mississippi, long described by nostalgic writers and historians as 'The Father of Waters', has been surrounded by an aura of romance, old-fashioned chivalry and charm. It could also be truthfully described as a sewer of social pollution, a convenient rendezvous for thugs, and a haven for horse-thieves. The towns which sprang up along its banks were rife with lawlessness, and every form of 'Southern Comfort' was available.

Those who feared that if violence were not tackled quickly it would become uncontrollable and so-called civilization would degenerate into a welter of debauchery, tended to view the steamboat as the 'carrier of carrion', or a 'floating hell'. The fact that the boats also carried cargoes, inspired trade along the river and encouraged the passage of honest citizens, counted little when set against one's chances of being robbed, injured and occasionally killed by the villainous cut-throats who infested the river-boats and the river-side. On occasion, sedate business men, the very pinnacle of respectability at home, once aboard quickly succumbed to the lure of the gamblers, pimps and prostitutes. Perhaps it was the feeling of being cut off from the world or the illusion of freedom from responsibility that affected them, but whatever the reason, many fell victim and

learned the hard way that gambling and fast women was a fool's game.

The belief that 'if a man owned a bar on a popular packet, it was better than possessing a gold-mine', led few men to riches; many more found early graves. Bar-tenders, skilled at mixing the latest cocktails for the Easterners and mint juleps for the Southerners, were equally adept at fixing a 'Mickey Finn' for the unwary tenderfoot. Alexander Marjoribanks spent some time on steamboats, and recalled in 1853 that drinking went on freely 'among the coloured as well as the white people, some presents of rum in bottles having been sent from the cabin passangers to some of the Negroes on the lower deck, and these getting drunk, became vociferously pious in their potations, and sang, with great fervour, and in full chorus, the Methodist hymn – *We are bound for the land of Canan*.'

Gambling, however, outstripped any other form of 'relaxation' as a 'national pastime' and the problems it created were long-lasting. With time, the onrush of civilization and the establishment of law and order, it was controlled but never eradicated. Consequently, on the river-boats, where it continued to flourish long after the Civil War, it was common to see notices warning 'gentlemen' that they played cards at their own risk. George Devol, one of the most famous of all the Mississippi gamblers, observed that 'every man who is not a professional gambler, is inevitably bound to get up a loser'. He was right, for despite severe punishments, duels fought over debts of honour abounded; the Deringer and the Ace of Spades were a formidable combination.

The 'gambling fraternity' was virtually classless; gentlemen of quality casually brushed shoulders with workers and roustabouts, but any man who failed to redeem his 'note' could expect no mercy. Retribution was swift, and under the guise of a 'debt of honour, sir', one man could literally murder another with impunity. Occasionally there was a violent reaction if an attempt were made to redeem an alleged debt by force. In Vicksburg, Mississippi on 4 July 1835 a gambler named Cabler threatened the life of one of the city's volunteer militia, and went after him with a gun and a knife. Fortunately, his friends intervened, grabbed Cabler, disarmed him and tied him to a tree. He was then whipped and tarred and feathered. Fellow gamblers reacted by killing one of the citizens, and an infuriated mob then lynched five gamblers in reprisal.

A similar situation existed out West, but did not reach fruition until the late 1860s when the railroads brought with them the dregs of humanity, the 'sporting' element to the boom towns and cattle towns. As early as 1855, Frederick L. Olmsted had written in his *A Journey Through Texas*, that there were 'probably in Texas about as many revolvers as male adults'. An exaggeration, perhaps, but it is a fact that in parts of the state, young men became accustomed to handle firearms almost as soon as they could walk, and in view of the state's violent origins it is not surprising!

Texas originally was a part of the Spanish territory which embraced most of the southern part of the present day United States. The intrusion of the French into the area prompted the Spanish to reinforce their territorial claims. In 1689 in co-operation with the Catholic Church, they sent an expedition into the region from Mexico with the object of strengthening their grip and establishing missions. They got rid of the French, but the Indians continued to cause problems. Following the Louisiana Purchase in 1803 and the increasing influx of whites from the northern regions, Spain realized that if she wished to retain her possessions she would have to fight for them.

The first Americans to enter what is now Texas probably did so to hunt or because they were adventurous. The land appealed to many of them and they stayed. Armed for the most part with single-shot muzzle-loading muskets, rifles and shotguns, they were a formidable crowd. The growth of the white population led eventually to the war of 1836, when would-be 'Texians' (as they were known) fought superior Mexican forces. The heroic 'last stand' of the men at the Alamo was followed shortly by the Americans' victory at San Jacinto which delivered Texas from the Spanish yoke. But something else was established in Texas – a reliance upon firearms to settle personal and community disputes.

It has been argued that the revolver revolutionized fighting, bringing a greater strength to the individual who, despite his physical stature, when so armed was the equal of all comers. This certainly applied to Texas! By the early 1830s and well into the 1840s, firearms of all types were regularly imported into Texas from as far away as Europe, but it was Colt's revolver which proved most popular, especially with the Texas Rangers.

Elsewhere we have noted that by the early 1850s California and the people of Kansas and Nebraska territories were also familiar with the use (and mis-use) of the revolver and other weapons. During the Civil War it was the turn of places like Nevada to experience the problems of firearms in the hands of violent men. The discovery of gold at Grasshopper Creek, a tributary of the Beaverhead River in Washington Territory, lured thousands to the region, many of them seeking escape from the war-torn East and the declining Californian strikes. The town of

Bannack sprang up and the lawless element grew so large that to control them a tough individual named Henry Plummer was elected sheriff. His efforts to control the endemic robberies proved almost futile, and the reason was revealed when it was discovered that he was in fact the leader of the gang which had been preying upon coaches, mining-company vehicles and anything else that carried 'dust'. Retribution was swift, members of the gang were rounded up, and together with Plummer himself, were hanged by the local vigilantes.

Montana also witnessed the final act in the tragic career of a man who could have been one of the West's great figures. This was the notorious Joseph Alfred 'Jack' Slade, who evidently enjoyed his reputation as a man 'more feared than the Almighty'. A former soldier in the Mexican War, saloon-keeper, gambler and, for a period, line superintendent for the freight-company, Russell, Majors & Waddell, he was small in stature, but formidable in a fight. His failing was the demon drink; once he got himself 'liquored up' no one was safe. Despite several warnings from the local vigilantes, Slade finally went too far, and on 10 March 1864 they hanged him.

The end of the Civil War gave thousands the longed-for opportunity to relinquish the

Above: Jesse Woodson James from a photograph made in Nebraska in 1874 or 1875. The Robin Hood of America (as some call him) spent a short time towards the end of the Civil War as a guerrilla under Quantrill, and then became a train and bank robber. A sufferer from trachoma, he was considered by many to be paranoid. Jesse's Schofield Smith & Wesson is now in a private collection. (Author's Collection)

gun and return to the plough, but for ex-guerrillas and others whose lives had depended upon their wits and skill with a gun, the West was the ideal place to go. Jesse and Frank James were among those who blamed the Civil War for their treatment at the hands of the authorities who 'forced them' to continue a life of crime. As America's foremost 'Robin Hood', Jesse's reputation as the robber of the rich to support the poor has long since become a part of folklore. The truth is that both he and his brother Frank were little more than common criminals who robbed anyone if it were profitable.

The brothers were born to the Reverend Robert and Zerelda James in Clay County, Missouri; Jesse Woodson James in 1847 and his brother, Alexander Franklin James, in 1843, but it was Jesse who was to become the dominant figure when the pair reached maturity.

When Jesse was three his father left for California where he died, and his mother married a Dr. Reuben Samuel in 1855. At the outbreak of the Civil War in 1861, the family supported the South and Frank joined Quantrill's guerrillas. In 1864 Jesse joined 'Bloody Bill' Anderson and participated in the Centralia massacre when the band murdered 24 unarmed Union soldiers. In 1865 Jesse tried to surrender under a white flag, but because he was a guerrilla he was shot at and seriously wounded. He recovered, however, and within a year he and his brother Frank had begun a career of bank and train robberies that was to last for nearly fourteen years.

By the early 1870s Jesse James was already a frontier legend, and his gang's methods were so efficient that the Pinkerton Detective Agency was brought in to track them down. The Pinkertons, however, overplayed their hand when two men (alleged to be members of the agency) threw a flare into the home of Jesse's mother in January 1875. The explosion killed Jesse's young half-brother, and his mother lost an arm. Many Missourians, who secretly admired the brothers' activities, especially against the railroads, believed that the attack on the Samuels' home was an act of reprisal. Even Jesse and Frank were surprised by the reaction of the public whose demands that the entire gang be granted amnesty were almost met by the State legislature, until common sense overcame romanticism.

In 1876 Jesse and Frank attempted to rob the bank at Northfield, Minnesota but their plan went wrong. A number of people (both gang members and civilians) were killed, and the hunt was on again. Following further robberies, the State of Missouri finally decided enough was enough and offered rewards of $5,000 each for Frank and Jesse

Below: Robert N. Ford, the 'dirty little coward that shot Mr. Howard' (Jesse's *alias* in St. Joseph), photographed some time afterwards. It is unlikely, but just possible, that the pistol in his hand is the one he used. He himself was murdered ten years later. (Author's Collection)

James. Two gang members, Charles and Robert Ford, made a deal with the Governor, Thomas Crittenden, to assassinate Jesse. On 3 April 1882 Robert Ford visited the home of a certain 'Mr. Howard' (Jesse's alias) in St. Joseph, Missouri, and shot him in the back as he stood on a chair straightening a picture. Frank gave himself up four months later. Ford escaped any family revenge, but was killed ten years later. Frank, stood trial for murder and robbery, both in Missouri and Alabama, but was never convicted. He died in 1915.

Equally notorious was Henry McCarty, alias William Bonney, alias Henry Antrim, alias 'Billy the Kid'. The 'Kid's' origin has been disputed for generations, but historian Jack DeMattos finally tracked him down. He was born in New York City on 17 September 1859, the son of Patrick Henry McCarty and Catherine Devine McCarty. His father died in the early 1860s and his mother moved West with her young family (another son, Joseph, and a daughter, Bridget) eventually reaching Wichita, Kansas and later, Silver City, New Mexico. Mrs. McCarty remarried, to a man named William Antrim (Henry's occasional alias), and after her death in 1874, young Henry got into one scrape after another. He adopted the name William Antrim when he worked as a farmhand and later as a cowboy, and because of his age and small size he was soon given the nickname 'the Kid'.

His first reported killing occurred in 1877 when he shot dead a blacksmith named Frank P. Cahill who had bullied him. From then on his life was spent among the cattlemen of New Mexico, and for a time he worked for John Chisum, the cattle baron, and later for the Englishman, John Tunstall. When the Lincoln County cattle war broke out (as a result of a feud between rival ranchers and merchants) the Kid was soon involved. When Tunstall was murdered in 1878 Billy the Kid set out to revenge him, but he gradually became more and more involved with rustlers. Attempts were made to persuade him to give up his life of crime; at one point a pardon was suggested if he would testify in court. He agreed to be arrested, but the men against whom he was to testify escaped, and as a consequence of the lax attitude towards him inspired by the Governor, Billy was able to leave Lincoln, where he was being held in a store-room,

Below: Henry McCarty, *alias* William Bonney — 'Billy the Kid'. Despite claims that he killed 'a man for every one of his 21 years', his 'tally' is closer to six. The original of this photograph was a tintype, which is reported to have been destroyed in a fire shortly after being copied. The tintype process provides a reverse or 'mirror' image, which is why so many people assumed that the 'Kid' was left-handed. (Author's Collection)

without interference when he complained that his pardon was long overdue.

Billy the Kid was soon engaged once more in rustling, and the Governor (General Lew Wallace who was even then working on his classic *Ben Hur*) ordered that he be taken dead or alive, a sentiment heartily endorsed by most of the cattlemen. At one point, Billy was captured, but escaped after killing two guards. Finally, on 14 July 1881, he met his end at Pete Maxwell's ranch when sheriff Pat Garrett shot him dead in the bedroom.

If Jesse James and Billy the Kid were prone to violence and murder, Robert Leroy Parker, alias George Leroy Parker, alias Butch Cassidy, was by comparison almost a saint. Born in 1866 near Circleville, Utah, he ran away with a rustler named Mike Cassidy and adopted his name – the 'Butch' was a reminder of a brief period working in a butcher's shop at Rock Springs, Wyoming. Captured in 1894, Cassidy was jailed in Wyoming, but in 1896 on his promise that he would never 'worry Wyoming again', he was pardoned. Whether that story is true or not is hard to say, but certainly he never committed any more robberies in Wyoming.

Later, in company with a number of equally notorious characters, including Harry Longbaugh (the 'Sundance Kid'), Ben Kilpatrick (the 'Tall Texan') and Harry Tracey, he established a reputation as a train robber and as leader of the 'Wild Bunch', or 'Hole in the Wall Gang', a reference to a hide-out located in a rugged area known as Brown's Hole, at the junction of Utah, Wyoming and Colorado.

During the years that he led the gang, Butch never shot or killed anyone which, for such a character, is exceptional to say the least. But the rapidly changing world of the West in the 1890s, when the telephone and the telegraph was being used to advantage against criminals, soon convinced the gang that their days were numbered. Those that were not killed or captured made themselves scarce. Cassidy and Sundance, accompanied by a girl named Etta Place, decided to quit the United States. Historians now believe that they first took ship to England where Butch visited some family members at Preston in Lancashire, before embarking for South America where they resumed a life of crime. It has been claimed that they were killed in a fight with Bolivian troops in 1911, but the families of both men insist that they survived and returned to the United States where they remained in obscurity. Be that as it may, the legend of Butch Cassidy will long outlive the man.

The West, therefore, presenting as it did a vast tract of land, largely unsettled and thinly populated, was a haven for all manner of wild characters who quickly responded to the opportunities proffered.

12
PERIL ON THE PLAINS

Two hundred and fifty miles from Atchison we . . . discovered the bodies of murdered men
[whom] . . . the Indians had left most barbarously mutilated. These discoveries . . . caused
us to be ever on the alert for an attack. – Theodore Davis, Harper's Weekly, 21 April 1866.

TO cross the Great Plains during the early and middle years of the nineteenth century called for hardy individuals, animals and vehicles, for apart from the warlike Indians, there were also natural hazards which took a great toll of man and beast. When Lewis and Clark, Zebulon Pike and others, confirmed that there was a route from East to West, many determined people were prepared to follow in their footsteps. The war with Mexico added the territory of California to the United States and this, together with the simultaneous discovery of gold in the region (and the subsequent discovery of gold and silver in Colorado and Nevada) encouraged migration. To protect the migrants from the Indians, the Government established military posts in strategic positions, but many of these were isolated and afforded only a limited protection. The chance of a new life and the possibility of striking it rich tended to diminish the dangers in the minds of the adventurous and soon the land routes were crowded with settlers and gold-seekers.

The majority travelled in trains of huge, lumbering wagons drawn by teams of oxen. Horses had been tried, but oxen proved better-suited to a vehicle that at best could make only two miles an hour and perhaps twelve miles a day. The wagons were based on the Conestoga wagon which had been developed in the Conestoga River Valley in Lancaster County, Pennsylvania early in the eighteenth century. The bed of the wagon, some 42 inches wide, was very deep and bowed downwards in the centre like a boat; the front and rear panels were also sloped in boat fashion. Protection from the elements was provided by Osnaburg cloths, or canvas, stretched over eight or sixteen wooden hoops. The wheels at the rear were slightly larger than those at the front, and all had iron tyres. From a distance the white-topped wagons had the appearance of ships and, in fact, were referred to as 'prairie schooners'.

Most of the 'trains' assembled at Independence, Missouri where they were organized under the command of a wagonmaster. Guides were hired, and as many guns were carried as was thought necessary. It was a hard trek of many months to reach the end of the Oregon or Santa Fe trails, and storms, drought, disease and Indian attacks were always likely. It was essential to arrive at their destination before the onset of winter, so if a wagon broke down its occupants might be left behind unless friends were able to take them in. Indian attacks were never so frequent as depicted by film-makers, but when one occurred there was no question of forming a circle. If the occupants were well armed they were usually able to drive their attackers off, for the Indians rarely fought face-to-face unless they had the advantage. At night, there was always a strong guard to protect the stock and the travellers.

Prior to the Mexican war communication between East and West was limited, and depended for the most part on sea routes. In 1849, for instance, a letter from New York to San Francisco had first to be taken from New York by the United States Mail Steam-Ship Company to Panama, transferred by pack-animal or freight-wagon across the Isthmus, and picked up again by the Pacific Mail Steam-Ship Company. Contracts for this service had been drawn up in 1847, and by 1850 the service was being run on a monthly basis. In 1851, however, it was increased to twice monthly with the aid of a Government subsidy of $724,350 per annum. Postage rates were reduced from forty to six cents a half ounce. Fare-paying passengers, however, paid $500 from New York to San Francisco, but plans were already afoot to improve the overland routes.

This was the era of the stage-coach which in some areas lasted well into the 1890s, despite competition from the railroads. In 1850 the first contract to transfer mail from the Missouri River to Salt Lake City went to

Left: A romanticized impression of a fight between troops and Indians. The sabre was not used during the Indian wars, and Indians would never face a cavalry charge. (Author's Collection)

Samuel H. Woodson of Independence, Missouri. A monthly stage-coach service was provided across a route 1,200 miles long and through some of the roughest country known. By the middle and late 1850s a number of similar companies were operating from such centres as Leavenworth, Kansas, St. Louis and Independence, establishing routes to Santa Fe, New Mexico, Denver, Colorado Territory, and on towards Salt Lake and the California coast. Freight-companies, notably Russell, Majors & Waddell; Jones, Russell & Co.; and Jones & Cartwright, all located in Leavenworth, ran freight routes principally to Denver and Santa Fe.

Various coaches were used, the most famous being the Concord, manufactured by the Abbot-Downing Company of Concord, New Hampshire. It was so designed that the centre of gravity was kept equi-distant between the wheels, and there was provision for nine inside and two outside passengers, and ample space for baggage, valuables and mail. When the coach was fully-loaded for a journey that might cover more than 600 miles, the passengers were said to be 'accommodated', but they soon learned just what that meant.

The drivers and conductors (shotgun guards) on the early stage-coaches (and indeed their counterparts on the huge lumbering freight-trains pulled by oxen) were a very tough bunch, armed to the teeth and prepared to shoot first if they thought that their coach, passengers or mail were in danger. In July 1850 the *Missouri Commonwealth*, a paper published at Independence, carried this description of a Concord stage-coach and its protection:

'The stages are got up in elegant style, and are each arranged to convey eight passengers. The bodies are beautifully painted, and made water-tight, with a view of using them as boats in ferrying streams. The team consists of six mules to each coach. The mail is guarded by eight men, armed as follows: each man has at his side, fastened in the stage, one of Colt's revolving rifles, in a holster below one of Colt's long revolvers, and in his belt a small Colt's revolver, besides a hunting knife; so that these eight men are ready, in case of attack, to discharge 136 shots without having to reload. This is equal to a small army armed as in the ancient times, and from the looks of this escort, ready as they are either for offensive or defensive warfare with the savages, we have no fears for the safety of the mails.'

Mules are hardier than horses and were used in rough country, but once the going got easier, the faster horse took over. Of the Colt revolvers mentioned in the foregoing account, the 'long revolver' was the six-shot Dragoon; the 'small' revolver was either the five-shot Baby Dragoon or perhaps the 1848–49 pocket-pistol complete with rammer. These, together with the six-shot rifle, gave each man seventeen shots, making a total of 136 for eight men as stated.

Richard Burton, ex-Indian Army officer, and celebrated African explorer, was, as we have previously noted, a devotee of Colt's revolvers. He, too, went West in 1860 and his book, *The City of the Saints and Across the Rocky Mountains*, published in 1862, gives a graphic picture of the West and its people. He boarded a stage-coach at St. Joseph, Missouri, bound for Salt Lake and paid $175 for the trip. After detailing his items of clothing and other personal requirements, he continues:

'For weapons I carried two revolvers: from the moment of leaving St. Jo. to the time of reaching Placerville or Sacramento the pistol should never be absent from a man's right side – remember it is handier there than on the other – nor the Bowie knife from his left. Contingencies with Indians and others may happen, when the difference of a second saves life: the revolver should, therefore, be carried with its butt to the fore, and when drawn it should not be levelled as in target

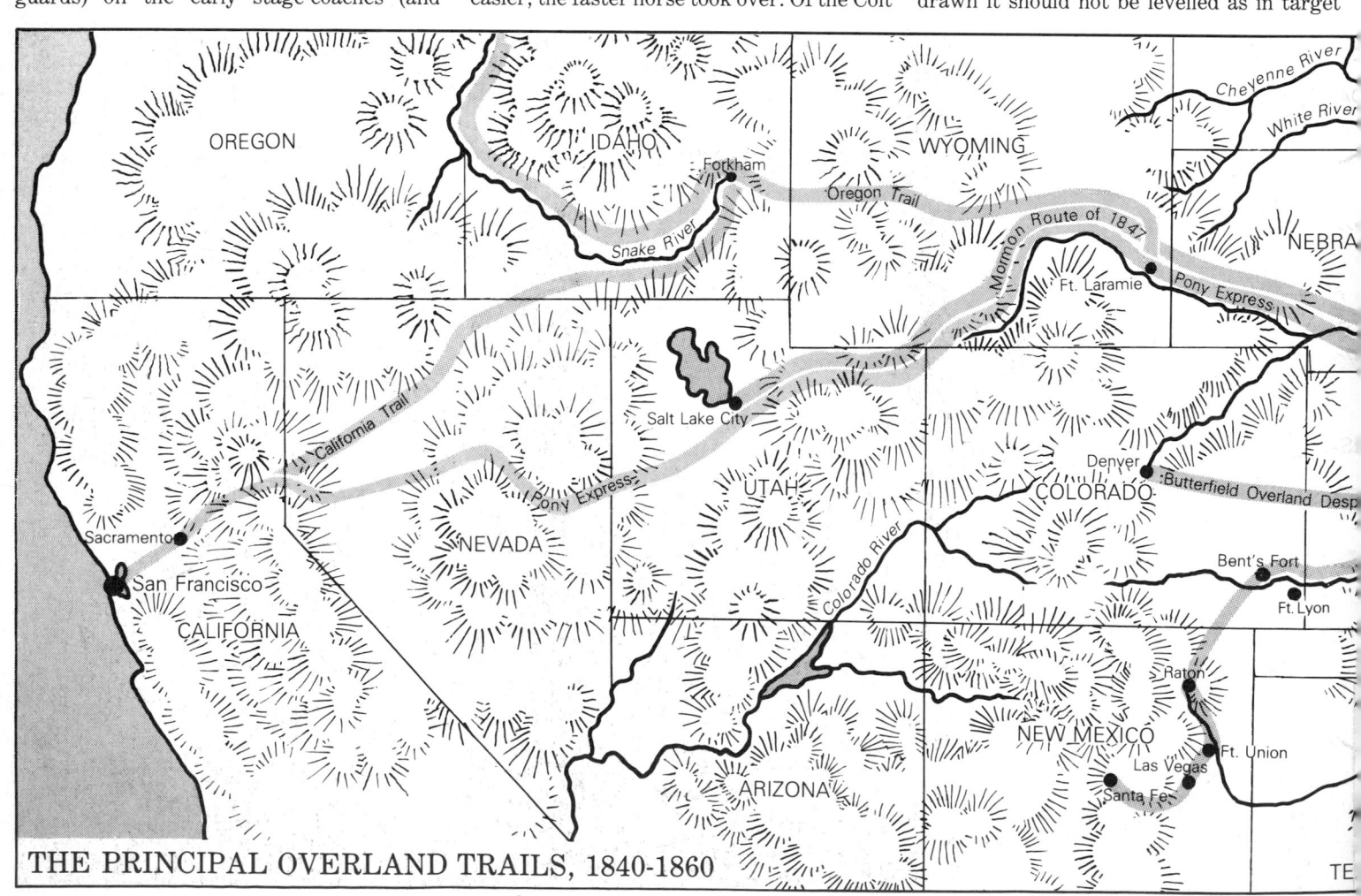

THE PRINCIPAL OVERLAND TRAILS, 1840-1860

practice, but directed towards the object, by means of the right forefinger laid flat along the cylinder whilst the medius draws the trigger. The instinctive consent between eye and hand, combined with a little practice, will soon enable the beginner to shoot correctly from the hip; all he has to do, is to think that he is pointing at the mark, and pull. As a precaution, especially when mounted upon a kicking horse, it is wise to place the cock upon a capless nipple, rather than trust to the intermediate pins. In dangerous places the revolver should be discharged and reloaded every morning, both for the purpose of keeping the hand in, and to do the weapon justice. A revolver is an admirable tool when properly used; those, however, who are too idle or careless to attend to it, had better carry a pair of "Derringers". For the benefit of buffalo and antelope, I had invested \$25 at St. Louis, in a "shooting iron" of the "Hawkins" [sic] type, – that enterprising individual now dwells in Denver City, – it was a long top-heavy rifle, it weighed 12 lbs., and it carried the smallest ball – 75 to the pound – a combination highly conducive to good practice. Those, however, who can use light weapons, should prefer the Maynard breech-loader, with an extra barrel for small shot; and if Indian fighting is the prospect, the best tool without any excep-

Above: A group of plainsmen fighting off an Indian attack. From a sketch by Remington. (Author's Collection)

Below: 'Pilgrims on the Plains'. Families heading West found plenty of game and water, but were sometimes attacked by Indians. (Author's Collection)

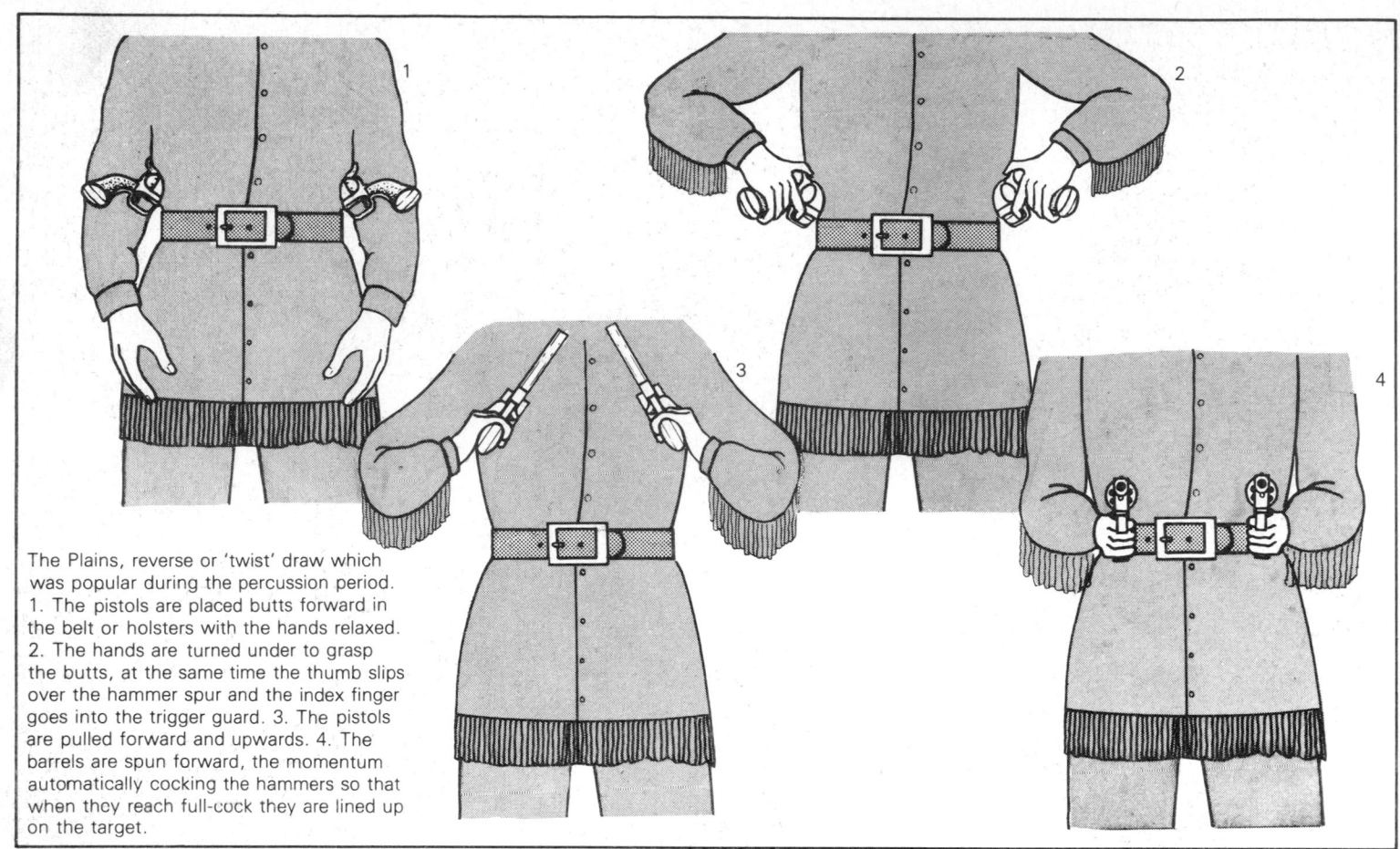

The Plains, reverse or 'twist' draw which was popular during the percussion period. 1. The pistols are placed butts forward in the belt or holsters with the hands relaxed. 2. The hands are turned under to grasp the butts, at the same time the thumb slips over the hammer spur and the index finger goes into the trigger guard. 3. The pistols are pulled forward and upwards. 4. The barrels are spun forward, the momentum automatically cocking the hammers so that when they reach full-cock they are lined up on the target.

tion, is a ponderous double-barrel, 12 to the pound, and loaded as fully as it can bear with slugs. The last of the battery was an air-gun to astonish the natives, and a bag of various ammunition.'

Burton's description of the Plains 'twist' or 'reverse' draw is interesting, but I find it difficult to accept his suggestion that one should lay the index finger along the cylinder. The index finger must be used if the operation is to be performed properly and at speed. In essence, the thumb is slipped over the hammer spur, the index finger goes into the guard, and the pistol is pulled and spun forward so that the weight of the barrel cocks the weapon; at this point the barrel is dead in line with the target. To have attempted such a manoeuvre without using the index finger would have proved disastrous.

Burton also gives a graphic description of a typical bull-train driver or 'ripper' as some called them. He says that he dressed in a variety of clothes from buckskins to flannel and cotton shirts, heavy pants or buckskins thrust into cowhide wellington boots, and on his head a sombrero that could assume almost any shape or form. Occasionally, the individual appeared looking more Indian-like than the real thing. Some men also wore green goggles as protection from the dust and glare of the sun. But without exception a 'broad leather belt supports on the right a revolver, generally a Colt's Navy or medium size [pocket-pistol] (when Indian fighting is expected, the large Dragoon pistol is universally preferred); and on the left, in a plain black sheath, or sometimes in the more ornamental Spanish scabbard, is a buckhorn or ivory-handled Bowie-knife. In the East the driver partially conceals his tools; he has no such affectation in the Far West: moreover, a glance through the wagon-awning shows guns and rifles stowed along the side.'

Burton's earlier reference to discharging his revolver daily focuses attention upon the problem faced by gun owners of the time: the salt-laden black powder tended to get damp and required constant attention. Misfires were common, and since safety was important, most revolvers were carried butt forward rather than along the thigh as with later weapons; if the pistol discharged accidentally, the ball would miss the wearer. The old-timers preferred the 'twist' or 'reverse' draw not only because it was safer, but once mastered it was much faster than a cross or hip draw.

Passengers on the coaches were also expected to play their part in defending themselves. Should the driver shout 'Indians', they knew that the coach would pick up speed to try to outrun them. The cry 'turn out!' meant that they should leap from the coach and prepare either to defend it or help push it up some particularly steep slope.

Indian attacks, a plains hazard that had been common for many years, had increased during and immediately after the Civil War because of the lack of frontier troops, so travellers had to exercise great care when in hostile areas. The *Harper's Magazine* artist, Theodore Davis, who made a trip along the Butterfield Stage route in 1865, and published his account of it in 1867, mentioned an incident which took place at Downer's Station, Kansas, on the day before his arrival. Although the Indians had professed friendliness, but 'like a rattlesnake, may be trusted only when his fangs are removed; otherwise, it is well to give him a wide berth or be prepared to kill him on sight', the passengers were wary. The Indians asked to shake hands, which was done, and then they drove up some mules they had recently scattered. Suddenly, the Indians attacked, killing a messenger (guard) and capturing two stocktenders. The survivors raced to a buffalo wallow and prepared to fight to the death. A passenger gave this account of what happend when the Indians attacked:

'They formed a circle about us, riding dexterously and rapidly; occasionally one more bold than the rest would come within range of our revolvers, but he was careful to keep his body on the side of his pony away from us. Arrows came from all directions; a rifle or revolver bullet would whistle past us or strike the earth near. It was evidently

Above: James Butler 'Wild Bill' Hickok from a photograph taken in about 1873 when he was a member of Buffalo Bill's theatrical show. Despite the costume (which was similar to that used by some men on the plains) Hickok's pose is not entirely 'theatrical'. The knife is a prop, but the position of his two Colt Navy pistols is authentic. (By courtesy of the Kansas State Historical Society)

Top right: The stage-coach drawn by six horses is a familiar feature of most Western films. This still comes from perhaps the most famous Western of all – John Ford's 1939 *Stagecoach* which was shot on location in Monument Valley. (Author's Collection)

Above right: This sketch from *Harper's Weekly* in 1867 is an accurate representation of the use of mules instead of horses over rough country. Attacks by Indians were common, but well-armed passengers and crew usually managed to drive them off. (Author's Collection)

their purpose to permit us to exhaust our ammunition, when they would be able to take us alive. Of this fact we were painfully aware and only fired at them when we were sure of a good shot. This kept them at a distance. The Negro blacksmith was armed with a Ballard rifle, with which he was a capital shot. He bravely exposed himself to obtain a shot, and came near losing his life by so doing. A bullet struck him in the head, when he fell, as we supposed, dead. I took his rifle, rolled the body up to the edge of the wallow to serve as a breastwork to shoot from, and commenced to fire. I had made several shots in this way, and had the rifle across his neck with a dead aim on an Indian when the darkey came to and remarked, "What you doin dar, white man?" thus discovering to us the fact that he was anything but a "gone coon dis time". He had been deprived of speech and power of motion by the shot, but was fully aware of what was going on about him. He was not disposed to regard the use of his body as a breastwork as altogether a pleasing performance.

'While we were fighting from the wallow, we could plainly see the Indians that still remained about the adobe, at work torturing the stock-herders that they had succeeded in capturing alive.

'One poor fellow they staked to the ground, cut out his tongue, substituting another portion of his body in its place. They then built a fire on his body. The agonized screams of the man were almost unendurable; about him were the Indians dancing and yelling like demons. The other stock-herder was shoved up to look at the barbarous scene, the victim of which he was soon to be, but they reserved him until nightfall, evidently hoping that we might be added to the number of their victims.

'There could not have been less than a hundred and fifty Indians in the entire party – that is, those who were about us and those near the adobe . . . Had there been a possible chance to rescue the stock-herders, we should have attempted it. When darkness came the Indians withdrew, and as soon as we were convinced of the fact, we followed their example, going, it is unnecessary to remark, in the other direction. Chalk Bluffs we found deserted and the station burning. Then we heard the coach coming and came to it. The Indians would have probably taken you in if we had not.'

That sort of experience was just one of the many 'diversions' faced by those who embarked upon a mode of travel that was uncomfortable, occasionally nauseating (when the coach swung violently upon its leather thoroughbraces) and always exhausting. A far cry from the romantic scene depicted in most Western films!

The stage-coach and freight-wagon were, however, too slow for those determined to improve communications, and by 1859 plans were already afoot to span the country by means of the telegraph. Before this could be established, however, a much more spectacular means of communication was organized. It was by no means a new idea, having been used in various forms since ancient times, but its Western innovation led to world-wide fame and a continuing admiration as one of the West's most spectacular legends – The Pony Express.

The demand for faster communications led, in 1859, to the culmination of plans by Russell, Majors & Waddell, proprietors of the Leavenworth & Pike's Peak Express Company. In February 1860 the firm became the Central Overland California & Pike's Peak Express Company, and organized a fast pony service between California and the middle West. The Pony Express began operations on 3 April 1860, and provided an eight- to ten-day service between St. Joseph, Missouri and Sacramento, California. Stages or exchange stations were set up nine to fifteen miles apart. The riders were expected to ride three different animals between three different stations and cover about thirty-three miles per trip. In an emergency they might be called upon to ride longer distances. The riders were young, light-weight and tough enough to withstand the rigours of hard galloping over hard country. It was a very dangerous job, and the following terse advertisement which appeared in the San Francisco newspapers early in 1860 described the type of rider required:

'WANTED'

'Young, Skinny, wiry fellows, not over 18. Must be expert riders willing to risk death daily. Orphans preferred. Wages $25 a week.'

There was no shortage of applicants.

Richard Burton states that the riders were 'mounted upon active and lithe Indian nags'. Perhaps some were, but most of the animals were small, sturdy but very fast Mexican ponies, ideal for hilly and mountainous country. Advertisements asking for grey mares 'from four to seven years old, and not to exceed fifteen hands high, well broke to the saddle', also appeared in the Leavenworth and San Francisco papers.

Specially-made light-weight saddles and stirrups were used and a specially-designed mail bag, the *mochila*, which had four *cantinas* or hard leather pockets which could be locked, was provided for the mail. The *mochila* (probably derived from a Basque word meaning errand-boy) fitted over the saddle by means of two holes through which the saddle horn and cantle protruded. Letters were written on tissue paper and charged at $5 in gold per half ounce or less, and those who insisted upon weighty letters paid as much as $27.50 for the privilege. Telegrams, too, could be carried and were charged at $6.90 for a ten-word message and twenty cents for each additional word.

Speed was of the essence: two minutes were allowed for a change of horses at relay stations, but so adept were the riders that even as they reached the exchange point they were half out of the saddle, the *mochila* clutched in their hands . . . a leap to the ground, a dash to the waiting pony, held ready by one of the stock-tenders, the *mochila* slung into place . . . grasp the reins, a slap on the rump, or a loud 'giddap!' and as the pony broke into a run, the rider raced alongside sprang effortlessly into the saddle and sped on his way. This most spectacular form of mounting a horse became famous, and Buffalo Bill Cody used it with considerable effect in his 'Wild West' 23 years later. In England in May 1888 one of Cody's per-

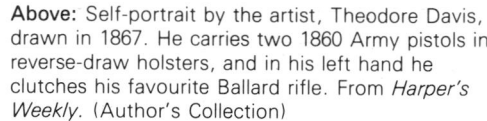

Above: Self-portrait by the artist, Theodore Davis, drawn in 1867. He carries two 1860 Army pistols in reverse-draw holsters, and in his left hand he clutches his favourite Ballard rifle. From *Harper's Weekly.* (Author's Collection)

Left: A group of Kansas settlers fighting off an Indian attack. From a steel engraving on a Union Military Scrip for $50, issued in June 1867, as compensation for damage caused by General Sterling Price's raid in 1864. (Author's Collection)

Top right: Passengers on an overland mail-coach camping for the night, hold a 'council of war' in preparation for an Indian attack. Note the assortment of weapons. Sketch by Theodore Davis, from *Harper's Weekly.* (Author's Collection)

Above right: On 12 October 1861 the *Illustrated London News* published this romantic sketch of a Pony Express rider. He looks more like a stable lad from Newmarket Racecourse than a 'young, skinny, wiry fellow'. However, it did give the British public some idea of what was involved. Of greater interest, of course, is the artist's inclusion of a Colt revolving carbine of the type originally issued to the Pony riders. (Author's Collection)

Russell was called to Washington to account for the crisis because the company had received a substantial amount of Government money in connection with their mail franchise. Watching events was Ben Holladay, who had lent the company a considerable sum of money and held the first mortgage. Then on 16 April it was announced in the San Francisco *Daily Herald* that:

'Messrs Wells Fargo & Co., have received a transfer of the Pony Express and everything referring thereto from Mr. W. H. Russell, and the first thing they do is, to advertise a material reduction in the charge for conveying letters. Hereafter, until the 1st of July next, half ounce letters will only be charged $2 each, the letters to be enclosed in ten cent government envelopes, and the postage to be prepaid. The Pony will leave the office of Wells, Fargo & Co., on Wednesday and Saturday of each week . . .'

By 1 July the rates had been further reduced. Letters weighing a half ounce or less were $1, and for every additional ounce or fraction of an ounce, an additional $1. Telegrams sent to Fort Kearney on a Monday and Friday morning could connect with the Pony leaving St. Joseph on Wednesdays and Saturdays. By October, however, even Wells, Fargo were having difficulty in keeping the Pony Express running, and their trans-Missouri Pony Express service (which has never received the same publicity as the original organization) was itself the victim of progress. On 24 October 1861 the Western Union overland telegraph line was completed from Omaha, Nebraska Territory, to California via Salt Lake City, and shortly afterwards the Government mail contracts for the Pony Express were officially terminated. Wells, Fargo continued to run short Pony routes until the mid 1860s, but their own stage-coach routes took precedence, and it is this part of the company's history which is best remembered. In March 1862 Ben Holladay finally took over the stage-coach routes of Russell, Majors & Waddell and renamed the company The Overland Stage Lines. It was the end of an episode characterised by heroism and devotion to duty that became a byword.

The youngsters who rode the Pony Express knew that each time they set out from one station they had no guarantee that they would reach the next, but they relied on a minimum of weapons, weight, of course, being the prime consideration. At first they carried two Colt's Navy revolvers and either a carbine or a Colt's revolving carbine or rifle. The rifles and carbines were soon discarded, together with one of the pistols, but some riders carried a spare loaded cylinder in a specially-made pouch on the pistol belt. Even this extra weight was begrudged by

formers, an ex-Pony Express rider, successfully beat off the challenge of some fine English thoroughbreds in a ten-mile relay race at Manchester, with thirteen changes of horses, simply because he could change horses in seconds, whereas his English rival stuck to the more conventional method.

The Pony Express rider, at full gallop and crouched over the neck of his steed, was a colourful figure. Coach passengers and others eagerly watched for him and admired his horsemanship. Mark Twain in *Roughing It* recalled the effect a Pony Express rider had upon himself and his companions when their stage-coach driver alerted them:

'"Here he comes!"'

'Every neck is stretched further, and every eye strained wider. Away across the endless dead level of the prairie a black speck appears against the sky, and it is plain that it moves. Well, I should think so! In a second or two it becomes a horse and rider, rising and falling, rising and falling – sweeping toward us nearer and nearer – growing more and more distinct, more and more sharply defined – nearer and still nearer, and the flutter of the hoofs comes faintly to the ear – another instant a whoop and a hurrah from our upper deck, a wave of the rider's hand, but no reply, and man and horse burst past our excited faces, and go winging away like a belated fragment of a storm.

'So sudden is it all, and so like a flash of unreal fancy, that but for the flake of white foam left quivering and perishing on a mail sack after the vision had flashed by and disappeared, we might have doubted whether we had seen any actual horse and man at all, maybe.'

By April 1861, however, Russell, Majors & Waddell were in serious financial straits, and their vast freighting empire was at stake.

Above: A contemporary view of the Pony Express rider, from an original oil painting. (By courtesy of the Kansas State Historical Society)

the company, but the riders were determined to protect the mail at all costs.

Apart from defending stage-coaches, wagon trains and, for a short period, the Pony Express, the frontier army was faced with the daunting task of keeping the entire frontier safe, but because it was never large enough to provide adequate protection for all, civilians organized themselves into volunteer groups. Some were officially attached to the army, others were formed for the duration of hostilities only. On the Plains, during the late 1860s, particularly in Kansas and Colorado, when Indian hostility was at its height, bands of civilian 'scouts' were organized into militia, much to the relief of people living in outlying areas.

During the Civil War, the Indians, largely unchecked, had endangered the frontier settlements. The Sioux, Kiowa, Arapaho and Cheyenne menaced the Plains, while in New Mexico and Arizona the Apaches carried out hit-and-run attacks on white settlements. The army viewed the situation with concern, and when Washington decided to take a firm hand, it prepared itself for a hard time.

Most of the Indian veterans wanted peace, but the young braves were anxious to flex their muscles, prove their manhood and test the army's strength. In 1867 Washington ordered Lieutenant-General William Tecumseh Sherman, commanding the Division of the Missouri, to take action, and he in turn ordered Major-General Winfield Scott Hancock, Commander of the Department of the Missouri, to take the field against the Indians in Kansas, with the object of persuading them to return to their reservations. Unfortunately, when the Indians found themselves confronted by six com-

panies of Custer's 7th Cavalry; seven companies of the 37th Infantry Regiment, and a battery of the 4th Artillery, they panicked and fled, leaving a trail of burned settlements behind them. In reprisal, Hancock had their villages burned and ordered Custer in pursuit. After months of marching and counter-marching, little had been achieved, but a semblance of peace was restored with the signing of a treaty at Medicine Lodge.

By August 1868, however, the Indians were again on the warpath, and General Philip H. Sheridan, who now commanded the Division of the Missouri, ordered the 7th Cavalry to Fort Larned and went there himself to hold a council with the Indians, though with little success. On 16 August William 'Medicine Bill' Comstock, one of the best of the Plains scouts, was murdered as he left the camp of the Cheyenne Chief Turkey Leg, where he had been trying to persuade the chief to control his braves and to determine whether the whites had been stirring up trouble. Sheridan now declared that he had had enough. Most frontier dwellers felt the same, and when reports of Indian depredations reached Hays City and other railroad towns, they swiftly organized groups of men to fight. Soon they were joined by outlying settlers who feared for their families' lives.

On 19 August, the Hays City 'First Independent Company of the State Militia' was formed, with Deputy U.S. Marshal John S. Park as its captain, and Matthew Bouton and Chauncey B. Whitney (who was murdered at Ellsworth in 1873 by Ben Thompson's brother Billy) as his lieutenants. Indian attacks on stage-lines and freighting outfits

were now a daily occurrence, so Sheridan took a train ride to Fort Harker where he saw evidence of the 'murders by Indians'. When he reported this to General Sherman he was ordered to 'compel' the Indians to remove themselves south of the Kansas border and, if necessary, to kill those who resisted. Sheridan realized that this would lead to war, but he hoped it could be confined to local action.

With only 2,600 men in the District of the Upper Arkansas, of whom 1,800 were employed protecting forts, railroads and stage-lines, Sheridan had only 800 troops available to conduct an offensive. Sherman was not keen on state militia, but Sheridan decided to form his own. On 24 August he ordered Brevet Colonel George A. Forsyth, a major of the 9th Cavalry Regiment, to hire fifty 'first class hardy frontiersmen to be used as scouts against the hostile Indians . . .' Forsyth was to command, with Lieutenant Beecher as his second in command.

Scouts, guides and couriers employed by the U.S. Army were normally very well-paid. They came under the jurisdiction of the Quartermaster General's Department, and were hired and fired by the resident post quartermaster or his assistant. A good man could command $100 a month, but the average wage varied between $50 and $75 per month, depending on the man's position or worth. Bearing in mind that a private soldier received the princely sum of $13 (later reduced to $11 due to economies) per month, it is easy to see why there was no love lost between 'civilians' and the military.

Although most of the hired men owned their own horses and weapons, they could be supplied with them by the Quartermaster's Department. It was common for scouts and guides to carry one or two revolvers on their belt and, if available, one or a pair of spare pistols in saddle holsters. Some men also carried a rifle or carbine slung across their shoulders or in army-style saddle 'buckets'. But in place of the thoroughbred horses depicted in Western films, most of them rode mules, their own or the army's. Mules were more sure-footed than horses, in the wilderness of scrub and gopher-holes and had greater stamina and speed in rough country. California Joe (Moses E. Milner) swore by his mule, and his great friend James Butler 'Wild Bill' Hickok, once undertook a dangerous journey by mule from Fort Hays to Fort Harker in April 1867, to carry a message requesting supplies. Armed with two Colt's Navy revolvers and a carbine, Wild Bill reckoned his mule could cover the sixty miles by daylight unless diverted by Indians. He summed-up his chances by stating that he reckoned he was 'good' for at least a dozen of them before they got him!

Forsyth's scouts, however, did not come within the normal category of army scouts, being basically frontiersmen recruited for a specific task. For this they were paid $1 a day plus 35 cents per day maintenance for the horse. The volunteers were signed up as 'Quartermaster's employees' to justify the issue of a Spencer repeating rifle and 140 rounds of ammunition, together with a Colt 1860 Army revolver and thirty rounds. Seven days' emergency rations were also issued and a four-mule pack train carried 4,000 cartridges, together with medical supplies, salt, coffee and other camp equipment. Abner 'Sharp' Grover was appointed chief guide. His presence caused some concern among the men, however, because he had been with Comstock when he was killed, and despite being severely wounded himself had made his escape. Some believed that he had in fact murdered Comstock and blamed the Indians. The company's surgeon was Dr. John Mooers, assistant surgeon at Fort Hays.

Forsyth's company set out for Fort Wallace where they arrived on 5 September. Here they were given a further supply of ammunition – 100 rounds for each revolver and 400 for the rifles, together with an additional ten days' rations. On the 8th they set off for Sheridan, then the end of the line for the Union Pacific Railway, Eastern Division, where they learned that some men had been killed by Indians. Later the company reached the Arickaree Fork of the Republican River, which Forsyth later described as the Delaware Fork in his letters to Fort Wallace requesting assistance.

On the 17th, they were attacked by a large number of Sioux and Cheyenne. Reports as to the number of Indians involved numbered between 400 and 900, but the actual number was probably somewhere between the two. The Indians, in addition to their usual lances and bows, were armed with an assortment of firearms, some of them up-to-date .44 Henry and Spencer rifles; a few also carried pistols.

Their leader was the famous Cheyenne war chief, Roman Nose, said to be six feet three inches tall. He was dressed for war, painted, and he rode his horse bareback, his toes tucked into a horse-hair rope tied around the animal, which he controlled by a simple bridle attached to its lower jaw. His commands were preceded by the sounding of an army bugle, which at first deceived the defenders into believing that a relief force was on its way.

After the first attack had been repulsed, Forsyth and his men retreated to an island in the centre of the dried-up riverbed. Some supplies were lost, but they managed to save some ammunition and tools which enabled them to dig in. Here they repelled a number of attacks during which Lieutenant Beecher was killed, Forsyth severely wounded and Surgeon Mooers mortally wounded – he died a day or so later. During one of the mass charges, Roman Nose was also killed, and as the day drew to a close, the riverbed was littered with dead Indians and horses. The scouts had 24 dead and wounded.

Late in the evening, Jack Stilwell and Pete Trudeau slipped out of camp and across the river with a dispatch for Fort Wallace, and on the evening of the 19th, scouts A. J. Piley and Jack Donovan left on a similar mission. Forsyth's message of the 19th described the state of his men and he added:

'The Cheyennes numbered four hundred and fifty (450) alone, or more. Mr. Grover says they never fought so before they were splendidly armed with Spencer and Henry rifles. We killed at least thirty-five of them & wounded many more, besides killing & wounding a quantity of their stock. They carried off most of their killed during the night but three of their men fell into our hands. I am on a little island & have still plenty of ammunition left. We are living on mule & horse meat and are entirely out of rations. If it was not for so many wounded I would come in & take the chances of whipping them if attacked. They are evidently sick of their bargain . . .'

Forsyth urged that no fewer than 75 men be sent to relieve him, plus ambulances (coaches or wagons specially fitted out for more comfortable transportation of the sick) and wagons, and suggested that the post commander bring 'a 6 pdr. Howitzer with you. I can hold out here for 6 days longer if absolutely necessary but please lose no time.'

Stilwell and Trudeau reached Fort Wallace three days after leaving Forsyth, and Donovan and Piley soon afterwards. The army wasted no time; nine days after the fight had begun the besieged men heard the shrill note of a cavalry trumpet and Captain Louis H. Carpenter led troopers of the 10th Cavalry into action against the Indians. The Cheyenne and their allies withdrew, still firing, and soon afterwards, Colonel Bankhead, in command of Fort Wallace, arrived with wagons, ambulances and medical supplies. The Battle of the Arickaree (commonly called Beecher's Island in honour of the young officer who died there) was over, but the courage of those who took part has become a Western legend. Some of the survivors later joined Lieutenant Silas Pepoon to become a unit of the 'Pepoon Scouts'.

General G. A. Custer remarked on several occasions that the well-armed state of the Indians was partly the fault of the officials in government who made sure that they were. In his book, *My Life on the Plains*, published in 1874, he recalls his meeting with Pawnee Killer, Bull Bear and other chiefs in 1867. The warriors he notes, were bedecked in war bonnets and feathers and carried the usual bows and lances.

'In addition to these weapons, which with the hunting-knife and tomahawk are considered as forming the armament of the warrior, each one was supplied with either a breech-loading rifle or revolver, sometimes with both – the latter obtained through the wise foresight and strong love of fair play which prevails in the Indian Department, which, seeing that its wards are determined to fight, is equally determined that there shall be no advantage taken, but that the two sides shall be armed alike; providing, too, in this manner the wonderful liberality of our Government, which not only is able to furnish its soldiers with the latest improved style of breech-loaders to defend it and themselves, but is equally able and willing to give the same pattern of arms to their common foe. The only difference is, that the soldier, if he loses his weapon, is charged double price for it; while to avoid making any such charge against the Indians his weapons are given him without conditions attached...'

Reaction to the Indian was very much divided. Contemporary reports are biased according to the state of relations at the time, but it is evident that no white man fully trusted the Indian who, for his part, had no good reason to trust the whites! On both sides, however, there were those who did their best to try and bring about some form of co-existence. It was a hard land and its peopled learned the hard way that a gun was a necessity – and when you needed it, you needed it in a hurry.

13
THE BUFFALO HUNTERS

I used a big fifty-calibre Sharps' rifle. It shot a hundred and twenty grains of powder, and the bullets were an inch and a quarter long. When one of these big leads would hit a buffalo, whether it hit the right place or not, it would make him sick. It wouldn't be long before I put another into him. – George W. Brown, a Kansas pioneer.

THE Great Plains, parts of Texas, the northern part of the United States towards Canada and, to a very limited extent, the eastern states, were home to the bison, a shaggy-haired, hump-backed, species of ox. Early visitors had mistaken it for the kind of buffalo found in India and Africa, but by the time the error was realized, the name 'buffalo' was in common use and as such the animal has been immortalized. Just how many of these animals there were is not known. Conservative estimates of thirty million in 1850 are usually stretched to sixty. More important is the significance of the buffalo in the Red-White relationship during the latter half of last century.

The buffalo was vital to the North American Plains Indian. From it he obtained meat; its hide provided robes, rugs and tepee coverings; its sinews, intestines and bones were fashioned into numerous domestic implements. The white man, however, saw the buffalo as yet another barrier to the eventual civilizing of the continent, and its removal was inevitable. The extermination was not accomplished by one generation; the slaughter really started during the post Civil War period, with the coming of the railroad and the springing up of townships, in the midst of the buffalo ranges.

There were two main herds: the northern and the southern. The southern herd was found in Kansas, Nebraska, parts of Texas,

southern Wyoming and Indian Territory (now called Oklahoma); the northern herd ranged across the Dakotas, Montana and northern Wyoming. Being a migratory animal, the buffalo 'follered the feed', as the old-timers would say, and although afflicted by poor eyesight, hearing and scent, the buffalo had an uncanny ability to do the most unpredictable things. Although the bulls fought one another over their cows and 'territories', experts believe that it was the cows that tended to be dominant and become leaders. The reaction of the buffalo to attack, depicted in most books as similar to a raging bull elephant, and mentioned elsewhere in this present study, was disputed by the last of the old buffalo runners, Frank Mayer, who died in 1954 age 104. In his classic, *The Buffalo Harvest*, he expressed doubt that any buffalo would turn upon its hunter; rather, he would run.

Mr. Mayer should have known, but I am sure that there were instances when the animals did attack their tormentors. I can recall comments made when I saw my first buffalo in Nebraska and later in the Custer State Park in 1965, followed by a visit to the small herd at Fort Hays, Kansas. I was greatly impressed by the creatures' majestic bearing and almost benevolent appearance, but I was glad a stout fence stood between myself and a formidable female named 'Calamity Jane', who, with her aptly named mate, 'Wild Bill', ruled the small herd at the fort. 'Wild Bill' had his moments and could be 'ornery', I was told, but 'Calamity' was a terror, and very dangerous. Everyone took great care to keep out of her way!

The huge herds depicted in most books and films were rarely seen except during migration. For the most part the animals split up into small groups, usually composed of a number of bulls, cows and calves. A stampede often increased the numbers when a herd joined another in a blind panic and thundered across the prairie destroying anything in its path. Stampedes were uncommon, but the migratory marches posed problems. According to the Junction City, Kansas, *Union* of 2 November 1867:

just west of Ellsworth, a 'train was intercepted by a whole herd of buffaloes and compelled to halt until they had crossed the track . . . for three miles the buffaloes pushed along parallel with the train, heedless of many shots fired among them, and finally swept across the track, ahead of the locomotive, fairly worsting the iron horse by bringing him to a halt'. Even the Texas longhorns *en route* for the Kansas cow towns were forced to halt when the mighty buffalo rumbled past.

During the building of the transcontinental railroads, the contractors found that the cheapest means of feeding the army of workers was to provide them with buffalo meat, and they hired a number of men to secure the supply. The Union Pacific Railway, Eastern Division (the U.P.E.D.) was built across Kansas between 1867 and 1870. In 1867 several hunters were hired, the most notable being William F. Cody, alias 'Buffalo Bill'. For eighteen months he supplied buffalo meat, and when his contract expired in May 1868, by his own reckoning he had killed 4,280 buffaloes.

In his *Life*, published in 1879, Cody described how, armed with his favourite rifle, 'Lucretia Borgia', and mounted on his best horse, 'Brigham', he would ride into a herd of buffalo, and once among them, would remove his horse's bridle. 'The moment the bridle was off', he wrote, 'he started at the top of his speed . . . and within a few jumps he brought me alongside the rear buffalo. Raising "Lucretia Borgia" to my shoulder I fired, and killed the animal at the first shot. My horse then carried me alongside the next one, not ten feet away, and I dropped him at the next fire. As soon as one buffalo would fall, Brigham would take me so close to the next, that I could almost touch it with my gun. In this manner I killed eleven buffaloes with twelve shots.'

Frank Mayer, however, was not much impressed by this form of slaughter. He noted that the buffalo had short legs, a huge body and was easily outpaced by a good horse. But the 'sport' had its attraction in that the innumerable prairie dog holes, down which an unwary horse could easily step, break a leg and pitch its rider into the path of one or more charging buffalo, made it hazardous, but that was all. And the practice of riding into a herd and using a pistol on the animals (as did Hickok on occasion, and so depicted by Catlin in the 1850s) might have been spectacular, but it was not very practicable.

The real slaughter of the buffalo began about five years after the end of the Civil War. No one knew how many of the animals there were, and many assumed that there were 'millions of 'em', and that the supply would never cease. An estimated 10,000 men, including some very tough characters,

were engaged in hunting the buffalo between 1870 and 1880. Some were ex-mountain men, who had seen the demand for beaver pelts disappear in the early 1860s, but the majority of them were ex-soldiers, storekeepers, farm-hands and others lured by the prospect of quick riches. But hides were fetching only $2 or $3 each, so if they were lucky, they netted about $2,000–$3,000 per year. Out of these earnings came expenses: food and camp supplies, a good skinner, a couple of horses or mules and a stout wagon.

The market for buffalo hides was prompted by a lack of suitable cow hides rather than a deliberate policy of extermination. For years the leather industry had

obtained its hides from the pampas of South America, but by about 1870 the supply had begun to dwindle and anxious contractors were looking elsewhere. Some hides were obtainable from Australia, where the cattle industry was as yet in its infancy, and others from the United States, but despite the enormous number of longhorn and domestic cattle, the demand could not be met. In 1870 an English tannery made a contract with a Leavenworth company; delighted with the quality of the leather, they placed further orders. The British War Department also examined buffalo hide and found that it was ideal for the manufacture of horse harness for the artillery, and they became regular

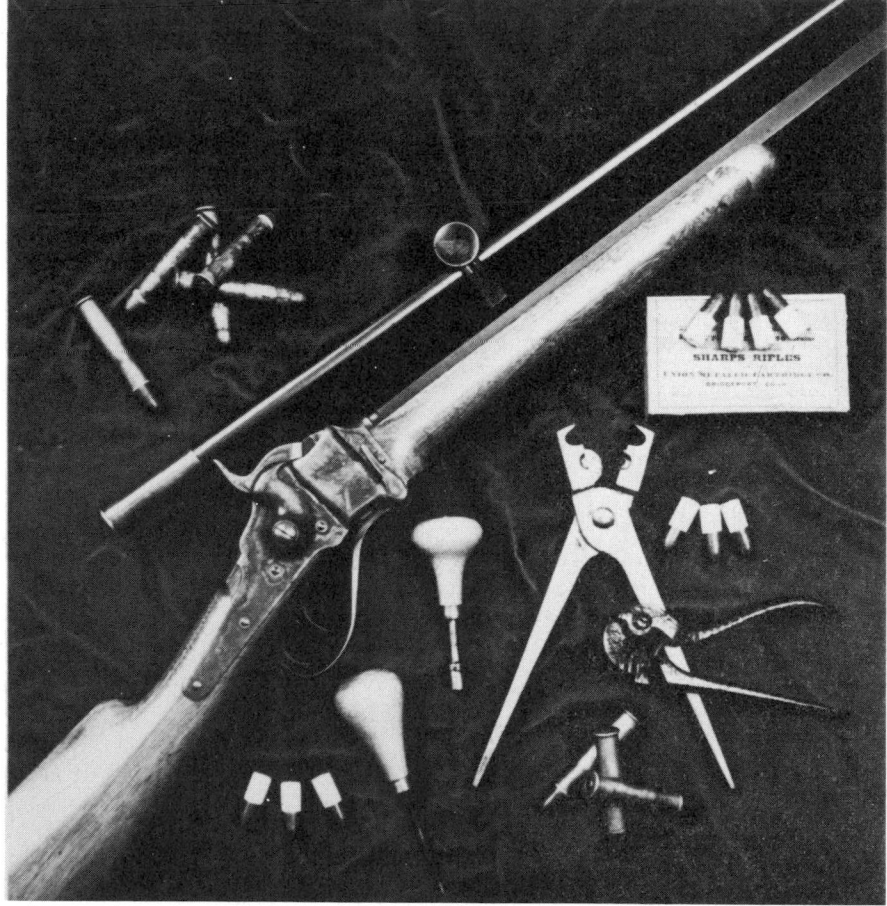

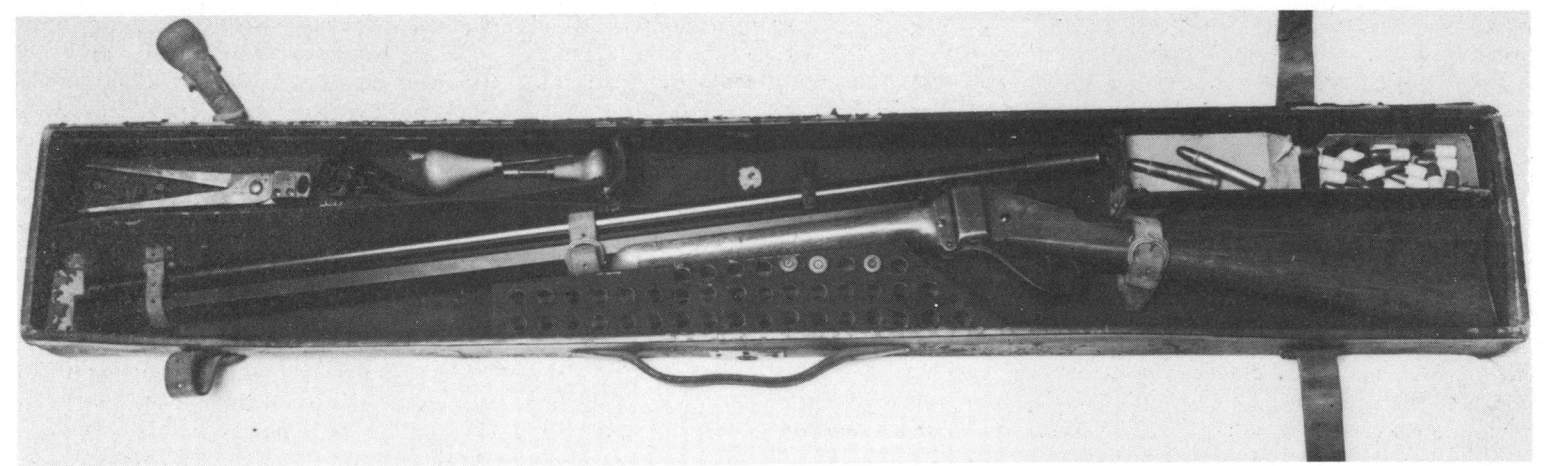

Far left: William 'Bill' Tilghman (left) is one of the most famous of the old-time peace officers. He bears a striking resemblance to the young Joel McCrea. He and his friend James Elder were photographed in about 1872 when they were both working as buffalo hunters. Tilghman is holding a Sharps' rifle and what appears to be a cleaning rod. Note the cartridge belt containing ammunition for the Sharps. (Author's Collection)

Left: A fine Sharps' Model 1874 sporting rifle, serial No. C53900, complete with accessories, some patched bullets and a box of original ammunition. It is alleged to have once belonged to Jay Gould, the telegraph and railroad financier of the 1880s – America's version of the 'robber baron!' (By courtesy of Frank N. Graves, Junior; photograph by Don Beardslee)

Below left: A group of buffalo stuffed and mounted, and displayed to give an impression of their natural habitat. (By courtesy of the late Earle R. Forrest)

Top: The Jay Gould rifle in its case, complete with accessories and bullets. Many of these rifles were carried to and from the buffalo ranges in such cases. This one weighs thirteen pounds. (By courtesy of Frank N. Graves, Junior; photograph by Don Beardslee)

Below right: A sacred white buffalo. This animal, named 'Big Medicine', was, until its natural death in 1959 or 1960, the sacred white buffalo of the Flathead Indians in Montana. Such creatures have long been revered by the Plains Indians. The animal is now mounted and on display at the Montana State Museum at Helena. (By courtesy of the late Earle R. Forrest)

customers. Soon buffalo hides were in demand from both American and European firms and the rush was on.

It has been claimed with some truth that although the United States Government never stated as much publicly, it was not averse to the disappearance of the buffalo if this led to the subjugation of the Indian and forced him to remain on his reservations. Mayer and others have intimated that various army officers never denied this – indeed, if a hunter ran short of ammunition (or claimed that he had) he had only to approach the commander of an army post to be supplied with some. Most of it was in .45–70 calibre, which the hunters usually broke up, melted the bullets for recasting and either replaced the military powder with better commercial loads, or traded it for supplies.

Treatment of the hides was very important, because a spoiled skin was unsaleable. In the early days only cows were shot because their hides were softer and more pliable and there was always the chance of finding an elusive 'silk'. A silk was a very special hide with long silky-like hair which commanded a higher price than the normal hides. The rarest of all was a 'White Buffalo' hide which was thought to be invaluable; to the Indian it had a spiritual value beyond price. Skinning was a filthy job, and one that required a lot of

skill. Few hunters relished struggling to remove a 150-pound hide in one piece. Once removed the hides were pegged out flat, flesh side up, and allowed to dry for a few days before being rolled up in bundles of ten and loaded on wagons for removal to a shipping point. It was hot, tiring work, and if the rewards were not high, they were guaranteed. Skinning was made worse in summer by the thousands of flies that plagued buffalo and hunters alike. Blood from the slaughtered animals caked up clothing as it dried, and the mixture of blood, burnt powder, sweat and tallow raised a stench that made it prudent to approach the hide men from an upwind direction.

The Indians had hunted the buffalo for centuries. Prior to the introduction of the horse into America, they used to stampede the animals into a trap, which invariably meant running them over a cliff. Later, from the back of a fast, agile pony, a bow and arrow or lance was used; but when the white man arrived with his guns, other and more scientific methods were tried. We have noted that 'running' buffalo from the back of a horse was not very successful, and once it was found that the buffalo did not stampede if one of its number suddenly keeled over, the use of the 'stand' took a deadly toll. When an animal went down its companions sniffed at it, prodded it and attempted to push it back upright. The runners saw that they were too stupid to realize what was happening and were able to slaughter them all.

According to Mayer and others, one could not afford to get too close to a herd; at ranges under 200 yards the heavy boom of the gun could cause a stampede. And Mayer was particularly scathing of artists who depicted buffalo runners despatching their prey from a prone position. Fired close to the ground, the report of the gun would reverberate and could 'spook' the herd into motion. So the 'stand' or rest stick began to be used. It consisted of two pieces of hard wood bolted or lashed together close to the top leaving a 'V'-notch or cross about thirty

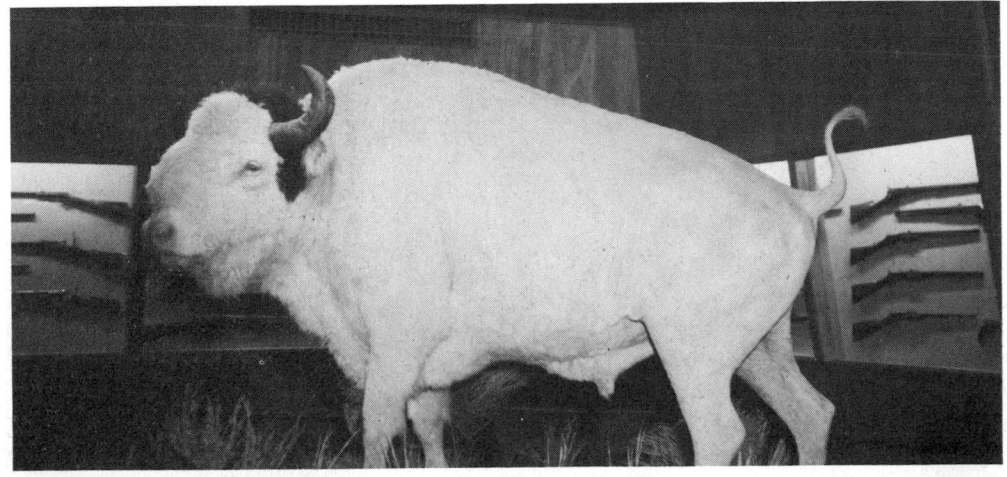

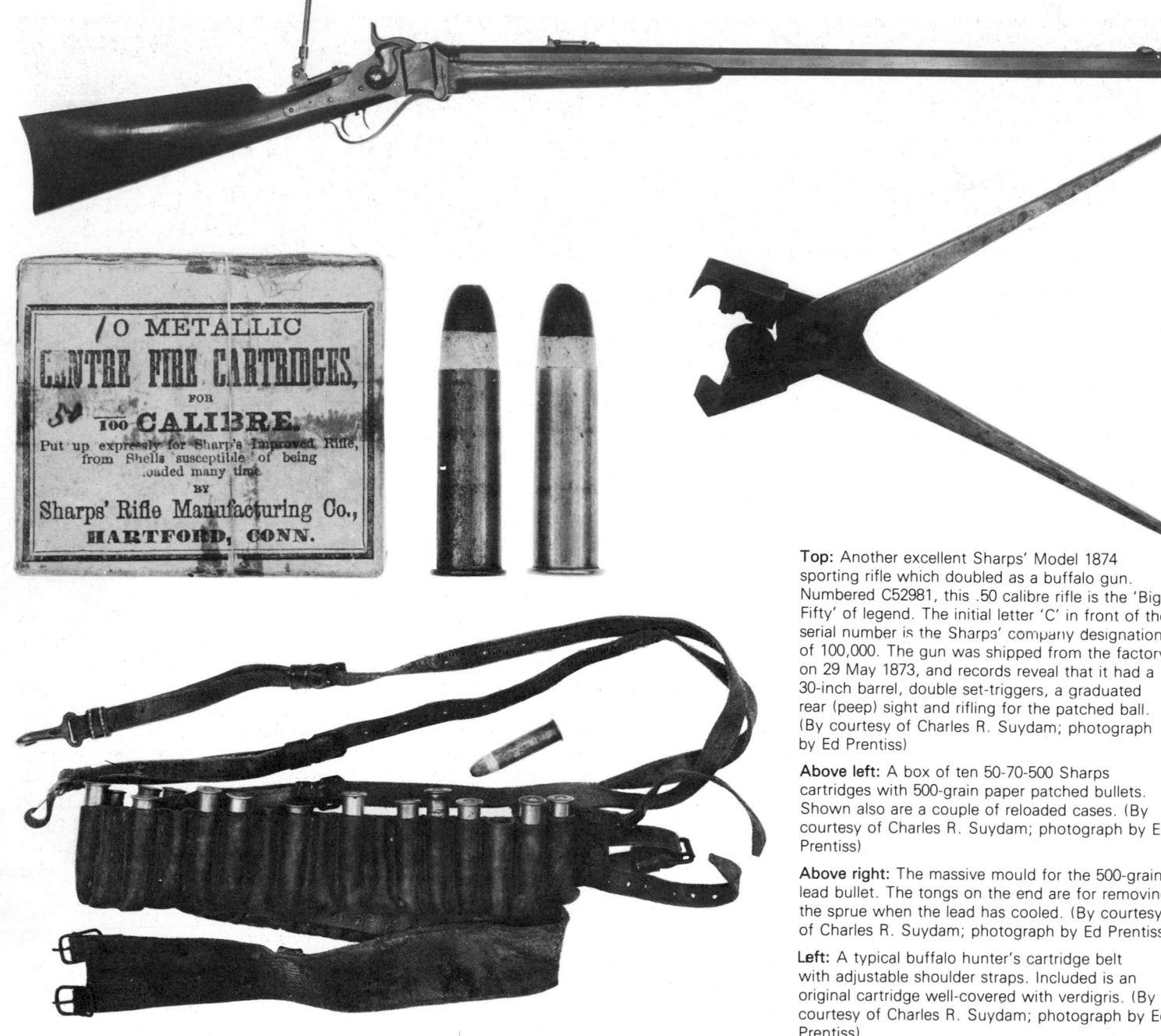

Top: Another excellent Sharps' Model 1874 sporting rifle which doubled as a buffalo gun. Numbered C52981, this .50 calibre rifle is the 'Big Fifty' of legend. The initial letter 'C' in front of the serial number is the Sharps' company designation of 100,000. The gun was shipped from the factory on 29 May 1873, and records reveal that it had a 30-inch barrel, double set-triggers, a graduated rear (peep) sight and rifling for the patched ball. (By courtesy of Charles R. Suydam; photograph by Ed Prentiss)

Above left: A box of ten 50-70-500 Sharps cartridges with 500-grain paper patched bullets. Shown also are a couple of reloaded cases. (By courtesy of Charles R. Suydam; photograph by Ed Prentiss)

Above right: The massive mould for the 500-grain lead bullet. The tongs on the end are for removing the sprue when the lead has cooled. (By courtesy of Charles R. Suydam; photograph by Ed Prentiss)

Left: A typical buffalo hunter's cartridge belt with adjustable shoulder straps. Included is an original cartridge well-covered with verdigris. (By courtesy of Charles R. Suydam; photograph by Ed Prentiss)

inches above the ground in which one rested the barrel of the rifle. The sticks were set into the ground and held steady by the shooter's left hand.

The reader may be puzzled by the use of the word 'runner' but that was how the men described themselves. They may have been (and still are) called 'buffalo hunters' by everyone else, but among themselves they were runners. To be called a 'hunter' on the plains implied one who shot any kind of game from jack-rabbit to deer, so the individual who referred to another as a 'buffalo hunter' was branded a tenderfoot. It was rare for a man to hunt alone because the task of stalking, shooting, skinning and transporting meat and hides was too much for one person to handle. Therefore, it was necessary for

every hide-hunter to be backed up by at least one skinner and a wagon that followed him as he shot his way through a herd.

The guns of the buffalo men varied. In the immediate post-war years many relied upon military Springfields, Henrys, Ballards, Spencers and Sharps. Buffalo Bill's 'Lucretia Borgia' was a .50–70 calibre Springfield converted from muzzle-loading to accept the Allin system, which included a long firing-pin, and was often mistakenly called a 'needle gun'. Cody boasted that his rifle could throw a ball twice the weight of the military version and, if it hit the vital spot, kill a buffalo at 600 yards.

Of the other military arms, the Spencer carbine was all right at short range but useless at normal buffalo range. The same

could be said for the Henry, and even military-converted .50–70 Sharps carbines proved inadequate. The Ballard rifle was better adapted to the task, but its ejector caused problems and the professionals soon discarded it. In the end it was a choice between the Remington and the Sharps. Both were produced in similar calibres, and apart from mechanisms and other refinements, were almost on a par. The Sharps, however, had the edge. Mayer recalled that there were many camp-fire debates as to the relative merits of each. The Remington was available in .44–70 and .44–90 calibre and chambered for bottle-necked cartridges. Sharps also produced this type of cartridge, but the straight-sided version was more popular, and Mayer said he preferred it. His

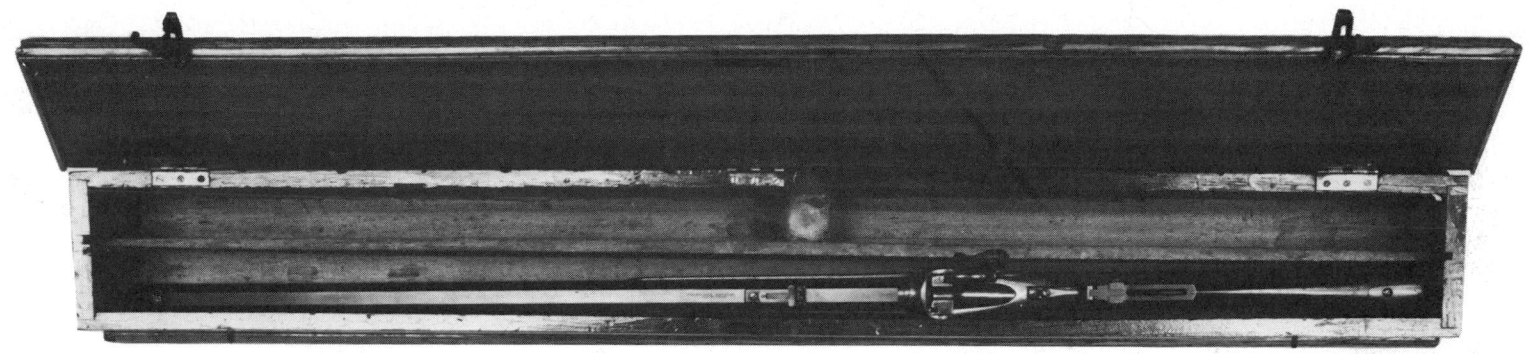

Above: The Sharps' original case which has been with it since 1874. The items shown in these photographs are now quite rare. (By courtesy of Charles R. Suydam; by Ed Prentiss)

ultimate choice was the Sharps because he preferred its action. The Remington's rolling-block breech was opened by a spur on the top, and it was a fast, efficient action, but the Sharps' falling breech-block activated by the trigger guard appealed to Mayer and to many others.

Buffalo rifles were on a par when it came to price. A good one cost anything from $100 to $300 depending on whether one wanted set-triggers, barrel length, telescopic sights (available with 10, 20, and 30 power) or other refinements. Mayer's first Sharps was purchased from Colonel Richard Irving Dodge, who parted with it for $125. It was of .40–90–420 calibre (that is, a .40 calibre bullet weighing 420 grains and backed by 90 grains of black powder), fitted with a walnut stock, a 32-inch barrel and having a total weight of twelve pounds. Along the barrel he mounted a 20 power telescopic sight made by A. Vollmer of Jena in Germany. He replaced the cross-hairs with upper and lower stadia hairs, which he set so that he could cover a vertical space of thirty inches at 200 yards.

Mayer used only the best powder to load his cartridges. Factory loads cost too much, and were rarely available on the buffalo ranges where it was necessary to have a plentiful supply of lead or pre-cast bullets, primers and other necessary tools. Mayer recalled that the two leading American brands of powder (Dupont and Hazard) although of good quality, tended to burn hot and dry which caked-up the barrels and necessitated constant cleaning. Various means were tried to remedy this, the commonest being to run cold water or urine through the barrel (the latter was well shaken up so that the ammonia could work on the bore), followed by hot water. The bore was then dried thoroughly and pulled through with a rag soaked in graphite tallow. Without this sort of attention, the accuracy of the gun was seriously affected.

Mayer solved the powder problem when he came across a can of English powder made by Curtis & Harvey. He also acquired the products of Pigou, and Laurence & Wilks. Their fine-grain powders burned 'moist' and developed much better energy than the American variety, so he used them for the remainder of his career. Purchased from Tyron of Philadelphia, he said they cost fifty per cent more than the American powder, but the increased price was worth it.

Mayer's experience with powder was shared by most of his contemporaries who were all concerned with quality in the pursuit of quantity. The tools available though crude by modern standards, were effective. A man who lacked the correct reloading dies was forced to improvise. To remove a spent primer or cap, the case was pushed into a hole, bored in a piece of hard wood, just large enough to accept the shell and hold it rigid. The spent primer was then removed by a 'cap awl'. A new primer was placed in position followed by the powder charge which was varied by trial and error until the desired quantity was achieved. A flat paste-board wad was then placed on top of the powder, followed by a $\frac{1}{16}$-inch disc made of beeswax and sperm oil which acted as a 'lubricator'. Finally, the bullet, which was also dipped in this same mixture, was placed in the shell and pressed home by a 'bullet seater', supplied by Sharps for $1 extra. For those who chose to patch the bullets with what the old instruction sheets termed 'trapezoid-shaped pieces of fine banknote paper', the 'bullet seater' was unnecessary because the ball was seated by hand pressure. Sharps also furnished empty brass cases for hand-loading at prices ranging from $22 to $32 per thousand, depending upon calibre and case length. It was the company's proud boast that some of their cases had been reloaded and fired in factory tests more than 500 times before being sold!

The Sharps company produced a number of fine weapons designed exclusively for buffalo hunting. The standard calibres were .40 and .45 with straight-sided cartridges, and the rifles were clearly marked to indicate the case length and calibre. The breech would bear the legend .40–1½; .40–2½; or .40–3½ (and similarly for the .45 calibre weapons). Mayer recalled that the rifling on the old Sharps varied in depth from four to five one-thousandths of an inch, but was shallower if paper patched bullets were used and seldom exceeded two and a half one-thousandths of an inch. He added that in calibres exceeding .45–50 there was a uniform twist of one in sixteen inches. Despite protests from the makers, guns supplied to special order had quicker or slower twists; in those days, of course, the customer was always right.

The accuracy and stopping-power of the old Sharps rifles were legendary, but by modern standards they would be considered weak. Muzzle velocity ranged between 1,400 and 1,500 feet per second with standard loads, but experimentation got them up to 2,000 feet per second. With properly adjusted telescopic sights and the right loads, the old-timers reckoned that they could hit anything they aimed at from 500 to 1,000 yards. At these ranges, many thought the Sharps .45–125–550 with patched bullets, was the best gun of them all. Mayer had seen 200 buffalo killed with one of these rifles at one stand, at between 300 and 600 yards with 200 shots, which was remarkable shooting by any standards.

The Sharps company provided standard as well as custom-made weapons. Barrel lengths ranged from 30 to 36 inches and were either round or octagonal, or a combination of both. The company also supplied set-triggers and special sights if required. The total weight of weapons varied from as low as ten pounds to as heavy as thirty pounds. The heavier guns, and particularly those supplied with telescopic sights were, of course, designed to be fired from a rest. The increased weights also allowed the use of more powerful and better-quality ammunition. The commonest calibres were the .45–70–420; .45–90–500; .45–100–500 and the .45–120–550. In about 1876 the company reintroduced the old Sharps trademark from the Christian Sharps era: 'Old Reliable', which was stamped on top of the barrel. Perhaps the most famous of all Sharps rifles was the celebrated 'Big Fifty', a massive weapon chambered for a .50–170–700 cartridge. Many believe that this was *the* buffalo rifle, but ironically, it arrived too late for the main slaughter, most of the

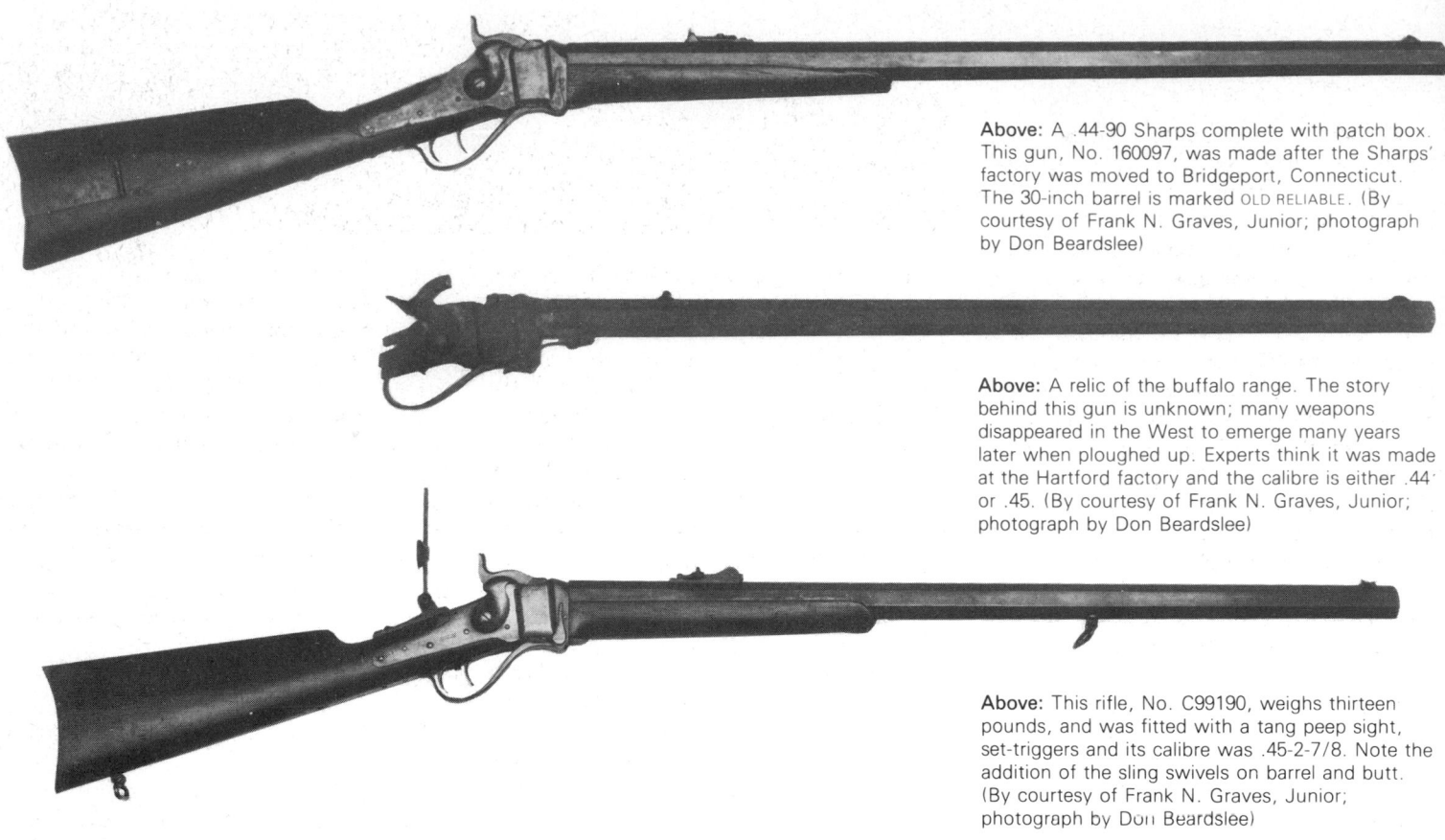

Above: A .44-90 Sharps complete with patch box. This gun, No. 160097, was made after the Sharps' factory was moved to Bridgeport, Connecticut. The 30-inch barrel is marked OLD RELIABLE. (By courtesy of Frank N. Graves, Junior; photograph by Don Beardslee)

Above: A relic of the buffalo range. The story behind this gun is unknown; many weapons disappeared in the West to emerge many years later when ploughed up. Experts think it was made at the Hartford factory and the calibre is either .44 or .45. (By courtesy of Frank N. Graves, Junior; photograph by Don Beardslee)

Above: This rifle, No. C99190, weighs thirteen pounds, and was fitted with a tang peep sight, set-triggers and its calibre was .45-2-7/8. Note the addition of the sling swivels on barrel and butt. (By courtesy of Frank N. Graves, Junior; photograph by Don Beardslee)

buffalo harvest having been reaped; but a few were used against the rapidly dwindling herds or against such game as the grizzly bear.

Contemporary recollections by buffalo hunters are few and eagerly sought. Therefore, the following letter* found among the effects of the late Joseph Bates of Wortham, Texas, a well-known collector of Sharps rifles, is a graphic account of a buffalo hunter's experience on the Texas plains near present-day San Angelo:

'Head of the North Concho
Saturday Dec. 30, 1876

'Dear Dave: I have not heard from you since I last wrote – nor from anybody else. I suppose there are letters for me somewhere, but they have not yet reached me.

'I have reached at last a primitive and wild country. It is part of the old Comanche hunting grounds. We are camped 60 miles up the North Concho from the Post and close by another camp of buffalo hunters. I have degenerated from a would be sportsman to a man who hunts for a living. Cas will tell you all the particulars I have not time now.

'I traded off my pony for a black pony and that pony I traded at the Post for a Sharps carbine .50 cal. and 16 cartridges or 14, I

*'A Buffalo Hunter's Letter', by Roger N. Conger, *The Gun Report*, August 1981. I am very much indebted to the Editor and Publisher for permission to reproduce this letter in full.

have forgot which. I could get no more in town – by town of course I mean Fort Concho. I have done no hunting yet having no ammunition. My partner does the hunting and I help skin and do the staking and cooking. I shot two buffalo out of a herd that came on me while I was skinning. There are lots of buffalo on all sides. The hunters are a different class of people than you have met in Texas – not akin to the cowboy – they are men who have hunted and trapped all over the west from the Black Hills south to Texas.

'The gun they swear by is Sharps .44 cal. just like yours, they shoot 90 grains powder, some use the .50 cal. and 120 grains. The best gun in this part of the country is a Sharps .40 cal. with 90 grains of powder, the ball weighs 420 grains. The hunter who has it says he can hit and kill a bull as far almost as he can see it. It holds up wonderfully. The .44 cal. day before yesterday loaded with 85 grns powder, 420 grns lead, shot through several bulls in succession at 500 yards.

'My partner shoots a Maynard .40 cal. ring ball 70 grns powder 340 grn lead. He shot a bull last week just to one side below the tail – the ball lodged in the tongue. The bull was 250 yards distant. Shooting from one side the balls mostly go through and frequently kill two at once. The Maynard seems to do as good work as the .44 cal. Sharps. The only objection my partner has to it is that it ought to shoot a patch ball. Shooting 20 or 30 times inside of half an hour leads the gun and pro-

bably wears it out sooner. The 40 cal. Sharps must be the Boss Gun. You see it shoots the same amount of powder as the 44 with a longer ball. The Winchester is a laughing stock among these men – they would not take one as a gift if they had to use it. These hunters ought to be pretty good authority for most of them have killed the Grizzly, the Cinamon Bear, which they say is about as bad – the Elk, the Blacktail Deer, the Panther, the Indian, the Greaser and ect. They are the company I have been in since I came to Texas, not excepting your own.

'If I cannot make a living in any other way I shall turn hunter and in the spring if I have enough money to get an outfit, that is, wagon, horses and ect. I shall start north through the Territories and hunt perhaps in the Black Hills. There will be a great deal of money in meat there selling to the miners and new Forts which are to be built. We have up to this evening 52 hides dry average from 35 to 55 lbs. cows from 15 to 30 lbs.

'No more time to write now – must make bread for tomorrow. My partner goes to town for ammunition and provisions – taking 30 hides – all that are dry. I hope he sells them for enough to pay for what we want to buy, for we have no money. I have written this letter by the light of a piece of cottom [*sic*] cord hanging out of a plate filled with buffalo tallow. Love to all. Yours very truly,

P. C. Bicknell

'P.S. We have a very comfortable wigwam or tepee built with poles and 10 hides – fire in the middle – very comfortable.'

Who Mr. Bicknell was or what became of him is not known, but his comments provide a fascinating glimpse into what was both a hazardous and (to some) romantic way of life.

By 1880 the buffalo was a rare sight; the runners off on some other pursuit, and the boom of the mighty Sharps scarcely heard. It had been a hectic era. Dodge City, known originally as 'Buffalo City' when it was started in 1872, had taken the lion's share of the hides and shipped them out east by the carload on the Atchison, Topeka and Santa Fe Railroad. When the hides were gone, there was a profitable but brief boom in bones for fertilizer or for refining sugar. But one facet of the slaughter that had angered the Indians and many whites, was the practice of slaughtering buffalo for their tongues and leaving the carcass to rot. The tongues were smoked and packed in barrels and were sold for about 25 cents each. Mayer recalled selling 1,000 tongues to the Carlton Club in London for $500. In 1880 it was estimated that there were less than 100 animals left, and it was then that Charles 'Buffalo' Jones stepped in and, with the help of other

equally devoted people, ensured the survival of the buffalo.

Curiously, as late as the 1930s when the animal had begun to breed in sufficient numbers to necessitate culling, there were few in authority who gave much thought to the manner in which the creatures should be slaughtered, and many suffered needlessly. The Denver Mountain Park were faced with this problem one Christmas when they decided to kill eight animals to feed the poor. Using modern high-powered rifles in such calibres as .35 Remington, .30–30 and .30–'06 (meaning .30 calibre U.S. Government Model 1906); the men detailed to do the job were using up to fifteen shots per animal to kill it. Outraged, the Mayor of Denver demanded: 'Go get an Indian!' Frank Mayer's comment (that which he could trust himself to put into print) was that an old-time buffalo runner should have been called in.

Failing that, someone could have at least got hold of the right rifle, preferably a Sharps.

Few bufffalo are killed today, and then only to cull a herd (although it is reported some are being bred for the table). Those that remain are fascinating creatures. Although confined in parks and reserves, they create the impression of majesty; a dignified aloofness, almost as if they are aware that they are a living monument to the time when the buffalo was Lord of the Plains.

Above: A top view of a Sharps telescope tube bearing the company's marking. These are rare, for they were usually supplied by outside contractors. (By courtesy of Frank N. Graves, Junior; photograph by Don Beardslee)

Below left: The Remington Creedmoor rifle price list, circa 1876. Note the different sights. (Author's Collection)

Below right: This woodcut shows the action of the rolling-block system which, as can be seen, was very strong. (Author's Collection)

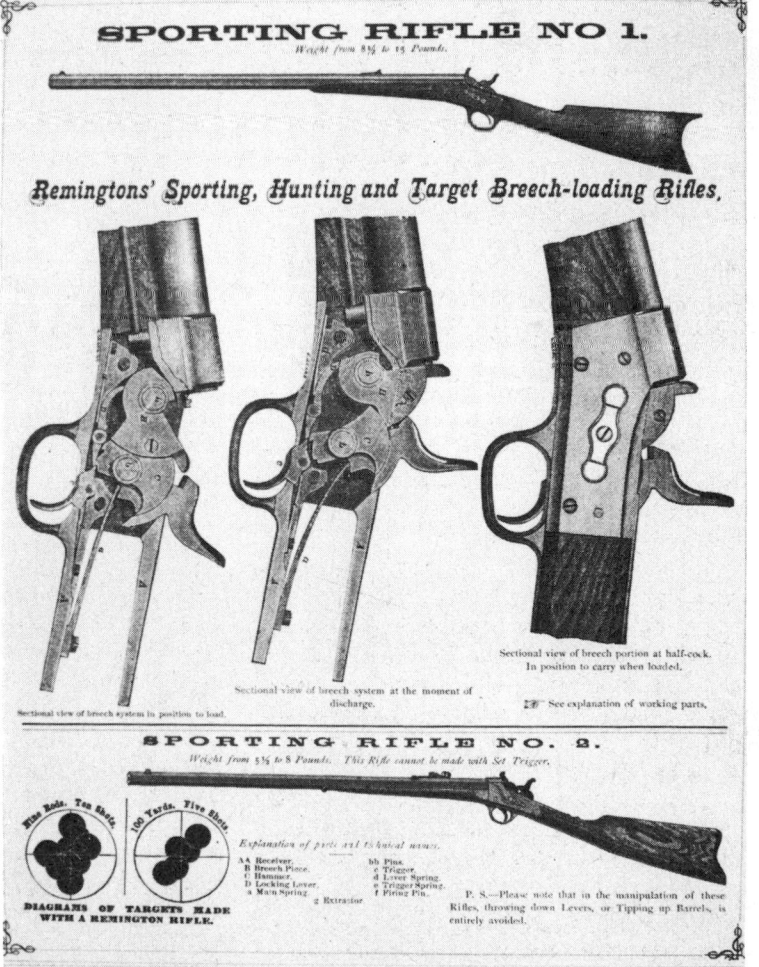

Above: Buffalo Bill Cody photographed on Staten Island, New York in the summer of 1886, with some of the Sioux and Pawnee Indians who formed a part of his 'Wild West'. At least two of those in the group accompanied him to London. Cody holds a fine 1873 Model Winchester with a pistol grip, and most of the Indians are armed with Colt Peacemakers. (Author's Collection)

Below left: Jessie Chisholm, the half-breed trader whose trail from Wichita to Texas became the principal cattle trail north. From a tintype made (or copied by) E. E. Henry of Leavenworth. (By courtesy of the Kansas State Historical Society)

Below right: Cowboys out on the range in Kansas in the 1880s. (By courtesy of the Kansas State Historical Society)

14
COWBOYS AND COW TOWNS

When you heard one or two shots, you waited breathlessly for a third. A third shot meant a death on Texas Street. – Stuart Henry.

ON 16 April 1887 the steam-ship *State of Nebraska* arrived at Gravesend from New York. Among its saloon and steerage passengers, the specially chartered vessel carried about 50 cowboys, 97 Red Indians, 180 horses, 18 buffalo, ten elk, five wild Texas steers, four donkeys, two deer and ten mules, together with an elk-riding Indian and other attractions. This colourful collection was supervised by William Frederick Cody, *alias* 'Buffalo Bill'. He had brought his newly-formed 'Buffalo Bill's Wild West' to London at the invitation of the organizers of 'An Exhibition of the Arts, Industries, Manufactures, Products and Resources of the United States' (soon to be known as 'The American Exhibition') to be held at Earl's Court, as part of Queen Victoria's Golden Jubilee celebrations.

Cody's 'Wild West' was formed in 1883, and was by no means the first of its kind. In the 1840s various 'exhibitions' had been staged using real buffalo and other Western attractions, and in 1872 his old friend Wild Bill Hickok had acted as Master of Ceremonies at a 'Grand Buffalo Chase' at Niagara Falls. Cody's venture, however, was by far the more successful. The exhibition (Cody never used the word 'show') was one of the most fascinating of its kind to be staged anywhere. It was completely authentic; the cowboys were right off the range, and many of the Indians had fought the United States Army, some of them were even present at 'Custer's Last Stand'. So, wherever the 'Wild West' appeared, it captivated its audiences.

Once Cody's troupe had settled in, a message came from Windsor to the effect that Queen Victoria would like to see the 'Wild West'. Some of the more exciting acts were staged at the castle for her benefit, but she was advised that it would be impossible to transport the whole company there, and she agreed to visit Earl's Court. This news caused considerable excitement because since Prince Albert's death in December 1861, she had scarcely ventured out in public; her willingness to do so now meant that she was once more prepared to face her subjects.

On the day that she visited Earl's Court, Queen Victoria amazed and delighted the Americans by rising from her seat and bowing as 'Old Glory' was carried past – the first time since the Declaration of Independence that a reigning British monarch had acknowledged the American flag. The Queen, of course, loved every moment, and the sheer spectacle of Buffalo Bill's 'Wild West' also won the hearts of his British audiences who had never seen anything like it. Indians in full war paint; unbelievable feats of horsemanship and, a rare experience, exhibitions of marksmanship in public. And it was here that Cody had problems.

When the *State of Nebraska* docked and Customs officials boarded, it was found that she was carrying many thousands of rounds of live ammunition. Although under-loaded, it was confiscated and in its place Woolwich Arsenal supplied blanks. For Buffalo Bill, Annie Oakley and others who were involved in target practice, however, specially-loaded cartridges containing ten or twenty grains of black powder and a quarter of an ounce of 7½ chilled shot were provided. When shooting at stationary targets twenty yards away, the shot pattern was about two inches, or about the diameter of the glass balls Cody and Miss Oakley regularly shot out of the air. Cody's Winchester was smooth-bore, but hitting glass balls from a galloping horse was no mean feat. But safety was paramount. In 1878 Cody had accidentally hit a small boy in the chest with a shot from his Winchester while on stage at a Baltimore theatre. Fortunately, the boy recovered and Cody invited him out to his ranch to recuperate. To avoid similar disasters, Cody arranged for the Union Metallic Cartridge Company to produce his stage cartridges with a five-grain powder load, but this was later changed to fifteen grains because the former were not 'strong enough'. As it was, an estimated 100 revolvers and Winchester rifles and carbines were brought in by the cowboys, and Woolwich Arsenal was kept extremely busy replenishing their ammunition. One wonders what would happen today should a similar event take place – in 1887 there were none of

the present firearms restrictions to contend with.

The British took cowboys and Indians to their hearts; they loved them. And for the cowboys in particular, to be treated to such adulation was not only unprecedented, but an experience few of them had had back home. The Europeans saw the cowboy as a romantic horseman, colourfully dressed, dashing and very brave. But for many Americans he was a ne'er-do-well, a desperado and an outlaw. Indeed, only six years before, following the Earp–Clanton feud in Tombstone, Arizona, where there had been friction and bloodshed between local ranchers, rustlers and citizens, President Chester A. Arthur, in his annual message to Congress in December 1881, had declared that 'armed desperadoes known as "cowboys"' were a menace to the peace of the Arizona Territory, and by the following May he had threatened martial law. Fortunately, it did not come to that, but the cowboy's now legendary status as the 'Knight Chivalric of the Plains' would have surprised his contemporaries, especially during the period from approximately 1865 until 1885.

Even the origin of the term 'cowboy' is controversial. During the period of this present study, it was usually hyphenated. Some researchers have even traced the term to Africa, but for our purposes it stems from the Tory (Loyalist) guerrillas in New York's Westchester County, who roamed the area stealing Patriotic (Rebel) cattle. These men often lured Patriots into traps with tinkling cowbells. The Patriots in turn were called 'skinners'. One is left with the distinct impression that both sides were a mixture of thieves and ruffians! Others, however, recall that in about 1766, during the period of the Stamp Act and the anti-Rent Rebellion in New York, the local Dutch colony described their rebellious tenants as 'cowboys'. It is not surprising, therefore, that the term was greeted with caution by the time the cattle trade was revived in the mid 1860s. It also explains how some writers confused Texas cowboys with 'drovers'. The 'drover' was the man hired by a rancher to drive a herd to market. The drover then engaged cowboys or 'hands' to assist with the drive, and appointed his own 'trail boss', or acted the part himself. Later, many of the ranchers took over these roles themselves, but during the heyday of the cattle drives (1867–1885), the drovers were highly respected among their kind.

One of the many that have written about the cowboy was the soldier, Richard Irving Dodge, whose understanding of the West and its peoples was much respected. In his classic *Our Wild Indians* (1882), he says:

'For fidelity to duty, for promptness and vigor of action, for resources in difficulty, and unshaken courage in danger, the cowboy has no superior among men.

'But there is something in his peculiar life which develops not only the highest virtues, but the most ignoble of vices. It is not solitude, for the shepherds of the Plains lead lives quite as solitary, and they are generally quiet, inoffensive persons. The cow-boy, on the contrary, is usually the most reckless of all the reckless desperadoes developed on the frontier. Disregarding equally the rights and lives of others, and utterly reckless of his own life; always ready with his weapons and spoiling for a fight, he is the terror of all who come near him, his visits to the frontier towns of Kansas and Nebraska being regarded as a calamity second only to a western tornado. His idea of enjoyment is to fill himself full of bad whiskey, mount his mustang, tear through the streets, whooping, yelling, flourishing and firing his pistols until the streets are deserted and every house closed, when with a grim smile of happiness he dashes off to his comrades to excite their envy by graphic pictures of his own exploits and the terror of the timid townspeople.'

As a class, cowboys were a strange mixture of the rough and the gentle. Most of them were born horsemen, whose talent for controlling cattle was legendary. Some, however, were itinerants who signed on for a drive to gather a little money or escape attention (for whatever reason) and were indifferent both to the job and their charges; few of these men lasted more than one season. But those who regarded the job as something to be proud of displayed a fierce independence and resentment of authority. And their spirit of comradeship was second to none. If someone intended to attack a cowboy, he knew that he might have to take on his companions as well. But the saga of the cowboy might never have reached its present status were it not for the economic crisis that afflicted the nation after the Civil War. In 1865 the cattle industry of the South, which had virtually halted during the conflict, faced a bleak future. During the war many thousands of cattle had run loose in the brush

country of Texas. The cost of rounding them up was prohibitive, partly because of the shortage of men – and there was no market for them. In the North beef was a luxury few could afford, but if it were available in plenty the price could be reduced thus creating markets and profits. The problem, how to get the meat to the masses?

The pre-war trails from Texas to Colorado, California, and the routes through Missouri and elsewhere had fallen into disuse. The growth of railroads after the war prompted speculators to begin thinking in terms of rail rather than trail movements of cattle, but the trans-continental rail link was as yet in the early stages of building, and other routes were in like position. Then, early in 1867 Joseph G. McCoy, a 29-year-old partner in the Illinois firm of William K. McCoy & Brothers, who had been active in the cattle business for some years, came up with the obvious solution: bring the cattle to the railroads. Following some fruitless visits to the headquarters of various companies he arrived at the small village of Abilene, Kansas, a track-side halt on the Union Pacific Railway, Eastern Division, then building through the state *en route* for Denver. He recalled it as a 'very small, dead place, consisting of about one dozen log huts, low, small, rude affairs, four-fifths of which were covered with dirt for roofing; indeed, but one shingle roof could be seen in the whole city. The business of the burg was conducted in two small rooms, mere log huts, and, of course, the inevitable saloon, also a log hut, was to be found.' But the lush surrounding grasslands were ideal for grazing cattle while awaiting shipment.

Kansas Quarantine Laws barred Texas cattle from much of the state for most of the year, so the only logical solution was to ship them by rail. McCoy approached the U.P.E.D. who decided to put in a 100-car switch (or siding) at Abilene, and orally agreed to pay him $5 a carload for all cattle shipped over their line. Within a very short time, McCoy had purchased 250 acres of land at the north-eastern end of Abilene, and constructed shipping pens, large enough to hold one thousand head of cattle. Handbills and messengers were dispatched to Texas inviting the drovers and cattlemen to bring their herds to Abilene. By August 1867 they were in business, and the first carload of cattle was shipped to Chicago on 5 September.

The cattle began their long march north from San Antonio, Houston, Austin and Waco, following a trail established some years before by Jesse Chisholm, a half-breed Indian trader who had settled at a place called Wichita (which later became a cattle town). All the cattle trails initially converged on the Red River and then separated. The

Right: Joseph G. McCoy, the father of the cattle trade, from a family portrait, circa 1870. McCoy never reaped a fortune from his efforts; when the Union Pacific Railway, Eastern Division, was renamed the Kansas Pacific Railway in March 1869, he claimed monies owed him by their predecessors. He won a court decision, but he was a broken man and never again enjoyed similar success. He died at Wichita in 1915. (Author's Collection)

Far right: A contemporary woodcut of cattle trains at Abilene in 1867 – 71; at the far right is the Drover's Cottage, a hotel-cum-meeting-place, and in the distance can be seen the shipping pens. (Author's Collection)

early Sedalia, Shawnee and Baxter Springs trails followed an easterly route; the Goodnight-Loving Trail turned west and north to Colorado and New Mexico and on to Wyoming; and the Western Trail wound up through Fort Griffin, crossed the Red River at Doan's Store, and on through the Nations (Indian Territory, now Oklahoma) to Dodge City and Oglalla. But the Chisholm Trail went straight north, passed Red River Station into Indian Territory, across the Washita, the Canadian, North Canadian and Cimarron rivers, and on to Wichita. Here it officially ended. Between Wichita and Abilene it was known either as 'McCoy's Extension', or 'The Abilene Trail'. By the mid 1870s the Chisholm and other trails were joined by the Ellsworth Trail (or 'The Texas Cattle Trail') and other routes.

Regardless of name or location, a cattle trail was a highway in its own right, sometimes up to six hundred yards wide; a sun-baked, hoof-packed track which, in some places, is still visible today. The life of a trail-driving cowboy was tough and dangerous. The constant threat of stampedes, storms, swollen rivers, sleepless nights, poor food and little rest, produced a breed of men who demanded their few pleasures when they wanted them and how they wanted them. Small wonder then that the inhabitants of towns such as Abilene, Wichita, Ellsworth or Dodge City feared the worst.

The significance of the railroad running through the centre of a cattle town can be gleaned from the following extract from the *Kansas State Record* of 5 August 1871:

'Before dark you will have an opportunity to notice that Abilene is divided by the railroad into two sections, very different in appearance. The north side is literary, religious and commercial, and possesses . . . [the town's newspaper, the] *Chronicle*, the churches, the banks and several large stores of various description; the south side of the [rail] road is the Abilene of "story and song," and possesses the large hotels, the saloons, and the places where the "dealers in card board, bone and ivory" most do congregate. When you are on the north side of the track you are in Kansas, and hear

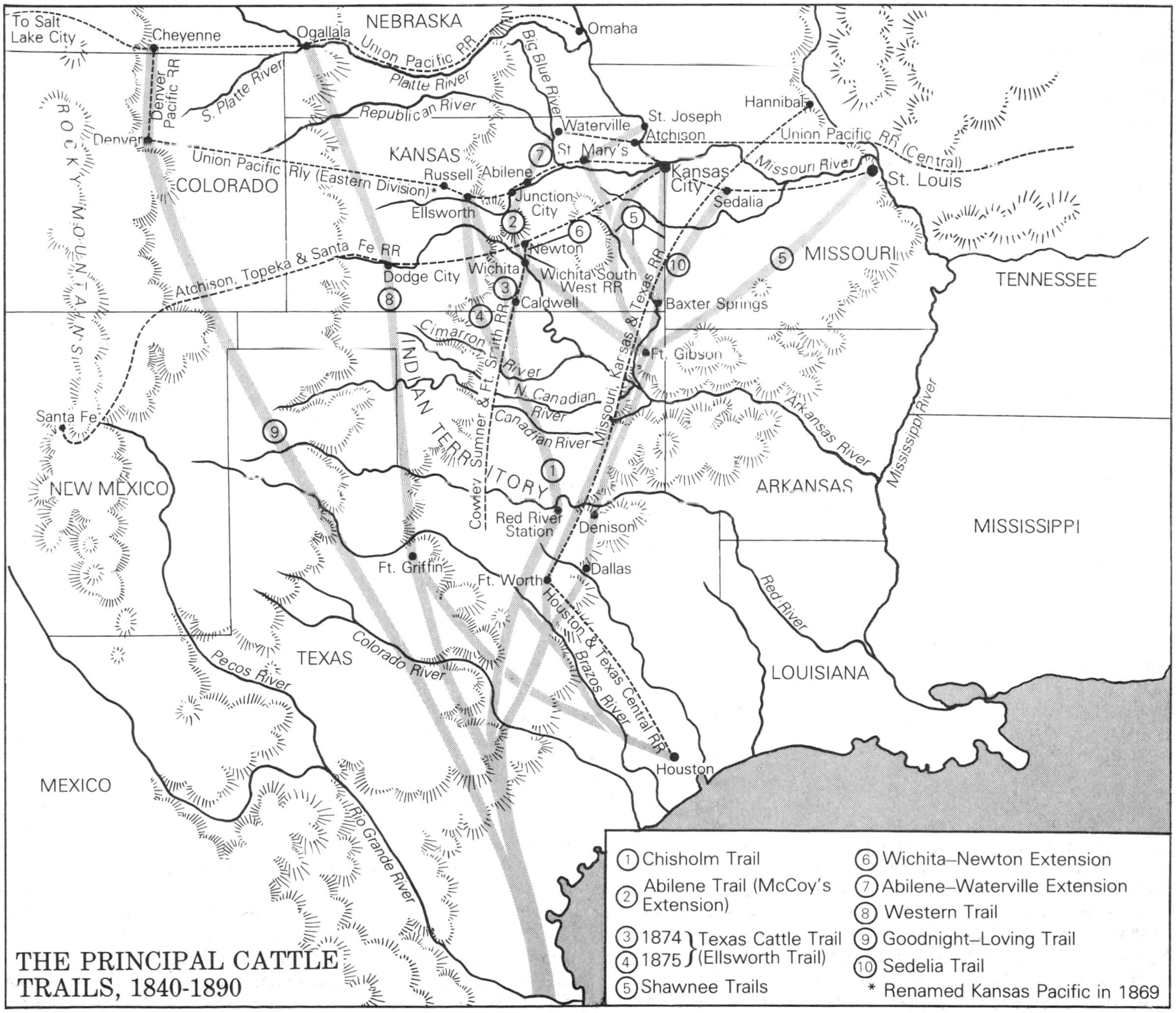

THE PRINCIPAL CATTLE TRAILS, 1840-1890

To Salt Lake City
Cheyenne
Ogallala
NEBRASKA
Omaha
Denver Pacific RR
S. Platte River
Union Pacific R.R.
Platte River
Big Blue River
Denver
Republican River
St. Joseph
Hannibal
Waterville
Atchison
Union Pacific RR (Central)
ROCKY MOUNTAINS
Union Pacific Rly (Eastern Division)*
KANSAS
⑦
St. Mary's
Kansas City
Missouri River
St. Louis
COLORADO
Russell
Abilene
Sedalia
Ellsworth
② Junction City
⑥
Newton
⑤
MISSOURI
Atchison, Topeka & Santa Fe RR
⑩
⑤
TENNESSEE
Dodge City
Wichita
Wichita South West RR
⑧
③
Caldwell
Baxter Springs
④
Cowley
Ft. Gibson
Cimarron River
INDIAN TERRITORY
N. Canadian River
Missouri, Kansas & Texas RR
ARKANSAS
Ft. Sumner & Ft. Smith RR
Canadian River
Arkansas River
Mississippi River
Santa Fe
⑨
①
NEW MEXICO
Red River Station
Denison
MISSISSIPPI
Ft. Griffin
Ft. Worth
Dallas
Red River
Houston & Texas Central RR
Brazos River
LOUISIANA
TEXAS
Colorado River
Pecos River
MEXICO
Rio Grande River
Houston

① Chisholm Trail
② Abilene Trail (McCoy's Extension)
③ 1874 } Texas Cattle Trail
④ 1875 } (Ellsworth Trail)
⑤ Shawnee Trails
⑥ Wichita–Newton Extension
⑦ Abilene–Waterville Extension
⑧ Western Trail
⑨ Goodnight–Loving Trail
⑩ Sedelia Trail
* Renamed Kansas Pacific in 1869

163

sober and profitable conversation on the subject of the weather, the price of land and the crops; when you cross to the south side you are in Texas, and talk about cattle, varied by occasional remarks on "beeves" and "stock". Nine out of ten men you meet are directly or indirectly interested in the cattle trade; five at least out of every ten, are Texans . . .

'At night everything is "full up." The "Alamo" [a famous saloon] especially being a center of attraction. Here, in a well lighted room opening on the street, the "boys" gather in crowds round the tables, to play or to watch others . . .

'It may be inferred from the foregoing that the Texan cattle driver is somewhat prone to "run free" as far as morals are concerned, but on the contrary, vice in one of its forms, is sternly driven forth from the city limits for the space of at least a quarter of a mile, where its "local habitation" is courteously and modestly, but rather indefinitely designated as the "Beer Garden." Here all that class of females who "went through" the Prodigal Son, and eventually drove that young gentleman into the hog business, are compelled to reside . . .

'Day in Abilene is very different. The town seems quite deserted, the "herders" go out to their herd or disappear in some direction, and thus the town relapses into the ordinary appearance of towns in general . . .'

After months on the trail, the cowboy reached the railhead town where the herd would be shipped East, anxious to cut loose as soon as possible. He hungered for the saloons, the brothels and the dance-halls; above all for company. And the gamblers, pimps and prostitutes were glad to accommodate him, and the opportunity to relieve him of his hard-earned cash, while the local police force turned a jaundiced eye on both factions. And well they might, for as we have already noted, every cowboy that came up the trail was armed. Some removed their pistols when they rode herd or performed other chores, but they were never far from a weapon, for it would have been unthinkable for a man to venture anywhere without one or two pistols in evidence. Most of the weapons were ex-military issue, mostly Colt's or Remington pistols "liberated" from the Yankees during the war. Some men, however, were armed with similar weapons, but which had been manufactured in Confederate arsenals. Any insult to his Confederate sympathies, and the Texan was liable to unlimber his artillery and start shooting at anything that moved. And it was this attachment to his pistols that caused most concern. Writing in the Topeka *Daily Commonwealth* on 15 August 1871, a correspondent noted that the Texas cowboy would use his revolvers 'with as little hesitation on a man as on a wild animal. Such a character

is dangerous and desperate, and each one generally has killed his man. There are good and even honorable men among them, but run-away boys and men who find it too hot for them even in Texas join the cattle drovers and constitute a large proportion of them. They drink, swear, and fight; and life with them is a round of boisterous gaiety and indulgence in sensual pleasure.'

The cowboy's addiction to weapons was both practical and traditional. In Texas, a white man never fought with his fists, he always used a gun or a knife, yet few cowboys were ever expert with a revolver. Many of them were passable shots with a rifle or carbine, but mastery of the revolver eluded them. This is not altogether surprising; the luxuries of plentiful ammunition and leisure to practise were denied them. The cowboy's pistol was really for his personal protection when away from the main herd, where he might have to shoot a snake, the occasional bear or a crazed or injured steer.

Paid-off at the end of the drive, the cowboy bought himself a complete outfit of new clothing (his trail-worn garments would be lice-ridden and fit only to be burned), which reflected his mood of gaiety: a stout corduroy fringed buckskin jacket and pants to match, or just the pants and a stylish jacket with facings. Next, a vast sombrero, and if the brim was as 'wide as an umbrella' so much the better. Around his neck was

knotted a silk bandanna or neckerchief and his feet were encased in a pair of very high-heeled boots of the finest kid, the tops perhaps decorated with the Lone Star. After a bath, a shave and a haircut the cowboy, dressed in his new finery, adjusted his six-shooters and was ready for his public.

The cleaned-up version of a 'Terrible Texan', with his ever-present six-shooters, would swiftly dispel any romantic illusions harboured by townsfolk. Law and order the cowboy ignored; for God he seemed to have little respect, and in manner he was judged profane, gross, vulgar and obscene. Although rarely molested, decent women

Below, far left: James M. Kellerman dressed in the correct cowboy gear for the period; Denver 1885. Note how the holster encloses all of the pistol except the butt and the triggerguard, and the narrow cartridge belt. (By courtesy of the Kansas State Historical Society)

Below, centre left: Earle R. Forrest spent his youth as a cowboy in Arizona and is photographed here in 1904 wearing authentic costume for the period His Colt Bisley is worn high on the hip in a drop-over holster. (Author's Collection)

Below left: Wild Bill at Fort Harker in September 1867 when he was a Deputy US Marshal. The two ivory-handled pistols are those referred to as having miraculous powers. (Author's Collection)

Below: An alleged photograph of Thomas James Smith, the first Marshal of Abilene in 1870. It came to light in the 1890s, and enough copies were sold to purchase a monument to his memory. (By courtesy of the Kansas State Historical Society)

avoided him; those who sought his company expected the worst. It was popularly supposed that he rarely ate good food, that his diet consisted almost entirely of 'chawing' tobacco and poisonous whisky – the latter of a quality that would make a 'rabbit fight a bulldog'. When drunk the cowboy had no hesitation in attacking any-one who offended him. And it was not unknown for bad blood to be settled by a shot in the back through door or window, the killer fleeing into the darkness. The cowboy did think twice, however, if confronted by the gun-fighting Marshals lined up against him. One look at such as Hickok, wandering about with his pair of pistols, was usually enough, though caution might fly when rot-gut whisky and a liquored-up bravado tempted a man to try his luck against a professional.

The gamblers and prostitutes who flocked to the cow towns were expert at relieving their customers of cash. Young men, scarcely out of their teens and inexperienced in the ways of women, fell easy prey to the 'painted doves'. Many a cowboy returned home broke and diseased after a session in one of the many cribs situated beside the saloons and dance-halls. Complaints could attract a bullet from her Deringer or a knife thrust from her saloon 'partner' or boss. Many of the women were as tough (or tougher) than their male companions. The terrible effects of their trade was hidden behind paint and powder, but their eyes reflected the depravity of their existence. The cowboy, driven by lust and in an alcoholic haze (and perhaps minus his trousers), stood little chance against a determined harlot drunk or sober!

Attempts to tame the 'murderous Texans' and curb the activities of the saloon set proved a daunting task. Abilene, which became the first and (with the exception of Dodge City) the most notorious of the cattle towns, suffered their antics for almost two years before action was taken to stop the rowdyism, general mayhem and sudden death. In 1869 the citizens applied to a probate judge for the incorporation of Abilene as a city. He granted them the status of 'third-class', which enabled them to hold elections, and by May 1870 they were able to appoint a Marshal.

The first Marshal (or Chief of Police) of Abilene was Thomas James Smith, a 40-year-old who is thought to have had some policing experience back East, but who was little-known on the frontier except for his part in the Bear River railroad riot of 1868, when the Union Pacific was building across Wyoming Territory, after which he was known as 'Bear River' Tom Smith. He estab-lished law and order in the town from June until November 1870. He had no reputation

as a gunfighter, but he would disconcert trouble-makers by knocking them down, drawing his pistol and threatening to shoot unless they surrendered their weapons. Tragically, he was murdered on 2 November while trying to arrest a wanted murderer. The man's companion came up from behind and all but decapitated Smith with an axe. Pursued by Smith's deputy and others, the pair were eventually captured and sentenced to long terms in the state penitentiary.

With the approach of the 1871 cattle season, the Abilene town council was in a panic. Attempts to find a replacement for Smith had failed, and despite the good job done by Smith's old deputy, James McDonald, they wanted a strong man in charge. On 11 April the council were advised by the Mayor, Joseph G. McCoy, that he had found such a one, and on the 15th the man was appointed Marshal. McCoy's choice was James Butler Hickok, whose reputation as 'Wild Bill' had made him a national celebrity. Some called him 'the Terror of the Plains', which he disliked, but his reputation proved effective when dealing with the Texans. Hickok never bluffed. He made it known that if a man wore a pistol and threatened him with it, he would draw his own and shoot to kill. Some claimed that without his pistols he would have been tame, but that was nonsense. He was well able to use his fists and proved it on one noteworthy occasion when he slugged it out toe-to-toe with a brawny mule-skinner. Few men gave Hickok the chance, however, so his survival depended upon being just that bit quicker in his reactions than his opponents. The fact that he was a good shot also helped, and not until his last weeks in office was he actually involved in a gunfight when, in front of the Alamo Saloon, he shot it out with a Texas gambler named Philip Coe. Michael Williams, a friend of Wild Bill's, tried to assist him, but was shot dead by the Marshal when he ran between the two men waving a pistol. Hickok's grief and rage at what happened, so frightened the Texans that they fled the town.

Early in 1872 the people of Abilene decided that they had had enough of the cattle trade and banned it, and the cattle men moved on to Wichita, then Ellsworth, Dodge City and finally Caldwell. Ellsworth, founded in 1867, and close to Fort Harker, became the haunt of buffalo hunters, teamsters and troopers. Long before it became a cattle town its violent reputation was a byword, but by the time the cattle business reached Ellsworth in 1871 the town had a council and a tough police force, all under the watchful eye of the county sheriff.

Newton, however, was not so fortunate. By August 1871 it had become another Abilene, having grown from a few shacks to a bustling community, boasting 23 saloons and dance-halls. One newspaper noted that it was doubtful if there were a dozen 'virtuous women' in the whole place. On 11 August 1871 the citizens voted on a proposal to issue $20,000 in county bonds to assist the building of the Wichita and Southwestern Railroad. During the day there was trouble between voters and some of the special police. One of these, Michael McCluskie (sometimes known as Art Delaney) and another special police-man, a Texan named William Wilson, came to blows and then shot it out. Wilson was killed, and his friends threatened McCluskie. For a time he kept away from town, but on the 19th he returned. The Texans ambushed him while he was playing cards in Perry Tuttle's saloon. When the smoke cleared, McCluskie was found to be mortally wounded, several other men were dead and a number, including innocent bystanders, were wounded. It was also claimed that several of the Texans were killed by a consumptive youth named Riley who had avenged his friend's death. Riley disappeared, but the shoot-out is remembered as the 'Newton General Massacre'.

From the summer of 1871 until the early months of 1872, a number of notable indivi-duals policed Newton and tried to tame the town. Among them were Tom Carson, a former deputy under Hickok at Abilene; James McDonald, another ex-Abilene lawman, and William L. Brooks, commonly called 'Billy' although some suggested it should have been 'Bully'. Newton's tenure as a cattle town was short and by 1872 Ellsworth was rapidly overtaking the place as the centre of the cattle trade. Soon Wichita, Dodge City and Caldwell were, in turn, to assume the mantle of 'Queen' of the cow towns.

Wherever they went, the carrying of fire-arms by Texans caused bitter arguments among citizens and councils alike. Many attacked the Texans in public and in print for being 'uncivilized' and too attached to their six-shooters. It was, it was argued, an open defiance of law and order, but the protests fell on deaf ears. When Smith had been appointed Marshal of Abilene the local paper, the *Chronicle*, declared that 'heretofore the Texans have not been inter-ferred with much, by the officers of the law in this locality when they killed each other', and the editor went on to demand that they now be subject to the law, firearms banned and state laws enforced. Brave words, but the difficulties were immense. The Kansas Statutes forbade the carrying of revolvers, pistols, knives and dirks by any former Confederate or 'Rebel' on Kansas soil. The problem, as any town Marshal could testify, was to implement the law, and this proved to be impossible. In some places notices were

put up banning firearms or demanding a toll (as was tried at Wichita), but to no avail. For every dozen or so men who would comply with the various ordinances, there were always the odd one or two who refused, and they became the targets for the gun-fighting Marshals.

The lone man of legend had no place in the real West, because every Marshal or Chief of Police was backed up by one or two full-time officers. During the summer months, when cattle drives were in progress, he could also hire extra men so that there were usually about five men available, which was still insufficient when one learns that during the height of a cattle season as many as 5,000 Texas cowboys could be in the vicinity at any one time! However, the state laws empowered a mayor to command the assist-ance of all males between the ages of 18 and 50.

Despite the circumstances which necessi-tated an armed police force, some editors, influenced perhaps by political opinion, occasionally demanded a reduction in arma-ment. In August 1873 the editor of the Ellsworth *Reporter*, in an attempt to emphasize how civilized the place was becoming, remarked:

'We protest against so much arming by our police. It may be well enough for our Marshal and his assistants to go armed, but one six shooter is enough. It is too much to have to see double-armed men walking our peaceful streets. It is not probable that any of the shotted revolvers will hurt anyone, for these are not the days of '67 and all people know. Don't let us by too big a show of derringers [*sic*], lead strangers to imagine that order is only to be maintained by the use of them. One pistol is enough and that should be concealed as much as possible.'

Ironically, only a few days later, Ben Thompson's homicidal brother William (generally called 'Billy'), cut loose with Ben's fine English shotgun (made by George Gibbs of Bristol) and mortally wounded County Sheriff Chauncey Whitney. Ben and his brother had been in dispute with fellow Texans and various members of the city police. Billy, the worse for drink, shot Whitney, who was friendly toward the brothers, when he tried to intervene in the row. Billy fired one barrel of the gun at him without provocation. Whitney's scream of agony sobered all who heard it. Ben, deeply shocked, told Billy that he had shot their best friend, but Billy shrugged it off. He said that he did not give a damn – he would have fired even had it been 'Jesus Christ'. Ben held everyone at bay with his shotgun as Billy made his escape, and he was then persuaded to give up his arms by Deputy Sheriff Edward Hogue, who promised him that the police would also be disarmed. Whitney died

in great agony several days later. In 1877 Billy was brought back to face trial, but he was acquitted on the grounds that the shooting was an accident. Curiously, in 1931, in his semi-fictional biography of Wyatt Earp, Stuart Lake claimed that it was Wyatt who made the arrest, but no contemporary account confirms this allegation.

The Texans, despite local ordinances, continued to carry pistols wherever they could. Many of them were fined and some suffered physical injury. In August 1873 three cowboys galloped up and down the main street of Wichita and a policeman ordered them to stop and disarm. There was a scuffle and the policeman hit one of them over the head with his Colt Navy pistol. It was later reported that the Texan might have suffered severe brain damage from the effects of the 'iron that fell upon him'. The editor of Wichita's *Weekly Beacon* also noted a slight panic when a Texan's pistol fell from its holster, struck the ground and went off, the ball lodging in the steps of an hotel. The cowboy, who happened to be galloping past

at the time, was as shaken as everyone else! On 30 July there had occurred an incident which posed problems for the paper and for the law: a mule, tied to a post and with its owner's pistol hanging from the saddle horn, suddenly decided to shake himself. The violent movement somehow cocked the pistol and it went off, putting a bullet into the dirt. When the pandemonium had subsided and it was realized what had happened, the editor of the *Beacon* gravely reported that since no city ordinances covered the carrying of pistols by mules, no action would be taken and no arrests made, and besides, the mule had gone back to sleep!

A serious cow town problem was the hostility between whites, blacks and Mexicans. During the period 1865–1873 there were few Negro cowboys; but later, when the trade became less lucrative they became more numerous as the whites dropped out. The Mexican vaquero (herdsman), however, had been very much a part of the cattle trade from the earliest days. In fact, much of the cowboy's way of life, his

dress, his equipment and his skills can be traced back directly to the horsemen of Spain and later, Mexico. But the Texans refused to accept him as an equal. The 'Texians', as many of them still preferred to call themselves, continued to 'Remember the Alamo' and the later war of 1846–48. The 'Mex' was a 'Greaser' first, last and always, and for their part, the Mexicans had nothing but contempt for the 'Gringos' and their way of thinking themselves superior; both factions did a lively trade in the swapping of lead or cold steel. Curiously enough, they could work together on a drive without fighting; until the job was done their skill transcended racial prejudice.

When the cattle trade departed, Abilene inherited a large Mexican population, but very little trouble ensued; with Wichita, the opposite was the case. The vaqueros, distrustful of American paper money (some of them thought it was Confederate) insisted on payment in silver or gold, and this led to friction. Even the newspapers were not averse to referring to the Mexicans as

Below, far left: William 'Billy' Brooks, Marshal of Newton, Kansas in 1872, who later appeared in Dodge City, where he killed a Santa Fe railroad yard master in a shoot-out during which both men fired three shots. Brooks was not popular and many called him 'Bully' Brooks. He and some others were lynched when caught rustling mules in 1874. He is wearing a pistol belt with some of the early cartridge loops. (By courtesy of the Kansas State Historical Society)

Below left: Benjamin 'Ben' Thompson, gambler and gunfighter from Texas. Ben, the son of a mariner, was actually born on 2 November 1843, in Knottingley, Yorkshire. The family emigrated to the United States just prior to the Civil War. He defended his brother Billy's homicidal actions on several occasions, most notably when Billy was drunk and shot their friend, Chauncey Whitney, at Ellsworth. Ben was killed from 'ambush' at the Vaudeville Variety Theatre, San Antonio, Texas on 11 March 1884. (Author's Collection)

Below right: Chauncey Whitney, ex Forsythe scout, town constable of Ellsworth and finally County Sheriff, who was gunned down by Billy Thompson on 15 August 1873. Ben Thompson engineered his brother's escape, but in 1877 Billy was brought back to face trial. He was acquitted on the grounds that the shooting was an accident. (By courtesy of the Kansas State Historical Society)

'diluted sons of Montezuma', or 'Mexican greasers', which did little to foster racial harmony! John Wesley Hardin, a one-time cowboy and credited with '40 notches', whom some thought to be a 'homicidal maniac' is reported to have killed eight Mexicans in 1871 after a row between rival outfits on the trail to Abilene. And when the Mexican, Juan Bideno, killed fellow Texan William Cohron, it was 'Wes' who pursued him to Sumner City and shot him between the eyes as he sat drinking coffee in a restaurant. Back in Abilene Wes, for no apparent reason, killed a trail boss named Charles Couger as he sat reading a newspaper. Wes then left town one jump ahead of Wild Bill.

Below: Wichita, Kansas in 1873. The wide streets are a feature of present-day mid-Western towns. (By courtesy of the Kansas State Historical Society)

Inset: John Wesley Hardin, said to be the most notorious of Texas's gunmen. Some credited him with 'forty notches', but there is no evidence of such a total. Captured and imprisoned in 1877 for the murder of a deputy sheriff some years before, he remained in jail until 1894 when he began practising law. His murder in 1895 was the culmination of a violent career. (Author's Collection)

The Texans were finally tamed – if one can believe that – when the cattle industry came to an end in the 1880s. The influx of 'nesters' on Government lands and the increased use of fencing (particularly barbed wire) spelled the end of the trail-driving era. By now organized legal processes were replacing local measures, and the successful control of gambling and the brothels contributed to the end of the wild and lawless days and did much to curtail the activities of the six-shooter virtuosos that had for so long held sway. As early as 1870 Abilene had tried to control an estimated 32 saloons and gambling hells by city ordinances, but the enforcing of them had not been easy. It was not lost on the city fathers that they gleaned a great revenue from such places – fines, licence fees and taxes – all of which kept the city's coffers full. Ordinary citizens avoided the dens of iniquity, which were normally separated from the respectable part of town by the railroad tracks. Efforts to enforce removal (as happened in Abilene in 1871 when the brothels were re-sited following a threat of a riot by the 'respectable ladies' of the town) occasionally led to bloodshed, but when properly negotiated usually led to mutual agreement.

Allegations by the gamblers and prostitutes of corruption among city officals and the police were rife, but they were usually exaggerated. When, in September 1871, the Abilene council purged the city of the 'cappers, pimps, and prostitutes' which 'infested' the place, Hickok was ordered to clear them out, and within days the trains to the East and West were crowded. The Texans tried all sorts of delaying tactics. The commonest was to buy up plots of land and build their own brothels and gambling halls, but they rarely succeeded. Once they had gone, however, the effect on the town's economy was soon felt and, as in the case of Abilene, led to a swift decline.

The part played by the gunfighting Marshals during the cattle-driving era has become folklore, but most of them would be surprised at the legendary status conferred on them. Some of them were professional policemen, others got the job because of a reputation and the ability to control the mob; the professional was the exception rather than the rule. Few of them were paid a great deal – in Abilene Smith started out at $150 per month which was raised to $225, the highest known cow town salary. Hickok received $150, plus a percentage of all fines imposed in court, and 50 cents for each stray dog he shot. Most Marshals or Chiefs of Police received $100 or $75, according to where they served. In some places, once the cattle season was over, the Marshal's salary was reduced to $50. To supplement their incomes policemen often held other jobs, often in saloons or gambling halls. Many would consider such activities to be prejudicial to the job in hand, but where better to be than among the very people one was hired to police? The welter of fact and fiction that has been devoted to the exploits of the cow town police has inspired some of the more lurid legends of that most sinister character of all – the gunfighter.

15

THE GUNFIGHTER

Whenever you get into a row, be sure not to shoot too quick. Take time. I've known many a feller to slip up for shootin' in a hurry. – Wild Bill Hickok, 1865.

THAT part-real, part-mythical character, immortalized in hundreds of books and films as 'the gunfighter', is now firmly established in American folklore. To his admirers he is a two-gun Galahad; the one-man judge, jury and executioner; his detractors compare his antics to the unpredictable behaviour of a mad dog. The truth, of course, lies somewhere between, and to establish the reality we must first understand the character in relation to his time and place.

The gunfighter evolved from the turbulence of the early frontier where the six-shooter prevailed and where, in the absence of a legal system, men used it to settle disputes or protect themselves or their families. Some men, however, would resort to the gun at the drop of a hat and survival demanded split-second reaction in a kill or be killed confrontation. Thus the ancient 'Code Duello' of sword and pistol found a new meaning among the 'pistoleers' of the West, where reputations were made and lost on the squeeze of a trigger. Some, and with good reason, believe that the six-shooter inspired an utter disregard for human life and elevated murder into a cold-blooded science.

By the late 1860s the habitual use of the six-shooter in parts of the West was already prompting a world-wide reaction, especially in England where the exploits of the gunfighting fraternity were little known or inaccurately reported; but the emphasis was directed more at the weapon itself than at those who abused it. On 22 October 1869 in reviewing the result of the Colt-Theur-Adams trial at Woolwich (when the Colt was soundly defeated), *The Daily Telegraph* added the following comments:

'In effect, these contending weapons [the Colt and the Adams] supply us with the latest and most effective outcome of that high art of Homicide which the race has been practising ever since the days of Tubal Cain. Humanity, always grateful for a murderous gift, has preserved the memory of the antediluvian blacksmith son of Zillah, because he forged the first sword and spear . . . The revolver, however, comes a little too late for any decisive use in warfare. It is for hand-to-hand combats, and it has been by this time pretty well distributed among all belligerent Christians; while everything points to the likelihood that in future battles will be decided mainly by strategy, artillery, and long-range weapons rather than at close quarters. The pistol is carried already by cavalry in many armies, and it did great work in the Indian mutiny and the American war; nor can anybody doubt that, when used for hand-to-hand fighting, a "Colt" or "Adams" has saved many a warrior and destroyed many another. It has, in truth, sent more heroes to Hades than people generally believe; but we do not think that it ever decided, or will ever decide a battle – although, of course, it is perfectly proper that the Government should find out which is the most effective form of the arm, and provide our soldiers with the best pattern.

'Duellists, travellers, and the rowdy bullies of the New World, enjoy the doubtful honour of having brought the pistol to its present sanguinary perfection. It is the weapon of the self-dependent man; and those who can find a "final cause" of good in rattlesnakes and poisonous drugs might cite a great many instances to prove that the pistol has furthered civilisation, and has been especially the arm of progress. With a six-shooter in his belt, the explorer goes alone in places where otherwise he would not dare to pass; and Africa has been to no insignificant extent opened by this key . . . A score of white men, with revolvers and plenty of ammunition, if they could keep clear of fever, might "destroy the balance of empire" anywhere among the sable monarchs of Central Africa. Unhappily, the drunken bully and gambler of America and Mexico has found the six-shooter convenient, and carries it more regularly than his tooth-pick. Some day, we hope, the Government of the United States, remembering what Thucydides says about the barbarity of people who "wear iron", will make it a punishable offence to carry a "Derringer" or a "Colt." But these blood-thirsty scoundrels complain of the revolver. It kills, but not immediately; its bullet is too small to paralyse; the victim dies by internal bleeding, but not before he has time to discharge his own battery. Hence those extraordinary encounters in the Western and Southern States, where a whole volley of shots is discharged before one of the wretched combatants succumbs . . .'

This anonymous correspondent was perceptive, particularly concerning the killing potential of the revolver, but his lack of first-hand knowledge of the place and of the people involved shows through. In one respect, at least, he was correct: the men who inspired the gunfighter legend had all 'killed their man'.

The gunfighter was an individual, and unlike his fictional counterpart, he was impossible to 'type'. The editor of the Kansas City *Journal*, writing on 15 November 1881, made this plain when he described the 'man-killer' as:

'. . . by no means a *rara avis*. . . He may be seen . . . in the congregations of the most aristocratic churches. He resides on "Quality hill", or perhaps on the East Side, or again in the five story buildings which bear in letters of living light at the doorway: "Furnished rooms for rent, 15c, 25c and $1.00 per night – reductions to regular lodgers." This ubiquitous individual may be seen almost anywhere. He may be found behind the bar in a Main Street saloon; he may be seen by an admiring audience doing the pedestal clog at a variety theater; his special forte may be driving a cab, or he may be behind the rosewood counters of a bank.

'If he has been here any great number of years, his "man" was

PROBABLY A PIONEER,

and he died in the interest of "law and order" – at least so the legend runs. And no one dares dispute the verity of the legend, for behold the man who executed a violator of the law without waiting for the silly formalities of a judge and jury, mayhap now sits in a cushioned pew at an aristocratic church, and prays with a regularity, grace and precision only equalled by his unerring arm [*sic* – ? aim] with a revolver, the great Western civilizer.'

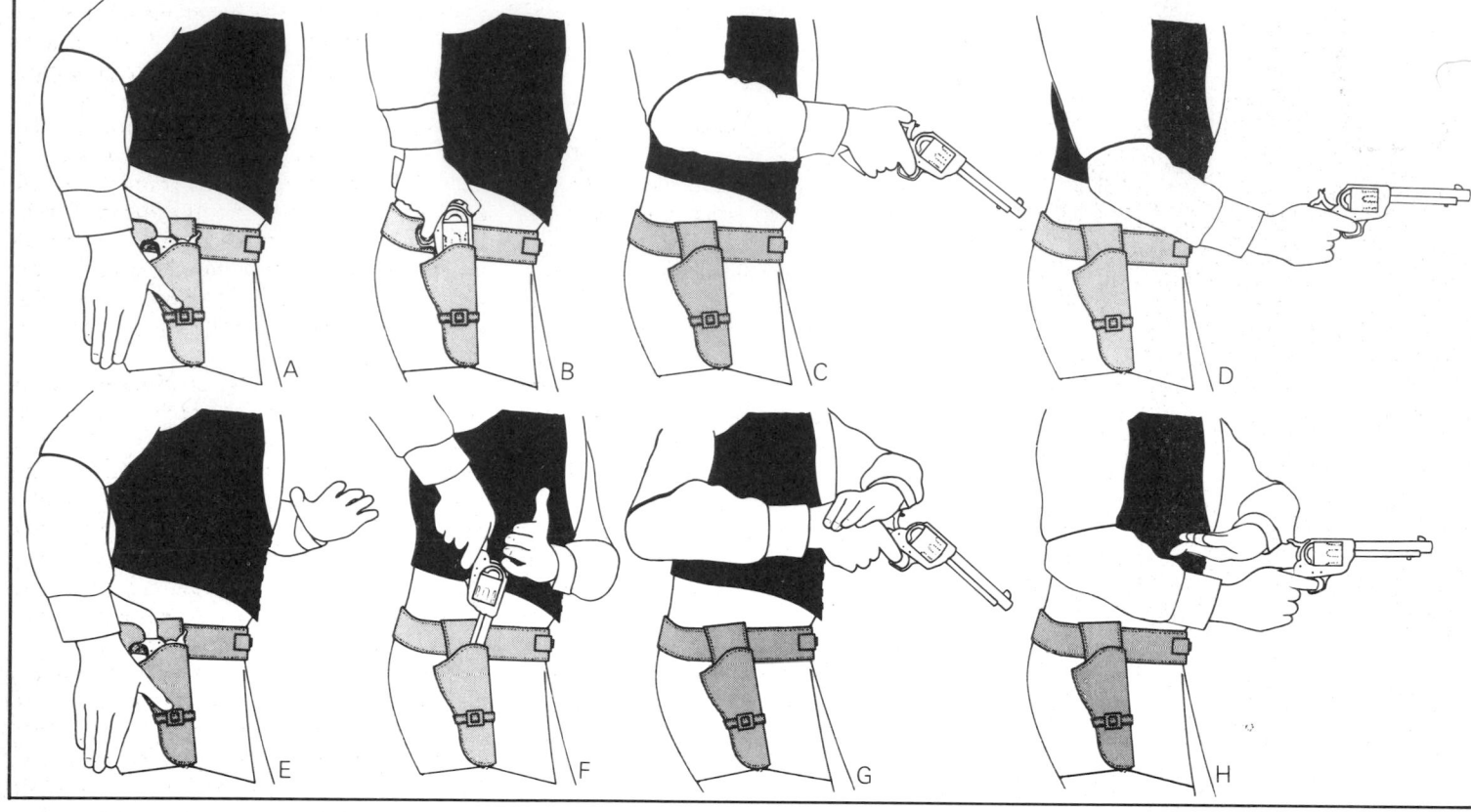

The fast draw. The hand is held slack (A) so that the butt of the pistol is between wrist and elbow. The hand grasps the butt, the index finger slips into the triggerguard and the thumb locks across the hammer spur (B). As the pistol is pulled, the thumb cocks the hammer (C) so that when the weapon is level (D) it only requires finger pressure to fire it. The fanner. The right hand is relaxed in the same position as a normal draw, but the left hand is placed across the body as shown (E). The hand grasps the pistol, the trigger finger squeezes the trigger back (F) or it is removed from the pistol or tied back. As the pistol is pulled and thrust forward, the left hand 'fans' the hammer spur (G) so that as the weapon comes level (H) the pistol is fired. By keeping the trigger back, the left hand can then 'fan' the remaining shots at great speed. Accuracy is, of course, much reduced.

The editor concluded by describing the "man-killer" as being quiet in demeanour, sober, thoughtful and sombrely dressed; he drank, but seldom got drunk; gambled but did not quarrel over a game; he was quiet – fatally quiet – and usually had blue or grey eyes, and in appearance was 'the last man on earth one would suspect of having notches on the butt of his pistol'. Contrary to popular belief, there is no reliable evidence that gunfighters notched their pistol butts.

Their contemporaries often called these men "shootists", but once this became confused with target and exhibition shooters, the more apt if sinister term 'man-killers' was adopted. Similarly, it has been suggested by recent writers that the term 'gunfighter' was invented by Hollywood. This is nonsense. I traced it back to 1874 and I believe it could be found even earlier, although it was not commonly used before 1900. Today, of course, we tend to call those who fought for law and order 'gunfighters' and those on the opposite side 'gun-men' – although today's society might prefer 'terrorists'.

Bat Masterson, a notable gambler and one-time sheriff, wrote about the 'man-killers' he claimed to have known, in a series of articles for *Human Life* in 1907. Bat intimated that being a good shot did not necessarily make one a gunfighter. Rather, it was a state of mind, and here the old-time pistolmen displayed characteristics and qualities which set them apart. For although the courage to 'step out and fight to the death with a pistol' was vital, it was not enough. It required cold-blooded nerve and the deliberation to place a vital shot in the face of flying lead. It was *that* which made a gunfighter! And for anyone unable to do that, it would be better to 'settle his personal differences in some other manner than by an appeal to the pistol'.

In the trans-Mississippi West between 1850 and 1900, an estimated 20,000 such men perished in personal shoot-outs, feuds and other community disputes. For it was an epoch of guns, guts and gore that has seldom been rivalled. The fact and fiction devoted to those highly controversial six-shooter virtuosos is quite bewildering. Our friend, the Kansas City editor, made it clear that the man-killers were a part of society, and the ordinary individual had little to fear from them. If it suited a community to employ such men as police, and their homicidal tendencies led to the swift removal of individuals who were a nuisance or a danger to the population, so be it, but the same people who hired these men also fired them with equal rapidity once the job was done, in order to preserve an 'aura of respectability'. Their moralizing and prejudice created problems for the erstwhile 'civilizers' in their midst. A favourite means of persuasion when a community decided it no longer needed the services of a gunfighter, was to charge him with 'vagrancy' which implied that he had no 'visible means of support'. Some took the hint and moved on, others bluffed it out, but the characterisation of the 'good bad-man' survives in fact and fiction.

Curiously, many of the men who achieved Western notoriety came from the East, from predominantly semi-civilized regions. Illinois, for example, laid claim to Wild Bill Hickok, Joseph 'Rowdy Joe' Lowe, Joseph A. 'Jack' Slade, Wyatt Earp and Bat Masterson (who was actually born in Canada, but spent his childhood in Illinois). Prior to the Civil War the State was a wilderness which rapidly became a largely farming community. As the 'frontier' moved farther West, so did many of the people. Claims that the gunfighter evolved from the Kansas–Missouri border conflicts of the 1850s are partly true, for as we have noted, he was found in most Western states, particularly California. After the Civil war, he became firmly established in the cattle

towns, mining camps, and railroad 'tent cities' which sprang up wherever 'civilization' followed in the wake of the tracks, cattle drives or the lure of gold.

In legend, the gunfighter's speed on the draw and deadly accuracy is paramount; it gives him purpose, power and prestige. In reality, such skill was not easily acquired, demanding as it did, hours of practice. Those who relied upon a pistol for survival were as careful in their choice of weapon as they were in its use. The Colt and Remington arms were the most favoured during the percussion period from 1836 until about 1876, but with the arrival of metallic ammunition the Smith & Wesson and the Colt Peacemaker proved the most popular. Even more formidable than the revolver, of course, was the sawn-off shotgun. Few men dared face another armed with such a terrifying weapon.

Accuracy, of course, varied from man to man, and one can disregard most of the legendary feats credited to various 'pistoleers' that would put the finest Olympics marksman to shame. Tests at ranges up to 450 yards have proved the accuracy of the old-time pistols at these distances, but few gunfighters cared for long-range shoot-outs – what happened at between five and fifteen feet was of much more concern to them.

The core of any pistol is its mechanism and if it is not in good order the weapon is virtually useless. Most gunfighters worked on the actions of their pistols, and some even removed the triggers in the belief that thumbing the action gave them the edge. There were even those who 'fanned' their shots; the pistol was gripped firmly in one hand, with the trigger squeezed, tied-back or removed altogether, and the hammer was operated by the palm of the other hand being brushed rapidly back against the hammer spur. Six shots could be fired at great speed, but fanning was never widely practised and has often been refuted, although by the 1880s it had already become part of the myth. On 27 April 1887 the Fresno, California, *Daily Evening Expositor* (citing the New York *Sun*) carried an amusing item on 'fanning the Hammer' based on an interview with ex-Sheriff Harry H. Whitehill. He explained the merits and demerits of the single-action and double-action revolvers, and described how he fanned the hammer of his 'single acting, old style pistol' at the same time suggesting that the reporter 'watch that tree'. He pulled his pistol, and before the 'words were well uttered, the handsome sheriff had got the drop on the growing timber, and six shots rang out in such rapid succession that they sounded like the explosion of a small pack of very large firecrackers. During the shooting Mr. Whitehill's left forefinger vibrated along the top of the pistol barrel from muzzle to breech. Six balls entered the tree about three inches apart. Pointing out that the pistol's trigger was tied back to the guard with a rawhide thong, the ex-sheriff continued: 'All I have to do with it . . . is to brush the hammer back as far as it will go with my left forefinger, while I hold the pistol firmly with my right hand. My right forefinger never goes near the trigger, but helps to hold the stock, and this makes my grip more firm and certain.' Anyone who has tried to 'fan' a single-action revolver with his forefinger in the manner described will know that it is almost impossible. The only way it can work is by using the *palm* of the other hand.

Curiously, Wyatt Earp, whose reputation as a man-killer, peace officer and gunfighter has undergone a great deal of 'revision' in recent years, has never been described as a great pistol shot, despite claims by his biographer, Stuart N. Lake (citing Bat Masterson) that armed with his 'Buntline Special' (more about this later) Wyatt could hit targets at any range from four to 400 yards. His speed was phenomenal and his contemporaries 'marvelled' at it. It was also suggested that in more than fifty gunfights Wyatt shot most of his victims through the arm or shoulder rather than through the stomach or the heart. He felt there was no need to kill them, and many people believed him to be too lenient and soft-hearted. This is ludicrous. Had Wyatt engaged in only a half dozen of those fights, his reaction would have been the same each time – if his life were threatened he, too, would have shot to kill.

Earp's biographer also credited him with the statement that top-notch gunfighters loaded their six-shooters with only five bullets to ensure against accidental discharge while the pistol was still in the holster. This was a reasonable precaution and one that was generally accepted. Unfortunately, Mr. Earp evidently forgot his own advice on one occasion. According to the Wichita *Beacon* of 12 January 1876:

'Last Sunday night [January 9], while policeman Erp [*sic*] was sitting with two or three others in the back room of the Custom House saloon, his revolver slipped from its holster and in falling to the floor the hammer which was resting on the cap, is supposed to have struck the chair, causing a discharge of one of the barrels [chambers]. The ball passed through his coat, struck the north wall then glanced off and passed out through the ceiling. It was a narrow escape and the occurrence got up a lively stampede from the room. One of the demoralized was under the impression that some one had fired through the window from the outside.'

Mr. Earp, however, proved on the few occasions when he did indulge in pistol practice upon others (notably the celebrated gunfight outside the O.K. Corral at Tombstone in October 1881) that he had what it took to swap lead.

Gunfighters were noted for their attention to detail and preferences for certain types of pistol. We have previously intimated that the double-action was not so popular as the single-action revolver, and the following anecdote from the Wichita, Kansas, *Daily Eagle* of 11 October 1884, citing the New Mexico *Globe-Democrat*, testifies to the truth of this. Their correspondent encountered a cowboy in an El Paso gun store, wandering about looking at the various weapons. The assistant offered him a brand-new Colt .45 double-action Army pistol, informing him that it was 'the newest thing out'. The cowboy's reaction was scornful: 'Ain't worth a row of beans. No man 'cept a tenderfoot want that kind of thing. Give me an old reliable all the time. Ye see, a man that's used to the old style is apt to get fooled – not pull her off in time – and then he'll be laid out colder'n a wedge.' The young man finally settled for a single-action pistol, paid for it and left.

Three years later, the Fresno *Daily Evening Exposition* of 27 April 1887, pointed out that every tenderfoot presumed that cowboys carried double-action pistols, or as some still called them, 'self-cockers'. That this was incorrect was explained by our friend the ex-sheriff:

'There was a time when these weapons were in high favor, but the cowboys soon found they were positively unhandy, instead of being a help to a man in a hurry. Now self-cocking pistols are boycotted. I'll bet that four-fifths of the cowboys in this territory [New Mexico] have gone back to the old style single acting pistols. Two years ago everybody had a double acting "gun", and wouldn't have any other.'

'Why? Don't they like the new style?'

'No. They discovered that, try as they would, they could not avoid deflecting the muzzle of the pistol to the right while pulling the trigger to raise the hammer. You see, all the power is applied from the right hand side of the trigger, where you put your finger in. Now, when you pull the trigger for the comparatively long period necessary to get the double acting hammer up, to the point where the spring is released, and it falls, you insensibly put a heavy pressure on the right hand side, and can't help slightly swaying the muzzle in that direction. When the double acting guns were in style here we used to notice that five out of every six men who got shot were wounded in the left side. Of these, about one half were shot so far to the left that the ball simply grazed their ribs. Another large percentage were shot on the innerside of the left arm.

HITTING THE DEAD CENTER.

'Now the cowboy prides himself on hitting the dead center of his opponent. It is always his wish to put the ball right at the juncture of the ribs above the stomach. This is not merely because they want to put on style, the placing of the forty-eight [*sic*] caliber ball right there prevents your man from "coming back at you". Now, as soon as the cowboys began to note this queer feature of the shooting, it became a matter of serious moment to them. They quickly found the fault to be in the self-cocker, which, by deflecting their muzzles, of course inclined the ball toward the left side of the man facing them in front. That settled the self-cocker. The fact that the cowboys were right is proven by the simultaneous disappearance of the new style pistol and the reappearance of the old style . . .'

We must accept that tongue-in-cheek yarn with great reservation, but the preference for the single-action pistol was very marked and those that depended upon it for survival took great care to see that it was properly looked after. As issued from the factory, the action tended to be crisp but hard, and it was common to have the mainspring eased or replaced by a weaker one. The trigger pull was also eased by working on the full-cock notch. A whetstone was occasionally used to slim this down, but any major work was given to a competent gunsmith. If one was not careful, either too much metal could be removed making the pistol 'hair-triggered', or the notch, no longer protected by the case-hardening treatment, chipped making the weapon useless except as a slip-hammer – that is, keeping the trigger squeezed or removed entirely and using the thumb to cock and fire the pistol. It was not accurate, but effective at close range.

Barrel length varied: the standard 7½ and 5½ inches of the Peacemaker, and the Remington's 7½-inch were popular, as was the 8-inch Smith & Wesson, but by the 1880s the length of barrel had become an important consideration. A holstered weapon with a 7½-inch barrel was one thing, but a concealed weapon needed a short barrel. When Bat Masterson started corresponding with the Colt company in the late 1870s, he ordered a 7½-inch pistol, ornately finished, with carved ivory stocks. By the 1880s, however, his tastes had changed and he now preferred plainer weapons. In March 1885 he ordered a 5½-inch pistol from Colt's and repeated the order in July, requesting that extra care be taken in their preparation. He liked his pistol to be easy on the trigger; the front sight to be higher and thicker than on ordinary pistols; the finish to be nickel and the grips of gutta-percha. All the other pistols he ordered had 4¾-inch barrels (the same length as the ejector housing), and as yet only one of them has come to light.

Most men took great care of their weapons. The climatic extremes of the West – great cold, heat and humidity – made it essential that all guns be kept clean and well-oiled, and ammunition checked regularly. The black powder of the time is generally considered to have been superior to that available today, but it was salt-laden and subject to damp. Richard Burton noted this when he advocated frequent discharging and reloading, and Wild Bill Hickok was also well aware of it. His friend in Abilene, Charles Gross, recalled that Hickok made a habit of emptying his pistols regularly and reloading them with care. Wild Bill moulded his own bullets. He carefully measured each charge, and before placing a cap on the nipple, checked with a pin or pricker that there was nothing inside the nipple channel, and that

the cap itself was a good one. Intrigued by all this Gross asked him if his pistols had got wet. 'No,' Hickok replied. 'But I ain't ready to go yet and I am not taking any chances – when I draw and pull I must be sure.'

The 'Cult of the Colt' has inspired many legends, perhaps the most famous being the 'Buntline Special'. This weapon was first publicised in 1930 in a series of articles written by Stuart N. Lake for *The Saturday Evening Post*, claiming that it was the chosen weapon of his hero, Wyatt Earp, and it has since become as controversial as Wyatt himself. According to Lake, Wyatt carried the 'Buntline' during the more prominent periods of his law-enforcement career, and in his role as a 'civilizer' frequently employed it to dispense justice with a well-aimed shot or by laying the barrel alongside some hapless cowboy's head and 'buffaloing' him into submission. Apart from the fact that hitting people over the head with barrel or butt could do as much damage to the pistol (relatively speaking) as to the recipient, most people seem to have accepted the legend of the 'Buntline Special' as though it were true.

It really started in 1928 or 1929 when Lake saw a long-barrelled Colt revolver in a private collection. The length of the barrel intrigued him: instead of the normal 7½ inches it was twelve inches long. Then, in October 1930 *The Saturday Evening Post* began a four-part series on 'Guns and Gunfighters' written by Stuart Lake. The 1 November issue contained information which surprised many of Wyatt's surviving contemporaries. According to Lake, Wyatt's fame in 1876 was such that Ned Buntline (E. Z. C. Judsen) actually came out to Dodge City to meet him. Wyatt and his companions, Charles Bassett, Bat Masterson, Bill Tilghman and Neal Brown, so inspired Ned with their tales of the raw West that in

Top right: Wyatt Earp and friends of the Dodge City Peace Commission of June 1883. They were formed to 'fight' the city administration of Dodge City. From left to right (Top row): W. H. Harris; Luke Short; Bat Masterson, and W. F. Petillon. Front row: C. E. Bassett; Wyatt Earp; M. F. McLain (or McLane), and Neil Brown. (By courtesy of the Kansas State Historical Society)

Right: A 'Buntline Special' with a 16-inch barrel and complete with skeleton stock. Ned Buntline had nothing at all to do with either the purchase or naming of these long-barrelled revolvers, but his name is now synonymous with the weapon. (By courtesy of R. Larry Wilson)

Far right: Luke L. Short (1854-93), the dapper gambler-gunfighter of Dodge City, Tombstone and Fort Worth. When he was thrown out of Dodge City in 1883, a number of his friends, among them Wyatt Earp and Bat Masterson, arrived in town and he was reinstated. Later, the group posed for a photograph, which was soon dubbed 'The Dodge City Peace Commission'. (By courtesy of the Kansas State Historical Society)

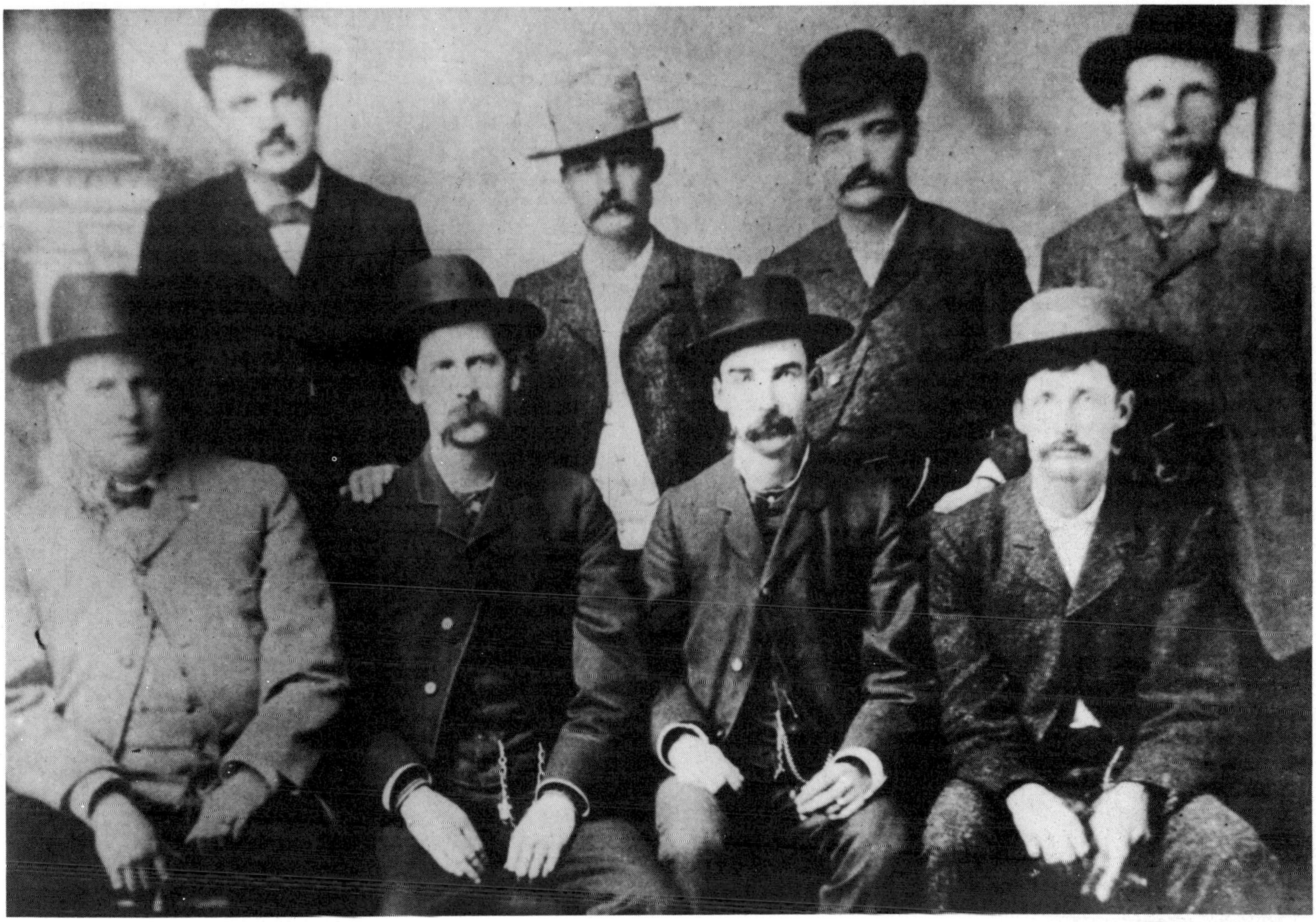

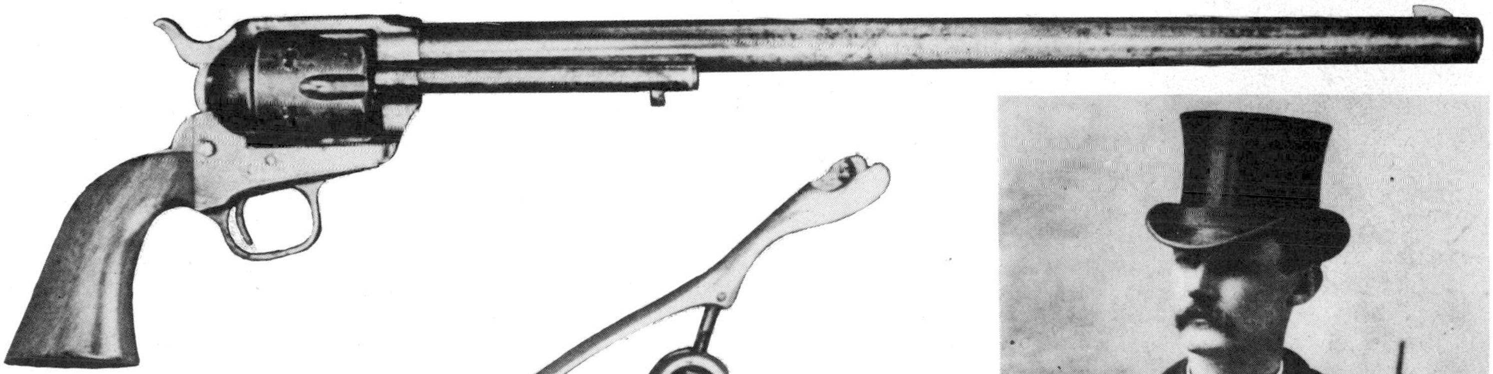

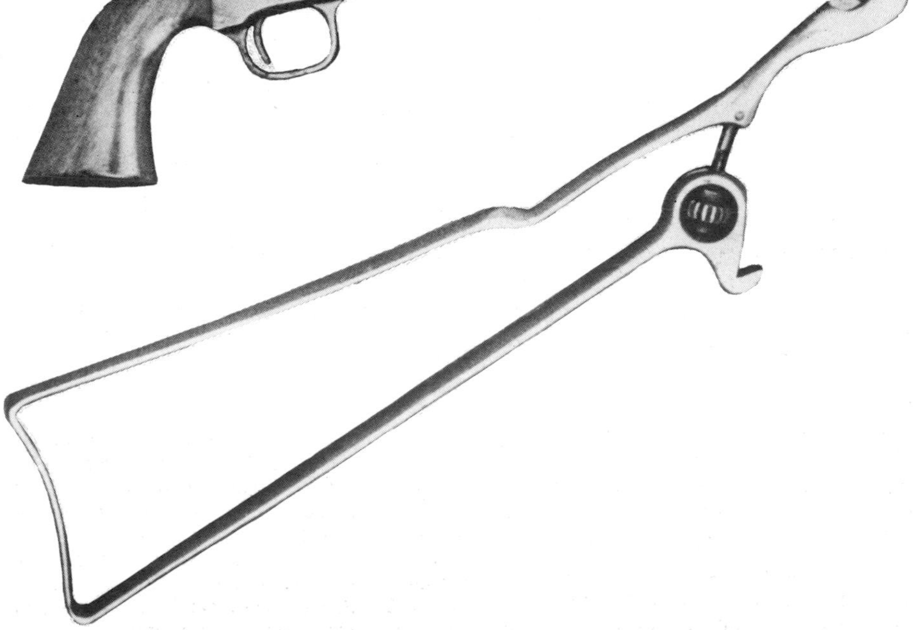

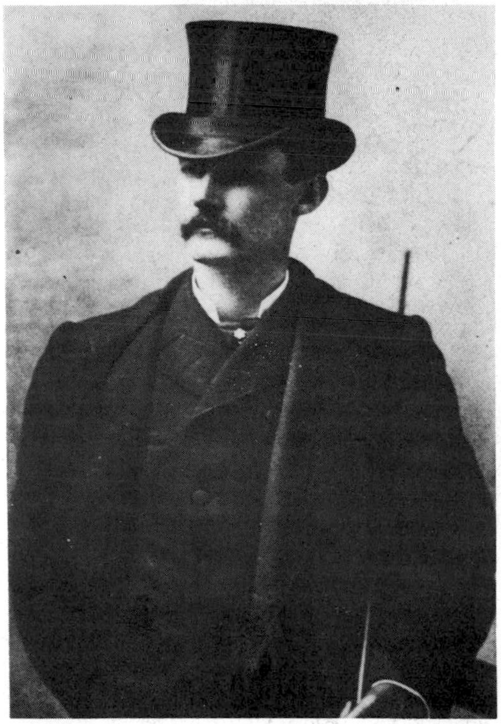

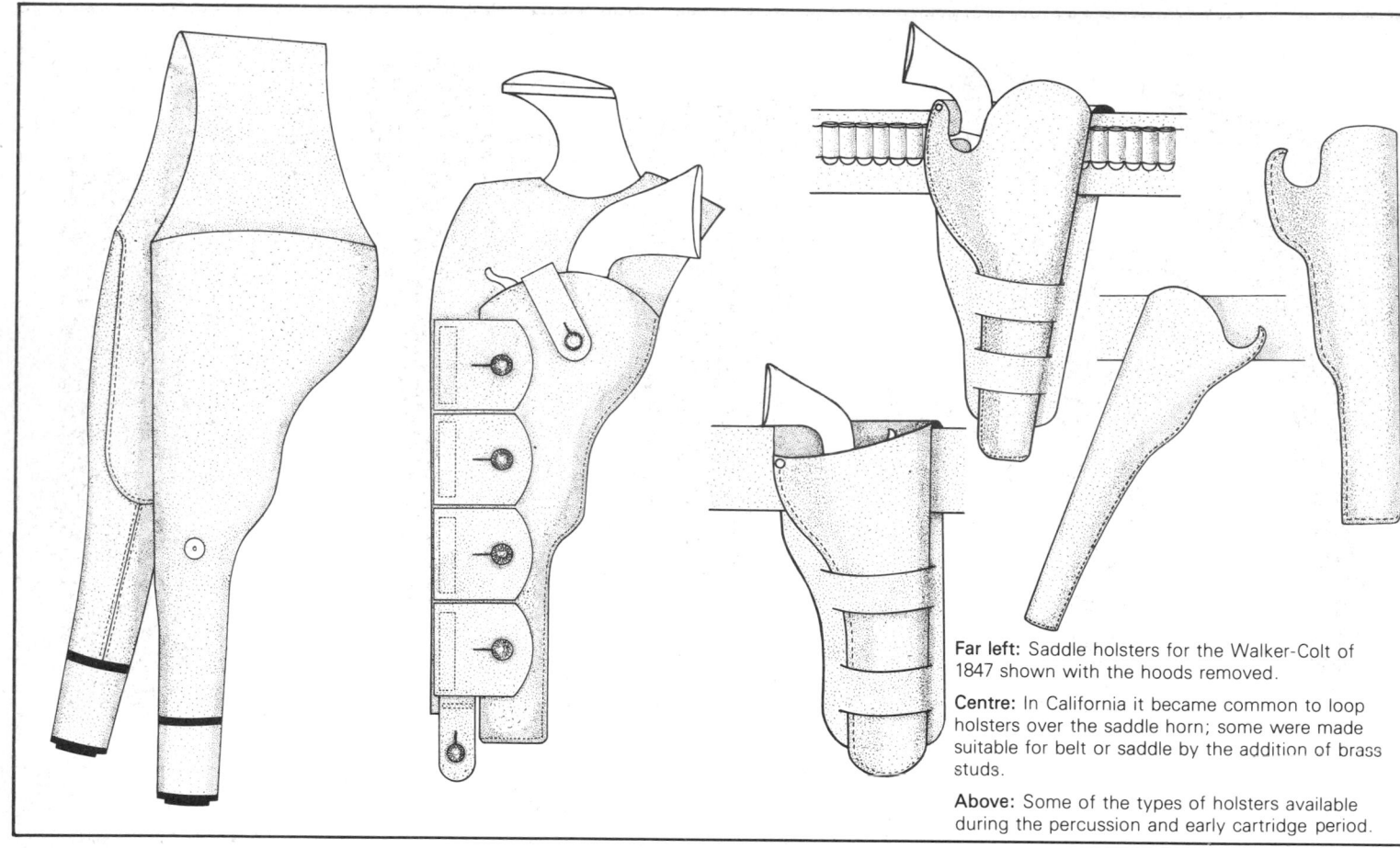

Far left: Saddle holsters for the Walker-Colt of 1847 shown with the hoods removed.

Centre: In California it became common to loop holsters over the saddle horn; some were made suitable for belt or saddle by the addition of brass studs.

Above: Some of the types of holsters available during the percussion and early cartridge period.

gratitude he sent to the Colt company and ordered five .45 calibre single-actions with 12-inch barrels. For each pistol he also ordered a dismountable walnut stock with a thumbscrew to attach it to the pistol. Each stock had the word 'Ned' carved deeply in the side and accompanying each pistol was a fine hand-tooled holster. Lake then claims that Buntline himself dubbed the pistols 'Buntline Specials'.

In 1931 the *Evening Post* articles were revised into book form as *Wyatt Earp, Frontier Marshal*, the text following the original articles closely. Lake says that Masterson and Tilghman cut their pistol barrels down to the standard length of 7½ inches, but Wyatt, Brown and Bassett kept theirs intact. Wyatt, apparently, had no difficulty in drawing his 'Buntline' at speed.

With time, of course, historians became more critical of the claims made by Lake and others, and began to investigate the elusive 'Buntline' weapon. The results were disappointing. It was true that Colt's began shipping extra-long pistols in 1876, and some of them were exhibited at the Philadelphia Centennial Exposition, but no trace could be found of any weapons ordered by Ned Buntline. What did come to light, however, was revealing. Presumably Lake was unaware that there had been some major changes in dismountable carbine stock design since the late 1850s. By 1876 the

wooden stocks which he described (and apparently identical to those issued in the Civil War) had been replaced by metal 'skeletonized' stocks which proved popular, especially in Europe. The serial range of the Peacemaker in 1876 was 28000 and about 31 pistols were produced with 10- and 16-inch barrels. Some of these were target weapons, fitted with special sights, flat top straps, and skeletonized stocks. By 1878 12-inch barrel lengths were also available, and one such weapon was ordered on 14 January 1881, by Frank Leslie, a noted desperado, army scout and peace officer, better known as 'Buckskin Frank' Leslie. Writing from Tombstone, he ordered a 'Colt's Frontier Model to take Winchester Cartridges 44 Cal. The revolver to have a twelve (12) inch barrel, browned, superior finished through out with carved ivory handle, also send scabberd [*sic*] or belt with everything complete for carrying & cleaning the pistol . . .' He did not, however, order a stock.

As for Wyatt Earp, in 1876 his reputation was strictly confined to Kansas, which makes it difficult to understand why Ned Buntline should hear of him in New York. But it was Ned himself who inadvertently debunked Lake's story. In July 1876 when he was supposed to have been in Dodge City, he was in fact at Stamford, New York, planning a special Fourth of July celebration, complete with fireworks. When news of Custer's

defeat at the Little Big Horn reached the East, Ned abandoned the idea. Instead, he and his wife visited the Centennial Exposition at Philadelphia, and in the August he went on his annual fishing trip. At no time during 1876, or indeed in 1875 or 1877, did he venture West to Dodge City.

Why then should Lake involve Buntline, or, for that matter, invent such a story? Several theories have been put forward. By the late 1920s Wild Bill Hickok remained the most popular of the Old West's gunfighters. His two ivory-handled Colt Navy revolvers were an important part of the legend which asserts that they were the gift of a Vice-President of the United States (Henry Wilson). They had, it was claimed, been presented to Hickok in 1869 by Wilson and friends at the completion of a guided tour of the plains. The story was a hoax, but the significance of the weapons remains. Clearly Lake viewed his hero, Wyatt Earp, as a man apart; someone special who deserved a unique firearm. So Lake invented the 'Buntline Special', and turned a hoax into history.

Out West the way the pistol was carried was a very personal thing. Some men simply thrust it into belt, trouser top or even coat pockets, but by and large most preferred some kind of holster and belt, and like so many Western accoutrements, the pistol holster owed its origin to the military; its

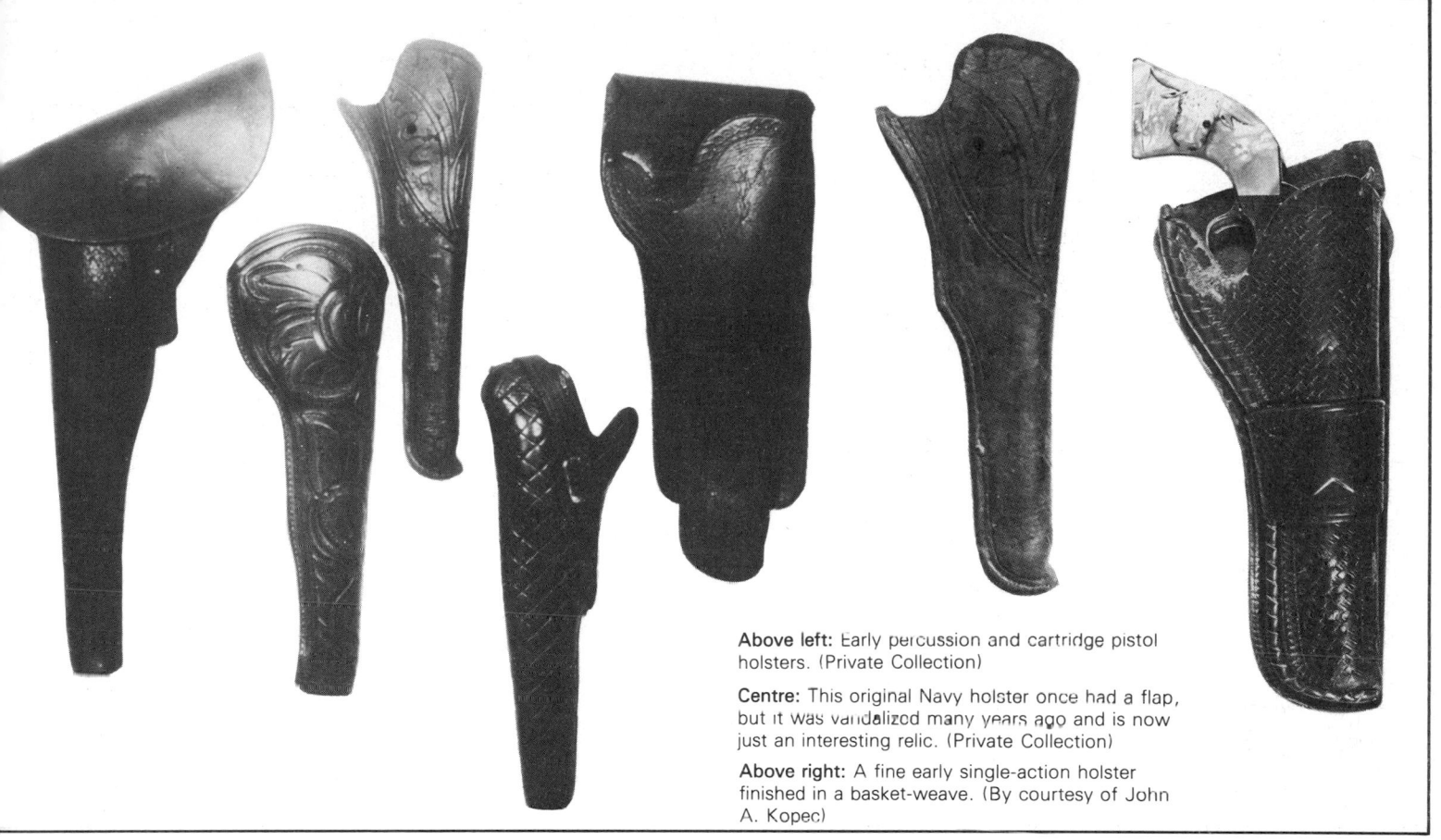

Above left: Early percussion and cartridge pistol holsters. (Private Collection)

Centre: This original Navy holster once had a flap, but it was vandalized many years ago and is now just an interesting relic. (Private Collection)

Above right: A fine early single-action holster finished in a basket-weave. (By courtesy of John A. Kopec)

evolution going back long before revolvers were thought of. For the purpose of this study, however, we will concentrate upon the late eighteenth and early nineteenth centuries when 'holster' meant an attachment to a horseman's saddle and contained one or two pistols. The term continued well into the 1850s when such pistols as the massive Colt–Walker Dragoon, designed for horseback use, were described as 'holster' pistols. Later, however, when Colt and others designed lighter and more practical 'belt' pistols, the term 'scabbard' came into common use, again because of the military. As late as the 1890s one still finds the word 'scabbard' in print when most people were using the more popular 'holster'. Today, of course, a scabbard refers to swords and bayonets, not revolvers.

Early belt holsters were cumbersome and were designed more for weapon protection than swift accessibility. The now familiar military flap holster appears to owe its origin (in England at least) to Charles F. Dennet, Colt's London Agent during the 1850s, and George Pays, an Oxford Street gunsmith and dealer. Their design, registered in 1855 but never patented, was generally adopted by the British military. An almost identical holster was adopted by the United States Army.

The early holsters were very light and were contoured to the shape of the pistol. In most cases the flap was an integral part of the holster, but occasionally it was added later. Some were fitted with metallic 'cups' on the muzzle end, but the majority were left plain. Most flap holsters were left-handed – that is they were made to be worn on the right hip so that the pistol butt poked forward. This enabled a cavalryman to draw his sword with his right hand and his pistol with his left. But disregarding the use of the sabre, a horseman could keep hold of his reins with his left hand and easily draw his pistol with his right, in an underhand or 'twist' draw – as we have mentioned elsewhere. It was safer than the later hip holsters; if the pistol fired accidently, the horse suffered and not the rider.

Civilian purchasers of the early percussion revolvers were quite happy to have the readily available flap holsters which, for most people, were practical: they kept the pistols clean, protected them from the elements, and there was little likelihood of losing the gun, a possibility with the open-top version. While the military holsters were made from hard leather which kept its shape, a number of the civilian types were made in much softer leather, some even from fine kid – although these couldn't have lasted very long. After the Civil War, however, when thousands of returned veterans retained military arms and equipment, the military-style holster was often modified by having the flap cut off. Soon, manufacturers all over the country (many of them practising saddlers) began producing open-top holsters of a set design or customized to individual requirements. Colours varied: the military favoured black, civilian tastes favoured brown or tan. Most holsters were finished plain, but some were finely tooled, sometimes with intricate designs. Stitched and riveted with wide belt loop attachments, they normally fitted tightly to a belt, and were adjustable to suit the wearer. Some men even stitched their holsters to the belt to ensure that the pistol butt remained in the same position whenever the gun was worn.

Styles of holster varied and over the years changed to conform with popular trends. The early versions of flap and open holsters gave way to a modification that allowed the trigger guard to be exposed by means of an 'S' curve cut in its top. The lower curve left the trigger guard exposed, the upper part covered the recoil shield, but left the hammer spur free. During the mid 1870s the percussion style of close-fitting holster was replaced by a version which had a 'skirt' or flap with slots cut into it through which the holster was thrust, leaving a loop at the top to fit over a belt. Holsters of this type became very popular because the pistol butt was well clear of the belt, and tilted slightly away from the wearer's side and out of the way of the shirt or other loose clothing.

The now familiar cartridge loops were introduced in the mid 1870s and were an immediate success on the frontier. Some men continued to carry two revolvers and slung them from one or two cartridge belts. But whether holsters were ever 'tied-down' in the traditional Hollywood manner is arguable. At the turn of the century, the 'buscadero' holster became very popular. This was favoured by the Texas Rangers, and an El Paso saddler named Sam Myers made a number of them for his many friends within the organization. The belt was wide and a long slit was cut along its length through which the holster was suspended. Today, thanks to Hollywood, the 'buscadero' is still one of the most popular styles and has been adopted by most fast-draw fanatics. The holster has come a long way since it was simply a means of carrying and protecting a pistol. In effect, the practical has given way to the theatrical.

Few expert gunfighters ever shot it out with one another. This had nothing to do with fear, they simply had no need to prove anything. Many of those who went up against such as Hickok were reputation-seekers, or were killed while resisting arrest. Some, of course, pulled pistols in the heat of the moment, in a quarrel over cards or women, but they were usually drunk. Most of the better-known gunfighters drank, but rarely to excess, for a man with a reputation was ever on his guard against his own and others' weaknesses when pent-up emotions so easily led to shouts, shots and death.

Romantics have hinted at a kind of 'Code of the West', but if it ever existed, it was ignored by the men who gunned down Hickok and Jesse James, both of whom were shot in the back. Among equals, however, there did exist a tacit understanding that both would be 'heeled' (armed) if things looked like getting out of hand, but, if a man of reputation learned that someone was out to kill him, he rarely postponed the encounter. The Hays City, Kansas, *Daily Sentinel* of 16 August 1876, in recalling the exploits of Wild Bill Hickok (who had just been murdered at Deadwood) noted that he never wasted time with braggarts – they put up or shut up 'Many a man has bit the dust when "hunting Bill", and many a man who has avowedly attempted to kill him, now lies with his toes upward . . . a man didn't say a thing unless he meant it; and after the thing was said, it was only a question of time as to who would be the chief mourner.'

The actual gunfight, that tense moment when death was imminent, is an essential part of the Western myth, and later we shall examine some of the classic encounters. Actually, of course, few gunfights took place in the traditional Hollywood face-to-face, draw-on-command manner. Rather, men

expecting trouble went into action gun in hand, or poised ready to draw and shoot. The more experienced gunfighter had the edge, for it was not speed on the draw that won gunfights, but a combination of skill, motivation and physical reaction.

Bat Masterson made this clear when he ignored speed in his recollections, and neither did he waste much time in discussing the old-timers' accuracy. He and others (notably Walter Winans, one of the greatest pistol shots of his day) considered the ability to make a 'possible' at 20 or 50 yards to be commendable, but that was not to say that the shooter would necessarily be ideal in combat. Few target shooters could shoot fast and accurately while being shot at themselves. As for the old-timers, despite the use of cut-away holsters, it is most unlikely that they paid much attention to speed in the sense of today's fast draw. When questioned about gun-fighting Wild Bill Hickok replied: 'Whenever you get into a row, be sure not to shoot too quick. Take time. I've known many a feller to slip up for shootin' in a hurry.' Hickok was really speaking of reaction time, but many of his contemporaries, particularly newspaper editors, confused speed of movement with reaction time. One editor noted in 1876 that Hickok's success was his 'ability to draw and discharge his pistols with a rapidity that was truly wonderful . . . being "out and off" before the average man had time to think about it'. Similar skills were attributed to a number of other gunfighters. But speed was secondary in a gunfight. For the man with the nerve, presence of mind and skill to draw, cock and fire while being shot at, a second could seem like an hour.

The old-time gunfighters would have viewed the modern fast-draw fanatics with some amazement. Their modern counterparts tend to regard speed as of the essence, and rely upon short-barrelled, finely-tuned pistols and crafted steel-lined, moulded-to-shape holsters. They are living in a fantasy world, but who can blame them? Not for them the gut-churning tension; the heart-stopping anticipation of a bone-crushing, tissue-tearing chunk of hot, soft lead that will kill or maim. Cocooned in the make-believe world of electric timers and wax bullets, fantasy can easily overtake reality. I have discussed this subject with a number of men who have swapped and stopped lead, and they fail to appreciate the romantic appeal of the 'fast draw'. These men are either serving police officers, F.B.I. Agents, or United States Marshals (who are still very active in the fight against crime). 'Speed is the last thing we think of,' declared one Marshal. 'Every effort is made to make an armed man give himself up without a shot, but if he refuses and wants to make a fight of it, then God help him – and us!'

Above: A gunbelt complete with cartridge loops, circa 1880. (Private Collection)

Below: An interesting open-top holster complete with hammer keep to prevent the weapon from falling out. (By courtesy of John A. Kopec)

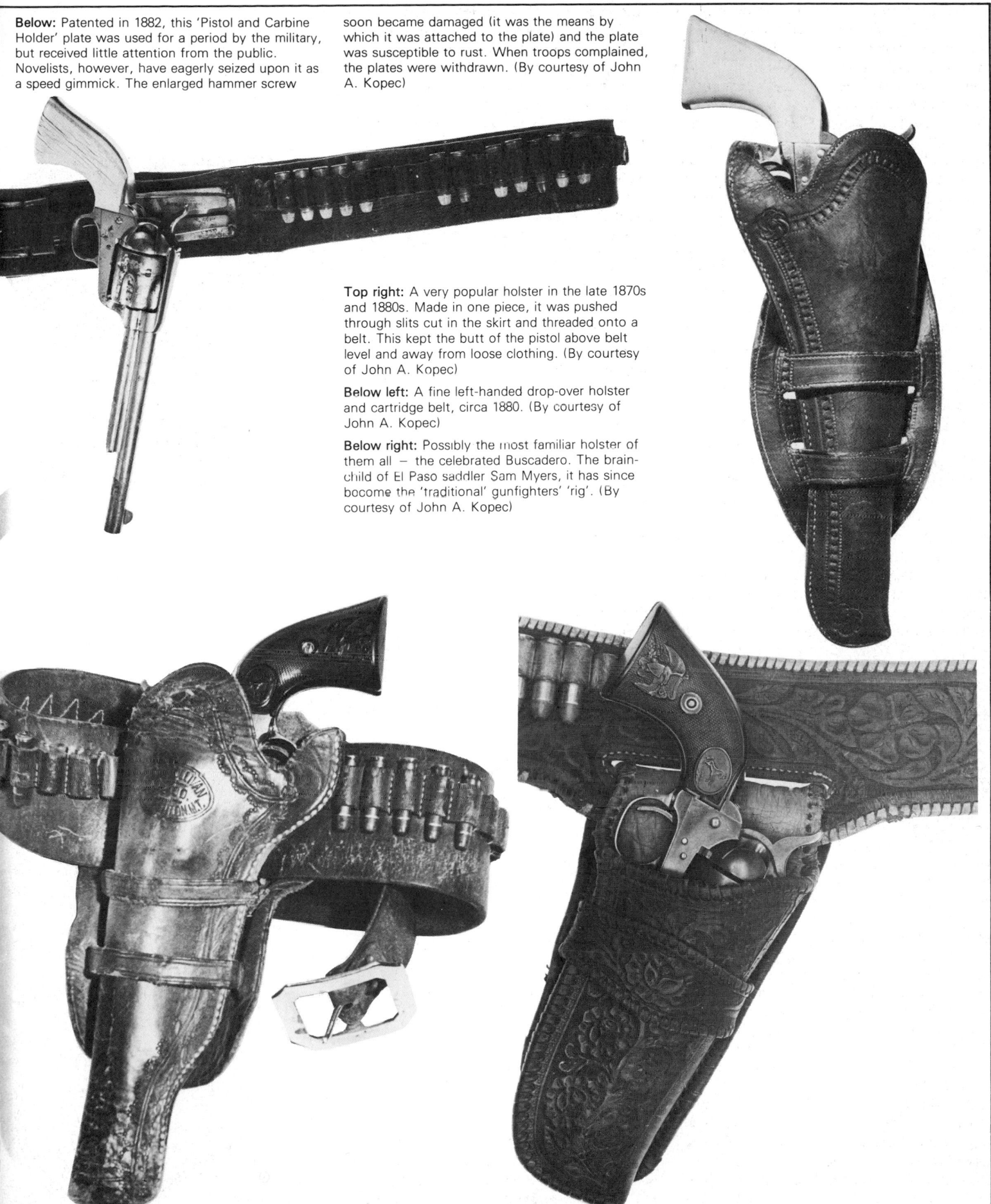

Below: Patented in 1882, this 'Pistol and Carbine Holder' plate was used for a period by the military, but received little attention from the public. Novelists, however, have eagerly seized upon it as a speed gimmick. The enlarged hammer screw soon became damaged (it was the means by which it was attached to the plate) and the plate was susceptible to rust. When troops complained, the plates were withdrawn. (By courtesy of John A. Kopec)

Top right: A very popular holster in the late 1870s and 1880s. Made in one piece, it was pushed through slits cut in the skirt and threaded onto a belt. This kept the butt of the pistol above belt level and away from loose clothing. (By courtesy of John A. Kopec)

Below left: A fine left-handed drop-over holster and cartridge belt, circa 1880. (By courtesy of John A. Kopec)

Below right: Possibly the most familiar holster of them all — the celebrated Buscadero. The brain-child of El Paso saddler Sam Myers, it has since become the 'traditional' gunfighters' 'rig'. (By courtesy of John A. Kopec)

PISTOL PRACTICE AND SIX-SHOOTER SHOW-DOWNS

'When I saw Billy Clanton and Frank McLowry draw their pistols, I drew my pistol . . .
The first two shots which were fired were fired by Billy Clanton and myself, he shooting at
me and I at Frank McLowry . . . We fired almost together. The fight then became general.'
– Wyatt Earp's evidence at the hearing in November 1881 after the gunfight outside the
O.K. Corral.

THE six-shooter inspired many myths and, in its way, perpetuated the exploits of that legendary band of 'pistoliferous personalities' who populated what we fondly call the 'Wild West' during the closing years of the nineteenth century. For the ability to hit seemingly impossible targets with unerring accuracy (and at speed) and be classed as a 'dead shot' was an important part of the gunfighter's myth. In reality, few gunfighters reached such dizzy heights, and those that came close were rarely called upon to demonstrate their skills at paper targets – somehow people had a bad habit of taking precedence!

Among the so-called 'dead shots' James Butler Hickok, alias 'Wild Bill' must rank high, for whatever one's conclusions may be concerning his alleged feats of arms, many regard him as the epitome of the Western gunfighter. Crediting him with more than a hundred 'notches' (the true figure is closer to ten) and the ability to outdraw and outshoot anyone on the frontier, Hickok's eulogizers have long overstepped the bounds of credibility, and one over-romantic biographer even dubbed him 'The Prince of Pistoleers'. That Hickok was a great pistol shot is not in doubt – the contemporary references to his skill, even if somewhat romanticised, are none the less based upon fact – but even he would have been embarrassed by some of the claims made in his name. One editor noted that his pistols were 'Colt's 'Navys, and in the rapid and wonderfully accurate use of them it is admitted he had no equal in the West. They were handsome, ivory-handled articles, and were always at that time [the late 1860s] swinging to his belt.' Three years after his death, these same pistols were the talk of the West when it was reported in the Cheyenne *Daily Leader* of 1 July 1879, that his grave had been robbed and the pistols stolen. The rumour was untrue, but the paper declared that the pistols were: 'made expressly for him and were finished in a manner unequalled by any ever before manufactured in this or any other country. It is said that a bullet from them never missed its mark. Remarkable stories are told of the

dead shootist's skill with these guns. He could keep two fruit cans rolling, one in front and one behind him, with bullets fired from these firearms. This is only a sample story of the hundred which are related of his incredible dexterity with these revolvers.'

From personal experience of 'plinking' as such shooting is called, I know that with practice one can indeed keep a can on the move with carefully placed shots, but one wonders if the word 'rolling' should be taken literally – in my experience, the cans tend to jump about rather than roll!

Those who had actually watched Hickok shoot, though enthusiastic, were a little less romantic about it. 'He never commenced a muss,' wrote another editor, 'but he was always in at the close, and as a general thing there was a procession to "Boot Hill" on the same day . . . Wild Bill was a great disciple of peace, and he frequently killed a man or two to preserve it . . . and the surprising celerity with which he could draw one of his "Colts" was a great peace promoter.' The writer concluded that anyone stupid enough to make threats against Hickok and fail to carry them through, ran the risk of being 'hunted up' and challenged, for the 'tribute to his bravery is not exaggerated. James B. Hickok was a cool, collected man; not a rough nor a desperado, but a brave man. His courage was never questioned.'

Some of the stories of Hickok's skill are beyond belief. It was claimed that he regularly shot coins out of the air; drove corks through the necks of whisky bottles; cut chickens' throats with bullets, and delighted in amusing a crowd by shooting a letter 'O' in saloon signs from fifty or 100 yards away. Those among his contemporaries who were prepared to comment when confronted by such stories admitted that his marksmanship was uncanny, but as W. E. Webb (who knew Hickok in Hays City) remarked in his book, *Buffalo Land* (1872): 'I do not believe, for example, that he could hit a nickel across the street with a pistol-ball, any more than an Indian could do so with an arrow. These feats belong to romance. Bill is wonderfully handy with his pistols, how-

Top left: Lined up for a 'morgue' photograph are the bodies of Grat, Bob and Bill Dalton, and at the right is Dick Broadwell after their unsuccessful attempt to rob two banks at once at Coffeyville, Kansas on 5 October 1892. (By courtesy of the Kansas State Historical Society)

Far left: Dr. John H. Holliday (1852 – 87) from a photograph published in *Human Life*, May 1907 (By courtesy of the Kansas State Historical Society)

Left: Frederick Remington's classic sketch 'A Fight in the Street', first published in *Century Magazine* in the 1890s. The two 'shootists' typify the 'gun-in-hand' approach to a fight rather than the more spectacular 'walk-and-draw' of fiction and film. (Author's Collection)

ever.' And Luther North, the brother of the famous Frank North, who commanded the Pawnee Battalion of Indian scouts, recalled that when shooting at targets Hickok never play-acted with hip shooting or similar nonsense. Rather, he 'was very deliberate and took careful aim closing his left eye'. Similarly, Charles Gross, who spent much time with Hickok in Abilene, recalled in the 1920s that he had often watched Hickok at target practice. On one occasion the pair rode out to some cottonwoods outside town where Hickok put up a piece of paper, about six inches by four inches with a black spot in the middle, at about navel height. He then paced off about twenty feet, turned, and ordered Gross to shout 'Draw!' Gross remembered that Hickok's movements were very quick and six shots were fired rapidly at the paper. Two bullets had entered the black spot and the others were scattered around it. He tried the same thing with his left hand, and although every shot was in the paper, none were in the spot, which did not seem to bother him. Wild Bill then turned to the wide-eyed Gross and said: 'Charley, I hope you never have to shoot any man, but if you do, shoot him in the guts, near the navel. You may not make a fatal shot, but he will get a shock that will paralyse his brain and arm so much that the fight is all over.'

In recent years, many attempts have been made to duplicate some of Hickok's alleged feats, with varying degrees of success. Debunkers have ridiculed some of the more incredible claims, but it is interesting to note that in the hands of an expert shot, a cap and ball revolver, properly loaded, may be slower than its modern counterparts, but is quite capable of 'putting 'em in the black' at ranges in excess of 100 yards. As for Hickok, perhaps Luther North best summed him up when he wrote: 'Wild Bill was a man of iron nerve and could shoot straight enough to hit a man in the right place when the man had a gun in his hand, and just between you and me, not many of the so-called Bad Men could do that.'

Bat Masterson wrote something of six-shooter skill when discussing the notable 'man-killers' he had known, but a lot of his remarks were directed to the pistols themselves. During his law-enforcement period in the late 1870s, he ordered a total of eight Colt Peacemakers for himself and friends. When he was paid to write a piece extolling the virtues of the Savage Arms Company's automatic pistols, however, he criticised the six-shooters of his youth. The percussion revolver he described as a 'monkey-wrench' and the later weapons as 'clumsy'. The man who could 'throw lead' accurately without taking sight had to be a 'born dead shot' or one prepared to practise long and hard. Bat's sense of humour was highly developed. He used to purchase old single-action pistols which he kept in the drawer of his desk for presentation to would-be collectors who pestered him for one of his guns. It is claimed that Bat carved notches in the butt before handing it over, poker-faced, and barely restrained himself from laughing as the over-awed individual all but bowed himself out!

Hickok, of course, was by no means alone in the alleged 'dead shot' stakes. The notorious Henry Plummer of Virginia City fame, was credited by Thomas Dimsdale, author of the classic *The Vigilantes of Montana*, with the ability to draw his 'pistol and discharge the five loads in three seconds'. Three seconds may seem an eternity to the modern fast-draw fanatic, but Dimsdale makes it clear that Plummer did not just pull his pistol at speed and risk a miss; he actually took aim.

Joseph A. Slade, whose contemporaries said was 'more feared than the Almighty', could shoot accurately and in haste, but on one occasion at least he allowed accuracy to take precedence. In *Roughing It*, Mark Twain recalls:

'Slade was a matchless marksman with a navy revolver. The legends say that one morning at Rocky Ridge, when he was feeling comfortable, he saw a man approaching who had offended him some days before – observe the fine memory he had for matters like that – and, "Gentlemen," said Slade, drawing, "it is a good twenty-yard shot – I'll clip the third button on his coat!" Which he did. The bystanders all admired it. And they all attended the funeral, too.'

Bat Masterson was obviously unaware of the U.S. Army tests which established that the Peacemaker had a mean absolute deviation of 3.11 inches at 50 yards when, in his article for the Savage Arms Company, he cast doubt upon the accuracy of some of the alleged top-notch 'shootists'. He recalled that Pat Garrett believed that if he himself could hit a 1½-inch bull's eye twice out of five shots at fifteen paces he would call it good shooting 'if I took careful aim and did my best'. Similarly, six-shooter exploits credited to the self-styled bad-man, Al Jennings (who took flight rather than risk a fight with Temple Houston when the latter shot it out with Al's brothers) was a joke among his contemporaries. One man recalled that Al could not have hit a barn door from the inside, and on the occasion when he was persuaded to fire ten shots at a gallon can twenty yards away he missed every time.

It is clear that being a good shot helped, but one's performance in an actual gunfight was the real test, because few of them were planned; most of them were spur-of-the-moment affairs precipitated by boredom, rot-gut whisky, feuds, gambling and disputes over women; all contributing to the final showdown when shouts were followed by shots.

The gunfight which inspired the 'walk and draw' shoot-out so beloved of novels and Hollywood films, was the encounter between Wild Bill Hickok and Davis Tutt in Market Square, Springfield, Missouri, on the evening of 21 July 1865. According to local gossip, the pair had been companions for some time and were a familiar sight as they meandered about Springfield, each armed with two revolvers, and celebrating their demobilization from military service. They were playing cards and fell out over a debt. Tutt claimed that Hickok owed him money from a previous game, which Hickok denied. Tutt then took Hickok's prize Waltham watch from the table and said that he would keep it until the debt was paid, adding that he intended to wear it the following day. Hickok replied that he had no wish to make a fuss in the house, but if Dave did wear that watch it would be a health hazard. Dave ignored him and walked out.

At about six o'clock a number of citizens were hanging about waiting to see what would happen; they were not disappointed. Tutt appeared at one end of the square and Hickok at the other. As they advanced towards each other, Major Albert Barnitz, commanding officer of the military post at Springfield, watched their progress, and only hours later wrote in his journal that both men opened fire 'simultaneously' when about 100 paces apart. Tutt missed, but Hickok's ball struck him in the chest and he died almost instantly. Barnitz immediately ordered Hickok's arrest and he was handed over to the civilian authorities. Charged with 'killing', which was later reduced to 'manslaughter', Hickok was tried on 5 August, but the jury believed that he acted in self-defence, and he was released.

The historical importance of this gunfight was two-fold: it established the now legendary face-to-face confrontation, and

made no reference to any form of 'fast draw'. In fact, it is possible that both men had their pistols in their hands when they stepped on to the square. The question of whether their pistols were holstered or in hand has been debated ever since. Hickok, of course, enhanced his already growing reputation.

A similar but less publicised event took place on 9 March 1877, at Cheyenne, Wyoming, when gamblers Charlie Harrison and James Levy shot it out after a dispute at a gaming table. The pair had been drinking heavily all evening, and the more they consumed the more belligerent they became, until finally Levy pulled a gun on Harrison. Charlie said he was not armed, but if Jim would wait until he got a pistol he would be glad to 'accommodate' him. They stepped into the street and Harrison hurried into the Senate Saloon to pick up a revolver. He emerged to find Levy waiting for him outside Frenchy's Saloon. Charlie promptly opened fire, but missed, and Levy shot back. Six more shots were exchanged before Harrison fell, struck in the chest. Raising himself, he fired once more but missed, and then fell back. Levy ran across the street, stood over him and deliberately fired another bullet into him before turning and hurrying away. A crowd gathered and a doctor was sent for. Levy's last shot had taken a circular tour from its point of entry in the right hip, across the stomach to lodge in the left hip. Despite expert advice, Charlie refused to allow the ball to be removed. He died two weeks later leaving his wife and daughter penniless.

The editor of the Cheyenne *Weekly Leader* echoed the views of most residents, when he condemned Levy's cowardly behaviour and the efforts of his gambler friends to get him bailed. 'The plea of self-defence might well be set up in Levy's behalf had he not done this, but we believe he should be made to

suffer the severest penalty of the law for thus carrying into effect an evident intention to kill his man.' Levy, who had obtained bail, promptly disappeared. This delighted those who thought themselves well rid of the 'pistoliferous gambler'. In 1907, Bat Masterson recalled that Harrison was a man of cool courage and nerve, but on that occasion his liquid intake must have affected his reasoning, for by shooting in a hurry he laid himself open to a man who remained cool – and callous.

Bystanders had a miraculous escape when a gunfight took place between Levi Richardson and Frank Loving, in the Long Branch Saloon at Dodge City on the night of 5 April 1879. Both men were well known locally; Richardson was a buffalo hunter turned freighter, with a reputation as a good shot with rifle or pistol and known for his quick temper. Frank Loving, known as 'Cock-Eyed Frank', on the other hand, was a very cool customer. The pair fell out when Richardson discovered that his lady friend preferred Frank. That evening both men sat at the same table for a few minutes, but were soon on their feet shouting insults at each other. Richardson pulled his pistol and Loving grabbed for his. Eye-witnesses recalled that at this point 'their pistols almost touched each other'. As Loving was pulling his .44 Remington 1875 Army revolver Richardson fired, but missed. Loving's first shot also missed, and he then ran behind the huge pot-bellied stove in the centre of the room. Both men then started chasing each other around the stove firing as they went. According to the *Ford County Globe* of 8 April, 'at it they went, in a room filled with people, the leaden missives flying in all directions. Neither exhibited any sign of a desire to escape the other, and there is no telling how long the fight might have lasted had not Richardson been pierced with bullets and Loving's pistol left without a cartridge. Richardson was shot in the breast, through the side and through the right arm. It seems strange that Loving was not hit, except a slight scratch on the hand . . .

Far left: Jeff Cooper and members of the Eaton Canyon Muzzle-loaders, emulating some of Hickok's alleged feats. The tests resulted in the conviction that some of the feats were possible, others possible but highly improbable, and some downright incredible! (By courtesy of Jeff Cooper)

Centre left: Jeff Cooper examines the results of some off-hand shooting with the 1860 Army at 50 yards. (By courtesy of Jeff Cooper)

Left: In February 1867, *Harper's New Monthly Magazine* published an article about 'Wild Bill' by Colonel George Ward Nichols, which purported to tell the true story of Wild Bill Hickok. Some of it was fiction, but by and large he was accurate. This woodcut depicts the moment after Hickok shot Tutt and then turned to his companions and said: 'Are you satisfied?' (Author's Collection)

Eleven shots were fired, six by Loving and five by Richardson.'

When Loving fired his last shot, Richardson had managed to get off one more shot before Deputy Sheriff William Duffy, who had been dodging the bullets, wrested the gun from him. Charlie Bassett, City Marshal, promptly disarmed Loving and in the scuffle, Richardson and Duffy fell to the floor. Richardson got to his feet, staggered a few steps and fell dead.

The bystanders' miraculous escape from injury was the talk of Dodge for weeks. The *Globe* commented: 'Gamblers as a class, are desperate men. They consider it necessary in their business that they keep up their fighting reputations, and never take a bluff. On no account should they be allowed to carry deadly weapons.' This advice would fall upon deaf ears, of course, for no gambler would tolerate any restriction on his right of 'self-defence'.

One of Dodge City's most famous shoot-outs occurred in 1884, between Dave Mather and Tom Nixon. Nixon was a notable buffalo hunter who was reputed to have ruined his Sharps' rifle (presumably through lack of cleaning) when killing 120 animals at one stand. Tom was an assistant marshal in Dodge, and engaged in a number of other activities. In 1883 he became a partner in the Bond & Nixon Saloon.

David Mather was said to be a 'very wicked man, a killer of killers', – a bad man to cross. Born on 10 August 1851 at Saybrook, Connecticut, he was of the wealthy Mather family whose members were to be found all over New England; but for various reasons he and his brother Joshuah Wright Mather had moved West. Both brothers achieved reputations, but it was Dave who was regarded as the more dangerous. He too had served as an assistant marshal in Dodge City for a short time before joining a man named Black to open the Mather & Black Opera House and Dance-hall. Local opposition and, so the partners believed, police interference prevented the dance-hall side of the business from prospering. Mather was convinced that Nixon was behind his problems, so he and his partner started selling their beer at less than the going rate of two glasses for 25 cents. Bond and Nixon, aided by the other saloon owners, lobbied the beer suppliers, and Mather and Black soon went 'dry'. Mather now made it known that he was out to get Nixon, who promptly shot at him when they met in the street. Fortunately for Mather, the ball missed, but struck a porch beam showering him with wood splinters, one of which embedded itself in his left hand.

On 19 July 1884 *The Democrat* reported that Nixon was promptly disarmed and taken to jail, adding: 'Mather claimed to have been unarmed, while Nixon claims Dave reached for his gun before he attempted to draw his own. Mather says he will make no complaint, but from all appearances the end is not yet.' Nixon was later released on bail to appear at the next sessions on a charge of assault 'with intent to kill'. When Nixon came up for trial, Mather refused to make a statement, so Tom was released. Later that day, 21 July, as Nixon stood on duty at the corner of Front Street and First Avenue, 'Mysterious Dave' came up behind him. 'Oh, Tom,' he called. As Nixon turned, Mather shot him four times, before he had a chance to draw his pistol. Bat Masterson was one of the first to reach him, but he was dead. Mather was arrested and later appeared on trial at Kingsley in Kansas. Nixon was deemed the original aggressor and some felt that he was a character the town 'could well do without', so Mather was acquitted, much to the 'approval' of the public gallery.

It was revenge that prompted Samuel Strawhun to attempt to murder Wild Bill Hickok at Hays City on 27 September 1869. A former army teamster and part-time courier, he was well known in Hays as a 'bad man', and one of several the local vigilance committee wished removed. In company with Joseph Weiss, a former Deputy U.S. Marshal who had 'done time' in the State Penitentiary, he tried to intimidate Alonzo B. Webster, a postal clerk (he later became mayor of Dodge City) who had been delegated by fellow vigilance committee members to order the pair out of town. When Webster delivered the written request to Weiss and Strawhun, they said they would 'come looking for him' the next day. On 23 July at about three o'clock, the two men entered his post office. According to the Ford County *Republican* of 20 April 1887:

'Webster had placed his pistol upon the head of a barrel under the counter, and was standing beside it. With an angry inquiry Weiss drew his pistol, but before he could carry out his murderous intention a bullet from Webster's pistol ended his career.

'The partner of Weiss, Sam Strawhorn [*sic*], who had remained outside, immediately fired at Webster through the window without effect, but fled and hid when Webster gave pursuit.

'Without delay the friends of Weiss organized to revenge his death and proceeded to the store for that purpose. Just at this juncture the tall form of Wild Bill appeared upon the scene, and when he swung himself into an easy seat upon the counter and said: "The boy had done right and that he would take the fight off his hands," the incident was over . . .'

Strawhun, however, bided his time and when, in August 1869, Hickok was elected acting sheriff of the county, he and his companions took action. On the night of 27

Above: David 'Mysterious Dave' Mather photographed when assistant Marshal of Dodge City — note the hatband! Dave and Tom Nixon fell out over a dispute connected with Mather's saloon business. Nixon took a shot at Dave who later ambushed him, but was found not guilty at his trial, on the grounds of provocation. (By courtesy of the Kansas State Historical Society)

Below: Dodge City, Kansas in 1873. Unfortunately, none of the characters has been identified. (By courtesy of the Kansas State Historical Society)

September they entered John Bittles' saloon and ordered drinks, but deliberately left the empty glasses in the street. They did this several times and the bartender found that he was rapidly running out of glasses. Strawhun threatened the life of anyone who retrieved them. Someone sent for Wild Bill. Whether Strawhun had planned it or not, he found himself face-to-face with Hickok. Realizing what the gang was up to, Hickok promptly gathered up the glasses and carried them into the saloon. The evidence is conflicting: some claim that Strawhun pulled a pistol hoping to catch Hickok unawares, others assert that he smashed a glass on the bar and tried to jab Hickok in the face with it. But Hickok was too quick for him: Strawhun died with a bullet in his brain. An eye-witness wrote a few days later: 'Too much credit cannot be given to Wild Bill for his endeavour to rid this town of such dangerous characters as this Stranhan [*sic*] was.' Hickok's reaction to Strawhun's threat is typical of the true gunfighter's instinctive 'shoot first and ask questions later' when faced by an armed man whose intention was to kill.

Dallas Stoudenmire was probably the best marshal El Paso, Texas, ever had during its turbulent period as a frontier cow town in the 1880s. He was appointed on 11 April 1881, and came with a good reputation as lawman, gunfighter, and ex-Texas Ranger. Utterly fearless, he stood six feet two inches tall, had hazel eyes, auburn hair and a granite jaw. In looks he was sombre, and his great height and reputation made him a for-

midable figure. Dallas had been appointed Marshal following a number of shoot-outs between local ranchers and Mexicans over alleged rustling, which had eventually involved the Rangers. In fact, Dallas's involvement in local feuds did not endear him to the criminal element, and when one evening an attempt was made on his life, instead of running for cover, he pulled his two short-barrelled, silver-plated, ivory-handled Smith & Wesson 'American' .44s, which he carried in his leather-lined hip pockets, and opened fire. A number of shots were exchanged before his assailants escaped in the dark, leaving him unhurt but with a bullet nick in the heel of his boot.

During his early months in office, Dallas fell out with the Manning brothers who ran most of the town's rackets, and he openly blamed them for the attempt upon his life. For some months an uneasy truce held sway and, in the view of the citizens, Dallas was a great Marshal. Many gifts were bestowed on him, and the town was quite peaceful but, perhaps from boredom, Dallas began to drink. Then, he announced that he was going to get married and his friends were delighted; perhaps at long last he would settle down to a domestic existence. When Dallas had left to get married, his brother-in-law, Doc Cummings, fell out with the Mannings and was killed by one of their bartenders. So it was with deep foreboding that James Gillett, a former deputy marshal (acting as Dallas's relief during his absence) broke the news that Doc was dead when the returning newly-weds got off the train.

Stoudenmire promptly declared war on the Mannings. Worried citizens managed to persuade both sides to sign a 'peace treaty' and although Dallas kept to the bargain, the strain took its toll, and he began drinking again. He would disappear for days at a time, leaving Gillett in charge. When it was announced that Dallas was leaving town anyway, the job was declared vacant. A number of people applied including Dallas and he got the job! It didn't last; he was forced to resign and Gillett (who later became a famous Texas Ranger) was appointed.

The feud with the Mannings was still simmering and on 18 September 1882 Dallas decided to have it out with them once and for all. Accompanied by his friend Walt Jones, a former policeman, he marched into their Coliseum Saloon to refute allegations made by them that he was seeking a fight. Inside were three of the Mannings: Jim standing at the bar; 'Doc' Felix playing billiards, and Frank, who had been sent for as soon as Dallas arrived. 'Doc' laid aside his cue and within moments he and Dallas were in a heated argument and both went for their pistols. Jones tried to interfere, but was pushed aside. His intervention was a mistake, for it gave 'Doc' time to pull his .44 double-action pistol and get off a shot which would have hit Dallas in the chest, but miraculously was stopped by his pocket-book and a wad of letters. Manning fired again and this time his shot hit Dallas in the left breast. Dallas staggered back, but managed to draw his pistol and shoot 'Doc' in the right arm, just above the elbow. 'Doc', by now

terrified of what would happen once Dallas drew a bead on him, lunged at him and threw his arms around him. Despite the pain in his elbow he managed to hang on, and locked together, both dripping blood, the pair staggered about the saloon in a *danse macabre*, until they stumbled into the street. Jim Manning rushed out with a .45 and opened fire. His first shot smashed a barber's pole, but his next was carefully aimed and it struck Dallas in the head, killing him instantly. 'Doc' disentangled himself from the dead man, and grabbing one of his pistols, began to beat him about the head with it until he was pulled away.

The Manning brothers were tried for murder, but as 'Doc' was acting in self-defence, and Jim was protecting his brother, no further action was taken. Old-timers believed that Dallas Stoudenmire was the victim of his own reputation, and that his hot-headedness, which had not been lessened by drinking, led to his downfall.

Three years later, El Paso witnessed yet another feud that led to a famous shoot-out. On 14 April 1885, the County Sheriff and City Marshal, together with their deputies, were away attending a murder trial. Charles M. 'Buck' Linn, a former Texas Ranger and part-time city gaoler, was acting city marshal. Linn was harmless when sober, but 'crazy' when drunk, and unfortunately, he chose that night to get drunk. His disposition was not improved when he learned that Sam Gillespie, a local citizen, had declared that Linn should be arrested and put on trial for pistol-whipping a friend who had cursed Linn when he locked him up for drunkenness.

Gillespie heard that Linn was looking for him with murder on his mind and hastily armed himself, making sure that Linn saw the gun in his hand. Reluctant to beat 'the drop', Linn retreated to the Gem Saloon, where he met his friend William P. Raynor, described by some as 'the best-dressed bad man in Texas', and at that time a gambler in the saloon. Linn poured out his story to Raynor, and the pair drowned their sorrows in drink. They then visited a number of saloons before returning to the Gem, where they had a row with a young faro dealer named Robert 'Bob' Cahill. Raynor and Linn separated, but not before George Look (a local businessman who had purchased Stoudenmire's pistols from the dead man's estate, and later wrote extensively about El Paso's early days) had warned the owner of the Gem Saloon, J. J. Taylor, to expect trouble. He had noticed that both Linn and Raynor had run out of money but were still getting drinks on credit.

Now things began to get complicated. A small theatre opened off the bar and it was filled with soldiers and others who had just arrived in town. Raynor suddenly appeared

in the doorway shouting for 'a son-of-a-bitch' who had come into town and offended him. Most people took the hint, and ducked under their seats or ran out. When Raynor saw Look and J. J. Taylor sitting in the audience, he holstered his pistol, removed his hat and bowed. Apologizing to everyone, he turned and left. The man Raynor was looking for kept out of the way.

Wyatt Earp was in the bar that night and his biographer, Stuart Lake, claims that Raynor tried to involve him in a fight, but Earp pleaded that not only was he unarmed, but he was unwilling to fight a glory seeker. Raynor next taunted a young cowboy who was wearing a white hat: 'Cowboy' Bob Rennick, refused to be drawn, but after Raynor had left the bar he brooded over the insults, grabbed a pistol from one of the dealers, stating: 'I have been imposed on enough and won't stand for it.'

At that moment Raynor charged back into the bar firing wildly. As everyone took cover, Rennick dropped to one knee, cocked his pistol and fired, hitting Raynor in the shoulder. He fired again this time hitting Raynor in the stomach. Raynor staggered

from the saloon, boarded a passing streetcar and collapsed on one of the seats, begging the other passengers to tell his mother he died 'game'. Rennick saw Raynor board the streetcar, but made no further attempt to attack him. Instead, he took the advice of George Look and crossed the Mexican border where he would be safe from Raynor's friends.

Buck Linn learned of his friend's death and immediately blamed Bob Cahill. He came roaring into the Gem determined on revenge. Warned of his coming, Cahill armed himself, but he had never been in a gunfight in his life and had no idea what to do. Lake credits Wyatt Earp with having advised Cahill that he should have his gun already cocked because Linn would 'come shooting'. Not to shoot until he was certain of a target and to aim for his belly, low, so that if the gun kicked up he would not shoot too high. Above all to, 'keep cool and take your time'. Cahill displayed remarkable courage and begged Linn to drop his gun. He refused and started shooting, but the liquor had taken its toll and he missed. Cahill shot him twice, once through the heart. Linn died instantly, and Cahill joined Rennick across the border. Raynor lingered for a few days and after his death, the two tyro gunfighters returned to face charges, but were acquitted in what became known as the 'Gem Saloon Shoot-Out'.

Probably the most famous gunfight of all took place on 26 October 1881, at Tombstone, Arizona, between the Earps, the Clantons and the McLaurys. The story is complicated and versions by today's historians of the actual sequence of events are as varied as they are numerous. One factor is common to all, however – the bitter animosity that existed between the antagonists. Wyatt Earp's reputation as a gunfighting policeman had been enhanced by his spell in Wichita and Dodge City, but when he arrived in Tombstone, Arizona in December 1879 he attracted little attention. Not until his political ambitions (he wanted to become county sheriff) involved him in local affairs did he become a force to be reckoned with by the local criminal element.

In Tombstone, Wyatt, his brothers Virgil, Morgan and James, and their respective wives soon settled into the way of the place, and Wyatt obtained employment as a shotgun messenger for Wells, Fargo. James, who had been crippled during the Civil War, did not become involved in later events, although Virgil and Morgan did. Virgil became City Marshal of Tombstone after the murder of the previous encumbent, and Wyatt augmented his own income by purchasing an interest in the Oriental Saloon, and running a faro game at a rival establishment, the Eagle Brewery. The Earps were later joined by Dr.

John H. 'Doc' Holliday, a tubercular dentist, reckoned by many of his contemporaries to be one of the meanest, ill-tempered men imaginable. His illness did little to improve his disposition, and he was given a wide berth.

Wyatt Earp did not like cowboys, no matter from which state they came, and he and his 'gang' soon fell foul of the local ranchers. He shared the opinion of the townsfolk that it was difficult to distinguish between an honest cowman and a rustler – the latter was a thriving local industry. Soon there was friction between the Earps and the Clanton–McLaury outfit of ranchers-cum-rustlers, and eventually Wyatt lost a prized horse which was traced to Billy Clanton. He claimed that he had purchased it legally. Later, six mules disappeared from an army post and were traced to the McLaury ranch, where the brands were being altered – it was claimed that the animals had been acquired honestly. When the Kinnear & Company stagecoach was held up on 15 March 1881, it was alleged by some that Doc Holliday was involved, and the murder of the driver, Bud Philpott, during the hold-up, aroused great anger, which was unfortunate in view of the rumours about Holliday.

Three men, Bill Leonard, Harry Head and Jim Crane, were accused by a fourth man, Luther King, of being the robbers. King had been captured by the Earps, who had formed a posse. He was handed over to Sheriff John Behan, but managed to escape from Tombstone. Later, Wyatt is reported to have tried to bribe Ike Clanton into betraying other members of the gang, but he refused. Then Virgil, in his capacity as a Deputy U.S. Marshal, arrested Behan's deputies Frank Stilwell and Pete Spence, in connection with the stage robbery, which did not endear the clan to Behan. The outcome was predictable: following a number of other incidents involving various members of both factions, the Clanton–McLaury gang made it known that they would eventually shoot it out with the Earps. On the morning of 26 October when they learned that Ike and Billy Clanton, Frank and Tom McLaury and Billy Claiborne were down at the O.K. Corral, the Earps decided to have it out once and for all.

Behan tried to stop the Earps, but they pushed him aside. Wyatt, Virgil, Morgan and Doc Holliday set off for the corral. The fight took place outside the corral in front of C. S. Fly's home and photograph gallery. The rights and wrongs of the shoot-out have been and will continue to be discussed interminably, for the whole affair is controversial. Here, however, is how Wyatt described the event when giving evidence before a preliminary hearing and reported by the Tombstone *Daily Nugget* of 17 November 1881:

'Billy Clanton and Tom McLowry commenced to draw their pistols; at the same time Tom McLowry threw his hand to his right hip, throwing his coat open like that (showing), and jumped behind a horse. I had my pistol in my overcoat pocket, where I put it when Behan told us he had disarmed the other parties. When I saw Billy Clanton and Frank McLowry draw their pistols, I drew my pistol. Billy Clanton levelled his pistol on me, but I did not aim at him. I knew that Frank McLowry had the reputation of being a good shot and a dangerous man and I aimed at Frank McLowry. The first two shots which were fired were fired by Billy Clanton and myself, he shooting at me and I at Frank McLowry. I do not know which shot was fired first. We fired almost together. The fight then became general.

'After about four shots were fired, Ike Clanton ran up and grabbed my left arm. I could see no weapon in his hand, and I thought at the time he had none, and so I said to him, "the fight has now commenced; go to fighting, or get away." At the same time I pushed him off with my left hand. He started and ran down the side of the building and disappeared between the lodging house and the photograph gallery; my first shot struck Frank McLowry in the belly; he staggered off on the sidewalk, but first fired one shot at me; when we told them to throw up their hands Claiborne held up his left hand and then broke and ran, and I never seen him afterwards until late in the afternoon; I never drew my pistol or made a motion to shoot until after Billy Clanton and Frank McLowry drew their pistols; if Tom McLowry was unarmed I did not know it; believe he was armed and fired two shots at our party before Holliday, who had the shotgun, fired at and killed him, if he was unarmed there was nothing in the circumstances, or in what had been communicated to me, or in his acts or threats that would have led me even to suspect his being unarmed; I never fired at Ike Clanton, even after the shooting commenced, because I thought he was unarmed; I believe then and believe now, from the facts I have stated and from the threats I have related, any other threats communicated to me by different persons, as having been made by Tom McLowry, Frank McLowry and Ike Clanton, that these men last named had formed a conspiracy to murder my brothers, Morgan, and Virgil, Doc Holliday and myself; I believe I would have been legally and morally justifiable in shooting any of them on sight, but I did not do so, or attempt to do so; I sought no advantage when I went, as a Deputy Marshal, to help disarm them and arrest them; I went as a part of my duty and under the directions of my brothers, the marshals; I did not intend to fight unless it became

necessary in self-defense or in the rightful performance of official duty; when Billy Clanton and Frank McLowry drew their pistols; I knew it was a fight for life and I drew and fired in defense of my own life and the lives of my brothers and Doc Holliday.'

Wyatt's pistol was a .44 calibre Smith & Wesson New Model No. 3, finely engraved and a present from John Clum, editor of the Tombstone *Epitaph*. When the brothers and Holliday started their walk toward the O.K. Corral, Wyatt had held the pistol beneath his coat, but later transferred it to his overcoat in which had been sewn a special canvas-lined wax-rubbed pocket designed for carrying a pistol and for getting it into action in a hurry. The other brothers carried Colt .45s as did most of their opponents. In addition to a pistol, Holliday was also carrying a Greener shotgun, allegedly ordered to his own specifications direct from W. W. Greener in Birmingham, England.

The fight did not end on 26 October 1881: Virgil was maimed for life on 28 November, when someone emptied the barrel of a shotgun into his arm as he left the Oriental Saloon, and on 17 March 1882 Morgan was murdered while he was playing pool in a saloon. The remaining brothers believed they knew who was responsible, and several men met untimely deaths. The killing continued. When Wyatt and Virgil accompanied Morgan's body to Tucson, where it was to be sent by rail to their parents' home in Colton, California for burial, they were confronted by Frank Stilwell, whom Wyatt believed was one of Morgan's killers. Wyatt shot him down in front of the Southern Pacific Railroad depot. Public opinion, however, and threats of arrest eventually drove the Earps out of Arizona. Despite the controversy, however, the legend of Wyatt Earp (aided considerably by Stuart Lake and the television series of the 1950s) is still very much alive, especially in Tombstone, the town that was 'too tough to die'.

By 1900 many of the old-time gunfighters were either dead or had reached the age when discretion becomes the better part of valour. A few, of course, refused to accept change, and continued to fight shy of civilization, spending their declining years in remote regions. As for the outlaws, those that managed to survive were forced to flee to new locations such as Central and South America. It was there that Butch Cassidy spent his last known years. But the Old West was going, and the farther it recedes, the greater our sense of nostalgia for it. We know that romance has long overtaken reality, but our fascination for those who tamed the West and survived is undimmed by the passing of time. They may be long gone, but they left behind a story which will be told and retold.

BIBLIOGRAPHY

The following books proved most useful in the preparation of this volume and some of them are cited in the text. The numerous newspapers and journals from which I have quoted are not listed here.

Blackmore, Howard L. *British Military Firearms, 1650–1850.* London, 1961

Boothroyd, Geoffrey. *The Handgun.* London, 1970

Burton, Captain Richard. *The City of the Saints and Across the Rocky Mountains.* London, 1862

Butler, David E. *United States Firearms: The First Century, 1776–1875.* New York, 1971

Connelley, William Elsey. *Quantrill and the Border Wars.* Cedar Rapids, Iowa, 1910

Corder, Eric. *Prelude to Civil War: Kansas–Missouri, 1854–1861.* London, 1970

Custer, General George A. *Life on the Plains.* New York, 1876

Description and Rules for the Management of the Springfield Rifle, Carbine, And Army Revolvers, Calibre .45. Government Printing Office, Washington, D.C., 1898

Dodge, Colonel Richard Irving. *Our Wild Indians.* London, 1882

Du Mont, John S. *Custer Battle Guns.* Fort Collins, Col., 1974

Edwards, William B. *The Story of Colt's Revolver.* Harrisburg, Penn., 1957

Edwards, William B. *Civil War Guns.* Harrisburg, Penn., 1962

Flayderman, Norman. *Flayderman's Guide to Antique American Firearms and their Values.* 3rd edn, Northfield, Ill., 1983

Frost, Lawrence A. (Ed.). *With Custer in '74: James Calhoun's Diary of the Black Hills Expedition.* Provo, Utah, 1979

Graham, Ronald, Kopec, John A., and Moore, Kenneth C. *A Study of the Colt Single Action Army Revolver.* Dallas, Texas, 1976

Hanger, Colonel George. *To All Sportsmen and Particularly Farmers and Gamekeepers.* London, 1814

Hanson, Charles E. Jr. *The Plains Rifle.* Highland Park, N.J., 1960

Jordan, Philip D. *Frontier Law and Order.* Lincoln, Neb., 1970

Lake, Stuart N. *Wyatt Earp, Frontier Marshal.* Boston, Mass., 1931

Lewis, Colonel Berkeley R. *Small Arms and Ammunition in the United States Service 1776–1865.* Washington, D.C., 1968

May, Robin. *The Gold Rushes.* London, 1977

Miller, Nyle, and Snell, Joseph W. *Why The West Was Wild.* Topeka, Kansas, 1963

Neal, Robert J., and Jinks, Roy G. *Smith and Wesson (1857–1945).* revd edn, New York and London, 1975

Ordnance Records (1776–1900). National Archives, Washington, D.C.

Parkman, Francis, Jr. *The Oregon Trail.* New York, 1849

Parsons, John E. *The Peacemaker and its Rivals.* New York, 1950

Parsons, John E. *Smith and Wesson Revolvers: The Pioneer Single Action Models.* New York, 1957

Peterson, Harold L., *The Book of the Gun.* London, 1962

Rosa, Joseph G. *The Gunfighter: Man or Myth?* Norman, Oklahoma, 1969

Rosa, Joseph G. *They Called Him Wild Bill: The Life and Adventures of James Butler Hickok.* Norman, Oklahoma, 1974

Rosa, Joseph G. *Colonel Colt London.* London, 1976

Russell, Carl P. *Guns on the Early Frontiers: A History of Firearms from Colonial Times through the years of the Western Fur Trade.* Lincoln, Neb., and London, 1980

Russell, Don. *The Lives and Legends of Buffalo Bill.* Norman, Oklahoma, 1960

Sage, Rufus B. *Rocky Mountain Life.* Chicago, Ill., 1857

Scoffern, John. *The Royal Rifle Match on Wimbledon Common.* London, 1860

Secrest, William B. *Dangerous Men: Gunfighters, Lawmen and Outlaws of Old California.* Fresno, Cal., 1976

Shillingberg, William B. *Wyatt Earp & the 'Buntline Special' Myth.* Tucson, Arizona, 1976

Steffen, Randy. *The Horse Soldier 1776–1943.* four vols, Norman, Oklahoma, 1977

Sutherland, Robert Q., and Wilson, R. Larry. *The Book of Colt Firearms.* Kansas City, Mo., 1971

Twain, Mark (Samuel L. Clemens). *Roughing It.* Hartford, Conn., 1872

Utley, Robert M. *Life in Custer's Cavalry: Diaries and Letters of Albert and Jennie Barnitz, 1867–1868.* New Haven, Conn., and London, 1977

Webb, Walter Prescott. *The Texas Rangers: A Century of Frontier Defense.* Austin, Texas, 1965

Webb, W. E. *Buffalo Land.* Topeka, Kansas, 1872

Williamson, Harold F. *Winchester: The Gun that Won the West.* London, 1978

Williamson, James J. *Mosby's Rangers.* New York, 1909

GLOSSARY

Aperture Sight: hole set in the centre of the rear sight, through which front sight is viewed.

Back Action Lock: during the late percussion period the mainspring (which on most arms was placed on the front of the lock) was moved to the rear, which made the fitting of such locks to small pistols much easier

Ball: lead spherical projectile generally called the 'bullet', used in muzzle-loading flintlock and percussion-lock arms

Ball Screw: device resembling a wood screw, threaded into the end of the ramrod and used to remove unfired balls from the barrel of a muzzle-loader

Barrel Key (or Pin): wedge-shaped bar or key pushed through the stock and passing through a slot set in the underside of the barrel to anchor the stock to the barrel. Sometimes a pin embedded in the wood of the stock was used

Black Powder: mixture of saltpetre (potassium nitrate), charcoal and sulphur which provides the propellent for muzzle-loading long arms, pistols and revolvers

Blueing: heat treatment by which a barrel, cylinder or other metal parts of a gun are finished. It is attractive and protects against rust

Blunderbuss: a weapon having a flared (bell-mouthed) muzzle, which flourished from the seventeenth to the nineteenth centuries

Boot: cover for flash pan of a flintlock rifle, usually made of water-resistant leather as a protection during wet weather

Bore: inside diameter of a barrel. In smooth-bore arms this is measured by the number of round balls that will fit it and can be cast from one pound of lead. When the barrel is rifled, the size of the bore is described as the calibre, and during the period covered by this book, it was calibrated in one hundredths of an inch

Box Lock: lock for muzzle-loader in which the mechanism is inside a metal box-like frame. The hammer is within the side plate of the box

Breech Plug: screw or gas-tight plug that is screwed into the end of the barrel to form the bottom or rear of the chamber of a single-shot long arm or pistol. The tang is normally attached to the plug

Browning: form of oxidation or controlled 'rusting' that predates blueing and acts as a protection and, if properly applied, creates a fine finish

Buckshot: favourite loading for sawn-off shotguns. A spherical shot that varied in size from .240 to .380, it was sometimes used in muzzle-loading pistols and rifles

Buffalo Chip: dried droppings of the buffalo. Settlers usually gathered these up for use as fuel for the fire

Calibre: diameter of the bore of a gun. Many are expressed in thousandths of an inch or in millimetres; but for our purpose we use the 19th century version in hundredths (i.e., .45 = 45 one hundredths of an inch)

Case-Hardening: heat-treatment of frames, hammers and other parts of the action or weapon whereby a tough surface hardness is imparted to prevent wear. The process usually leaves the part finished in a series of rainbow-like colours

Combustible Cartridge: cartridge used with muzzle-loading weapons. It consisted of the powder and ball contained in a prepared paper or foil casing. The paper is nitrated and 'consumed' when fired from the gun

Cone (or Nipple): screwed-in anvil for a percussion cap. A hole is drilled through the stem and through the threaded base so that the stem becomes a 'tube' upon which is placed the percussion cap. The flash from the cap when struck by the hammer is then transmitted straight to the main charge

Curly Maple: because of its 'striped' grain, this was the favoured wood for the early Pennsylvania or Kentucky rifle stocks

Damascus Barrel: this was formed by welding together strips of metal (often old nails and horseshoes were included). The metal was then hammered and forged around a mandrel the same diameter as the intended bore. When finished, the effect was of wavy lines or a grain all through the metal

Disc Primer: Christian Sharps' invention, it was designed to replace percussion caps. Fed from a magazine, the disc-like primers were placed on the nipple when the hammer was cocked

Flash Pan: pan or tray beneath the frizzen (or frizzel) that contains very fine powder. When the flintlock hammer struck the frizzen it sent sparks into the pan which ignited and flashed through a small hole direct to the main charge

Frizzen (or Frizzel): hardened steel plate (hinged and retained by a spring) against which the hammer of a flintlock struck to create sparks for ignition. The flint was held in the jaws of the hammer and had to be carefully knapped to ensure that it created sufficient sparks, and the flints were changed constantly

Fulminate of Mercury: Reverend Alexander Forsyth's experiments with various fulminates culminated in his use of this substance as a primer for firearms. It is highly combustible and needs careful handling

Gain Twist: rifling in the bore of a rifle or pistol that increased in the number of turns in the barrel as it reached the muzzle. During Colt's percussion period, he used both a right-hand and left-hand twist.

German Silver: this was really nickel silver and was an alloy of zinc, copper and nickel which appeared to be silver. It was greatly favoured for sights and fittings

Grooves: spiral channels cut into the rifling of a bore. The raised portions are the lands and the lower part the grooves. It is these that make the bullet rotate during flight and ensure its accuracy

Gunpowder: see Black Powder

Hair-Trigger: when a set-trigger is cocked, the pull on the front or main trigger is extremely light, and it can be adjusted to act with very little pressure. It was also a term applied to faulty actions where a cocked gun could go off without warning.

Half-Cock: first notch on the hammer of a percussion or early cartridge revolver, or the tumbler of a flint or percussion lock pistol. When drawn back to this position the scear rests in this notch so that the weapon cannot be fired by pulling the trigger, thus allowing the arm to be loaded or carried safely

Half-Stock: instead of being stocked to the full length of the gun to the muzzle, many of the mountain rifles (particularly the Hawken) were stocked only halfway along the barrel, leaving the remainder exposed, or taken up by the rammer

Hang-fire: not to be confused with a misfire when nothing happens. The gun does go off, but not at once. This is often described as 'slow ignition'

Minié Ball: the invention of Captain C. E. Minié of France in 1848, it was hollow-based and expanded into the rifling when fired. It was adopted by both the British and American armies (and other countries) and was the most common bullet of the American Civil War

Misfire: caused by dampness in the powder or failure of the propellent and/or primer; also see 'Hang-fire'

Musket: long-barrelled fully-stocked smooth-bore flintlock and early percussion lock arms in general use before the introduction of the rifle

Muzzle-Loader: the weapon is loaded by pouring powder down the barrel, followed by a patched ball and a rammer

(or a prepared cartridge). Percussion revolvers are also called muzzle-loaders, but in fact they are loaded not via the barrel but by means of the front of the chambers

Open Sights: sights on early rifles and revolvers. They usually consisted of a blade or pin forming the front sight and a 'V' notch forming the rear sight. Before squeezing the trigger, the shooter lined up the blade or pin of the front sight so that it appeared in the centre of the 'V' of the rear sight

Patch: cloth or leather disc used to form a gas-tight seal around muzzle-loading rifle balls. When greased it was forced into the rifling and served the dual purpose of ensuring accuracy of ball and lubricating the barrel

Patch Box: small compartment set in the side of the stock at the lower part of the butt. These were used to house spares and patches. Many of the lids were ornately finished

Patch Cutter: circular hollow tool that was placed over suitable material and struck with a hammer or mallet to cut out 'patches' for loading

Pepperbox: common name for the myriad multi-barrelled weapons that abounded during the 1840s and 1850s

Percussion Cap: copper 'cup' lined at its bottom with a fulminate of mercury paste. This was placed upon the nipple anvil and when struck by the hammer exploded and sent a flame into the main charge

Scear (or Sear): the tip of the trigger on a revolver which engages the notches or bents on the hammer, or a part of the

lock mechanism which operates between the trigger and the tumbler on a flint or percussion weapon with a lock plate

Set-Trigger: mechanism that allowed the shooter to lessen the pressure on the main trigger. There are two triggers: the second or rear trigger is pulled which sets up the main trigger and eases its pull. These were very common on target and hunting weapons

Skin Cartridges: form of combustible cartridge in which the powder and ball are contained in paper or animal intestine enclosed in nitrate-treated paper. Captain John Hayes, R.N., and Eley Brothers both produced versions of this form of cartridge which were widely copied

Swivel gun: piece of ordnance mounted on a turning pivot; eventually embracing muskets, blunderbusses or rifles on a swivel

Tang: normally attached to the breech-plug, the tang extended back from the breech into the stock and retained the long screw that held the barrel to the stock. Some rifle rearsights were fixed to the tang and were known as 'Tang Sights' and were of a folding type which also enabled the shooter to use conventional open or peep sights set into the barrel

Windage: this refers to the lateral adjustment made to a rear sight. The old-timers, however, had to judge cross-winds by watching their effect upon trees and scrub and allow for it

Worm: like the worm-screw, this device, similar to a corkscrew, was used to remove cleaning patches from the bore of muzzle-loading barrels

INDEX

ACKNOWLEDGMENTS

DURING the preparation of this volume a large number of people and institutions offered advice and assistance with illustrations, and without their help my task would have been impossible. I should like, therefore, to express my gratitude to the following who are listed alphabetically:

Fritz Baehr; Don Beardslee; Howard L. Blackmore; Lawrence Brooker; Lieutenant-Colonel William S. Brophy; Christopher Brunker of Christie's; David Burghoff; Emory Cantey, Jr.; Bert Cantwell (former U.S. Marshal); Arnold M. Chernoff; the staff of Connecticut State Library; Jeff Cooper; the late Sir William Charles Crocker; Paul and Penny Dalton (who prepared many of the illustrations); Anthony D. Darling; John Darwent; Peter DeRose; William Edmonds of Richard A. Bourne Co. Inc.; Robert W. Fisch, Curator of the West Point Museum; the late L. G. 'Pat' Flannery; the late Earle R. Forrest; Dr. Lawrence A. Frost, M.D.; Frank N. Graves, Jr.; the Editor and Publisher of *The Gun Report*; the late S. Basil Haw; Gregory Hermon; Ethel A. Hickok; Herbert Houze, Curator, the Winchester Museum; Jackson Arms, Dallas, Texas; David Jeffcoat; the Kansas State Historical Society; John A. Kopec; the staff of the Library of Congress; Herschel C. Logan; Dr. Richard C. Marohn, M.D.; Robin May; Andrew Mowbray; William H. Myers; Douglas A. Nie; Anthony North of the Department of Metalwork, Victoria and Albert Museum; the late John E. Parsons; Herbert Peck; Edward Prentiss; Jack L. Richardson (former U.S. Marshal); the staff of the Smithsonian Institution; Sotheby & Co., London; Judge Arthur J. Stanley, Jr.; Oscar 'Jay' Steerman; Robert Q. Sutherland; Charles R. Suydam; Nathan L. Swayze; Anthony Taylerson; Matthew E. Taylor; John Thorpe; the Wadsworth Atheneum; Messrs Wallis & Wallis; David Webb; Messrs Weller & Dufty, and R. Larry Wilson.